The Legal Doctrines of the Rule of Law and the Legal State (Rechtsstaat)

IUS GENTIUM

COMPARATIVE PERSPECTIVES ON LAW AND JUSTICE

VOLUME 38

For further volumes:
http://www.springer.com/series/7888

James R. Silkenat • James E. Hickey Jr.
Peter D. Barenboim
Editors

The Legal Doctrines of the Rule of Law and the Legal State (Rechtsstaat)

Springer

Editors
James R. Silkenat
Sullivan & Worcester LLP
New York, NY, USA

James E. Hickey Jr.
Hofstra University
Hempstead, NY, USA

Peter D. Barenboim
Asnis and Partners
Moscow, Russia

ISSN 1534-6781 ISSN 2214-9902 (electronic)
ISBN 978-3-319-05584-8 ISBN 978-3-319-05585-5 (eBook)
DOI 10.1007/978-3-319-05585-5
Springer Cham Heidelberg New York Dordrecht London

Library of Congress Control Number: 2014938031

Printed on acid-free paper

Springer is part of Springer Science+Business Media (www.springer.com)

Thank you to the World Justice Project (WJP), which originated in 2006 as a Presidential initiative of the American Bar Association. WJP, which has evolved into an independent, non-profit organization, leads "a global multidisciplinary effort to strengthen the rule of law for the development of communities of opportunity and equity". WJP's focused and sustained efforts have provoked important academic and practical interest in the relationship between the rule of law and legal state (rechtsstaat), which is reflected in this book.

James R. Silkenat
President (2013–2014), American Bar Association, Sullivan & Worcester LLP
James E. Hickey, Jr., Maurice A. Deane School of Law, Hofstra University
Peter D. Barenboim, Asnis and Partners

Acknowledgements

We would like to acknowledge the Series Editors, Mortimer Sellers and James Maxeiner, for both their chapter contributions to the book and their support of the book from the outset. We would also like to thank Springer's Senior Editorial Assistant, Diana Nijenhuijzen, for all her valuable assistance in bringing this book into production.

We give special thanks to Anna Ovcharenko for her research and her excellent substantive and editorial review and comments on a substantial portion of the book. We also acknowledge gratefully the participation and help of Paulina Brown and Elena Pribytkova.

We would also like to acknowledge the ABA Section of International Law and its current Chair, Gabrielle Buckley, and its immediate Past Chair, Bart Legum. We also want to acknowledge the leaders of the World Justice Project, Juan Botero, Bill Neukom and William Hubbard. A special acknowledgement goes to the President of the Federal Chamber of Lawyers of Russia, Eugene Semenyko, and the President of the Constitutional Court of the Russian Federation, Valery Zorkin, for their support of the major international Rule of Law and Legal State symposium held in St. Petersburg which contributed in a substantial way to the development of this book.

Finally, we thank all our chapter authors for the substance of their contributions and for their patience and cooperation and goodwill.

New York, NY, USA — James R. Silkenat
Hempstead, NY, USA — James E. Hickey, Jr.
Moscow, Russia — Peter D. Barenboim

Introduction

For several decades, there has been a growing and robust institutional, governmental, academic and legal interest in Rule of Law issues on many fronts. Less well-explored has been a focused dialogue examining the Rule of Law doctrine together with the Legal State (Rechtsstaat) doctrine, which is widely known in Europe. A premise for this book is that a meaningful and full appreciation of the Rule of Law doctrine may be advanced by also examining in juxtaposition the doctrine of the Legal State. Both legal doctrines are aimed fundamentally at helping to provide for societies some fundamental safeguards for human dignity and legitimacy for a state and its prescriptions. However, the doctrines, of course, may have different meanings and applications depending on the legal system and the socio-economic-cultural contexts in which they are invoked.

The 25 expert authors who are brought together to produce the 21 chapters of this book analyze variously the philosophical, legal, historical and political background and operation of both legal doctrines discretely and in relation to each other. This book, in Part I, explores the development of both the civil law conception of the Legal State (Rechtsstaat) and the common law conception of the Rule of Law from general, philosophical and legal perspectives. Part II examines the doctrines from a variety of specific applications and locations. A reader should find value not only in the individual chapters standing alone, but also in the work as a whole.

Our hope is that this book contributes significantly to the Rule of Law/Legal State literature and dialogue and that it provokes further discussion and understanding of both doctrines and their interrelationship in the years ahead.

James R. Silkenat
James E. Hickey, Jr.
Peter D. Barenboim
Editors

Contents

Part I General Perspectives on Rule of Law and the Legal State

1 **What Is the Rule of Law and Why Is It So Important?** 3
Mortimer N.S. Sellers

2 **On the Foundations of the Rule of Law and the Principle of the Legal State/Rechtsstaat** 15
Dietmar von der Pfordten

3 **Philosophical Foundations of the Principle of the Legal State (Rechtsstaat) and the Rule of Law** 29
Stephan Kirste

4 **Rule of Law (and *Rechtsstaat*)** 45
Martin Krygier

5 **The Rule of Law and Legal State Doctrines as a Methodology of the Philosophy of Law** 61
Dmitry Dedov

6 **Applying the Rule of Law to Contexts Beyond the State** 71
Matthias Kötter and Gunnar Folke Schuppert

7 **The Rule of Law as a Global Norm for Constitutionalism** 91
Francois Venter

8 **The Ill-Fated Union: Constitutional Entrenchment of Rights and the Will Theory from Rousseau to Waldron** 105
Aniceto Masferrer and Anna Taitslin

9 **The Measure of Law: The Non-instrumental Legal Side from the State to the Global Setting (and from Hamdan to Al Jedda)** 129
Gianluigi Palombella

10 **Rule of Law, Legal State and Other International Legal Doctrines: Linguistic Aspects of Their Convergence and Differentiation** ... 145
Yury A. Sharandin and Dmitry V. Kravchenko

Part II Specific Perspectives on the Rule of Law and the Legal State

11 **Freedom, Equality, Legality** ... 155
T.R.S. Allan

12 **The Rechtsstaat-Principle in Germany: The Development from the Beginning Until Now** ... 171
Paul Tiedemann

13 **The German Rechtsstaat in a Comparative Perspective** ... 193
Rainer Grote

14 **The Russian Judicial Doctrine of the Rule of Law: Twenty Years After** ... 209
Gadis A. Gadzhiev

15 **The Law Is a Causeway: Metaphor and the Rule of Law in Russia** ... 229
Jeffrey Kahn

16 **American Constitutional Analysis and a Substantive Understanding of the Rule of Law** ... 251
Robin Charlow

17 **Building a Government of Laws: Adams and Jefferson 1776–1779** ... 267
James R. Maxeiner

18 **Rule of Law v. Legal State: Where Have We Come from, Where Are We Going To?** ... 289
Nadia E. Nedzel

19 **The Rule of Law in the Middle East** ... 315
Hossein Esmaeili

20 **Waiting for the Rule of Law in Brazil: A Meta-legal Analysis of the Insufficient Realization of the Rule of Law in Brazil** ... 331
Augusto Zimmermann

21 **The Rule of Law and the United Nations** ... 349
Edric Selous and Giovanni Bassu

Editors ... 361

Contributors ... 363

Part I
General Perspectives on Rule of Law and the Legal State

Chapter 1
What Is the Rule of Law and Why Is It So Important?

Mortimer N.S. Sellers

Abstract This chapter considers the rule of law from within the rule of law tradition to clarify what the rule of law is, why it is so valuable, and how we can secure it. The rule of law in its original, best and most useful sense signifies the "*imperium legum*" of the ancients and enlightened modernity: "the empire of laws and not of men". This requires removing the arbitrary will of public officials as much as possible from the administration of justice in society. The rule of law implies constitutionalism, and all states and societies that struggle toward the rule of law are also working towards constitutional government, because well-constructed constitutions alone hold out the hope of controlling the governors as well as the citizens. Above all the rule of law requires an independent and self-confident judiciary, with power to interpret and apply the laws impartially, without fear or favor. The rule of law may be difficult to obtain, but its absence is never hard to perceive. Whenever power and naked self-interest can prevail against reason and the common good, the rule of law is not complete. The ultimate goal of every society and every legal system should be equal and impartial justice for all, free from oppression and arbitrary power.

1.1 Introduction

These reflections on the rule of law consider the rule of law from within the rule of law tradition. This chapter clarifies: (1) what the rule of law is; (2) what the rule of law requires of us; (3) where the rule of law comes from; (4) why it is so valuable; and (5) how we can secure it. Let there be no confusion about the subject matter of this inquiry. The rule of law in its original, best, and most useful sense signifies the "*imperium legum*" of the ancients, "the empire of laws and not of men" pursued by the early

M.N.S. Sellers (✉)
Center for International and Comparative Law, University of Baltimore, Baltimore, MD, USA
e-mail: msellers@ubalt.edu

J.R. Silkenat et al. (eds.), *The Legal Doctrines of the Rule of Law and the Legal State (Rechtsstaat)*, Ius Gentium: Comparative Perspectives on Law and Justice 38,
DOI 10.1007/978-3-319-05585-5_1,

humanists, by the partisans of liberal Enlightenment, and republican revolutions across the globe. This is not the later, positivist, more limited understanding of the rule of law as "*Rechtsstaat*," which has sapped the rule of law everywhere and caused so much confusion. The rule of law in its original and most natural sense is a pure social good, in which the legalism of the *Rechtsstaat* plays only a partial and supporting role. Societies that enjoy the rule of law are vastly better situated than those that do not. This makes the real rule of law (or its absence) the central measure dividing good from bad government everywhere. All law and political institutions can and should be evaluated to determine whether it or they advance the rule of law – or do not.[1]

Five main points should be made as plainly as possible at the outset. First, the definition: "rule of law" is the English translation of the Latin phrase "*imperium legum*", more literally "the empire of laws and not of men". This goes beyond the mere legalism of a "rule *by* law" or "*Rechtsstaat*", through which one man, or a faction, or a party rules through positive law to impose his or her or their will on others. Second, the rule of law – the *imperium legum* – requires of us that we remove the will of public officials as much as possible from the administration of justice in society. No executive, legislator, judge or citizen should enjoy arbitrary power to act against the public welfare. Third, the rule of law ideal arises from human nature, because all people seek justice through law and all law and governments claim – explicitly or implicitly – that the laws they promulgate serve justice in fact. From this it follows (fourth) that only the rule of law can secure stable justice in society, which makes the rule of law vastly important. So the fifth and greatest question is how to discover, create, interpret, and enforce the rule of law in such a way that law controls and governs the various private interests, not only of ordinary citizens, but also of the public officials who administer the state. All this follows from the original, once pervasive, and still the most useful understanding of the "rule of law" as "the empire of laws and not of men" – not simply the rule of men through law.

1.2 What the Rule of Law Is

The rule of law signifies "the empire of laws and not of men": the subordination of arbitrary power and the will of public officials as much as possible to the guidance of laws made and enforced to serve their proper purpose, which is the public good ("*res publica*") of the community as a whole. When positive laws or their interpretation or enforcement serve other purposes, there is no rule of law, in its fullest sense, but rather "rule *by* law" – mere legalism – in service of arbitrary power. The vocabulary here is important, because the concept of the rule of law enjoyed its fullest elaboration in tandem with related struggles for "liberty" and "republican government" against tyranny and oppression. The liberty ("*libertas*") of the ancients, the

[1] This chapter repeats and elaborates arguments also presented in M.N.S. Sellers, "An Introduction to the Rule of Law in Comparative Perspective" in M.N.S. Sellers and Tadeusz Tomaszewski, eds, *The Rule of Law in Comparative Perspective* (2010) at 1. Springer.

Enlightenment, and the republican revolutions of emergent modernity, signified protection by the law and government of all members of society against domination by other persons, or by states, or by the governments of states (where "domination" consists in the arbitrary control by one person or faction of another, without reference to the common good). The key here is the purposes for which positive laws and state action are created, interpreted, or enforced. The law may legitimately control us, but public officials must respect law's proper purpose, which is the common good of society as a whole, and not their own private interests.

When we have and maintain a legal system that serves the common good of society as a whole, then we have the rule of law (because the laws rule and not men), we have liberty (because the law prevents oppression), and we live in a republic (because government advances the "*res publica*" or "common good of its subjects"). The rule of law, liberty, and republican government are three facets of the same substantive good, secured only where the laws rule and protect us from tyranny and oppression. When positive laws and their interpretation and enforcement serve the public good, and prevent domination by any person or group of persons, then we have the "*imperium legum*", the rule of law in its fullest and best sense: "the empire of laws and not of men".

Persons may, of course, disagree about what serves the common good best. Nor should we forget that the "public good" ("*res publica*") also includes and protects the legitimate private goods and interests ("*res privata*") of separate individuals and groups. This raises the second-order question, how best to discover and preserve the common good through law: "What combination of powers in society, or what form of government, will compel the formation of good and equal laws, an impartial execution, and faithful interpretation of them, so that citizens may constantly enjoy the benefit of them, and be sure of their continuance."[2] The difficulty of answering this question should not obscure the central importance of the value that it seeks to advance. The rule of law is not simply one or a few or the most important of the techniques sometimes used to secure the "empire of laws and not of men," but rather the "*imperium legum*" itself. There is no rule of law unless the law itself rules, and regulates the private interests of those with power, so that they cannot act against the common good of society as a whole.

1.3 What the Rule of Law Requires of Us

The rule of law requires that we remove the private will of public officials as much as possible from the administration of justice in society. Private as well as public power should be regulated by law, to advance the common good. When acting in a public capacity our only concern should be the public good. When acting in a private capacity, the law should also limit our self-interest to protect the community as a whole. The concept of law embodied in the rule of law tradition therefore

[2] John Adams, *A Defence of the Constitutions of Government of the United States of America*, volume I (1787) at 128.

includes an element of impartiality that regulates the scope of public power. Legislators should legislate for the common good. To do otherwise would be "corrupt" (a term of art) and undermine the rule of law. Public officials should execute the laws in the light of the common good. To do otherwise would be "tyranny" (another term of art) and violate the rule of law. Judges should interpret the law to advance the common good. To do otherwise would be "arbitrary" (a third term of art) and violate their duty to society. The rule of law constrains the guardians of the law to serve the interests of the law, which is the interest of the whole, rather than any particular party or faction.

The rule of law requires fidelity to one overarching value, sometimes called "liberty," the state that obtains when law prevents domination by powerful interests, public or private. Note the limits of this requirement. The rule of law does not require that citizens always act in the public interest, but rather, that they do so when the law determines such deference to be necessary, in the light of the common good. Citizens may and properly should have and pursue private interests, but not at the expense of their public duties (which increase as they gain more authority). There can be a significant gap between the requirements of law and morality. The law determines what is *necessary* and therefore required to prevent domination and promote the public good. Morality reflects what is *useful* in advancing the good of society as a whole, but may not be required. Law has much the narrower jurisdiction.

The rule of law requires that laws be made and enforced only to serve their proper purpose, which is the common good or *res publica* of society as a whole. From this many other requirements follow, but always limited by the central purpose of the enterprise. For example, legal certainty is a great friend of liberty. Well-known and easily understood laws can be significant constraints on self-serving power. But legal certainty at the expense of the common good would defeat the purpose of law. Advocates of rule *by* law sometimes undermine the rule *of* law by legitimating the enactments of tyrants. Positive laws promulgated in the private interest do not satisfy the rule of law – although they may sometimes be an advance on otherwise unregulated tyranny. Promulgation and the other virtues of legal formalism often advance the empire of laws. But they are only secondary and contingent requirements of the rule of law, and not the thing itself.

1.4 Where the Rule of Law Comes From

The rule of law ideal arises in the first instance from human nature, because all people and all nations seek – or claim to seek – the rule of justice through law. All legal systems claim to be actually and normatively "legitimate," in the sense that they have the moral right to rule. This does not suggest that all such claims are true or sincere, but rather that they are made – implicitly or explicitly – by every existing system of law. The law's universal claim to obedience is dependent upon a prior claim to serve justice. Note the vagueness and procedural ambiguity of the first-order claim to legitimacy. Rulers may claim to find the law through sortition, or by virtue of their own infallibility, or (as Numa did) by direct consultation with God. The veracity (or not) of such claims is less significant than their unanimity. All legal systems depend on the assertion (explicit or implicit) that the laws do and should rule, and not men. All claim to implement the rule of law.

The law's claim to serve justice, rather than the interests of those in authority, arises from human nature and the realities of social power. People more readily submit to laws they perceive to be just, therefore all legal systems claim to realize justice in fact. These natural and universal origins of the rule of law explain the concept's latent appeal, but not its actual success. Beside the universal human desire for the rule of law is the historical rule of law tradition, through which lawyers, governments, and nations have sought to specify, implement, and ultimately to realize the rule of law in practice. This gives the world a basis for evaluating existing legal systems. It is not enough simply to assert the primacy of law. States must actually advance it. If "law" in practice were reduced to the simple self-interested commands of those in power, then the "*Rechtsstaat*" would be an instrument of oppression, and law itself no more than a weapon, to be wielded for good or ill by whosoever holds the sword of the state.[3]

The American John Adams,[4] followed the Englishman James Harrington,[5] in quoting the Florentine Donato Giannotti,[6] who divided the whole history of law and politics into a battle between two parties: those fighting for the rule of law (or government "*de jure*") and those fighting for the rule of certain particular men (or government "*de facto*").[7] This descent of authority, back from America and France to England, Venice, Florence, and ultimately Rome, illustrates the high points of the modern rule of law tradition, which sought to work out in practice what the rule of law requires in principle. The conflict between the "*de facto*" theory of law as the instrument of power, and the "*de jure*" conception of law as the product of reason and justice, has been the driving force of legal modernity, and the development of constitutional government throughout the world.[8]

1.5 Why the Rule of Law Is So Valuable

The rule of law is of vast and permanent value to any society, because only the rule of law can secure justice, by preventing tyranny and oppression. The Universal Declaration of Human Rights, approved by the General Assembly of the United Nations

---

[3] *See* Joseph Raz, "Authority, Law and Morality", 68 *The Monist* (1985) 285, 299.

[4] John Adams, *A Defence of the Constitutions of Government of the United States of America*, volume I (1787) at 126.

[5] James Harrington, *The Commonwealth of Oceana* (1659), ed. J.G.A. Pocock (1992) at 6.

[6] Donato Giannotti, *Libro della Republica de' Viniziani* (1540) in F. Diaz, ed. *Opere politiche* (1974).

[7] *Cf.* Cornelius Tacitus, *Annalium ab excessu divi Augusti libri* at I.2.

[8] *See* M.N.S. Sellers, *The Sacred Fire of Liberty: Republicanism, Liberalism, and the Law* (1998). Macmillan.

without dissent, recognized that "it is essential, if man is not to be compelled to have recourse, as a last resort, to rebellion against tyranny and oppression, that human rights should be protected by the Rule of Law."[9] More recently, the General Assembly identified "human rights, the rule of law and democracy" as "universal and indivisible core principles of the United Nations."[10] These ringing assertions, repeated or paraphrased by the European Convention on Human Rights,[11] the American Convention on Human Rights,[12] the African Charter on Human and Peoples Rights,[13] and numerous other regional agreements and national constitutions[14] illustrate the substantive moral component always present in appeals to the "rule of law". The "rule of law" in its best and usual sense implies the fulfillment of justice through law and the negation of arbitrary government.

The battle of the rule of law against arbitrary government takes place in every human society when those with power seek to expand their discretion, and their subjects resist. Nor are the advocates of unfettered power without arguments in their favor. The most learned apostle of despotism, Thomas Hobbes, denied any distinction between "right and wrong," "good and evil," "justice and injustice," beyond our separate and conflicting desires.[15] Hobbes had seen in the horrors of England's Civil War the indiscriminate misery of anarchy, "which is the greatest evil that can happen in this life."[16] From this it follows (he suggested) that we need an absolute and uncontested sovereign power to rule us and keep us safe.[17] The fear of anarchy is a powerful and compelling argument for despotism, and as a result the struggle for freedom usually begins with small and incremental advances, beginning with the simple call for written laws, to contain the discretion of those in authority, and only later even attempting to secure just and impartial laws, a much more difficult undertaking.[18]

The rule of law is so valuable precisely because it limits the arbitrary power of those in authority. Public authority is necessary, as Thomas Hobbes rightly observed, to protect against private power, but the rule of law keeps public authorities honest. The rule of law implies constitutionalism, and all states or societies that struggle

[9] *Universal Declaration of Human Rights* (December 10, 1948), Preamble.

[10] *See* U.N.G.A./RES/61/39, 18 December, 2006, on "The rule of law at the national and international levels". *Cf.* U.N.G.A./RES/62/70; U.N.G.A./RES/63/128.

[11] *European Convention on Human Rights* (4 November, 1950), Preamble.

[12] *American Convention on Human Rights* (22 November, 1969), Articles 8 and 9.

[13] *The African Charter on Human and Peoples Rights* (27 June, 1981), Articles 3, 6, and 7.

[14] *See*, for example, *Constitution of Russia* (12 December, 1993), Article 1; *Constitution of the Peoples Republic of China* (4 December, 1982), Article 5.

[15] Thomas Hobbes, *Leviathan* (1651) at I.vi.24; I.xiii.63.

[16] *Id.* at II.xxx.175.

[17] *Id.* at II.xviii.90.

[18] The famous story of the *decemviri* and the struggle for the rule of law in Rome was told by Livy in the third book of his history (*ab urbe condita libri* III.33ff). For similar developments in Athens, *see* Martin Ostwald, *From Popular Sovereignty to the Sovereignty of Law* (1986). University of California Press.

toward the rule of law are also working toward constitutional government, to control power with reason, or (more prosaically) make "ambition counteract ambition",[19] with the constant aim to "divide and arrange the offices in such a manner as that each may be a check upon the other – that the private interest of every individual may be a sentinel over the public rights."[20] The rule of law is valuable, because only the rule of law compels "the formation of good and equal laws, an impartial execution, and faithful interpretation of them, so that citizens may constantly enjoy the benefits of them, and be sure of their continuance."[21]

1.6 How to Secure the Rule of Law

The fundamental principle of the rule of law is so widely and universally accepted as to be almost a truism. The laws should rule, and not arbitrary power. The real difficulty arises in securing the rule of law in practice. The great constitutionalist, John Adams, observed that "in establishing a government which is to be administered by men over men", the greatest difficulty "lies in this: you must first enable the government to control the governed; and in the next place oblige it to control itself." This requires a "well-ordered constitution" so that justice could prevail "even among highwaymen," by "setting one rogue to watch another," so that "the knaves themselves may in time, be made honest men by the struggle."[22] Many of these necessary legal and political controls were as well-known (as John Adams expressed it) "at the time of the neighing of the horse of Darius" as they are today.[23] The basic guarantors of the rule of law include representative government, a divided legislature, an elected executive, and above all, an independent judiciary serving for extremely long and non-renewable terms in office.[24]

To recognize the necessary connection between the rule of law as an ideal and well-constructed constitutional government does not and should not be taken to imply that all states can or should maintain the same constitutional structures in practice. The social, historical, geographical and other circumstances in different societies will never be entirely the same necessarily, limiting what is appropriate, prudent and possible. Certain practices will never be justified, however, and certain standards and basic institutions will be shared by every society that aspires to attain "the government of laws and not of men." This brief investigation cannot and should not presume to offer a detailed formula for securing the real rule of law, but it can

[19] "Publius" [James Madison], *The Federalist* LI (February 6, 1788).

[20] *Id.*

[21] John Adams, *A Defence of the Constitutions of Government of the United States of America*, volume I (1787) at 128.

[22] John Adams, *A Defence of the Constitutions of Government of the United States of America*, volume III (1788) at 505 (Letter VII, December 26, 1787).

[23] *Id.*, Preface, at I.ii.

[24] *Id.*

help to establish a basic outline of the common elements necessary to any rule-of-law polity, including some of the exceptions and allowances that may be needed to establish the rule of law in fact, when history and governments are deeply set against it.

The rule of law will be best secured by stable constitutional government, because well-constructed constitutions alone hold out the hope of controlling the governors themselves. If the only legitimate purpose of government is to advance the common good, and to establish justice (which follows from the common good), then procedures will be needed to determine what the common good requires in practice, and adjudicate between rival conceptions of the public welfare. A rule of law constitution does this by so structuring public institutions and civic debate that private interests cannot usurp public power. This civic architecture of law and government has two main purposes: first, to secure good public officials, second, to make them rule well. The two are related, but one does not always follow from the other. Constitutionalism and the rule of law tradition recognize the inevitable fallibility of human judgment. No person is so well-placed or well-intentioned that she or he will not benefit from the checks and balances of a stable and constitutional rule of law.

1.7 Some Practical Requirements

The first necessary and inescapable desideratum of the rule of law is an independent judiciary. Judges must be secure and well-paid, so that they can apply the law without fear or favor. The great breakthrough in securing the rule of law in most societies occurs when judges attain tenure "*quam diu se bene gesserint*" (or during good behavior) rather than "*durante bene placito*" (at the whim of those in authority). This transition took place in England with the "Glorious Revolution" of 1688, confirmed by the Act of Settlement in 1701, which also prevented the executive from diminishing judicial salaries, once they had been established by law.[25] The Act of Settlement was a turning point in the progress of the rule of law, which made Britain the envy of other European nations.[26] Wherever judges do not enjoy secure tenure in their offices, their rulings are subject to improper influence and coercion.[27]

Judges secure in their salaries and tenure in office, who believe the law to be just, will do their best to uphold law's empire, not least because their own status and prestige depends upon the legal system's standing in society. This confirms the second great basis of the rule of law, which is that laws themselves should seek justice. Not only must judges apply the laws fairly, but the process of legislation must also attempt to advance justice, for its products properly to attain the status of "law."

---

[25] *Statutes of the Realm* VII, 636f.; 12–13 William III, c.2.

[26] *See*, for example, Voltaire [François-Marie Arouet], *Lettres Philosophiques* (1734), *Lettre* 8, *Lettre* 9.

[27] *See*, for example, Alexis de Tocqueville, *De la démocratie en Amérique* (Paris, 1835, 1840), volume I, part 2, chapter 8, for how even the elections of judges by the people poses a threat to the rule of law.

This is a complicated point. The concepts of law and fidelity to law imply a claim to justice.[28] The rule of law assumes a theory of law that separates law from the volition of those who serve it. Thus, pursuit of the rule of law also requires the maintenance of legislative procedures that will generate legislation for the public good, and not simply promote the private interests of those with power.

This link between the rule of law and a "common good" theory of justice is profound and essential. The "empire of laws and not of men" seeks a world of "equal" laws that serve all those subject to their control.[29] This absence of partiality is what sets government "*de jure*" apart from government "*de facto*" (to use the old terminology) and distinguishes "the empire of laws" from "the government of men."[30] But the question remains how to find "good and equal laws."[31] "Representative government" and "checks and balances" in the legislature (and the separation of both from the actual administration of justice) seem necessary precursors to "good and equal laws"[32] – and here we begin to reach the limits of the "essential" or "necessary" rule of law.[33]

1.8 Exceptions to the Rule of Law

John Stuart Mill advanced a theory of liberty and government, still extremely popular among statesmen, according to which some societies may not yet be sufficiently developed in their institutions and culture to support even such simple requirements of just government as the separation of powers between the executive and legislative powers, checks and balances in the legislature and administration of justice, or representative institutions in any branch of the government.[34] In circumstances such as these, perhaps "a ruler full of the spirit of improvement" may be "warranted in the use of any expedients that will attain an end perhaps otherwise unattainable."[35] But, there are offensive implications in making the judgment that certain peoples or nations are not yet capable of being trusted with political freedom and equality.[36]

[28] *See* M.N.S. Sellers, "The Value and Purpose of Law", 33 *Baltimore Law Journal* (2004) 145.

[29] *See* the citations to John Adams and Voltaire above; *Cf.* John Rawls, *The Law of Peoples with, The Idea of Public Reason Revisited* (1999), 71. Harvard University Press.

[30] *Supra*, notes 25–28.

[31] To use John Adams' felicitous description., *supra* note 2.

[32] *Id.* at I.1.

[33] For the concept of "necessary" law, *see* Emer de Vattel, *Le Droit des Gens ou Principes de la Loi Naturelle Appliqués à la conduite et aux affaires des Nations et des Souverains* (1758) at Preface pp. xx–xxi. His "voluntary" law is also "necessary," in the more natural sense of the terminology; *cf.* Christian Wolff, *Jus gentium methodo scientifica pertractatum* (1764).

[34] John Stuart Mill, *On Liberty* (1859) referred to "backward states of society in which the race itself may be considered as in its nonage."

[35] *Id.*

[36] And Mill was not shy in spelling these out. *id.*: "Despotism is a legitimate mode of government in dealing with barbarians."

Despotism in the common interest, even when pursued with a view to developing the higher faculties of those subject to its rule, is still despotism, and vulnerable to abuse.[37]

The dependence of the rule of law upon the institutions of representative government arises from the observation that government *by* any subgroup within the larger society will inevitably become government *for* the interests of that subgroup, above the others.[38] And even were the natural effects of self-interest somehow avoided, the laws of a benevolent despot would suffer from a very incomplete knowledge of the actual needs and circumstances of the citizens that all laws must actually serve, to be worthy of the name.[39] So, the concept of the rule of law implies an attempt to establish just laws, which, in turn, implies representative government, in order to achieve the degree of general knowledge and commitment to the common good necessary for an impartial legal system.[40] The rule of law entails the impartial pursuit of justice, which requires an equal concern for the welfare of all members of society.

While the rule of law without representative government may be a near impossibility, due to the fallibility of human nature, representative government by itself does not assure the rule of law, and may sometimes impede it. The earliest recorded musings about law and justice already distinguish "tyranny" from the rule of law, and contemplate the dangers of the tyranny of the majority, as well as by smaller factions.[41] The word "democracy" implied a sort of popular despotism for most of its history,[42] and the concept of "representative" government was developed to distinguish elected deliberative assemblies from more narrowly "democratic" governments.[43] Representative legislatures must be constructed to respect the rights of minorities, and will require the checks and balances of divided power to guide them away from populism and oppression.[44]

[37] *See* Philip Pettit, *Republicanism: A Theory of Freedom and Government* (1997). Oxford University Press.

[38] John Stuart Mill, *Considerations on Representative Government* (1861), chapter III.

[39] *See* James Bohman, *Public Deliberation: Pluralism, Complexity, and Democracy* (1996). MIT Press.

[40] *See* M.N.S. Sellers, "Republican Impartiality" in 11 *Oxford Journal of Legal Studies* (1991) 273.

[41] *See*, for example, Aristoteles, *Politika* IV.2.1 (1289 a 26 ff).

[42] So much so that Kant baldly stated that democracy was "im eigentlichen Verstande des Worts notwendig ein Despotism." Immanual Kant, *Zum ewigen Frieden* (1795).

[43] "Publius" [James Madison], *The Federalist* No. LXIII (March 1, 1788).

[44] This necessity is well expressed by James Madison ("Publius") in *The Federalist* No. 10 (November 22, 1787).

1.9 Conclusion

This short review of the primary attributes of the rule of law provides a brief reminder of the principles and institutions toward which nations and their peoples struggle, as they seek to create "an empire of laws and not of men." Establishing the rule of law requires constant attention to the "combination of powers in society" that will form the most impartial laws, for the benefit of everyone, without regard to the interests of those in power. These include representative government, a divided legislature, an elected executive, the separation of powers, and an independent and self-confident judiciary, with the power to interpret and apply the laws impartially, without interference (or influence) over actual cases by executive or legislative power.

The greatest threats to the rule of law differ at different times and places, but the underlying principle remains the same: to separate the law from arbitrary power. In many societies, custom and public opinion are the best and only constraints against despotism. More developed polities create written statutes to constrain those in authority. The single greatest advance towards the rule of law occurs when judges secure their independence from executive and legislative power. "Rule of law" states finally come into being with the emergence of constitutional government, provided that the constitution seeks justice and the common good through the checks and balances of divided governmental power, under the ultimate review of independent judges. These fundamental preconditions of an impartial legal system can be vastly improved upon and infinitely refined – but they are hard enough to achieve in themselves and do not entirely prevail under any existing polity.[45]

The rule of law may be difficult to obtain, but its absence is never hard to perceive. Whenever power and naked self-interest can prevail against reason and the common good, the rule of law is not complete. Government will always be needed to protect liberty against aggression and secure the many social goods that require large-scale collective action, but the rule of law constrains those in power to the purposes that justify their authority. Scholars may sometimes advocate partial departures from the rule of law, or its incomplete realization, or its different application in different societies, because of transient or unfortunate circumstances, but no one can deny that every departure from the rule of law is a denial of justice. The ultimate goal of every society and every legal system should be equal and impartial justice for all, free from oppression by arbitrary power.

[45] To give just one example, the United States still retains popular elections of sitting judges in many states of the Union.

Chapter 2
On the Foundations of the Rule of Law and the Principle of the Legal State/Rechtsstaat

Dietmar von der Pfordten

Abstract This chapter inquires into the foundations of the rule of law and the principle of the legal state/Rechtsstaat. This will be done in four steps: Firstly, it will be asked: What is involved in the obligation to use the specific means of law for political and administrative decisions? Secondly, an ethical grounding will be searched for both principles. After these two parts in which the common foundations of both principles are sought, a third step will consider more concrete applications, in which the two principles coincide. Finally, the fourth step inquires where the two concepts divide due to cultural particularities of the different national legal orders.

2.1 Introduction

The rule of law and the principle of the legal state/Rechtsstaat (État de droit, Stato di diritto, Estado de Derecho) are today widely accepted, both nationally and internationally.[1] The former is, for example, a core element of the British and American legal tradition, the latter is a fundamental principle of the German Constitution (Art. 20, 23 I 1, 28 I, 79 III Grundgesetz). The French and the Italian Constitutions only embody some main elements, but not the concept as such explicitly.[2] In international law, we find the rule of law and the principle of the legal state in the

[1] *See* in general: *The Rule of Law. History, Theory and Criticism*, Pietro Costa and Danilo Zelo eds (2007). Springer, Dordrecht. For a comprehensive survey on the literature on the legal state/ Rechtsstaat, *see* also Grzeszick, in: *Maunz-Dürig, Grundgesetzkommentar* (2013), Art. 20, VII. C. H. Beck, München and Katharina Sobota, *Das Prinzip Rechtsstaat: verfassungs- und verwaltungsrechtliche Aspekte* (1997). Mohr Siebeck, Tübingen.

[2] *See* Preamble, Art. 1 I, 5 I, 34, 64 I of the French Constitution. Art 1 II of the Italian Constitution says: "La sovranità appartiene al popolo, che la esercita nelle forme e nei limiti della Costituzione."

D. von der Pfordten (✉)
Philosophy of Law and Social Philosophy, University of Göttingen, Göttingen, Germany
e-mail: dpfordt@gwdg.de

J.R. Silkenat et al. (eds.), *The Legal Doctrines of the Rule of Law and the Legal State (Rechtsstaat)*, Ius Gentium: Comparative Perspectives on Law and Justice 38,
DOI 10.1007/978-3-319-05585-5_2, © Springer International Publishing Switzerland 2014

Preamble and Art. 2 of the Treaty on the European Union, in the Preamble of the Charter of the United Nations and in the Preamble of the Declaration of Principles of International Law Concerning Friendly Relations and Co-operation Among States in Accordance with the Charter of the United Nations.

Acceptance does not always mean realization, however. Because of ideological abuse and general overuse, the concepts/principles need some readjustment.[3] In order to help widen the acceptance and to shape the core meaning of these concepts and principles, this chapter inquires into the foundations of these principles. This will be done in four steps: Firstly, it will be asked: What is involved in the obligation to use the specific means of law for political and administrative decisions? Secondly, an ethical grounding will be searched for both principles. After these two parts in which the common foundations of both principles are sought, a third step will consider more concrete applications, in which the two principles coincide. Finally, the fourth step inquires where the two concepts divide due to cultural peculiarities of the different national legal orders.

2.2 The Form of Law

Both the rule of law and the principle of the legal state/Rechtsstaat demand that political and administrative decisions should – at least in serious cases – be made in the form of law.[4] But what is the implication of this requirement? What does the form of law add to the pure political or administrative decision? The answer depends on the philosophical question of what distinguishes law from pure politics and administration.

2.2.1 What Do Politics, Administrative Decisions and Law Have in Common?

To inquire into this distinction, it is necessary to first understand what politics, administrative decisions and law have in common. All three are not only natural but social facts, more precisely human actions and decisions in a wide sense which include individual and collective decisions and some intended consequences of

---

[3] Tom Bingham, *The Rule of Law* (2011), at 5ff. Allen Lane, London.

[4] Already Plato's shift from the wise but unbound philosopherking in the *Politeia* to the ruling of the laws in the *Nomoi* can be seen as an acknowledgement of the rule of law/legal state. See for a formulation of this demand also: Aristotle, *Politics* 1300b12ff.; John Locke, *Two Treatises of Government* II, § 3, at 137. *See* for a history of the rule of law and the Rechtsstaat: Pietro Costa, "The Rule of Law: A Historical Introduction", *in The Rule of Law. History, Theory and Criticism*, Pietro Costa and Danilo Zelo eds. (2007) at 73ff. Springer, Dordrecht. On p. 87 he shows that the concept of the Rechtsstaat emerged in Germany at the end of eighteenth century. France and Italy followed much later.

these decisions.[5] All three are human actions in two respects: as a general phenomenon and in all their singular manifestations. When a judge decides, he always performs a human action. When a public official issues an administrative act, he performs a human action. When a parliament votes for a statute, it performs a collective human action. If politics, administrative decisions and law, by conceptual necessity, are a form of human actions, they can only be understood if one takes into consideration the necessary qualities of human actions. What are the necessary qualities of human actions? Human actions are comprised of at least two necessary elements[6]: an aim or an intention, and some means (broadly conceived) to realize this aim.

2.2.2 *What Is the Aim of Politics, Administrative Decisions and Law?*

From the beginning of philosophy in ancient times up to the late Middle Ages, great emphasis was laid on quite specific and demanding aims in order to distinguish politics, and especially law, from other phenomena. For Plato and Aristotle, the aim of law and politics was the good, explained as justice, and, specifically for Aristotle, eudaimonia and the common good.[7] The means played no great role. Cicero, too, stressed justice as the aim of the law.[8] Thomas Aquinas then defined law as "an ordinance of reason for the common good, made by him who has care of the community, and promulgated".[9] So the necessary aim is the common good. Aquinas still mentions justice though, especially in respect of the positive law.[10]

In the seventeenth century, this emphasis on the specific aim of law and politics vanished. The good, justice, eudaimonia and common welfare were no longer considered to be the main aim of law and politics. The means became a primary consideration. Thomas Hobbes proposed a reduced but still quite specific aim of law and politics: self-preservation.[11] Furthermore, he stated that law in general consists

[5] Gustav Radbruch, *Rechtsphilosophie*, ed. Ralf Dreier and Stanley Paulson, (2nd edn. 2003): "Recht ist Menschenwerk." at 11, C. F. Müller, Heidelberg. See for the following: Dietmar von der Pfordten, "What is Law? Aims and Means" in: Archives for Philosophy of Law and Social Philosophy (ARSP) (2011) 97, at 151–168.

[6] For the necessity of an aim in every action *see* e.g. Aristoteles, Nicomachean Ethics 1094a1; John Searle, *Intentionality. An Essay in the Philosophy of Mind* (1983), at 107. Cambridge University Press, Cambridge, New York. Not all actions have the same aim, but specific types of actions like law can be specified by one uniform, albeit for obvious reasons quite abstract aim.

[7] Plato, *Politeia* 327a1, 433a; Aristotle, *Nicomachean Ethics* I 1, 1094a; V 1, 1129a; *Politics* 1328a36.

[8] Cicero, *De Legibus*, I, 29.

[9] Thomas Aquinas, *Summa Theologiae*, II-I, qu. 90. questioning the course of the queastio, these four elements are developed. The final definition is at the end in the answer to article 4.

[10] Thomas Aquinas, *Summa Theologiae*, II-II, qu. 57ff.

[11] Thomas Hobbes, *Leviathan* (1991), chap. 17, 1. Cambridge University Press, Cambridge.

of commands,[12] which were later interpreted by Austin as orders accompanied by sanctions for lack of compliance.[13] Locke assumed the preservation of property – understood in a wide sense to include life, liberty and ownership in material goods – as the main aim of law and politics.[14] The utilitarians still proposed a specific aim, but in a reduced form: maximizing happiness, understood as a collective effort to promote the individual and contingent states of pleasure and pain.[15] Kant defined law with respect to a liberal and very limited aim: Law comprehends the whole of the conditions under which the voluntary actions of any one person can be harmonized with the voluntary action of every other person, according to a universal law of freedom.[16] For Hegel, too, the aim of law is freedom.[17]

In the nineteenth and twentieth century, scepticism concerning necessary aims, value relativism, and a general positivism in the philosophy of science led to a nearly total dismissal of specific aims of law and politics and an almost exclusive reference to the means as the fundamental aspect of law. In England, John Austin characterized law as "sanctioned commands".[18] In Germany, Rudolf v. Jhering defined law in a purely formal way, namely, as the valid coercive norms of the state.[19] For him, norms and coercion are the crucial means of law. However, Jhering also proposes an aim of law, if only a relative and rather unspecific one: securing the fundamental conditions for the existence of a society.[20]

Hans Kelsen did not identify any specific aim of the law and the state. In his theory, law is distinguished from other social facts only by forming a hierarchical and dynamic system of coercive norms which confer validity on other inferior norms with a basic norm as the last necessary assumption and unifying ground of validity.[21] Law is differentiated from other similar social systems like morals only by its specific means: by the necessary use of coercion to guarantee obedience, and by its quality of being a dynamic system, that is, by the fact that the hierarchy of validity is based not upon correspondence in content but upon formal authorization.[22]

---

[12] Thomas Hobbes, *Leviathan*, chap 26, 1.

[13] John Austin, *The Province of Jurisprudence Determined* (1995), at 12, 21–37. Cambridge University Press, Cambridge.

[14] John Locke, *Second Treatise on Government* (1991), §§ 3, 6, 7, 123, 124. Cambridge University Press, Cambridge.

[15] Jeremy Bentham, *The Principles of Morals and Legislation* (1988), chap. 1, I at 1.

[16] Immanuel Kant, *Metaphysik der Sitten, Metaphyische Anfangsgründe der Rechtslehre*, § B.

[17] Georg Wilhelm Friedrich Hegel, *Grundlinien der Philosophie des Rechts oder Naturrecht und Staatswissenschaft im Grundrisse* (1970), works 7, § 40, p. 98, § 4, at 46. Suhrkamp, Frankfurt am Main.

[18] John Austin, *The Province of Jurisprudence Determined* (1995), at 12, 21–37. Cambridge University Press, Cambridge.

[19] Rudolf v. Jhering, *Der Zweck im Recht* (3rd ed. 1893), vol. 1, at 320.

[20] *Id.* at. 443. At 446, Jhering stresses the relativity of aims. At 511, both conditions are put together.

[21] Hans Kelsen, *Reine Rechtslehre* (1967), at 3, 196. Deuticke, Wien.

[22] Hans Kelsen, *Reine Rechtslehre* (1967), at 34. Deuticke, Wien.

H. L. A. Hart, too, finds the distinguishing feature of modern, developed law, "the heart of a legal system", only in means, namely, in a system of primary and secondary rules.[23] He identifies three forms of secondary rules: rules of change, rules of adjudication and a rule of recognition. The rule of recognition is in particular the necessary means to identify the other rules of law.[24] An aim of law is mentioned by him only in passing, and it is only a very unspecific aim, which holds for many other social facts. Hart says: "I think it quite vain to seek any more specific purpose which law as such serves beyond providing guides to human conduct and standards of criticisms of such conduct."[25] Joseph Raz, in his definition of law, omits the two-level requirement and adds "authority" as the decisive feature.[26] But "authority" is still another means – like norms, sanctions, and second-order rules. No one accepts authority as a final aim of law.

One of the few philosophers of law in the twentieth century who identified a specific and decisive aim of law (and, because of this, deserves of careful attention) was Gustav Radbruch. In a return to pre-modern roots, Radbruch proposed justice as the necessary aim or "idea" of law.[27] For him, justice (in a wider sense) encompasses three sub-aims[28]: justice as formal equality (formale Gleichheit), expediency (Zweckmäßigkeit), and the certainty of law (Rechtssicherheit).

What is the outcome of this brief history of attempts to identify a specific aim of politics and law? We have to look for aims of law and politics which satisfy two requirements: they must not be too abstract, for otherwise they would be worthless to distinguish politics and law from other human actions. Hart's proposal that law "governs human conduct" may be true, but it is much too abstract to serve as a specific aim of politics and law. Human conduct is governed by all kinds of things, including age, location, friendship, and the weather. At the same time, the proposed aims of politics and law must not be too specific if they are to hold for all kinds of politics and law, that is, if they are to serve as necessary conditions of the concepts of politics and law. For that reason, the good, justice, or equality, understood in a substantial way, could not be the conceptually necessary aim of politics and law. For, on the one hand, the good, justice, and equality have been, and still are, understood in very different ways. On the other hand, we assume that bad or unjust politics or law is still politics and law.

---

[23] H. L. A. Hart, *The Concept of Law* (2nd ed. 1997), at 98. Oxford University Press, Oxford.

[24] H. L. A. Hart, *The Concept of Law* (2nd ed. 1997), at 79. Oxford University Press, Oxford.

[25] H. L. A. Hart, *The Concept of Law* (2nd ed. 1997), at 249. Oxford University Press, Oxford.

[26] Joseph Raz, "Legal Positivism and the Sources of Law", in Raz, *The Authority of Law. Essays on Law and Morality* (1979). Oxford University Press, Oxford.

[27] Gustav Radbruch, *Rechtsphilosophie* (2nd ed. 2003), at 34. C. F. Müller, Heidelbereg.

[28] Gustav Radbruch, *Rechtsphilosophie* (2nd ed. 2003), at 54, 73. C. F. Müller, Heidelbereg.

2.2.3 What Is the Necessary Aim of Politics?

The necessary aim of politics is to act in representation of a community.[29] Even a dictator can be said to represent his people in a purely formal sense. This does not mean that this representation takes into account the interests of the represented. It requires only the general factual acceptance that somebody acts in the name of the people or the state. In distinction to other non-political communities the representation of political communities requires that the decisions of this representative can successfully claim to be the ultimate decision. That does not mean that the ultimate decision is always factually made by the representative of the political community. However, the representative of the political community claims effectively to decide who decides.

2.2.4 What Is Then the Necessary Aim of Law?

Law has the same basic necessary aim as politics and administration: to act in representation of a community. But beyond this first basic necessary aim, law has a second distinctive necessary aim (and, thus, necessary feature of its concept), namely the mediation between possibly contrary, conflicting concerns.[30] For instance, statutes mediate between various general concerns of people; judges' holdings mediate between interests in particular conflicts; administrative acts mediate between the specific wishes of individual citizens and/or the interests of the general public. Four elements of the necessary aim of law can be devised: (1) at least two concerns or interests, (2) which are contrary, (3) the possibility that these concerns may conflict and, (4) a form of mediation. What does this mean? There must be a weighing or considered decision between these possibly contrary concerns. That does not mean that law must be good or just in a perfectionist sense. The necessary condition is only that the entities which are of concern have to be taken into consideration in some way. If persons are murdered or if their homicide is ordered – that is, they are killed without a criminal inquiry or fair trial -, this cannot be law, because it does not mediate between actual or possible contrary concerns at all.

In this sense, killings in war are not law, though, of course, they may be allowed from the point of view of international law or ethics, for instance, as a means of self-defense. Similarly, for conceptual reasons the total disfranchisement of certain social groups cannot be law. Whether, for example, ancient slavery-"law" qualifies

---

[29] *See* Dietmar von der Pfordten, "Politik und Recht als Repräsentation", in *Recht und Politik*, Jan C. Joerden and Roland Wittmann eds., (2004), at 51–73. Steiner, Stuttgart.

[30] *See* Dietmar von der Pfordten, "What is Law? Aims and Means", in Archives for Philosophy of Law and Social Philosophy (ARSP) (2011) 97, at 151ff.

as law depends upon whether the concerns of the slaves were taken into account, even if only to a minimal degree. The conditions of law proposed here are relatively abstract and weak. Law cannot fulfill all or even the main demands of morality or ethics as its necessary aim. But it does have a conceptually necessary aim, without which it is impossible to identify a social fact as law. We may call this aim "justice" in some weak sense.

Now we can see what the form of law adds to politics and administrative decisions: Politics and administrative decisions can be reduced to a mere representation of the citizens by the rulers. So also the decisions of a dictator are both political and administrative decisions. These decisions can factually take into consideration all persons concerned with their interests. But this is contingent and not conceptually necessary. Here lies the main difference between politics/administration and law: When the form of law is used it is conceptually necessary that all persons concerned with their interests are taken into account. This does not guarantee a just or equal decision in a substantial sense. But it provides a first requisite for the chance of such a just and equal decision. It is therefore a crucial improvement for the individuals concerned.

So both the rule of law and the principle of legal state demand that politics and administrative decisions are made in the form of law. And this demand implies that all persons concerned with their interests are taken into account.

2.2.5 *What Distinguishes Law from Other Social Facts?*

By reference to this aim of mediation between possibly contrary concerns, we can distinguish law from many other social facts. But some social facts have the same or at least a similar aim or can at least have such an aim. This holds in particular for morals, politics, religion and non-moral conventions. Also these social facts will in reality often mediate between possible contrary concerns. Law can be distinguished from these social facts which have or can have the same or a similar aim by reference to its necessary and distinguishing means. What distinguishes law as a means from politics?

Law, in all its manifestations, is marked by a certain formality in its making, promulgation, or application, which simple political acts, for example, a decision in foreign politics, even in the form of a rule like the Monroe Doctrine or the Breschnew Doctrine, do not have.[31] So the distinctive feature of law in comparison to politics is its formality in all its singular instantiations (e. g. fixation in a document, certain procedures etc.). This formality lends support to legal certainty.

[31] *See* for a comprehensive study of the formality of law: Robert Summers, *Form and Function in a Legal System* (2006). Cambridge University Press, Cambridge. Summer's concept of formality is in many respects wider than necessary to distinguish law from politics.

The rule of law and the principle of the legal state demand therefore not only a mediation between possible contrary interests. They demand also that this mediation and decision is done in a formal and therefore more secure way. This is another crucial improvement by the rule of law and the principle of the legal state. But these requirements are hitherto purely conceptual. They explain only what takes place necessarily if we frame a political or administrative decision in legal form.

2.3 The Ethical Grounding of the Rule of Law

Having examined what it means to frame a political or administrative decision in legal form, it remains to be determined what justifies the demand for this form. So we do not yet know what justifies the demand to realize the rule of law or the principle of the legal state. In order to answer this question, the ethics of law must be considered.

Many theories are proposed within the realm of normative ethics. At least four competing groups of theories are especially prominent in the discussion: virtue ethics, utilitarianism or consequentialism, deontological ethics as represented most notably by Kantianism, and contractualism/discourse ethics. How should one orient oneself within this plurality of different approaches to normative ethics? There is one promising way to deal with the plurality of ethical theories. This possibility may be characterized as an "analytic-synthetic" method. The various theories can be analyzed into their elements and then assessed by comparing them with each other. If necessary, additional or modified elements may be added. Finally, they can be brought together by a synthesis. (I have tried to apply this method elsewhere and will here only present the core result).[32] All these theories embody what might be called the principle of normative individualism.[33] This principle has three parts:

1. Only individuals can be the ultimate point of reference of any justification of obligations and hence the justificatory source of law, morals and ethics. Collective entities such as nations, peoples, societies, communities, clans, families, or eco-systems, etc. cannot fulfill this function of last justification.
2. In the last instance, justifications of actions or decisions have to take into account all individuals affected by an action or decision, i.e., all "moral patients". We may call this the "all-principle" of normative individualism.
3. All individuals have to be taken into account prima-facie equally.

If normative individualistic ethics demands that all individuals have to be taken into account prima-facie equally as ultimate source of justification, then this holds true also for political and administrative decisions. Therefore, political and

[32] Dietmar von der Pfordten, "Five Elements of Normative Ethics – A General Theory of Normative Individualism", in: *Ethical Theory and Moral Practice* (2012) 15, at 449–471. deGruyter, Berlin, New York; Dietmar von der Pfordten, *Normative Ethik* (2010).

[33] *See* for a mentioning of individualism: Norberto Bobbio, L'Età dei Diritti, in: *L'Età dei Diritti* Norberto Bobbio ed. (1997), at 59. Einaudi, Torino.

administrative decisions have to be framed in a form which secures that all individuals are considered prima-facie equally with their interests. The best form we know that is able to realize and secure this is law, because law is by definition, as stated above, the form of human action which mediates between possibly conflicting interests and secures this mediation by its specific formality. Thus, normative individualistic ethics demands that political and administrative bodies use the form of law. So the rule of law and the principle of the legal state are justified by the ethical principle of normative individualism.

2.4 The Core in Which the Rule of Law and the Legal State/Rechtsstaat Coincide

Beyond this basic justification of the rule of law and the principle of the legal state, the principle of normative individualism can be used to specify the core in which the rule of law and the principle of the legal state coincide.

If individuals are the ultimate source of justification according to the first part of the principle of normative individualism, then these individuals should be assigned the highest value by the law: This justifies the first and most important part of the rule of law. It is already included in a personally limited form in the Magna Charta from 1215:

> 39. No free man shall be seized or imprisoned or stripped of his rights or possessions, or outlawed or exiled, or deprived of his standing in any other way, nor will we proceed with force against him, or send others to do so, except by the lawful judgment of his equals or by the law of the land. 40. To no one will we sell, to no one deny or delay right or justice.[34]

This important part of the rule of law was famously identified by A. V. Dicey in the following formulation: "We mean, in the first place, that no man is punishable or can be lawfully made to suffer in body or goods except for a distinct breach of law established in the ordinary legal manner before the ordinary courts of the land."[35] Normative individualism also explains why Dicey states the right to personal freedom as the first and foremost application of the rule of law that is the core of the individual human rights.[36] Similarly, the principle of the legal state/Rechtsstaat contains the individual human rights.[37] One has to admit that this was

---

[34] *See* Tom Bingham, *The Rule of Law* (2011), at 10. Allen Lane, London.

[35] A. V. Dicey, *Introduction to the Study of the Law of the Constitution* (10th ed. 1959), at 188. Macmillan, London.

[36] A. V. Dicey, *Introduction to the Study of the Law of the Constitution* (1959), at 206. Macmillan, London. See Tom Bingham, *The Rule of Law* (2011), at 66ff. Allen Lane, London. *See also* Danilo Zolo, "The Rule of Law: A critical reappraisal", in *The Rule of Law. History, Theory and Criticism*, Pietro Costa and Danilo Zelo eds., (2007) at 8. Springer, Dordrecht.

[37] BVerfGE 33, 367 (383); 34, 269 (286); 84, 90 (121); 111, 307; Christoph Degenhart, *Staatsrecht I. Staatsorganisationsrecht*, (29th. ed. 2013), at 60. C. F. Müller, Heidelberg; Grzeszick, in: *Maunz-Dürig*,

not the case in the nineteenth century, that is, at the beginning of the development of the principle of the legal state/Rechtsstaat. However, it was a development in the Weimar Republic and especially after World War II. Previously, the Rechtsstaat was only understood formally, now it is also materially understood.[38] To this corresponds a "thin" or a "thick" definition of the rule of law. Like the Rechtsstaat, the rule of law is now not only thin but thick.[39] That means it also includes such human rights as the right to life, the prohibition of torture, the prohibition of slavery and forced labor, the right to liberty and security, the right to a fair trial, the right to respect for private and family life, the freedom of thought, conscience and religion, the freedom of expression, the freedom of assembly and association, the right to marry and the protection of property etc.

If, according to the third part of the principle of normative individualism, all individuals shall be taken into account equally, this justifies Dicey's second part of the rule of law: "We mean in the second place, when we speak of the rule of law as a characteristic of our country, not only that with us no man is above the law, but (what is a different thing) that here every man, whatever be his rank or condition, is subject to the ordinary law of the realm and amenable to the jurisdiction of the ordinary tribunals."[40] The principle of the legal state/Rechtsstaat embraces the general principle/right that nobody is above the law and everybody is subject to the ordinary law.[41]

Dicey's reference to the Magna Charta and other historical documents of the British constitution as well as the historical process of the enactment of the constitution in the USA show another implicit demand of the rule of law which is also a demand of the principle of the legal state: the principle of constitutionalism. Both the rule of law and the principle of legal state require that the most important decisions of the political community are made in the form of a legal constitution which is superior to every other legal, political and administrative act.[42]

Law can fulfill its aim to mediate between possible conflicting interests and its function as a mean to be formal better if it does not only consist of singular case solutions, that is, singular contracts, singular judicial judgments or singular municipal

Grundgesetzkommentar, Art. 20, VII, nr. 37; Schnapp, in: *Grundgesetzkommentar* Bd. 1, v. Münch and Kunig eds. (6th ed.2012), Art. 20, Nr. 37.

[38] Christoph Degenhart, *Staatsrecht I. Staatsorganisationsrecht* (2013), at 60. C. F. Müller, Heidelberg.

[39] Tom Bingham, *The Rule of Law* (2011), at 66ff. Allen Lane, London.

[40] A. V. Dicey, *Introduction to the Study of the Law of the Constitution* (1959), at 193. Macmillan, London. *See* Tom Bingham, *The Rule of Law* (2011), at 55ff. Allen Lane, London. *See also* Danilo Zelo, "The Rule of law. A critical reappraisal", in *The Rule of Law. History, Theory and Criticism*, Pietro Costa and Danilo Zelo eds., (2007) at 7. Springer, Dordrecht.

[41] *See* Art. 20 II Grundgesetz and § 1 BGB. BVerfG NJW 1993, at 997 (998).

[42] *See* Tom Bingham, *The Rule of Law* (2011), at 25ff. Allen Lane, London; Klaus Stern, *Das Staatsrecht der Bundesrepublik Deutschland, Band 1, Grundbegriffe und Grundlagen des Staatsrechts, Strukturprinzipien der Verfassung* (2nd ed. 1984), § 20 III 4, at 784, 787f. C. H. Beck, München.

orders. There have to be general legal norms that is rules/laws, too.[43] So, both the rule of law and the principle of the legal state/Rechtsstaat embrace the demand to frame at least important legal decisions in a general form. Legal systems have developed different ways to attain this form of generality. One of the oldest ways is the system of precedents where several judgments form a general legal solution in the common law. Another way is the development of customary law which is realized, for example, by several singular contracts. A third way are statutes which are issued by a parliament or the executive. Written constitutions are a fourth modern form to attain this aim of generality of the law.

A mediation between possibly conflicting interests by the law takes into account the concerns of the individuals which are at stake only if it is not retrospective. This holds strictly for all forms of criminal trial. Nobody is able to obey duties and prohibitions if these do not exist before the action. So, there shall be no punishment without law (nullum crimen sine lege, nulla poena sine lege). This rule is both part of the rule of law and part of the legal state/Rechtsstaat (see Art. 103 II Grundgesetz).[44]

In order to mediate between possibly conflicting interests well and so take into account all individuals concerned, the formality of the law must include some additional requirements, such as accessibility/publication, consistency, clarity, definiteness. This is true for both the rule of law and the legal state/Rechtsstaat.[45]

While Dicey largely neglected the separation of powers and saw all sovereignty vested in parliament, nearly all modern interpreters have emphasized that the rule of law includes the principle of the separation of powers.[46] If politics and law are two different social forms, they have to be also distinguished institutionally. And, if law has to include general norms, one should distinguish the production of these general norms and their application. So we get the classical trias of executive, legislative and judiciary. Within English history, the distinction is between executive and judiciary. The legislative emerges later. The principle of the legal state/Rechtsstaat includes as an initial core element this separation of powers.[47]

If the existence of an independent judiciary is required, it must be accessible to the citizens and must give the citizens effective and fair legal protection. This is stated both by the rule of law and the principle of the legal state (see Art. 19 IV of

[43] *See* Friedrich Carl v. Savigny, *System des heutigen Römischen Rechts*, Bd. I, (1840), at 9f.; H. L. A. Hart, *The Concept of Law* (2nd ed. 1997), at 21ff. Oxford University Press, Oxford; Lon Fuller, *The Morality of Law* (2nd ed. 1969), at 46ff. Yale University Press, New Haven.

[44] *See* for the rule of law: Tom Bingham, *The Rule of Law* (2011), at 73ff. Allen Lane, London.

[45] *See* for accessibility Tom Bingham, *The Rule of Law* (2011), at 37ff. Allen Lane, London; *see* for clarity, definiteness and consistency: Christoph Degenhart, *Staatsrecht I. Staatsorganisationsrecht* (2013), at 142. C. F. Müller, Heidelberg.

[46] T. R. S. Allan, *Law, Liberty, and Justice. The Legal Foundations of British Constitutionalism* (1993), at 3, 48ff. Clarendon Press, Oxford.

[47] *See* Art. 20 II 2, III Grundgesetz; BVerfGE 3, 225 = BVerfG NJW 1954, 65 (66); Grzeszick, in: *Maunz-Dürig, Grundgesetzkommentar*, Art. 20, V, at nr. 2; Klaus Stern, *Das Staatsrecht der Bundesrepublik Deutschland, Band 1, Grundbegriffe und Grundlagen des Staatsrechts, Strukturprinzipien der Verfassung*, § 20 III 4, at 784, 792ff.

the German Grundgesetz).[48] A fair legal procedure includes several elements: the freedom from political or other external influence on the judges, the equal hearing of all parties (audiatur et altera pars), the search for comprehensive evidence, the application of the law via the acknowledged methods, the openness of the trial for the public, no inordinate delay of the trial, the principle of the "natural judge" (a judge predetermined by law), and no ad hoc courts etc.

While Dicey's original explications of the rule of law can be linked to the principle of normative individualism very easily and clearly, some modern definitions of the rule of law lost this clear linkage to normative individualism. This holds, for example, for the proposal of Lord Bingham: "The core of the existing principle is, I suggest, that all persons and authorities within the state, whether public or private, should be bound by and entitled to the benefit of laws publicly made, taking effect (generally) in the future and publicly administered in the courts."[49] Here, the individual is not any longer emphasized as a last resort for justification and the highest value of the law. On the contrary, individuals and authorities, that is collectives, seem to be placed on a somewhat equal level. This seems to be a very dangerous and unjustified modification compared to the initial formulation of Dicey.

2.5 Concrete Applications in Which the Rule of Law and the Principle of the Legal State Divide

Some more concrete applications of the rule of law and the principle of the legal state can neither be derived from the aim and mean that is the form of law (mediation of possibly conflicting interests, formality) nor – with one notable exception referred to below – from the ethical principal of normative individualism. Consequently, they are peculiar to specific legal orders and cannot be assumed as implications of a unified transnational rule of law/principle of the legal state. They are part of specific historic developments in different legal orders, different cultures and different times as demonstrated in the following examples.

The tying to a specific legal order holds for the third part of Dicey's understanding of the rule of law as it is applied in the United Kingdom. That is, the general principles of the constitution are the result of judicial decisions and not a result of a constitutional assembly.[50] Dicey states immediately that this judge-centeredness is peculiar to English constitutional law because of the common law tradition. This is different under many other constitutions and cannot be assumed to apply universally.

The principle of the legal state/Rechtsstaat is, by contrast, more centered on the formal constitution and the formal statute. It contains the requirement of a formal

[48] *See* Tom Bingham, *The Rule of Law* (2011), at 37ff., 90ff. Allen Lane, London. Christoph Degenhart, *Staatsrecht I. Staatsorganisationsrecht* (2013), at 164ff. C. F. Müller, Heidelberg.

[49] Tom Bingham, *The Rule of Law* (2011), at. 8. Allen Lane, London.

[50] A. V. Dicey, *Introduction to the Study of the Law of the Constitution* (1959), at 196. Macmillan, London.

that is written constitution.[51] And it contains the two doctrines of the necessity of the statute (Vorbehalt des Gesetzes) and the primacy of the statute (Vorrang des Gesetzes).[52] The doctrine of the necessity of the statute (Vorbehalt des Gesetzes) holds that every administrative act with negative consequences for human rights needs to be justified by a formal statute of a parliament.[53] The Bundesverfassungsgericht has stated, that essential decisions have to be made by a parliament (Wesentlichkeitstheorie).[54] The doctrine of the primacy of the statute (Vorrang des Gesetzes) holds that every statute of a parliament is primary to all judgments and administrative acts. It is clear that these doctrines are the consequences of a statute-centered legal system like the German system and the French and Italian ones but not of a common/case law system like the American and the British system.

This centeredness on the formal statute has in the legal state/Rechtsstaat also some consequences for the relationship to administrative rules (Verordnungen) and municipal and other public rules (Satzungen). According to Art. 80 of the German Grundgesetz, all administrative norms (Verordnungen) need some formal authorization by formal statutes. As a consequence of the bad experiences with Art. 48 of the Weimarian Constitution where blank authorizations lead to an avoiding of the parliament by the Nazis in the so called "enabling act" (Ermächtigungsgesetz), Art. 80 I S. 2 of the Grundgesetz strictly limits this authorization of the executive and administration. The scope of the authorization must be precisely determined in content (Inhalt), purpose (Zweck) and extent (Ausmass). Municipal norms (Satzungen) by cities and counties are limited to municipal matters which are part of the local autonomy. If they collide with human rights, they need some authorization by formal statutes, for example, in the case of local taxes. The same holds for other public norms, e. g. the norms (Satzungen) of public professional corporations.[55]

The principle of the legal state/Rechtsstaat also contains the principle of proportionality (Verhältnismäßigkeit). It holds that legal norms must be effective (Geeignetheit), they must use the most modest means (Erforderlichkeit) and purpose and means must be proportional (Angemessenheit, Verhältnismäßigkeit im engeren Sinn).[56] These are quite universal principles of rationality which are in principle also applicable in the systems of the rule of law. But they have to be implemented by political or legal decisions because they are not mere logical or conceptual requirements.[57] If individuals are the ultimate source of justification according to the principle of normative

---

[51] Grzeszick, in: *Maunz-Dürig, Grundgesetzkommentar*, Art. 20, VII, at nr. 30.

[52] BVerfGE 58, 257 = BVerfG NJW 1982, 921 f.; Grzeszick, in: *Maunz-Dürig, Grundgesetzkommentar* (2012), Art. 20, VI, at nr. 72ff., 99, VII, at nr. 26.

[53] Grzeszick, in: *Maunz-Dürig, Grundgesetzkommentar*, Art. 20, VI, at nr. 117. Christoph Degenhart, *Staatsrecht I. Staatsorganisationsrecht* (2013), at 329, 331. C. F. Müller, Heidelberg.

[54] BVerfGE 49, 89 (126).

[55] German Bundesverfassungsgericht, BVerfGE 33, 125 (158f.).

[56] Christoph Degenhart, *Staatsrecht I. Staatsorganisationsrecht* (2013), at 157ff. C. F. Müller, Heidelberg. *See*, *Verhältnismäßigkeit*, Oliver Lepsius ed. (2014), forthcoming.

[57] *See* for such an implementation in the European Union: Art. 52 of the Charter of Fundamental Rights of the European Union.

individualism, then these individuals should be protected by the necessity to take into consideration their interests, which is prescribed by the principle of proportionality.

Beside these differences in form, procedure and proportionality there also exists one very central material difference between the rule of law and the principle of the legal state/Rechtsstaat. This is the protection of human dignity. The Anglo-Saxon legal tradition does not explicitly include the protection of human dignity as such, but only some main applications of it: the prohibition of torture, slavery etc. Human dignity is neither found originally in the common law, nor in the American Declaration of Independence, including the Bill of Rights of the American Constitution. The European Convention of Human Rights from 1950 which was heavily influenced by the United Kingdom does not contain a protection of human dignity but only partial norms like the prohibition of torture, slavery and degrading treatment. And even in Lord Bingham's recent book, *The Rule of Law*, human dignity is not mentioned.[58]

This is different for Continental Law. After the U.N.'s Universal Declaration of Human Rights put human dignity into prominence in 1948, many European Countries followed sooner or later, for example, the German Grundgesetz 1949 in Art. 1: "Human dignity is inviolable." (Die Würde des Menschen ist unantastbar). The protection of human dignity is also found in many other constitutions.[59] Finally, the Charter of Human Rights of the European Union articulated the protection of human dignity in the preamble and Art. 1: "Human dignity is inviolable. It must be respected and protected." This adoption has also consequences for the principle of the legal state. If the principle of the legal state is not only understood formally any more but also materially, as we saw above, then it includes all human rights. But if it includes all human rights, then it must contain also the first and most important of these human rights: the protection of human dignity.[60]

Human dignity is not only a historical or cultural particularity. It is a main result of normative individualism because it expresses human autonomy that is the relationship between the second and first order concerns of human beings.[61] So if the rule of law is not only thin but thick and does include all human rights, it must consequently be further developed to include also the protection of human dignity.

---

[58] One exception in legal philosophy is Lon L. Fuller who mentions human dignity: Lon Fuller, *The Morality of Law* (1969), at 162. Yale University Press, New Haven.

[59] *See* Paul Tiedemann, *Menschenwürde als Rechtsbegriff. Eine philosophische Klärung* (3rd ed. 2012), at 51. Berliner Wissenschafts-Verlag, Berlin.

[60] *See also* Klaus Stern, *Das Staatsrecht der Bundesrepublik Deutschland, Band 1, Grundbegriffe und Grundlagen des Staatsrechts, Strukturprinzipien der Verfassung* (2nd ed. 1984), § 20 III 1, at 781. C. H. Beck, München.

[61] *See* Dietmar von der Pfordten, *Normative Ethik*, (2010) at 74ff. Steiner, Stuttgart; Dietmar von der Pfordten, "Some Remarks on Human Dignity", in *Human Dignity as a Foundation of Law*, Winfried Brugger and Stephan Kirste eds. (2013), at 13–23; Dietmar von der Pfordten, "On the Dignity of Man in Kant", in *Philosophy* (2009) 84, at 371–391.

Chapter 3
Philosophical Foundations of the Principle of the Legal State (Rechtsstaat) and the Rule of Law

Stephan Kirste

Abstract The aim of this paper is to establish freedom as an embracing concept of the legal state and the rule of law. At times, especially by positivist scholars on the continent and i.e. Dicey in England, 'legal state' and 'rule of law' have been interpreted as seemingly antagonistic conceptions. If a broader concept of law is applied, the opposition between the two principles can be overcome. From this philosophical point of view they can be understood as two formulations of a common goal, distinct in some results and institutional settings, but united in a core value. For this purpose I understand law as a system of norms the enactment and enforcement of which is organized by procedures, which are themselves subject to norms. Because of this structure, law addresses freedom and is at the same time an expression of freedom. As a norm, law addresses freedom by directing the choice between alternative actions; these norms open and limit areas for the enactment, adjudication and enforcement of norms and actions. Accordingly, the principle of the legal state and the rule of law base public authority on legal freedom. Both principles can thereby be intrinsically connected to democracy. Against the narrative of antagonistic principles, my article will sketch how the development of the concept of the legal state is heavily indebted to the rule of law and has only towards the end of the nineteenth century gone a separate path.

S. Kirste (✉)
Department of Legal and Social Philosophy, Faculty of Law, Paris Lodron University of Salzburg, Salzburg, Austria
e-mail: stephan.kirste@sbg.ac.at

J.R. Silkenat et al. (eds.), *The Legal Doctrines of the Rule of Law and the Legal State (Rechtsstaat)*, Ius Gentium: Comparative Perspectives on Law and Justice 38,
DOI 10.1007/978-3-319-05585-5_3,

3.1 The Common Goal of the Rule of Law and the Principle of the Legal State

One does not have to trace the common roots of the rule of law and the principle of the legal state back to Antiquity in order to justify them.[1] The assumption that both are strictly distinct principles is itself a historical side product of the late nineteenth and early twentieth century theory of public law positivism ("Staatsrechtspositivismus");[2] a product that was adopted by Anglo-American scholars as well.[3] When the principle of the legal state was elaborated between the aftermath of the French Revolution and the German revolution in 1848/9, it was clear that, just like under the British rule of law, the German state, too, should be a limited state that serves freedom. Freedom was thus the common goal of both, the rule of law and the limited state.[4] Freedom is also the root back to which, in both conceptions, their respective limiting principles were traced.

3.1.1 Mutual Influences

Authors on both sides of the Canal found historic roots for the necessity of Government founded on and limited by laws in Germanic traditions.[5] Whereas in the United Kingdom the rule of law continuously developed from the Norman times and is expressed in the great declarations beginning with the Magna Carta Libertatum in 1215, its nucleus can be found in the Holy Roman Empire of German Nations; but

---

[1] Brian Tamanaha *On the Rule of Law. History, Politics, Theory.* (2004), 7 ff. Cambridge: Cambridge University Press.

[2] Differences were emphasized, for example, by Horst Dreier " Rechtsstaat" in *Enzyklopädie Philosophie.* H.J. Sandkühler Ed. (2010) 2265–2272. Hamburg: Meiner.

[3] From the British perspective, *see* Gianluigi Palombella "The Rule of Law and its Core" in Gianluigi Palombella and Neil Walker *Relocating the Rule of Law* (2009) 17 ff. Oxford and Oregon: Hart Publishing.; from the American perspective, *see* Michael Rosenfeld "Rule of Law versus Rechtsstaat" in *Menschenreche und Bürgerrechte in einer vielgestaltigen Welt,* Peter Häberle and Jörg Paul Müller eds. (2000) 49–71. Basel, Genf, München: Helbig & Lichtenhahn; from the German perspective, see Ernst-Wolfgang Böckenförde, "Entstehung und Wandel des Rechtsstaatsbegriffs" in Ernst-Wolfgang Böckenförde, *Recht-Staat-Freiheit.* (1991) 143–169 Frankfurt/Main: Suhrkamp; for a closer association of the two principles *cf.* Neil MacCormick "Der Rechtsstaat und die Rule of Law" in *Juristenzeitung* (1984) pp. 65–70.

[4] *Cf.* von Hayek, who equates "Rule of Law" and "legal state", thus we read "Rechtsstaat" in the German translation, wherever rule of law is used in the English original, Friedrich Hayek (1944): *Road to Serfdom.* London 1944, S. 75 f., 85 f.

[5] von Gneist traces the "Rechtsstaat in England" back to "Carolenean institutions" ("karolinische Grundeinrichtungen"), Rudolf von Gneist *Der Rechtsstaat und die Verwaltungsgerichte in Deutschland.* (1879) 37; *cf.* also the differentiated picture Tamanaha *supra* note 1 at 23 f. where he applies a very broad term of "rule of law"; for a more coarse picture *see* Samuel J. M. Donnelly "Reflecting on the Rule of Law: Its Reciprocal Relation with Rights, Legitimacy, and Other Concepts and Institutions" in *Annals of the American Academy of Political and Social Science* No. 603 (2006), pp. 37–53, p. 42 ("The English-speaking countries of the world are renowned citadels of the rule of law").

they never formed a very coherent principle. Government too was bound by natural law and the basic laws of the Empire; these did not, however, have the character of individual or group rights designed to serve freedom. That the "law makes the king" to foster the reasonableness and justice of his decisions is at the core of the rule of law.[6] The Staufer Emperor Frederic II. also accepted limitations to his government; they stemmed, however, from the transcendent forms of natural law and reason, whereas the laws that founded and limited the king in Bracton's view, came from the incarnated natural law in the form of laws, customs and court rulings.[7] In the continental tradition, the limitation of government remained mostly outside the realm of positive laws. In England, the natural law received, on the contrary, an institutionalized and historical form as the not (necessarily) written rule of law. This distinction was famously made by Lord Chief Justice Edward Coke (1552–1634), who emphasized the different rationalities of natural law and the rule of law.[8] The "fixed rule of law" provided a much more precise "golden metwand" (Coke) than any natural law could. This form required experience and artistry as the basis of legal argumentation – and not philosophical reasoning – as Edmund Burke put it later, thereby following Coke.[9] The laws as expressions of historical processes and covenants together with the artistry and artfulness of their interpretation provided the exclusion of arbitrariness in government. The result did not necessarily contradict natural law and reason, but achieved its goals in a form tested and established by history. Accordingly, William Blackstone (1723–1780) could rightfully hint at the similarities of both, the continental limiting of government by natural law and the rule of law tradition:

> *Nec regibus infinita aut libera potestas* [kingly power is neither free nor unlimited], was the constitution of our German ancestors on the continent. And this is not only consonant to the principles of nature, of liberty, of reason, and of society, but has always been esteemed an express part of the common law of England, even when prerogative was at the highest[10]

At the turn of the nineteenth century, the many descendants of the "German ancestors" did not want to rely merely on natural law. To some of them, the independence of the former North-American Colonies and their Constitutionalism as well as the French Revolution had proven that the time had come for a transformation of natural law into the founding documents of government. Later, as the demand for the positive form of the rule of law arrived at the Continent, the expectations for its realization rested not so much with the courts or the administrations but with the state as a legal person. "Come to England and study England", claimed Friedrich Murhard (1778–1853), who praised the English rule of law as an ideal

---

[6] Henry of Bracton II *De Legibus et Consuetudinibus Angliae*. George E. Woodbine Ed. (1922) 33 Yale: Yale University Press ("quia lex facit regem … Noluit enim uti viribus, sed iudicio").

[7] Ernst H. Kantorowicz, *Die zwei Körper des Königs. Eine Studie zur Theologie des Königs*. (1999) 164 f. u. 163. Stuttgart: Klett.

[8] Case of Prohibitions, 12 Co Rep 64, [1607] EWHC KB J23, 77 ER 1342, zit. nach http://www.bailii.org/ew/cases/EWHC/KB/1607/J23.html, last checked Dec. 15th 2013.

[9] Edmund Burke II *The Works of Edmund Burke with a Memoir* (1836) 461.

[10] William Blackstone, *Commentaries on the Laws of England, 3rd ed.* (1768) 233 f.

model of a monarchy "under the sovereign rule of law" with the strongest respect for the rights and liberties of the individual.[11]

Although he shied away from the idea of a revolution, Immanuel Kant marks the beginning of the discussion of the principle of the legal state.[12] He defined law through freedom and even based, and limited, the state with respect to freedom. A "State (Civitas)" properly understood, is "the union of a number of men under juridical Laws".[13] Only then would the state be a republic, if it had a representative government, the powers of which were separated between and administered by the different institutions of legislation, administration and jurisdiction. All use of public authority should be intrinsically justified by freedom. He expanded his concept on the relations of states, inspiring contemporary calls for an international rule of law. It is remarkable enough that the first author to write a monograph on the principle of the legal state, Robert von Mohl, was inspired by both, Kant and the British tradition of the rule of law. A scholar of comparative law, Mohl intensely studied the laws of England before he wrote his book on the "Rechtsstaat" which influenced all further discussions about the principle. He claimed that "in modern times the idea of the legal state belonged mostly to the English"[14] – obviously without distinguishing the idea of the legal state from the rule of law. In particular, he praised English liberties as models for German fundamental rights.[15] However, the "master piece" of the rule of law was, from his point of view, the American Constitution[16] for it combined "highest respect for the laws with the uppermost freedom of individual behavior" and the representation of the people with the necessary authority of the state.[17]

The longer and the more successfully the American Constitution was interpreted and applied by the US Supreme Court, the more the American understanding of the rule of law supplanted the English understanding. When Carl Josef Anton Mittermeier (1787–1867) called on the people to "read the American Constitution!", he did not only intend to observe the achievements of the Supreme Court for the

---

[11] Friedrich Murhard "Englands Verfassung" in *Staats-Lexikon oder Encyclopädie der Staatswissenschaften*, Hrsg. V. C.v. Rotteck u. C. Welcker, Fünfter Band, (1837), S. 84–171 at 161 ("Die Rechte und Freiheiten des Individuums nehmen in Englands Grundgesetzen den ersten Platz ein, und die Engländer sind so stolz und eifersüchtig auf ihre so lange behaupteten Rechte und Freiheiten, daß König und Parlament, ohne mit Gewißheit vorauszusehende größte Gefahren, es nicht würden wagen können, sie anzutasten").

[12] For a deeper analysis of the history of the principles of the rule of law and the principle of the legal state, *cf.* Stephan Kirste, "Die Rule auf Law in der Deutschen Rectsstaatstheorie des 19 Jahrunderts", in *Jahrbuch fur Recht und Ethik* (2013) 23 ff. Berlin: Duncker & Humblot.

[13] Georg Wilhelm Friedrich Hegel *Philosophy of Right*. (2001), Transl. by S.W. Dyde, § 45, at 165. London: George Bell and Sons.

[14] Robert von Mohl *Die Geschichte und Literatur der Staatswissenschaften Erster Band*. (1855), quotation transl. by Stephan Kirste, 33.

[15] Robert von Mohl *Die Geschichte und Literatur der Staatswissenschaften, Zweiter Band*, (1856) 4.

[16] Robert von Mohl, "Story, J., Commentaries on the Constitution of the United States, with a preliminary review of the Constitutional History of the Colonies and States, before the Adoption of the Constitution". in *Kritische Zeitschrift für Rechtswissenschaft und Gesetzgebung des Auslandes* No. 7 (1835) 1–25, p. 17.

[17] *Von Mohl supra* note 14 At 519.

improvement of the rule of law based on its "enormous powers", but also the improvements for the freedom of the people.[18]

Later in the nineteenth century, another important scholar, Rudolf von Gneist (1816–1895), contributed to the elaboration of the principle of the legal state by extensively analyzing the "English Freedom".[19] Whereas von Mohl was primarily influenced by the natural law tradition, von Gneist was more interested in the institutional framework of the rule of law. He found the idea of self-government – in the German transformation of "self-administration" – an important check in the balance of powers and a form of the realization of positive freedom. Self-government and the rule of law, this was about what could be achieved in the nineteenth century German Reich.[20] In accordance with Josef Anton Mittermaier he trusted in the consciousness of the people ("Volksbewußtsein") as the "guarantor" of freedom and the "legal state"[21] and less in the constitution. Participation of the people in government and in courts would then be the "security and bond" of private liberties.[22]

[18] Quoted from Horst Dippel, *Die amerikanische Verfassung in Deutschland im 19. Jahrhundert. Das Dilemma von Politik und Staatsrecht*. (1994) 164. Meisenheim/Glan.

[19] Eduard Fischel, *Die Verfassung Englands*. Berlin (1862) 32 ff. The German-American, Hans Lieber, has it that "englisch-amerikanische Freiheit sich vor Allem durch entschiedenes Streben, die Unabhängigkeit des Einzelnen zu kräftigen, und durch das Gefühl des Selbstvertrauens auszeichnet ... die Individualität ist fast vernichtet im Absolutismus (mag er nun monarchischer oder demokratischer Art sein), während höchste Freiheit (nach englisch-amerikanischer Anschauung) die Individualität eines Jeden ans Licht und die besondere Thätigkeit von Jedem, nach seinem Gutdünken, in die freiest Bewegung bringt. Unabhängigkeit auf der höchsten, mit Wohlfahrt und breiter volksthümlicher Sicherung der Freiheit verträglichen Stufe ist das grosse Ziel englisch-amerikanischer Freiheit, und Selbstvertrauen ist die Hauptquelle, woher sie ihre Kraft schöpft", Hans Lieber "Beilage, Englische und Französische Freiheit" in Mittermaier, Carl Joseph Anton *Die englische Staatsverfassung in ihrer Entwicklung nach der neuesten Schrift von E. S. Creasy* (1849) 23–40, at 29.

[20] Paul Kahn, *The Cultural Study of Law: Reconstructing Legal Scholarship* (1999) 15 f. Chicago and London: Chicago University Press. ("The rule of law is not just the sum total of the statutory and regulatory output at any given moment; it is also understood as a process of evaluating and creating new laws that corrects the deficiencies of what came before ... The state of law ... stand opposed simultaneously to the divine and to the merely natural. The perfect image of this set of ideas may be that of the signing of the Mayflower Compact, which we imagine stripped of its theocratic context. On one side of the Atlantic appeared the false claim to a politics of divine will; on the other side appeared nature as wilderness without political order or history. History begins with a communal act of will, imposing a reasonable order on self and polity. This is the beginning of law's rule").

[21] "Die durch den Zwischenbau [der Selbstverwaltung, SK] geschaffenen Garantien des 'Rechtsstaats' sind aber wesentlich vollständig; es fehlt darin kaum ein Glied, welches zum Schutz des individuellen Rechtskreises im Staat erforderlich scheint. Es liegt darin vor Allem die Realität der sogenannten Grundrechte ...", von Gneist *supra* note 5 at 60 and at 37 "aus England ... im Gegentheil nur die Wahrheit zu entnehmen, dass die politische Freiheit nicht anders als in ununterbrochener Anknüpfung an das überkommene Recht des Landes zu gewinnen ist, und dass die erstrebte Freiheit. nach englischem Vorbild nur dadurch entstehen kann, wenn jedes Volk seine Verwaltungsorgane in gleichem Sinne der Stetigkeit mit der heutigen Ordnung der Gesellschaft verbindet".

[22] Lieber, *supra* note 19. At 31.

3.1.2 *Conceptions of the Opposition of the Rule of Law and the Principle of the Legal State in the Positivistic School of Public Law*

The positivistic school of public law ("Staatsrechtspositivismus") in Germany distinguished the theory of constitutional and statutory laws, separating it methodically from the legal argumentation in private law and conceptually both from social and from such philosophical ties as historical developments or natural law.[23] Richard Thoma (1874–1957), for example, understood the principle of the legal state as a clear and firm demarcation line between the state and the spheres of individual freedom in the civil society.[24] Influenced by debates about the German nation, this school also distinguished the principles of German law from the principles of other traditions. Warnings, not to copy the US-American or British tradition of the rule of law had already been articulated in the 1848 debates in the Paulskirchen Parliament, but only in the late nineteenth century did they become prevalent. Even Georg Jellinek (1851–1911), generally much in favor of the American constitutionalism, emphasized the positivist indifferentism of the English and American laws towards any content.[25] Jellinek was positivist also in his assumption that the state is prior to the law and that laws only constrain its supreme powers. The rule of law became a rule of laws.[26] He was interested in the primacy of the constitution over the laws, the idea of the recognition of natural rights in a positive form and their democratic legitimation in the United States, the system of checks and balances, the authority of the courts, and, in particular, in the US Supreme Court.[27] More than other scholars, his perspective sheds light on the potential of law not only to protect freedom, but also to be an expression of freedom. Up until today, German conceptions of this freedom, however, tend to emphasize its public character, namely the political autonomy of the people, and not its form as an individual right. Some scholars still hold the positivist assumption that the difference between the rule of law and the legal state with respect to the "distinction between civil society and state" consists in the fact that the rule of law would permeate society and state, whereas the principle of the legal state would protect the separation of society and state.[28]

---

[23] Dreier *supra* note 2. At 2265 and 2267.

[24] *Id.*

[25] Georg Jellinek, *Gesetz und Verordnung. Staatsrechtliche Untersuchungen* (1887) 3 ("Mit dem Worte 'law' wird ununterschiedlich Alles bezeichnet, was aus den verschiedensten Rechtsquellen kommend den mannigfaltigsten Inhalt haben kann").

[26] And for this particular conception, Palombella *supra* note 4 at 20, is indeed correct, claiming that "law is not the constraint but rather the 'form' of the state's will".

[27] Georg Jellinek, *Ein Verfassungsgerichtshof für Österreich* (1885) 55 f. He draws the conclusion from this, at 60 "Ein Bundesstaat ohne Verfassungsgericht ist kein Rechtsstaat im vollen Sinne", see also Georg Jellinek, *Verfassungsänderung und Verfassungswandlung* (1906) 16 f.; for further problematization of a Constitutional Court: Georg Jellinek *Allgemeine Staatslehre* (3rd ed. 1959) 615.

[28] Böckenförde *supra* note 4 at 143 ff.; Palombella *supra* note 4 at 17 f.

Obviously, legal doctrine did not end its development at the age of state legal positivism. The "constitutional state" ("Verfassungsstaat"), which is receptive to supranational and international norms, is the present form of the legal state. Laws are not merely forms in which a state, preexistent to the constitution would express itself. The state rather fulfills supreme constitutional demands. These constitutional obligations are imposed for the sake of freedom. From the point of view of freedom, the principles of the rule of law and the legal state do not seem as distinct as the positivist assumption suggested. If the legal state does not only paternalistically provide laws for presumably immature people – recall the nineteenth century constitutional monarchies – the participation of the people in the creation of these laws also has to be guaranteed. This democratic state must be founded on freedom. If democracy shall not become a despotic form of government, it must be founded and limited by preexisting fundamental rights. Neither does the legal state exist before the constitution, nor is positive law, legitimated by the legal subject, valid without the state. Both have to be founded through individual freedom. This common goal of both principles is expressed in Art. 2 of the Treaty on European Union which mentions as European values in the German wording "Menschenwürde, Freiheit, Demokratie, Gleichheit, Rechtsstaatlichkeit und die Wahrung der Menschenrechte" and in the official English version "human dignity, freedom, democracy, equality, the rule of law and respect for human rights".

3.2 The Foundation of the Rule of Law and the Legal State in Freedom

3.2.1 The Form of Law

Can this common assumption about the foundation of the rule of law and the legal state in law and of law in freedom be justified philosophically? In order to show that it can, I will reconstruct both principles from the form of law.

Modern law can be understood as a system of norms.[29] A norm is law if its enactment and enforcement are subject to other norms. Norms are sentences containing an obligation. They aim at regulating human behavior by commands, prohibitions or permissions. Norms become positive by enactment, the conclusion of a contract or other forms of recognition. This voluntary act is the facticity that raises the question whether it is law or just an act of arbitrariness. An arbitrary command may contain a norm. What distinguishes it from law is that the legal norm is being enacted in an organized procedure. This norm-setting procedure is again regulated by

[29] For the following *cf.* Stephan Kirste *Einführung in die Rechtsphilosophie* (2010). Darmstadt, 87 ff.; Stephan Kirste "The Human Right to Democracy as the Capstone of Law" in: *Human Rights, Democracy, Rule of Law and Contemporary Social Challenges in Complex Societies*. Hrsg. v. B. A. Rocha, K. Salgado, M. C. Galuppo, M. Sette Lopes, Th. B. Silva dos Santos u. a. Belo Horizonte (2013), S. 103–120, IV.

the respective norms for legislation, procedural law for courts and administrations and contract law. Constitutions, laws, statutory instruments, international and private contracts are kinds of legal norms in this sense. Accordingly, the setting of a norm is a necessary condition for its positivity. However, it is not a sufficient condition of a norm's legal form. In order to be law the respective norm must be enacted in a normatively ordered procedure. This definition of law avoids the narrow association of state and law and permits the analysis of legal pluralism, namely the pluralism of different sources of law, which is characteristic for the rule of law as well as for the legal state in a supra-national and international legal environment.[30]

Some authors consider the enforcement of norms or the general efficiency of a legal order a necessary condition of law. Indeed, many legal norms can be distinguished from moral or conventional rules by their enforcement. On the one hand, this is not true for all legal norms and on the other hand, there are other social norms that can react with sanctions on their violation. Many norms of international law cannot be enforced by public authorities. The debate about humanitarian interventions shows that the question if and how the violation of human rights should be enforced and sanctioned requires a decision between alternative forms to make them efficient.[31] An impolite and insulting behavior in a conversation as a violation of a conventional rule can result in a termination of communication as a sanction to this insult. If other norms and conventions can also be enforced and if different forms of enforcement are possible, then enforcement itself is not a distinctive feature of law. What distinguishes the mere use of force such as torture, brutal punishment, war and others from legal enforcement is that the enforcement of legal norms is organized in legal procedures, justified and limited by other norms: the enforcement laws. Accordingly, it is not the facticity of their enforcement that bestows norms their legal character, but that they are enforced in procedures organized by norms. Necessary and sufficient conditions for a norm to be law then are the normative regulation of its enactment and enforcement.

Because of the normative organization of the enactment and enforcement of its norms, law is not a mere facticity, but evaluates and regulates the possible actions for its genesis and realization. Law can therefore include the criteria for its validity and does not need to shift them to other normative systems, thereby transgressing the dichotomy of facticity and validity. Legal orders themselves concretize the general concept of law and specify the criteria for legal validity of their respective norms. Accordingly, legal validity signifies the matching of a legal norm into the system of a concrete legal order. To refute possible objections, it should be emphasized here that this concept of legal validity does not imply anything regarding the moral or social validity of law.

As a normative system, law aims at controlling free actions. In contrast to force or subconscious control, norms presuppose that their addressees are capable of acting alternatively and determining one of the alternatives as preferable. They also

---

[30] Palombella, *supra* note 4 at 21, 24.

[31] Dietrich Murswiek, "Souveränität und humanitäre Intervention" in: *Der Staat* No. 35 (1996) 31–44.

enable freedom by permitting legal possibilities for action. The reflective structure of law provides the possibility that legal norms are expressions of freedom, but not the actualization of this possibility.

These normative systems determine the content of the legal obligations (demands, prohibitions, permissions) and the legitimation of them. In morality, the regulation of behavior follows self-commitment, because there is no external power to bind the individual moral consciousness. Moral norms have to be accepted by the individual in order to have practical relevance for its action. This is the basis for his autonomy, understood as the ability to act according to self-determined laws. Only law can legitimately enforce norms against the will of its addressee. If the law merely enforces its norms without giving the addressee any influence on its establishment, he is subjected to a heteronomous regulation of his behavior. This basic model (*model of security*) of law secures the enforcement of its commands, but shifts the legitimation of them to other normative or social systems. The respective norm can be legitimate, but this legitimation stems at least in part from extra-legal factors such as the authority of the ruler, a moral justification of its content or positive consequences of the norms for the common good etc. However, the addressee of the obligation of these norms is deprived of the influence he has with respect to moral norms: Regarding moral norms, the individual can decide whether or not to accept this norm as a guideline for his or her action.[32] Now, the complexity of law can be increased if the individual is given the possibility to decide about the foundation of obligations. Contractual obligations are legitimate if the partners of contracts act upon their private autonomy. Generally binding rules are, in this sense, legitimate if they are expressions of the wills of the addressees of these norms (*model of autonomy*).

Both, the security model and the autonomy model of law concern only law (and not other normative systems, e.g., morality). They are distinguished by the differentiated use they make of the conceptual potentials of law. Different specifications of the concept of law with respect to the legitimation of its norms between the two models are possible. A legal order following the model of autonomy, including the individual at each step of the enactment and enforcement of its norms, is then more differentiated than a system in the security model. Autocrats that submit the use of force to certain procedures, but protect norms which serve their own interest only, are over-simplistic then, because they shift the problems of norm-justification and justice to other normative and social systems.

[32] Hannah Arendt. *On Revolution* (1990) 130. München: Pieper. ("Tyranny, as the revolutions came to understand it, was a form of government in which the ruler, even though he ruled according to the laws of the realm, had monopolized for himself the right of action, banished the citizens from the public realm into the privacy of their households, and demanded of them that they mind their own, private business. Tyranny, in other words, deprived of public happiness, though not necessarily of private well-being, while a republic granted to every citizen the right to become 'a participator in the government of affairs', the right to be seen in action").

3.2.2 Freedom and Law

If norms are aimed at freedom, because they regulate the choice between alternative actions and if law orders the choice between regulatory and enforcement alternatives of these norms, then freedom is at the core of legal regulation.

Individual self-determination, viewed in this way, is the central meaning of the modern concept of freedom.[33] In a negative sense, freedom means the independence of the self from heteronomy. The positive meaning of freedom is the ability of the self to determine the motives of its action. This dimension is also called "autonomy." The individual is free in his actions if the motives for them are self-determined – autonomous and not originating from any heteronomous influence. Accordingly, freedom is not a given attribute, but a quality the individual has to produce itself by transforming the external facts into one's own. The individual is free if and insofar as the self is not something objectively given, but produced by him on the basis of an autonomous choice among different motives. Legal freedom, then, is the possibility for a person to determine his own action not being subjected to any other person. This freedom is especially secured when legal norms provide individual rights. An individual right is a norm that puts an obligation on the addressee of the right and gives the subject of the right a claim to the fulfillment of this obligation.[34]

The subject of this right cannot naturalistically be understood as a human being. The attribution of an individual right rather transforms the human being into a legal person by making it the subject of the right and the point of attribution of its claim. Law reconstructs the natural human being as a legal person by the individual rights it attributes him or her. The individual constructs itself as free by morality and is recognized in its social identity by the autonomy of people. This implies a free decision whether to recognize the individual as a legal person or not. And indeed the Nazis and other totalitarian regimes misused this factual freedom to deny human beings this recognition. Since this denial would render the individual a mere object of the state, his or her dignity demands the recognition of all individuals as legal persons.[35] This right to be acknowledged as a legal subject is the basis of all further rights. All further human rights reconstruct the human being as a legal person more concretely. Understood as opportunities to express ones freedom in law, they strengthen his or her state of being free. This way, not only the legal form is an expression of freedom, but also the individual right and the legal subject.

If a right is attributed to a person, this person is legally free in a negative sense, because he or she can avert illegal infringements of his or her freedom. The person is also free in a positive sense, because, within the sphere of freedom guaranteed by the right, that person can determine his or her actions autonomously. If laws

---

[33] Böckenförde, *supra* note 4 at 42.

[34] Stephan Kirste "§ 204. Die naturrechtliche Idee überstaatlicher Menschenrechte" in *Handbuch des Staatsrechts*, Vol. 10 P. Kirchhof und J. Isensee Eds. (2012) 1–30 and marginal note 1. Heidelberg: C.F. Müller; Robert Alexy *A Theory of Constitutional Rights*. (1996) (original: Theorie der Grundrechte. Frankfurt/Main. 1996), 120 ff.

[35] *Cf.* Art. 6 UDHR: "Everyone has the right to recognition everywhere as a person before the law."

would stop specifying the persons' potentials at this stage, freedom would only be realized in the sense of the security model: the subject is free with respect to the protection by this right, but not with respect to its foundation, justification and interpretation. In the words of Georg Jellinek: the *status subiectionis*, *status negativus* and *status positivus* are secured.[36] According to this model, the law has indeed only an instrumental function for the security of freedom.[37] At the same time the positive freedom of persons is limited, because they are not part of the founding of their rights.

In the conclusion of a contract, positive freedom is guaranteed by the private autonomy of the parties. The mutual obligations and rights are expressions of autonomy of the contracting parties. If their enactment would remain within the security model, these rights would not be expressions of the subjects' positive freedom.[38] Rights would be granted in a paternalist way to the advantage of the individual, but without his or her consent.[39] Obligations would be heteronomous. The justification of these rights and duties would stem from social consequences and moral values, but not from legal grounds. Positive freedom of the individual is guaranteed only if he or she can participate in the creation of the individual rights and duties.[40] Thus, for the realization of positive freedom deliberation, decision and interpretation of human rights have to be organized in public discourses, which are open to the participation of all subjects of these rights and duties.[41] Without negative human rights, law is self-contradictory, since it is necessarily directed towards freedom; without active human rights in the *status activus*, the catalogue of human rights is incomplete. Both are necessary and sufficient conditions for the reconstruction of law on

[36] Winfried Brugger "Georg Jellineks Statuslehre: national und international. Eine Würdigung und Aktualisierung anlässlich seines 100. Todestages im Jahr 2011" in *Archiv des öffentlichen Rechts* No. 136 (2011) pp. 1–43, at 1 ff.

[37] Böckenförde, *supra* note 4 at 42. (Human rights declarations "sind zumeist aus dem Streben nach Befreiung von staatlicher Übermacht und die Freiheit mißachtendem Recht entstanden. Doch schon an ihnen zeigt sich, daß zwischen Freiheit und Recht ein notwendiger und begrifflicher Zusammenhang besteht: Freiheit muß, damit sie Bestand und Sicherung erhält, als Recht formuliert und anerkannt werden").

[38] With respect to the concept of human rights, they are indivisible. *See*, Robert Alexy "Die Institutionalisierung der Menschenrechte im demokratischen Verfassungsstaat" in *Philosophie der Menschenrechte*, Stefan Gosepath, Georg Lohmann Eds. (1998) 244–264, p. 261 Frankfurt: Suhrkamp; nineteenth century constitutionalism has shown, however, that the realization of the two aspects of autonomy can fall apart.

[39] For the concept of paternalism as benevolent action towards another without his will, *cf.* Stephan Kirste "Harter und Weicher Rechtspaternalismus unter besonderer Berücksichtigung der Medizinethik" in *Juristenzeitung* (2011) 805 ff.

[40] Georg Jellinek Die Entstehung der modernen Staatsidee. In: *Schriften und Reden*, Vol. 2. (1911) 45–63, 53 f. ("Frei ist derjenige, der niemand unterworfen ist als sich selbst; das ist die zweite weltgeschichtliche Nuance der Freiheitsidee in der neueren Geschichte. Neben den liberalen tritt der demokratische Freiheitsgedanke").

[41] Heiner Bielefeldt, *Philosophie der Menschenrechte. Grundlage eines weltweiten Freiheitsethos* (1998) 107 f. Darmstadt: Wissenschaftliche Buchgesellschaft.

the basis of freedom.[42] The active status of political autonomy as the basis of a right to democracy then rounds up the legal status.[43]

Legal freedom is thus only fully realized if it is not only protected by individual rights, but if these rights are also expressions of autonomy. This autonomy again is realized, whenever the individual actively participates in the enactment of norms in the broadest sense – in the framing of a constitution, in legislation, the enactment of administrative statutes, the interpretation of his rights and duties in forensic trials or in the conclusion of contracts.

A particular legal order that does not only protect and limit freedom, but in which the enactment of its norms is organized in a participatory way, builds the complete structure of law on freedom. Freedom is then not only a protected and limited value but the protections and limitations are themselves expressions of freedom. Law may be defined as a norm the enactment and enforcement of which is regulated by other norms. A legal order realizes the potentials of freedom contained in the concept of modern law, if the enactment and justification of its norms are expressions of self-determination, just as the enforcement of its norms respects the freedom of the persons concerned, and if it delimits the freedoms of the citizen in a just way and enables freedom, where the individual is incapable of doing so himself. Because the legal form itself is not conceptualized as external to freedom, but rather derived from the concept of freedom, it needs no further legitimation. The reflective structure of law does not only organize this freedom, but also the freedom to decide between alternative norms and alternative modes of enforcing the norms. If a legal order makes only minimal use of the potentials of freedom in the concept of law, because, e.g., an autocratic ruler enforces unjust norms, the freedom of its subjects has to find a way to articulate itself outside the law. This would weaken it. However, if in the autonomy model the enactment and enforcement is organized in a way that the people concerned can deliberate and decide about their rights and duties themselves and can realize their freedom in the adjudication and enforcement of them as much as possible, then this legal order realizes the potentials of the concept of modern law and strengthens its structure.[44]

[42] To make it clear: A limited government may obey the rule of law without being democratic (*see* Brian Tamanaha "A Concise Guide to the Rule of Law" in Gianluigi Palombella and Neil Walker *Relocating the Rule of Law*. (2009) pp. 3 ff., 13. Oxford and Oregon: Hart Publishing). However, it does not realize its potentials with respect to freedom then.

[43] At the international level *cf.* 67/1 Declaration of the High-level Meeting of the General Assembly on the Rule of Law at the National and International Levels, I, 5 ("We reaffirm that human rights, the rule of law and democracy are interlinked and mutually reinforcing and that they belong to the universal and indivisible core values and principles of the United Nations").

[44] *Aristotle* already knew that, although he considered democracy to be unrealistic for his time: "… a fundamental principle of the democratic form of constitution is liberty – that is what is usually asserted, implying that only under this constitution men participate liberty, for they assert this as the aim of every democracy … And one is for a man to live as he likes; for they say that this is the function of liberty, inasmuch as to live not as one likes is the life of a man that is a slave. This is the second principle of democracy" (Aristotle *Politics* Engl. Transl. by H. Rackham (1967) VI, 2, 1317a 40-b 17, at 489–491).

3.3 Legal Freedom, the Rule of Law and the Principle of the Legal State

As a legal person, the individual has a generally recognized status for his or her freedom that is, on the one hand, protected by laws and in a democratic state, and on the other hand, also is the expression of legal autonomy.[45] Since the discovery of "The King's two Bodies"[46] – the natural and the legal – in medieval times, legal scholars and philosophers have tried to reconstruct government and state as a legal person as well. After the concept of the legal person had been applied in canon law for centuries and, beginning in the nineteenth century, also in civil law, the concept was applied to public law and in particular to the state later in the nineteenth century. First restricted to the fiscal government, the concept of the legal person later became a focus of all competences and duties attributed to the state. Georg Jellinek claimed that the state together with his legal order created itself as a legal person by self-obligation. Hans Kelsen (1881–1973) finally conceived of the state as a mere personification of the law. Here, indeed, "the law makes the king".[47]

The concept of the state as a legal person permits the understanding of the relationship between the individual legal person and the state as a legal person as a purely legal relationship and as the basis of public authority. Natural, moral or other possible forms of freedom and rights have to be reconstructed by constitutions and laws in order to become legally relevant.[48] In this transformed validity, they have all the legitimation the constitution and constitutional laws can provide. All claims and duties have to be articulated by constitutions, laws and fundamental rights, constituting a "Government of laws and not of men" (Art. 30 Mass. Constitution). The constitution, supranational and public international norms and the laws regulate the form of government. The systematic relation of these pluralistic legal sources is changing and their hierarchy and the criteria to solve their collision is still a matter of debate. All institutions of government receive their legitimation from the constitution or the legal order (hierarchy of norms) as supreme norms. They are supreme,

[45] This is all a metaphysical concept (in this sense *see* Palombella *supra* note 4, at 19), but a mere legal construction; although the concept of the legal person had metaphysical roots in the concept of "persona moralis" (*see* Pufendorf and others), it is decisive that these metaphysical roots were decidedly cut off by scholars like Friedrich Carl von Savigny; *cf.* Stephan Kirste, "Dezentrierung, Überforderung und dialektische Konstruktion der Rechtsperson" in *Verfassung – Philosophie – Kirche* (Festschrift für Alexander Hollerbach zum 70). Geburtstag. Hrsg. v. J. Bohnert, Chr. Gramm, U. Kindhäuser, J. Lege, A. Rinken u. G. Robbers (2001) 319–361, at 335 ff. Berlin: Duncker & Humblot.

[46] Kantorowicz *supra* note 7.

[47] *Cf. supra* note 6.

[48] This does not preclude that in a moral sense, in England "the law of the constitution, the rules which in foreign countries naturally form part of a constitutional code, are not the source but the consequence of the rights of individuals, as defined and enforced by the Courts", Albert Venn Dicey *Introduction into the Study of the Constitution* (1915) 120.

because they are expressions of the constituent power or the constitutionally unrestricted public autonomy of the people.[49]

The constitution and laws compatible with the constitution lay the fundaments of all public authorities and limit the extent of their powers. This means that all government is founded on a constitution (be it written, laid down in several constitutional laws or unwritten)[50] and acts upon laws that have a higher authority if they have the legitimation of the parliament. These rules govern the actions of the state as well as of the people:[51] it must therefore "be capable of guiding the behavior of its subjects".[52] To be able to do that, these laws must not be retroactive and have to be determinate in order to provide a secure orientation of actions and expectations.[53] This government is limited by fundamental rights. Infringements of these rights are only legitimate if they are proportionate.[54] If a government acts outside these limitations – ultra vires – or violates the liberties of the people in another way, it is liable for this action and responsible for the actions of its civil servant officers. This limitation does not merely apply in relation to the citizens, but also to the government itself. The "inner" sphere of state and government are no legally free areas like the French *droit administrative* or the former German "*besonderes Gewaltverhältnis*" ("special factual power relationship"[55]).[56] It may only act on the basis of its competences rendered to them and within the framework of the constitution. In this perspective, not only functional checks and balances or the distinction of powers comes into focus, but also aspects of federalism: The federal state, regionalism,

[49] Alexander Hamilton, James Madison, John Jay, *The Federalist*, G. W. Carey, Ed. (2001), § 49, at 261. Indianapolis: Liberty Fund; Dieter Grimm "§ 1. Ursprung und Wandel der Verfassung" in *Handbuch des Staatsrechts der Bundesrepublik Deutschland*, J. Isensee, P. Kirchhof Eds. 2–45 and marginal note 28. (The idea of a constituent power does not preclude limitations by other (moral, natural) norms or rights, but only by the former or future constitution).

[50] In the constitutional state the state does not, legally speaking, exist "before" or outside the law, but is founded on the law and receives its legal identity from it.

[51] Insofar the German tradition speaks of the "principle of the legal state in a formal sense", this understanding comes close to Tamanaha's concept of "the rule of law in a thin sense", *see* Tamanaha, *supra* note 42.

[52] Raz calls this "the basic intuition from which the doctrine of the rule of law derives", Joseph Raz (1979): The Rule of Law and Its Virtues. In: *The Authority of Law: Essays on Law and Morality*. Oxford 1979, p. 214. Oxford: Oxford University Press.

[53] *See* Dicey *supra* note 48. At 120 ("man may with us be punished for a breach of law, but he can be punished for nothing else"). This is pretty much the content of the old rule: "nulla poena sine lege praevia".

[54] David Beatty, "Law's Golden Rule" in Gianluigi Palombella, and Neil Walker *Relocating the Rule of Law* (2009) 99–116. Oxford and Oregon: Hart Publishing.

[55] Due to the concept that the legal person can only act legally "outside" itself, the German doctrine of public law, presupposed a merely factual relationship of civil servants, pupils in public schools, soldiers or inmates. As far as this special relationship was concerned they were supposed to have either no or only limited protection by constitutional rights; Dicey correctly criticized this an the French concept of "administrative law" *of his time* as being incompatible with the rule of law, Dicey *supra* note 48. At 120.

[56] Gernot Sydow *Parlamentssouveräntität und Rule of Law* (2005) 10 f. Tübingen: Mohr.

devolution or self-administration and self-government activate the autonomy of the people to take part in the enactment and administration of their rights. The constitutional and legal foundation and limitation of government is controlled by independent courts and judges. In their procedures, the individual legal persons have a hearing, because, in the interest of their active freedom, the interpretation of their rights should consider their views. Individual participation of the people in different forms, in trials, self-administration and self-government, equal democratic participation in the perspective of the rule of law or the legal state add to the system of checks and balances. In this sense, laws regulate the content of public authority and of public actions.[57]

Accordingly, the rule of law and the legal state as founding principles of the state can be reconstructed from freedom. Analyzed from this perspective, the formalistic and legalistic interpretation of the principle of the legal state by legal positivism yields an understanding of the parliamentary statutes as expressions and safeguards of freedom. Particular legal orders may, of course, further specify them and distinguish these principles from fundamental rights, democracy, and separation of powers.[58] But in a philosophical perspective, it remains relevant to recognize the focal point of all these structural principles of government or state in the idea of freedom. This does not imply that democracy and justice are necessary parts of the rule of law or the principle of the legal state. In particular, the constituent powers are free to give these principles a more narrowly defined meaning. The reconstruction in the light of freedom shows, however, the links of a public government, based and limited by the law with these values.

With this perspective of freedom, the rule of law and the principle of the legal state on the one hand and justice on the other, are no contradictions,[59] because the former is to be understood in the perspective of the latter and because the elements of justice are not only equality and dignity, but also freedom.[60] Both, the rule of law and the legal state serve freedom as an element of legal justice.

[57] Some authors distinguish this "thick concept of the rule of law" (Tamanaha *supra* note 42 at 4) or "materieller Rechtsstaat" ("legal state in a material sense") from the formal principle.

[58] Dreier *supra* note 2. At 2268.

[59] After the Re-Unification of Germany, one of the East German civil rights activists, Bärbel Boley, claimed: "Wir wollten Gerechtigkeit und bekamen den Rechtsstaat" ("We wanted to achieve justice, but received the legal state instead"), quoted by Ingo von Münch "Rechtsstaat versus Gerechtigkeit" in *Der Staat* No. 33 (1994) 165–184. At 165.

[60] Kirste *supra* note 29. At 125, 132 ff.

Chapter 4
Rule of Law (and *Rechtsstaat*)

Martin Krygier

Abstract In all its many versions, the rule of law has to do with the relationship between law and the exercise of power, particularly public power. As an ideal, it signals that law can and does well to contribute to articulating, channeling, constraining and informing – rather than merely serving – such exercise. Beyond that, what it rules out, what it allows, what it depends on and indeed what it is, are all matters of disagreements that stem from differences among political and legal histories and traditions, but also reflect dilemmas and choices that recur, in different forms and weights, in many such histories and traditions. This entry is concerned with these enduring themes, dilemmas and choices, as they occur within particular traditions, especially the common law 'rule of law' tradition', on the one hand, and the Continental Rechtsstaat tradition, on the other.

From the last quarter of the twentieth century, the rule of law has come to occupy an increasing amount of discursive space, not only among lawyers, for whom it had been an old theme, but also among promoters of economic development, human rights, democratization, state-building, political and legal reform. Increasingly, it is alleged, the rule of law is a key ingredient in the attainment of all these good things and others. As one author has observed,

> Among a plethora of development and security agencies, a new "rule of law consensus" has emerged. This consensus consists of two elements: (1) the belief that the rule of law is essential to virtually every Western liberal foreign policy goal – human rights, democracy, economic

This article will be published in *The International Encyclopedia of Social and Behavioral Sciences*, second edition, W. Darity Jr editor in chief, Copyright Elsevier 2015.

M. Krygier (✉)
Gordon Samuels Professor of Law and Social Theory, University of New South Wales, Sydney, Australia

Adjunct Professor, Regulatory Institutions Network, Australian National University, Canberra, Australia
e-mail: m.krygier@unsw.edu.au

J.R. Silkenat et al. (eds.), *The Legal Doctrines of the Rule of Law and the Legal State (Rechtsstaat)*, Ius Gentium: Comparative Perspectives on Law and Justice 38,
DOI 10.1007/978-3-319-05585-5_4, © Springer International Publishing Switzerland 2014

> and political stability, international security from terrorist and other transnational threats, and transnational free trade and investment; and (2) the belief that international interventions, be they through money, people, or ideas, must include a rule-of-law component. (Call 2007, 4)

In this transformation, the rule of law has gained a great deal in modishness but less, actually nothing, in clarity. But clarity was never the concept's strong suit. Like many other important moral, political and legal ideals, among them democracy, justice and liberty, its meaning, scope, conditions and significance are all highly, perhaps essentially contested (Waldron 2002). And like those ideals, not only are there enduring common themes but also common axes of argument and disputation that pervade discourse on the rule of law. As suggested elsewhere (Krygier 2011, 69), these contests do not render such concepts meaningless or useless. On the contrary, some of them are the most important we have. We will not resolve those contests, here or anywhere, but it might be possible to clarify a few of them and suggest why they – and the rule of law – are important.

The concept of the rule of law embodies ideals that have figured in political and constitutional discourse at least since Aristotle, who contrasted 'the rule of the law' with 'that of any individual'. Those ideals have varied, so too the strategies to achieve them and the verbal formulation of them. They revolve around enduring themes and concerns, however, the character of which is nicely captured by Otto Kirchheimer's laconic observation that:

> for all the differences in historical roots and particular legal traditions their common denominator lies in the simple thought that the security of the individual is better served when specific claims can be addressed to institutions counting rules and permanency among their stock-in-trade than by reliance on transitory personal relations and situations. Beyond that, a good part of their common success probably lies in the mixture of implied promise and convenient vagueness. (Kirchheimer 1996, first published 1967, 244)

In all versions, the rule of law has to do with the relationship between law and the exercise of power, particularly public power. As an ideal, it signals that law can and does well to contribute to articulating, channeling, constraining and informing – rather than merely serving – such exercise. That takes us some distance from those who see law simply as one of the means by which power is exercised, neither better nor worse than any other. For there are lots of ways to exercise power; partisans of the rule of law insist that it helps us block some of them, including many of the worst of them (see Rundle 2009), and to channel others in salutary directions and ways. But what it rules out, what it allows, what it depends on and indeed what it is, are all matters of disagreement. This is so for several reasons, often stemming from differences among political and legal histories and traditions, but also reflecting dilemmas and choices that recur, in different forms and weights, in many such histories and traditions.

4.1 Law and State

These days, and in contemporary language, the words 'law' and 'state' are rarely far apart. However, it was not always and everywhere so, and even now it makes a difference whether the connection is seen as necessary or contingent, even more so whether it is seen as a conceptual rather than an historical connection. A clue to this comes from the terms used in various languages. In particular, there is an obvious semantic difference between 'rule of law,' the term used in English, and those found in many European languages to cover some, but not all, of the same terrain. Each of these has a context and a history that cannot be ignored or simply elided, but in a host of European languages there is one thing commonly built into the concept, which is missing from the English phrase: the State. Whether it is *Rechtsstaat* (German: (state of law; law-governed state)), *état de droit* (French), *statto diritto* (Italian), *estado de derecho* (Spanish), *państwo prawa* (Polish) or *pravovoe gosudarstvo* (Russian), law is inextricably connected to the state. It is the subject – grammatically and ontologically – of each rendition. However, the rule of law does not mention the state. This is not an accident.

The concept of the state is not part of English constitutional jurisprudence, while in Australia and the United States it refers to what Germans would call *Länder* (see MacCormick 1984, 65). More deeply, the English tradition was long pluralistic in its conceptions of the sources of law (Rosenfeld 2001), with multiple cumulative and competing authoritative sources, among them custom, court decisions and statutes. Indeed, while the common law courts were long agents of the Crown, some of the mythologically most powerful contests in the English rule of law tradition, particularly the constitutional struggles of the seventeenth century, pitted them against successive wearers of that Crown, even at the cost of the head of one of those (Charles I); what might in other countries be called the head of State.

According to the common law tradition, popular custom, an antient collection of 'unwritten maxims and customs' (Blackstone [1765–9] 1979, vol. 1: 17) was long seen as a primary source of law, and '[t]he only method of proving, that this or that maxim is a rule of the common law, is by shewing that it hath been always the custom to observe it' (Blackstone [1765–9] 1979, vol. 1, 68). That custom was evidenced (rather than made, it was claimed) by another non-legislative source, the judgments of courts in particular cases brought to them. This was the 'common law' (Krygier 1998), which seventeenth century partisans of the rule of law preferred to the commands of the King; 'Law established by customary practice, law that was not the creation of will, command, or sovereignty, was a restraint on government – a restraint on discretionary power (Reid 2004, 12). True, the courts were the King's courts, but the law they adjudicated was not, in the main, considered to be the King's creation. It was not just an instrument with which the Crown and the state could direct activities and control public policy. For the King, like his subjects, was subject to 'the law of the land.'

Deliberate, secular, purpose-guided, prosaic (not sacred) legislation, as Max Weber observed, is a central and distinctive characteristic of modernity in law (see Weber 1968, 760–68). Today, of course, in its exponential rush since the eighteenth century (see Lieberman 1989), legislation has swamped custom and even judicial decisions as a quantitatively primary and increasingly imperious source of law, in the common law world as elsewhere. However, the notion that the rule of law draws upon sources other than legislative fiat, that the judiciary is a fundamental guardian of it, and that all, even the most powerful, are and should be subject to it, goes deep in the common law tradition and has not lost resonance. It was expressed in many ways over centuries, but the canonical connection between the term 'rule of law' and those thoughts came to displace other descriptors, primarily as a result of the hugely influential late nineteenth century work by. A.V. Dicey (1961 (first published 1885)). Dicey's formulations distilled (and in some respects distorted) a very old English legal tradition.

No parallel existed in the nineteenth and early twentieth century *Rechtsstaat.* The term was coined only at the very end of the eighteenth century (Heuschling 2002, 29), to capture a new phenomenon, the modern State with its monopoly of force. That state was the subject of this concept, and also the legal source of law. The *Rechtsstaat* ruled *by or through* law, whereas other states, such as the *Machtstaat* (state of power) or *Polizeistaat* (police-state) (see Raeff 1983) might dispense with it and exercise power in other ways. What was distinctive of a *Rechtsstaat* was not that the state was subject to law that had other sources and independent guardians, but that it acts in a *rechtlich* way; 'according to some nineteenth century (and early twentieth-century) constructions, there is a relation of near-identity between the state and its law … within the system of rule the law is the state's standard mode of expression, its very language, the essential medium of its activity' (Poggi 1978, 102). That is how we recognize it as a *Rechtsstaat,* as distinct from any other type of state. There was no conceptual space to say to the State what Sir Henry Bracton already said in the thirteenth century:

> The king has a superior, namely God. Also the law by which he is made king. Also his *curia,* namely the earls and barons, because if he is without bridle, that is without law, they ought to put the bridle upon him. (quoted in Reid 2004, 11, and see Palombella 2010, *passim*)

That is an important rule-of-law claim.

4.2 Arbitrary Power: Uncontrolled or Unruly

That the law should rule even over the most powerful people and institutions is a very old theme in the English legal tradition. The rule of law is commonly contrasted with *arbitrary* exercise of power; that, above all, is the evil that the rule of law is supposed to curb. This leads to another difference, this time masked rather than revealed by semantics. For arbitrariness is itself an ambiguous concept. Is it, for example, 'uncontrolled interference' or 'interference that is not subject to established rules' (Pettit 2012, 58)? These are two of several (see Richardson 2002, chapter 3) conceptions of the concept. They have particular relevance to law; the former commonly being referred to as 'government *under* law', the latter as 'government *by* law.' If one had to choose, there are strong arguments to favor the former over the latter (see Pettit 2012), but ideally one would encounter the first always, and in exercises of public power the second as well. Not everyone opposed to 'arbitrary power' has had both these senses in mind, however.

As we saw, the common law tradition, from at least the thirteenth century until well into the eighteenth, maintained that the king was subject to a law that he had not made, indeed that made him king. For the king, for anyone, to ignore or override that law was to act arbitrarily (see Reid 2004; Palombella 2010). Liberties, and procedures to protect them such as habeas corpus and due process, were enshrined in that law, and encroachment on such liberties was barred, even to the monarch, by the law. That that law was often *not* expressed in clear, prospective, general rules (see Maitland 1965, first edition 1908, 383), today regarded as the essence of the rule of law, was not to the point (Reid 2004). Indeed, given the customary, dynamic, fluxful, and evolutionary character of the common law as theorized by its adepts, it was beside the point (see Postema 1986, chap. 1). The issue was that it was superior.

From the eighteenth century, however, law came to be viewed increasingly as the direct or indirect product of the political legislator, the 'sovereign', and in English law there was, at least arguably until very recently as a result of EU membership, no legal superior to the sovereign legislator. The conception of the rule of law gradually became more preoccupied with the character of the rules that the sovereign enacted: they should be clear, prospective, consistent, etc.

Shocked by this downgrading of the notion of a law superior to the sovereign, and by what they regarded as their own 'arbitrary' treatment by the British sovereign Parliament (Reid 2004), the American colonists first staged a revolution, and then a pathbreaking innovation: a written constitution binding on the legislator, and in due course routinely overseen by an independent Supreme Court, whose decisions also came to be seen as binding on the legislator. This was a novel way of vindicating a very old principle. In England, old conceptions persevered, but in increasing tension with the legislative bias of modernity.

On the Continent, things were different. A *Rechtsstaat* was not just any sort of state, as we have seen, but one which operated on the basis of legal rules configured in particular ways. '[S]ituated at the heart of the theory of the *Rechtsstaat* is the question of the arbitrariness of power, of the potential violence inscribed in all relations of domination, whether private or public' (Heuschling 2002, 42). However, partisans of the *Rechtsstaat* did not envisage a law superior to the state, a basis for appeal to some higher notion or other source of law. Law was a characteristic of the *Rechtsstaat,* but it was also its *product*. The non-arbitrary *rechtlich* quality of the state was a matter of the degree to which its edicts took the form of general rules that conformed to specific formal criteria and were supposed, in particular, to guarantee certainty and predictability. In this understanding, '[t]he *Rechtsstaat* means that the law is the structure of the State, not an external limitation to it. … Liberty is a consequence not truly a premise of the law. The authority vested in this conservative aristocratic state protected civil liberties as a service offered through the State' (Palombella 2010, 11–12).

The notion that state agencies must comply with a law above the State, only came with the development of written and legally binding constitutions, particularly in reaction to the Nazi calamity in the middle of the last century. Until then, although 'it was in the state's interest to promote its self-limitation through self-binding to legal norms' (Loughlin 2010, 320), and the people's interest too, it was up to the state to bind itself (*Selbstbeschränkung*). Whereas the common law tradition frequently, and in the seventeenth century vociferously, conceived of individual rights as protected by the courts *against* the Crown, no such opposition existed in the German conception of the *Rechtsstaat* (see Rosenfeld 2001, 1319), which, as Leonard Krieger shows, projected 'older national assumptions which made the idea of liberty not the polar antithesis but the historical associate of princely authority' (Krieger 1957, 5). The contrast is deep. As Gozzi observes:

> In Germany … the doctrine of the *Rechtsstaat* precludes the possibility of the primacy of law over the state. Indeed, it is precisely in the relationship between law and state – which in the German case is settled with the primacy of the state – that the most significant feature of the doctrine of the German *Rechtsstaat* emerges. Conversely, the English doctrine of the government of law is most clearly distinguished by grounding the rule of law on the superiority of law as proclaimed by the courts of justice. (Gozzi 2007, 238)

From the point of view of those subject to the exercise of power, both its control and its manner of exercise, government under and by law, are important. But they are not the same. A state could be controlled but act under decrees with quite particular targets, kept secret from citizens, or inconsistent with each other, or retrospective, or without any decrees, let alone laws, at all. It could, conversely, be uncontrolled but act through promulgated, clear, consistent etc. laws. In either case, something significant would be lacking. For where arbitrariness in either of these senses is linked with significant power, it at the very least raises the reasonable apprehension that it will tend to: threaten the *liberty* of anyone subject to it; generate reasonable and enduring *fear* among them; and deprive citizens of sources of reliable sources of expectations of, and *coordination* with, each other and with the state. And as Lon Fuller (1969) and Jeremy Waldron (2011a) have emphasized, it threatens the *dignity* of all who find themselves mere objects of power exercisable at the whim or caprice of another.

These are four good reasons to value reduction of the possibility of arbitrary exercise of power (see Krygier 2011, 79–81). There may well be many others, such as those that commend themselves to many economists, having to do with the alleged contribution of the rule of law to economic development (Dam 2006). To the extent that the rule of law can help deliver such reductions, this is reason to value it. This is not, of course, merely a negative matter of removing evils, but can be expressed positively. A society in which law contributes to securing freedom, confidence, coordination and dignity, is some great and positive distance from many available alternatives. There are other things we want from law, and many more things we might want in a good society, but ways of serving these values are goods immeasurably harder to attain without institutionalizing constraints on arbitrariness, in both these senses, in the exercise of power.

For some thinkers, speculating in these ways about what good might flow from reducing arbitrariness in the exercise of power, what it might be *for,* takes us beyond the analytical task of understanding what the rule of law *is*; for others it doesn't get us close to what matters. The former favor 'thin' accounts; the latter lard their accounts of the rule of law with more ingredients and of different kinds. These are often known in the literature as 'thick' accounts of the rule of law.

4.3 Thin or Thick

Apart from questions of control versus character of law, writers on the rule of law often distinguish between 'thin' or 'formal,' on the one hand, and 'thick', 'substantive', or 'material' conceptions of it, on the other. The former limit themselves to formal properties of laws and legal institutions, that are purported to constitute the rule of law. The latter require substantive elements from a larger vision of a good society and polity – democratic, free-market, human rights respecting, or some such – to be present.

The first tack is favoured by modern analytical jurists. They have often adopted (Hart 1967, 273–74) or extended (Raz 1979; Walker 1988) Lon Fuller's eight principles of what he called 'the morality of law' as defining characteristics of the rule of law, even when they disagreed with him over whether they deserved to be called moral principles. According to Fuller (1969), these were that there must be rules, these must be publicly available, prospective, understandable, consistent, possible to perform, sufficiently stable for citizens to orient their actions by them, and administered in ways congruent with their terms. There is controversy over whether there is any reliable connection between such thin principles and substantive values beyond them (see Krygier 2010, 114–20) but whatever the view on that, on a thin conception those further values are something other than the rule of law.

Again, the *Rechtsstaat* has oscillated between thick and thin through its 200 years of evolution. It was first theorized by German liberal constitutional and administrative theorists, prominent among them Karl Rotteck, Karl Theodor Welcker and Robert von Mohl, seeking to characterize a legal order in terms of values it served (those values in their turn to be realized *in* and not *against* the state). The post-Nazi *Rechtsstaat* returned to, and richly amplified, a normative characterization based on the fundamental value, inscribed in the first article of the German Basic Law of 1949, of human dignity. However, in between times, after the failure of the 1848 revolutions and particularly under and after Bismarck, its late nineteenth century and early twentieth century versions were pared of normative adhesions, and strictly devoted to elaborating the formal components of a legal order that might properly be called a *Rechtsstaat.*

Not only legal philosophers, but also legal comparativists (see Peerenboom (ed.) 2004) tend to favour 'thin' versions of the concept, what might be called rule-of-law-lite: easier to identify and able to travel further, because it carries less baggage. Many governments, too, particularly authoritarian ones, prefer to be assessed against thin formal criteria, easier to satisfy than thick morally demanding ones. Today international businessmen, unwilling to buy into controversial questions about democracy, human rights and other large values in, say, Singapore and China (with both of which they might want to do business), often prefer a formal, thin, conception too.

Many, however, find thin conceptions quite inadequate. Ronald Dworkin, for example, was skeptical of conventional 'rule book' conceptions of the rule of law, which insist that 'so far as is possible, the power of the state should never be exercised against individual citizens except in accordance with rules explicitly set out in a public rule book available to all … Those who have this conception of the rule of law do care about the content of the rules in the rule book, but they say that this is a matter of substantive justice, and that substantive justice is an independent ideal, in no sense part of the ideal of the rule of law' (Dworkin 1985, 11). He, by contrast, regarded the rule of law as incorporating an ideal and an eminently positive and substantive one, 'the ideal of the rule by an accurate public conception of individual rights' (Dworkin 1985, 11–12).

The sociologist Philip Selznick had a more complex combination of thin and thick. He agreed with those political realists who stressed the importance of strict legality as a restraint on, and saw the rule of law as a precious protection against abuse of, power (Selznick 1992, 174). On the other hand, he insisted that there was a 'larger promise of the rule of law,' and this 'thicker, more positive vision speaks to more than abuse of power. It responds to values that can be *realized,* not merely protected, within a legal process. These include respect for the dignity, integrity, and moral equality of persons and groups. Thus understood, the rule of law enlarges horizons even as it conveys a message of restraint' (Selznick 1999, 26).

In Germany, the circumstances which moved prevailing conceptions of the *Rechtsstaat* from thin to thick were more dramatic than those that preoccupied Dworkin and Selznick. Indeed they were tragic. Already in the Weimar Republic, Hermann Heller rejected the legal positivist, formalistic, conception of the *Rechtsstaat* as crystallized by his contemporary, Hans Kelsen, which could accommodate any state. He argued for one that insisted that only a democratic state, that depended upon and then institutionalized fundamental ethical principles, was a *Rechtsstaat* (for the debates between Carl Schmitt, Kelsen and Heller, which centred on the nature of the *Rechtsstaat,* see Dyzenhaus 1997). Though Heller died in 1933, he already saw fascism as the great threat to such a state. His nightmare became real in the ensuing years.

In the perspective of German post-Nazi retrospection and introspection, thin conceptions came to seem not merely inadequate, but on their own positively dangerous. The *Rechtsstaat* embodied in post-War German jurisprudence thus embodies a strong commitment to fundamental rights and to the dignitarian premise of its 1949 *Grundgesetz* or Basic Law (see Grote 1999), grounded in its unamendable Article I. This proclaims that 'Human dignity shall be inviolable. To respect and protect it shall be the duty of all state authority.' Particularly through the interpretations of the Federal Constitutional Court, this has spawned a rich jurisprudence of fundamental rights that characterizes the modern German understanding of the *Rechtsstaat,* or as it is frequently expanded (and at times complicated) to join the social welfare state (*Sozialstaat*), the *sozialer Rechtsstaat.*

There are problems at the extremes. What is gained by defining down a concept that bears so much normative resonance, in terms that ignore any interrogation of what its point might be, and simply focus on the characteristics of institutions and practices? Particularly when it is not clear whether the characteristics chosen by 'thin' theorists relate as much to what law does and should do in the world, as they do to lawyers' unevenly informed intuitions and guesses about these matters. Again, what of the exercise of power by extra-legal forces, social networks? If they are free to act arbitrarily, capriciously, whatever the law says, does it make sense to insist that nevertheless the rule of law exists because certain formal elements of a legal order are present? Excessively thin conceptions often seem urgently in need of a feed.

Yet, conversely, accounts that purport to be thin as a rake are often rather plumper than intended, particularly where – as is frequently the case in well-intentioned first world interventions in benighted countries – they embody parochial suggestions as to what features of familiar legal orders generate rule-of-law friendly results. When packages of legal *bric-à-brac* are asked to travel, it often turns out that they work very differently or not at all where they land (see Krygier 2011). It might also turn out that institutions and practices of sorts not known in the homes of confident rule of law exporters perform adequately in their own homes, even if they look quite strange to visitors. Whether they do or not should be a matter of investigation, not overbearing legalistic assumption. Too often, however, imported assumptions about the working of legal institutions, based on distant histories, traditions, institutions and practices, have been smuggled in and then re-sold as though of universal applicability. When they fail to 'take' is it because the rule of law is a false ideal, or because what has been exported is not the rule of law itself but parochial institutions taken to be necessary for values that might yet be reached, and need to be reached, in other ways?

Partisans of thin versions, on the other hand, often associate the thickness insisted on by moralists with a combination of parochialism and imperialism about values and institutions. Why should we assume, either as a matter of fact or of value, that all cultures value the same things from law? Meta-ethical disputes this raises are too large to be resolved here, but there is another worry about too thick an account of the rule of law. As Joseph Raz has argued, 'thick' conceptions have a tendency to wash away all distinction between the rule of law and anything else we might want. That lays them open to the criticism that '[i]f the rule of law is the rule of the good law then to explain its nature is to propound a complete social philosophy. But if so the term lacks any useful function. We have no need to be converted to the rule of law just in order to discover that to believe in it is to believe that good should triumph' (Raz 1979, 211).

Such criticism points up another inadequacy of the choice on offer: the dichotomy between a spare and formalistic thinness, on the one hand, and a pudgy confection of everything we'd like to find in a good society, does not exhaust the field. There is space for values particularly associated with the exercise of power, what might be called distinctively *legal* values were it not for the fact that the differences between them and other values are unlikely to be categorical, but rather matters of focus, shades and degree. Many legal orders bear and transmit long histories of observation, experience and reflection upon the pathologies of unconstrained and/or capricious exercise of power and on what might be done to avoid or moderate such pathologies. Legal orders typically embody and generate values related to what they do, both in their animating principles and ideals, and in the complaints they provoke when their practices flout the sources of their legitimacy (see Selznick 1999; Waldron 2011a). These have included such values as due process or natural justice, ideals of fair treatment and notice, and in particular legal traditions much more. They have to do with treating a subject of power with the respect due to a person, rather than a 'rabid animal or a dilapidated house' (Waldron 2011a, 16). The rule of law might well be argued to be incomplete to the extent that some such power-related values, that have to do with how to arrange and transact potentially harmful interactions between it and its subjects (too often treated as objects), are dishonored. Attempts to vindicate such values, often implicit in many legal principles and traditions if not all legal rules, might be considered a service to the rule of law, even if they go beyond purely formal aspects of laws and notwithstanding that they might fall short of justice more holistically conceived. On one view, the special disease, to which the rule of law is part of a remedy, is the propensity of power unconstrained to be exercised in arbitrary ways. It is a widespread disease.

4.4 Anatomy or Teleology

More fundamental than contests over the fleshiness of the rule of law is one over whether we should begin with focus on its anatomy – the institutional features one should expect to find in such a creature – or its point – the reasons one is concerned with this rather than something else. The long common law tradition was not fixated on specific institutions, even less the precise character of legal rules. As Reid demonstrates, it was all too murky: 'Ironically, the medieval constitutional law out of which today's rule of law developed would not have met the requirements of clarity or precision. There was always an air of indefiniteness, a smoky vagueness surrounding this all-embracing restraining "law" of English constitutionalism. Even its authority as law was shrouded in immeasurability' (Reid 2004, 16). But the common law tradition was clear on one thing: 'It was, Viscount Bolinbroke said in the eighteenth century, a matter of curbing power and not of the type and structure of government. Whether power was vested in a single monarch, in "the *principle Persons of the Community*, or in the *whole Body of the People*," was immaterial. What mattered was whether power was without control. "Such Governments are Governments of *arbitrary Will*,' he contended" (Reid 2004, 42). Bolinbroke would likely be puzzled by the rule of law toolkits carried by UN and World Bank rule of law promoters throughout the world today; uniform in character, diverse in application, apparently universal in application. Why are *those* particular institutions sacrosanct? What is the *point*? How has the point influenced the kit? Even for those of us who have left the mythologies and hagiographies of common law theory long behind, these are not bad questions.

Similar choices are also found in the *Rechtsstaat* tradition. The early propagators of the concept were not legal anatomists but proto-liberals in the main, many influenced by Kant, seeking to establish an order of citizens equal before the law, whose personal autonomy and property were protected by the law. A state was a *Rechtsstaat* to the extent that it achieved these tasks, not because it had this or that particular form. As von Mohl put it, 'the objective of the *Rechtsstaat* is not logically entwined with a particular form of government; on the contrary, every arrangement of public power which guarantees the right and the development of all human activities, is admissible' (quoted in Heuschling 2002, 59; my translation from Heuschling's French). These writers were explicit that what mattered was achieving what they conceived to be the point of the rule of law, not whether it exemplified a particular form of institutional architecture. That understanding did not continue through the century, but was supplanted by a formalistic, anatomizing conception, stressing the positivistically characterized features of a state, that qualified it to be declared a *Rechtsstaat.*

On the teleological account, however, the rule of law cannot adequately be explicated by a list of features of legal institutions, rules or practices. For the rule of law occurs when and to the extent that there is a social *achievement* to which law contributes. If we say, for example, that there were lots of laws under Stalin and a lot of rule, but there was not much rule of law, we are not saying something controversial, and you wouldn't have to know much about Dicey or Fuller to agree. So at least among the legally and philosophically unwashed, the rule of law has something to do with what the law does, rather than simply with what it has been somewhere declared to be.

Moreover, if the law is enlisted to do things we associate with the rule of law but the mission fails, we might say that there was an attempt to achieve the rule of law, but it was unsuccessful: laws were of the sorts we associate with the rule of law, everyone was trying, but they were overborne, for whatever reason. To say the rule of law exists in a society is to imply an accomplishment; among its partisans a valued accomplishment: an ideal to which law is taken to contribute has been approached.

On this view, the rule of law is not a natural entity like a tree, simply awaiting scientific description, or even a man-made contrivance like *a* rule of law in a statute book, which might be identified by pointing to it. It exists to the extent that a certain state of affairs, one in which power is exercised in relatively non-arbitrary ways, exists in the world. Law is supposed to contribute, though it will never do so on its own. The aspiration or ideal is satisfied only *insofar as* some purpose or goal for law is realized. While such an achievement could in principle be thought value neutral or even valueless, and has been, the rule of law also has partisans – today perhaps, even too many – who think it valuable, an ideal for law. If we value that ideal we should of course seek to identify what might be necessary to generate it. But that is a second step. Without some principle of selection even if only tacit, we won't find a bunch of legal bits and pieces waiting 'out there' and recognizable as the rule of law.

The teleological contention is, then, that to understand what the rule of law requires we need to start by reflecting first on its *point* rather than, as is more common, with an enumeration of purportedly defining legal-institutional *features*, whether they be particular institutions such as common law courts (Dicey 1961), particular formal qualities of rules, such as prospectivity, clarity, etc., or even traditions and procedures, such as defences, *habeas corpus,* and so on (Waldron 2011a), though the last is getting closer to explicit concern with the specific point of the rule of law.

At first blush, this looks like a repetition of the distinction between thin and thick, and it is true that anatomical accounts of the rule of law are often 'thin', since they focus on delineating the characters of legal institutions. But there are two differences. First, particularly among rule of law promoters, it is rare that anyone has thin *ambitions,* more commonly they just have confused ideas of what the rule of law is about. Rule of law promotion, after all, is ostensibly an attempt to enlist the rule of law to do good in the world, not just to build replicas of institutions from home. However rule of law promoters are often restricted by the conventional identification of the rule of law, or *Rechtsstaat,* with a particular box of tricks, and proceed to try to vindicate some purpose with an *a priori* catalog of what is needed to achieve it, rather than an openness to the possibility that they might need to learn some new tricks. Awareness that one should start with the end, as it were, rather than purported means, might avoid a lot of grief over transplants that fail to do what is expected of them: promote the rule of law.

Moreover, the distinctions between thin versus thick, on the one hand, and anatomical versus teleological, on the other, do not occupy the same plane. A teleological account is not necessarily normatively thick; it might occupy itself with a small point, say predictability in the legal environment. How normatively enriched the point of the rule of law might be is a legitimate matter of debate, but it is a debate on the teleological plane. On that plane, the question is not, first of all, how much normative weight the concept carries but where one should start to think about the rule of law – by enumerating a set of purported (and typically universal) features or by asking what it is might be good for. Since it is hard to know what features matter unless one has sorted out what they are for, the suggestion here is to start with the end.

4.5 Legal or Socio-legal

If one is concerned with underlying values that inspire commitment to the rule of law, this has significant and somewhat paradoxical implications for where one should look to vindicate whatever one decides such values to be. For the search to redeem them is likely to de-center law itself. After all, it is in principle an open, and likely variable, matter what in the world best minimizes arbitrariness in the exercise of power, and the same might be said of any other values that we imagine law helps vindicate. Yet if ends matter, then it is not clear that one should *assume* that law is always key to achievement of the animating values of the rule of law, even less the state. This is so, whatever the values one has in mind, and it will be all the more so as one ramps up the values one associates with the rule of law. A good society is quite an achievement, and law only a small, if precious, contributor.

This applies at virtually every level. If arbitrary power is to be feared, then wherever power is powerful enough to be fearful, rule of law concerns are relevant. Thus, preoccupation with the state is not always appropriate, in circumstances where many of the sources of restraint on arbitrary power, many dangers flowing from it, and many of the goods accomplished by its curtailment, lie outside the state, and many of the means of achieving those goods lie outside the law as well (see Krygier 2011, 85–91).

If that is the case, it is not obvious that the familiar institutions associated by legal anatomists with the rule of law will always be the best to wield. Law will never accomplish much in the world on its own, and a key accompaniment of investigation of the rule of law should be, but rarely has been, study of what else is needed, beside and beyond, law, to attain its ends.

On this view, law should be viewed, not as the always-necessary centerpiece of power-taming policy to which other measures are subordinate or supplementary addenda, but as one implement among several, of varying significance, in some respects and circumstances of potentially unique importance, but dependent for its success on many other things, and perhaps not more important for the achievement of its own goal than they. Similar reflections apply, but all the more, to the State of the *Rechtsstaat.*

There is something to be said for the legal pluralism embodied in the old common law tradition, and squeezed out by the rise of the contemporary state: in principle in the *Rechtsstaat,* and by the statophilic tendencies of modernity more generally. Even with its dominance, and especially where it is 'failed', 'fragile' or 'transitional', the state is never the only game in town. That is a sociological platitude, but it should have more bearing on legal platitudes than it has. Lawyers will naturally, habitually, focus their attention on state and legal agencies, but those interested in promoting the values that underpin the rule of law and make it worthwhile will need to look further afield.

If the foregoing considerations are plausible *within* existing nation states, they must be all the more compelling for anyone who wants, as many today do, to speak about an emerging 'international rule of law' (Palombella 2009; Waldron 2011b). For whatever that might mean, there is no international *Staat* to be its lawgiving and enforcing source. It might be a matter of argument whether it is a good idea to seek to extend the rule of law to the international sphere, but it would seem a strange truncation of the argument simply to rule out a non-state-centered rule of law *by definition.*

This suggests the need for a sociological awareness and sensibility not especially common among lawyers, whether rule-of-lawyers, or *rechtsstaatlich* ones. There will be other sectors of a society altogether that influence the extent to which the values at the heart of the rule of law will be attained. Paradoxically, in order to reach those values we will have to look far beyond the institutions we have most conventionally associated with them.

That does not make either the law or the state unimportant. However, it might enable us to see their importance in perspective, give due weight to other phenomena that might need enlisting to serve such goals, and release us from the hold of a mantra, whether 'rule of law' or *Rechtsstaat,* which in their modish ubiquity threaten to obscure the valuable, indeed precious purposes for which they were pushed into the fray, instead promiscuously to serve virtually any purpose you want to name.

References

Blackstone, William. 1979. *Commentaries on the laws of England.* Chicago: University of Chicago Press.

Call, Charles T. 2007. Introduction. In *Constructing justice and security after war*, ed. Charles T. Call. Washington, DC: United States Institute of Peace Press.

Dam, Kenneth W. 2006. *The law-growth nexus: The rule of law and economic development.* Washington, DC: Brookings Institution Press.

Dicey, A.V. 1961. *Introduction to the law of the constitution*, 10th ed. London: Macmillan.

Dworkin, Ronald. 1985. Political judges and the rule of law. In *A matter of principle*, ed. Ronald Dworkin. Cambridge, MA: Harvard University Press.

Dyzenhaus, David. 1997. *Legality and legitimacy. Carl Schmitt, Hans Kelsen and Hermann Heller in Weimar*. Oxford: Oxford University Press.

Fuller, Lon L. 1969. *The morality of law* (Rev. ed.). New Haven: Yale University Press.

Gozzi, Gustavo. 2007. *Rechtsstaat* and individual rights in German constitutional history. In *The rule of law. History, theory and criticism*, ed. Pietro Costa and Danilo Zolo, 237–259. Dordrecht: Springer Verlag.

Grote, Rainer. 1999. Rule of law, Rechtsstaat and "Etat de droit". In *Constitutionalism, universalism and democracy: A comparative analysis*, ed. Christian Starck, 269–306. Baden-Baden: Nomos Verlagsgesellschaft.

Hart, H.L.A. 1967. Problems of philosophy of law. In *The encyclopedia of philosophy*, vol. 5, 264–276.

Heuschling, Luc. 2002. *État de droit, Rechtsstaat, Rule of law*. Paris: Nouvelle Bibliothèque de Thèses, Éditions Dalloz.

Kirchheimer, Otto. 1967. The *Rechtsstaat* as Magic Wall. In *The rule of law under Siege. Selected essays of Franz L. Neumann and Otto Kirchheimer,* ed. William E. Scheuerman, 243–263. California: University of California Press, 1996.

Krieger, Leonard. 1957. *The German idea of freedom*. Chicago: University of Chicago Press.

Krygier, Martin. 1998. Common Law. In *Routledge encyclopedia of philosophy*, 10 vols, vol 1, ed. Edward Craig, 440–446. London: Routledge.

Krygier, Martin. 2010. The Hart-Fuller debate, transitional societies and the rule of law. In *The Hart-Fuller debate in the twenty-first century*, ed. Peter Cane, 107–134. Oxford: Hart Publishers.

Krygier, Martin. 2011. Four puzzles about the Rule of Law: Why, What, Where? And Who Cares? In *Getting to the rule of law*, ed. James E. Fleming, 64–104. New York: New York University Press.

Lieberman, David. 1989. *The province of legislation determined*. Cambridge: Cambridge University Press.

Loughlin, Martin. 2010. *Foundations of public law*. Oxford: Oxford University Press.

MacCormick, D. Neil. 1984. Der Rechtsstaat und die rule of law. *Juristenzeitung* 50: 65–70.

Maitland, F.W. 1965. *The constitutional history of England*. Cambridge: Cambridge University Press.

Palombella, Gianluigi. 2009. The rule of law beyond the state: Failures, promises, and theory. *International Journal of Constitutional Law* 7(3): 442–467.

Palombella, Gianluigi. 2010. The rule of law as institutional ideal. In *Rule of law and democracy*, ed. L. Morlino and G. Palombella. Leiden: Brill.

Peerenboom, Randall (ed.). 2004. *Asian discourses of the rule of law*. London: RoutledgeCurzon.

Pettit, Philip. 2012. *On the people's terms. A republican theory and model of democracy*. Cambridge: Cambridge University Press.

Poggi, Gianfranco. 1978. *The development of the modern state*. Stanford: Stanford University Press.

Postema, Gerald. 1986. *Bentham and the common law tradition*. Oxford: Clarendon.

Raeff, Marc. 1983. *The well-ordered police state: Social and institutional change through law in the Germanies and Russia, 1600–1800*. New Haven: Yale University Press.

Raz, Joseph. 1979. The rule of law and its virtue. In *The authority of law*, ed. Joseph Raz. Oxford: Clarendon Press.

Reid, John Philip. 2004. *The rule of law*. De Kalb: Northern Illinois University Press.

Richardson, Henry S. 2002. *Democratic autonomy. Public reasoning about the ends of policy*. Oxford: Oxford University Press.

Rosenfeld, Michel. 2001. The rule of law and the legitimacy of constitutional democracy. *Southern California Law Review* 74: 1307–1352.

Rundle, Kristen. 2009. The impossibility of an exterminatory legality: Law and the Holocaust. *University of Toronto Law Journal* 59: 65–125.

Selznick, Philip. 1992. *The moral commonwealth*. Berkeley: University of California Press.

Selznick, Philip. 1999. Legal cultures and the rule of law. In *The rule of law after communism*, ed. Martin Krygier and Adam Czarnota, 21–38. Aldershot: Ashgate/Dartmouth.

Waldron, Jeremy. 2002. Is the rule of law an essentially contested concept (In Florida)? *Law and Philosophy* 21(2): 137–164.

Waldron, Jeremy. 2011a. The rule of law and the importance of procedure. In *Getting to the rule of law*, ed. James E. Fleming, 3–31. New York: New York University Press.

Waldron, Jeremy. 2011b. Are sovereigns entitled to the benefit of the international rule of law? *The European Journal of International Law* 22(2): 315–343.

Walker, Geoffrey de.Q. 1988. *The rule of law. Foundation of constitutional democracy*. Carlton: Melbourne University Press.

Weber, Max. 1968. *Economy and society*, vol. II. New York: Bedminster Press.

Chapter 5
The Rule of Law and Legal State Doctrines as a Methodology of the Philosophy of Law

Dmitry Dedov

Abstract This chapter examines the doctrines of rule of law and the legal state in a human rights context. Specifically, it includes a philosophical analysis of the doctrines' utility for the protection of basic human rights values have been confirmed in a practice of the European Court of Human Rights.

5.1 Some Theoretical Issues

Understanding the rule of law and legal state doctrine is controversial and theoretical views may differ deeply from the reality.

One may proclaim the rule of law to be a vague term. Others apply it to any legal system regardless of the extent of acknowledgement of democratic values stating that it is sufficient if a legal norm is precise, possesses a general nature and addresses everyone to the same extent. This statement comes from a formal approach that is close to positivism. The functional approach is based on the scope of powers of the authorities in question: the lesser is the freedom of discretion, the stronger is the rule of law.

The understanding of the rule of law as something not allowing the abuse of state power looks more interesting. In such a case, one usually adds that the rule of law means that the state cannot position itself above society, and no one can be above the law.

It is fascinating how one doctrine can combine these contradictory ideas. But is it really possible? The answer should be yes, given the presumption of fairness of a statute that been approved by a legislature. An important point here is that the presumption of fairness of statute does not mean an absolute impossibility to prove

---

D. Dedov (✉)
European Court of Human Rights, Strasbourg, France
e-mail: Dmitry.Dedov@echr.coe.int

J.R. Silkenat et al. (eds.), *The Legal Doctrines of the Rule of Law and the Legal State (Rechtsstaat)*, Ius Gentium: Comparative Perspectives on Law and Justice 38,
DOI 10.1007/978-3-319-05585-5_5, © Springer International Publishing Switzerland 2014

the opposite, given the general nature of the legal norms and the necessity to clarify their meaning and their general conception in order to understand whether it is applicable in a particular situation. Since it is possible to prove the unfairness of statutes (which happens all the time in court practice), the doctrines are susceptible to combination.

There is one more understanding of the rule of law that is usually forgotten. The supremacy of law means that law prevails over statutes. This fact brings up unlimited cognitive possibilities for understanding the essence of law as equity. In ancient Greece and considerably later in the USA, slavery was a routine thing (*Dred Scott v. Sandford*, 60 U.S. 393 (1857)). This is why, according to the Soviet theory of law, the legal order that is typical for any socioeconomic period is always fair for its time. Such an understanding of a fair legislative act contradicts the doctrine of the rule of law, declines the necessity to cognize the law and thus impedes the development of law. This cognition happens by the virtue of doubts that first arise among the minority, then become universally recognized and eventually result in annulment of an old norm. The legal order cannot be modified with a wave of a magic wand, and the economic relations won't change in the absence of appropriate technological development. This could look so natural aside from the utopian concepts of numerous philosophers, including Karl Marx.

The statement that positivism impedes development of law has been made on purpose. To put it differently – "it doesn't allow the law to develop". Society does not develop the law on purpose. To the contrary, the law develops in the society's perception of law. It is a natural process related to the people's ideas about what a fair legal order contributing to the well-being of the society should look like.

It is not a mistake to say that the legal state doctrine almost has the same meaning. As it usually happens, two different legal systems (the common law system and the civil law system) give different names to a doctrine in question while they move in the same direction purporting to prevent abuse of power and arbitrariness and to impose limits on politics in accordance with short-term interests.

From the viewpoint of the philosophy of law, the prevention of arbitrariness means not only an ideal model but also a certain methodology. Truth be told, currently the desire to prevent the abuse of power and arbitrariness remains only a good intention. That is the point at which the fundamental principles come into play. Fundamental principles abound and their content sometimes intertwines, which makes the doctrine hard to understand and sometimes results in implementation mistakes and a failure to understand the essence and necessity of these principles. These fundamental principles include:

- the principle of proportionality, where rights and freedoms are limited due to publicly important goals;
- the principle of legal certainty;
- the principle of reasonable expectations;
- the principle of prevention of retroactivity of a legislative act that imposes limitations on rights and freedoms of individuals;
- the principle of prevention of the conflict on interests;

- the principle of formal equality;
- presumption of innocence and bona fide;
- the principle of due administration;
- the principle of legality (where individual rights and freedoms can be restricted only by the virtue of law) or the principle of due legal process;
- the principle of non-discrimination;
- the principle of due cautiousness and diligence;
- the principle of consistency (the analogy of law);
- the principle of reality, actuality and importance of the rights and interests subject to protection;
- the principle of hierarchy of interests, i.e. the interest possessing a more important, a high priority meaning for the society comparing to the other conflicting interest.

Other principles not listed have a similar essence. For example, the principle of respect of the fundamental rights and freedom is a cornerstone of the *Rule of Law* and the *Legal State* recognizing universal values in the course of the development of the society. Other principles address protection of these values and have been formed in the course of scientific (methodological) analysis.

These values are important in order to simplify the system and facilitate the methodology of the application of these principles. It is always helpful to keep in mind something more general and fundamental than the aforementioned basic principles of law. In order to do that, one must find something that impedes abuse and arbitrariness. Immanuel Kant accepted that moral law exists inside every human being. He used the famous Biblical formulation: do unto others as you would have others do unto you. However strong is the motivation, this formula proved to be insufficiently efficient to be applied in all cases.

Thus, for practical purposes, these values should be used together with more powerful factors that had been underestimated from the viewpoint of the philosophy of law. The question is – what are the key factors of efficiency of the doctrine of rule of law and doctrine of the legal state? Iain Stewart distinguishes among these two doctrines stating that the *Legal State* doctrine is contained in the codified legislation while rule of law may be found mostly in the courts' decisions.

These differences are based on the distinctions of two legal systems, but their gradual convergence has become well-known. The United States and the countries of continental Europe are democratic states. They represent European legal tradition, so there are no grounds for sharp demarcation. Moreover, given the fact that courts embody the first factor of efficiency of both doctrines (that is even more applicable to the rule of law doctrine).

In the course of analysis of the rule of law doctrine the definition "law" is construed both as statute law and as precedent law.[1] This understanding arises from the content of this definition and does not depend only on its formal expression. This means that

[1] *See* Sunday Times v. the United Kingdom (no. 1), 26 April 1979, §47; Kruslin v. France, 24 April 1990, §29; Casado Coca v. Spain, 24 February 1994, §43.

law includes statutes and any other rules of behavior, customs and judicial legal reasonings (that is, everything that affects the behavior standards in the society).[2]

So, these are the courts that attach the live content to the statute norms. That is where the statutes translate from the abstract into a custom (i.e. a rule which fairness has been proved by the practical experience). The Russian legislation resembles a corporation where the management allocates all the company operations into separate procedures establishing the order of communication between the employees, their duties and rights as well as the periods of realization of separate stages of these procedures. The idea is beautiful but half of these procedures do not work since the existing experience of communications between the employees and informal practices are not taken into account. Many procedures are simply useless. Many norms are usually referred to as "dead," "sleeping," "empty," or "reference rules."

Courts are also important to increase the efficiency of these doctrines. They are vital for gradual (evolutional and not revolutionary) development of law as well as for extension and elaboration of meaning of legislative acts. Since a court decision results directly from the human activity, courts possess a will for application of general principles of law that emphasizes the court's special importance. By all means, there can be a situation where such mechanism will not work, for example, where court's independence or impartiality has been affected.

Courts possess certain disadvantages. They become engaged only after a problem or conflict has arisen. In the event of interpretation of a legal norm from the viewpoint of its fairness, a new court interpretation will apply prospectively only for further disputes. As for possible problems with judicial independence, they are insignificant when compared to the general level of efficiency of the judiciary. In order to maintain this level of efficiency, judges must constantly learn how to apply these general principles. And here the interpretation of the statute norms by a Parliament may be helpful. The Parliamentary Assembly of the Council of Europe and the Council of Ministers are most active in this realm. They pass recommendations and resolutions on the issues of human rights policy, which are considerably broader than the sphere where the European Convention on Human Rights (hereinafter referred to as Convention) applies. At present, there are hundreds of such "interpretations". But despite the efforts to train judges, it must be taken into account that judges are human beings and they make mistakes. However, the statistical analysis shows that the number of errors in any system, including judiciary, does not exceed 2 %.

Apparently, the representatives of the legislative and executive power often act differently. They interfere into court activities directly or by the means of public statement of their position relating to a pending case. Account must be taken that the interference into court activities does not happen all the time. Usually, this happens only as far as high profile cases are concerned and the number of such cases is not large, so it will not be a problem to devise some sort of additional control by society in order to maintain normal operation of the judiciary.

[2] *See also* De Wilde, Ooms and Versyp v. Belgium, 18 June 1971, §93; Leyla Şahin v. Turkey, §88; Sud Fondi S.r.l. and Others v. Italy, §§107–108, 20 January 2009.

By and large, it is very difficult to secure the maximum efficiency of the judiciary from the viewpoint of the *Rule of Law* doctrine. The difficulty is compounded because the objective laws of evolution demonstrate that only a few judges possess the ability to development the law. That ability depends upon an academic approach to the problem in question by formulating and systematically analyzing the problem from the position of the conflicting interests, social goals and universal human values. It also depends upon the ability to predict the consequences of such decision. This task is not for everyone. If the society frowns on rude behavior or on bribe-giving and bribe-taking and, on the contrary, welcomes respect for others, then most individuals seek to comply with these rules.

In order to make correction of errors a routine matter, another efficiency factor may be helpful – a custom as a behavior standard. Any case of noncompliance with these standards becomes public, and such inconsistency will be immediately stopped by public opinion. In such a situation, both lawmakers and judges start to work in good faith, and their professional knowledge and skills become very helpful. This phenomenon is usually referred to as moral norms. However, it should be emphasized that the characteristic of a custom or a behavior standard is respected and followed by the majority of the society and not by a small group of high-minded intellectuals. It is vital not only to declare high moral ideals, but also to follow them. That was the problem of the Russian society both under the Soviet rule (when the entire regime possessed a declarative nature) and today, when the representatives of the authorities constantly find themselves in the middle of countless scandals.

5.2 Practical Issues

Professor Dicey, the inventor of the definition *Rule of Law,* applied it only to the situation of bringing up criminal charges and only in cases of breach of a precisely formulated rule. This axiom is still true today. Moreover, it is now a universally recognized principle of international law that has been included into a number of international agreements. However, sometimes even this rule cannot maintain its balance to compare to the rule of law as a doctrine of constant improvement of legal system in order to protect public interests. Let us track the evolution of this approach with the example of Article 7 of the Convention, "No punishment without law". This article states:

1. No one shall be held guilty of any criminal offence on account of any act or omission which did not constitute a criminal offence under national or international law at the time when it was committed. Nor shall a heavier penalty be imposed than the one that was applicable at the time the criminal offence was committed.
2. This article shall not prejudice the trial and punishment of any person for any act or omission which, at the time when it was committed, was criminal according the general principles of law recognized by civilized nations.

Here is the current position of the European Court for Human Rights regarding Article 7.

The guarantee envisaged by Article 7 of the Convention (which is an essential element of the rule of law) has an important position in the conventional system of human rights protection, especially because Article 15 allows no deviations from this requirement, even in the time of war or another emergency situation. This rule is construed and applied in accordance with its subject and goals in a way that provides efficient guarantees of protection against arbitrary prosecution, conviction and punishment.[3]

In the case *S.W. v. the United Kingdom* (where the issue was whether the punishment for rape applies to conjugal relations) the European Court for Human Rights clarifies its position in paragraph 35:

> Accordingly, as the Court held in its Kokkinakis v. Greece judgment of 25 May 1993 (Series A no. 260-A, p. 22, para. 52), Article 7 (art. 7) is not confined to prohibiting the retrospective application of the criminal law to an accused's disadvantage: it also embodies, more generally, the principle that only the law can define a crime and prescribe a penalty (nullum crimen, nulla poena sine lege) and the principle that the criminal law must not be extensively construed to an accused's detriment, for instance by analogy. From these principles it follows that an offense must be clearly defined in the law.
>
> This requirement is satisfied where the individual can know from the wording of the relevant provision and, if need be, with the assistance of the courts' interpretation of it, what acts and omissions will make him criminally liable. The Court thus indicated that when speaking of "law" Article 7 (art. 7) alludes to the very same concept as that to which the Convention refers elsewhere when using that term, a concept which comprises written as well as unwritten law and implies qualitative requirements, notably those of accessibility and foreseeability (see also *Kokkinakis v. Greece*, 25 May 1993, § 51; *Tolstoy Miloslavsky v. the United Kingdom*, 13 July 1995, § 37).

However clearly drafted a legal provision may be, in any system of law, including criminal law as a public law realm, there is an inevitable element of judicial interpretation. There will always be a need for elucidation of doubtful points and for adaptation to changing circumstances.

This is vital because from the viewpoint of the rule of law the progressive development of any area of law by the means of judicial law-making is a universally recognized element of legal tradition. Thus, as the European Court for Human Rights has put it, article 7 of the Convention cannot be construed as prohibiting the gradual explanation of the criminal liability rules by the means of occasional judicial interpretation, given that the result of this development complies with the nature of the crime and could be reasonably pre-determined (*Streletz, Kessler and Krenz v. Germany*, § 50).

Bearing in mind that crimes and appropriate punishments must be precisely envisaged by the law, such an approach prohibits extension of the realm of existing offenses by the acts that earlier were not considered as criminal.

But such approach also may imply an opposite trend. If legal norms always possess a general nature, their formulations are not always precise. Here the standard method

---

[3] S.W. v. the United Kingdom *and* C.R. v. the United Kingdom, 22 November 1995, §34 and §32 respectively; Kafkaris v Cyprus, §137, 12 February, 2008; Scoppola v. Italy (no. 2), §§92–101, 17 September, 2009; Kasymakhunov and Saybatalov v. Russia, §§76–78, 14 March, 2013.

of regulation is the use of general definitions and categories instead of making up an exhaustive list. It means that many statutes inevitably are formulated in words that are more or less ambiguous, and their interpretation and implementation depends on use. So, in any legal system even the most elaborated legal norm, including criminal law norms, may inevitably become the object of judicial interpretation. Apparently (though certainty is most desired here) it may make the norm in question so strict that it will impede the compliance of the laws with the changing situation.

This approach has become especially clear in *Soros v France*, on which the Court's Chamber ruled on October 6, 2011. A famous investor and philanthropist, the author of the idea of the Open Society (which precisely complies with the doctrines of the rule of law and legal state), George Soros was nevertheless convicted by a French court for insider trading in 1990. On September 12, 1988, he held a meeting in New-York with a group of investors. After the meeting a banker from Switzerland informed him of his idea to purchase together with other investors the stocks of a huge French bank in the form of a friendly acquisition offer. Soros declined and on September 19, 1988, spent 50 million USD on the stocks of four recently privatized French companies, including stocks of the bank in question. Between September 22 and October 17, 1988, his hedge-fund, "Q.F.," additionally purchased the stocks of this bank for 11.4 million USD on the stock markets of Paris and London. Several days after the purchase "Q.F." sold some stocks of the bank, and George Soros earned the profit amounting to 2.28 million USD, including 1.1 million on the French market.

In February of 1989, the controller of the French stock market initiated an investigation into the selling of the bank stocks during the period from June 1 to December 21, 1988, searching for evidence of insider trading of stocks. When some suspicious operations were spotted, the controller reported the results of this investigation to the prosecutor. In 1990, criminal charges were brought against Soros and other individuals suspected of insider trading of stocks. He was accused of buying the bank's stocks by using confidential information on the alleged acquisition of the bank.

In the course of investigation Soros insisted that the prosecution was illegitimate due to the ambiguity and unpredictability of the norms of criminal legislation applicable to insider trading. He stated that in the light of provisions of article 10-1 of the Decree № 67-833 of September 28, 1967, his behavior could not be considered a crime at the moment of the purchase of stocks. Nonetheless, the court ruled that Soros was guilty of insider trading and imposed a fine of 2.2 million euro.

Soros appealed and the Paris appellate court upheld the judgment. The Court of Cassation pointed out that the purchase of stocks on the London stock market cannot be referred to insider trading under the French law (that's where the court missed the principle of consistency, whereas the problem arises from the court's jurisdiction and not from the content of the prohibition) and transferred the case back to the Paris appellate court. The latter then considerably diminished the amount of the fine and took into consideration only the operations made on the Paris stock market.

When seeking remedy in the European Court for Human Rights, Soros invoked Article 7 of the Convention asserting "there is no punishment without law." He pointed out that the key criminal elements of the insider trading were not precise enough at the moment of his conviction according to the insider trading definition contained in Article 10-1. This article applies only to the employees of professional businessmen who have business relations with a company in question.

The court made a point that considering general wording in the criminal legislation its provisions are not always clear. Moreover, the court confirmed that the level of predictability depends to the considerable extent upon the content of the legal norms, on the spheres of its application and on the status of the individuals whom the law addresses. Given the subject of transaction in this case, the businessmen who possess information must be very cautious in their activities. Also they should take special measures to evaluate their risks. The court took into consideration that the definition of the "insider trading" contained in the legal norms was too general and that the parties had agreed with a concrete wording "purporting realization of their professional or other responsibilities".

The French courts found that the law was precise enough in order to make George Soros aware of the fact that he should refrain from investing into the stocks after receiving of the information in question at the time of his refusal to take part in the friendly acquisition of the bank.

Though George Soros was the first person who had no professional or contractual relations with the bank in question and was nevertheless prosecuted for insider trading in France, the European Court of Human Rights found that the French authorities did not depart from the principle of predictability of law, since in the absence of precedent of any sort the national courts failed to come up with any sort of legal reasoning on this point.

The ECHR emphasized that George Soros was an institutional investor who was well-known in the business community as a participant of many large international financial projects. Given his status and experience, he could not have been unaware of the fact that his decision to invest into the bank stocks involved the risk of committing a crime known as insider trading. In the absence of an appropriate precedent one should be especially cautious in such cases (the principle of due cautiousness and diligence was unexpectedly applied in a criminal case instead of the proof of existence of criminal intent).

The ECHR ruled that there was no breach of Article 7 of the Convention due to unpredictability of law. The vote was a slender 4 to 3. Could Dicey assume that such thing could happen? The result directly contradicts his axiom but at the same time fully complies with general applicable legal principles. All things considered, this is a fair judgment. These circumstances demonstrate clearly that the rule of law doctrine is very flexible and has a high potential for further development.

The minority of three judges who came up with dissenting opinions indicated that the legal norms were too imprecise and ambiguous to distinguish between legitimate and illegitimate activities. These judges concluded that the result was the decrease of the level of protection against arbitrary interference as well as the breach of provisions of Article 7 of the Convention.

One way or another, the inside trade constitutes damage to public interests, contradicts the spirit of capitalism, and no one will avoid liability for such activities. If we take a look at the United States response to the crisis of Internet companies in

1998–1999, when the investors had lost their money and got no legal remedy, we will see that in twenty-first century the situation has become dramatically different, and investment banks paid hundreds millions of dollars in fees for their manipulation of the security market. That is an indicator of the efficiency of the rule of law doctrine.

5.3 Conclusion

A comparison of the concepts of the rule of law and legal state reveals that both concepts may coincide in certain interpretations, especially when they refer to the role of a statute approved by a legislature as opposed to the restrictions of rights and freedoms made through illegal arbitrary decisions of the executive bodies. This is a fundamental principle of the contemporary legal order that had been created many years ago.

But even this was not sufficient. Somehow it has turned out that statutes are not always fair. In order to give this conclusion a binding effect, it is necessary to use the national highest court as a part of the state machinery. That is, the statute is fair unless it has been proved otherwise. This approach permits two conclusions to be made: (1) there is a presumption of fairness of statutes and, (2) statutes must comply with a professional juridical perception of fairness (of law). The second conclusion looks more provocative and implies a deeper insight. It means that law prevails over statutes, and the law is the truth that must be constantly comprehended. This truth involves not only formal juridical categories, it also includes the whole set of social, economic and political problems of the modern society and calls for a response to the fundamental questions on how the society can maintain its welfare and how it may survive.

So both concepts make up a necessary methodology for protection of basic values (freedom, mutual respect, tolerance, pluralism) that has been confirmed in a concrete case of the European Court of Human Rights. This is a separate strategy that deserves attention, since protection of these values have not yet become a general standard for the use of powers of authority and force in general.

Chapter 6
Applying the Rule of Law to Contexts Beyond the State

Matthias Kötter and Gunnar Folke Schuppert

Abstract By focusing on two recent developments, the authors of this chapter argue that rule of law principles can provide a general yardstick to evaluate even these norm-building processes that occur beyond the state. First, various discourses on governance in contexts beyond the state have started to integrate non-state legal structures into the rule of law concepts illustrated in terms of constitutional law, law and development, and global governance, generalizing the criteria under which non-state law can assume the same quality as the rule of law. And second, there is an increasing tendency in contexts "beyond the state" to use experiences subsumed under the rule of law as a normative yardstick to measure non-state processes of setting and enforcing norms, as well as the quality of those norms. Distanced from its origin as a principle of state law, the rule of law functions here as a general standard for legitimate and effective rule-making.

6.1 The Rule of Law Paradigm

Fifteen years ago, in 1998, Thomas Carothers propagated the "Rule-of-Law Revival," and recent development debates point to one thing: the "revival" has transformed into a rule of law paradigm. More than ever before, the rule of law is considered the

---

The chapter summarises results of our research within the Berlin Research Cluster SFB700 "Governance in Areas of limited Statehood" that is funded by the German Research Foundation. The translation from German was done by Sophie Perl.

M. Kötter (✉) G.F. Schuppert
Rule of Law Center, WZB Social Science Center Berlin,
Berlin Research Cluster "Governance in Areas of Limited Statehood",
Berlin, Germany
e-mail: koetter@wzb.eu; schuppert@wzb.eu

J.R. Silkenat et al. (eds.), *The Legal Doctrines of the Rule of Law and the Legal State (Rechtsstaat)*, Ius Gentium: Comparative Perspectives on Law and Justice 38,
DOI 10.1007/978-3-319-05585-5_6, © Springer International Publishing Switzerland 2014

key to sustainable political and economic development in society. As Carothers put it: "The rule-of-law promises to move countries past the first, relatively easy phase of political and economic liberalization to a deeper level of reform."[1]

To contain and check the exercise of authority, to ensure the rule of justice rather than of individual caprice, and to render ruling bodies institutionally and normatively compatible with international governance structures—it is with these promises that the rule of law has become an international model for nonviolent, effective system-building and conflict resolution. This is the basis of "Rule of Law Promotion" (Sect. 6.2.2), *the* central policy in international development cooperation today. Conceptually, this policy draws on the same domestic constitutional debates over the rule of law that it itself has initiated in certain countries. At the same time, the policy cannot be separated from a shift toward the law and the concept of the rule of law in international relations and discourses on global governance, tied to the search for legitimate and stable structures.[2] The discussion of authority and governance in relation to a bundle of issues and principles conventionally associated with the rule of law has increasingly become the *lingua franca* among actors in these loosely linked political fields.

Rule of law means that the exercise of authority occurs by way of the law. But which societal conditions must be satisfied in order for the rule of law to exist and which individual normative demands does the rule of law imply? Debates over the rule of law have always revolved around these central questions without ever generating a single, generally accepted answer.[3] Instead, the spectrum of answers ranges from "thinner," mainly formal definitions to "thicker," highly substantive conceptions of the rule of law.[4] However, scholars tend less and less to derive concrete legal guarantees from the concept. Instead they place stronger emphasis on formal standards such as good lawmaking (see Sect. 6.3).[5]

The elasticity of the rule of law concept leaves room to accommodate cultural, political, and economic preferences, opening the discourse to legal understandings that differ from the Western tradition. To this effect, the acknowledgement of a minimum normative standard suffices in order to maintain a connection to the rule of law. At the same time, the fuzziness of the rule of law makes it difficult to distinguish it precisely from other normative concepts such as human rights,

---

[1] Thomas Carothers, "The Rule of Law Revival", 77 *Foreign Affairs* (1998) 95–106 at 98.

[2] Bernhard Zangl and Michael Zürn, "Make Law, Not War. Internationale und transnationale Verrechtlichung als Baustein für Global Governance", in *Verrechtlichung. Baustein für Global Governance?* Bernhard Zangl and Michael Zürn eds. (2004) Bonn: Dietz 12–45; Bernhard Zangl, "Judizialisierung als Bestandteil internationaler Rechtsherrschaft: Theoretische Debatten", in *Auf dem Weg zu internationaler Rechtsherrschaft? Streitbeilegung zwischen Politik und Recht*, Bernhard Zangl ed. (2009) Frankfurt: Campus 11–36.

[3] Brian Tamanaha, *On the Rule of Law* (2004) Cambridge University Press; Rachel Kleinfeld, *Competing Definitions of the Rule of Law: Implications for Practitioners*, Carnegie Papers No. 55, Carnegie Endowment for International Peace (2005).

[4] Tamanaha, *supra* note 3. At 91.

[5] Gunnar Folke Schuppert, "New Modes of Governance and the Rule of Law: The Case of Transnational Rule Making", in *Rule of Law Dynamics*, Michael Zürn, André Nollkaemper, and Randall Peerenboom eds. (2012) Cambridge University Press 90–107 at 104.

democracy-building, constitutionalization, or good governance. Each of these concepts carries its own meaning. However, there can be considerable overlaps depending on how the rule of law is defined.

Despite the difficulty of defining the rule of law and delineating it from other concepts, two aspects can be identified as its core structures: First, the rule of law requires that the exercise of authority and the resolution of societal conflicts occur by way of the law; and second, the rule of law provides concrete, normative standards with regard to the setting, enforcement, and quality of legal norms. The rule of law's point of reference is typically state law—that is, legal norms created and enforced by state institutions. As Brian Tamanaha put it: "The notion of the rule of law is typically applied to state law, and sometimes to international law."[6] The evolution of the rule of law was linked to the development of modern statehood, still reflected in the continental European understanding of *Rechtsstaat* or *état de droit* (literally, the state of law). It finds similar expression in the British tradition of common law, which is not set by state institutions but rather passed down through society and recognized by the courts in order to become official law and thus be included in the rule of law.

For the law to rule supreme, however, it is not enough for a state to exist, create laws, and operate courts; the factual validity of the law is essential as well. Therefore, rule of law assumes that the state factually maintains control over the production and enforcement of the law. As Laura Grenfell writes, "The modern concept of the rule of law is based on two assumptions: first, the existence of a modern state and, second, that within this modern state paradigm the state is sufficiently strong and organized to enjoy a monopoly of law."[7] According to this understanding, conditions of weak statehood or transnational contexts without effective state law represent gaps in the rule of law. However, these contexts are not necessarily governance gaps in terms of lacking structures to build systems or resolve conflicts. Other "informal" forms of governance often determine the rules of the game[8] but are omitted from discussions on the state-centered rule of law.

Regarding the inclusion of non-state legal structures in the rule of law, a conceptual shift has begun in recent years that this chapter investigates by focusing on two aspects. First, various discourses on governance in contexts beyond the state have started to integrate non-state legal structures into the rule of law concepts illustrated in terms of constitutional law, law and development, and global governance, generalizing the criteria under which non-state law can assume the same quality as the rule of law. Second, there is an increasing tendency in contexts "beyond the state" to use experiences subsumed under the rule of law as a normative yardstick to measure

[6] Brian Tamanaha, "The Rule of Law and Legal Pluralism in Development", 3 *The Hague Journal on the Rule of Law* (2009) 1–17.

[7] Laura Grenfell, *Promoting the Rule of Law in Post-Conflict States* (2013) Cambridge University Press at 4.

[8] Gunnar Folke Schuppert, "Law Without the State? A 'New Interplay' between State and Non-State Actors in Governance by Rule-Making", in *Governance without a State*, Thomas Risse ed. (2011) Columbia University Press 65–86; Matthias Kötter, "Non-State Justice Institutions", SFB-Governance Working Paper Series No. 34 (2012).

non-state processes of setting and enforcing norms, as well as the quality of those norms. Distanced from its origin as a principle of state law, the rule of law functions here as a general standard for legitimate and effective rule-making.

Taken together, the two aspects of this conceptual shift demonstrate that the rule of law as a normative yardstick is in no way limited to state contexts and state law. If we assume that the creation of legal systems requires norm-building processes to "be guided by the application of universal rules or at least justified in terms of universal principles,"[9] then the rule of law becomes the repository for these principles.

6.2 Extending the Rule of Law to Non-state Legal Structures

For quite some time now, various discourses have started to include non-state legal structures in contemplations of the rule of law. We will first examine national rule of law discourses in constitutional law, which are fundamentally dominated by a state-centered understanding of the rule of law. However, when non-state legal norms in certain regions or for certain groups of people carry as much weight as state law, these can often contribute to the rule of law, for example with the inclusion of customary law in the South African legal system.

6.2.1 Discourses in Constitutional Law: Rule of Law as a Constitutional Principle

As a topos in the legal discourses of constitutional states, the rule of law—like its German equivalent, the *Rechtsstaatsprinzip* (state of law principle)—is a constitutional principle based on numerous provisions that shape state structures and the exercise of public authority through the mechanisms and procedures of the state's legal system. These rules also contain requirements of a constitutional (statutory) law. In her comprehensive analysis, Katharina Sobota distinguishes 142 provisions that together comprise the German constitutional principle of *Rechtsstaat*.[10] These include such fundamental tasks as the institutional separation of powers, the basic principles of the law's supremacy and restraint, the right to a fair trial, and the guarantee of effective protection of the law in court—and only in rare exceptions in a different form[11]—against all forms of public violence. The points also include the precision and predictability of the law, as well as protection against retroactive

[9] Jeremy Waldron, *The Rule of Law in Contemporary Liberal Theory*, 2 *Ratio Juris* (1989) 79–96 at 81.

[10] Katharina Sobota, *Das Prinzip Rechtsstaat. Verfassungs- und verwaltungsrechtliche Aspekte* (1997) Tübingen: Mohr.

[11] Like, for example, by a parliamentary commission: German Federal Constitutional Court, Decision of 15 December 1970 (2 BvF 1/69, 2 BvR 629/68, 308/69).

decisions. According to the German understanding of constitutional law, the rule of law principle is not a specific guarantee but rather a structural principle that guides the entire constitution.[12] The rule of law principle requires the primacy of the law as a means of making and protecting societal order and resolving conflict between private parties. This requires legal certainty, which is only possible when the law is identifiable, predictable, and reliable.[13]

In terms of content, there is little variation in the applications of the rule of law in different legal orders.[14] The national legal discourses with their own respective historic foci draw on the same canon of topics related to the rule of law, often making reference to the rule of law's (supposedly) common development as a principle of official justice in the modern state. Thus, German constitutional law applies the rule of law principle above all in its dimension of freedom and state containment, through provisions restricting the exercise of executive power—as evidenced in recent security debates, for example.[15] The French *état de droit* similarly refers to an array of constitutional duties that the Conseil d'État is obliged to carry out. In these cases, rule of law refers primarily to constitutional statehood.[16] Meanwhile, the British understanding of the rule of law—like the original conception based on A. V. Dicey—emphasizes the aspect of equality, that is, equal application of the law by the executive state organs and the courts.[17]

Rule of law's concentration on the state is not only confined to Western European legal orders. In the United States, the rule of law centers on the duty of state institutions and state law to serve the People in a formalized system of societal self-government. All persons including executive offices are bound to the law, and this presumes transparency of the law, fair procedure, and equal application of the law. In Russia, the constitution interprets the outdated concept of *pravovoe gosudarstvo* as a law-based state (Art. 1, Par. 1 of the Constitution of the Russian Federation). This derives from the primacy of the *sakon* (закóн: law, *lex*), issued by the state legislation and

[12] Philipp Kunig, *Das Rechtsstaatsprinzip. Überlegungen zu seiner Bedeutung für das Verfassungsrecht der Bundesrepublik Deutschland* (1986) Tübingen: Mohr; *id.*, "Der Rechtsstaat", in *Festschrift 50 Jahre Bundesverfassungsgericht*, Peter Badura and Horst Dreier eds. (2001) Tübingen: Mohr 421–444.

[13] Andreas von Arnauld, *Rechtssicherheit. Perspektivische Annäherung an eine idée directrice des Rechts* (2006) Tübingen: Mohr.

[14] Rainer Grote, "Rule of Law, Rechtsstaat and 'Etat de droit'", in *Constitutionalism, Universalism and Democracy: A Comparative Analysis*, Christian Starck ed. (1999) 269–306; Stefan Martini, "Die Pluralität von Rule-of-Law-Konzeptionen in Europa und das Prinzip einer europäischen Rule of Law", in *Normative Pluralität ordnen*, Matthias Kötter and Gunnar Folke Schuppert eds. (2009) Baden-Baden: Nomos 303–344.

[15] Matthias Kötter, *Pfade des Sicherheitsrechts* (2008) Baden-Baden: Nomos; and the articles in Gunnar Folke Schuppert, Wolfgang Merkel, Georg Nolte, Michael Zürn eds., *Der Rechtsstaat unter Bewährungsdruck* (2010) Baden-Baden: Nomos.

[16] Arthur Dyevre, "The Rule of Law in France", in *Understandings of the Rule of Law in various Legal Orders of the World*, Rule of Law Working Paper Series No. 14, Matthias Kötter and Gunnar Folke Schuppert eds. (2010), *available at* http://wikis.fuberlin.de/download/attachments/21823972/Dyevre+France.pdf.

[17] Martini, *supra* note 14. At 312.

therefore a direct reflection of the sovereign will of the people. All other norms must comply with the *sakon* to guarantee that they also represent the will of the people.[18] The rule of law's orientation toward the state is also propagated in the more recently formed constitutions of Africa and Asia, where providing the institutional preconditions for public authority exercised by way of the law has been a principal purpose of all state-building efforts. Meanwhile, in Islamic countries, the rule of law—because of its relation to the state—is often portrayed as standing in opposition to rule based on Islamic law, which distances itself from the state.[19]

This focus on the state causes problems when non-state legal norms replace state law as the decisive "rules of the game," when system-building and conflict resolution occur regionally or among certain groups based on culturally transmitted or religious laws because state institutions lack the capacity to enforce state law. To overcome the collisions and normative conflicts that result from parallel systems of state and non-state law, societies worldwide have developed various models of connecting the two and incorporating culturally transmitted or religious laws into state law to varying degrees under the umbrella of the constitution.[20] Almost all of these models maintain the primacy of state law and the rule of law, meaning that other norms are only recognized within the framework circumscribed by state law.

In Germany, for example, the right of the churches to regulate their own affairs by means of church law is guaranteed by German Basic Law but only "within the limits of the law that applies to all".[21] This reservation entitles the courts to protect fundamental constitutional provisions and—as in other conflict-of-laws situations—hold up the "ordre public".[22] A similar system applies to native tribes in the United States, which are allowed to set and enforce their own laws on their own land ("Indian territory") according to the principle of tribal sovereignty. At the same time, the federal government has imposed limits on autonomous self-regulation through "native american law", shaped for the most part by Supreme Court decisions.[23]

---

[18] Ilja Skrylnikow, "Understanding of the Rule of Law in Russia", in *Understandings of the Rule of Law in various legal orders of the World*, Rule of Law Working Paper Series Nr. 8, Matthias Kötter and Gunnar Folke Schuppert eds. (2009), *available at* http://wikis.fu-berlin.de/download/attachments/22347909/Skrylnikow+Russia.pdf.

[19] Hatem Elliesie, "Rule of Law in Islamic modeled States", in *Understandings of the Rule of Law in various Legal Orders of the World*, Rule of Law Working Paper Series No. 13, Matthias Kötter and Gunnar Folke Schuppert eds. (2010), *available at* http://wikis.fu-berlin.de/download/attachments/69533704/Elliesie+Islamic+modeled+States.pdf); id., "Binnenpluralität des Islamischen Rechts. Diversität religiöser Normativität rechtsdogmatisch und -methodisch betrachtet", SFB-Governance Working Paper Series (2013), (forthcoming).

[20] Brynna Connolly, Non-State Justice systems and the State: Proposal for a Recognition Typology, 38 *Connecticut Law Review* (2005) 239–294; Miranda Forsyth, A Typology of Relationships between State and Non-State Justice Systems, 56 *Journal of Legal Pluralism*, 67–112; and Kötter, *supra* note 8. At 16.

[21] Article 140, German Basic Law, in conjunction with article 137 of the Weimar Constitution.

[22] German Federal Constitutional Court, Decision of 4 June 1985 (2 BvR 1703, 1718/83, 856/84).

[23] William C. Jr. Canby, *American Indian Law in a Nutshell* (5th ed. 2009) St. Paul, MN: Thomson/West.

Both of these systems assume that state law is valid and can be enforced when needed. In places where state law cannot be enforced, however, it is impossible to impose limits on other actors' regulatory autonomy; here, state law only maintains authority on paper. Because of this, the South African constitution takes a slightly different approach. In order to protect the cultural rights of its African communities, it declares traditional customary law to be part of the official legal order and recognizes customary courts as part of the official court system.[24] Recognition exists under the condition that traditional norms can be reconciled to the rest of the constitution and the rule of law, understood here as a synonym for constitutional statehood.[25] This applies to both formal requirements and human rights guarantees. The integration of customary courts into state jurisdiction gives the Constitutional Court the ultimate interpretive authority on the compatibility of legal norms and their resulting decisions—regardless of whether customary or state law is involved. Legal certainty requires individual rules to be predictable and reliable whether they are set by statutory law, common law, or customary law. When customary law does not fulfill the same strict, formal standards as state law (e.g., in carrying out a trial or in issuing a verdict in written form), the discrepancies are temporarily tolerated to some extent in order to foster recognition of traditional law, but are also presented for public discussion to encourage normative equalization.[26]

Rather than emphasizing the primacy of state law to which non-state norms are subordinate, South Africa gives weight to the role of non-state norms as long as they represent equivalents to state law; de facto, they are effective regulatory norms in the areas of system-building and conflict resolution. The rule of the law can therefore be exercised through non-state legal norms as well, as long as they fulfill the qualitative standards that rule of-law principles require of state law. In normative terms, non-state law must also fit into the rest of the legal system; in South Africa this means that customary law is nominally subject to the same constitutional standards as state law. Thus, South Africa represents a departure from a concept of law and the rule of law based solely on the state.

The extension of the rule of law to non-state law is not only a South African phenomenon. New constitutional orders have adopted this approach as well, for example in East Timor and South Sudan, which have modeled themselves more or less explicitly after South Africa.[27] The conceptual expansion goes beyond the

---

[24] Jan C. Bekker and Christa Rautenbach, "Nature and Sphere of Application of African Customary Law in South Africa", in *Introduction to Legal Pluralism*, Christa Rautenbach, Jan C. Bekker, Nazeem M. I. Goolam eds. (3rd ed. 2010) Durban: LexisNexis at 39.

[25] Francois Venter, "South Africa as a 'Diceyan *Rechtsstaat*'", in *Understandings of the Rule of Law in various legal orders of the World*, Rule of Law Working Paper Series No. 18, Matthias Kötter and Gunnar Folke Schuppert eds. (2011), *available at* http://wikis.fuberlin.de/download/attachments/173736195/Venter+South+Africa.pdf.

[26] *See* Matthias Kötter, "Anerkennung fremder Normen im staatlichen Recht als normatives und kognitives Problem", in *Extra-disziplinäres Wissen im Verwaltungsrecht*, Ino Augsberg ed. (2013) Tübingen: Mohr 63–98 at 94.

[27] Laura Grenfell, *supra* note 7.

framework of constitutional law to include development cooperation and rule of law promotion, discussed below in terms of the indicators used to assess the rule of law.

6.2.2 Development Policy Discourses: The Rule of Law as a Model and Yardstick

Development policy debates over the last 10 years have largely centered on rule of law promotion—a concept that aims to restructure the governments and legal systems of precarious states according to the model of the Western constitutional state. At its core, this approach hopes to lay the institutional foundations for constitutional rule in the areas of legislation, administration, and justice. The rule of law concept serves as both a model and a measuring tool with which to assess state systems and governance. Thus, the rule of law has become increasingly integral to the concept of good governance, which has shaped international development discourse since the early 1990s and takes the rule of law as one of its pillars.[28]

As a transnational model of statehood, the rule of law facilitates agreement among the various development cooperation actors on the local, national, and international levels—governments, international organizations, scholars, think tanks, NGOs—with regard to legitimate rule. Rule of law is based on a canon of topics and arguments that frame this process of compromise and agreement in a way that is acceptable to everyone. A globally accessible mode of communication—a kind of *lingua franca*—has emerged in international development cooperation under the banner of the rule of law to describe the "correct" way to structure societies and governance.

For societies in which system-building and conflict resolution have not taken place by way of or according to the law, the rule of law also entails an agenda of reform or a modernization program following the model of Western constitutions and their justice systems. Rule of law promotion often includes establishing institutions as one component of comprehensive state-building efforts. However, empirical evaluations show that such programs seldom meet with success, and the creation or transfer of effective legal orders and court systems is often prone to failure.[29] "State law regulatory gaps" can be attributed in large part to the persistence of culturally rooted institutions and their functionality in terms of system-building and conflict resolution.[30]

---

[28] Matthias Kötter, "Wie viel Recht steckt in Good Governance?", SFB-Governance Working Paper Series No. 58 (2013).

[29] Noah Coburn and John Dempsey, "Traditional Dispute Resolution and Stability in Afghanistan", U. S. Institute of Peace (USIP) (2010), *available at* http://www.usip.org/publications/traditional-dispute-resolution-and-stability-in-afghanistan (2014-03-29).

[30] Brian Tamanaha, *supra* note 6.

In order to assess the extent of the rule of law (already) in place in a given country and to identify "regulatory gaps," measuring instruments and scales of evaluation have been developed in recent years whose importance for the field of international development policy cannot be overstated.[31] "Rule of law by indicators"—a thematic variation on "global governance by indicators"—is designed to provide an empirical foundation for policy-making while simultaneously generating benchmarks of success.[32] However, the rule-of-law concepts cited in various indices have little theoretical foundation and differ markedly from each other.[33] In the World Bank's *Worldwide World Governance Indicators* (WGI) and the *Bertelsmann Transformation Index* (BTI), for example, the rule of law is measured as a subdimension in a broader index to evaluate the quality of democratic governance. Only the *Rule of Law Index*, published annually by the World Justice Project since 2010, exclusively assesses the rule of law and uses the following indicators:

1. Limited government powers
2. Absence of corruption
3. Order and security
4. Fundamental rights
5. Open government
6. Regulatory enforcement
7. Civil justice
8. Criminal justice

The eight indicators in the *Rule of Law Index* focus on state institutions and state law. They are supposed to measure the degree to which the exercise of authority occurs in accordance to the law. More recently, however, the World Justice Report's conceptualization of the rule of law has undergone a shift toward non-state, "informal" structures of order and conflict resolution. In the 2012 report, "informal justice" was added as a ninth factor to the list above with the following explanation[34]:

> Factor 9 concerns the role played in many countries by traditional, or "informal," systems of law—including traditional, tribal, and religious courts as well as community-based systems—

---

[31] Peter Thiery, Jenniver Sehring, and Wolfgang Muno, "Die Messung von Rechtsstaatlichkeit", in *Interdisziplinäre Rechtsforschung zwischen Rechtswirklichkeit, Rechtsanalyse und Rechtsgestaltung*, Josef Estermann ed. (2009) Beckenried: Orlax 211–230; Wolfgang Merkel, "Measuring the Quality of Rule of Law: Virtues, Perils, Results", in Zürn et al. *supra* note 5, 21–47.

[32] Christine Arndt and Charles Oman, "Uses and Abuses of Governance Indicators", OECD Development Center (2006). Armin von Bogdandy and Matthias Goldmann, "The Exercise of International Public Authority Through National Policy Assessment. The OECD's PISA Policy as a Paradigm for a New International Standard Instrument", 5 *International Organizations Law Review* (2008), 241–298; Kevin Davis, Angelina Fisher, Benedict Kingsbury, and Sally E. Merry eds., *Governance by Indicators* (2012) Oxford University Press; Kevin E. Davis, Benedict Kingsbury, and Sally E. Merry, "Indicators as a Technology of Global Governance", 46 *Law and Society Review* (2012) 71–104.

[33] Wolfgang Merkel, *supra* note 31. At 47.

[34] Mark D. Agrast et al., *The WJP Rule of Law Index 2012*, The World Justice Project (2012) at 17.

in resolving disputes. These systems often play a large role in cultures in which formal legal institutions fail to provide effective remedies for large segments of the population or when formal institutions are perceived as remote, corrupt, or ineffective. This factor covers two concepts: (1) whether traditional, communal and religious dispute resolution systems are impartial and effective; and (2) the extent to which these systems respect and protect fundamental rights.

The additional indicator points to the specific functions of non-state structures for order and conflict resolution and asks how compatible these structures are with international legal standards. To what extent non-state systems contribute to the rule of law in the same way that state law does, initially emerges as an empirical question.[35] The knowledge gained through these empirical findings will change the general understanding of the rule of law and encourage the inclusion of non-state legal institutions in the rule of law model and policy-making efforts. Impulses in this direction appear elsewhere as well, for example when Brian Tamanaha tries to avoid the rule of law's "state law thrust" by not confining his definition specifically to state law; here, rule of law dictates that "government officials and citizens are bound by and abide by the law." As Tamanaha writes, "This generic quality allows it to be applied more broadly to other forms of law."[36]

At the same time, it is important to examine the requirements and limitations involved in expanding the rule of law to include non-state regulatory forms. The *Rule of Law Index* ascribes significant conflict resolution capacities to non-state legal systems in situations where state institutions cannot access broad portions of the population or are generally considered ineffective and corrupt. Contributions by non-state legal systems to the rule of law can then be measured in terms of their impartiality, effectiveness, and commitment to guaranteeing human rights. In order to contribute to the rule of law, non-state legal systems are subject to much stricter standards than state law; they must be factually valid, effective, and respectful of human rights. The conceptual discussions here are still in their early stages.

6.2.3 Global Governance Discourse: The Rule of Law as a Building Block of Global Governance

Even in international and transnational contexts beyond the state and the state law, scholars increasingly use the rule of law to generate standards by which to measure norm-building processes.

---

[35] *Id.* In a footnote, the authors of the World Justice Report address the limitations of this endeavor: "Significant effort has been devoted during the last 3 years to collecting data on informal justice in a dozen countries. Nonetheless, the complexities of these systems and the difficulties of measuring their fairness and effectiveness in a manner that is both systematic and comparable across countries, make assessments extraordinarily challenging. Although the WJP has collected data on this dimension, it is not included in the aggregated scores and rankings".

[36] Tamanaha, *supra* note 6. At 6.

In the field of international relations and global governance, a twofold shift has occurred in the meaning of the rule of law. On the one hand, the concept has become increasingly consolidated as a topos of international law, relating to a whole array of general international legal principles. On the other hand, expanding the perspective to include global governance has revealed many different formal and informal institutionalized forms of social coordination beyond clearly delineated state entities. Taken together, these developments in addressing contexts beyond the state call into question whether the rule of law can apply to non-state (legal) norms, and which requirements this recognition would imply.

In international law, the rule of law has increasingly established itself as a legal principle in its own right as well as a yardstick with which to evaluate state action.[37] Similar to the rule of law principle in domestic constitutional law, the rule of law is understood here as a structural principle that shapes international law, encompassing numerous individual guarantees that derive from various legal sources. The rule of law refers to an adherence to and enforcement of international treaties, as well as the strengthening of international law as such. It manifests itself in a prohibition of violence and the basic principle of peaceful dispute settlement.[38] Especially within the United Nations, long-term developments have led to an increasingly strong commitment to rule-of-law principles. The most recent step so far was the *Declaration of the High-level-Meeting of the General Assembly on the Rule of Law at the National and International Level*, ratified by the General Assembly on September 24, 2012. The Declaration includes 42 points addressing topics such as limited authority, peaceful conflict resolution, the guarantee of legal certainty, and universal access to the law.

One major deficit in international rule of law lies in the underlying difficulty of enforcing international law due to a lack of comprehensive political authority or coercive power in the international legal system.[39] For the most part, international law is a system of treaties and custom. Its binding power depends on the will of the contracting parties to comply and the mutual expectation that the stated obligations will in fact be respected.

However, beyond the formal structures of the international arena, phenomena of non-state norm production exist as well through standard-setting processes and other forms of informal lawmaking. From a juristic point of view, these phenomena can be understood as part of "transnational law,"[40] and they pose similar questions

[37] Helmut Aust, Georg Nolte, "International Rule of Law and the Rule of Law at the National Level", in Zürn, Nollkaemper, and Peerenboom, *supra* note 5. At 67.

[38] *Cf.* Thomas Kleinlein, *Konstitutionalisierung im Völkerrecht. Konstruktion und Elemente einer idealistischen Völkerrechtslehre* (2012) Heidelberg: Springer at 542.

[39] Stefan Oeter, "Chancen und Defizite internationaler Verrechtlichung. Was das Recht jenseits des Nationalstaats leisten kann", in Zangl and Zürn, *supra* note 2, 46–73 at 52; Kleinlein, *supra* note 38. At 548.

[40] Philipp C. Jessup, *Transnational Law* (1956) at 2 uses "the term 'transnational law' to include all law which regulates actions or events that transcend national frontiers. Both public and private international law are included, as are other rules which do not wholly fit into such standard categories."

to informal lawmaking processes in the national context regarding the rule of law: Can informal legal structures established in the framework of global governance by globally active state and non-state actors contribute to the rule of law? And to what extent can rule-of-law principles provide a yardstick with which to measure the formation of legitimate, informal legal norms that adhere to international law?

In the global governance debate, the role of the law and rule of law principles have garnered increasing attention.[41] In their 2004 paper, "Make law, not war," Zangl and Zürn summarize the development of international and transnational juridification as a core element of global governance. At the heart of this development is peaceful conflict settlement following legal standards according to legally regulated procedures. More and more, the review and revision of decisions in cases of conflict have become functions of the courts or court-like judicial institutions. The formation of a combined regime of legal norms and judicial institutions—the basic structure of all formal definitions of the rule of law—has become especially pronounced in the increasing judicialization of dispute settlement within the World Trade Organization (WTO), which serves as an international model. Bernhard Zangl justifiably observes an "internationalization of the rule of law" through judicialization.[42]

As a result, the processes of setting and enforcing norms in the arena of global governance must adhere to rule of law standards in order not only to create a system of rules governing action, but also—on a second level, as a regime of "second-order rules" (see Sect. 6.3.2)—to establish and institutionalize adequate structures to enforce these norms. Judicialization in this sense refers to the development of binding legal rules and legal procedures to implement the law. In addition to simply regulating relations between the various actors, there must be a qualitative "something else" in the form of secondary codification that outlines the application and enforcement of the rules. This trend manifests itself in the marked expansion of international courts and the growing importance of court-regulated dispute settlement procedures.

6.2.4 Summary

All three discourses addressed in this section start with a state-centered understanding of the rule of law, which is then challenged by the non-existence of effective state law in certain areas; in its place, other, non-state forms of system-building and conflict resolution emerge that seem to serve as functional equivalents (in terms of rule of law standards). In their own ways, all three discourses refer to these

---

[41] Zangl and Zürn, *supra* note 2; Michael Zürn, "Global Governance", in *Governance-Forschung. Vergewisserung über Stand und Entwicklungslinien*, Gunnar Folke Schuppert ed. (2005) 121–146.

[42] Bernhard Zangl, *Die Internationalisierung der Rechtsstaatlichkeit. Streitbeilegung in GATT und WTO* (2006) Frankfurt: Campus.

non-state legal structures in order to expand the scope of the rule of law. Thus, the rule of law concept has undergone a significant conceptual shift that, considering its function, seems inevitable. If the rule of law denotes the exercise of authority and settlement of societal dispute by way of the law and guarantees these things as an overriding legal principle, then it must be able to accommodate legal norms beyond the laws set by the state.

Three requirements must be met in order for non-state legal norms to be recognized under the rule of law. They must: (1) perform legal functions, contributing to system-building and conflict resolution; (2) be factually valid, in most cases requiring adequate enforcement institutions; and (3) normatively and institutionally reflect a general understanding of justice. Only with this last requirement is it possible to avoid associating the rule of law with forms of injustice serving as functional equivalents of justice. With this definition, the rule of law can be used as a global yardstick for norm-building processes beyond the state.

6.3 The Rule of Law as a Global Yardstick, Even and Especially in Contexts Beyond the State

This section addresses a second observation: the experiences of legitimate and effective governance subsumed under the rule of law can be applied as a normative yardstick to evaluate both the non-state processes of setting and enforcing norms, and the quality of those norms. This development is illustrated through the example of transnational standard-setting.

6.3.1 The Growing Significance of the Rule of Law in Discussions on the Legitimation of Governance Beyond the Nation-State

A single topic dominates the discussion in political science today: the legitimation of authority in the postnational constellation.[43] Since "modern rule" primarily refers to the rule of the law, the legitimacy debate is forced to include the legitimation of non-state regulatory systems and international legal regimes. Therefore, all normative systems necessarily require justification, as Rainer Forst and Klaus Günther have argued.[44] And, if normative systems require justification, then they need the

[43] Michael Zürn, "Perspektiven des demokratischen Regierens und die Rolle der Politikwissenschaft im 21. Jahrhundert", 52 *Politische Vierteljahresschrift* (2011) 603–635; Anna Geis, Frank Nullmeier, and Christopher Daase eds., *Der Aufstieg der Legitimitätspolitik* (2012) Baden-Baden: Nomos.

[44] Rainer Forst and Klaus Günther, "Die Herausbildung normativer Ordnungen. Zur Idee eines interdisziplinären Forschungsprogramms", in *Die Herausbildung normativer Ordnungen. Interdisziplinäre Perspektiven*, Rainer Forst ed. (2011) Frankfurt: Campus 11–32.

support of a convincing justification narrative. On the level of nation-states, this is the constitution. It regulates and legitimizes the establishment of national law, the values it is obliged to follow, and the limits of legal regulation. It makes sense to want to transfer the constitution's legitimation potential to the international level; hence the general fascination with the concept of constitutionalization which enables the possibility of "zoning up" a recognized and proven justification narrative to the transnational or international level.[45]

However, a different approach is warranted. Drawing on Bernhard Zangl's analysis of the emerging international principle of exercising authority by way of the law (*internationale Rechtsherrschaft*),[46] we propose differentiating between three constitutionalization processes that are all grounded in basic principles of a constitutional order: human rights, democracy, and the rule of the law. While all three principles are of equal normative value, their degrees of realization often differ sharply depending on political reality, dictating that they should be separated analytically by treating them as three different legitimation narratives. In the rule of law legitimation discourse, this entails being able to use the rule of law principle as a normative yardstick, even—and indeed, especially—for normative systems beyond the state.

6.3.2 Rule of Law Principles as "Second-Order Rules"

Rule of law principles can easily serve as a normative yardstick if they are seen as so-called "second-order rules." Common in legal theory, this distinction between primary and secondary rules was outlined by Robert S. Summers for the context of the rule of law[47]:

> The principles of the rule of law differ from principles of ordinary "first order law." Principles of ordinary first order law apply directly to determine legal relations between immediate addressees of such law. … Unlike such "first order" principles, the principles of the rule of law are what might be called *"second order" principles*. … Principles of the rule of law are about first order law in the sense that they are general norms that direct and constrain how first order law is to be created and implemented.

Michael Zürn and Bernhard Zangl agree with this differentiation and apply it to the judicialization processes discussed above[48]:

---

[45] Christoph Möllers, "Verfassungsgebende Gewalt—Verfassung—Konstitutionalisierung", in *Europäisches Verfassungsrecht. Theoretische und dogmatische Grundzüge*, Armin von Bogdandy ed. (1st ed. 2003) Berlin: Springer 1–57; Kleinlein, *supra* note 38; Mattias Kumm, "Kosmopolitischer Staat und konstitutionelle Autorität. Eine integrative Konzeption Öffentlichen Rechts", in *Verabschiedung und Wiederentdeckung des Staates im Spannungsfeld der Disziplinen*, Der Staat Beiheft 21, Andreas Voßkuhle, Christian Bumke and Florian Meinel eds. (2013) Berlin: Duncker&Humblodt, 245–266.

[46] Zangl, *supra* note 2. At 27.

[47] Robert S. Summers, "The Principles of the Rule of Law", 74 *Notre Dame Law Review* (1999) 1691–1712 at 1692f.

[48] Zangl and Zürn, *supra* note 2. At 21, with further reference to HLA Hart, *The concept of law* (1994), and Paul F. Diehl, Charlotte Ku, Daniel Zamora, "The Dynamics of International Law: The

> Judicialization processes are characterized ... by the institutional definition of so-called 'secondary rules.' Wherever the setting, implementation, and enforcement of rules do not follow previously defined procedures ... it is impossible to really speak of the law. Thus, a sophisticated legal system requires both primary and secondary rules.

Keeping this in mind, rule of law principles can be conceived as manageable "second-order rules" that function as a normative yardstick in the three areas below.[49] The rule of law principle provides clear secondary rules for:

1. *Lawmaking*: "In other words, these rules determine how the lawmaker should create legal norms so that they can be legally binding. ... They are indispensible to the legal system!"[50]
2. Certain *qualitative demands* of lawmaking: if legal rules are to function as the central steering instrument of a democratic constitutional state,[51] they must contain a certain level of clarity and precision and be free of contradiction.
3. *Law enforcement*: Rules of this kind are also essential for law enforcement in modern societies: "The effectiveness and societal relevance of a legal order largely depend on the extent to which it is capable of guaranteeing its own realization. At the same time, the dimensions and limitations of a coercive power deemed acceptable reflect the fundamental values of a society."[52]

If it is accepted that the principle of the rule of law represents a bundle of "second-order rules," it is important to test whether its effectiveness is limited to state law—in which case it may even be redundant in developed constitutional states—or whether it is in fact more effective in the area of non-state norm formulation. From a regulatory science perspective, this is indeed the case.

6.3.3 *Rules for Rule-Making: The Example of Non-state Standard-Setting*

Once one departs from the context of state law and enters the other "world of rules," it quickly becomes clear that secondary rules have enormous importance for non-state rule-making. What is needed from the perspective of regulatory science is a set of "rules for rule-making."[53] In the area of non-state standard-setting, a kind of code

Interaction of Normative and Operating Systems", 57 *International Organisations* (2003) 43–75.

[49] Nico Krisch, *Beyond Constitutionalism. The Pluralist Structure of Postnational Law* (2010) Oxford University Press; *cf.* Zangl, *supra* note 46. At 28.

[50] *Id.* At 29.

[51] Gunnar Folke Schuppert and Christian Starck eds., *Das Gesetz als zentrales Steuerungsinstrument des Rechtsstaates. Symposion anläßlich des 60. Geburtstages von Christian Starck* (1998) Baden-Baden: Nomos.

[52] Karin Nehlsen von-Stryk, "Grenzen des Rechtszwangs: Zur Geschichte der Naturalvollstreckung", 193 *Archiv für die civilistische Praxis* (1993) 529–555 at 530.

[53] Schuppert, *supra* note 5. At 100.

for non-state rule-making has emerged. As Harm Schepel reports,[54] nearly all significant standard setters have developed so-called "standardization standards," formulating minimum standards that can achieve consensus among the participating actors. Among them Schepel lists the following[55]:

1. Elaboration of draft standards in technical committees with a balance of represented interests (manufacturers, consumers, social partners, public authorities);
2. A requirement of consensus on the committee before the draft goes to
3. A round of public notice and comment, with the obligation on the committee to take received comments into account, and
4. A ratification vote, again with the requirement of consensus rather than mere majority, among the constituency of the standards body, and
5. The obligation to review standards periodically.

The "Code of Good Practice for Standardization" from the International Standard-Setting Organization[56] offers one example of a self-regulatory formulation of secondary rules in the area of standard setting. Especially crucial is rule 3.1, which explicitly states that these "second order rules" apply to any kind of standardization, whether at the state, non-state, international, or local level:

> 3.1 This code is intended for use by any standardizing body, whether governmental or non-governmental, at international, regional, national or sub-national level. …
>
> 4.1 Written procedures based on the consensus principle should govern the methods used for standards development. Copies of the procedures of the standardizing body shall be available to interested parties in a reasonable and timely manner upon request.
>
> 4.2 Such written procedures should contain an identifiable, realistic and readily available appeals mechanism for the impartial handling of any substantive and procedural complaints.
>
> 4.3 Notification of standardization activity shall be made in suitable media as appropriate to afford interested persons or organizations an opportunity for meaningful contributions. …
>
> 4.6 All standards should be reviewed on a periodic basis and revised in a timely manner. Proposals for the development of new or revised standards, when submitted according to appropriate procedures by any materially and directly interested person or organization, wherever located, should be given prompt consideration. …
>
> 6.1 Participation in standardization processes at all levels shall be accessible to materially and directly interested persons and organizations within a coherent process as described in this clause.

[54] Harm Schepel, *The Constitution Of Private Governance: Product Standards In The Regulation Of Integrating Markets* (2005) Oxford: Hart Publ.

[55] *Id.* At 6.

[56] ISO/IEC Guide 59 (1994).

The material above may be summarized in two main points.

First, the area of non-state norm-setting has produced "rules for rule-making" that satisfy exactly the same function as we attribute to the rule-of-law principles when talking about the state. These "standards for standardization" are nothing more than secondary rules that guide the process of setting standards and therefore present certain procedural and organizational requirements to which the process must comply. From a regulatory science perspective, which does not limit itself to the legal order of the state but rather includes a variety of normative regulatory systems, it is easy to conclude that these are, in fact, rule-of-law principles—an unsurprising epiphany considering that the Anglo-Saxon understanding of the rule of law was never exclusively confined to the state. In this respect, the rule of law concept shares its power to relativize the state with the concept of *governance*, whose usefulness derives from its capacity to address institutional arrangements and regulatory structures beyond the state from a functionalist perspective.[57]

Second, it is important to note that applying rule of law principles to non-state regulatory systems necessarily ties in to the legitimation discourses mentioned above: "second-order rules" formulate conditions and requirements under which non-state norms such as "standards" and "codes of conduct" become legitimate norm-setting processes that can expect to garner general compliance. This need for legitimation in non-state rule-making becomes especially important when regulatory systems not only "look … like lawmaking"[58] but are, in fact, functional equivalents to state law.

6.3.4 Norm-Setting in Place of the State: Filling the Regulatory Gap

The existence of regulatory gaps becomes especially obvious in two constellations: first, in areas where the state takes a position of regulatory abstinence and uses the self-regulation of private actors to relieve itself of regulatory duties; second, in "denationalized" arenas in which the state has no regulatory authority. Two examples illustrate this equivalence.

The first example is the "fate" of a German non-state takeover code containing rules prescribing the behavior of bidding and target companies in the context of public company takeovers.[59] Written by the German Exchange Experts Commission (BSK) in 1995 and modeled after the British City Code on Takeovers and Mergers of

[57] Thomas Risse, "Governance in Areas of limited Statehood", in Risse ed. *supra* note 8, 1–35 at 9; Michael Zürn and Mathias Koenig-Archibugy, "Conclusions II: The Modes and Dynamics of Global Governance", in *The Modes of Governance in the Global System*, Mathias Koenig-Archibugy and Michael Zürn eds. (2006) Houndsmills: Palgrave Macmillan, 236–254 at 236.

[58] Schepel, *supra* note 54. At 6.

[59] Steffen Augsberg, *Rechtsetzung zwischen Staat und Gesellschaft. Möglichkeiten differenzierter Steuerung des Kapitalmarktes* (2003) Berlin: Duncker&Humblodt.

1968, the body of rules aimed above all to protect the investor but also tried to secure and support a functioning market by ensuring transparency and equal opportunity[60]:

> In a growing and interwoven global economic system in which national regulations increasingly orient themselves toward the expectations of a real or fictive international "financial community," the takeover code can be seen as an attempt to introduce international standards to Germany on a voluntary basis in order to improve Germany's reputation as a financial center.

The special thing about this document is its adoption to a great extent by the German legislation—following proposed guidelines from the European Union—through the Securities Acquisition and Takeover Act ("Wertpapiererwerbs- und Übernahmegesetz") of January 1, 2002. The passage of this law illustrates "a normative regulatory technique by which former mechanisms of self-regulation are taken over by the state and transformed into law."[61]

The second example arises from standardized terms of contract. Standardization is not only limited to technical things such as paper formats (letter, legal etc.) or the sizes of screw threads[62]; it can also apply to contractual conditions. The rapid proliferation of standardized terms of contract—especially in the areas of insurance and transportation—reflects on the one hand a need for standardization in industries with strong ties to the world economy, and on the other a general reticence of lawmakers to exercise regulation, resulting in a "regulatory gap"[63]:

> The emergence of special standard contracts, standard clauses or standard contract forms for international commerce depended upon several circumstances. In principle, the interest in a standardization of the contractual bases was more intense the more the given branch was involved in world commerce. Just as on the level of individual States, the companies took pains to achieve an international standardization of their contractual bases if State regulations were lacking or were deemed ineffective or outdated. … The less the State regulated the law of individual branches, the more did non-state regulations of commercial and legal transactions become widespread.

Tilmann Röder proposes four functions performed by the standardization of contract terms:

- Power (asymmetrical influence over the content of contract terms)
- Communication
- Legal certainty
- Filling in gaps and making progress

Examining these functions, there can be no doubt that the practice of standardization is also a process of norm formation. Standardized contracts influence the behavior

---

[60] *Id.* At 279.

[61] *Id.* At 289.

[62] Miloš Vec, *Recht und Normierung in der Industriellen Revolution. Neue Strukturen der Normsetzung in Völkerrecht, staatlicher Gesetzgebung und gesellschaftlicher Selbstnormierung* (2006) Frankfurt: Klostermann.

[63] Tilmann J. Röder, *From Industrial to Legal Standardization, 1871–1914: Transnational Insurance Law and the Great San Francisco Earthquake* (2012) Leiden: Martinus Nijhoff at 293f.

of market actors, who depend on their reliability and use them as a point of orientation; whatever agreements they contain serve as the authoritative body of rules, substituting, developing, or entirely circumventing existing statutory law. It is a form of rule-making, a new structure of norm formation that contemporary legal experts hardly acknowledge. Röder summarizes as follows[64]:

> Standard clauses and contracts were preformulated without relation to concrete business transactions as the uniform legal bases for large numbers of future contracts. In this respect, their origin is reminiscent more of the legislative process than of the usual business contract process.

Both examples vividly illustrate that non-state bodies of rules in the area of transnational commerce operate as functional equivalents to state law. Such bodies of rules not only "feel like they are close to the law"[65]; they *are* de facto the law. However, if non-state norm-setting substitutes for state lawmaking in certain contexts, it follows that the production process of these rules should be held to the same standards as the creation of legal principles. This essentially clears the path for the application of rule of law principles. As Harm Schepel aptly puts it, this expansion of usage entails a "normative borrowing between the public and private spheres".[66]

6.4 Conclusion

This chapter has shown that in contexts "beyond the state," where state institutions do not have a monopoly on the setting and enforcement of rules, non-state entities produce (legal) norms that can fulfill the functions of the rule of law. The rule of law's expanded scope beyond state law manifests itself in all three discourses addressed here: constitutional law, law and development, and global governance. When non-state norms contribute to system-building and conflict resolution, when their validity has institutional foundations, and when they normatively and institutionally reflect a general understanding of justice, it is productive to recognize them as the rule of law. At the same time, informal legal norms that replace state law as its functional equivalent must be measured according to the same standards as state law. In this sense, rule of law principles can provide a general yardstick to evaluate even these norm-building processes that occur beyond the state.

[64] *Id.* At 291.

[65] Oliver Lepsius, "Standardsetzung und Legitimation", in *Internationales Verwaltungsrecht. Eine Analyse anhand von Referenzgebieten,* Christoph Möllers, Andreas Voßkuhle, and Christian Walter eds. (2007) Tübingen: Mohr 345–374 at 347.

[66] Schepel, *supra* note 54. At 6.

Chapter 7
The Rule of Law as a Global Norm for Constitutionalism

Francois Venter

Abstract The rule of law is widely used (and sometimes cynically abused) in domestic and international constitutional discourse, occasionally with clear meaning, more often obscurely. When mention is made of constitutionalism (an equally imprecise term), the rule of law is almost always invoked. Constitutionalism purports to reflect good values, and so does the rule of law, but listing these values comprehensively to the satisfaction of all would be an impossible quest. Nevertheless, due to the universality of the notion of reciprocity, agreement that human dignity and non-arbitrariness are the most essential characteristics of the rule of law, is attainable. The rule of law offers a *tertium comparationis* particularly useful for constitutional comparison.

7.1 Introduction

Lawyers, and perhaps even more so constitutional lawyers, have a highly flexible vocabulary. The suppleness of their terminology has through the centuries contributed to such (sometimes joking) characterizations of the legal profession as: does a lawyer say what he means and mean what he says? It is unfortunately true that many lawyers have abused, and will in future abuse the flexibility of language to state poor cases. One would, however, hope that is not the case in legal scholarship. Scholars are subject to the discipline of their peers, who will censure the work of one among them who abuses language to further some interest, academic or otherwise.

The research reflected in this chapter was made possible by the generous support of the National Research Foundation and the Alexander von Humboldt Foundation.

F. Venter (✉)
Faculty of Law, North-West University, Potchefstroom, South Africa
e-mail: Francois.Venter@nwu.ac.za

J.R. Silkenat et al. (eds.), *The Legal Doctrines of the Rule of Law and the Legal State (Rechtsstaat)*, Ius Gentium: Comparative Perspectives on Law and Justice 38,
DOI 10.1007/978-3-319-05585-5_7,

And yet, constitutional scholarship is constrained by language speckled with embarrassingly vague, though otherwise revered concepts such as democracy, human rights, constitutionalism, dignity, justice and the rule of law. Legal scholarship is, alas, not an exact science. It uses expressions, sometimes defining or redefining them to justify a particular application, sometimes simply assuming (or hoping) that those that read or hear it, attach approximately the same meaning to the words. This is an unsatisfactory situation, but one that cannot be circumvented.

Where does this leave scholarship on the rule of law? To attach a particular meaning to the phrase requires taking into account its history and usage, then to position it in the broader context of constitutionalism. Its utility then may be considered for the purposes of constitutional comparison and to draw some conclusions regarding its merits and limitations. These are the steps that are traced below.

7.2 Employment of the Notion

No doubt other chapters in this book will provide an authoritative philosophical and conceptual history of the rule of law.[1] There can also be no doubt that a range of equivalent and relatively similar notions are available, including the German *Rechtsstaat* and *Verfassungsstaat*, the French *l'Etat de droit* and/or *l'Etat légal*, the Italian *stato di diritto*, the Spanish *estado constitucional* or *estado de derecho*, etc.

The use of the term (or its equivalents) in constitutions and international instruments is widespread. Some examples:

The third paragraph of the United Nations Universal Declaration of Human Rights states:

> Whereas it is essential, if man is not to be compelled to have recourse, as a last resort, to rebellion against tyranny and oppression, that human rights should be protected by the rule of law

What this means in the UN context was defined in 2004 by the Secretary General:[2]

> The "rule of law" is a concept at the very heart of the Organization's mission. It refers to a principle of governance in which all persons, institutions and entities, public and private, including the State itself, are accountable to laws that are publicly promulgated, equally enforced and independently adjudicated, and which are consistent with international human rights norms and standards. It requires, as well, measures to ensure adherence to the principles of supremacy of law, equality before the law, accountability to the law, fairness in the application of the law, separation of powers, participation in decision-making, legal certainty, avoidance of arbitrariness and procedural and legal transparency.

---

[1] A slight effort in this direction is to be found in Francois Venter, "South Africa: A Diceyan *Rechtsstaat*?", 57 *McGill Law Journal* (2012) 721–747.

[2] *The rule of law and transitional justice in conflict and post-conflict societies,* UN Security Council S/2004/616, 23 August 2004, par III 6.

The final paragraph of the preamble to the 1950 European Convention for the Protection of Human Rights and Fundamental Freedoms (ECHR)[3] reads:

> Being resolved, as the governments of European countries which are like-minded and have a common heritage of political traditions, ideals, freedom and the rule of law, to take the first steps for the collective enforcement of certain of the rights stated in the Universal Declaration

The age-old rift between European civil law and English common law scholarship have until recently isolated rule of law teaching from continental thinking on the concept of the *Rechtsstaat*. The two notions developed under fundamentally different assumptions, but they addressed broadly speaking a similar area, leading many European writers to use the term "rule of law" when they write in English about *Rechtsstaatlichkeit*.[4] In the German text of the ECHR, "rule of law" appears as "Rechtsstaatlichkeit." The reason for this dichotomy lies in the fact that the two terms are mutually untranslatable to or from English and especially the Germanic languages. Some English writers, however, tend to simply ignore the *Rechtsstaat*. In one of the finest recent dissertations on the rule of law, Trevor Allan[5] in his "liberal" theory of the rule of law (apparently unconcerned with continental constructions), extracted from compared common law systems a number of characteristics that are very similar to those of the *Rechtsstaat*, though described in different terms. Thus, he speaks of the "internal morality" of the law reflected in the rule of law, which comes very close to what continental scholars would refer to as an "objective normative system of values" characteristic of the *Rechtsstaat*.[6] Had Allan extended his comparative work beyond common law systems to the rich continental theory of the *Rechtsstaat*, there can be little doubt that his contribution would have been even more impressive.

In the documents reflecting the work of the Conference on Security and Co-operation in Europe (CSCE) and later the Organization for Security and Co-operation in Europe (OSCE), references to the rule of law, frequently in the phrase "human rights, the rule of law and democracy" abound. Some of the areas identified for "strengthening" the rule of law, and therefore reflecting the nature of

---

[3] Text available at e.g. http://www.echr.coe.int/Documents/Convention_ENG.pdf German version available at e.g. http://conventions.coe.int/Treaty/ger/Treaties/Html/005.htm

[4] A recent example among many can be found in the official translation of a judgment of the German *Bundesverfassungsgericht* BVerfG, 2 BvR 2661/06 of 6 July 2010, par 81: The phrase "Zu den wesentlichen Elementen des *Rechtsstaatsprinzips* zählt die Rechtssicherheit" was translated as "The major elements of the *principle of the rule of law* include legal certainty" (italics added).

[5] Trevor Allan, *Constitutional Justice: a liberal theory of the rule of law* (2001). Oxford: Oxford University Press.

[6] A *locus classicus* in this regard is the *dictum* of the German *Bundesverfassungsgericht* BverfGE 39, 1 (on abortion in 1975) where the Court stated (par 41):

> Nach der ständigen Rechtsprechung des Bundesverfassungsgerichts enthalten die Grundrechtsnormen nicht nur subjektive Abwehrrechte des Einzelnen gegen den Staat, sondern sie verkörpern zugleich eine objektive Wertordnung, die als verfassungsrechtliche Grundentscheidung für alle Bereiche des Rechts gilt und Richtlinien und Impulse für Gesetzgebung, Verwaltung und Rechtsprechung gibt.

the phenomenon as it is understood in the OSCE, are:[7] the independence of the judiciary; effective administration of justice; right to a fair trial; access to court; accountability of state institutions and officials; respect for the rule of law in public administration; the right to legal assistance and respect for the human rights of persons in detention; honouring obligations under international law; adherence to the principle of peaceful settlement of disputes; prevention of torture and other cruel, inhuman or degrading treatment or punishment; efficient legislation and an administrative and judicial framework in order to facilitate economic activities, trade and investments; the protection of the natural environment; the provision of effective legal remedies; the observation of rule of law standards and practices in the criminal justice system, and the fight against corruption.

The term "rule of law" also crops up in many current national constitutions. A search of the database of *Oceana's Constitutions of the Countries of the World Online*,[8] indicates that 95 of the 125 current constitutions contained in the collection use the expression "rule of law," sometimes surprisingly, given the condition of constitutional affairs in some of those countries. Examples are:

The Constitution of the Islamic Republic of Afghanistan, 2004 which expresses in its preamble the desire of the people of Afghanistan to "[f]orm a civil society void of oppression, atrocity, discrimination as well as violence, based on rule of law, social justice, protecting integrity and human rights, and attaining peoples' freedoms and fundamental rights." The Constitution of the Republic of Angola, 2010 contains various references to the rule of law, including article 2 that elevates the rule of law to a fundamental principle and article 6.2 which provides that "[t]he state shall be subject to the Constitution and shall be based on the rule of law, respecting the law and ensuring that the law is respected." The Constitution of Bosnia and Herzegovina, 1995 provides in Article I 2 that "Bosnia and Herzegovina shall be a democratic state, which shall operate under the rule of law and with free and democratic elections." The Constitution of the People's Republic of China, 1982 provides in Article 5: "The People's Republic of China exercises power in accordance with the law and establishes a socialist country under the rule of law." The Constitution of the Federal Democratic Republic of Ethiopia, 1995 states in its preamble that the nations, nationalities and peoples of Ethiopia are "[s]*trongly committed,* in full and free exercise of our right to self-determination, to building a political community founded on the rule of law …" Section 18(1a) of the Constitution of the Republic of Zimbabwe (inserted in 2009) provides that "[e]very public officer has a duty towards every person in Zimbabwe to exercise his or her functions as a public officer in accordance with the law and to observe and uphold the rule of law."

[7] Par. 4 of the OSCE's Ministerial Council's Decision No. 7.08 "Further Strengthening the Rule of Law in the OSCE Area" MC. DEC/7/08 of 5 December 2008.

[8] Under subscription accessible at http://www.oceanalaw.com/default.asp

On the assumption that the idea of the rule of law can be understood to be limited to legality, its appearance in Islamic constitutions should not be surprising. After all, Shari'a law is what makes a constitution Islamic:[9]

> If Islamic civilization, culture, or state ever constituted a regime of any kind, it was one of nomocracy. There has never been a culture in human society so legally oriented as Islam … we have come to realize – more than ever – that Islamic law was not merely a legal system that resolved conflicts and negotiated social and economic relationships (the role normally assigned to law in the West), but that it was in addition a theological system, an applied religious ritual, an intellectual enterprise of the first order, a cultural pillar of farreaching dimensions and, in short, a world-view that defined both Muslim identity and even Islam itself.

Tamanaha[10] identified three themes usually encountered in the rule of law tradition, viz. government limited by law, formal legality and rule of law, not man. However, he does not subscribe to the idea that the rule of law is an unqualified "universal good":[11]

> Saying that there are legal limitations on the government does not say what those limits are; the requirements of formal legality specify the form but not content of the laws; the 'rule of law, not man' says that government officials must sublimate their views to the applicable laws but does not specify what those laws should be.

Considering the breadth of application of the term, one might easily lose all hope of pinning down some clear and circumscribed meaning to be attributed to "the rule of law." But there must be a reason for its popularity. It has obviously attained the status of a *chiffre*, a code for desirable conduct on the part of the state. It indicates, admittedly in widely divergent ways, something which is constitutionally, legally and politically good. The key question is however how one can contain its meaning as one can contain a fluid in a bowl that does not leak or spill, without producing a new and contestable definition.

One way of going about the containment of the rule of law would be the often-repeated exposition of its roots in the work of the famed English constitutional lawyer, Albert Venn Dicey, in the expectation that it would have developed into a mature doctrine in Britain.[12] In fact, one might expect to find some clarity from the fact that the British Constitutional Reform Act of 2005 provides in section 1 that it does not adversely affect "the existing constitutional principle of the rule of law." Referring to this provision, Lord Bingham pointed out in 2006 that the courts have

[9] Wael B. Hallaq, " 'Muslim Rage' and Islamic Law", 54 *Hastings Law Journal* (2003) 1705–1719, at 1707–1708.

[10] Brian Z. Tamanaha, *On the Rule of Law – History, Politics, Theory* (2004) Chapter 9. Cambridge: Cambridge University Press.

[11] *Id.* at 140.

[12] In *The Queen on the Application of Corner House Research and Campaign Against Arms Trade v The Director of the Serious Fraud Office and BAE Systems PLC* [2008] EWHC 714 (Admin), counsel for the government however pointed out that there 'continues to be debate about the meaning and scope of the rule of law' (par 61).

"routinely invoked" the rule of law, "[b]ut they have not explained what they meant by the expression, and well-respected authors have thrown doubt on its meaning and value" (referring to Raz, Finnis, Scklar, Waldron and Tamanaha).[13] He then launched into an exposition of his understanding of the "principle of the rule of law" which should serve as an iconical contribution, at least in British constitutional law.

According to the late Lord Chief Justice, the core of the rule of law is "that all persons and authorities within the state, whether public or private, should be bound by and entitled to the benefit of laws publicly and prospectively promulgated and publicly administered in the courts." He then, with acknowledgement of other authoritative commentators and sources, set out a series of sub-rules, providing further content, albeit with some qualifications. These rules are:

- the law must be accessible and so far as possible intelligible, clear and predictable.
- questions of legal right and liability should ordinarily be resolved by application of the law and not the exercise of discretion.
- the laws of the land should apply equally to all, save to the extent that objective differences justify differentiation.
- the law must afford adequate protection of fundamental human rights.
- means must be provided for resolving, without prohibitive cost or inordinate delay, bona fide civil disputes which the parties themselves are unable to resolve.
- ministers and public officers at all levels must exercise the powers conferred on them reasonably, in good faith, for the purpose for which the powers were conferred and without exceeding the limits of such powers, thus reflecting the "well-established and familiar" grounds of judicial review.
- Adjudicative procedures provided by the state should be fair.
- the existing principle of the rule of law requires compliance by the state with its obligations in international law.

With some hesitation, Lord Bingham added to this that, despite some views to the contrary, the rule of law requires democracy,

> it seems to me that the rule of law does depend on an unspoken but fundamental bargain between the individual and the state, the governed and the governor, by which both sacrifice a measure of the freedom and power which they would otherwise enjoy.

7.3 From Rule of Law to Constitutionalism

When dealing with the rule of law, the idea of constitutionalism is not far away. Conversely, descriptions of constitutionalism almost always invoke the rule of law. In an insightful survey of the meanings attached to constitutionalism, Catá Backer[14]

---

[13] Lord Bingham, "The Rule of Law", 66 *The Cambridge Law Journal* (2007) 67–85.

[14] Larry Catá Backer, "Theocratic Constitutionalism: An Introduction to a New Global Legal Ordering", 16 *Indiana Journal of Global Legal Studies* (2009) 85–172, at 99–101.

points out that a search for common values lies at the heart of the universalist form of constitutionalism, the rule of law sometimes serving the purpose of a shorthand for such values and even for governmental systems. The values he refers to include both process rights, whereby the power of the state is required to be founded on legitimately enacted law (legality), and the substantive protection and promotion, employing the law, of "a set of foundational communally embraced substantive norms" required of the state. The governmental systems that he associates with the rule of law include democracy, citizenship and human rights based on the point of departure that human dignity is the fundamental value that is protected by constitutionalism.

Accepting that it is difficult to pin a stable meaning to the rule of law, it may be even more challenging to determine the meaning of "constitutionalism." In a contribution aimed at making the discussion of constitutionalism more transparent, Vorländer[15] identified the following approaches to or versions of constitutionalism: societal constitutionalism, creeping constitutionalism, compensatory constitutionalism, pluralistic constitutionalism, multilevel constitutionalism (containing the notion of a constitutional compromise or settlement), cosmopolitan constitutionalism, and global constitutionalism (with variations in the form of transnational constitutionalism, where mention is made of a constitution of mankind and global civil constitutions). Among those propounding state (as distinct from international) constitutionalism, he identified apologists for sovereignty and the national state, theorists on identity and homogeneity and an approach that considers it possible for the principles of modern democracy to be maintained only in the context of a state-structured order. Vorländer, however, suggests an alternative view which empathizes on the one hand with the statist insistence on the normativity of a constitution, but also accepts spreading extra-statal constitutionalism to be emergent constitutionalizing processes.[16]

Constitutionalism in the "national" context has a longer history[17] than the more recent idea of global constitutionalism. Brugger and Sarlet[18] reduced it, with reference to the constitutions of the USA, Germany and Brazil to three core elements: democracy, *Rechtsstaat* and consensually agreeable common welfare goals (*konsensfähige Gemeinwohlziele*). Backer[19] says –

> Constitutionalism is a system of classification, the principal object of which is to define the characteristics of constitutions, which is used to determine the legitimacy of a constitutional system either as conceived or implemented, based on the fundamental postulate of rule of law and grounded on values derived from a source beyond the control of any individual.

---

[15] Hans Vorländer, "Die Verfassung vor, nach, über und unter dem Staat. Die Konstitutionalismusdebatte in der Suche nach einem anderen Verfassungsbegriff", in *Erzählungen vom Konstitutionalismus*, Helena Lindemann et al. eds. (2012) at 23–42. Baden-Baden: Nomos.

[16] *Id.* at 31.

[17] *Cf.*, for example, Charles Howard McIlwain, *Constitutionalism: Ancient and Modern* (1947). Ithaca: Cornell University Press.

[18] Winfried Brugger and Ingo Wolfgang Sarlet "Moderner Konstitutionalismus am Beispiel der US-Verfassung, des Grundgesetzes und der brasilianischen Verfassung: eine rechtsvergleichende Perspektive" in 56 *Jahrbuch des Öffentlichen Rechts der Gegenwart* (2008) 613–638.

[19] Backer, *supra* note 14. At 93.

According to Schwöbel,[20] "global constitutionalism" has become one of the most discussed areas of international law, although the academic debate reflects a range of visions of the idea. She considers it generally assumed that constitutions can exist beyond the nation state, that there is a certain homogeneity in the international sphere and that global constitutionalism is a universal idea. She however finds that global constitutionalism does not have content and that no predetermined values or common principles characterize it. She therefore proposes an organic global constitutionalism which is to be flexible, non-universal, non-existent, but holding a promise for the future.

Klabbers[21] also acknowledged the spreading discourse on global constitutionalism, describing it as a response to the fragmentation of international law concerned with placing limits on the activities of international organizations by subjecting them to "standards of proper behaviour." Constitutionalism debates were going on (in 2004) in the UN, the EU, the WTO, the IMF and World Bank, the European Court of Human Rights and the International Criminal Court. Significantly, for present purposes, he included in his concept of constitutionalism,[22]

> such things as democracy and transparency, … a premium on free expression, due process and participation on the basis of equality, and [it] would encompass the exercise of authority in accordance with some version of the rule of law, be it limits internal to the organization (emanating from its own documents) or external to the organization (subjecting it to general international law and human rights standards).

No doubt, therefore, that the rule of law is an integral part of the international discourse on constitutionalism seen both from the intra-statal and the extra-statal perspectives.

7.4 The Essence of the Rule of Law in the Context of Constitutionalism

Rule of law and constitutionalism go hand in hand, but they are different notions. As we have discovered, neither lends itself to water-tight characterization although both are being used extensively in international instruments, national constitutions, scholarly literature and jurisprudence. However, to conclude that one is dealing here with concepts so ephemeral that they either completely defy definition, or that their meaning is so broad that one might legitimately attach any significance of one's choice to them, will amount to conceptual defeatism. It is possible to extract enough

---

[20] Christine E. J. Schwöbel, "Organic Global Constitutionalism" 23 *Leiden Journal of International Law* (2010) 529–553. Joseph Weiler (cited by Vorländer, *supra* note 15. At 24, note 13) calls it an "academic pandemic".

[21] Jan Klabbers, "Constitutionalism Lite", 1 *International Organizations Law Review* (2004) 31–58.

[22] *Id.* at 33.

of the essence of each in order to work with meanings that would satisfy most (although never all) users. This extrusion of meaning will however have to be minimalist in order to maximise the numbers of participants in the discourse.

An obvious prerequisite for the rule of law is the existence of law, but stumbling blocks on the road to broad consensus immediately present themselves: the question of the legitimacy of the law-giver and the quality of the law itself.

Can a law making capital punishment compulsory on conviction for adultery, proclaimed by a dictator or absolute ruler that came to power by means of a *coup d'etat* or patricide, be said to conform to the rule of law? To say that it does, would obviously be counter-intuitive for at least three reasons: the illegitimacy of the law-giver, the disproportionality of the punishment and the deprivation of judicial discretion. Would it make a difference if the law was adopted by a freely elected legislature and then subjected to a popular referendum before it was put into effect? Again, many will still consider the death penalty for adultery to be unacceptably harsh and the exclusion of the trial court's jurisdiction to decide on an appropriate punishment objectionable, thus contradicting the rule of law.

These examples highlight three indisputable elements of the rule of law: (1) the legitimacy of the authority of the source of law must not be compromised; (2) the law must be fair; and, (3), the judiciary must be independent. To state it this simply is however misleading, because each of these seemingly uncomplicated elements involve a range of ensuing issues, many of which are concerned with value-laden considerations. To name a few of these considerations: democracy (in the form of contested, fair and open election) is the most obvious determinant of uncompromised authority of a law-giver; the determination of the fairness of a legal rule involves justice, which is a highly contested normative concept; judicial independence is a multi-faceted phenomenon concerned with *inter alia* the selection and appointment of judges, their tenure, and the limits of their jurisdiction. The value-laden issues surrounding the rule of law therefore ineluctably elicit subjective considerations which can abruptly close down the channels of communication between discussants with divergent perspectives.

Turning to constitutionalism, the term seems to imply that the existence of a constitution is essential. What should we however understand "a constitution" to be – necessarily a consolidated, written document and only one which establishes superior legal norms? Can constitutionalism prevail in a state which does not have a constitution made in the image of, for example, the German *Grundgesetz* or the US Constitution? Can one speak of constitutionalism in a state whose structural arrangements (the establishment, empowerment and limitations of the organs of the state) are contained in legislative instruments that are not strictly protected against amendment, but where a political and legal culture exists in which public opinion has an important effect on executive and legislative governance, where the judiciary is independent from the government and the legislature and is considered to deliver fair judgments, and citizens perceive themselves to be free and equal? If the response to these questions is positive, it once again immediately gives rise to secondary issues: how can, given the global trend towards pluralism in the citizenry, an ordinary and unentrenched statute or set of otherwise authoritative documents provide sufficient means to curb the human tendency to abuse power for subjective gain?; is electoral democracy guaranteed to be an effective instrument for public opinion to steer the actions of the governors, and if so, which kind of democracy is required in the range from direct to proportional democracy?; how can the judges be constrained to maintain fairness in the face of contentious litigation, especially in hard cases involving the balance of power within the state and the exercise of authority over individuals in the public interest as perceived by the authorities?; which of the range of notions concerning the freedom and equality of individuals must be promoted by the state and all its organs?

These and many more factors that complicate a reductionist understanding of the rule of law and constitutionalism threaten to rob the widespread discourse in which the notions are freely employed of its relevance and cogency, but their prominence continues unabated. What can then be done to promote clarity in this matter?

It helps to acknowledge that there is no place where the rule of law prevails in a pristine form. Inspired politically, the motives of lawgivers are hardly ever beyond reproach. Law as an artefact of human society is never perfect and adjudication of questions of law is typically controversial, especially from the perspective of the losing party. The purity of the rule of law in any legal order is therefore relative and it can vary in the course of time and political adjustment.

It is also useful to accept the normality of the variability radiating from each of the essential elements of the rule of law that brings about different applications of those elements and therefore of the notion itself. To illustrate: whether a legislature is elected in single-member constituencies or proportionally does not as such determine its legitimacy; a law on sales tax may be fair in one economy, but not in another; in one legal culture judges appointed on the advice of the bar may be more independent than judges appointed in another system on the advice of a constitutional commission.

Acceptance of the idealistic nature and the variability of the rule of law takes us a step closer to containing this elusive juridical artefact, but more is needed. If there is to be a meaningful conversation about it, participants will have to have common ground regarding the normative assessment of the conditions being measured in terms of the rule of law. Such common ground can be found, to a limited extent, in structural considerations, like the proper management of elections, free and public parliamentary debating procedures and guaranteed judicial tenure. Agreement on the need for structures of a particular nature may however not be enough: common acceptance of the desirability of specific value-determined considerations will enhance the scope of utility of the rule of law significantly.[23]

Global constitutionalism, in both of its guises, constitutional and extra-statal, can provide us with values whose acceptance is growing, regardless whether it is founded in popular support or in the pressures of the international community on states and their governments to conform to the values that have gained global acceptance.

[23] Difficulties that are encountered when the value-laden notions of the rule of law and constitutionalism are newly introduced in legal orders from which the relevant values were absent before, are clearly demonstrated in the contributions in Wojciech Sadurski, Adam Czarnota and Martin Krygier eds, *Spreading Democracy and the Rule of Law? – The Impact of EU Enlargement on the Rule of Law, Democracy and Constitutionalism in Post-Communist Legal Orders* (2006). Dordrecht: Springer.

What we are dealing with when we distinguish between posited norms, principles and values is in itself a vast subject fraught with terminological and conceptual confusion.[24] Thus, the concepts "values"[25] and "principles" are sometimes used interchangeably.[26] Regarding the notion of a "constitutional value", a working description is as follows:[27]

> As an abstract concept, it indicates a standard or a measure of good. A constitutional value may therefore be deemed to set requirements for the appropriate or desired interpretation, application and operationalization of the constitution and everything dependent thereupon. If something were not to conform to the standards of a particular constitutional value, it would mean that the standards of a lower, different, conflicting or extra-constitutional measure is being applied, which would therefore lead to unconstitutional results.
>
> … constitutional values are distinguishable but related to principles in the sense that the principles of the constitution would be founded in and give expression to the values. E.g. the principle that the law must be applied fairly and equitably, is founded in and gives expression to the values of justice and equality. Thus understood, a constitutional value provides an ethical foundation for constitutional norms, whereas a constitutional principle equips us with a more concrete, though still broadly phrased, guideline for appropriate constitutionally sanctioned conduct.

Drawing up a watertight list of value-determined considerations relating to the rule of law is impossible, but extracting the most important ones, hardly presents a difficulty. Broad agreement can be expected if the following characteristic elements are associated with the rule of law:

- Human dignity, i.e. acceptance that the individual person has inherent dignity.
- Non-arbitrariness, i.e. acceptance that the fairness of actions performed in the exercise of public authority must be capable of and subject to open, rational explanation.[28]

---

[24] *Cf.* e.g. Ralf Poscher, "The Principles Theory – How many theories and what is their merit?" published in the internet in 2009 at http://ssrn.com/abstract=1411181, and Raul Narits, "Principles of Law and Legal Dogmatics as Methods Used by Constitutional Courts", XIII *Juridica International* (2007) 15–22 and the broad range of authorities they refer to. A related theme emerging from German literature, e.g. Uwe Volkmann, "Leitbildorientierte Verfassungsanwendung", 134 *Archiv des öffentlichen Rechts* (2009) 157–196, at 157–196, is what might be called notions guiding the application of constitutions.

[25] Iain Benson argues (Iain T. Benson, "Do 'values' mean anything at all? Implications for law, education and society", 33 *Journal for Juridical Science* (2008) 1–22, at 1–22) that the term obfuscates rather than furthers clarity of meaning and that "virtue" is to be preferred above "value".

[26] *E.g.* in Armin von Bogdandy's description of Tomuschat's proposed international system in Armin von Bogdandy, "Constitutionalism in International Law: Comment on a Proposal from Germany", 47 *Harvard International Law Journal* (2006) 223–242, at 223–242 (italics added):

[T]he constitutional character of the international system is understood as enshrining and securing (though not always successfully) *fundamental legal values*. The *principles* of Article 2 of the U.N. Charter and the core of international human rights enshrine those *values*.

[27] Francois Venter, *Global Features of Constitutional Law* (2010) at 56. Nijmegen: Wolf Legal Publishers.

[28] Mathilde Cohen, "The Rule of Law as the Rule of Reasons", 96 *Archiv für Rechts- und Sozialphilosophie* (2010), 1–16 e.g. represents the thesis that a substantial (as opposed to a procedural) definition of the Rule of Law should require the giving of reasons by legal decision-makers as a central component of the notion.

Despite the potential of a wide range of justifications that might be produced for the universal merits of these elements, their validity is founded in the essence of reciprocity (dealing with others as you want them to deal with you). The soundness of reciprocity, generally expressed as "the golden rule", is universally accepted in essence, although not identically motivated, ranging from the major philosophies (beginning with Confucianism) and religions (including Judaism, Christianity and Hinduism). Although some philosophers such as John Locke rejected it (as will cynical postmodernists), the golden rule manifests itself intuitively as a universal truth.[29] It hardly requires justification to state that the golden rule results in acceptance of both the inherent dignity of a person and the need for fair, non-arbitrary government.

7.5 Rule of Law as *Tertium Comparationis*

No existing constitutional order, however autochthonous, was born without being conceived by more than one constitutional parent, midwifed by active local and often foreign participants and developed under the scrutiny of a community of critical international onlookers whose influence, though seldom precisely measurable, is omnipresent. However, the compelling justification for doing constitutional comparison is to be found in more than historical path dependence.

Despite the absence of a recognizable or identifiable project undertaken by some global authority, it can hardly be denied that constitutional lawyers around the globe share terminologies, dogmatic frameworks and a style of verbalization of matters constitutional.[30] This naturally does not mean that we are in general agreement on profoundly important points of departure, but our language is mutually understood: thus, for example, socialists, African communitarianists and Western individualists have divergent aspirations for the state, but they all agree in general terms what we are talking about when we refer to e.g. the state, government, adjudication, decentralization and the law.

It is important when doing constitutional comparison to be explicit in choosing a reason for undertaking it and to make a careful choice of systems that are to be compared.[31] From this follows a decision regarding the question what the chosen material should be compared with. Here, we encounter the useful notion of the

---

[29] *See,* for example, Jeffrey Wattles, *The golden rule* (1996). New York; Oxford: Oxford University Press and Imer B. Flores, "Law, Liberty and the Rule of Law (in a Constitutional Democracy)" in Imer B. Flores & Kenneth E. Himma, *Law, Liberty, and the Rule of Law* (2013) Chapter 6. Dordrecht; Heidelberg: Springer.

[30] As an example which hardly requires elaboration beyond the title, see e.g. W.U. Fan "Legal Reasoning in Chinese and Swiss Appellate Judgments – Exploring China's Path Toward Rule of Law", 2 *Tsinghua China Law Review* (2009) 19–78. Fan naturally finds and describes vast contrasts and incompatibilities, but is able to describe the materials in the two systems in similar conceptual terms.

[31] Venter, *supra* note 27. At 51–61.

tertium comparationis, which suggests the identification or choice of an abstract standard against which the compared material extracted from two or more sources is measured, weighed or reflected. Especially for comprehensive comparative projects, this is an effective mechanism with which to enhance objectivity and comparatists often employ it without expressly voicing it.

Constitutional comparison at the deepest level will tend to be related to a deeply paradigmatic *tertium comparationis*. Where the foundations of systems (or materials within systems) are investigated, a comparative framework of normative principles and values can hardly be avoided. Recognition of the usefulness of doing so seems to be on the ascendant.[32] This is where human dignity and non-arbitrariness present themselves as vehicles for employment of the rule of law as a comparative measure of constitutional good.[33]

Using the rule of law to measure compliance of legal orders purporting to incorporate the rule of law with the underlying values, quickly show up their shortcomings. An example is Sarka's conclusion at the end of an analysis of Russian constitutionalism:[34]

> What Max Weber had called sham constitutionalism would give way to real constitutionalism where political institutions are subordinated to the rule of law

7.6 Conclusion and Proposals

The rule of law can clearly be a source of confusion when the meaning in which one uses it is not outlined. Critics of the conduct, processes or systems of others can also use it as an instrument of chastisement or disparagement on the assumption that the critics' conception of the rule of law is dominant or superior. Finding commonly acceptable meaning in the notion for it to be useful over a broader spectrum, requires the elimination of as many of its potential elements as may rupture consensus. Given the overwhelming occurrence of references, constitutional and extra-statal, to the rule of law, it is essential to extract as many elements as possible on which consensus is possible in a specific setting. Put differently, what is needed for the

---

[32] *See*, for example, Mayo Moran in her chapter in *The Migration of Constitutional Ideas* Sujit Choudhry ed. (2006) at 233–255, *inter alia* where she concludes at 255:

Increasingly, constitutional regimes are suggesting that constitutional values exert a distinctive kind of influential authority over private law and common law. But the very terms of this relationship which of necessity disaggregates force and effect and simultaneously posits that effects and not simply rules may be mandatory poses a serious challenge to the traditional account of legal authority.

[33] If one were able in specific circumstances to agree on further value-determined elements of the rule of law, they might be added usefully.

[34] Richard Sakwa "Constitutionalism and Accountability in Contemporary Russia: The Problem of Displaced Sovereignty" *in Russia and its Constitution* Gordon B. Smith and Robert Sharlet eds. (2008) at 21. Leiden: Nijhoff; *see also, supra* note 24.

promotion of universal acceptance of the rule of law, at least as a point of departure, is reductionism. Distilling only structural components such as the binding force of the law, generality of law or *nullum crimen sine lege*, however important these may be, and putting them on a checklist, may deprive the rule of law of its deeper normative value. This, however, raises the grave difficulty of finding values defensible as common to humanity.

A possible route to consensus on a reductionist view of the rule of law is the one via the (mostly equally contested) conception of constitutionalism. The value of constitutionalism in this context is to be found in its expanding popularity as a standard of legitimacy. The logic can summarily be worded as follows: both the rule of law and constitutionalism have (despite the lack of precise and generally acknowledged delimitation of the contents of either) attained the status of conditions universally recognized as desirable; constitutionalism is the broader conception, giving expression under one umbrella to various rather elastic elements such as democracy, due process and human rights, difficult to reduce across divergent perspectives; the rule of law is subsumed into constitutionalism as one of its elements that can be reduced to a universalized value-determined essence.

The demerits of the rule of law lie in the huge potential of its users to allocate too much or too little meaning to it, and its attractiveness for being commandeered for one or the other dogmatic purpose. The momentous merit of the rule of law is to be found in the expression of its reduced essence (serving both as a standard of measurement and as foundation for constitutional structuring and procedures): human dignity and non-arbitrariness.

Chapter 8
The Ill-Fated Union: Constitutional Entrenchment of Rights and the Will Theory from Rousseau to Waldron

Aniceto Masferrer and Anna Taitslin

Abstract This chapter revisits the key theses of Georg's Jellinek's *Declaration of the Rights of Man and of Citizens: A Contribution to Modern Constitutional History* [1895]. The objective of this chapter is to expose the 'umbilical cord' that linked the notion of 'constitutional' rights and the will theory, on one side, and the internal incompatibility of notion of 'inalienable rights' with the will theory – reflecting an unabated conflict of the doctrines of parliamentary supremacy and constitutional rights, on another side. These doctrines are part of both 'continental' and 'common law' traditions. Our intent is also to reflect on the shared groundwork of the doctrine of sovereignty of Hobbes, Austin (and Dicey), on one side, and Rousseau, on another side. Our more particular thesis is that 'neo-Benthamite' positivists, as Waldron, assailing adjudication as being 'undemocratic', seem to return to the Rousseauan position, with all its flaws.

8.1 Introduction

This chapter has a twofold focus: first, the idea of *constitutional* recognition and protection of fundamental rights, *raison d'être* of the modern constitutional state, and second, the notion of parliamentary legislative supremacy. Both these doctrines

This study has been undertaken in the context of the research project entitled "La influencia de la Codificación francesa en la tradición penal española: su concreto alcance en la Parte General de los Códigos decimonónicos" (ref. DER2012-38469), financed by the Spanish 'Ministerio de Economía y Competitividad'.

A. Masferrer (✉)
Faculty of Law, University of Valencia, Valencia, Spain
e-mail: aniceto.masferrer@uv.es

A. Taitslin
College of Law, The Australian National University, Acton, ACT 2602, Australia

The School of Law, The University of Canberra, Bruce, ACT 2601, Australia
e-mail: anna.taitslin@gmail.com

J.R. Silkenat et al. (eds.), *The Legal Doctrines of the Rule of Law and the Legal State (Rechtsstaat)*, Ius Gentium: Comparative Perspectives on Law and Justice 38,
DOI 10.1007/978-3-319-05585-5_8,

are part of both 'continental' and 'common law' traditions. Our intent is to reflect on the shared groundwork of the doctrine of sovereignty of Hobbes, Austin (and Dicey), on one side, and Rousseau, on another side.

More specifically, this chapter revisits the key theses of Georg's Jellinek's *Declaration of the Rights of Man and of Citizens: A Contribution to Modern Constitutional History* [1895]. Jellinek (1851–1911), a prominent German legal positivist, berated the idea of constitutionally entrenched 'natural' rights. His main target was the French Revolution *Declaration of the Rights of Man and of Citizen* (1789), which he contrasted with the English *Bill of Rights* (and the American bills of rights insofar as they confirmed what they inherited from the mother-country). According to him, a striking difference (between the two approaches to rights) was that "in the one case the institutions preceded the recognition of rights of the individual, in the other they followed after". Another Jellinek 'French' target was Rousseau's vision of the state, as an expression of general will (*volonté générale*), which, in his view, contained no constraints on power of the state, and, hence, was irreconcilable with an idea of inalienable natural rights.

Jellinek, however, consciously or not, overlooked the dependence of the idea of constitutional entrenchment of rights upon Rousseau's vision of *contrat social*, embodied by the legislative will. The idea of legislative supremacy is not confined to the French. In England, it is associated with Dicey's doctrine of parliamentary supremacy. Dicey's position, though, was complicated by his 'common law' version of the rule of law. Jellinek enlisted Dicey's notion of the rule of law (as an opposite of arbitrary rule) in support of his own concept of *Rechtsstaat* as 'self-limitation'. Dicey, just as Jellinek, was no admirer of constitutional rights and held that rights were better protected by the common law remedies and the checks on the crown's powers. Our last reference is to Waldron, a modern protagonist of the parliamentary supremacy and 'normative' positivism, who offers the 'will' critique of the *adjudication* of constitutional rights.

The objective of this chapter is to expose the 'umbilical cord' that linked the notion of 'constitutional' rights and the will theory, on one side, and the internal incompatibility of notion of 'inalienable rights' with the will theory (reflecting an unabated conflict of the doctrines of parliamentary supremacy and constitutional rights), on another side. The more particular thesis is that 'neo-Benthamite' positivists, as Waldron, assailing adjudication as being 'undemocratic', seem to return to the Rousseauan position, with all its flaws.

8.2 Jellinek's Concept of Rechtsstaat as Self Limitation of the State[1]

The notion of *the rule of law state* [*der Rechtsstaat*] was, probably, coined by Robert von Mohl.[2] His early vision was informed by a Humboldt-like affirmation of the spontaneous human development. For him, a *Rechtsstaat* could have one purpose

[1] *See also* Murray Raff and Anna Taitslin, "Private Law in the Shadow of Public Law. A Legacy of 20th Century Marxism and the Soviet Legal Model", *Archive fur Rechts- und Sozialphilosophie*, Beihefte (2012) at 157, 171–173.

[2] Gottfried Dietze, *Two Concepts of the Rule of Law* (Liberty Fund, 1973) at 20, 23 (Dietze noted Mohl's shift with time to less liberal position).

only: to order the people's living together in such a way as to support and promote every member of society in the freest and most comprehensive possible use of all his abilities.[3] This hopeful vision somewhat faded later on.[4] Still, even for the older Mohl, to confine the state's rationale to welfare of the community [rather than individuals] was to misunderstand the character of the *Rechtsstaat*.[5]

In comparison, Mohl's contemporary, Julius Stahl, already saw the rule of law state as a state acting in a legal form (setting the boundaries of its actions) and providing for the free ambit of the citizen according to law.[6] A generation later, Carl Friedrich Gerber, and his pupil Paul Laband, sought to separate legal analysis from political or sociological content. Gerber was a student of Georg Puchta, a prominent member of the Romanist faction of the German Historical School. For Puchta, the law itself was a system.[7] This approach could be traced to a founder of the Historical School Savigny, who looked at the classical Roman law as an ideal system of private law. Gerber transferred the conceptual legal (*begriffsjuristisch*) method of the Romanists to the emerging discipline of public law, so both public and private law could be defined through systematically coordinated concepts.[8] For Gerber, individual rights already were the public law effects.[9] For Laband, similarly, private law rights emanated from public law: 'basic rights' were protected only insofar as their violations required clear statutory permissions, and they were the subject of adjudication.[10]

For a pupil of Laband, Georg Jellinek, in the same vein, "the general rights of subjects were to be found essentially only in the form of the duties on the part of the state, not in the form of definite legal claims of the individual".[11] Jellinek's emphasis

---

[3] Robert Mohl, *Die Polizeiwissenschaft nach den Grundsatzen des Rechtsstaates*, [*Police Science according to the Principle of the Rule of Law State*], 1st ed. (1832) at I, 7 (cited in Dietze, *id.*, 23 note 35).

[4] Later, to Mohl, the state had already "the purpose of realizing the total interest [*Gesamt-Lebensansicht*] of the people", 2nd ed. (1844) at I, 7 (cited in Dietze, *supra* note 2. At 23.). In the third edition of 1866, at I, 12–13, Mohl assumed that the state created general "establishments and institutions which benefit all those who want to move to certain direction." (Dietze, *supra* note 2. At 23.).

[5] Dietze, *supra* note 2. At 23.

[6] Friedrich Julius Stahl, *Philosophie des Rechts II*, Part 2; Dietze, *supra* note 2. At 26.

[7] Armin Bogdandy, "The Past and promise of doctrinal constructivism: A strategy for responding to the challenges facing constitutional scholarship in Europe" 7 (3) *International Journal of Constitutional Law* (2009) 372–373.

[8] Gerber developed his vision most fully in *Grundzüge eines Systems des deutschen Staatsrechts* (1865).

[9] Pietro Costa, "The Rule of Law – Historical Introduction", in *The Rule of Law. History, Theory and Criticism* (Pietro Costa and Danilo Zolo, eds,) (2007) at 95, *available at* www.springerlink.com/content/u5j51tx50u285248/fulltext.pdf.

[10] Paul Laband's concept of public law was elaborated in his *Das Staatsrecht des deutschen Reiches* (1876–82).

[11] Georg Jellinek, *The Declaration of the Rights of Man and of Citizens: A Contribution to Modern Constitutional History* [1895], transl. by Max Farrand (1901), *available at* http://oll.libertyfund.org/title/1176.

Hans Kelsen had attended Jellinek's seminar in Heidelberg. However, as Costa noted, in case of Kelsen, "[h]aving founded the rule of law on the hierarchical relationship between the constitution and legislation, the link with any prior definition of individual rights (endemic to the former development of the 'rule of law') has been severed and the rule of law acquired a purely formal dimension." (Costa, *supra* note 9, at 115).

on the *duty* of the state to limit its own powers was critical to his vision of the rule of law state. The state, thus, has a faculty of *self-limitation* (*Selbstbeschrankung*), ordaining the laws for itself and limited by the rights that it recognises in others. The state, hence, separates its own domain from that of private action. So certain individual rights (such as freedom of conscience, press, meetings and so on) form a sphere free of state intervention.[12]

In his *Declaration of the Rights of Man and of Citizens* [1895], Jellinek distinguished the *Bill of Rights 1689* (together with the *Habeas Corpus Act 1679*, the *Petition of Rights 1628* and the *Magna Charta Libertatum 1215*), as embodying 'inherited from their fathers "old, undoubted rights of the English people"', from the bills of rights of American colonies, which set precepts that stood 'higher than the ordinary lawmaker' with the judge watching over 'the observance of the constitutional limitations by the ordinary legislative power'. Jellinek's chief contrast, however, was between the English *Bill of Rights* and the American bills of rights with the French Revolution *Declaration of the Rights of Man and of Citizen* (1789). He used the English *Bill of Rights* historical vision of the Englishmen's liberties (linked by him to the alleged "old Teutonic" concept of the state self-limitation)[13] to support his notion of self-limitation of the state, which was at the root of his concept of *Rechtsstaat*:

> And so we find only ancient "rights and liberties" mentioned in the English laws of the seventeenth century. Parliament is always demanding simply the confirmation of the "laws and statutes of this realm"... there is no reference whatever to the important fundamental rights of religious liberty, of assembling, of liberty of the press, or of free movement. And down to the present day the theory of English law does not recognize rights of this kind, but considers these lines of individual liberty as protected by the general principle of law, that any restraint of the person can only come about through legal authorization...[14] The theory, founded in Germany by Gerber, and defended by Laband and others, according to which the rights of liberty are nothing but duties of the government, sprang up in England, without any connection with the German teaching, from the existing conditions after the conception of the public rights of the individual as natural rights, which was based on Locke and Blackstone, had lost its power.[15]

[12] Georg Jellinek, *Allgemeine Staatslehre [General Theory of State]*, (3rd ed., Springer, 1922) 419–420.

[13] This appeal to the English liberties as having "Teutonic" roots could be (somewhat paradoxically) seen as an attempt to universalize the allegedly uniquely Germanic notion of right (advocated by Otto Gierke). This point seems to be (obliquely) made by Duncan Kelly in his "Revisiting the Rights of Man: Georg Jellinek on Rights and the State", 22 (3) *Law and History Review* (2004) 66). Still, Jellinek's recurrent appeal to Teutonic inheritance of liberties, though not untypical of the beliefs of assimilated German Jews of his time, sounds rather poignant in the face of the twentieth century history, with Jellinek's two own children (Dora and Otto) perishing in the Nazis' hands four decades later.

[14] At this point, Jellinek directly referred to Dicey, *Introduction to the Study of the Law of the Constitution* (3rd ed., 1889).

[15] Georg Jellinek, *Declaration of the Rights of Man and of Citizens [1895]*, Chapter *VI: THE CONTRAST BETWEEN THE AMERICAN AND ENGLISH DECLARATIONS OF RIGHTS*, *available at* http://oll.libertyfund.org/title/1176/104826/1940437.

...there arose out of the English law, old and new, that was practised in the colonies, the conception of a sphere of rights of the individual, which was independent of the state, and by the latter was simply to be recognized. In reality, however, the declarations of rights did nothing else than express the existing condition of rights in definite universal formulas. That which the Americans already enjoyed they wished to proclaim as a perpetual possession for themselves and for every free people. In contrast to them the French wished to give that which they did not yet have, namely, institutions to correspond to their universal principles. Therein lies the most significant difference between the American and French declarations of rights, that in the one case the institutions preceded the recognition of rights of the individual, in the other they followed after...The Americans could calmly precede their plan of government with a bill of rights, because that government and the controlling laws had already long existed.[16]

Magna Charta declares that the liberties and rights conceded by it are granted "*in perpetuum*". In the *Bill of Rights* it was ordained that everything therein contained should "remain the law of this realm forever". In spite of the nominal omnipotence of the state a *limit which it shall not overstep is specifically demanded and recognized in the most important fundamental laws*. In these nominally legal but perfectly meaningless stipulations, the old Teutonic legal conception of the state's limited sphere of activity finds expression. The movement of the Reformation was also based on the idea of the restriction of the state. ... The new defining of the religious sphere and *the withdrawal of the state from that sphere* were also on the lines of necessary historical development. So the conception of the superiority of the individual over against the state found its support in the entire historical condition of England in the seventeenth century. The doctrines of a natural law attached themselves to the old conceptions of right, which had never died, and brought them out in new form [italic added].[17]

This liberty accordingly was *not created but recognized*, and recognized in the *self-limitation of the state* and in thus defining the intervening spaces which must necessarily remain between those rules with which the state surrounds the individual. What thus remains is not so much a right as it is a condition. The great error in the theory of a natural right lay in conceiving of the actual condition of liberty as a right and ascribing to this right a higher power which creates and restricts the state [italic added].[18]

Jellinek insightfully observed that Rousseau's vision of the state, as an expression of general will (*volonté générale*) which implied no inherent constrain on power of the state, made (through *Contrat Social*) the state the master of even all possessions of its members.[19] Jellinek was also right to point out Rousseau's effective rejection of the natural rights.[20] Jellinek's critique of the constitutional natural rights, as prone to be unsupported declarations, such as the assertion that all men were by nature free

---

[16] *Id.*, Chapter *VIII: THE CREATION OF A SYSTEM OF RIGHTS OF MAN AND OF CITIZENS DURING THE AMERICAN REVOLUTION*, *available at* http://oll.libertyfund.org/title/1176/104832/1940484.

[17] *Id.*, Chapter *IX: THE RIGHTS OF MAN AND THE TEUTONIC CONCEPTION OF RIGHT*, *available at* http://oll.libertyfund.org/title/1176/104835/1940496.

[18] *Id.*, Chapter *IX: THE RIGHTS OF MAN AND THE TEUTONIC CONCEPTION OF RIGHT*, *available at* http://oll.libertyfund.org/title/1176/104835/1940505.

[19] *Supra* note 15, available at http://oll.libertyfund.org/title/1176/104826/1940437. Even 'Natural Law' codifications of the late eighteenth – early nineteenth century, supplanting the stateless *ius commune* of the medieval Europe, reflected the state (public law) sanction of private law.

[20] *Id.*, Chapter *II: ROUSSEAU'S CONTRAT SOCIAL WAS NOT THE SOURCE OF THIS DECLARATION*, *available at* http://oll.libertyfund.org/title/1176/104814/1940368.

and equal in the slave states,[21] justly highlighted the crucial role of the *existing* conditions of rights.

However, the Natural law theory had nothing to do with giving effect to the natural rights by means of public law. Natural rights (that, as Jellinek noted,[22] in Locke were confined to property, to which liberty was included)[23] were "inalienable" because they arise from the natural capacities of man (to act rationally and appropriate external things). According to Locke, all persons were "equal and independent, *no one ought to harm another in his life, health, liberty or possessions*" [italic added].[24] Natural law, by definition (as arising from the state of nature), confined itself to the private law sphere, outside of the state interference.[25]

Jellinek's contribution was to underline the concept of the rule of law as 'non-interference' of the state with the *residual* sphere of private liberties, left free from the state intervention (including by the way of positive definition of individual rights), as the better protection for individual rights than the Declarations of Rights.

8.3 Dicey's Notion of the Rule of Law

Jellinek's vision of *Rechtsstaat* bears a visible similarity to Dicey's concept of *the rule of law*. Dicey listed three meanings of rule of law under the English constitution. First, "no man is punishable… except for a distinct breach of law established in the ordinary legal manner before the ordinary Courts of the land. In this sense the rule of law is contrasted with every system of government based on the exercise by persons in authority of wide, arbitrary, or discretionary power of constraint".[26] Second, not only "no man is above the law", but also (what is not the same) "every man, whatever be his rank or condition, is subject to the ordinary law of the realm and

[21] *Id.*, Chapter *VIII: THE CREATION OF A SYSTEM OF RIGHTS OF MAN AND OF CITIZENS DURING THE AMERICAN REVOLUTION*, available at http://oll.libertyfund.org/title/1176/104832/1940482.

[22] *Id.*, Chapter *VI: THE CONTRAST BETWEEN THE AMERICAN AND ENGLISH DECLARATIONS OF RIGHTS*, *available at* http://oll.libertyfund.org/title/1176/104826/1940437.

[23] John Locke, *Two Treatises of Government [1690]*, Thomas Hollis ed. (1764), Chapter V: Property, § 27: "every man has a *property* in his own *person*"[italic added], *available at* http://oll.libertyfund.org/title/222/16245.

[24] *Id.*, Chapter *II: Of the State of Nature, § 6; available at* http://oll.libertyfund.org/title/222/16245/704312.

[25] On the nineteenth-century American debate about the provinces of public law ('written law') and private law ('unwritten law') outside of the state interference, *see* Aniceto Masferrer "The Passionate Discussion among Common Lawyers about postbellum American Codification: An approach to its Legal Argumentation" 40 (1) *Arizona State Law Journal* (2008) 173–256; Aniceto Masferrer, "Defense of the Common Law against postbellum American Codification: Reasonable and Fallacious Argumentation", 50 (4) *American Journal for Legal History* (2008–2010) 355–430.

[26] Albert Venn Dicey, *Introduction to the Study of the Law of the Constitution* [1885], (8th ed., Macmillan and Co, 1931) at 183–184.

amendable to the jurisdiction of the ordinary tribunal".[27] Third, the general principles of the constitution (for example, the right to personal liberty, or the right of public meeting) are "the result of judicial decisions determining the rights of private persons in particular cases brought before the Courts".[28]

Dicey's rule of law notion (like Jellinek's) was based on the rejection of arbitrary (unlimited) rule, with no one being above the law. Unsurprisingly, Jellinek explicitly referred to Dicey to support his own views.[29] Both Jellinek and Dicey contrasted the English notion of rights with the constitutional Declarations of the Rights. Both believed that individual rights were no less secure under the English ['unwritten'] constitution than under the [written] constitutions with declarations of rights. Both stressed the importance of pre-existing institutions (conditions) for the protection of rights. For both, the success of the American bills of rights was linked with the colonies' English inheritance (with Jellinek emphasising that, aside from the right to religious freedom, the core rights were already brought with the colonists from the mother-country).

Thus, for Dicey, "[t]here is in the English constitution an absence of those declaration or definitions of rights so dear to foreign constitutionalists."[30]

> The [French] Constitution of 1791 proclaimed liberty of conscience, liberty of the press, the right of public meeting, the responsibility of government officials. But there never was a period in the recorded annals of mankind when each and all of these rights were so insecure...as at height of the French Revolution.[31] ... the Englishmen...fixed their minds far more intently on providing remedies for the enforcement of particular rights or (what is merely the same thing looked at from the other side) for averting definite wrongs, than any declaration of the Right of Man or of Englishmen. The Habeas Corpus Acts declare no principle and define no rights, but they are for practical purposes worth a hundred constitutional articles guaranteeing individual liberty.[32] Where...the right to individual freedom is part of the constitution because it is inherent in the ordinary law of the land, the right is one which can hardly be destroyed without a thorough revolution in the institutions and manners of the nation.[33]

Hence, like for Jellinek, the *Petition of Rights* (1628) and the *Bill of Rights* (1689) were for Dicey 'judicial condemnations of claims or practices on the part of the Crown', which were thereby proclaimed illegal; in a similar vein, the American Declarations of Rights had 'the distinct purpose of legally controlling the action of the legislature', in contrast to *Déclaration des droits de l'Homme et du Citoyen*.[34]

---

[27] *Id.*, 189.

[28] *Id.*, 191.

[29] *Supra* note 15.

[30] Dicey, *supra* note 26. At 192.

[31] *Id.*, 194.

[32] *Id.*, 195.

[33] *Id.*, 197. According to Dicey (at 204), "Personal freedom ...is secured in England by the strict maintenance of the principle that no man could be arrested or imprisoned except in due course of law, i.e. ... under some legal warrant or authority, and... it is secured by the provision of ...redress for unlawful arrest or imprisonment by means of a prosecution or an action, and deliverance from unlawful imprisonment by means of the writ of habeas corpus".

[34] *Id.*, 195, note 1.

Dicey's rule of law perspective was, though, different from the one of Jellinek, in the authentically common law emphasis on adjudication. According to Dicey, the common law checked the state's arbitrary power through the authority of judges, "invested with the means of hampering or supervising the whole administrative action of the government, and of at once putting a veto upon any proceeding not authorised by the letter of the law".[35]

Dicey's definition of the rule of law, however, confined "self-limitation" of state power to the executive power. Dicey's notion of the legal state, thus, placed no formal restriction on the Parliament's legislative power. This is a rather controversial aspect of Dicey's notion of the rule of law, a result of the Austinian positivism,[36] as well as of the seventeenth century doctrine of sovereignty.

There are competing interpretations of Dicey's presumption of legislative supremacy of the parliament. One is to modify this presumption by asserting implicit constraint on the legislature through judicial interpretation of the statutory laws.[37] Dicey himself placed the courts at the centre of his concept of the rule of law. Indeed, according to him, the English constitution was 'a judge-made constitution', being 'the fruit of contests carried on in the Courts on behalf of the rights of individuals'.[38] But it is hard to ignore Dicey's explicit statements regarding parliamentary supremacy.[39] Another interpretation is to point to the political, rather than legal, limitations on the legislature, implicit in the principle of democratic representation.[40]

---

[35] *Id.*, 218.

[36] Dicey, though, in contrast to Austin (*Jurisprudence*, I (4th ed., John Murray, 1873) at 253), did not see Parliament as a 'trustee' for the electorate (Dicey, *supra* note 26. At 72–73). Nevertheless, by distinguishing political and legal sovereignty, Dicey (at 73) recognised the electors as the predominant part of the political sovereign power. Recently, Eleftheriadis and Duzenhaus brought the attention to Austin's influence on Dicey; *see* Pavlos Eleftheriadis, "Parliamentary Sovereignty and the Constitution", *Oxford Legal Research Paper Series,* Paper No. 45/2009 (October 2009), 22 and David Dyzenhaus, "Austin, Hobbes, and Dicey", *24 Can. J. L. & Jurisprudence* (2011) 411, 418–419. As Eleftheradis noted at 23, Dicey's "account of parliamentary sovereignty employs the same idea of the 'sovereign' as the author of voluntary directives that through the force of their irresistible power create the legal order as a whole".

[37] *See* Emilio Santoro, "The rule of law and the 'liberties of the English': the interpretation of Albert Venn Dicey", in *The Rule of Law, supra* note 9. At 166. Santoro underplays the conflict between these two Dicey's assumptions by arguing that "Parliament, acting as a legislative body, has limited itself to ordering and incorporating the jurisprudential output of the courts. When it has performed a creative role in the process of incorporating law into the constitution, it has done so in its role as High Court of the country, not as legislative organ". *Cf.* Dicey, *supra* note 26. At 192 (but in the context of comparison of written and unwritten constitutions): "[s]uch [English constitutional] principles… are…mere generalisations drawn either from the decisions or dicta of judges, or from statutes, which, being passed to meet special grievances, bear a close resemblance to judicial decisions, and are in effect judgments pronounced by the High Court of Parliament."

[38] Dicey, *supra* note 26. At 192.

[39] *Infra* notes 43 and 45.

[40] The possibility of the subjects to resist the laws of a sovereign posed, in Dicey's view, the external limit to the sovereign's real power (Dicey, *supra* note 26. At 74). The internal limit was for Dicey (at 77) in "the moral feeling of the times and the society". For Dicey (at 81), "the essential property of representative government is to produce coincidence between the wishes of the sovereign and the wishes of the subjects; to make it, in short, the two limitations on the exercise of sovereignty absolutely coincident."

Furthermore, Dicey's assumption of the supremacy of the legislative Parliament underlined his contrast of the (English) 'flexible' constitution with the 'rigid' ones.[41] He opposed rigid constitutions as preventing a gradual innovation (and, thus, being essentially undemocratic).[42] He, though, favourably distinguished the American constitution from the French one, by noting that the former provided the only adequate safeguard against unconstitutional legislation by making the judges the guardians of the constitution,[43] while the latter over-estimated the effect produced by general declaration of rights, opposing any intervention by the judges in the sphere of politics.[44] Dicey's observation again underscores the tension between the assumptions of the parliamentary supremacy and of the judge-made law.[45] Notwithstanding his notion of the rule of law, his doctrine of parliamentary supremacy had sealed the fate of Coke's once popular 'common law constitutionalism'.

8.4 The Groundwork of the Will Theory

The roots of Dicey's doctrine of parliamentary supremacy could be traced to the early modern notion of Sovereign. A seemingly Positivist doctrine, at a closer look, transpires to be a Natural law Social Contract legacy. This uncomfortable truth can be uncovered through a textual comparison of the relevant passages by the doctrine's celebrated protagonists. We start by introducing the original Bodin's notion of sovereignty. Next, after extensive quotations from Hobbes, Rousseau, Bentham and Austin, we reflect on the similarities and differences in their visions. Finally, we provide an overview of the French doctrine of sovereignty, as developed under Rousseau's influence, as well as the notion of 'inalienable' rights of the French *Declaration of the Rights of Man and of the Citizen* (1879).

---

[41] *See* Dicey *supra* note 26. At 122–123. "A 'flexible' constitution is one under which every law of every description can legally be changed ...in the same manner by one and the same body... A rigid constitution is one under which certain laws generally known as constitutional or fundamental laws cannot be changed in the same manner as ordinary laws."

[42] Dicey, *supra* note 26. At 126.

[43] Dicey noted that, in contrast to England, where functions of "judicial department" might be modified by an Act of Parliament, in the United States, the Federal judiciary could not be deprived of single right by Congress (Dicey, *supra* note 26. At 152). Moreover, according to Dicey (at 156), the Supreme Court as the final Court of Appeal, had an authority to pronounce on the constitutionality of legislation, passed by Congress or by the legislature of a state.

[44] Dicey, supra note 26. At 132–133.

[45] *Cf* Bingham's critique of Dicey's separation of legal and historical analyses (Lord Bingham, "Dicey revisited" *Public Law* (2002) 39 at 42. *See also*, J.W.F. Allison, *English Historical Constitution*, (Cambridge University Press, 2007) at 162–165; P.P. Craig, "Dicey: unitary self-correcting democracy and public law" 106 *LQR* (1990) 105 at 106 ff.

8.4.1 The Notion of Sovereign

Modern Founding Father: Jean Bodin

The concept of the Sovereignty is a creation of the Western legal tradition and the result of a long development, particularly from the Middle Ages to the sixteenth century,[46] being thenceforth developed by many authors. As Jellinek once remarked, it was difficult to find a concept subject to more debate.[47] It is not surprising, then, that this notion may have suffered from imprecision and changed meaning over time.

The first modern definition of sovereignty was coined by Jean Bodin (1530–1596): "*Maiestas est summa in cives ac subditos legibus solute potestas*" (*Six libres de la république* (1576), book I, ch. VIII).[48] Sovereignty, in this view, is the original, independent and inalienable power of the state. Sovereignty is a part or essence of the unity and of the power of the state. According to Bodin, "[t]he sovereignty is the absolute and perpetual power of a republic". In reality, however, this translates to "the right government of various families". Nevertheless, "without the sovereign power which unites all the members and parts of it and all the families and colleges in one body, [it] ceases to be republic."[49]

Bodin's definition of *souveraineté* or the *summa potestas* as a power over citizens and subjects, that is not itself bound by law, has laid a foundation for a theory according to which sovereignty is a supreme power that is permanent, indivisible and, at least theoretically, without legal responsibility.[50] However, Jean Bodin never proposed the notion of unlimited sovereignty, as he believed that it should never transgress the boundaries imposed by divine law, natural law and *ius gentium*.[51] Besides, Bodin seemed to separate the private and public spheres, so that the sovereign's power might be limited by the private property of subjects, as he repeated after Seneca: "*ad reges potestas omnium pertinet, ad singulos proprietas*" (to kings power over all belongs; to individuals, property) and "*omnia rex imperio possidet, singuli dominio*" (a king possesses all within his power; an individual has dominion over his property).[52]

---

[46] *See also*, Aniceto Masferrer and Juan A. Obarrio, "The State Power and the Limits of the Principle of Sovereignty: An Historical Approach", *Post 9/11 and the State of Permanent Legal Emergency: Security and Human Rights in Countering Terrorism*, Aniceto Masferrer ed. (Springer, 2012) at 15–51.

[47] G. Jellinek, *Teoría General del Estado* (Albatros, 1954) at 447.

[48] On the importance of Bodin's work for the doctrine of sovereignty see J.A. Maravall, *Teoría del Estado en España en el siglo XVI* (Centro de Estudios Constitucionales, 1997) at 15.

[49] Jean Bodin, *Los Seis Libros de la República*, I. 2 (Tecnos, 1986).

[50] *Six livres*, 1:223 (I:VIII).

[51] *See*, Masferrer and Obarrio, *supra* note 46.

[52] Bodin, *Methodus ad facilem historiarium cognitiones* (1565), 205; Bodin, *Six livres*, 1:223 (I:viii); Edward Andrew, "Jean Bodin on Sovereignty" 2 (2) *Republics of Letters: A Journal for the Study of Knowledge, Politics, and the Arts* (June, 2011), *available at* http://rofl.stanford.edu/node/90. To compare Bodin and Hobbes *see* Charles McIlwain, "Sovereignty in the World Today", 2 *Measure* (1950) 110–7, *available at* http://www.potowmack.org/mcilwain.html; W. A. Dunning, "Jean Bodin on Sovereignty", 11 *Political Science Quarterly* (1896), 82–104.

8.4.2 *Hobbes, Rousseau, Bentham and Austin: The Sources*

Thomas Hobbes

Leviathan (1651)

Chapter XVII

> *The only way* to erect such a common power, as may be able to defend them from the invasion of foreigners, and the injuries of one another...*is to confer all their power and strength upon one man, or upon one assembly of men, that may reduce all their wills, by plurality of voices, unto one will*: ... to appoint one man, or assembly of men, to bear their person... *and therein to submit... their judgements to his judgement. ... it is a real unity of them all in one* and the same person, *made by covenant of every man with every man...* as if every man should say to every man: I authorise and give up my right of governing myself to this man, or to this assembly of men, on this condition; that thou give up, thy right to him, and authorise all his actions in like manner.[53] This done, the multitude so united in one person is called a COMMONWEALTH; in Latin, CIVITAS. This is the generation of that great LEVIATHAN...And in him consisteth the essence of the Commonwealth; which... is: *one person, of whose acts a great multitude...have made themselves every one the author*, to the end he may use the strength and means of them all as he shall think expedient for their peace and common defence. And he that carryeth this person is called sovereign, and said to have sovereign power; and every one besides, his subject.

Chapter XVIII

> That he which is made sovereign maketh no covenant with his subjects before hand is manifest; because either he must make it with the whole multitude, as one party to the covenant, or he must make a several covenant with every man. With the whole, as one party, it is impossible, because as they are not one person: and if he make so many several covenants as there be men, those covenants after he hath the sovereignty are void; because what act soever can be pretended by any one of them for breach thereof is the act both of himself, and of all the rest... Besides, if any one or more of them pretend a breach of the covenant... there is in this case no judge to decide the controversy...and every man recovereth the right of protecting himself by his own strength, contrary to the design they had in the institution.

Jean-Jacques Rousseau

Du contrat social (1762)[54]

I. VII: The Sovereign

> ...the act of association comprises a mutual undertaking between the public and the individuals, and that *each individual, in making a contract, as we may say, with himself,* is bound in a double capacity; as a member of the Sovereign he is bound to the individuals, and as a member of the state to the Sovereign. ...it is consequently against the nature of the

---

[53] In his Conclusion and Review of *Leviathan*, Hobbes noted that "this promise may be either expresse, or tacite: Expresse, by Promise: Tacite, by other signes... yet if he live under their Protection openly, hee is understood to submit himselfe to the Government".

[54] Translated by G. D. H. Cole (1782) [italic added], *available at* http://www.constitution.org/jjr/socon.htm.

body politic for the Sovereign to impose on itself a law which it cannot infringe… *there neither is nor can be any kind of fundamental law binding on the body of the people – not even the social contract itself.*

…the social compact… tacitly includes… that whoever refuses to obey the general will shall be compelled to do so by the whole body.

II.I: That Sovereignty Is Inalienable

Sovereignty, being nothing less than the exercise of the general will, can never be alienated, and that the Sovereign, who is no less than a collective being, cannot be represented except by himself: the power indeed may be transmitted but not the will …

II.II That Sovereignty Is Indivisible

…sovereignty is indivisible; for will either is, or is not, general; it is the will either of the body of the people, or only of a part of it. In the first case, the will, when declared, is an act of Sovereignty and constitutes law: in the second, it is merely a particular will, or act of magistracy—at the most a decree.

II.IV The Limits of the Sovereign Power

If the state or city is nothing but a moral person whose life consists in the union of its parts, and if its most important concern is for its own preservation, it must have a universal force to move and place each part in the way that is most advantageous to the whole. *Just as nature gives each man absolute power over all his members, the social compact gives the body politic absolute power over all its members… it is this power which, under the direction of the general will, is called 'sovereignty'.*

But as well as the public person, we have to consider the private persons who compose it, and whose life and liberty are naturally independent of it. So now there's the matter of clearly distinguishing: the citizens' rights from the sovereign's, and the citizens' duties as subjects from their natural rights as men.

Agreed: *each man alienates by the social compact only the part of his powers, goods and liberty that are is important for the community to control… the sovereign is sole judge of what is important.* Any service a citizen can give to the state should be performed as soon as the sovereign demands it; but the sovereign on its side can't impose upon its subjects any fetters that are useless to the community. Indeed it can't even want to do so, because there's no reason for it to want to, and 'Nothing can happen without a cause' applies under the law of reason as much as it does under the law of nature.

Jeremy Bentham

Of Law in General (1789)

Sovereign is

that person or assemblage of persons to whose will a whole political community are … supposed to be in a disposition to pay obedience and that in preference to the will of any other person…[O]f the power of all subordinate power-holders the ultimate efficient cause is the command or allowance of the Sovereign: of the power of the Sovereign himself the constituent cause is the submission or obedience of the people.[55]

[55] *Quoted in* Hart, *Essays on Bentham* (1982) at 220–1; J. Bentham, *Of Laws in General*, H.L.A. Hart, ed., (Athlone Press, 1970) at 18.

Constitutional Code (1822–1832)[56]

I.XV.II

The supreme authority in a state is that on the will of which the exercise of all other authorities depends.[57]

I.XV.III

By the sovereignty is meant the supreme constitutive authority: in virtue of which, immediately or unimmediately, the people exercise...the locative and...dislocative[58] function in relation to the possessors of all the several other authorities in the state.

John Austin

The Province of Jurisprudence Determined (1832)

Lecture V

The existence of law is one thing; its merit or demerit is another. Whether it be or be not is one enquiry; whether it be or be not conformable to an assumed standard, is a different enquiry. A law, which actually exists, is a law, though we happen to dislike it, or though it vary from the text, by which we regulate our approbation and disapprobation.[59]

Lecture VI

If a *determinate* human superior, *not* in a habit of obedience to a like superior, receive *habitual* obedience from the *bulk* of a given society, that determinate superior is sovereign in that society and that society (including the superior) is a society political and independent.[60]

An independent political society is divisible into two portions: namely, the portion of its members which is sovereign or supreme, and the portion of its members which is merely subject (...). An independent political society governed by itself, or governed by sovereign body consisting of the whole community, is not impossible: but the existence of such societies is so extremely improbable...[61]

But in many of the societies whose supreme governments are popular, the sovereign or supreme body (or any numerous body forming a component part of it) exercises through representatives, whom it elects and appoints...Where a sovereign body ... exercises through representatives the whole of its sovereign powers; it may delegate those its powers to those its representatives... 1. It may delegate those its powers to those its representatives, subject to a trust or trusts. 2. It may delegate those powers to those its representatives, absolutely or unconditionally.[62]

---

[56] The work was left unfinished. J. Bentham, *Constitutional, Code* F. Rosen, J.H. Burns, eds. (Clarendon Press, 1983) Vol 1.

[57] Bentham started this section "Authorities in a State" with a reference "to the French phrase *autorités constituées*...in English, the constituted authorities."

[58] To appoint and remove. *See also* J. H. Burns, "Bentham on Sovereignty: An Exploration" 24 *Northern Ireland Legal Quarterly* (1973) 133–416.

[59] John Austin, *The Province of Jurisprudence Determined* [1832], Wilfrid E. Rumble ed., (Cambridge University Press, 1995) at 157.

[60] *Id.*, 166–167.

[61] *Id.*, at 183.

[62] *Id.*, at 192.

One can, almost immediately, see a notable similarity between the definitions of sovereignty of Hobbes and Rousseau: both, in line with Bodin, held that the whole power of multitudes resided in sovereign. Austin's vision of the sovereign body delegating of all its powers unconditionally to its representatives, is, again, not far apart. There is also an apparent disparity between Hobbes and Rousseau: while Hobbes envisioned the sovereign as a separate (and unaccountable) 'person' from the multitudes,[63] Rousseau 'collapsed' sovereign into the whole body (as if envisioning something like 'deliberative democracy').[64]

Austin, as noted by Dicey, seemed to separate (somewhat illogically) a sovereign body from the representatives, to whom it delegated its own powers. There is, too, an evident difference between, Hobbes and Rousseau, on one side, and Austin, on another side. Austin did not attempt to justify the sovereignty, or law more generally, as it was, by the appeal to some (hypothetical) original contract of society. Already in Bentham, the sovereign is defined independently of the 'fiction' of Social Contract, as a matter of fact (of "obedience of the people"). Here lays the crucial distinction between Legal Positivism and Natural law.

Moreover, Hobbes and Rousseau's visions of Social Contract (and a post-contract society) shared with Legal Positivism the presumption of submerging of the whole power of society in the sovereign. As a result, any Natural (or pre-political) Rights were irrelevant in political (post-contract) society. Hence, any post-contract rights could only come into being as a (new) grant of the Sovereign. In a sense, any natural, or alienable, rights are sort of contradictions of terms within Hobbes and Rousseau's vision of Social Contract as a formation of the Sovereign. As Hobbes put it, those who join into Social Contract are to "reduce all their wills … unto one will". Sovereignty, as explained by Rousseau, is "nothing less than the exercise of the general will". Moreover, no law can bind this Sovereign. As a result of such Social Contract, nothing is beyond this Leviathan's reach.

Unsurprisingly, Hobbes and Rousseau lacked any meaningful notion of private law (as distinct from public law). Only the Natural law theories, which assumed the persistence of natural rights in the post-contract society, could account for the existence of autonomous private law. Thus, the hostility of Hobbes to the common law was rather "natural".[65] Hobbes' "residual" approach to liberty,[66] and the notion

---

[63] On the notion of this 'artificial' person see Quentin Skinner, "Hobbes and purely Artificial Person of the State" 7 (1) Journal of Political Economy (1999) 1–29; *cf.* Runciman, "Debate: What kind of person is Hobbes' State. A reply to Skinner", 8 (2) Journal of Political Philosophy (2000) 268–78. On Hobbes generally, see Quentin Skinner, *Hobbes and Republican Liberty* (Cambridge University Press, 2008); Perez Zagorin, *Hobbes and the law of nature* (Princeton University Press, 2009).

[64] On Rousseau' 'inalienable' general will see Robin Douglass, "Rousseau's Critique of Representative Sovereignty: Principled or Pragmatic?" 57 (3), *American Journal of Political Science* (2013) 735–747.

[65] Austin's interest in the Roman law (as a source of the basic legal concepts) might explain his more liberal stand towards the common law. Similar outlook could be discerned in German positivism (as discussed with respect to Jellinek).

[66] *See* CA Gearty, in his 'Escaping Hobbes: liberty and security for our democratic (not anti-terrorist) age' LSE Legal Studies Working Paper No. 3/2010 (*available at* http://ssrn.com/abstract=1543121) at 8.

of law as an expression of the sovereign will and, hence, as the Sovereign's command, naturally, led to the idea of rights as legislative grants.[67]

In sum, the doctrine of sovereignty is a legacy of the early modern concept of sovereign from the Social Contract Natural law theories of Hobbes and Rousseau. Through Hobbes, this Social Contract notion of sovereign was submerged within the positivist concept of law as derived from the Sovereign's will, with the sovereign seen as the 'source' of the whole law.

8.4.3 Sovereignty and the Will Theory: The 'French' Doctrine

Rousseau effectively originated the dogma of supremacy of the legislature,[68] whose laws were regarded as the expression of the general will.[69] Rousseau presented the notions of sovereignty and legislation as being interlinked.[70] In this vein, legislation being the expression of the general will carried with it the force of democratic legitimacy. Rousseau defended "a form of government that places the law *supra* man" and warned that "liberty is impossible in a state in which the body entrusted to apply it has the right to make it speak according to its fancy, for then it could enforce its most tyrannical desires as law". According to Rousseau, 'a free people' "obeys nothing but the laws, and thanks to the force of laws, it does not obey men". 'A people' "is free, whatever form its government takes when it sees in him who governs not a man but the organ of the law. In a word, liberty always follows the fate of the laws, it reigns or perishes with them, I know nothing more certain".[71]

---

[67] *See* M. Loughlin, *The Idea of Public Law* (Oxford University Press, 2003) at 86. According to Loughlin, for Hobbes "individual rights-bearers do not possess rights because they are inscribed in nature or because they can be understood to be expressions of human reason, but only because they have been conferred by the sovereign's legislation". For the contrary view of Hobbes' civil law as remained anchored in the pre-political reality, *see* M. Rhonheimer, "*Auctoritas non veritas facit legem*: Thomas Hobbes, Carl Schmitt und die Idee des Verfassungsstaates", 86 *Archiv für Rechts- und Sozialphilosophie* (2000) 484; M. Rhonheimer, *La filosofia politica di Thomas Hobbes: coerenza e contradizzioni di un paradigma* (Armando, 1997); N. Bobbio, "Hobbes e il giusnatulaismo", 17 *Rivista Critica di Storia della Filosofia* (1962) 470.

[68] Raymond Carré De Malberg, *La loi expression de la volonté générale. Etude sur le concept de la loi dans la Constitution de 1875* (1931); On Rousseau generally, *see* Richard Fralin, *Rousseau and Representation: A Study of the Development of His Concept of Political Institutions* (Columbia University Press, 1978); Joshua Cohen, *Rousseau: A Free Community of Equals* (Oxford University Press, 2010).

[69] Rousseau, thus, rejected the Roman law principle that the will of the monarch had force of law (*quod principi placuit legis habet vigorem: Institutiones Justiniani* 1.2.3.6) and his actions were not constrained by law (*princeps legibus solutus est*: *Digesta Justiniani* 1.3.31); *see also* D. Wyduckel, *Princeps legibus solutes. Eine Untersuchung zur Frühmoderne Rechts- und Staatslehre* (Duncker und Humblot, 1979).

[70] Jean-Jacques Rousseau, *El contrato social o Principios de Derecho Político* (Cormon y Blanc, 1762) at 29.

[71] Jean-Jacques Rousseau, *Lettres écrites de la Montagne, Lettre VIII, Ouvres complètes de la Bibliothèque de La Pléiade*, v. III (Gallimard, 1964) at 842.

Rousseau's presumption of the subjection of all public power to the will of the people or the principle of legislative supremacy had rested on Bodin's principle of sovereignty. Moreover, the same presumption underlined the idea of safeguarding fundamental rights (which in the French Revolution context meant individual rights).[72] According to this principle, ultimate power did not reside in the monarch (or the institution of the monarchy) but in the people (popular sovereignty).[73] The evolution of the principle of sovereignty passed through the stages until the nation became seen a bearer of the sovereignty of the state exclusively.[74]

According to Rousseau, sovereignty was indivisible (only differentiation among the functions of government was possible). This idea was to have an enormous influence on the posterior French thought. From a political perspective, Rousseau distinguished between the "will" and the "force" of the people. While the notion of will corresponded to the functions of the legislature (whose task it was to determine the will of the nation and to enact legislation in accordance with this will), "force" was the province of the executive power (who carried out the mandates of the law and, if necessary, forcibly executed them). It has been noted that "a consequence derived from the superiority of the legislature was the inexistence of any hierarchy between the Constitution and ordinary law, the latter was the expression of the general will and the former simply another law, one that served to codify certain principles regarding political relations".[75]

Another important contributor to the French theory of sovereignty was Abbé Sieyès (1748–1836), who distinguished between the "constituent power" and the "constituted power".[76] According to Sieyès, the constituent power was a source of

---

[72] Regarding the concept of natural law in the Constitutions of the United States and France, *see* Eduardo García de Enterría, *La lengua de los derechos. La formación del Derecho Público europeo tras la Revolución Francesa* (Alianza, 1994) at 145–152. With respect to the declarations of rights in the French constitutional texts, *see* Leon Duguit, *Manual de Derecho constitucional* (Francisco Beltrán, 1937) at 203 ff. A synopsis of the evolution of the concept of individual rights prior to the French Revolution can be found in García de Enterría, *id.*, 47–96. On connection between law and rights in the French Revolution *see* García de Enterría, *id.*, 114–124, and J. Varela Suanzes, "Derechos y libertades en la historia constitucional, con especial referencia a España" in *Política y Constitución en España (1808–1978)* (Centro de Estudios Políticos y Constitucionales, 2007) at 109–119.

[73] On replacement of the sovereignty of the monarch by national sovereignty in the French Revolution *see* García de Enterría, *id.*, 102–114.

[74] A. Papell, *La monarquía española y el Derecho constitucional europeo* (Editorial Labor, 1980) at 15–16.

[75] Rafael Jiménez Asensio, *El constitucionalismo. Proceso de formación y fundamentos del Derecho constitucional* (2003) at 71.

[76] Emmanuel Joseph Sieyes, *What is the Third Estate?* [1789], available at http://www.fordham.edu/HALSALL/mod/sieyes.asp; *see also* Marco Goldoni, "At the Origins of Constitutional Review: Sieyès' Constitutional Jury and the Taming of Constituent Power" (September 14, 2011), available at SSRN: http://ssrn.com/abstract=1927162; L. Corrias, *The Passivity of Law. Competence and Constitution in the European Court of Justice* (Springer, 2011) at 25–55; Ramón Maíz, "Nation and Representation: E.J. Siéyès and the Theory of the State of the French Revolution", Working Paper No. 18 (1990); Joel Colón-Ríos, "The Legitimacy of the Juridical: Constituent Power, Democracy, and the Limits of Constitutional Reform" 48 *Osgoode Hall Law Journal* (2010) 200.

the constitution (the constitution-making power). The constitution was the first and highest juridical norm, the rule of recognition for the whole legal and political system. Thus, the constituent power was not merely about writing and enacting a constitution, rather a power that established political community, by creating and institutionalizing its members (citizenship), the relationships among them (basic rights), and political authority bound by the requirements of constitutionalism (the constituted power).

To put it simply, whereas the assembly in charge of drafting and promulgating the constitution is the constituent power, all other powers emanating from the approved constitutional text, such as the legislative, the executive and the judiciary, were the constituted powers. However, the fact that national sovereignty resided more in the former than in the latter did not impede the legislature acquiring supremacy over the executive and the judiciary, both theoretically and in practice. Even accepting that all state powers emanated from national sovereignty, if the legislature, given its representative character, embodied sovereignty more than any other state power, it followed that once the constitution had been passed and the bodies invested with state power had been constituted, the legislature and the laws it passed would be unequalled in authority.

Added to this, the French Constitution did not have the status of a law: its precepts were not legally binding unless they became the object of legislation.[77] French Constitutionalism, thus, was characterized by the marked supremacy of the legislature over the executive and, above all, the judiciary.

It was the legislature as a constituted state power invested with national (not popular, as Rousseau suggested) sovereignty that assumed the role of a protagonist. Firstly, since the Constitution lacked the status of a supreme law, it was not subject to interpretation and application by the courts in particular cases. Thus, the courts could not regard any laws to be hierarchically inferior to the Constitution. It was therefore impossible to question their consistency with the Constitution. Secondly, since laws were seen as the expression of the general will, the courts were unable to declare any law passed by the legislature a nullity (even though, strictly speaking, the legislature was a "constituted" rather than "constituent" power). Finally, at the end of the *Ancien Régime*, there was a general antipathy towards both the traditional parliaments, which had served as higher jurisdictional organs, and the judges, who had often exercised their power in the arbitrary manner (in the King's name).[78] Unsurprisingly, "the members of the [National] Assembly acted in the conviction... that legislation was the complete expression of the law, and that only legislation

[77] On the normative value of constitutions and judicial review in the continental legal tradition, *see* Juan Manuel López Ulla, *Orígenes constitucionales de control judicial de las leyes* (Tecnos, 1999) at 27 ff., 39–53 (and in the case of Spain 54 ff.; in the case of France, *see* Javier Pardo Falcón, "Notas sobre la historia del control de constitucionalidad en Francia hasta la aparición del Consejo Constitucional", *Revista de Estudios Políticos* 72 (1991) 243–258; for an overview of the notion of a Constitution as a legal norm, *see* Eduardo García de Enterría, *La Constitución como norma y el Tribunal Constitucional* (Civitas, 1981) at 49–61.

[78] Concerning the Parliaments and their function in the French juridical tradition, *see* Cristina García Pascual, *Legitimidad democrática y poder judicial* (Alfons el Magnànim, 1997) at 56 ff.

could express the aims of law and that as a consequence, only legislation could create law. The role of the judge was reduced therefore, to the servile application of legislation to each case that came before him".[79]

Owing to Sieyès distinction between constituent and constitutive powers, Rousseau's doctrine of popular sovereignty had been transformed into the notion of parliamentary sovereignty (with the national legislature, as a constituted power, fused with the legislative constituent power).[80] This relation between national sovereignty, the separation of powers and the principle of legislative supremacy in French constitutionalism can be summed up as follows[81]:

1. Parliamentary sovereignty, and therefore the supremacy of legislation (while the Constitution, even when "rigid", was no more than a text which outlined the political organization of the state);

[79] R. Carré de Malberg, *Teoría general del Estado* (2nd ed., FCE-UNAM, 1998) at 663. On the French revolutionaries' opinions concerning the judiciary, the Napoleonic Code and the School of Exegesis, *see* García Pascual, *id.*, at 104–113. At the 18th November 1790 session of the National Assembly Robespierre declared: "We should eliminate the term 'law of precedent' from our language. In a State that possesses a Constitution and legislation the law of the courts is nothing more than legislation itself, and therefore legal precedent should always be identical to legislation."

[80] Richard Price attacked the idea of 'legislative supremacy' (and, effectively, Sieyès distinction between 'constituent power' and 'constituted power') from the American perspective. He maintained that government is a Trust, so all its powers are "a delegation for gaining particular ends" and "all delegated power must be subordinate and limited." According to Price, then, "[n]othing, therefore, can be more absurd than the doctrine …with respect to the omnipotence of parliaments."; *see* Richard Price, *Observations on the Nature of Civil Liberty, the Principles of Government, and the Justice and Policy of the War with America* (9th ed., 1776), *Sect. II: Of Civil Liberty and the Principles of Government, available at* http://oll.libertyfund.org/title/1781/94817/2137427.

Joseph Priestley, who criticized the policy of his native Great Britain regarding the American colonies, viewed 'natural rights' as a limit on the governmental power. Joseph Priestley, *An Essay on the First Principles of Government, and on the Nature of Political, Civil, and Religious Liberty* (2nd ed., 1771), *SECT. I: Of the nature of Civil Liberty in general, available at* http://oll.libertyfund.org/title/1767/93214/2087462.

[81] Article 2 of the 3rd Title (Of Public Powers) of the Constitution of 1791 stated: "The Nation, from which all power emanates, cannot exercise power except by delegation. The French Constitution is representative: the representatives are the legislative body and the King". Among the powers that emanated from the nation were the legislative power (Article 3), the executive power (Article 4) and the judiciary (Article 5). In Clavero's opinion, the Constitution of 1791 did not establish a system of the separation of state powers but rather a system that merely distinguished them from one another (Bartolomé Clavero, *Evolución histórica del Constitucionalismo español* (Tecnos, 1984) at 22), in a way similar to the distinction effected in Spain by the Decree of the 24th of September 1810 (Bartolomé Clavero, *Manual de historia constitucional de España* (Alianza, 1989) at 26). In comparison, the Constitution of the United States of America (1787) would organize the State by separating the legislative bodies (article I, Sections 1–10) from the executive (article II, Sections 1–4) and the judiciary (article III, Sections 1–3). In fact, the American Constitution was concerned primarily with the organization and structuring of State power and omitted the express recognition of fundamental rights and liberties, a matter that was dealt with in the first ten articles of the amendment to the Constitution that was passed 4 years later, on the 15th of December 1791. Concerning the normative value of the North American Constitution and its judicial control, *see* López Ulla, *Orígenes constitucionales de control judicial de las leyes* (Tecnos, 1999) at 27 ff., 32–39.

2. The existence of a strong executive power that was kept in check, at least initially, by the legislative power, not by the judiciary; and
3. The judiciary was an auxiliary to the legislature. It was not able to intervene in the affairs of either of the other two state powers. It could not declare the nullity of a law in a case of its inconsistency with the Constitution (as the Constitution did not have a normative status).

8.4.4 Constitutional Entrenchment of 'Natural Rights'

The same notion of national sovereignty, embraced by the French Revolution, provided the justification for the constitutional entrenchment of 'natural' rights. *La Déclaration des droits de l'Homme et du Citoyen* (1879) proclaimed the principle of national sovereignty in the following terms: "The principle of all sovereignty resides essentially in the nation. No body nor individual may exercise any authority which does not proceed directly from the nation" (Article 3).[82]

The Preamble to the Declaration affirmed that "The representatives of the French people, organized as a National Assembly … have determined to set forth in a solemn declaration the natural unalienable and sacred rights of man". The Declaration proceeds with the avowal of "natural rights" (liberty, property, security, and resistance to oppression) as the aim of any political association (Article 2), but these rights, at a closer look, appear to be at mercy of the law. The law is proclaimed to be "the expression of the general will", with everyone partaking in it directly or indirectly, by means of representation (Article 7). The sovereignty is vested in the nation (Article 3). Hence, the general will of the will of the nation. "The law", then, is to place a limit to liberty and "natural rights" (Article 4), provide for the punishment (Article 8) and so on. The law, though, is to prohibit only the actions "harmful to society" (Article 5) and to provide for the "strictly and obviously necessary" punishments (Article 8). But it is for the general will to decide what is harmful (or necessary).

It may look that a constitutional declaration of 'natural' and 'inalienable' rights was a rather remarkable result of the victorious doctrine of sovereignty, according to which everything could only come about as a result of its 'grant'. But this is just an apparition. The Declaration, if anything, only strengthened the doctrine of sovereignty.[83]

---

[82] *Available at* http://www.constitution.org/fr/fr_drm.htm. For a concise history of national sovereignty from a French perspective, *see*, Maurice Hauriou, *Principios de Derecho público y constitucional* (Comares, 2003) at 268–306. In a somewhat similar vein, the first North American constitutional texts enshrined the principle that "all power is vested in, and consequently derived from, the people" (Article 2 of the Declaration of Rights of Virginia (12 June 1776), granting the people the power to dissolve the political ties that connected them to other nations (The Preamble to the Declaration of Independence (4 July 1776), and gave them the faculty to promulgate and sanction their own Constitution (The Preamble to the Constitution of the United States of America (1787)).

[83] While modern constitutional texts contain a growing list of fundamental rights (with 'rights' being at the heart of the modern constitutionalism), such rights might not only be theoretically vulnerable, due to the doctrine of legislative sovereignty, but also they are under the continuous practical threat from the executive power. On the relationship between the state's power and the

As Jellinek rightly noticed, "the conception of an original right, which man brings with him into society and which appears as a restriction upon the rights of the sovereign, is specifically rejected by Rousseau."[84] Within the Rousseauan doctrine of legislative sovereignty as an expression of general will, there was no mechanism to nullify laws violating 'constitutional' rights. Unsurprisingly, the fruit of this doctrine, the Declaration, placed the law above man and his supposedly 'inalienable' rights, proclaiming man being free *because* of the supremacy of the law. In this Rousseauan vision, rights became merely a creature of the law,[85] as the law was the expression of the general will that could not be dissented from. As a result, no right was anymore beyond the reach of (public) law, with all rights deriving their whole legitimacy from the exercise of the sovereignty.

8.5 Waldron's "Democratic" Positivism: Rousseauan Revival?

8.5.1 Critique of Adjudication of Constitutional Rights

Dicey overlooked that even within 'rigid' constitution, with the constitutionally entrenched rights, adjudication itself could become a matter of controversy. Under such rigid constitution, the (supreme) court is able to revise and adapt rights, potentially contentiously (outside of representative institutions). This point was made by Jeremy Waldron.[86] Waldron offers a positivist solution to the problem of the disagreement about the rights: to agree on the authority to decide the conflict. He professed to getting this solution from Hobbes (*Leviathan*, Chapter XVIII), who

---

rule of law, *see* Aniceto Masferrer, "The Fragility of Fundamental Rights in the Origins of Modern Constitutionalism. Its Negative Impact in Protecting Human Rights in the 'War on Terror' Era", *Counter-Terrorism, Human Rights and the Rule of Law: Crossing of Legal Boundaries in Defence of the State*, A. Masferrer and C. Walker, eds. (Edward Elgar, 2013).

[84] Georg Jellinek, *Declaration of the Rights of Man and of Citizens* [1895], Chapter *II: ROUSSEAU'S CONTRAT SOCIAL WAS NOT THE SOURCE OF THIS DECLARATION, available at* http://oll.libertyfund.org/title/1176/104814/1940368*; see* particularly Jean-Jacques Rousseau, *The Social Contract and Discourses*, Chapter *4 'The limits of the sovereign power', available at* http://oll.libertyfund.org/title/638/71005. For the contrary view (defending the compatibility of Rousseau's Social Contract with natural rights), *see* G.D. H. Cole, "Introduction" to Jean-Jacques Rousseau, The Social Contract and Discourses by Jean-Jacques (1923), *available at* http://oll.libertyfund.org/title/638/70974/1686826.

[85] For the critique of the assumption that rights must be embodied in a legal or constitutional text for them to be guaranteed by the judicial system, *see* A. Masferrer, 'El alcance de la prohibición de las penas inhumanas y degradantes en el constitucionalismo español y europeo. Una contribución histórico-comparada al contenido penal del constitucionalismo español y alemán' in *Presente y futuro de la Constitución española de 1978* (Tirant lo Blanch, 2005).

[86] "A right-Based Critique of Constitutional Rights" 13 *Oxford Journal of Legal Studies* (1993), 18–51.

likewise pointed out, that the people needed a sovereign namely because they disagreed.[87] Waldron, in contrast to Hobbes, supports majoritarian decision-making on the basis of, in his view, *the* fundamental right to political participation. Waldron appeals to Rousseau, as the author of the ideal of the community through participation on equal terms with others in the framing of laws.[88] Waldron also asks: "how is the *Bill of Rights* to be made responsive to changing circumstances and different opinions in the community over time about the rights we have and the way they should be formulated?"[89] In his view, "the justices do undertake the task of altering the way in which the document is interpreted and applied, and the way in which individual rights are authoritatively understood—in many cases with drastic and far-reaching effects".[90] Waldron's logic is clear: in the circumstances of disagreement about the values, why the judiciary should be a better judge than the rest of us?[91] To restate it in Waldron's words: "moral issues concerning individual and minority rights [are] to be addressed directly as moral issues."[92]

Waldron, though, might recently have a slight change of heart. As noted by Dyzenhause, Waldron now confines his opposition to judicial review both to 'strong form judicial review' (rather than its weak form)[93] and to the society with 'democratic institutions', independent judiciary and the commitment to individual and minority rights.[94] Hence, the societies without the rule of law might, presumably,

---

[87] *Id.*, 32.

[88] *Id.*, 38.

[89] *Id.*, 41.

[90] *Id.*

[91] *Id.* This, in Waldron's view, is true also with respect to ordinary legislation "If a majority of judges in the House of Lords, for example, strikes down legislation passed by majoritarian processes in parliament, then the voting powers of a few judges are being held to prevail over the voting powers of the people's representatives." (*id.*, 44).

[92] J. Waldron, "Do Judges Reason Morally", in *Expounding the Constitution*, G. Huscroft ed. (2008) at 54. For the contrary view, *see* W.J. Waluchow, "Constitutional Morality and the Bills of Rights", in *Expounding the Constitution*, G. Huscroft ed. (Cambridge University Press, 2008), 65–92, who, at 89, points out that a judge's task "is to respect and enforce the true commitments of the community's constitutional morality in reflective equilibrium," stressing "the role of legal judgments in shaping the principles of the community's constitutional morality."

[93] *See* D. Dyzenhaus, "The Incoherence of Constitutional Positivism", in: *Expounding the Constitution*, G. Huscroft ed. (Cambridge University Press, 2008) at 142–144, 147–148. *See* also J. Goldsworthy, "Judicial Review, Legislative Override, and Democracy" in *Protecting Human Rights*, T. Campbell, J. Goldsworthy and A. Stone eds. (Oxford University Press, 2003) 263, 267–268. Both Goldsworthy and Dyzenhaus regard Waldron's focus on strong form judicial review as misconceived.

[94] *See* J. Waldron, "The Core of the Case against Judicial Review" 115 *Yale Law Journal* (2006) 1346, 1360. (1) democratic institutions in reasonably good working order, including a representative legislature elected on the basis of universal adult suffrage; (2) a set of judicial institutions, again in reasonably good order, set up on a nonrepresentative basis to hear individual lawsuits, settle disputes, and uphold the rule of law; (3) commitment on the part of most members of the society and most of its officials to the idea of individual and minority rights; and (4) persisting, substantial, and good faith disagreement about rights (i.e., about what the commitment to rights actually amounts to and what its implications are) among the members of the society who are committed to the idea of rights. *See also* Dyzenhaus, *id.*, 140–141.

benefit from judicial review. But this concession not only goes against the whole tenor of his enquiry to define the issue in general terms but also begs the question (why those lacking the rule of law might need judicial review).

If the only difference between Rousseau's and Dicey's perspective is in the latter's attachment to the common law notion of the rule of law', then maybe this rule of law vision does matter?

In his early paper, Waldron makes much of the characteristics of legislature, discovered him in Locke: "the Soul that gives Form, Life, and Unity to the Commonwealth".[95] This sounds very Rousseauan, doesn't it? At the same time, in comparison with the supporters of deliberative democracy, Waldron's explicitly accepts that the disagreements about the common good is a part of life, and sees voting as a valid way to deal with disagreement.[96]

Owing to this emphasis on disagreement, Waldron is able to put forth an ingenious argument for Positivism (or, more precisely 'normative positivism'), enlisting Hobbes (!) among his allies. Hence, he says that "it was better for reasons of peace, stability, or predictability if the legality of putative rules of law could be determined by individual citizens without those citizens having making value judgements… concerning the content of the putative norms".[97]

But everything comes at a price. Waldron's 'normative positivism' seems (in comparison with Hart) to be a step back to Austinian positivism, with its Hobbesian Sovereign, now cloaked as a parliamentary majority, as the only source of a law. Waldron, just as Rousseau before him, does not seem to see a danger of having the whole state power vested in the legislature. This assumption of supremacy of the legislature is supported by a normative vision of 'participatory democracy'. This vision differs from Rousseau's by the explicit endorsement of the *parliamentary* majoritarianism (but the same might be said about the post-Rousseau French theory of sovereignty). Moreover, the majority decision, advocated by Waldron,[98] was a practical solution to the issue of general will even for Rousseau.[99] If anything, Rousseau's original vision of majoritarian direct voting was only more 'participatory',[100] also according to the utilitarian ideal of equality (one man – one vote).

So why, if the only remaining inalienable "right" is the right to political participation, would it protect the liberties and interests of citizens any better than the French model? Reference to "dignity", which has even less obvious formal content

---

[95] John Locke, *Two Treatises on Government* (Cambridge University Press, 1970) at 425 (3d ed., 1698) Second Treatise, at 212); Jeremy Waldron, "The Dignity of Legislation" 54 *Maryland. Law Rev.* (1995) 633.

[96] J. Waldron, "Legislation, Authority and Voting" 84 *The Georgetown Law Journal* (1996) 2185, 2188–2189.

[97] J. Waldron, "Kant's Legal Positivism" 109 *Harvard Law Review* (1996) 1535, 1541.

[98] *Id.*, 2203.

[99] SC IV.II. To reconcile 'majority' decision with 'general will' Rousseau introduced the distinction between 'will' and 'opinion': a minority has other opinion (but the same will); *see* Douglass, *supra* note 64. At 742.

[100] *See* Douglass, *supra* note 64. At 744.

than "right", does not help to alleviate the persistent fears about the Positivist notion of law as a posited rule. No vestige of 'pre-political life', not only of 'natural rights' but of any non-public law (such as autonomous common [private] law) or anything like Dicey's notion of the rule of law, could exist within this vision. As A.W.B. Simpson memorably observed, Positivism could only reduce the common law to "the set of rules by codification, coupled of course with a deliberate reduction in the state of judiciary and some sort of ban on law reporting".[101]

Waldron's case against the bills of rights rests on his thesis that the courts are not best to judge in cases of moral disagreement.[102] But, if Simpson is correct, the real issue is not about the bills of rights. The issue at stake is infeasibility of any autonomous role for the judiciary within Rousseau-Waldron's perspective. More crucially it is about a place for any non-posited law, which is not a result of 'legislative' will, such as the common law. Waldron's appeal to democratic societies as the only proper object of his critique of the adjudication of rights, merely underscores Jellinek's acumen of seeing through the American declarations of rights to its true source: the common law rule of law, as uncovered by Dicey.

8.6 Conclusion

This chapter argues that the idea of 'inalienable' rights is incompatible with Rousseau's notion of unlimited sovereignty.[103] The effect of Rousseau's doctrine was not to bury absolutism but rather to shift its center, by replacing an absolute monarch with a legislature, as an expression of fictitious but unlimited 'general will'. It endowed a revolutionary totalitarianism with a veneer of democratic legitimacy.[104] The French doctrine might be seen as an extreme case, but it is hard to deny its kinship with Hobbes' no less radical vision. For Hobbes, just as for Rousseau, Social Contract would result in formation of the Sovereign that subsumed the will of all in society. Neither Bentham nor Austin had anything against this vision of a

[101] A. W. B. Simpson, Oxford Essays in Jurisprudence, Second Series (2nd ed., Oxford University Press, 1975) at 99.

[102] Waldron, *supra* note 94. At 1380–1382. In Waldron's view, while the judges' moral reasoning might be constrained, for example, by textual formalism, legislatures, in contrast, would take into account the full range of moral reasons.

[103] Leon Duguit, *Manual de Derecho constitucional* (Francisco Beltrán, 1937) at 133.

[104] J. Ballesteros, *Repensar la paz* (2006) at 115: "In effect, totalitarian democracy is possible and the revolutionary Convention proved that; it arose in an environment in which the general will was believed to serve as a supreme principle, and individual rights were subordinated to the will of the collective entity. This conversion of the general will into an absolute principle led to the logical necessity of eliminating dissenters, who were seen almost as delinquents". Cf. Leon Duguit, *Soberanía y libertad* (Francisco Beltrán, 1922) at 214: "Rousseau... is often cited as the inspiration for the liberal Declaration of Rights promulgated in 1789, when... he is the originator of all doctrines of dictatorship and tyranny, from the Jacobin doctrines of 1793 to the Bolshevik doctrines of 1929"; *see also* J. L. Talmon, *Los orígenes de la democracia totalitaria* (Aguilar, 1956) at 41 ff.

mighty Sovereign, but just clothed it in a Positivist 'value free' vocabulary. Dicey's doctrine of parliamentary supremacy, in effect, originates from the same source as the French one.

The merit of pre-Kelsen, German Positivism, like one of Jellinek, was to delimitate a space to private law, left free from a public law interference. Jellinek found an ally in Dicey. He understood Dicey's 'common law' notion rule of law (and the historical success of the common law countries in protecting the individual liberties) as being congenial to his own vision of the rule of law as self-limitation of the state. But he overlooked incompatibility of this (common law) notion of the rule of law with Dicey's doctrine of parliamentary supremacy.

Waldron's critique of adjudication of constitutional rights could be seen as a continuation of the line of critique going back to Dicey and Jellinek, highlighting the inherent incompatibility of constitutional rights and Rousseau's doctrine of sovereignty. But, in a more general sense, Jellinek's criticism of *French Declaration of the Rights of Man and of the Citizen* underlined the futility of a notion of the rule of law within the Rousseauan's will theory. This may ring a bell for the modern normative positivists, like Waldron.

Chapter 9
The Measure of Law: The Non-instrumental Legal Side from the State to the Global Setting (and from Hamdan to Al Jedda)

Gianluigi Palombella

Il n'y a point de plus cruelle tyrannie que celle que l'on exerce à l'ombre des lois et avec les couleurs de la justice.

Montesquieu

Abstract This chapter maintains that when the law lives up to the ideal of the "rule of law" (RoL), it is organized in such a way as to display two internal sides, in mutual tension, concurring in the legal order as a whole. This notion of RoL is contrasted with the rule *by* law and the albeit precious principle *of legality*, seen through historical and comparative lens. As the analysis shows, for the RoL to surface, a part of the law should not be under the jurisgenerative power of the sovereign. This feature of duality (in the same sense as the medieval jurisdictio and gubernaculum couple) represents a scheme that prevents domination from being perpetrated through the monopoly of law. In the extra State setting, it holds true as well, as different patterns can show, from the Hamdan case at the US Supreme Court to Al Jedda at the ECtHR. It means that sheer exercise of democratic sovereignty should not be sufficient for justifying infringement of international law and that the sovereign exercise of rule-making by the UN Security Council cannot per sé unconditionally override fundamental rights. Finally, being different from sheer respect for human *rights* or *democracy*, and dealing with the configuration of *law,* it would be even too narrow the assumption that the RoL boils down to benefit only individuals (against States that should not "be entitled" to its "benefits").

G. Palombella (✉)
Faculty of Law, University of Parma, Parma, Italy
e-mail: gianluigi.palombella@unipr.it

J.R. Silkenat et al. (eds.), *The Legal Doctrines of the Rule of Law and the Legal State (Rechtsstaat)*, Ius Gentium: Comparative Perspectives on Law and Justice 38,
DOI 10.1007/978-3-319-05585-5_9,

9.1 Introduction: A Genuine Rule of Law Question

In the famous US Supreme Court case of *Hamdan v. Rumsfeld*, the Military Commissions used by the US President Bush in Guantanamo Bay were declared unconstitutional, because sentences and executions were carried out "without previous judgment pronounced by a regularly constituted court, affording all the judicial guarantees which are recognized as indispensable by civilized peoples'".[1] Moreover, by creating such military commissions, the US President had used a power which is not "implied" in times of war, and should have been conferred upon him by the Congress. This is why the Court affirmed, with confident solemnity, that "in undertaking to try Hamdan and subject him to criminal punishment, the Executive is bound to comply with the Rule of Law that prevails in this jurisdiction".[2]

This case is worthy of citation here because, although the two steps are connected, the decision of the Court is recognising on the one hand that the judicial rights of Mr Hamdan and international law obligations must be respected (fundamental principles of law recognised by civilised nations) and on the other hand that the separation of powers has been infringed. However, the relevance of rights and international norms is here granted by their inclusion within the laws of the land. Democracy and the separation of powers (the "structural" aspect) are at the heart of the justificatory arguments, denying presidential power a blank check, thereby making the *Hamdan* case decision "democracy forcing."[3] This is confirmed through the concurring opinion of Justice Breyer.[4]

Given the mixed rationale of the Supreme Court decision, the Congress was asked to legislate on the matter. The result was the Military Commissions Act (MCA) in October, 2006. Many MCA provisions "are incompatible with the international obligations of the United States under human rights law and humanitarian law." [5]

---

[1] 548 U.S. 557 (2006), at 631-2. According to the Supreme Court, the Uniform Code of Military Justice "conditions the President's use of military commissions on compliance not only with the American common law of war, but also with the rest of the UCMJ itself, insofar as applicable, and with the 'rules and precepts of the law of nations' ... including, *inter alia*, the four Geneva Conventions signed in 1949. .... The procedures that the Government has decreed will govern Hamdan's trial by commission violate these laws" (548 U.S. at 613). According to the Court, the Geneva Conventions – and the requirements of Common art. 3- are "judicially enforceable" *because* are part of the law of war (art. 21 of UMCJ). Reference is to *The Geneva Convention Relative to the Treatment of Prisoners of War*, August 12, 1949, art. 3 § 1(d).

[2] 548 U. S. at 635.

[3] Jack Balkin wrote: "What the Court has done is not so much countermajoritarian as *democracy forcing*. It has limited the President by forcing him to go back to Congress to ask for more authority than he already has, and if Congress gives it to him, then the Court will not stand in his way." (*Hamdan as a Democracy-Forcing Decision*, June 29, 2006 at http://balkin.blogspot.com/2006/06/hamdan-as-democracy-forcing-decision.html last visit June 2013.

[4] "Where, as here, no emergency prevents consultation with Congress, judicial insistence upon that consultation does not weaken our Nation's ability to deal with danger" by trusting constitutional "faith" in "democratic means" (548 U. S.577 at 636).

[5] *Cf.* the list of violations in *Special Rapporteur on the promotion and protection of human rights and fundamental freedoms while countering terrorism*, Martin Scheinin: United Nations Press Release, October 27, 2006. at http://www.unog.ch/unog/website/news_media.nsf

The MCA contradicts "the universal and fundamental principles of fair trial standards and due process enshrined in Common Article 3 of the Geneva Conventions."[6]

This being, however, a consequence of the "Rule of law in this jurisdiction", the question arises whether a matter like basic rights and the rule of International law can be reserved to *democracy* as such. Of course, the latter is just one among the ideals that western constitutional polities cherish. Should the legal duty to provide individuals with the minimum guarantees universally recognized by the most fundamental rules of international law, be wiped away by a majority vote of the United States Congress?

This is a genuine rule of law question. The reason for the emergence of the rule of law as a principle and an ideal in our legal civilization has to do with the service of legality, its autonomy, its non-instrumental function, and its conceptual separability *vis à vis* the albeit legitimate exercise of sovereign normative power; regardless of whether its holder can show democratic credentials or otherwise.

This chapter sets out the features of the principle of legality, the rule by law, and the rule of law, extending their rationale beyond the State. The last section concludes with a short analysis of the ECtHR decision in *Al Jedda*, as an example of the practicability and normative import of the notion of rule of law (RoL) that is proposed and defended here.

9.2 The Rule of Law as Legality Principle?

At one level of meaning the RoL may be intended to protect the linkage between constituencies and the law, ethos and a legal order. The RoL is here a jurisdiction related notion. Among its famous templates, for example, Montesquieu, "L'esprit des lois". Starting with a huge amount of data and experience among diverse peoples, Montesquieu came to an intuition: laws are "relations" that result from the combination of social, cultural, geographical factors, commerce, economy, manners and costumes, as much as from the sound (or unsound) role played by political rule. Not a naturalist, Montesquieu explains in this sense law, as a situated notion, under general rationales: not simply its ultimate belonging in nature or will. And, in turn, even polities live up to the "principles" that "set [them] in motion", and make their structure to "act".[7] Public passions towards common institutions are a functional, objective element of the complex system. One can take this pattern to fairly reflect some part of our received ideas on law, made of the "relations" connecting diverse contextual vectors, a fabric embedded in the "nature of things"[8]; and the general "esprit des lois" takes shape as such a "whole" re-composing.[9] Accordingly, laws

---

[6] *Id.*

[7] Ch. L. de Secondat, Baron de Montesquieu, *The Spirit of Laws* (Thomas Nugent, Cincinnati, R. Clarke & Co., 1873) vol. I, 22 ff.

[8] *Id.* at, *Pref.*, at XXXII.

[9] This is suggested by E. Ehrlich, "Montesquieu and Sociological Jurisprudence" 26 *Harvard Law Review* (1916), 582, at 589.

are hardly detachable from what they are supposed to regulate.[10] One can say that a version of that conception can conservatively recall the "Burkean" mode, within which the Courts are to reflect the "whole experience of a nation".[11]

This conception sometimes – unfortunately and somewhat misleadingly- becomes a reinforcement of a rigid, will based, self-referential notion of law. It works externally as well, through deciding, by coherent interfacial constitutional rules, the general attitude toward – and the legal force and status that domestic law can assign to – conventional or customary international law, Treaties and general principles. It is, in brief, the "rule of law in this jurisdiction".

A second fashion of the latter conception of the rule of law can be less ethically or socially embedded, but still of much weight, in current theories. It dictates again a jurisdiction-relative conception, but builds upon the importance of abiding by the law, and sticking to its alleged determinacy, by making law count through interpretive restraint, through exegetical attitudes, less inclined to replace meaning with teleology or similar evolutionary openness. That is in the words of his famous champion, US Supreme Court Justice, Antonin Scalia: the rule of law as a law of rules.[12]

There are a host of expected consequences of making law count, in this very sense. Serving certainty and submitting public powers to the pre-established rules, is a necessary premise of a liberal state, of the separation of powers. It seems to grant the *legality principle*: that is, the very idea that the exercise of power depends on laws' conferral, and is submitted to limiting rules. The legality principle is tantamount to protecting *non-arbitrariness*. Here is the core of its virtue. From this point of view it is sometimes legitimated because allegedly convening the ethos of a nation, and fidelity to its law[13]; *non-arbitrariness* can be defended as coherence of rules' fabric, either as an expression of a State constitution, of its life world, or formally, given the above recalled service that formality or textuality provide.

In the European doctrines, the service of legality was precisely intended through the idea of a 'legislative State'. According to the German sociologist, Max Weber,[14] the nature of the legislative state was granting predictability of public powers' action and providing each citizen with legal certainty under the formal rationality of a rule-based method of social control (instead of any other methods, arbitrary, casual, violence based, etc.).

[10] Accordingly, "something is right not just because it is a law; but it must be a law because it is right" (Montesquieu, *Cahiers,* Paris, Grasset, 1951, p. 135.). One should note how even in this perspective the law is not a matter of mere 'will'.

[11] Oliver Wendell Holmes, in *Missouri v. Holland*, 252 U.S. 416, 433 (1920) and see R. Post, "The Challenge of Globalization to American Public Law Scholarship", in *Theoretical Inquiries in Law*, (2001), 2:323, at 326 ff.

[12] Antonin Scalia, "The Rule of Law as a Law of Rules", 56 *University of Chicago Law Review* (1989) 1175.

[13] One can cite the famous dictum adopted from Roman civilization, in the European continental State in XIX and XX centuries: *dura lex sed lex*.

[14] Max Weber, *Economy and Society*, vol 2, edited by G. Roth and C. Wittich, Berkeley, CA: University of California Press, 1978, p. 82.

Yet, the RoL can be misinterpreted if reduced to a kind of legality principle and ultimately, it could not explain the difference, if any, between the rule of law *sans phrase* and the rule of law as a jurisdiction dependent notion.

To overcome this perspective, one might look first at the telling semantics of the Rule *of* law, one to be clearly differentiated from a rule *by l*aw, which is often still used, unconvincingly, as equivalent.

A mainstream conviction is endorsed by Tamanaha:

> The rule of law, at its core, requires that government officials and citizens be bound by and act consistently with the law. This basic requirement entails a set of minimal characteristics: law must be set forth in advance (be prospective), be made public, be general, be clear, be stable and certain, and be applied to everyone according to its terms. In the absence of these characteristics, the rule of law cannot be satisfied.[15]

Despite its claim to encapsulate the 'core' of the rule *of* law, such a definition only describes the core of the rule *by* law. One must take the mentioned requisites as necessary for the *law to exist,* as it is aptly shown in Lon Fuller's famous list of the eight features that law requires in order to be law.[16] Of course, that does not detract from the evidence that legality of itself, the rule by law, obviously makes a huge difference *vis à vis* arbitrariness and crude violence, as Max Weber himself taught. Not by chance, given the constraining logics of legality, the German Nazi *legal* order, notwithstanding its instrumental service to the regime, was better suspended in order to get rid of albeit procedural limitations, and to effectively achieve some of the regime's objectives.[17]

But still the rule *by* law is hardly our normative ideal (the one that the Rule *of* law can be referred to). It conforms instead with what Thomas Hobbes described as the means of social ordering by the sovereign, the Leviathan, that does rule *by t*he law: it sets up rules, public competences, and organized procedures in stable and prospective ways.[18] The requirements for the law to exist do not automatically mean that the RoL is actually realized; its rationale needs that those requisites be effective, and nonetheless *per se* insufficient for the RoL to be properly achieved (as explained below, Sect. 9.3).

A further argument, referring to the relation between law and the political process, can reinforce this tenet. A widespread perspective, like the one endorsed by Stephen Holmes, looks at the RoL from the view that law is, after all, (just) an instrument: it all depends on how power is socially distributed whether the law will result as just

---

[15] Brian Z. Tamanaha, "A Concise Guide to the Rule of Law", in G. Palombella and N. Walker, *Relocating the Rule of Law,* Oxford: Hart Publishing Company (2009) at 3.

[16] Martin Krygier has graphically called similar notions "anatomic", in his "The Rule of Law: Legality, Teleology, Sociology" in *Relocating the Rule of Law*, edited by Gianluigi Palombella and Neil Walker (2009) at 47 ff. Law must be general, public, non retroactive, non-contradictory, comprehensible, possible to perform, relatively stable, and consistently followed by officials and administrators (L. Fuller, *The Morality of Law*, 2nd ed. New Haven: Yale University Press (1969, ch. 2).

[17] Ernst Fraenkel described this as the Nazi "Doppelstaat": *The Dual State. A Contribution to the Theory of Dictatorship* [1941], transl. E. A. Shils, (1969) at, 56 ff.).

[18] Thomas Hobbes, [1651]. *Leviathan*, edited by M. Oakeshott. (1946) (chaps. 26–28).

or unjust, serving liberty or oppression.[19] Accordingly, as the argument goes, only a democratic polyarchy can make the difference. Now, there is hardly a way, within such a perspective, to draw a line between *rule of law* and *rule by law*.

On the contrary, should we achieve the first and get beyond the second, law would emerge with some functional autonomy *vis à vis politics,* and would cease to simply reflect its decisional arm. The question about the RoL is not tantamount to asking about the organization of governmental power, and cannot coincide with the structure/quality of the Sovereign. Distinctively, it is the question about the organization and role *of law* itself, in its *additional* value. A quality turn makes the law not *only* an instrument of social groups, but in some part *also* an authority irreducible to sheer manageability at their own whim.

9.3 Normative/Institutional History

Accordingly, behind the *by/of* alternative there is some *institutional* difference, that can be understood if we analyze the institutional embeddedness of the RoL. specifically, This section turns to reconstruct the original sense of the RoL and its normative meaning (as such everlasting). But *before* that, it is necessary to explain in the same methodological attitude, what the sense of legality in continental Europe was taken to imply. This is a significant test.

9.3.1 The Sense of Legality in Continental Europe

Before the totalitarian decades, the legal state (*Etat de Droit, Stato di diritto, Rechtsstaat*) and the so called 'thin' conception of the alleged RoL held the central place in Continental Europe. First, despite being the current translation for the English "rule of law", the European expressions are not 'equivalent', not least because they do not refer to the law but to the State. That is, they refer to a determinate institutional system, a configuration of power, in a certain range of times. By contrast, the RoL spans diverse historical settings, and should not be frozen necessarily in any contingent State configuration. The focus is upon the European State *before* its *constitutional* transformations in the aftermath of the II World War. Despite its non-arbitrariness, some of its features are compatible with those recently resumed under the oxymoron "the authoritarian rule of law", labeling the Singapore regimes.[20]

---

[19] Stephen Holmes, "Lineages of the Rule of Law.", in *Democracy and the Rule of Law*, edited by J. Maravall and A. Przeworski. Cambridge: Cambridge University Press (2003) 19–61 at 49–51.

[20] Jothie Rajah, *The Authoritarian Rule of Law. Legislation, Discourse and Legitimacy in Singapore*, Cambridge: Cambridge University Press (2012).

More in detail, as F. J. Stahl[21] and the German public law doctrine worked out the concept of *Rechtsstaat*, the State was to act under precise and fixed mechanisms, and pre-defined rules, thereby self-limiting its own power through the law. Beyond enlightened paternalism, it appeared to move from the law of power to the power of law. The *Rechtsstaat* means that law is the structure of the State, but not a limitation to it. Liberty is a consequence and not truly a premise of the law. In its overall European meaning, it included both the separation of powers and the principle of legality, which requires that no authority can exist that is not created and conferred by legislation. The priority of legislation can both formally grant individual rights and subordinate them. The independent role of the judiciary was trusted rigidly to respect the legislative will. Legislation turns out to be the authentic voice of the State, expressing its will: it is not the constraint but rather the "form" of the State's will.[22]

Both "La loi" in France and *die Herrschaft des Gesetzes* in Germany are the ultimate source of the law. This "legislative state" is generated by the hierarchical supremacy of legislation, lacking equally relevant sources, protagonists and actors on the (institutional) scene. This impinges upon the relationship with rights. According to Georg Jellinek,[23] citizens hold "public subjective rights" on the ground that the latter result from a self-obligation of the State. There is almost nothing real, including rights, unless it is contained in legislation. The tension between individuals and public power could only be "decided" by legislated law. Despite (or because of) being a sound incarnation of the Rule *by* law, such a law-based state was based neither on "Rule of law" nor on the practice of modern constitutionalism (cf. 1787 American Constitution).

As shown in the following section, the fact that some rights might even be actually protected by the law is not the litmus test in the RoL discourse. The point relates instead with independent legal sources. The declaration of independence of rights (and individuals' prerogatives) from State legislation was written only with the contemporary Constitutions, that is during the twentieth-century: the constitution – not legislation – created that 'independence', long awaited on the continent. Constitutional rules and principles granted fundamental rights and other countervailing principles as high a rank as the democratic principle, preventing the exercise of the second from being endowed with the legal power to discretionally decide the fate of the first. Prior to this, the logic of the RoL could not be developed.

9.3.2 *The Original Sense of the Rule of Law*

Contrary to a *Rechtsstaat* (or a *Stato di diritto*), understood as a peculiar form of the *State*, the RoL as an ideal presupposed that, in part, positive law was beyond the disposal or "will" of the King, or the sovereign power. Its ideal can be shown as one

---

[21] Friedrich J. Stahl, *Philosophie des Rechts*, vol. II, *Rechts- und Staatslehre auf der Grundlage christlicher Weltanschauung* (1870) 137 ff. *See* the term from Ludwig v. Mohl, *Die Polizeiwissenschaft nach den Grundsätzen des Rechtsstaates*, I-III, (1832).

[22] The importance and dominance of legislation was also a product of the process of codification of law which took place in continental Europe from the seventeenth through twentieth centuries.

[23] Georg Jellinek, *System der subjektiven öffentlichen Rechts* (1892, 1919^2).

based upon a relationship between two essential western law domains developed within the medieval tradition and evoked through the couple *jurisdictio – gubernaculum*: justice and sovereignty. "For in *jurisdictio,* as contrasted with *gubernaculum*, there are bounds to the King's discretion established by a law that is positive and coercive, and a royal act beyond these bounds is ultra vires. It is in *jurisdictio*, therefore, and not in 'government' that we find the most striking proof that in medieval England the Roman maxim of absolutism was never in force theoretically or actually."[24]

In the line which unites Henry de Bracton (cf. the pair *gubernaculum/jurisdictio*) with Edward Coke (cf. Bonham's case), the U.S. Federalist Papers and ultimately U.S. judicial review, we find —despite their differences – evidence of a general unitary logic.

There is a plurality of sources going together to make up the intrinsic diversity of the law of the land. It allows for rights to be retained and emerge with an autonomous aspect.

The law certainly also reflects Parliamentary sovereignty. However, sovereignty is complex, shared between Crown, Lords and Commons, and the law has a wider purpose. As a matter of fact, law includes a main second pillar, the common law and the Courts, the ultimate interpreters of the legal system as a whole.

The complexity of legal achievements in the diverse denominations of common law, precedents, customary law, conventions and rights, is entirely relevant to the "rule of law." The latter is a "founding" element of itself, to the extent that Dicey recognized certain English features: no man can be punished for what is not forbidden by law; legal rights are determined by the ordinary courts; and "each man's individual rights are far less the result of our constitution than the basis on which that constitution is founded".[25]

But this endows the constitution and the RoL with the historical content of liberties, which is part of positive law, not abstract claims from natural law (or, say, organic) doctrines. This feature stands at odds with the self-reference of the formalist idea of legality, the final turn of the *Rechtsstaat*.

As Giovanni Sartori noted, "the Rule of Law does not postulate the State, but an autonomous law, external to the State: the common law, the case law, in sum the judge made and jurists' law. Therefore, there is a 'rule of law' without the State; and more exactly it does not require the State to monopolize the production of law."[26] However, while the reality of a Stato di diritto is the self-subordination of the State

---

[24]Charles McIlwain, *Constitutionalism: Ancient and Modern*, Ithaca: Cornell University Press (1940) at 85 and *passim* (elaborating on the pairing of jurisdictio and gubernaculum).

[25]Albert V. Dicey, *Introduction to the Study of the Law of the Constitution*, edited by E. C. S. Wade, VIII ed. (1915), *Reprinted*. New York: Macmillan (1982). *Introduction*, p. LV). As Dicey wrote, *id* at 21): "[W]ith us … the rules that in foreign countries naturally form part of a constitutional code, are not the source but the consequence of the rights of the individuals, as defined and enforced by the Courts."

[26]Giovanni Sartori, "Nota sul rapporto tra Stato di diritto e Stato di giustizia" in *Rivista internazionale di filosofia del diritto*. Milano: Giuffrè. (1964) at 310.

by its own law, in the case of the rule of law, the State is subordinated to a law which is not its own.[27] Again, the roots of these differences are in medieval times, as MacIllwain, Haskins[28] and others have shown.

In conclusion, the meaning of the RoL is better understood through its enduring continuity with its own past: the concurrency of sources of law is requisite to create a virtuous "tension" within the justice-government coupling. Beyond the legitimate expression of sovereign will, there is a part of the law belonging in the land, protecting its positive idea of justice and giving liberties their due: it is the part formed through judicial decisions, the common law and conventions. On the other hand, there is the gubernaculum, which embraces instrumental aims and government policies. The ultimate power of a polity could avail itself of the law only in part: that which is under its sovereign prerogative. If there must be law which remains at the disposal of the sovereign, another side of law is not, and the sovereign is thus bound to be deferential.

In principle, then, despite legality being effective under the purview of the Sovereign's idea of the common good, it is implied that where the RoL is absent, justice, or the "right," has no shield. It becomes mere 'morality' and fades outside the positive order, altering the balance between *gubernaculum* and *jurisdictio*, and undermining a reliable premise for the RoL.

Eventually, in *moral* terms, the institutional shift from rule *by* law to the rule *of* law has a possible representation, in terms of consequences. Being the moral import of the RoL generally designated through the idea of liberty, here the point is not the sheer *fact* that the law by the sovereign does not actually interfere arbitrarily on individuals' and minorities' spheres. On the contrary, at issue is that such an interference could not be made legal by a sovereign's rule, precisely because it has to be considered illegal due to a law that the Sovereign lacks the legal power to overwrite. Those spheres are placed outside of the ultimate (legal) control of the Sovereign, however gracious he might happen to be. The borders of the Englishman's home are legally safe, and not contingently so, from arbitrary interference, accordingly, due to the existence of "another" law. In the logic of the RoL (its scheme) such a duality of law has a decisive role, and affects its general form, one that can encompass a wider spectrum of political regimes, regardless of centuries.

When this situation applies, it is not improper to describe the ideal of the RoL as a specific asset of liberty, that is under a *non-domination*[29] principle, since liberty itself is not made to depend from contingent law of the prince, but on a law beyond its disposal.

---

[27] *Id. at* 311.

[28] *Cf.* McIlwain, *supra* note 24, at 90. *See* George Haskins, "Executive Justice and the Rule of Law: Some Reflections on Thirteenth-Century England.", in *Speculum* 30, 1955, 536 (the medieval "rights and remedies of the common law came to be identified with the rule of law itself.").

[29] Not being under someone else's control: The meaning suggested is borrowed from the theory elaborated by Phillip Pettit, in *Republicanism: A Theory of Freedom and Government*, Chicago: Chicago University Press (1997) where it is adopted in a rather different (not referred to law) context.

9.4 On the Rule of Law as an Extra-State Question, and Its "Benefits"

As discussed above, such a normative meaning exceeds the mere fact of complying with the rules that apply in one jurisdiction or the other. It is rather the opposite: it is the law "in this jurisdiction" that should be measured against the parameter of the RoL, one that interrogates the very configuration of legality, and its legal 'non domination', liberty serving, structural scheme. In this regard, it works as a measuring function as much as other normative ideals, democracy and human rights do in our present legal civilization.

When freed from a single jurisdiction-dependent notion, the RoL projects onto a supra-state setting, in so far as we choose to adopt its consequences in managing the tensions among different legal orders.

First, it is to be considered how the above mentioned scheme or rationale of the RoL can be referred to the domain of International Law; after that, a judicial case shall be discussed as an example of how relations *among legal orders* should better be arbitrated through reference to a RoL measure (Sect 9.5, below).

Once we recognise that constitutional States can realise a balanced duality of legal 'sides', and good enough to fulfil in their domestic order, the RoL, that means for instance that an unlimited exercise of "democratic" power is prevented, and even the Sovereign lacks (unless the present system is cancelled) a legal monopoly. Such a duality should emerge in the international legal order as well. Beyond unrestrained States' power to negotiate their own interests, in the traditional view of International Legal Order as 'conventional', an "other international law" has developed to include human rights law out of the 1948 Universal Declaration of Human Rights; or, among many others, the International Covenant on Civil and Political Rights (1966), or The Convention Against Torture and Other Cruel, Inhuman or Degrading Treatment or Punishment (1984). And not least, environmental law, or humanitarian law, in times of war, through the Hague Convention (1899 and 1907), the Geneva Conventions (1949, and 1977 Protocols) and their exemplary common Article 3 (mentioned in the case at the start of this chapter), that was defined in 1986 *Nicaragua* judgment by the International Court of Justice (ICJ) as one incorporating "elementary considerations of humanity."[30] Albeit slowly, a corpus of general norms of international law is increasingly thought of as *jus cogens*.[31] Thus, a "community" law has enriched the contents of international law, a "super partes law", and the principle that there are rules, beyond the conventional consent. All those create an "other side" to international law, that clearly prefigures a "non instrumental" aspect of legality. Founded on this "duality," even the International legal order has developed an embryonic structure like rule of law, one that can aspire to be a *measure* of civilisation *vis à vis* States' behaviour and the diverse entities and regimes of supranational nature as well.

[30] *Nicaragua v. United States of America, Merits*, Judgment of 27 June 1986, ICJ Reports 1986, par. 218. The Court recalled its first use of the expression in the *Corfu Channel Case* (*United Kingdom v. Albania*, 9 April 1949).

[31] *See* A. Cassese, *International Law*, 2nd ed., Oxford: Oxford University Press (2005) at 294, and 310.

One can assume that in the relations between domestic and international orders the ultimate nature of mutual obligations rests on the substantive *acquis* of contents that they share. This goes somehow beyond the obligation stemming from *pacta sunt servanda* meta-rule, which might boil down to respecting consented rules, whatever. The positive allegiance to an international order is, in the more recent transformations, better seen as framed also by convergence on shared community interests and values. The 'new' legal commitments, like those just recalled, seem to weave an international law that gains a higher force *vis à vis* the mere will of the Masters of Treaties. Those commitments generate, as mentioned, an "other" international law, and accordingly a 'duality" in law's sides of which the RoL general scheme consists (as explained in this chapter).

Moreover, the idea that domestic democracy is not the final judge of whichever question internally, goes hand in hand with the assumption that *mutatis mutandis*, powerful States, even in international intercourses, cannot take their whim as the ultimate (external) legislator. The recognition of the RoL principle, proclaimed internally, is unsuited to a double standard, and hard to dismiss (consistently) when participating in a common wider order whose RoL features are enshrined and entrenched in the same sense.

Confrontations among diverse legalities stably happen between States in the international order, between international organisations and global 'regimes' on one side and national law and Courts on the other. Accordingly, the RoL is to be conceived as a frame to locate mutual intercourses and confrontations, a parameter that displays as well an *interfacial* function, in so far as those very relationships are thought of as having a legal nature. If there is a "legality" holding in the *intercourses* among orders of different nature and levels, even in those relations the duality and the non domination principle (in the legal sense of the notion) as described above have a potential to develop.

Different constitutional arrangements in diverse States, however, (whether making IL general principles of higher constitutional rank or affording Treaties with legislative, supra-legislative strength, etc) do not change the point that interconnections between matters of external *independence* (concerning the external action of States) and internal sovereignty (concerning their action within their own internal sphere) – think of the environment and human rights especially, or commitments in international trade to abstain from protectionist provisions – have made it rather contradictory to maintain that the rule of law can stand alone, "in this jurisdiction". Less than ever, there is a watertight separation among RoL in each different orders, unless it is used as a shield, a self referential normative closure, thus with a meaning that narrows to the parochial one, generally objected to in the first sections of this chapter.

For intuitive reasons, the very fact that the ideal of the RoL has started to be set in concrete through the duality enshrined even in the International legal order, ends up *benefiting all the actors or subjects,* that would otherwise fare worse without it. In so far as individuals are considered and protected through international law provisions (but they can also be targeted by supranational authorities) or in so far as weaker States are allowed to make countervailing legal claims against power, the desirability of the RoL connects to the functioning of an objective state of affairs, to legal institutions' design as a whole, more than only to the protection of individual justice, or to a 'benefit' exclusively reserved to individuals. This follows from the systematic nature of RoL one that also concerns as well fairness and avoidance of specific domination through law in the relations among legalities of different nature, reach, power, and social embeddedness (like, for example, global regimes as UNCLOS, WTO, ISO, ICANN, *vis à vis* regional orders, the EU, national States, IL Order *stricto sensu*).[32] When different orders confront each other appealing to law, they need a stage of fairness where law is not reduced to the rule of the more powerful. This principle stems from the Rol as a normative ideal, one that is all but identifiable with some unilateral parochial use of legality (like when it is simply equated with the democratic will of a people).

The RoL is not to be viewed in a straightforward identity with, say, human rights, precisely inasmuch as it cannot be equated either with the single value of the pursuit of democracy. The latter are, not by chance, listed separately, with an autonomous strength and bearing a separate rationale *vis à vis* the RoL itself. Although the RoL, a democratic society, and a respect for human rights are in consequential terms, to be seen as mutually reinforcing, each being a strong bedrock for the increasing establishment of the others, the RoL focuses upon the quality/configuration of legality, providing the scheme of law's duality. There is, in a sense, a *systematic* character of the configuration of the legal universe that separates the point of the RoL from the important question of one and each individual's justice case, and matters in a *specific* modality through the ideal of the RoL. It is true only in part that States should not be "entitled to the benefits of the rule of law"[33] while individuals are. Although truly nothing can be justified, in its ultimate *raison d'etre*, unless for the sake of human beings, nonetheless in a legal universe even the claims from distinct legal orders (international law or domestic law, etc.) can have an inherent value *vis à vis* each other. Inherent value does not necessarily preclude from serving further values or even more fundamental ones (justice to individuals, for ex.). An inherent value deserves to be considered as such: the existence of something else that one can regard as even more 'fundamental' does not detract from it, nor contradicts its worthiness of protection, benefits and respect. The benefits from the RoL, in a sense, need to be multifaceted.

9.5 The Dynamics of Rule of Law and the Lesson from *Al Jedda* (ECtHR)

The RoL can be construed in confrontational steps among legal orders. However, it cannot avoid the question of consistency between principles embraced externally and those enshrined internally. Some of those principles, either construed by the epistemic community of national, supranational courts, or shared through domestic

---

[32] On these issues, at length in my "*The Rule of Law in Global Governance. Its construction, function and import,* The Straus Institute for the Advanced Study of Law and Justice (2010).

[33] With regard to Jeremy Waldron, "Are Sovereigns entitled to the benefits of the Rule of Law?" in 22 *European Journal of International Law* (2011), 315–343.

constitutions, international charters and conventions, are actually practiced as bridges among different confronting orders, between global regimes (the WTO and the WHO, the SC and ECHR, and so forth).[34] Although an analysis of that progress exceeds the scope of this chapter, in order to close the circle opened in its introduction, the *Al Jedda* case at the ECtHR shall be mentioned. That decision does not embrace simply an adversarial, self-referential point of view, that is, the single European Convention's regime for the individual, human rights' protection. Its argumentation, although without mentioning it, interprets the RoL and its implications as a general and shared principle within the common supranational legal setting (in which the Security Council is included).

The Grand Chamber of the ECtHR found, in *Al-Jedda v United Kingdom,*[35] that indefinite detention without charge of Al Jedda (dual citizen British/Iraqui) by the UK in a Basra facility controlled by British forces was unlawful and infringed his rights to liberty under art. 5 of the ECHR. The significance of the argumentative strategy adopted by the Grand Chamber marks an innovative step.

The ECtHR rejected the opinion upheld by the House of Lords in the proceedings that had decided Al Jedda in UK (before he applied to the ECtHR): a universally reputed author, champion of the rule of law, Lord Bingham[36] had asserted in the House of Lords' judgment, that the treatment reserved to Al Jedda derives from the unavoidable compliance with the UN Security Council Resolution 1546, requested under Art. 103 of the UN Charter.[37] This is the argument of conformity to the rule of international law, centered upon *respect for the RoL* as a matter of hierarchy of rules in the international order[38]; that is, one that cannot be objected against even if implying human rights infringements.

The ECtHR neither took such a path, nor did it resort to another and famous reasoning adopted in the *Kadi* case by the European Court of Justice. In that decision, the ECJ found that fundamental rights of Kadi had been actually infringed by a EU regulation in order to implement a Security Council resolution against him. According to the ECJ, however, those rights are not simply part of a well founded individual claim, they are pillars of the European primary law[39]: RoL in the European

---

[34] There is here developing an intensive amount of work taking account of the elaboration by Courts and scholarship, *See* Ch. Brown, *A Common Law of International Adjudication*, (2007); S. Cassese, *I Tribunali di Babele*, Roma, Donzelli (2009).

[35] European Court of Human Rights, *Case of Al-Jedda v. The United Kingdom*, Application no. 27021/08, 7 July 2011 (*Al Jedda*).

[36] Tom Bingham,, *The Rule of Law*. London: Penguin Books (2011).

[37] *See id* at para 35: at 11: "Emphasis has often been laid on the special character of the European Convention as a human rights instrument. But the reference in article 103 [UN] to 'any other international agreement' leaves no room for any excepted category, and such appears to be the consensus of learned opinion".

[38] That kind of appeal to the RoL in the international legal order, resonates in the 2005 decision of the European Court of First Instance in the *Kadi* case (21 September 2005, Case T-315/01 *Kadi v Council and Commission*).

[39] ECJ, Joined Cases C-402/05 *P, Yassin Abdullah Kadì and Al Barakaat International Foundation v. Council & Commission*, (2005), E.C.R. II-3649, Judgment of 3 September 2008.

order requires that internal regulations are unlawful, regardless of a Security Council mandate, when they violate the fundamental norms of Community law.

Now, as one can see, what the RoL is deemed to command in one path (House of Lords, Al Jedda) is contrary to what RoL commands in the other (the ECJ in Kadi). There was a third alternative available, though: in a less strict interpretation, the ECJ Kadi decision can be taken as an appeal to the Security Council, aiming to grant compliance in the future if it can guarantee some equivalent protection of human rights of the targeted individuals. Seen in this way, it represents more than a vindication of the "Rol in this EU jurisdiction", namely a pattern of RoL beyond the State, with promising potential in the relationship among legalities (the UNSC and the EU).[40]

By walking an original path, different from those just mentioned, *Al Jedda* (2011) can now be understood as further contributing the theoretical profile of the RoL. In proclaiming the unlawfulness under the ECHR, art 5 (1), of indefinite detention without charge, the ECtHR reasons by taking on its shoulder a more comprehensive interpretive pattern (which overcomes as well the Kadi decision even understood in its better light).

The Court refers to the RoL as a principle whose consistency is not a matter for each separate regime/order of law to internally (self) assess; the judges reason around it as an issue and a model ultimately controlling the interactions among the respective orders. They do not put in the forefront the issue of the supremacy through Art 103 of the UN Charter, but at the same time they appear to carefully consider both the reasons of the sovereign Security Council and the rights protected by the Convention.

The ECtHR refuses to agree that the unlawful indefinite detention *was commanded or authorized* by the SC resolution. To the contrary, it finds that under the relevant resolution, the security task assigned to the UK could not be considered an authorization (and less than ever an obligation) to preemptively and indefinitely detain Al Jedda, without judicial review, and lacking necessity.

Accordingly, it does not ask the question about which is the most powerful law in international *hierarchy*. Although this choice (*i.e.* not asking/not answering) is believed a kind of prudential withdrawal from the core issue of the 'last word' & ultimate authority in international law, therein lies its strength, and its deep value. The Court raises an argument not of 'sources' but of integrity and meaning of the law, in the wider and plural, supranational order. The issue is no longer which is the higher to rule, whether the UN Security Council or the European Convention, in 'pyramidal' terms, but which meaning can be ascribed to the *whole system* of relevant law, included that from the Security Council. Such a meaning should be made to cohere with the normative context where it is placed. As the Courts states, Art 1 of the UN Charter "provides that the United Nations was established to 'achieve international cooperation in … promoting and encouraging respect for human rights

[40] *See,* Gianluigi Palombella,"The Rule of Law beyond the State: Failures, Promises, and Theory", 7, *International Journal of Constitutional Law* 442 – 467.(In that article I started my analysis on one of the issues in the present chapter).

and fundamental freedoms'. Article 24(2) of the Charter requires the Security Council, in discharging its duties with respect to its primary responsibility for the maintenance of international peace and security, to 'act in accordance with the Purposes and Principles of the United Nations'".[41]

Thus, a considered insight in the relevant legal system emphasizes the import of that 'other' side of the international legality that should be an obligation for the Council, and the Assembly of States themselves, to fulfill and protect. It cannot be really *presumed* that Security Council imperatives are to be conceived either in isolation or as unconditional, regardless of any *other law.* In fact, for the Court, "in interpreting its resolutions, there must be a presumption that the Security Council does not intend to impose any obligation on Member States to breach fundamental principles of human rights".[42] Human rights seem to escape a sheer source-hierarchy, bearing a countervailing, autonomous strength, in the interpretive scope, even *vis à vis* the ultimate security authority. Accordingly, "the Court must therefore choose the interpretation which is most in harmony with the requirements of the Convention and which avoids any conflict of obligations".[43]

Now human rights law is a meaningful check on the Security Council. Eventually, in a last statement, the Court seems to raise the point that the law of human rights enjoys an *equally* concurring weight: therefore, should the Security Council want to impose a rupture in the fabric of UN law, this could result only from "clear and explicit language" (§ 102) against international human rights law. This last point brings, ultimately, an argument *per absurdum,* in so far as there can hardly be integrity of the system, and convincing interpretation, that would beyond dispute allow for that. Here lies the challenge which leads to the denial that a *legitimate* international law norm can be conceived that shall undermine the basis of *duality* of the RoL.

Naturally, one can recall the principle of legal civilisation that an extensive, beyond the text, interpretation (of the resolution, in our case) can be used only in favour of the less powerful or the accused person. But more importantly, how can the 'sovereign' authority of the Security Council *explicitly phrase* an order of direct negation of fundamental basic human rights (that is, outside state of necessity)? How could it be defended as unconditionally legitimate, that is, holding- in the UN system- an unassailable seal of legality? While the ECtHR commits itself to comply – in principle- with any Security Council resolution, it requires, against human rights, only explicit terms: but those very terms could hardly be worded, without making the resolution apparently unlawful, that is, equally explicitly, illegitimate in the integrity frame that the Court itself has aptly drawn.

Or this – should one wish to disagree with the view of *Al Jedda* presented here – would be the sense of a reasoning intended to live up to the ideal of the RoL that is maintained in this chapter.

---

[41] ECtHR, *Al Jedda,* para 102 (and the para 44 that is premised to it).

[42] *Id.*

[43] *Id.*

Chapter 10
Rule of Law, Legal State and Other International Legal Doctrines: Linguistic Aspects of Their Convergence and Differentiation

Yury A. Sharandin and Dmitry V. Kravchenko

Abstract This chapter concerns the linguistic problems of translation of similar (but not the same) international legal doctrines, particularly doctrines of rule of law and legal state. Moreover, authors argue that the doctrines, while they should not be confused, should nonetheless be compared in order to define accurately both of them.

The Rule of Law is the only mechanism so far devised to provide impartial control of the use of power by the State.
08.10.2009 Resolution of the IBA Council

There is a paradox at the heart of the rule of law. That ideal demands certainty and condemns ambiguity in the law. But that is great uncertainty and alleged ambiguity in the ideal itself. Firm adherents are locked in great disagreement about what the rule of law really is.
From Ronald Dvorkin's speech at 02.03.2012 Venice Commission Conference: "The Rule of Law as a Practical Concept"

Legal State, historically originating from the German Rechtsstaat—probably, the highest achievement of the German legal philosophy,—is a term seen in the texts of many national constitutions, and its definition can vary in some details due to the particularity of each national legal system.
Peter Barenboim, from the book "The Interrelationship between the Rule-of-Law and the Legal State doctrines as the Main Question for Philosophy of Law and Constitutionalism"

Y.A. Sharandin (✉)
Federal Assembly of the Russian Federation, Moscow, Russia
e-mail: ysharandin@yandex.ru

D.V. Kravchenko, Ph.D.
Asnis and Partners, Moscow, Russia
e-mail: dmitriy-kravchenko@yandex.ru

J.R. Silkenat et al. (eds.), *The Legal Doctrines of the Rule of Law and the Legal State (Rechtsstaat)*, Ius Gentium: Comparative Perspectives on Law and Justice 38,
DOI 10.1007/978-3-319-05585-5_10,

10.1 Introduction

Today, nobody doubts the serious impact that globalization processes have on national law. The problems of convergence, differentiation, and competition between different legal systems existing in the world are being discussed by leading politicians, legal practitioners, scientists, and philosophers. One of the clearest indicators of this was the discussion of many of the world's legal issues at the Third International Legal Forum in St. Petersburg specifically in the context of the rule of law – the doctrine, which the Russian Federation adopted in accordance with its international obligations, and which originates from the Anglo-Saxon legal system.

Many of the world's leading legal scholars openly admit that there is still no globally uniform understanding of the rule of law as such, which is particularly interesting against the background of creation and operation of international institutions charged with the task to incorporate this doctrine into national legal systems. Evolving expert evidence shows that the rule of law principle is subject to different interpretations not only in its original, Anglo-Saxon understanding, but also in connection with its global meaning. It seems that today's "global" rule of law already differs quite significantly from the "Anglo-Saxon" rule of law. It is impossible to transfer a certain fundamental legal concept in a purely mechanical fashion to be applied to other countries. Moreover, many experts now argue that the Rule of Law doctrine can and should be perceived and interpreted through juxtaposition with its main "rival" legal doctrine – that of the legal state (and vice versa). Therefore, this chapter is only a preliminary presentation of the issue of such juxtaposition. This issue is in great need of both comprehensive and versatile analysis, which includes legal, historical, philosophical, geographical, socio-cultural aspects and many other considerations.

10.2 The Problem of Definition

Until recently, the problem of the comparative study of the Legal State and the Rule of Law doctrines has not meaningfully been investigated. This is largely due to linguistic difficulties and confused translations. In today's globalized world, the linguistic accuracy of the international professional communication and interpretation of international documents is becoming increasingly important. In March 2013, the world's largest news agencies, by having incorrectly translated the statements of Pyongyang, addressed to South Korea, almost declared a war against the latter on behalf of North Korea. Similarly, translators of legal texts can often have quite an impact on the international legal processes.

It is only in the last decade that lawyers seem to have noticed that the Rule of Law and legal state doctrines are different in essence, thus finding out that a state respecting rule of law does not automatically become a state respecting a legal state doctrine (and vice versa). Specialists have paid attention to the fact that quite often the rule of law was translated wrong into Russian as *Verkhovenstvo zakona* (i.e. "the supremacy of statute law"). This linguistic misnomer appears in some of the conceptual normative legal acts currently in effect in Russia –for example, in the Federal Law "On the Public Prosecution in the Russian Federation". Still, both the accuracy of each word when naming such fundamental principles and a most careful and thoughtful understanding of each of their components are of a paramount importance for the legal development of a state, as well as for that of the entire international community. Each aspect of such legal doctrines may become a decisive factor, as it was negatively demonstrated by the Nazi Germany, which preferred to "overlook" some elements of the Legal State doctrine that were "uncomfortable" to them. The effect was to distort the originally benign doctrine beyond any recognition.

Therefore, the fact that many international experts have now come to realize the multifaceted nature of the legal world and the need to distinguish between various legal doctrines is most welcome.

One of the first serious attempts to raise the problem of linguistic confusion between the legal state and the rule of law doctrines was undertaken by the Parliamentary Assembly of the Council of Europe.

The 2007 PACE resolution,[1] initiated by Erik Jurgens from the Netherlands (by the way, one of the authors of this article was among those who discussed and adopted it), provides:

> Despite a general commitment to this principle, the variability in terminology and understanding of the term [the rule of law], both within the Council of Europe and in its member states, has elicited confusion. In particular, the French expression "Etat de droit" (being perhaps the translation of the term "Rechtsstaat", known in the German legal tradition and many others) has often been used but does not always reflect the English language notion of the "rule of law" as adequately as the expression "prééminence du droit", which is reflected in the French version of the Statute of the Council of Europe, in the preamble to the European Convention on Human Rights (ETS No. 5) and in the Strasbourg Court's case law.
>
> The Parliamentary Assembly draws attention to the fact that in some recent democracies in Eastern Europe, the main trends in legal thinking foster an understanding of the "rule of law" as "supremacy of statute law", in Russian "verkhovenstvo zakona". "Rule of law" should, however, be translated into Russian as "verkhovenstvo prava", just as "rule of law" is correctly translated into French as "prééminence du droit" and not as "prééminence de la loi". (Similarly, the words "Recht" and "droit" in "Rechtsstaat"/"Etat de droit" should be translated into Russian as "pravo".) Translating the "rule of law" as "verkhovenstvo zakona" gives rise to great concern, since in some of these countries certain traditions of the totalitarian state, contrary to the "rule of law", are still present both in theory and in practice. Such a formalistic interpretation of the terms "rule of law" and "Etat de droit" (as well as "Rechtsstaat") runs contrary to the essence of both the "rule of law" and "prééminence du droit". Certainly, in these cases there is an inappropriate lack of consistency and clarity when translating into the legal terms used in member states.

[1] The Principle of the Rule of Law. Resolution of the Parliamentary Assembly of the Council of Europe # 1594 (2007).

In his Explanatory Memorandum to this document, Erik Jurgens also notes:

> What is clear is that in Western Europe the variations of "Rechtsstaat" / "Etat de droit" have long been used as an analogue of the "rule of law", while both of these terms were not the latter's exact translation… The interpretation of these national legal terms may not include all the elements of the rule of law in the form, in which it is understood and interpreted by the European Court of Human Rights.

The Annex to the Memorandum contains references to the decisions of international courts, which exemplify the terminology confusion during translation. Thus, in the Decision of the ECHR of March 22, 2001 in the case of "K.-HW v/Germany", the "State governed by the rule of law" is rendered into the second official language – French – as the "Etat de droit".[2]

Thus, Erik Jurgens at once raised two issues important to PACE: (1) the correct translation of the names of the international legal doctrines and their interrelationship; and (2) the use of an incorrect translation by non-legal regimes for the sake of self-justification.

This topic was further developed by the European Commission for Democracy through Law (the Venice Commission). For example, in the text of its 2009 Report on "The Rule of Law and the Rechtsstaat" the Venice Commission notes that these two doctrines largely overlap and, therefore, cannot be easily separated from each other. The document also states:

> Both notions pursued and pursue similar aims, in particular the prevention of arbitrary governmental power
>
> Differences:
>
> - Mainly due to the differences between Common law conceived as judge made law and Civil law based on statutes, respectively the inductive method of the Common Law in contrast with the deductive method of the Civil Law
> - Rechtsstaat links law more closely to the state
> - Rule of law in Dicey's original conception was driven by his campaign against administrative discretion (which he equated with arbitrariness) and a separate system of public law (which he saw as giving special protection to public officials).

The issues of the interrelationship between the rule of law and legal state doctrines were reflected in other documents of the Venice Commission. Thus, in its Report on the Rule of Law,[3] it states:

> Although the terminology is similar, it is important to note at the outset that the notion of the "rule of law" is not always synonymous with that of "Rechtsstaat", "Estado de direito" or "Etat de droit" (or the term employed by the Council of Europe: "prééminence du droit"). Nor is it synonymous with the Russian notion of "Rule of the laws/of the statutes" (verkhovenstvo zakona), nor with the term "pravovoe gosudarstvo" ("the law-governed state") (see para. 4).

---

[2] The Principle of the Rule of Law. Report. Committee on Legal Affairs and Human Rights. Rapporteur: Mr Erik JURGENS, Netherlands, Socialist Group. 6 July 2007. Doc. 11343.

[3] Report on The Rule of Law, adopted by the Venice Commission at its 86th plenary session (Venice, 25–26 March 2011).

One should note that in this text we see a link only to the preferential correctness of applying the term "prééminence du droit" as an analogue of the "rule of law." This means that the Venice Commission in 2011 still did not fully understand the clear-cut position developed by the Council of Europe 4 years earlier. After the 2007 Resolution of the Council of Europe the European Court of Human Rights did start using the term "prééminence du droit". This is seen, for example, in its decisions of 10.01.2013 in the case Agnelet v. France (para. 57), of 29.06.2011 and in the case Sabeh El Leil v. France (para. 46), etc. That is, one witnesses obvious ambiguity in the interpretation of the terminology, begging further clarification, even in the framework of the European Court of Human Rights.

The Venice Commission Report, in the section dedicated to the analysis of the genesis of these legal concepts, also indicates that:

> The Rechtsstaat concept focuses, by definition, much more on the nature of the state. Whereas the rule of law emerged from courtrooms, the Rechtsstaat emerged from written constitutions... The Rechtsstaat was defined in opposition to the absolutist state, with unlimited powers conferred on the executive. Protection against absolutism had to be provided by the legislature rather than by the courts alone (para.13).
>
> The French approach can be foreseen in the Declaration of the Rights of Man and the Citizen (1789). The notion of Etat de droit (which followed the positivistic concept of Etat legal) puts less emphasis on the nature of the state, which it considers as the guarantor of fundamental rights enshrined in the Constitution against the legislator... The Etat de droit connotes (judicial) constitutional review of ordinary legislation (para.14).
>
> The rule of law has been interpreted variously, but it must be distinguished from a purely formalistic concept under which any action of a public official, which is authorized by law, is said to fulfil its requirements. Over time, the essence of the rule of law in some countries was distorted so as to be equivalent to "rule by law", or "rule by the law", or even "law by rules". These interpretations permitted authoritarian actions by governments and do not reflect the meaning of the rule of law today (para. 15).

However, the same report states:

> [I]t seems that a consensus can now be found for the necessary elements of the rule of law as well as those of the Rechtsstaat which are not only formal but also substantial... (para. 41).

Such terminology ambiguities cannot create successful preconditions for finalizing the definitions of such concepts as the "rule of law" and its analogues, the "Rechtsstaat" and its analogues, "pravovoye gosudarstvo", etc. Moreover, the fact that the rule of law doctrine tends to be understood in different ways complicates this situation ever further. In the Venice Commission Report, the rule of law is defined by the following six elements:

(1) Legality, including a transparent, accountable and democratic process for enacting law
(2) Legal certainty
(3) Prohibition of arbitrariness
(4) Access to justice before independent and impartial courts, including judicial review of administrative acts
(5) Respect for human rights
(6) Non-discrimination and equality before the law (para. 41).

The World Justice Project defines the "rule of law" as necessarily possessing the four following features:

(1) the government and its officials and agents as well as individuals and private entities are accountable under the law;
(2) the laws are clear, publicized, stable and just, are applied evenly, and protect fundamental rights, including the security of persons and property;
(3) the process by which the laws are enacted, administered and enforced is accessible, fair and efficient;
(4) justice is delivered timely by competent, ethical, and independent representatives and neutrals who are of sufficient number, have adequate resources, and reflect the makeup of the communities they serve.[4]

Nevertheless both the Parliamentary Assembly of the Council of Europe and the Venice Commission do indicate the need for distinguishing between the "rule of law", "Etat de droit", and other doctrines. At the same time, the United Nations Organization continues translating the "rule of law" into French as before, while completely disregarding the new European findings.[5] For example, in the autumn of 2012 the UN General Assembly adopted the "Declaration of the High Level Meeting of the General Assembly on the rule of law at the National and International Levels". The French and Spanish translations[6] of this Declaration reduce the "rule of law" concept to that of the "Rechtsstaat" (or "legal state") – i.e. "Etat de droit" and "Estado de derecho", respectively. The Russian translation of this term appeared to be correct – "verkhovenstvo prava". This gives one an idea as to the quality of translations from the UN "core" English into the "non-core" languages, all of which retain their official status. This example demonstrates the need for further work as a practical matter to clarify the differences between the international legal doctrines.

10.3 Conclusion

The "rule of law" and the "legal state" terms were and, in many cases, still are translated incorrectly. In some cases, this may be ascribed to a mere incompetence of the interpreter. In other cases this hides a direct political intent, allowing a state

[4] *See* http://worldjusticeproject.org/what-rule-law

[5] In Russia, the only noteworthy source mentioning this problem was Peter D. Barenboim's book entitled "*The Interrelationship between the Rule of Law and the Legal State Doctrines as the Key Issue of the Legal Philosophy and Constitutionalism*", Moscow, LOOM, 2013, p. 46.

[6] The problems identified in the Russian translation of this Declaration have already been reviewed – *see*, e.g.: D.V. Kravchenko, D.M. Kiryukhin, "A Legal-linguistic Approach to International Documents: Translation Errors (using the example of the Declaration of the High Level Meeting of the General Assembly on the Rule of Law at the National and International Levels)", in *The Problem of Mutual Understanding of International Legal Doctrines*. Collection of articles, E.G. Tarlo and D.V. Kravchenko eds (2013) at 168–177. Loom.

government to create variations on a theme of the state's easily adoptable (and, therefore, easily malleable) statutes, which thus can "comfortably" supplant the demanding general concept of law. In any case, the inaccuracy of translation reduces the possibilities to explore usefully the potential separation/convergence of these doctrines, and—in many cases—the quality of how well these legal principles are secured.

In this regard, the system of international and national documents, reinforcing international legal doctrines, requires a thorough audit to verify the correctness of terminology and identification of contradictions. The authors of this chapter share the position of V.D. Zorkin, President of the Constitutional Court of the Russian Federation, which he expressed at the Third International Legal Forum in St. Petersburg, saying that today the contradictions in the application of international principles deserve a most thorough analysis.

In addition, neither the rule of law nor the legal state doctrine have been adequately studied and/or defined. The definition of the rule of law without regard to other international doctrines in today's globalized world cannot be complete. The interpretation of the rule of law and the legal state today cannot be done properly without studying both of these doctrines and their historical origins, or without understanding the degree of their interpenetration and interdependence. Taking the work of the Venice Commission as an example, the first timid attempts have been undertaken to achieve contemporary interpretation of both doctrines, together with their interrelationship and distinctions. However, this work needs to be proactively pursued on all levels, including that of the European Court of Human Rights. For this purpose, it becomes necessary to unite the international legal community in a joint effort to conduct a comprehensive, multi-polar and well-balanced research of the formulated challenges.

Part II
Specific Perspectives on the Rule of Law and the Legal State

Chapter 11
Freedom, Equality, Legality

T.R.S. Allan

Abstract The rule of law is both a legal principle, central to judicial reasoning and adjudication, and a political ideal underpinning and illuminating constitutional democracy. It should not be identified with a narrowly formal conception of law. It is not merely a set of precepts for ensuring that statutes are correctly framed and capable of being accurately applied to particular cases. The rule of law is rather a commitment to governance in accordance with principles of justice, reflecting a stable legal tradition built on respect for human dignity and equality. Exercise of discretionary administrative powers must meet demanding standards of fairness and rationality; the proceedings of courts, tribunals, and official agencies must satisfy principles of natural justice or procedural fairness. And the civil and political liberties associated with democracy are also key constituents of the rule of law. Ideals of freedom, equality, and legality are closely linked; and these ideals cannot stand with assertions of "sovereignty", whether by government or Parliament.

11.1 Introduction

The rule of law is both a political ideal and a constitutional doctrine. In English law, the rule of law expresses a general principle of constitutionalism, associated not only with procedural fairness and the impartial administration of law but also with ideas of human dignity and respect for persons. Although A. V. Dicey famously identified *two* basic principles of British constitutional law—the "rule of law" was honoured alongside the doctrine of "parliamentary sovereignty"—it is

T.R.S. Allan (✉)
Faculty of Law, University of Cambridge, Cambridge, UK

Pembroke College, Cambridge, UK
e-mail: trsa2@cam.ac.uk

J.R. Silkenat et al. (eds.), *The Legal Doctrines of the Rule of Law and the Legal State (Rechtsstaat)*, Ius Gentium: Comparative Perspectives on Law and Justice 38,
DOI 10.1007/978-3-319-05585-5_11,

the former that arguably has the greater claim to foundational status.[1] While the precise meaning and full implications of Dicey's doctrine of the rule of law remain controversial, the principle serves to root English common law in a conception of legality having close links, at a philosophical level, with fundamental values of liberty and equality. The rule of law is at the same time both a doctrine of British constitutional law, developed by the courts in elaborating the traditional common law, and a general principle of constitutional government, wherever it exists. In working out the implications of the rule of law, case by case, the judges attempt to make sense of the ideal of constitutionalism in the context of British legal and political institutions and practice. There is no clear distinction between political ideal and legal principle: legal doctrine evolves by the elaboration of legal precedent, seeking always to bring public law closer to the connected ideals of freedom, equality and legality that history and practice exemplify, at least when favourably interpreted.[2]

According to Dicey, the rule of law meant that in England no one was above the law, exempt from its ordinary requirements: "every man, whatever his rank or condition, is subject to the ordinary law of the realm and amenable to the jurisdiction of the ordinary tribunals".[3] Taken together with his insistence that the "supremacy or the rule of law" excludes "the exercise by persons in authority of wide, arbitrary, or discretionary powers of constraint",[4] Dicey's principle is usually understood as an affirmation merely of *formal* legality, or formal equality before the law. There should be general rules (rather than ad hoc commands) faithfully applied to particular cases. It is a common criticism that formal equality is perfectly compatible with the imposition by law of unequal or even oppressive burdens or constraints, making invidious distinctions between persons or groups. The context of Dicey's discussion, however, makes clear that the formal equality secured by the consistent application of law to everyone, whether private citizen or public official, is only the route to a larger, more substantive equality of legal principle. The British constitution was said to be "pervaded by the rule of law" in the sense that such "general principles" as the right to personal liberty or right of public meeting were "the result of judicial decisions determining the rights of private persons in particular cases brought before the courts".[5] The consistent application of general principles of law, as these are explored and refined in the elaboration of the common law, achieves a broader constitutional equality: general rules and principles of law must be fairly to applied to everyone, according to all the circumstances; and the distinctions drawn between different persons or

[1] A. V. Dicey, *Introduction to the Study of the Law of the Constitution*, first published 1885 (10th ed. 1964; Macmillan, London, 1959).

[2] The dependence of legal interpretation on recourse to moral and political principle is a central theme of my book, *The Sovereignty of Law: Freedom, Constitution, and Common Law* (OUP, Oxford, 2013).

[3] Dicey, *supra* note 1. At 193.

[4] *Id.* 188.

[5] *Id.* 195–196.

cases must be justified before independent judges, committed to an ideal of respect for persons and the demands of human dignity.[6]

The British constitution is essentially a *common law constitution*. Its content is the product of a continuing effort, over many generations, to achieve a satisfactory reconciliation between the potentially conflicting doctrines of the sovereignty of Parliament and the rule of law. As a common law doctrine, parliamentary sovereignty is itself subject to judicial interpretation: any challenge to the authority of an Act of Parliament or controversy over its proper meaning must be resolved by the courts, invoking the resources of general constitutional principle. As courts of *law*, the judges must interpret British legal and political practice in the light of general notions of legality: there is a complex interweaving of settled British tradition and general moral or political principle. In affirming the right of personal liberty as an integral part of the common law, the courts draw not only on general principle but on the well-established practice of invoking habeas corpus as a remedy against unauthorized deprivations of freedom. Dicey wrote that in England "the right to individual liberty is part of the constitution, because it is secured by the decisions of the courts, extended or confirmed as they are by the Habeas Corpus Acts".[7] The Acts reinforced an existing common law remedy, enabling the courts to maintain in practice the tradition of personal liberty that constitutional principle affirmed. In extending common law principle to protect other fundamental rights, such as those of free speech, conscience and association, the courts have worked out the implications of a general commitment to the rule of law. Even when public officials or agencies are granted extensive discretionary powers, conferred by Act of Parliament, it is assumed that the exercise of such powers should respect established common law rights. Any limitations of rights, inimical to legal tradition, must be subject to rigorous justification: there must be a reasonable accommodation of conflicting rights and interests, disallowing extravagant restrictions of freedom, unnecessary to the governmental aim envisaged.

When the rule of law is treated as a mainly *formal* idea, securing merely formal equality before the law, its connection with liberty consists primarily in the absence of unregulated discretion. If citizens and officials alike are bound by the law as officially announced or declared, the individual can be assured that, provided he complies with the law himself, he will enjoy a sphere of independent action: he will not be subject to the arbitrary will of others. When the law consists of general rules, which are published, intelligible, prospective, and enforced in accordance with a reasonable interpretation of their meaning, it provides clear guidance on how to act without the risk of interference or domination by powerful officials. Retrospective laws, punishing actions that were lawful when undertaken, are a grave offence against legality: they deny the respect for persons that animates the ideal of the rule of law. The formal or procedural dimension of the rule of law includes those principles of "natural justice" or fairness that ensure that the law is accurately administered.

[6] *See* Allan, *The Sovereignty of Law*, *supra* note 2, ch. 3; *see also* Allan, *Constitutional Justice: A Liberal Theory of the Rule of Law* (OUP, Oxford, 2001).

[7] Dicey, *supra* note 1. At 197.

A court, for example, must be composed of impartial judges, having a duty to listen to the representations of anyone accused of wrongdoing. A court or tribunal must apply the law to the facts as they are correctly understood; and it must also adjudicate between competing interpretations of the law, allowing reasonable challenges to official assumptions or assertions about the correct meaning of relevant legal rules.

Dicey's notorious opposition to the exercise by officials of broad discretionary powers reflects the threat such powers inevitably pose to the rule of law: the individual is governed not by rules, previously enacted, but by the less predictable judgements of those in authority, based on their present opinions about what would best serve the public interest (or their current conception of the public interest). Recognizing the inevitability of a degree of official discretion, in practice, English common law has developed the formal requirements of the rule of law into a more comprehensive doctrine: the principles of fair procedure have been extended to those of *due process*. When legal rules confer powers on public officials, there are principles of legality that operate as safeguards against abuse: statutory powers must be exercised only for legitimate public purposes, implicit in the statutory scheme. Such powers must not become a means of employing coercion against people whose actions or aspirations are considered mere hindrances to public policy, if they are otherwise perfectly lawful. Even when a public authority may lawfully impose restrictions on a citizen's liberty, in exercise of discretionary powers, the damage done to individual rights or interests should be a proportionate response to the public need: the infliction of *disproportionate* harm on individuals, even when interference is legally authorized, betrays a contempt for the dignity and well-being of those concerned.

The fundamental idea of equality before the law cannot be limited to the impartial application of general rules. It must encompass administrative or executive authority, allowing independent courts to appraise the justification offered for the distinctions drawn between persons by officials in the exercise of discretionary power. In that essential respect, administrative discretion must meet standards of legality similar to those implicit in legal process and intrinsic to the rule of law. When the courts apply and develop the common law, they apply a pertinent principle of equality: like cases should be decided alike. That general principle does not, of course, provide criteria of likeness or similarity. The courts must draw on more specific principles of law to justify the distinctions drawn between particular cases. We expect those principles, however, to be morally justified; they must amount to a coherent philosophy of constitutional government with roots in legal tradition, reflecting ultimate values of liberty and justice. Even if administrative decisions, by contrast, are typically based on general considerations of public policy, that policy must be even-handedly applied: there must no discrimination between persons or groups inconsistent with a coherent and plausible account of the public interest. Public policy must be enforced within the constraints of law and legal process. The validity of particular decisions—whether those of courts or government officials—finally depends on the implicit theory of legitimate government that underpins, and qualifies, their authority.[8]

[8] For further argument, *see* Allan, *The Sovereignty of Law*, *supra* note 2, ch. 3.

11.2 Freedom, Equality and Due Process

A citizen who enjoys the protection of the rule of law is free to live according to his own ideas about what makes a good life, subject only to the similar freedom equally granted to other citizens. He may make and execute personal plans and projects, developing and pursuing private aspirations; he enjoys an immunity from arbitrary interference, whether by public officials or other persons—interference at whim, outside or beyond the limits of coercion permitted by ascertainable general legal rules. The rule of law is a bulwark of freedom in the sense of *independence*: no one is at the mercy of ad hoc or *ad hominem* intervention in his affairs, but may enjoy the security afforded by the impartial administration of the law, according to its published or readily accessible requirements.[9] It does not matter that influential public officials (or other private citizens) may dislike or condemn the citizen's beliefs or projects or actions because they have no power to interfere unless it is conferred by law, publicly and clearly announced beforehand and enforced, in disputed cases, by impartial courts, independent of Parliament or executive Government. There is, then, the reasonable assurance that any threat or exercise of force, inimical to the citizen's interests but beyond the limits of any lawful authority, will be met with judicial resistance. The courts will confine official coercion within determinate legal and constitutional boundaries.

The basic idea of the rule of law as a guarantee of freedom, in the sense of independence, finds clear expression in John Locke's account of constitutional government. Freedom is not, as sometimes supposed, freedom from legal constraints but is rather "to have a standing rule to live by, common to every one of that society":

> A liberty to follow my own will in all things where that rule prescribes not, not to be subject to the inconstant, uncertain, unknown, arbitrary will of another man, as freedom of nature is to be under no other restraint but the law of Nature.[10]

Freedom under the law is the antithesis of subjection to official *discretion*, which renders a person vulnerable to interference at the will or pleasure of others—public officials or agencies, left free to discriminate between persons as they choose. Even if such discrimination is not malicious, biased against disfavoured persons, it may nonetheless reflect questionable opinions about the public interest—opinions that have not been publicly challenged and defended in the course of the deliberation that precedes the enactment of general rules. Governance under law entails a separation of powers between Parliament, which frames and enacts the general rule, and the judiciary that applies that rule to particular cases. Official discretion, unconstrained by general rule, disrupts that separation, making the citizen's freedom precarious:

> The [pertinent] conception of freedom under the law ... rests on the contention that when we obey laws, in the sense of general abstract rules laid down irrespective of their application to us, we are not subject to another man's will and are therefore free. It is because the

[9] *Compare* Nigel Simmonds, *Law as a Moral Idea* (OUP, Oxford, 2007).

[10] John Locke, *Two Treatises of Government,* originally published 1690, (1924), II, para 22.

> lawgiver does not know the particular cases to which his rules will apply, and it is because the judge who applies them has no choice in drawing the conclusions that follow from the existing body of rules and the particular facts of the case, that it can be said that laws and not men rule.[11]

It is a familiar objection to the emphasis on enacted general rules that the implementation of public policy, especially economic or social policy, may in practice require resort to official discretion. Dicey and Hayek are often criticized for failure to acknowledge the benefits of flexibility that the conferment of discretionary powers on officials may bring: public policy may be adapted to unforeseen or changing circumstances, permitting state agencies to distinguish between persons or groups according to the demands of their specific tasks or functions. It would be foolish, however, to ignore or deny the real threat to liberty that such discretionary powers present; they leave the citizen at the mercy of the judgement of public officials, who may have little incentive to allow even reasonable objections to thwart their pursuit of their own policy agendas. There is a danger of oppression or unfairness, even when officials are well intentioned and act in good faith in (what they deem) the public interest.

The principle of the rule of law requires that a grant of official discretion should be no greater than strictly necessary for the tasks in view: the scope of a power must be confined by its proper purposes, as those purposes are ascertained by interpretation of the empowering statute. In the event of dispute the relevant purposes must be determined by an independent court, whose construction of the statute will be binding on the executive government.[12] Legal constraints cannot be limited to matters of scope, however, but must extend to the *manner of exercise* of discretionary power. Freedom as independence requires not only governance according to clear and published rules, which limit the exercise of official discretion in particular cases, but the enforcement of rigorous standards of due process. The principle of due process lies at the heart of the rule of law. It demands that every assertion of coercive state power be justified as an accurate and defensible application of general rules to the particular instance in view. Principles of procedural fairness or natural justice must be supplemented by constraints of *rationality or reasonableness*: the powers in question must be employed only for legitimate purposes, there being a convincing connection between ends and means. While the ultimate decision may be a matter for the public official or agency, the courts have an important constitutional role in circumscribing the lawful field of choice. A decision must be based on relevant considerations alone, disregarding any matter that (in the final judgement of the court) is irrelevant or extraneous to the statutory function.[13]

There is here a close analogy with the criminal trial, in which a person accused of an offence is entitled to a fair hearing before an unbiased judge (or judge and jury) on the basis of proper evidence, adduced according to established legal

[11] F. A. Hayek, *The Constitution of Liberty* (Routledge & Kegan Paul, London, 1960), at 153.

[12] *See*, for example, *Padfield v Minister of Agriculture, Fisheries and Food* [1968] AC 997.

[13] *See*, especially, *Associated Provincial Picture Houses Ltd v Wednesbury Corporation* [1948] 1 KB 223.

standards. The precept *nulla poena sine lege* is central to the rule of law: no one should be punished for an offence on the basis of conduct that had not been clearly prohibited in advance. The general law erects a barrier between the citizen and oppressive interference by prosecutors or other state officials, desirous of punishing him for lawful action inimical to current government policy or speech critical of the conduct of public affairs. There must be rules of evidence and procedure that operate to forestall the conviction of innocent defendants, mistakenly accused of crimes they have not in fact committed. A fair trial is one in which both prosecution and defence have equal opportunity to present evidence and argument relevant to the charge; and the judge must be even-handed and impartial. No one can be properly convicted of an offence unless the twin requirements of the rule of law are satisfied. First, there must be a *general rule*, made and announced in advance of the behaviour impugned; and, second, *due process* must be satisfied in the application of that rule to the particular case.

The "bill of attainder", invoked in earlier centuries by the English Parliament, is the paradigm instance of violation of the rule of law. Such an Act provides for the punishment of a named individual (or group of individuals) who has incurred the displeasure of the legislature: the enactment flouts the separation of powers, Parliament acting as legislator, prosecutor and judge. A bill of attainder represents the antithesis of the rule of law in two main respects. First, the named offender is denied the protection of a *general rule*, prohibiting specific conduct in advance of his actions and applicable to anyone who may commit the offence delineated. Secondly, the offender—or victim—is deprived of the benefit of a *fair trial*, in which there is an impartial investigation of all the circumstances to ascertain whether or not he is guilty of the conduct proscribed. Depriving its victims of the protection of the rule of law, a bill of attainder is a "law" only in name: in substance it is only a vindictive *measure*, which a court should repudiate as an affront to constitutional principle. When legal form is abused to attain ends which infringe the point and spirit of the rule of law, as a basic safeguard of liberty, a court should stand firm against the abuse. Otherwise, it ceases to act, in substance, as a court of *law*.[14]

Analogous to a bill of attainder, and hence equally an affront to the rule of law, is a measure that, while permitting a judicial trial, distorts the ordinary criminal law for the purpose of ensuring the punishment of particular individuals. In *Liyanage*, the Judicial Committee of the Privy Council struck down the Criminal Law (Special Provisions) Act 1962, enacted by the Parliament of Ceylon (Sri Lanka), as a breach of the division of powers implicit in the Constitution (conferred by the Ceylon (Constitution) Order in Council 1946 and Ceylon Independence Act 1947).[15] The 1962 Act was designed to punish the participants in an attempted *coup d'etat*: it created a new criminal offence retrospectively and provided for a minimum sentence of 10 years' imprisonment and mandatory forfeiture of property. It also purported to authorize certain breaches of ordinary criminal procedure and to sanction the receipt

[14] For further discussion, *see* Allan, *Constitutional Justice*, *supra* note 6, at 146–157, 244–246; Allan, *The Sovereignty of Law*, *supra* note 2, at 140–143.

[15] *Liyanage v R* [1967] 1 AC 259.

in evidence of confessions that were otherwise inadmissible. The changes applied only to the trial of these defendants and ceased to operate afterwards. Accepting the contention that the statute constituted an interference with the functions of the judiciary, the Judicial Committee held it invalid as a "legislative plan *ex post facto* to secure the conviction and enhance the punishment" of particular individuals.[16] Although the court invoked the formal entrenchment of judicial power—constitutional amendment requiring a special two-thirds majority vote in Parliament—the case stands, more generally, as an illustration of judicial resistance to an attack on the basic idea and structure of the rule of law.

The detention without trial of foreign suspected terrorists, under the (British) Anti-terrorism, Crime and Security Act 2001, presents a more remote analogy with the bill of attainder, but nonetheless illuminates the central features of the rule of law. The Home Secretary was empowered to order the detention of any foreign national whom he suspected of being a terrorist, but whose deportation (under immigration rules) would expose him to the risk of torture or inhuman treatment abroad—a risk that could not be assumed consistently with the requirements of Article 3 of the European Convention on Human Rights, having domestic legal force under the Human Rights Act 1998.[17] The British Government made an Order purporting to derogate from Article 5 of the Convention, which would otherwise preclude detention without trial. Derogation was permitted by Article 15 in time of war or "other public emergency threatening the life of the nation", but only to the extent "strictly required by the exigencies of the situation". The House of Lords, as final court of appeal, held that even if there were truly a public emergency, no such extraordinary measures were "strictly required": the Order was therefore invalid and the suspects' detention breached Article 5.[18]

The legislation amounted to a form of irrational discrimination between foreign nationals and British citizens because there could be no justification for singling out the former, who otherwise enjoyed a limited right of residence, for such special treatment. The threat of terrorism came not only from foreign nationals but also from certain British citizens, known to support Al-Qaeda but who were not subject to any similar regime of preventative detention. If it were unnecessary to apply such special measures to British nationals, who in some cases posed a similar threat, it was difficult for the Government to show that they were necessary in the case of foreigners. The measures were not "strictly required" in the sense that they were not proportionate to the severity of the consequences for those affected. In the result, those detained were deprived not only of the fair trial necessary to satisfy the full demands of due process—an impartial adjudication to determine the truth of the allegations made against them—but also the protection of a general rule, applicable to all those who presented the same kind of danger to national security.

The example shows that the rule of law is not satisfied by mere *formal* equality before the law—the equal subjection of everyone, private citizen and public official,

[16] *Id.* 290.

[17] Convention for the Protection of Human Rights and Fundamental Freedoms (Rome 1950).

[18] *A v Secretary of State for the Home Department* [2004] UKHL 56.

to the law of the land—but extends to a more demanding *substantive* equality. The distinctions drawn between persons, or between groups of persons, as regards their treatment by public authorities, must be defensible and legitimate—capable of justification, when challenged, by reference to a tenable view of the public good, consistent with prevailing governmental policy and general constitutional principle. If we identify personal liberty as an important constitutional value, which normally prohibits preventative detention, we must respect that value in all cases: arbitrary distinctions between persons, unrelated to the public good, are impermissible. The generality secured by adherence to general rules, faithfully and consistently applied, is a species of *equality*—the fundamental equality of status of citizens and, ultimately, of all those subject to the power of the state. The ideal of equality is a reflection of respect for human dignity, acknowledging inherent limits on the authority of the state—limits intrinsic to its legitimacy.

Acknowledging the fundamental idea of equality, Lord Bingham quoted Justice Jackson's celebrated defence of equality as a principle binding on American local and federal governments:

> The framers of the Constitution knew … that there is no more effective practical guaranty against arbitrary and unreasonable government than to require that the principles of law which officials would impose upon a minority must be imposed generally. Conversely, nothing opens the door to arbitrary action so effectively as to allow those officials to pick and choose only a few to whom they will apply legislation and thus to escape the political retribution that might be visited upon them if larger numbers were affected. Courts can take no better measure to assure that laws will be just than to require that laws be equal in operation.[19]

We can see clearly here how the rule of law constitutes a bridge between law and justice. It does not impose any specific conception of justice, which will be dependent to a considerable degree on local tradition and democratic choice; but it holds public authorities to a *coherent scheme of justice*, fairly and consistently applied to everyone. Differential treatment of persons or groups must be justified on the basis of reasons all could acknowledge as compatible with a genuine public good, capable of eliciting broad assent. Democracy itself is in this way linked to the rule of law, in the sense that equal citizenship is more fundamental than simply an equal voice in political affairs: a political majority must respect the rights of minorities, whose interests are entitled to fair consideration in deliberations over justice and public policy.

In the House of Lords, Lord Bingham directly addressed the objection that it was undemocratic for the courts to interfere in a matter concerned with national security, rejecting a submission that the court should defer to Government and Parliament, as "democratic institutions", when reviewing the legality of the regime of preventative detention. Bingham rightly affirmed that "the function of independent judges charged to interpret and apply the law is universally recognized as a cardinal feature of the modern democratic state, a cornerstone of the rule of law itself".[20] Admittedly,

---

[19] *Railway Express Agency Inc v New York* (1949) 336 US 106, 112–13.

[20] *A v Secretary of State for the Home Department* [2004] UKHL 56, para 42.

the court must have regard to the proper "demarcation of functions", as regards the division of responsibility between governmental organs, and it must sometimes acknowledge a disparity in "relative institutional competence". While conceding that the existence of a public emergency (within the meaning of Article 15) was a matter of "pre-eminently political judgement", having regard to the complexity of the necessary appraisal of risk, the court accepted responsibility for determining the propriety of the distinction made between nationals and foreigners. Questions of fundamental equality, as regards the application of basic constitutional rights, are finally matters for judicial decision as an integral part of upholding and enforcing the law.

11.3 Parliamentary Sovereignty, Legality and Constitutional Rights

If the rule of law enforces basic standards of due process and constitutional equality, even the legislation of a representative legislature must respect its demands. Governance by law entails compliance with the principles of the rule of law. There cannot, then, be a "sovereign" Parliament, exempt from all constraints on the current will of a majority of its members. The English doctrine of "parliamentary sovereignty", which on its face suggests the opposite, must be interpreted instead as a principle of *legislative supremacy*: Parliament enjoys a broad law-making power, superior to any other body, but subject to compliance with the ultimate safeguards for the citizen provided by the rule of law. In *Anisminic*, the House of Lords was not precluded from quashing an erroneous administrative decision by the purported ouster of jurisdiction contained in the Foreign Compensation Act 1950.[21] Parliament had provided, in section 4, that no determination of the Foreign Compensation Commission should "be called in question in any court of law"; but it was held that, by exceeding its proper jurisdiction, the tribunal had failed to make a genuine "determination" within the meaning of that provision. Its "purported determination" could be quashed as part of the court's inherent authority to enforce the law, including the legal limits on any powers conferred by Parliament on an administrative tribunal. Parliament could not, in practice, insulate the exercise of an administrative power from judicial oversight: to permit an immunity from judicial review would be to leave the citizen at the mercy of a potentially arbitrary power.

Governmental discretion must be exercised in a manner that satisfies the demands of due process and equality, making all proper allowance for the legitimate needs of the public interest and the related distinctions between persons and groups. The specification of the public interest, however, must always accommodate constitutional principle: there are fundamental rights and safeguards implicit in a democratic constitution founded on the rule of law. There must be no political interference,

[21] *Anisminic Ltd v Foreign Compensation Commission* [1969] 2 AC 147.

for example, with the judicial system; the process of law must not be tainted by extra-legal considerations, irrelevant to the truth or soundness of legal claims of right or accusations of wrong. When a British Home Secretary was empowered by Parliament to decide the minimum term of imprisonment for a young offender, convicted of murder, the courts rightly held that the minister must display standards of propriety similar to those required of judges.[22] While such an offender was formally subject to indefinite detention "at Her Majesty's pleasure", in substance the "tariff" sentence imposed by the Home Secretary represented the real punishment. The imposition of punishment being a quintessentially judicial procedure, it was not permissible for the minister to succumb to the pressure of public opinion—led by a hostile press—in favour of a disproportionately harsh sentence. The minister should be guided, instead, by judicial advice about generally applicable standards: he must not be influenced by "public clamour".[23]

Admittedly, Parliament had chosen to confer the sentencing power on a government minister rather than the judges (as the two dissenting judges pointedly observed); but the court held that his exercise of a "classic judicial function" posed a threat to the constitutional separation of powers. Parliament must be taken to have intended that he should not act "contrary to fundamental principles governing the administration of justice".[24] When even the legislation of a "sovereign" Parliament is subject to independent judicial interpretation, regulated by the standards of due process and fundamental equality intrinsic to the rule of law, the citizen's liberty is made resistant to assertions of arbitrary power. No one is subject to state coercion except in accordance with legal rules and principles, enforced against errant public officials by impartial and independent courts of law. Threats to the public welfare must be addressed by means of general rules, applicable to all citizens according to published and defensible criteria. When rules give way to discretion, individual cases must be fairly governed by general principles, curtailing the scope for political action that reflects popular hostility or prejudice. A genuine liberty is freedom to act within the law even when others, however justifiably, may strongly disapprove; and breaches of the law must be punished proportionately, according to recognizable criteria, faithfully and consistently applied.

The "principle of legality" in English law is often understood as having only presumptive force, capable of being overridden by explicit parliamentary enactment. A strong presumption in favour of settled common law rights, underpinning the liberties of the citizen, is vulnerable (on that view) to the expression of an unambiguous contrary legislative will. In *Simms*, Lord Hoffmann suggested that legislation should always be treated as "intended to be subject to the basic rights of the individual", at least in "the absence of express language or necessary implication to the contrary".[25] Rather than conceding that Parliament might override basic constitutional rights, in breach of the rule of law, however, we should insist that there must

[22] *R v Secretary of State for the Home Dept, ex p Venables and Thompson* [1998] AC 407.

[23] *See*, further, Allan, *Constitutional Justice*, *supra* note 6, at 142–148.

[24] *ex p Venables and Thompson* [1998] AC 407, 526.

[25] *R v Secretary of State for the Home Dept, ex p Simms* [2000] 2 AC 115, 131.

be an appropriate accommodation between individual rights and the broader public interest—an accommodation that reflects the dual imperative of democratic deliberation and decision and respect for legal principle. Fundamental rights such as freedom of speech or association or privacy are undeniably abstract in nature. A right's application to particular cases entails reflection on its rationale and pertinence to the context in view. There is no *infringement*—and hence no need for overriding—if the right is accorded all proper respect compatible with reasonable governmental action, directed to legitimate public ends.

The legality of a rule that permitted a prison governor to read and intercept a prisoner's correspondence—its compatibility with the rule of law—depended on the reasons for such interference.[26] A general power conferred by the Prison Act 1952 to make rules for the purposes of prison management and discipline could not justify whatever restrictions the Home Secretary chose to authorize, regardless of content. It could not, in particular, justify interference with a prisoner's right of access to his lawyer for confidential legal advice. The confidentiality bestowed by the rules of legal professional privilege, at common law, was an established feature of the more fundamental right of access to the courts: legal advice was a necessary step towards the institution of proceedings to vindicate legal rights. While there might be a limited power to inspect correspondence to ensure that it was genuinely seeking legal advice, there could be no wider power of interference: no *justification* could be shown for any greater intrusion into ordinary legal privilege. Even if the right might be curtailed by "necessary implication"—restrictions implicit in the statutory scheme or language—the minister bore a heavy burden of justification: "the more fundamental the right interfered with, and the more drastic the interference, the more difficult becomes the implication".[27]

There is here a general principle of *proportionality*, inherent in the recognition of fundamental rights and so implicit in the rule of law. There could be no assertion of any general power to read and intercept a prisoner's legal correspondence unless the government could show why such a power was necessary, and hence implicit in the grant of powers of prison management and discipline. The question was "whether there is a *self-evident and pressing need* for an unrestricted power to read letters between a prisoner and a solicitor" and to stop them if considered objectionable. If no such "objective need" could be established to the court's satisfaction, the power did not exist.[28] Parliament is presumed to confer no wider powers to encroach on basic constitutional rights, such as the right of access to the courts, than are strictly necessary for the public purposes in view. To override a fundamental right in other circumstances is to violate the rule of law: such governmental action would exhibit a contempt or indifference to rights inconsistent with the respect for persons that constitutes the whole point and value of the rule of law.[29]

---

[26] *R v Secretary of State for the Home Dept, ex p Leech* [1994] QB 198.

[27] *Id.* 209.

[28] *Id.* 212 (emphasis added).

[29] *See*, further, Allan, *The Sovereignty of Law*, *supra* note 2, at 255–259.

A principle of proportionality brings the court uncomfortably close to matters of policy-making, which fall chiefly within the jurisdiction of Parliament and government. The court must be satisfied that the advancement of proper statutory purposes really justifies the specific restriction of rights under review. The executive government must normally demonstrate that no less restrictive or intrusive interference with individual rights would suffice to achieve the relevant public ends; and there must be an overall proportionate *balance*: those public ends must be capable, in principle, of justifying what may be a serious interference with constitutional rights. Naturally, a court must have regard to administrative expertise and experience: it may sometimes be necessary to defer to a public authority's own judgement of the urgency of the public interest or the feasibility of different strategies to accomplish particular tasks. The court's independence from both public authority and private citizen is nevertheless a crucial foundation for impartial judgement. The balance of public and private interests must not be left to the unfettered determination of a public agency, focused wholly or largely on implementation of its own policy agenda.

The rule of law is not compatible with state action that is indifferent or hostile to the fundamental rights that lie at the heart of the liberal-democratic constitutional tradition. These rights include not only the civil liberties necessary to democratic self-government, such as the freedoms of speech and assembly, but also those rights, such as privacy or personhood, that affirm our conception of the independent citizen, free to pursue a life of his own making subject only to the similar freedoms of others.[30] Such rights may be curtailed or qualified by statute only when a strong case of necessity can be made on grounds of pressing public interest; and there must be a right of recourse to judicial review to determine reasonable complaints of unconstitutional action. The executive government must act within the authority conferred by Parliament, narrowly interpreted by the courts to exclude any power to violate constitutional principle. The English "principle of legality" must have more than merely prima facie force, dependent on presumptions of parliamentary intent that might be displaced by explicit statutory enactment. While there is usually no difficulty in reconciling statutory purpose and constitutional principle, it may sometimes be necessary to "read down" or qualify the statutory language to forestall an infringement of the rule of law. By requiring the court to read statutes compatibly with the European Convention on Human Rights, whenever such a construction is "possible", the (British) Human Rights Act 1998 affirms a basic principle of settled common law: competent statutory interpretation must forge an accommodation between statutory purpose and constitutional principle, attuned to all the circumstances.[31]

The fundamental right to natural justice or due process—the right to a fair hearing conducted by an independent and impartial court or tribunal, bound by rules and

---

[30] *Compare*, Ronald Dworkin, *Freedom's Law: The Moral Reading of the American Constitution* (OUP, Oxford, 1996), at 15–35.

[31] *See* Allan, "Parliament's Will and the Justice of the Common Law: The Human Rights Act in Constitutional Perspective" 59 *Current Legal Problems* (2006), 27–50.

principles of law—provides a clear example. Although the precise requirements of a fair hearing may vary according to the nature of the power being exercised and the gravity of the consequences for individuals, they must be adequate in all the circumstances to safeguard affected rights and interests. An appeal against the cancellation of a licence cannot be expected to meet the high procedural standards of a criminal trial; but the appeal must still be conducted fairly, having regard to the seriousness of the loss of a licence for the person concerned. There must be appropriate opportunities to make representations and to challenge adverse evidence. When disclosure of confidential information poses a risk to national security, or some other important dimension of the public interest, the court may be obliged to adapt the ordinary requirements of fair procedure; but there are limits to how far such adaptation can legitimately go. Unless, in particular, a person knows the charges or allegations against him, in reasonable detail, any attempt to answer or rebut them will plainly be futile.

In a case where a suspected terrorist had been made subject to a "control order" under the (British) Prevention of Terrorism Act 2005, sharply curtailing his ordinary liberties, the House of Lords held that the suspect had been denied the fair judicial hearing to which he was entitled. The Home Secretary's decision to make an order was subject to judicial review under the Act; and his decision could not, it was held, properly be based mainly on "closed materials", withheld from the suspect on grounds of national security.[32] Following the guidance of the European Court of Human Rights, applying the European Convention in a similar context, it was held that a person could not have a fair hearing unless he were told the case against him in sufficient detail to allow him to respond. Lord Scott acknowledged the high importance accorded to natural justice by English common law; and Lord Hope affirmed that requisite disclosure or notice was a requirement of the rule of law. Although the statutory rules appeared on their face to forbid the disclosure of information detrimental to national security, they were "read down" (under the Human Rights Act 1998) to preserve constitutional principle. The prohibition on disclosure of sensitive material was made subject to an implicit proviso, permitting disclosure when necessary to ensure a fair trial.

11.4 Conclusion

When the rule of law is narrowly interpreted as a formal or procedural principle, requiring published general rules to be accurately applied to particular cases, its requirements may sometimes surrender to competing considerations of justice or public policy. A retrospective enactment may be necessary, for example, to remedy an earlier procedural or jurisdictional defect. Or, it may be thought that government by general rule should sometimes make way for administrative discretion, allowing officials to discriminate between persons or cases, according to the needs of public

[32] *Secretary of State for the Home Dept v AF (No 3)* [2009] UKHL 28.

policy, in a manner that general rules would preclude. It may even be said that it is wrong to give too much weight to the rule of law, being merely one value among others, which may sometimes be more pressing. According to Joseph Raz, the rule of law has only prima facie force:

> It has always to be balanced against competing claims of other values … Conformity to the rule of law is a matter of degree, and though, other things being equal, the greater the conformity the better— other things are rarely equal. A lesser degree of conformity is often to be preferred precisely because it helps realization of other goals.[33]

I have argued, however, that the formal precepts of the rule of law make up only one part of a larger, more complex ideal of constitutional government. There are principles of legality that govern the exercise of administrative discretion. Such principles of rationality and proportionality cannot be applied in the abstract: their application invokes a richer, more substantive conception of the rule of law. While the rule of law cannot simply be equated with any specific theory of justice or rights, it nevertheless demands the consistent application of established rights to everyone, without unfair discrimination. Any plausible conception of freedom or equality will embrace such fundamental rights as those to freedom of speech and conscience, freedom of association and movement, privacy or personhood, personal liberty and fair trial, in addition to those civil rights associated directly with self-government, such as rights to vote and to stand for public office. The precise content and contours of these rights will vary from jurisdiction to jurisdiction, reflecting local history and legal tradition. When the rule of law is in place, however, these rights will amount to a coherent philosophy of freedom, applicable to everyone according to general criteria, publicly acknowledged and open to uninhibited challenge and debate.[34]

Ronald Dworkin's theory of law as "integrity" has a similar character, reflecting a broad and substantive conception of the rule of law. His "model of principle" is explicitly contrasted with a "rule-book" model of political community, in which the law consists only of specific rules, adopted as a means of compromise between antagonistic interests or points of view. Dworkin's model of principle assumes a deeper, more comprehensive understanding of a shared commitment to constitutional governance:

> It insists that people are members of a genuine political community only when they accept that their fates are linked in the following strong way: they accept that they are governed by common principles, not just rules hammered out in political compromise. Politics has a different character for such people. It is a theatre of debate about which principles the community should adopt as a system, which view it should take of justice, fairness, and due process … Members of a society of principle accept that their political rights and duties are not exhausted by the particular decisions their political institutions have reached, but depend, more generally, on the scheme of principles those decisions presuppose and endorse.[35]

---

[33] Joseph Raz, *The Authority of Law: Essays on Law and Morality* (Clarendon Press, Oxford, 1979), at 228.

[34] *See*, further, Allan, *Constitutional Justice*, ch. 9; and Allan, *The Sovereignty of Law*, ch. 8.

[35] Ronald Dworkin, *Law's Empire* (Fontana, London, 1986), at 211.

Chapter 12
The Rechtsstaat-Principle in Germany: The Development from the Beginning Until Now

Paul Tiedemann

Abstract The constitutional principle of freedom of action is the normative axiom from which the Rechtsstaats-principle must be understood. It requires not that the exercise of freedom, but that the restriction of freedom is what must be justified. The Rechtsstaat-principle from its beginnings in the nineteenth century until now has experienced two modifications. The *formal* Rechtsstaat, where the original idea from the nineteenth century is handed down, is distinguished from the *material* Rechtsstaat, and the *social* Rechtsstaat (Bodo Pieroth, "Historische Etappen des Rechtsstaats in Deutschland", JURA (2011), 729). However, these three conceptions are not meant as alternatives. The elements of the formal Rechtsstaat are also elements of the material Rechtsstaat and the elements of both can also be found in the theory of the social Rechtsstaat. Since the 1990s, another evolutionary step, which may be termed "*green* Rechtsstaat (The expression "green Legal State" is in Germany not customary as a constitutional concept. So far it was only used in polemic intention to criticize green politicians, *cf.* Dirk Maxeiner, "Grüner Rechtsstaat", *available at* http://www.achgut.com/dadgdx/index.php/dadgd/article/gruener_rechtsstaat/)" may also be observed. This concept is not an alternative to the earlier conceptions of Rechtsstaat. It only adds just another element.

Judge at the Administrative Court Frankfurt am Main, honorable Professor at Justus-Liebig-University Giessen and adjunct Professor at Özyeğin University, Istanbul. The author thanks James E. Hickey Jr. for the review of the text in terms of grammatical, stylistic and orthographic mistakes. All remaining errors are the author's sole responsibility.

P. Tiedemann (✉)
Department of Law, Justus-Liebig-University, Giessen, Germany
e-mail: paul.tiedemann@recht.uni-giessen.de

J.R. Silkenat et al. (eds.), *The Legal Doctrines of the Rule of Law and the Legal State (Rechtsstaat)*, Ius Gentium: Comparative Perspectives on Law and Justice 38,
DOI 10.1007/978-3-319-05585-5_12,

12.1 Introduction

The expression, Rechtsstaat (literally, Legal State), was coined in the nineteenth century. It was born of the initiative of Christian Theodor Welcker and denotes originally a state that is ruled by the rational volonté general.[1] In the nineteenth century, the opinion prevailed that it was not possible to derive the rationality of the law by pure rational philosophical thinking. Rather, one saw it as the task of the ruler, to help rationality to break through by creating positive statutory laws – statutes.[2] From the beginning, the sense and the function of the Rechtsstaat-principle was safeguarding and protecting individual freedom through positive laws. Statutes are written laws published in general accessible law gazettes and therefore available to everybody who can read.

It is necessary to stress that the Rechtsstaat-principle, due to the German tradition, is very different from the state-theoretical thinking in France. Traditionally, in France the idea of Rousseau prevails according to which individual freedoms of citizens can only be guaranteed by a very narrow connection between legislation and the will of the people. Therefore, it is the legislative monopoly of the democratically elected Parliament that ensures adequate protection of individual freedom.[3] In contrast, the idea of the Rechtsstaat-principle is due to the fact that all democratic movements of the nineteenth century have failed in Germany. There was always a monarch who was the source of legislation and the influence of parliaments was limited to more or less extensive rights to consultation or consent. The Rechtsstaat-principle should explain how it is possible to protect individual freedom of the citizens against the absolute power of an autocratic regime despite the absent of democratic control. The Rechtsstaat was considered on the one hand as an alternative to the patronizing police-state of the seventeenth and eighteenth century and on the other hand as an alternative to the democratic peoples-state of French provenance.[4]

The question of popular sovereignty and democracy did not play any role in the nineteenth century idea of the Rechtsstaat-principle. Robert von Mohl, one of the most prominent legal academics of the time, held the opinion that the question of democratic participation was secondary and only a matter of expediency, because it had no relevance for the character of the State as a Rechtsstaat.[5] This special feature of the German idea of Rechtsstaat makes this concept even today interesting for those countries where the economic development and an increasing middle class

[1] Carl Theodor Welcker, *Die letzten Gründe von Recht, Staat und Strafe: philosophisch und nach den Gesetzen der merkwürdigsten Völker rechtshistorisch entwickelt* (1813) [new printed 1964], *available at* http://books.google.de/

[2] Carl v. Rotteck, *Lehrbuch des Vernunftrechts und der Staatswissenschaften* vol. 1 (1829) at 77, *available at* http://books.google.de/

[3] Constance Grewe, "Die Grundrechte und ihre richterliche Kontrolle in Frankreich", 29 *Europäische Grundrechte-Zeitschrift* [EuGRZ] (2002), 209.

[4] Robert v. Mohl, *Encyklopädie der Staatswissenschaften* (1859) at 326, *available at* http://books.google.de/

[5] *Id.*

demand the guarantee of freedom and where there is little hope for democracy.[6] On the other hand, however, it has now also been proven that democracy alone cannot secure freedom. Freedom is always the freedom of minorities. But it is the Rechtsstaat-principle and not the principle of democracy, which protects minorities.

The Rechtsstaat-principle from its beginnings in the nineteenth century until now has experienced two modifications. The *formal* Rechtsstaat, where the original idea from the nineteenth century is handed down, is distinguished from the *material* Rechtsstaat, and the *social* Rechtsstaat.[7] However, these three conceptions are not meant as alternatives. The elements of the formal Rechtsstaat are also elements of the material Rechtsstaat and the elements of both can also be found in the theory of the social Rechtsstaat. Since the 1990s, another evolutionary step, which may be termed "*green* Rechtsstaat[8]" may also be observed. This concept is not an alternative to the earlier conceptions of Rechtsstaat. It only adds just another element.

12.2 The Formal Rechtsstaat

The reason based concept of law was constituted on the idea that there are substantive criteria of proper law which every rational human could be aware of and which therefore must be recognized also by the absolute monarch. The positivist conception, asserted in the nineteenth century, decided against substantive criteria of proper law. It is based instead on the idea of "justness through procedure and structure."

The formal Rechtsstaat-principle is based on the following basic idea: "Anybody may do and omit whatever they want – as long as it is not prohibited in the forms of the Rechtsstaat." This basic idea was nowhere implemented in constitutions or statutes of the nineteenth century. Although it was articulated for the first time in a formulation of the draft *General Legal Code for the Prussian States* of 1791 (Allgemeines Gesetzbuch für die Preußischen Staaten), which stated (Intro. § 79): "The statutes and regulations of the state may not limit the natural freedom and the rights of the citizens more than it is demanded by the common ends." The draft never entered into force, but was withdrawn by the Prussian king. Only in Article 2 of the Grundgesetz (Basic Law) of the Federal Republic of Germany (GG) of 1949 was the basic idea of the Rechtsstaat-principle expressed. However, the drafting history of the clause shows, that its fundamental importance was generally still not clear at that time. One of the first proposed drafts of the clause did express the idea

[6] Vgl. He Weifang, "Die schwierige Reform des Justizwesens in China", in *Wie China debattiert. Neue Essays und Bilder aus China*, Barbara Unmüßig and Kartin Altmeyer eds (2009) at 101ff., *available at* http://www.boell.de/downloads/wie_china_debattiert.pdf; Chen Hongmei, "The Idea of Government by Law in Harmonious Society – Procedure Just", in *Global Harmony and Rule of Law*, Papers of the IVR 24th World Congress Beijing, vol. 1 (2009) at 117. Beijing: China Law Society.

[7] Bodo Pieroth, "Historische Etappen des Rechtsstaats in Deutschland", JURA (2011), 729.

[8] The expression "green Legal State" is in Germany not customary as a constitutional concept. So far it was only used in polemic intention to criticize green politicians, *cf.* Dirk Maxeiner, "Grüner Rechtsstaat", *available at* http://www.achgut.com/dadgdx/index.php/dadgd/article/gruener_rechtsstaat/

in very clear words: "Human beings are free. They may do and omit whatever does not violate the rights of others and does not disturb the constitutional order of the community." However, in the version of the Basic Law that came finally into force the expression "freedom to do and to omit" was replaced by the more unclear and dark wording "Everyone has the right to the free development of their personality". The Federal Constitutional Court, however, was not impressed by these nebulizing "ceremonial words" and clarified in 1956 in one of its most famous decisions that Article 2, paragraph 1 of the Basic Law guarantees the "general human freedom of acting", and that this is exactly what was meant in the former draft by the "freedom to do and to omit whatever they want". The constitutional principle of freedom of action is the normative axiom from which the Rechtsstaats-principle must be understood. It requires not that the exercise of freedom, but that the restriction of freedom is what must be justified.

The formal Rechtsstaat-principle protects and ensures the freedom of action: (1) by mechanisms of hampering of power; (2) by particular formal conditions for statutes; (3) by the principle of the legality of public administration and justice; (4) by the principle of legislative reservation; (5) by the principle of public liability; and (6) by the independent judicial power.

12.2.1 Hampering of Power by Separation of Powers

The basic idea of the formal Rechtsstaat is to domesticate the state, when it appears as a liberty-threatening power. The means of domestication are statutes.

Domestication by statutes demands first the internal separation of legislative and executive powers. The separation of legislative and executive powers is not only mere division of labor. It is rather a mechanism of mutual hampering. It consists both of the institutional and personal separation of the conceptional, and of the realizing aspects of rule. Conceptional rule is the monopoly of the legislative power while concrete realization is the task of the executive power. Hampering is caused by the fact that the institution which has the power to determinate the general aims and means of rule does not have the power to realize those aims and means in a particular case. It may not take hold of certain real persons. In contrast, the institution that has the power of taking hold of a single individual, may not determine the goals and means of rule.

The separation of power tends also to improve the rationality of rule. The legislator has always to keep in mind the general consequences and results of its legislation and not the rather random consequences in a particular single case. The executive power on the other hand has a wider capacity for optimizing the efficiency of rule because it is relieved from the burden of general planning. Rationality of rule is in itself a contribution to the safeguard of freedom because it protects against senseless and arbitrary restriction of freedom, i.e. it protects against sacrifices of freedom that are not connected with a common benefit.

12.2.2 Formal Conditions of Statutes

There are three formal conditions for statutes. First, statutes have to be abstract and general. Second, they have to be sufficiently clear in meaning. Third, statutes may not be retroactive and they have to be trustworthy.

From the conceptional function of legislation, it follows that statutes, if they intend to infringe the freedom of citizens, always have to be abstract and general. (Article 19 Abs. 1 GG).[9] A legal norm is abstract if it is not related to a certain locality or temporally fixed action or omission but only to actions or omissions that are described in general terms. A legal norm is general if it obligates or entitles an indefinite multitude of individuals. Those affected by the legal norm – i.e. those whose rights and obligations are created by the norm- are not determined individually, but only by general properties that meet a variety of people. This requirement serves not only the purpose of hampering of power by separation of legislative and executive power. It also safeguards equal treatment and reduces the risk of arbitrariness. At the same time, the infringement of freedom is made more difficult because the legislator can never reduce the freedom of a certain single person without reducing the freedom of all those who share the same general properties.

The addressees of legal norms can only obey the laws if the content of the norms is sufficiently clear and understandable.[10] Citizens can only estimate and calculate the space of freedom in which they can develop and realize their own life plans if the statutes show clearly the limits of freedom. Therefore, a sufficiently clear meaning of statutes is an essential condition of a Rechtsstaat.

In order to make statutes sufficiently clear, it is necessary that the legislator uses descriptive language and if possible adopts legislation without evaluative concepts. Only by the means of descriptive concepts is it possible to make sure that the statutes and not the users of the norms determine the legal facts that triggers legal consequences.

Unfortunately, the German legislator has used increasingly evaluative terms and the courts have not declared such statutes unconstitutional because of lack of sufficient precision.[11] This tends to lead to a weakening of the Rechtsstaat-principle. Evaluative terms lead to an unacceptable move of power from the statutes to those who exercise executive or judicial power. An example is § 131 of the German Penal Code. According to that norm, anyone will be punished who distributes scriptures that "describe cruel or otherwise inhuman violence against humans [...] in a way that expresses glorification or playing down of such violence". The norm suggests that violence is something that can have the property of "cruelty" or of being "inhuman otherwise". In fact these expressions do not describe a property of violence or of depictions of violence. They only express that among all kinds of violence there are some which are evaluated negatively. It is not the statute itself that evaluates certain

[9] Bundesverfassungsgericht (BVerfG), Dec. of 07.05.1969 – 2 BvL 15/67 –, BVerfGE 25, 371 [396].

[10] BVerfG, Dec. of 23.06.2010 – 2 BvR 2559/08 –, BVerfGE 126, 170, Rn 71.

[11] BVerfG, Dec. of 23.06.2010 – 2 BvR 2559/08 –, BVerfGE 126, 170, Rn 73.

kinds of violence as cruel or inhuman. In contrast, the statute leaves this evaluation to those who use the statute to exercise executive power – i.e. to the individual police officers, prosecutors and judges. The more insensitive the policeman feels, the less likely he will pursue a case. The more sensitive the judge feels, the more likely he will convict the offender. In either case the decision, about what is punishable and what is not, is not the decided by the statute but of the user of the statute. The decision of those users is not predictable and therefore it remains unclear what is prohibited and what is not.

Evaluative terms have to be distinguished from so-called "indeterminate legal concepts".[12] It is common to cite as examples of indeterminate legal concepts particular abstract concepts like ability, suitability, efficiency, reliability, common benefit, darkness, danger, risk etc. However, this can be the case for concepts like "mother" or "father" as well. In fact, almost every concept of our ordinary language is in a certain way indeterminate. Very often such concepts are not only equivocal but also vague. In particular, vagueness is a problem because it calls into question in a case whether or not a certain legal norm is applicable. Therefore, legal interpretation is needed and unavoidable. The Rechtsstaat-principle does not demand *complete* clarity but only *sufficient* clarity of the legal language of a statute. A concept is sufficiently clear if there are many cases in which the concept is certainly applicable (positive candidates) and if there are also many cases in which the concept is certainly not applicable (negative candidates). In addition to those clear cases, there might be some cases in which the applicability of the concept is uncertain. In such a situation, it is possible to determine an appropriate interpretation of the concept by comparing the certain cases with the uncertain case. By this approach, it is possible to develop good arguments to decide the question in a rational manner. The question of sufficient clarity involves a lot of difficult problems beyond the scope of this chapter. However, it can be stated that there is an always problematic tension between the Rechtsstaat-principle and the nature of our language in which the statute must always be expressed.

Human beings under the Rechtsstaat-principle are not subject to restriction of their freedom except as described in statutes. Thus, it is necessary that the statutes logically and temporally anticipate the behavior that is regulated by them. That means that the state is not authorized to deteriorate the legal position of the citizens retrospectively. The prohibition of retroactive effects of a statute shows the most important function of the formal Rechtsstaat-principle. This is legal security. The regularity of government action should allow the citizen to adjust his behavior in the frame of the law. The frame of law defines the scope of freedom in which the citizen can behave rationally. Legal security allows long-term life plans that can calculate with the valid norms of the law and shows the scope of discretion in which everyone can organize their lives. It is obvious that this function of the formal

[12] Koch, Hans Joachim. 1979. *Unbestimmte Rechtsbegriffe und Ermessensermächtigungen im Verwaltungsrecht*. Frankfurt: Metzner; Ogorek, Regina. 2008 (2nd ed.). *Aufklärung über Justiz. Richterkönig oder Subsumtionsautomat. Zur Justiztheorie im 19. Jahrhundert*, Frankfurt: Klostermann; Bundesfinanzhof (BFH), Jud. of 05.10.1984 – III R 192/83 –, BFHE 142, 505.

Rechtsstaat-principle is an indispensable condition of economic productivity, technique, trade, commerce and therefore of common and individual prosperity.

For the same reason, the formal Rechtsstaat-principle also calls for the respect of legitimate expectation. According to the Rechtsstaat-principle, the legislator may introduce neither a new statute with retroactive effect nor a statute with future effect, if by former statutes is already established the legitimate trust that a certain relevant legal position will remain in future as it is today. So, a legal norm that guarantees economic or tax privileges for a certain period of time in order to motivate a certain kind of investment may not be changed until the end of this period.[13] A current example of this is the guarantee of the *Act Concerning the Priority of Renewable Energy* (EEG), according to which anyone who has set up a photovoltaic system in 2009 and supplies energy in the public electricity supply systems is entitled to a payment of 31,94 Ct/kwh for the time period of 20 years (§ 32 EEG).[14] Meanwhile, the amounts of energy have been reduced drastically. But this reduction does not apply to those facilities that have been built under the scope of the EEG 2009.

12.2.3 Legality of the Public Administration and Judiciary

The separation of powers demands also the principle of legality of public administration and judiciary. Clear statutes are only useful and effective, if those who practice executive power, feel bound by the laws and are willing and able to respect them. This is why disregard of the statutes by administrative authorities or individual officers must not remain unpunished. However, the legality of the administration can hardly be implemented by sanctions alone. Even sanctions must be executed by civil servants or judges of a higher rank and thus the willingness of officials must exist to adhere to the statutes. The formal Rechtsstaat-principle can therefore only work in countries where an appropriate culture of legality is firmly established in the minds of civil servants and judges at all levels. This cannot be achieved without early ethical education and a common sense of respect for individual freedom and responsibility for the public benefit.

However, people will only be willing to internalize the ethos of legality when their engagement experiences the appropriate social recognition. This manifests itself in a reasonable salary, which makes people economically independent, provided it is high enough to immunize against corruption. The realization of the Rechtsstaat depends though not only from certain regulations in constitutions and statutes. The enlargement of the European Union particularly in the recent years was faced with significant problems, because too much attention focused on the content of the statute and too little attention on the above mentioned "soft" conditions of a legal culture.

---

[13] BVerfG, Dec. of 23.03.1971 – 2 BvL 17/69 –, BVerfGE 30, 392.

[14] BGBl 2008 I 2074.

The principle of legality embraces also the aspect of the primacy of statutes. That means that the public authorities have to orientate their actions in the first line at the statutes. Only if in a certain situation there does not exist a statute then the administration is free to determine the rules of its actions itself. This principle is especially true for those areas of public administration, which are not dealing with reduction and withdrawal of freedom, but with the provision of public services and benefits. The primacy of the statutes in the area of *granting administration* is a means of constitutional protection of freedom, because it excludes arbitrariness and ensures equal treatment.[15]

12.2.4 Legislative Reservation

The axiom of freedom says that no public authority has so to speak "by nature" the right to reduce, to revoke, or to deprive the freedom of the citizen. The state has this right only if it is conferred on him by statutes. Therefore, the state may only intervene in the freedom of the individual insofar there is a law that allows that act of power.

The classic application of the formal Rechtsstaat-principle is therefore the *intervening administration*, i.e. the exercise of state power, which is connected to a restriction of individual freedom. Interventions do not only consist of prohibitions of certain actions. It is also possible that they consist in any other state activity that leads in consequence to a factual reduction of individual freedom. This is the case if public authorities publish warnings about individuals and their activities (e.g. about food of a certain supplier)[16] or about the alleged harmful machinations of, say, a particular psycho-sect.[17]

According to the classical conception, the formal Rechtsstaat has only the function to protect against interventions with individual freedoms that are caused by the state. It was not considered that powerful private agents also should be able to reduce or to deprive the freedom of their fellow citizens. According to the classical conception, everybody has to tolerate and to endure the activities of non-state-agents insofar their behavior is not prohibited by statute. As long as there is no statute that prohibits the behavior, the rule applies that everybody may do or omit whatever they want.

In 1978, the Federal Constitutional Court, however, modified this axiom of freedom. The axiom of freedom does not apply any longer if private agents make use of their freedom in a way that intervenes in the freedom of a large, possibly inestimable large, number of citizens and changes their general conditions of life in

[15] The primacy of law also has an important function in the frame of representative democracy. It ensures, namely, that the exercise of rule can be steered by the Parliament through the means of law. This is the reason why the executive power may only spend money in the frame of the yearly budget act. However, this context has nothing to do with the Legal State Principle.

[16] BVerfG, Dec. of 26.06.2002 – 1 BvR 558/91 u.a. – "Glykol", BVerfGE 105, 252.

[17] BVerfG, Dec. of 26.06.2002 – 1 BvR 670/91 – "Osho", BVerfGE 105, 279.

a very intense and probably irrevocable way. Such a use of freedom is not covered by the axiom of freedom because it is by nature not compatible with the freedom of everybody else. It cannot be understood as a regular free development of one's personality but rather as a kind of illegitimate rule over the community in a way that fellow citizens cannot escape from. Only the (legal) state is entitled to exercise such a power and no private agents. "Fundamental and essential" decisions of this kind may only made by the legislative power of the state. For this new element of the Rechtsstaat-principle, the term "Wesentlichkeitstheorie" (Essentiality-theory) has become established in constitutional doctrine. In the scope of the Wesentlichkeitstheorie the axiom applies that "everything is prohibited that is not expressively allowed by statute". It is interesting to see that in the scope of the Wesentlichkeitstheorie the axiom of freedom thus is turned into its opposite. That seems to be paradox. Nevertheless, it is a consequence flowing from the formal legal-state-thinking. The Federal Constitutional Court first applied the Wesentlichkeitstheorie in a judgment concerning the so called "peaceful use of nuclear power".[18] Another example is the cultivation of genetically modified plants.[19]

The principle of legislative reservation applies only in the area of *intervening administration* and not in the area of *granting administration*. If the state grants benefits to individuals, it is not reducing or depriving individual freedom. In contrast, it enlarges the scope of individual freedom. The principle of legislative reservation however applies if the state's activity consists not only in a benefit but if there is a compulsory connection with duties. If for example, the statute provides that every employee is obliged to be a member of pension insurance scheme (intervention in freedom), then the conditions for the grant of pension and the rules governing the amount and duration of pension (benefit) must be regulated by statute. If, on the other hand, the state provides subsidies to individuals to build photovoltaic facilities on the roof of their houses then a statute is not needed. However, without an entitlement granted by statute there is no legal claim to a subsidy about which the individual could sue in court. There is only a legal claim to equal treatment if an individual thinks that he or she has been discriminated against compared to other citizens.

12.2.5 State Liability

The idea that the Rechtsstaat-principle also includes the recognition of state liability for unlawful acts of officials, still has not really been accepted in Germany. This is hard to understand because from the Rechtsstaat-principle follows the guarantee that state power may only be exercised in accordance with the statutes. Therefore, illegal exercise of state power that leads to a damage of property, life or limb

[18] BVerfG, Dec. of 08.08.1978 – 2 BvL 8/77 – "Kalkar I", BVerfGE 49, 89.

[19] Hessischer Verwaltungsgerichtshof (VGH Kassel), Dec. of 06.11.1989 – 8 TH 685/89 –, NVwZ 1990, 276.

demands compensation.[20] In Germany, the doctrine instead prevails that the state as such is not able to act unlawfully. Unlawful conduct is therefore considered to be the conduct of its officials and must not be attributed to the state. Damage claims can therefore only be directed against the officials concerned according to private law and requires his personal fault.[21] In the nineteenth century the very famous specialist of administrative law, Otto Mayer, already advocated that the wrongful conduct of officials should be attributed to the State. However Mayer failed to find the crucial and winning argument in favor of his opinion, namely the appeal to the Rechtsstaat-principle. Instead, he relied on vague ideas of "justice and equity".[22] The codified law follows this approach until today. It established in § 839 BGB (Civil Code) the civil liability of civil servants for culpable injury of the duties of his office. The Basic Law has adopted this nineteenth century view. It does not provide for primary liability of the state, but only an assumption of debts by the state (Article 34 GG). The original liability claim remains in private law and depends on the fault of the civil servant. The victim merely no longer bears the risk of insolvency. The Federal Constitutional Court did not also see the connection between Rechtsstaat-principle and state liability. Instead, it holds the opinion that direct state liability cannot be derived from the Grundgesetz. It did not understand that state liability can clearly be derived from the Rechtsstaat-principle which is a constitutional principle of the Grundgesetz.[23] An Act on State Liability that was launched by the Federal Parliament in 1981[24] was declared unconstitutional on grounds that it lacked responsibility for legislation.[25]

12.2.6 Requirements for the Judiciary

The efficiency of the principle of legality of the public administration demands not only compensation for damages caused by unlawful actions but also and above all judicial protection against unlawful acts of the state. Unlawful actions of administrative bodies need not necessarily rise to the level of an abuse of power. It can also follow from a wrongful interpretation of the statute. Disputes between the public authority and the citizens about the correct interpretation of the statutes occur quite often. The interpretation of the private individual as well as the interpretation of the public administrative body is strongly influenced by partisan interests. Therefore,

---

[20] Wolfram Höfling, "Vom überkommenen Staatshaftungsrecht zum Recht der staatlichen Einstandspflichten", in *Grundlagen des Verwaltungsrechts* vol. III, Hoffmann-Riem/Schmidt-Aßmann/Voßkuhle eds. (2009), § 51 Rn 15. Munich: C.H. Beck.

[21] *Id.*, § 51, Rn 12ff.

[22] Otto Mayer, *Deutsches Verwaltungsgericht* vol. II, (3rd ed. 1924) at 295. Berlin: Duncker & Humblot.

[23] BVerfG, Jud. of 19.10.1982 – 2 BvF 1/81 –, BVerfGE 61, 149 [198].

[24] Staatshaftungsgesetz of 26. 06. 1981 (BGBl I S 553).

[25] BVerfG, Jud. of 19.10.1982 – 2 BvF 1/81 –, BVerfGE 61, 149.

the Rechtsstaat-principle demands an independent and impartial judicial power in order to decide legal conflicts between the state and the citizen.[26]

Before the failed German revolution of 1848/49, there was in Germany no judicial protection against unlawful or lawless interventions in the freedom of individuals. Only the one who enjoyed special privileges or stipulated claims, could sue the state in a regular civil court. Only in the 1860s did a development start toward judicial protection against interventions in the sphere of private freedom by establishing special law courts that were separated from the "ordinary" civil courts.[27] They were called *Administrative Courts*. The judges had the same status and the same privileges as the judges in ordinary courts but they were very experienced in administrative law and they had to act according to a different procedure order. The idea of a separate administrative judiciary was very successful in Germany because the judicial protection against administrative acts follows different premises and different rules than the judicial protection in civil law cases. The Civil Court's approach does not start with the axiom of freedom but with a positive basis for a claim whether it is a claim in contract or tort or unjust enrichment. It also always has only the subjective rights of litigants in \view and not the public interest in the legality of the administration as well. Therefore, the Civil Court follows the principles of adversarial proceedings and not the principles of inquisitorial proceedings like the Administrative Courts do.

The principle of comprehensive judicial protection against administrative acts was completed by Article 19 Sec. 4 GG, according to which everyone who claims to have been injured in their rights by public authorities has access to a judicial court (so called guarantee of recourse to the courts). Due to this rule, it is unconstitutional to exclude certain kinds of disputes between public authorities and citizens from judicial protection. There is no act and no activity of any public authority that is excluded from the recourse to the courts.

Judicial control of legality requires the clear distinction between the political act of legislation and the result of this act (the statute itself). After its entry into force, the legal norm must be emancipated from politics and it must obtain an autonomous status.[28] This autonomy requires that the legal norm must be interpreted and applied only according to judicial criteria and not according to political criteria. The difference is essentially that the interpretation of the statutes must not only be based on the intentions and motives of the legislator, but also on how the statute has to be understood from the perspective of the citizen.

---

[26] Otto Bähr, *Der Rechtsstaat, eine publizistische Studie* (1864) at 71; *available at* http://books.google.de/

[27] *Cf.* Wolfgang Rüfner, "Verwaltungsrechtsschutz im 19. Jahrhundert vor Einführung der Verwaltungsgerichtsbarkeit", 16 *Die Öffentliche Verwaltung* [*DÖV*] (1963), 719; Christian-Friedrich Menger, "Zur Geschichte der Verwaltungsgerichtsbarkeit in Deutschland", 16 *DÖV* (1963), 726; Georg Christoph von Unruh: "Die Einrichtung der Verwaltungsrechtspflege als rechtsstaatliches Problem", 28 *DÖV* (1975), 725.

[28] Dieter Grimm, "Stufen der Rechtstaatlichkeit. Zur Exportfähigkeit einer westlichen Errungenschaft", 64 *Juristenzeitung* [JZ] (2009), 596 [599].

The Rechtsstaat-principle requires also certain standards for court proceedings.[29] In particular, the judge must ensure a fair trial. This means, for example, that a lawyer shall be assigned to a claimant in order to ensure "equality of arms" and to balance his professional and legal inferiority toward the authorities.[30] The citizen and his lawyer have the right to be heard in full. The judges are obliged to deal with the submissions of the parties and use the submissions in their considerations.[31] This consideration must be transparent in the written reasons for the judgment.[32] The guarantee of recourse to the courts includes also the right to effective judicial protection. This comes about by the suspensive effect that is triggered by a legal action in front of the Administrative Courts (§ 80 Administrative Court Procedure Act). [33]

The judiciary can only be a relevant factor in the context of the Rechtsstaat, if decisions of the courts are also observed and followed by the administrative authorities. In that regard, the Rechtsstaat-principle requires not only the binding of the administration to the statutes, but also the binding of the administration to the Court. More than the binding to the statutes depends the binding to the court decisions. However, courts have no means to force civil servants in administrative bodies to obey court decisions. Thus, civil servants must feel bound to follow court decisions as a matter of professional ethos. In some countries, legal-state deficits are primarily caused by relevant ethical deficits in this regard.[34]

The Legal-State-Principle requires not only the legality of the executive power but also the constitutionality of the legislative power. The legal-state principle must be respected not only in the application, but also during the creation of statutes. In order to ensure this respect, a constitutional court must have the capacity and authority to control the constitutionality of the statutes. In Germany, the constitutional jurisdiction was (under strong American influence) only established under the Grundgesetz.

12.3 The Material Rechtsstaat

The attribute "formal" was only added to the Rechtsstaat-principle when it came to the distinction between the "formal" from the "material" Rechtsstaat.[35] Originally, the attribute "formal" was meant in a pejorative sense. The material Rechtsstaat should be the preferable worthy alternative. Today, the formal as well as material elements are seen as integral parts of the Rechtsstaat-principle.

---

[29] BVerfG, Dec. of 26.04.1988 – 1 BvR 669/87 u.a. –, BVerfGE 78, 123.

[30] BVerfG, Dec. of 08.10.1974 – 2 BvR 747/73 –, BVerfGE 38, 105.

[31] BVerfG, Dec. of 19.05.1992 – 1 BvR 986/91 –, BVerfGE 86, 133.

[32] BVerfG, Dec. of 19.05.1992 – 1 BvR 986/91 –, BVerfGE 86, 133.

[33] BVerfG, Dec. of 20.12.2012 – 1 BvR 2794/10 –, EuGRZ 13, 76.

[34] Vgl. Klaus Kreiser/Christoph K Neumann, *Kleine Geschichte der Türkei* (2nd ed. 2009) at 485. Stuttgart: Reclam.

[35] Friedrich Darmstaedter, *Die Grenzen der Wirksamkeit des Rechtsstaates. Eine Untersuchung zur gegenwärtigen Krise des liberalen Staatsgedankens* (1930) [reprint 1971], at 194ff. Aalen: Scientia.

12.3.1 Material Versus Formal Rechtsstaat

The idea that formal and material Rechtsstaat thinking were the exact opposite to each other depends in terms of methodology from the appearance of the so called free-law doctrine (Freirechtslehre). The agents of this movement or doctrine claimed that the postulate of legality could not be met because it was impossible to gather the authoritative law from the wording of a statute. As a result of this doctrine the statutes as such were not considered as the law but only what the judges had in mind about the content of the law.[36] The free-law doctrine, which is thus far supported by a strong minority of academics and high judges,[37] gained influence only after the First World War. This was due to the fact that many legal rules no longer fitted with the unique, disastrous, economic situation caused by the lost war, by the collapse of import flows, by the broad social impoverishment and by hyperinflation. The written statutes stipulated conflict resolutions, which appeared to produce intolerable injustices. In this conflict between the binding to the statutes and a sense of justice, the Supreme Court (Reichsgericht) developed a case law that was rather orientated on equity than on the "formal" ties with the written statutes. The judges decided according to their own sense of justice and ignored the wording and the sense of the statutes.[38] The Supreme Court later attempted to introduce a rule that judges may only ignore the wording of the statutes if the law concerned is in conflict to the rules of the Constitution and constitutional basic rights.[39] The taboo was broken by this brief free-law episode. The idea of judicial independence from the statutes served in the later years of the Weimar Republic as an argument that the anti-democratic forces encouraged to make biting criticism and polemics against the formal Rechtsstaat.[40] The formality of the Rechtsstaat-principle was accused of failing to distinguish between justice and injustice and only to guarantee legal certainty but not justice. Therefore, they called for a "just state" instead of "formal Rechtsstaat."[41]

---

[36] Hermann Kantorowicz, *Der Kampf um die Rechtswissenschaft* (1906), [reprint 2002] at 34. Baden-Baden: Nomos.

[37] Winfried Hassemer, "Rechtssystem und Kodifikation: Die Bindung des Richters an das Gesetz", in: *Einführung in die Rechtsphilosophie und Rechtstheorie der Gegenwart*, Kaufmann/Hassemer/Neumann eds. (7th ed. 2004) at 260. Heidelberg: C.F. Müller UTB; Günter Hirsch, "Zwischenruf. Der Richter wird's schon richten", 39 *Zeitschrift für Rechtspolitik* [ZRP] (2006), 161; Günter Hirsch, "Die Auflösung des Bayerischen Obersten Landesgerichts", 59 *Neue Juristische Wochenschrift* [NJW] (2006), 3255 [3256].

[38] Knut Wolfgang Nörr, *Der Richter zwischen Gesetz und Wirklichkeit. Die Reaktion des Reichsgerichts auf die Krisen von Weltkrieg und Inflation, und die Entfaltung eines neuen richterlichen Selbstverständnisses* (1996). Heidelberg: C.F. Müller.

[39] Reichsgericht [RG], Dec. of 25.01.1924 – III 882/22 –, RGZ 107, 315 [316f.]; Jud. of 01.03.1924 – V 129/23 –, RGZ 107, 370 [376]; 107, 370; Jud. of 04.11.1925 – V 621/24 –, RGZ 111, 320 [322].

[40] Ernst Forsthoff, *Der totale Staat* (1933) at 13: "Der reine Rechtsstaat, das heißt der Staat, der sich existenziell erschöpft in einer Rechts- und Ämterordnung, ist der Prototyp einer Gemeinschaft ohne Ehre und Würde." – Otto Koellreutter, *Deutsches Verfassungsrecht* (1935) at 54f.: "Im nationalsozialistischen Rechtsstaat gibt es nicht nur positive Rechtsquellen, sondern die oberste Rechtsquelle ist die nationalsozialistische Rechtsidee, die im Rechtsgefühl des Volkes zum Ausdruck kommt."

[41] Heinrich Lange, *Vom Gesetzesstaat zum Rechtsstaat* (1934) at 20ff. Hamburg: Hanseatische Verlagsanstalt.

In the first years after World War II, this approach was still very influential in Germany. However, the formal principles were no longer supposed to be replaced by the "higher" values of Nazi origin, but rather by the "higher" values of Catholic natural law.[42]

12.3.2 The "Objective Value Order of the Grundgesetz"

The Federal Constitutional Court clearly rejected these approaches in 1959.[43] According to this approach, it is not allowed to consult natural law ideas or other ideas of values as a source of law. On the other hand, this does not mean that material values cannot play any role and that only formal criteria are relevant. Rather, the constitution of the Grundgesetz itself contains material values. The basic rights of the constitution are not only considered rights of defense against state interference. And the catalogue of basic rights in the Constitution must also be considered as "an objective value order that as a constitutional principle is applicable to all areas of the law."[44] This value order rules not only the legal relationship between citizen and state but also the relationship between citizens. It influences not only the interpretation of the public law (administrative law) but also the interpretation of the civil and penal law. Furthermore it restricts the scope of discretion of the legislator. While the formal Rechtsstaat-principle subjects only the public authorities and law courts to the rule of statutes, the material Rechtsstaat-principle subjects every power including the legislative power and the civil sector to the constitutional value order. The legislator may not issue legal norms which are incompatible to the "value deciding basic norms of the Grundgesetz"[45] The citizens can defend themselves against the unreasonable demands of their fellow citizens which are incompatible to the constitutional value order.

By this judgment, the turn to the material Rechtsstaat-principle was accomplished. It is important to understand that this principle is not in contrast or opposite to the attributes of the formal Rechtsstaat-principle. The latter is rather enriched with criteria of material justice. While the criteria of the formal Rechtsstaat can only guarantee legal certainty, the material Rechtsstaat has to protect legal certainty as well as material justice, insofar as it is embraced by the basic rights of the constitution.[46]

---

[42] Hermann Weinkauff, "Der Naturrechtsgedanke in der Rechtsprechung des Bundesgerichtshofs", 13 *Neue Juristische Wochenschrift* [NJW] (1960), 1689; Hans Ulrich Evers, "Zum unkritischen Naturrechtsbewusstsein in der Rechtsprechung der Gegenwart", 16 *Juristenzeitung* [JZ] (1961), 241; Arthur Kaufmann, "Zur rechtsphilosophischen Situation der Gegenwart", 18 *Juristenzeitung* [JZ] (1963), 137 [140]; *see also* Wolfgang Fikentscher, *Methoden des Rechts in vergleichender Darstellung* vol. III (1976) at 332ff. Tübingen: J.C.B. Mohr (Paul Siebeck).

[43] BVerfG, Dec. of 29.07.1959 – 1 BvR 205/58 – BVerfGE 10, 59 [81].

[44] BVerfG, Jud. of 15.01.1958 – 1 BvR 400/51 – "Lüth", BVerfGE 7, 198 [205].

[45] BVerfG, Dec. of 17.01.1957 – 1 BvL 4/54 – "Steuersplitting", BVerfGE 6, 55 [72].

[46] Later, the Federal Constitutional Court overstretched the objective value approach and turned it upside down. It derived the value order namely not only from the basic rights but also from other norms of the constitution. The effect was not the protection of freedom but the reduction of freedom.

12.3.3 The "Barrier-Barriers"

According to the formal Rechtsstaat-principle, the axiom of freedom stands within the limits of the abstract-general written statute. Freedom is so to speak subjected to the *barriers of the statutes*. However, due to the material Rechtsstaat-principle the statutes themselves are subjected to barriers, namely the barriers of the constitutional objective value order that is based on the catalogue of constitutional basic rights. So, there are barriers of the barriers. In constitutional doctrine, it has become customary to speak of *barrier-barriers*.

Statutes can only restrict freedom if they are compatible with the constitutional catalogue of basic rights. Therefore, it is always necessary to check the compatibility of the statutes with the constitution. The competence to check is only in the courts and not in the administrative bodies. The administrative authorities have to obey the statutes whether or not they are constitutional or unconstitutional. The strict binding of administrative bodies to the wording of the statutes is acceptable because the citizen concerned has always the constitutional right to sue about the administrative act and to claim that it is based on unconstitutional statutes. The regular courts are authorized to declare legal norms as invalid because of unconstitutionality if the legal norm concerned is not issued by the Parliament but only by self-governing bodies or by the government. If parliamentarian statutes are in question, the courts have to put forward the case to the Federal Constitutional Court if they have serious concerns that the statute concerned is unconstitutional (Article 100 GG).[47]

The standards to check statutes are different and depend upon the basic right concerned. So, some basic rights provide for their restriction by statute (e.g. Article 8 Sec. 2 GG: outdoor assemblies), while others do not contain such a legal reservation (e.g. Article 4 Sec. 1 GG: Freedom of religion and conscience). Those basic rights can only be limited by other constitutional basic rights (immanent constitutional barriers).[48] Some basic rights may only be restricted by so called "qualified" statutes (e.g. Article 6 Sec. 3 GG: The right to family togetherness of parents and children may only be restricted if the parents fail and the children threatened with neglect.). This chapter does not address all the modifications of legal reservation in detail. Only two examples are presented.

The first example involves the Freedom of Opinion (Article 5 GG) which may only be restricted by a "general" statute. Due to the case law of the Federal Constitutional Court, the word "general" in this context does not only mean the regular requirement that freedom restricting norms have to be abstract and general. Rather, "general"

E.g. it derived from the constitutional empowerment of the Federation to set up armed forces that the functionability of the armed forces was a constitutional value. This alleged value could then be used to justify the limitation of the freedom of conscience of military service objectors, *cf.* BVerfG, Dec. of 26.05.1970 – 1 BvR 83/69 –, BVerfGE 28, 243: Jud. of 24.04.1985 – 2 BvF 2/83 u.a. –, BVerfGE 69, 1 [22].

[47] However, the regular courts also have a competence to overrule formal laws if they are contrary to the law of the European Union. But this issue is not discussed here further.

[48] BVerfG, Jud. of 24.04.1985 – 2 BvF 2/83 u.a. –, BVerfGE 69, 1 [22].

means in Article 5 GG that it is not allowed to prohibit certain opinions by statute but it is only possible to restrict the right to free opinion by a statute that does not have the task to regulate and to oppress opinions. The task of the statute must rather be different. The statute must be dedicated to the aim to protect any other object that has nothing to do with opinions.[49] For example, the statute which prohibits teachers and students from expressing *any* political or religious opinion in school and from displaying political or religious symbols is such a general statute. The target of such a statute is obviously not the suppression of a particular political or religious opinion because the expression of *every* political and religious opinion is prohibited. The target is rather to ensure peace in the school. However, such a legitimate purpose is still not sufficient to consider the statute as constitutional. In any case, it is rather necessary to weigh up the interest in the free expression of opinions and the competitive legitimate good (here, peace in the school) in order to find out which interest is more important. If there is, for example, a conflict between the interest of a leaseholder to express his political opinion by sticking posters on his window on the one side and the competing interest of a landlord on the other side who does not want to tolerate the different opinions of his leaseholder, then the leaseholder's interest to express his opinion is more important than the landlord's interest to suppress opinions that he does not share. On the other hand, peace in the school can be weighted more than the freedom to express one's opinion inside the school because peace in the school is a public good and teachers and students do not lose the opportunity to express their opinions outside the school.[50]

Since in the last instance it is the office of the courts to judge these considerations, the courts in general and the Federal Constitutional Court in particular gain in strong power. Therefore, in polemical intention, it is occasionally customary to speak of the "Richterstaat" (literally "Judge-State") instead of "Rechtsstaat".[51]

The second example refers to the restrictions of the freedom of profession (Article 12 GG). The Federal Constitutional Court has developed a so called *three-step-theory* to this.[52] If the statute concerned refers only to the mere way of practicing a particular profession (e.g. the duty to display prices on the product in a shop) any reasonable consideration of the common interest can legitimate the restriction. If the statute concerned refers to the conditions under which it is only allowed to practice a particular profession at all, then only personal conditions can be required (e.g. special education, exams) but not any other criteria (e.g. limited admissibility in order to protect competitors). Such personal conditions can only be required if this is necessary in order to protect important common goods (e.g. health). The total prohibition of a profession is only possible in extreme, extraordinary cases, in particular

[49] BVerfG, Jud. of 15.01.1958 – 1 BvR 400/51 – "Lüth", BVerfGE 7, 198.

[50] Amtsgericht Freiburg, Jud. of 17.03.1987 – 10 C 4904/86 –, WuM 1987, 144; opposite opinion: Landgericht Aachen, Jud. of 25.11.1987 – 7 S 294/87 –, WuM 1988, 53.

[51] Z.B. Hans Maier, "Dritte Gewalt und Grundgesetz – nach vierzig Jahren", 68 *Deutsche Richterzeitung* [DRiZ] 1990, 4; Bernd Rüthers, "Rechtswissenschaft ohne Recht?", 64 *Neue Juristische Wochenschrift* [NJW] (2011), 434.

[52] BVerfG, Dec. of 11.06.1958 – 1 BvR 596/56 –, BVerfGE 7, 377.

if the practice of the profession would lead to serious dangers for an eminent important common good (e.g. trade with weapons of war).

In cases where particular basic rights do not demand special requirements to the purpose of the restricting statute and also in the case where no particular basic right is concerned but only the general rule of the freedom of action (Article 2 Sec. 1 GG), it is not sufficient that the legislator creates a simple abstract-general prohibition act. Rather, in these cases it is also necessary to check in detail whether the restrictions can be justified. The standard for this check is the proportionality principle.[53] It requires a legitimate purpose and means that are suitable, necessary, and proportional. The courts have to examine whether these conditions are met.

A further *barrier-barrier* is the so called *essentiality-guarantee*. Under Article 19 Sec. 2 GG, it is in any case not allowed to restrict or to infringe the *essence* of a basic right. However, it has not been clarified – either by the case law of the Constitutional Federal Court or by doctrine – what is meant by *essence*. It is reasonable to assume that a basic right may never be restricted in a way that there is "nothing left" for the person concerned. A good example is life imprisonment. The imposition of life imprisonment leads to the result that the basic right of freedom from imprisonment (Article 2 Sec. 2 sen. 2 GG) no longer exists for the prisoner. This is an infringement of the essence of this right. The Federal Constitutional Court decided in 1977 that life imprisonment is not compatible with the Constitution, if the person concerned does not have a realistic chance to become free by appropriate behavior and personal development. That chance must be guaranteed by enforceable law and not left only to a prospect of pardon.[54] The Court, however, did not refer to the essentiality-guarantee but argued on the basis of the Human-Dignity Principle (Article 1 Sec. 1 GG). However, it seems not very convincing and it would have been much more insightful if the Federal Constitutional Court would have relied on the essence-guarantee.

With that, the last and strongest barriers-barrier is addressed, which is provided by the material Rechtsstaat-principle, namely the principle of human dignity (Article 1 Sec. 1 GG).[55] This barrier-barriers applies only to those basic rights that are codifications of human rights. Human rights are subjective rights that can be derived from human dignity.[56] Human dignity does not refer to the freedom of action but to the freedom of will, i.e. the personhood of persons. Personhood is the capacity of self-determination on the basis of a person's own considerations and reflections. Human rights are rights that protect the personhood of persons and not merely the freedom of action.[57] The Grundgesetz contains many basic rights whose

[53] BVerfG, Dec. of 16.03.1971 – 1 BvR 52/66 –, BVerfGE 30, 292 [316].

[54] BVerfG, Jud. of 21.06.1977 – 1 BvL 14/76 – "lebenslange Freiheitsstrafe", BVerfGE 45, 187.

[55] *Cf.* Paul Tiedemann, *Menschenwürde als Rechtsprinzip. Eine rechtsphilosophische Klärung* (3rd ed. 2012). Berlin: Berliner Wissenschafts-Verlag.

[56] *Cf.* Preamble of the International Covenant on Civil and Political Rights of 19.12.1966 (UNTS 999, 171).

[57] *See also*, Paul Tiedemann, "Human Dignity as an Absolute Value", *in Human Dignity as a Foundation of Law, ARSP-Beiheft*, Winfried Brugger †/Stephan Kirste eds. (2013), 25. Stuttgart: Franz Steiner.

infringement is never at the same time a violation of human dignity. This is true in other contexts like the freedom of profession (Article 12 GG), the right to freedom of movement (Article 11 GG), and the right of petition (Article 17 GG). Whereas the Essentiality-Guarantee is applicable for every basic right, the Human-Dignity Principle is only applicable for those which embrace at least partly a human right. On the other hand, basic rights which do not contain human rights can be replaced through a narrower wording or they can completely be abolished by the constitution-amending legislator.[58] In this case, the Essentiality-Guarantee is dropped. Human rights on the other hand are beyond the reach of the constitution-amending legislator because they embody the Human-Dignity-Principle and this principle falls under the so called *eternity-clause* of Article 79 Sec. 3 GG. It is unchangeable.

12.4 The Social Rechtsstaat

Just as the concept of material Rechtsstaat was originally a polemical counter-concept to the concept of formal Rechtsstaat, the term "sozialer (social) Rechtsstaat" owes a lot to an originally skeptical attitude to freedom. The expression "sozialer Rechtsstaat" appears for the first time in 1921 at Poloty/Schneider, who from a socialist point of view demanded the renunciation of the idea of "pure Rechtsstaat" and the replacement through the idea of the "social Rechtsstaat" or "social state".[59] In the drafting process of the Grundgesetz, a member of Parliamentarian Council, Hermann von Mangoldt, made the proposal to characterize the Federal Republic of Germany as a "social Rechtsstaat".[60] Finally, the Parliamentarian Council chose a different formulation, namely the formula of the "social federal state" (Article 20 Sec. 1 GG). The expression "social Rechtsstaat" appears only in Article 28 Sec. 1 GG, where it is ruled that the constitutional order in the Lander has to follow the principles of the "social Rechtsstaat in the meaning of the Grundgesetz". However, it remained uncertain what principles could be meant. Neither the text of the Grundgesetz nor the protocols about the drafting process reveals what actually was meant by the attribute "social". The Parliamentarian Council has not made the slightest resolution of the uncertainty.[61]

The academic doctrine held first the opinion that the expression "social" is an empty formula ("substanzlosen Blankettbegriff") that contains no substantial content and is therefore open to unlimited interpretation.[62] Ernst Forsthoff introduced the

---

[58] The Grundgesetz can be changed by a 2/3 majority in each of the both chambers of Parliament.

[59] Robert Piloty/Franz Schneider, *Grundriß des Verwaltungsrechts in Bayern und dem Deutschen Reiche* (5th ed. 1930) at 2. Leipzig: Deichert.

[60] W. Weber, "Die verfassungsrechtlichen Grenzen sozialstaatlicher Forderungen", in 4 *Der Staat* (1965), 409, 411.

[61] *Id.*

[62] Wilhelm Grewe, "Das bundesstaatliche System des Grundgesetzes", 4 *Deutsche Rechtszeitung* (1949), 349, 351.

concept of *precaution for existence* ("Daseinsvorsorge") that has become a key concept in order to describe the social Rechtsstaat.[63] Here, the state is no longer understood as a huge threat of human freedom which has to be brought under control by the means of the formal and material Rechtsstaat-principle. Rather, quite more important sources of danger are considered, in particular such as private economic power but also illness, age, and handicaps. The state is less considered as a mechanism of potential power abuse and oppression than a powerful means of protection against the threats of individual fate or of powerful non-state-agents. The expression, "social Rechtsstaat", serves therefore the purpose to entrust the state with the duty to ensure the existence of the citizens. Following this idea, Hans Peter Ipsen has developed a new type of constitutional concept. He coined for this type the term, *state-goal-provision* ("Staatszielbestimmung"). A state-goal-provision is a constitutional clause by which the state is empowered to achieve the goals that are described in the clause.[64] Due to Ipsens doctrine, a state-goal-provision clause "Social State" rules "the aim and responsibility of the state to shape the social order".[65] This view has prevailed in German constitutional doctrine. However, it engenders several serious reservations.

First, it is not clear why the Constitution should entrust the state with the task and responsibility to shape the social order. The state can do so without being instructed by the Constitution. The responsibilities of the federal state and the Lander is not based on the principle of specific conferment of powers but on the principle of Competence over competence. Due to this principle the Lander and – in the frame of its legislative competence – the Federation can take responsibility for any aim or subject. Federation and Lander are therefore authorized to conduct social policy. The social state clause adds nothing to this.

Second, the Social-Legal-State clause cannot prevent the state from not acting in social matters. If it does nothing there is nobody who could sue the state because of it. The Social-Rechtsstaat clause does not determine who should exactly be responsible for certain targets. Are the Lander responsible or the Federation? And within the Federation or the Lander, which organs have to take care of what aspects of the social order? Which authority can be sued because it has not fulfilled its task? Obviously, the Social-Legal-State clause answers none of these questions. Only the specific statutes can deliver an answer.

Finally, the Social-Rechtsstaat clause cannot fix certain targets because the expressions "social" and "social order" are much too vague to describe exactly what the state should do. Which social order should to be approached, a neo-liberal one, a socialist one, a market economy system or rather a state-trading system or

[63] Ernst Forsthoff, "Begriff und Wesen des sozialen Rechtsstaats", in 12 *Veröffentlichungen der Vereinigung Deutscher Staatsrechtslehrer* (1954), 8.

[64] Hans Peter Ipsen, "25 Jahre Grundgesetz", 27 *Die Öffentliche Verwaltung* (1974), 289 [294]; vgl. Karl-Peter Sommermann, *Staatsziele und Staatszielbestimmungen* (1997).

[65] Hans Peter Ipsen, "Enteignung und Sozialisierung", in 10 *Veröffentlichungen der Vereinigung Deutscher Staatsrechtslehrer* (1952), 74.

something different? These questions show that shaping of the social order is in the first instance the subject of social policy and not a constitutional issue.

It is very interesting to note that the Social-Rechtsstaat clause has had absolutely no relevance in German case law. One of the classical examples of a judgment that dealt with this principle was the decision of the Federal Administrative Court of 1954 according to which public assistance to the poor is not only to be carried out in the public interest but in the first instance in the interest of the persons concerned. They have an enforceable right to economic support in the case of existential poverty.[66] However, this judgment was not only justified with the Social-Rechtsstaat-principle but primarily with the Human-Dignity principle. In some cases, the Federal Constitutional Court declared statutes as unconstitutional which excluded particular individuals from the social solidarity. However, also in all these cases the court did not derive the conclusion from the Social-Rechtsstaat-principle but from the Human-Dignity principle. The court mentions the Social-Rechtsstaat-principle very often but only as a topos of no relevance. It functions rather as a rhetoric strengthening of judicial reasoning.[67]

The marginal role of the social attribute clearly shows that the attempt to construct the social element as a part of the Rechtsstaat-principle has failed. The Rechtsstaat-principle is in fact a negative principle. It can only tell us what the state may not do, not what it should do. The concept of Sociality on the other hand refers to anything positive, to something that the state should do. However, the decision about what the state positively should do is the subject of the political process that is influenced and determinated by democratic elections and ballots.

12.5 The "Green" Rechtsstaat

The expression "grüner (green) Rechtsstaat" is not customary in the German constitutional doctrine. I introduce this term in order to point to a new development that deals with a further enrichment of the Rechtsstaat-principle. This development started only in the mid-1980s. Whereas the state-goal-provision doctrine was developed in order to interpret the little word "social" in the expression "Social Rechtsstaat" in Article 28 GG, there was since the 1980s more and more awareness that this doctrine may not only be relevant to interpret the given constitution but that state-goal-provision clauses can also be used to introduce new state goals by amending the constitution. So, in February 1984, the SPD faction in the German Parliament demanded an amendment to the constitution to implement a state-goal-provision clause concerning the protection of environment.[68] The German reunification in

[66] BVerwG, Jud. of 24.06.1954 – V C 78.54 –, BVerwGE 1, 159.

[67] BVerfG, Dec. of 10.11.1998 – 2 BvL 42/93 – "Kinderexistenzminimum I", BVerfGE 99, 246; Dec. of 13.02.2008 – 2 BvL 1/06 – "Kinderexistenzminimum II", BVerfGE 120, 125; Jud. of 09.02.2010 – 1 BvL 1/09 u.a. – "Hartz IV", BVerfGE 125, 175.

[68] BT-Drs. 10/974 v. 08.02.1984.

1989/90 brought a further impulse. The Unification Treaty of 1990 provided that the legislative bodies should deal with considerations for adding new state-goal-provisions in the Constitution.[69] Finally in 1994 a new clause was inserted to the Constitution with the following wording: "The state, also in its responsibility for future generations, protects the natural foundations of life and the animals in the framework of the constitutional order, by legislation and, according to law and justice, by executive and judiciary." (Article 20a GG)

With that, a new state-goal-provision was created that, like the Social-State clause, formulated only a very general and vague goal that could not be enforceable as such. In any case, the new clause implies new limits of state power. The state may not pursue political objectives that are contrary to the protection of the natural foundations of life. Public policies that jeopardize this goal can only be constitutional if a precise, comprehensible and transparent assessment was done, which is – within certain limits – amenable to judicial review. So, for example, the Higher Administrative Court Weimar has declared a municipal statute about the compulsory connection and usage to a district heating system null and void because it did not provide for exemption of property owners who had their own system for generating heat from renewable energy sources (solar collectors). Such legislation was incompatible with the state goal of Article 20a GG.[70] Unfortunately in more important cases, the new state-goal-provision clause has been mostly ignored. It is interesting to note that the German decision to exit from nuclear power was only a political one and not a legal one based on the environmental state-goal-provision clause.[71]

Nevertheless, the new state-goal-provision clause concerning the protection of the foundations of life can be understood as the constitutional manifestation of the Green-Rechtsstaat-principle. It does not explain exactly what the state has to do in order to protect the foundations of life. But it contains above all a negative provision according to which the state is not allowed to adopt any policy that is obviously contrary to the protection of the foundations of life. It is clear that the natural foundations of life belong to the most relevant conditions of individual freedom. One can hardly imagine a greater impairment of individual freedom as that which is brought about by destroying our livelihood and for example, measures that make our conventional habitat uninhabitable.

The further development of the state-goal-provision "foundations of life", in particular in the state of Hesse, shows, however, the risk that is connected with an extensive use of state-goal-provisions in general. In Hesse we find an example of how state-goal-provisions can be abused.

---

[69] Art. 5 des Vertrages zwischen der Bundesrepublik Deutschland und der Deutschen Demokratischen Republik über die Herstellung der Einheit Deutschlands v. 31.08.1990 – BGBl. 1990 II 885.

[70] Oberverwaltungsgericht Weimar, Jud. of 24.09.2007 – 4 N 70/03 –, 4 *Contracting und Recht* [CuR] (2008), 102.

[71] Annika Breithhardt, "Germany plans to shut all nuclear reactors by 2022", *available at* http://www.reuters.com/article/2011/05/31/us-germany-nuclear-idUSTRE74Q2P120110531

In 1991, the people of Hesse amended a new state-goal-provision in the Constitution of Hesse (HV) which is very similar to that of Article 20a GG.[72] Article 26a HV states: "The natural foundations of human life are under the protection of the state and of the municipalities."

In 2001, the Landessportbund Hessen (Hessian Association of Sports) started a campaign intended to make the environmental state-goal-provision ineffective if interests of the sport are affected. To this end, it claimed publicly and in front of all political parties to implement another state-goal-provision in the Constitution in order to protect "sports". The purpose of this campaign became clear in a letter of the president of the Association to the Hessian Prime Minister: "After 1991, an environmental protection clause has found input in the Hessian constitution, the inclusion of the sport a decade later would establish the necessary equality of arms."[73] The environmental protection clause was considered to be a weapon against sports and the sports officials wanted to get equal arms in order to protect their interests more effectively. They awarded their own private and particular interests the same status as the public interest on the foundations of life. And they were successful. The political parties were enthusiastic about the proposal because it was an effective means to distract from serious political problems.[74] Citizens in a constitutional ballot were requested to vote in favor or against "sports". And it is not surprising that the overwhelming majority voted in favor for sports. Nobody understood the true motivation behind the proposal and nobody understood the constitutional function of state-goal-provisions. Nobody realized the true function and aim of the proposal and that it should not support sports but should waken the environmental state-goal-provision. In September 2002, Articles 62a HV came into force, according to which "sports enjoy the protection and care of the state, the municipalities, and the associations of municipalities."[75]

Now the equality of arms is established! In a conflict between the protection of the foundations of life and the protection of sports, the constitutional weight of the former is so to speak paralyzed by the constitutional weight of the latter. This example shows how carefully state-goal-provisions must be dealt with. They should be used of it only in very rare and extreme relevant situations (like the protection of the foundation of life) and only after very intensive public discourse.

---

[72] GVBl. Hessen 1991 I 101.

[73] Brief des Präsidenten des Hessischen Sportbundes Dr. Rolf Müller an den hessischen Ministerpräsidenten Roland Koch v. 28.11.2011 – *available at* http://www.landessportbund-hessen.de/presse/archiv/2001/11/28/sport-als-staatsziel-in-die-verfassung/

[74] Hessischer Landtag Drucksache 15/3579 v. 29.01.2002.

[75] GVBl. Hessen 2002 I 628.

Chapter 13
The German Rechtsstaat in a Comparative Perspective

Rainer Grote

Abstract This chapter focuses on the historical features of the German concept of "Rechtsstaat" as it developed in the second half of the nineteenth century. It examines how the original concept was transformed under the influence of the Basic Law following World War II. The question how the concept of "Rechtsstaat" relates to similar yet different concepts in other legal systems like the Anglo-American rule of law and the French "principe de legalité" is also addressed. The chapter also deals with the question how far the influence of the "Rechtsstaat" can be perceived in the modern thinking on the rule of law in the era of globalization.

13.1 The Origins of the German Rechtsstaat in the Nineteenth Century

The concept of Rechtsstaat was first developed in nineteenth century Germany.[1] From there it migrated in the early twentieth century to France[2] and other parts of continental Europe.[3] In its original version, the concept of Rechtsstaat was the doctrinal attempt to domesticate the powers of the monarchical state by restricting their exercise to the protection of life, liberty and property of the members of society.

[1] On the origins of the term *see* U. Scheuner, "Die neuere Entwicklung des Rechtsstaats in Deutschland", in: *Hundert Jahre deutsches Rechtsleben, Festschrift zum 100jährigen Bestehen des Deutschen Juristentages*, vol. 2 (1960) at 229. C.F. Müller.

[2] In France the term "Etat de droit" was popularized by Raymond Carré de Malberg, a prominent law professor who taught at the University of Strasbourg and was intimately familiar with the German debate on the Rechtsstaat (between 1871 and 1918 Strasbourg had been part of the German Empire), *see* R. Carré de Malberg, *Contributions à la théorie générale de l'État*, vol. 1 (1920) at 488 et seq. CNRS.

[3] Namely to Italy ("Stato di diritto"), Spain ("Estado de derecho") and Russia ("Prawowoje gosudarstwo"), *see* R. Gosalbo-Bono, "The Significance of the Rule of Law and its Implications for the European Union and the United States", *University of Pittsburgh Law Review* (2006) 72, 229, 245; A.-C. Pereira Menaut, "Rule of Law o Estado de Derecho" (2003) at 34. Marcial Pons.

J.R. Silkenat et al. (eds.), *The Legal Doctrines of the Rule of Law and the Legal State (Rechtsstaat)*, Ius Gentium: Comparative Perspectives on Law and Justice 38,
DOI 10.1007/978-3-319-05585-5_13, © Springer International Publishing Switzerland 2014

This emphasis on the preservation of individual autonomy underpinned the highly influential definition of the lawful state given by Immanuel Kant, the most prominent Enlightenment philosopher in Germany. According to Kant, the founding principles of a state governed by the laws of justice were the freedom of every member of society as a human being, the equality of every man with all other men as a subject and the independence of each member of a commonwealth as a citizen.[4] Such a state would involve the citizens, either directly or through their representatives, in the making of the laws which they had to observe as members of society, so that in effect they were subject to no laws other than those which they had chosen to give to themselves.[5]

The theory of the lawful state marked a radical departure from older notions of the state which had seen its main *raison d'être* in the realization of transcendental moral or religious values.[6] The new theories essentially limited the state to the purpose of securing individual liberty and private property as the material basis for individual autonomy, rejecting the far-reaching policing powers the monarchical state had claimed for itself in order to provide for the material and spiritual well-being of its subjects. They quickly became the basis for a wide-spread reform movement in post-Napoleonic Germany which called for a secular, liberal state based on the recognition of fundamental rights like freedom of movement, economic liberty and freedom of the press, constitutional guarantees for the independence of the courts, and trial by jury. The term Rechtsstaat was increasingly used in this debate as shorthand for the liberal reform program of the monarchical state.[7]

The reform movement achieved some limited progress in the member states of the German Bund where constitutions enacted after 1815 usually provided that laws regulating the rights of the individual were subject to the approval of the legislative assembly before they could come into force. Hopes of adopting a liberal constitution for the whole of Germany, however, were frustrated when the revolutionary movement of 1848/49, seeking to establish a German nation state based on popular sovereignty, foundered on the resistance of the reactionary forces led by Austria and Prussia. When a German nation state was finally established in 1871, it was based on a federation of the royal houses of the German principalities under the leadership of Prussia – Austria had been driven out of Germany as a result of its defeat in the war with Prussia in 1866 – rather than on the vote of the German people. While the Bismarckian constitution of 1871 made some efforts to accommodate liberal and democratic aspirations, notably by creating a national Parliament (the *Reichstag*)

---

[4] Immanuel Kant, *Über den Gemeinspruch: Das mag in der Theorie richtig sein, taugt aber nicht in der Praxis* (1793), *II: Vom Verhältnis der Theorie zur Praxis im Staatsrecht (Gegen Hobbes)*, at 41.

[5] Kant, Über den Gemeinspruch, *supra* note 4, at 46–48.

[6] E.W. Böckenförde, "Entstehung und Wandel des Rechtsstaatsbegriffs", in *Recht, Staat, Freiheit* (1992) at 143, 145. Suhrkamp.

[7] The most prominent of these liberal scholars in the first half of the nineteenth century was Robert von Mohl who used the concept to establish binding limits on the far-reaching police powers of the monarchical state, *see* R. von Mohl, *Die Polizei-Wissenschaft nach den Grundsätzen des Rechtsstaats*, 2 vol. (1832/33).

elected on the basis of universal suffrage, it consciously departed from the tradition of 1848/49 in many other respects, most importantly by foregoing a constitutional bill of rights (the aborted constitution of 1849 had contained a detailed bill of rights).

The failure of the 1848 revolution also had a major impact on the further development of the concept of Rechtsstaat. While the concept had originally been conceived in order to protect and promote the ideal of individual autonomy, it was now increasingly redefined in purely formal terms. According to this view, the Rechtsstaat had nothing to do with the purpose and the content of the state but was exclusively concerned with the methods and means of their realization.[8] At the same time, the rise of legal positivism as the dominant method of legal scholarship also in constitutional and administrative law further undermined any material interpretation of the idea of "Rechtsstaat." This was most evident with regard to fundamental rights. Whereas they had formerly be seen as fundamental principles legitimizing and directing all state activity, they were now widely regarded as juridically superfluous declamations whose programmatic purpose had largely been fulfilled with the codification of the most important basic freedoms like freedom of profession and trade and freedom of the press by ordinary statute.[9] Not surprisingly, fundamental rights were increasingly supplanted by the concept of "public subjective rights" which the legislature could largely fashion at will.[10]

The end of the nineteenth century thus witnessed the gradual transformation of the concept of "Rechtsstaat" into a mere principle of legality. This meant that while the legislature was still subject to the provisions of the Constitution in the exercise of its legislative powers, these requirements were of a purely formal and procedural character. The focus of the revised concept of Rechtsstaat was clearly not on the (elected) legislature, but on the administration which was still firmly under the control of the monarch.[11] The administration was not only subject to the limits imposed on its action by the legislature, it also needed express statutory authorization for any measure which interfered with personal liberty or private property. Decisions taken by the administrative authorities in individual cases could be attacked for illegality before specialized administrative law courts whose independence was guaranteed in terms similar to those which applied to the ordinary courts. The main endeavor of legal scholarship in this period was the development of general principles of administrative law which would provide the individual with an adequate protection against the potential abuse of the powers conferred on the administrative authorities.[12]

[8] F.J. Stahl, *Die Philosophie des Rechts nach geschichtlicher Ansicht* (3rd ed., 1856) at 137.

[9] G. Lübbe-Wolff, "Safeguards of Civil and Constitutional Rights. The Debate on the role of the Reichsgericht", in *German and American constitutional thought – contexts, interaction and historical realities*, H. Wellenreuther ed. (1990) at 354. Berg.

[10] Georg Jellinek, one of the leading German scholars of the time, proclaimed that constitutionally guaranteed civil rights were thus nothing more than special reformulations of the general principle that the state authorities may not unlawfully curtail the liberty of the individuals, *see* Jellinkek, *System der subjektiven öffentlichen Rechte* (1892).

[11] Böckenförde, Rechtsstaatsbegriff, *supra* note 6, at 156.

[12] The paradigmatic character of administrative law for this version of the Rechtsstaat was widely recognized at the time. Otto Mayer, who is considered to be the pioneer of the doctrinal analysis of

13.2 The Transformation of the Rechtsstaat After World War II

The period after World War II has witnessed a radical break with the formal notions of Rechtsstaat that had dominated the debate at the turn of the century and had survived the constitutional upheaval at the end of the First World War, which resulted in the demise of the Empire and the establishment of the Weimar Republic, largely intact.[13] By contrast, the experience of Nazism which used the parliamentary and administrative machinery at its disposal to dress even some of its most outrageous policies in the trappings of formal legality,[14] dealt a fatal blow to the positivist concept of Rechtsstaat as a system in which public power is exercised by the competent organs in accordance with the legally prescribed procedures. In response to these excesses, the Basic Law, the constitution of the Federal Republic of Germany, marks a fundamental shift towards a substantive ideal of the Rechtsstaat. While the formal aspects of the Rechtsstaat have not been abandoned, they are complemented by a number of substantive values and principles which direct all forms of state action, be they legislative, executive, or judicial.[15]

The Basic Law refers to the principle of Rechtsstaat explicitly only in the provision which deals with the constitutional order in the federal states, the Länder. According to Article 28, para. 1 the constitutional order in the Länder must conform to the principles of a republican, democratic and social state governed by the rule of law within the meaning of the Basic Law. Art. 28 functions as a "homogeneity" clause, i.e. its basic function is to ensure that the structure of the constitutional order in the Länder closely mirrors that of the Federation. It follows from this that the Rechtsstaat must also be seen as one of the defining elements of the constitutional order of the Federation. Consequently the Basic Law expressly incorporates some of its most important formal and procedural aspects, like the principle of legality (Art. 20, para. 3), the right to a fair hearing before the courts (Art. 103, para. 1), or the prohibition of retro-active criminal laws (Art. 103, para. 2). Other requirements, like legal certainty and predictability, and the ban of retroactive legislation outside

---

modern German administrative law, captured this general impression by stating: "Der Rechtsstaat ist der Staat des wohlgeordneten Verwaltungsrechts" (The *Rechtsstaat* is the state of the well ordered administrative law), *see* O. Mayer, *Deutsches Verwaltungsrecht* (1924) at 58. Duncker & Humblot.

[13] In the preface to the 3rd edition of his treatise "Deutsches Verwaltungsrecht" which was published in 1924 Otto Mayer emphasized this continuity by stressing the resilience of administrative law, and thus the core of the Rechtsstaat in its prevailing positivist interpretation, against the fundamental changes which had occurred in the previous years at the political and constitutional level: "Verfassungsrecht vergeht, Verwaltungsrecht besteht."

[14] A particularly repulsive example is the infamous Nuremberg race laws adopted in the form of ordinary statutes, which deprived Jews of their German citizenship and prohibited sexual relations between Jews and so-called "Aryans", *see* A. Rethmeier, *"Nürnberger Rassegesetze" und Entrechtung der Juden im Zivilrecht* (1995). Lang.

[15] *See* R. "Grote, Rule of Law, Rechtsstaat and "Etat de droit"", in *Constitutionalism, Universalism and Democracy – A comparative analysis*, C. Starck ed. (1999) at 269, 285–292. Nomos.

criminal law are directly derived from the principle of Rechtsstaat as such.[16] The separation of powers, which is expressly prescribed in the second sentence of paragraph (2) of Article 20, also constitutes an important element of the German concept of Rechtsstaat, designed to prevent the abuse of political and administrative power through a set of elaborated power-sharing arrangements.[17]

The most important feature of the Rechtsstaat of the Basic Law, however, is its transformation from a merely formal concept focusing on organizational and procedural safeguards into a concept based on a substantive ideal of justice. Art. 20, para. 1 of the Basic Law explicitly commits the legislative and other authorities of the Federal Republic to the goal of social justice, although it leaves the political bodies a wide discretion in the determination of the economic and social policies which are required to achieve this goal. This constitutes a major shift away from a narrow concept of liberty which focuses on the right of individuals to be left alone by the government to a broader notion of individual freedom that takes into account the economic and social conditions in which this liberty thrives and recognizes a legitimate role for the state in promoting the welfare of its citizens by providing vital public services in areas like education, health, housing and transportation.[18] Even more importantly, Art. 1, para. 1 of the Basic Law establishes the respect for, and the protection of, the dignity of man as the guiding principle of all state action. In direct response to the collectivist doctrines of fascism and other totalitarian ideologies, the provision states unambiguously that the state is not an institution created for its own sake or for the exclusive benefit of a specific ethnic or racial group or social class at the expense of all others. It is, rather, a political and social organization designed to serve the needs of its members defined by their most fundamental quality of human beings and regardless of their ethnic, religious, gender, political or social affiliation. The question whether the legal principles limiting the exercise of state power are of an "objective" nature or are merely the expression of the sovereign will of the state, as the theory of "autolimitation" which had dominated previous debates on the foundations of the Rechtsstaat had assumed,[19] has lost its relevance under the Basic Law. Art. 1, para. 2 acknowledges inviolable and inalienable human rights as the basis of every community, of peace and justice in the world, thereby recognizing the universal and extralegal character of those rights which exist prior to, and irrespective of, their official recognition by the state.[20]

---

[16] H. Schulze-Fielitz, Art. 20 (Rechtsstaat) para. 45, in, *Grundgesetz-Kommentar*, vol. 2, H. Dreier ed. (2nd ed., 2006). Mohr Siebeck.

[17] *Id.*, para. 67.

[18] Already in the nineteenth century some proponents of a substantive interpretation of Rechtsstaat like Robert von Mohl had tried to integrate the ideal of social justice into the concept, *see* M. Stolleis, *Geschichte des öffentlichen Rechts in Deutschland*, vol. 2(1992) at 259–60. C.H. Beck.

[19] G. Jellinek, *Allgemeine Staatslehre* (3rd ed., 1914) at 370–71.

[20] C. Starck, "Entwicklung der Grundrechte in Deutschland", in *Der demokratische Verfassungsstaat* (1995) at 156. Mohr Siebeck.

In a remarkable departure from the prevailing fundamental rights conceptions in the Weimar Republic and the Empire, the Basic Law stresses the legally binding and enforceable nature of the constitutionally guaranteed rights. Art. 1, para. 3 provides that the fundamental rights guaranteed in the following articles shall bind the legislature, the executive, and the judiciary as directly enforceable law. This provision makes it clear that the fundamental rights are to be used not only in the judicial review of acts done by administrative bodies or by the judiciary, but also in the assessment of the constitutionality of rules and laws adopted by Parliament itself. Furthermore, the Basic Law provides that in no case may the essential content of a basic right be encroached upon by any branch of government (Art. 19, para. 2). Finally, it tries to make sure that the very essence of fundamental rights cannot be abolished by way of future constitutional amendments. Art. 79 declares, among other things, amendments to the Basic Law which affect the basic principles laid down in Articles 1 and 20 of the Constitution are inadmissible in any circumstances. Thus, the guarantee of the inviolability of human dignity contained in Article 1 of the Basic Law, which constitutes the basis for each of the more specific fundamental rights guarantees contained in the following articles, is protected against any kind of constitutional change.

The Basic Law makes sure that the binding effect of the fundamental rights on all branches of government, and especially on the legislature, does not remain a mere programmatic principle. The Basic Law guarantees the right to have recourse to the courts to any person who claims that his/her rights, including his/her fundamental rights, have been violated by public authority (Art. 19, para. 4). Should the appeal to the ordinary courts be unsuccessful, the individual concerned may also bring his/her case before the Constitutional Court. A special individual complaints procedure, which has been given constitutional rank by the reform of January 29, 1969 (Art. 93, para. 1 clause 4), allows individual citizens – as well as corporate bodies and other legal persons entitled to fundamental rights protection – to bring a claim that their fundamentals rights have been violated by an act of public authority (which includes parliamentary statutes) before the Constitutional Court after they have exhausted the remedies available to them in the ordinary courts.

By emphasizing the duty of all state authority to respect and protect human dignity, the Basic Law has set up, in the words of the Federal Constitutional Court, an "objective order of values" based on the supreme value of the dignity of man.[21] In this capacity, fundamental rights do not only confer specific right guarantees on individual citizens protecting their individual freedoms against any form of government interference, they act also as fundamental principles of an objective character which serve as guidelines in the process of creating, interpreting and applying law. This reconceptualization, first undertaken by the Federal Constitutional Court in its famous decision in the *Lüth* case,[22] has transformed the

[21] BVerfGE (Decisions of the Federal Constitutional Court) 7, 198 (205). For an English translation see Decisions of the Bundesverfassungsgericht – Federal Constitutional Court – Federal Republic of Germany, Volume 2/Part 1, Freedom of Speech, Nomos 1998, 1 – *Lüth Case*.

[22] *Id.*

fundamental rights of the Basic Law from mere "negative" principles, limiting the scope of action of state authorities with regard to individual liberties, to "objective values" which oblige the competent organs to take into account fundamental rights in all fields of legislation, administration and adjudication and to create the best conditions possible in the circumstances for their effective enjoyment. The legislature must make sure that the ordinary legislation in the different fields of law – administrative law, criminal law and private law – gives full effect to the contents of the relevant fundamental rights provisions. On the other hand, the administrative bodies and the judiciary must apply the law in the light of the fundamental rights guarantees of the Basic Law.

Such a requirement may be self-evident with regard to the rules of administrative and criminal law, which traditionally deal with specific forms of state interference with the rights of individual citizens (right to liberty, right to property etc.). But it also applies to the application and interpretation of private law. This is important, because in the German system fundamental rights are not directly binding on private persons, a conclusion which can be derived directly from the wording of Art. 1, para. 3. As the case-law of the Federal Constitutional Court demonstrates, however, the fundamental rights of the Basic Law have nevertheless a substantial influence on the shaping and application of private law rules in their function as objective values or principles. The legislature is constitutionally bound to enforce the authority which the Basic Law has on the civil law system through explicit protection clauses and equality-promoting rules. The judge on the other hand has to interpret the relevant law, and especially the open-ended clauses in private law codifications, in the light of the fundamental rights guaranteed in the Basic Law.[23]

Another important aspect of the interpretation of fundamental rights as objective principles is the duty of the state to provide for an effective protection of fundamental rights (*Schutzpflichten*). This requires protection of basic rights not against the state but *by* the state. The State has a constitutional duty to protect individuals against the infringement of their most basic rights like life and liberty by other private parties, especially through the enactment and effective enforcement of criminal law provisions. This jurisprudence was developed in the abortion cases where the question arose whether the state was under a constitutional duty to secure the protection of the unborn even by means of penalizing the conduct of women seeking an abortion, if no other remedy was effective. The Court answered this question in the affirmative. While the state authorities, and in particular the legislature, enjoy a certain margin of appreciation in choosing the adequate means to protect the life of the unborn child, these may not be manifestly inadequate or insufficient. In the case of the unborn child this implies,

[23] In the *Lüth* case (BVerfGE 7, 198), the Constitutional Court held that the sentencing of the petitioner to pay compensation for the damages caused by his appeal to boycott a film of Veit Harlan, a director who had been heavily involved in the antisemitic propaganda of the NS regime (SEE COMMENT ON P. 4), by the ordinary courts in application of the relevant tort law provisions of the German Civil Code had not taken sufficiently into account the significance of free speech on issues of public interest in a democratic society, and thus violated the petitioner's right to freedom of expression.

according to the Court, that abortion must in principle be illegal and has to be punished accordingly.[24] Although the jurisprudence on protective duties is in principle applicable to other basic rights, its main focus has been on the rights to life and physical integrity.[25]

This pervasive influence of fundamental rights in the German constitutional and legal order has greatly reduced the significance of the Rechtsstaat as an autonomous concept. Fundamental rights are no longer considered as mere programmatic principles which are given substance only through their implementation by the legislature. Instead they are directly applicable normative standards which form an "objective order of values" that binds all branches of government and is enforced through an elaborate judicial machinery with the Federal Constitutional Court at its apex. The rise of fundamental rights as a shorthand for the substantive ideal of justice has profoundly affected the doctrinal understanding as well as the practical application of the concept of Rechtsstaat. For example, the requirement of a statutory basis for executive action (*Vorbehalt des Gesetzes*) had historically been regarded as an objective principle of constitutional law which determines the scope of the subordination of the administration to Parliament. But today the decisive criterion whether a specific measure is subject to this requirement is to be found, according to the well-established case law of the Federal Constitutional Court, in its significance for the exercise of fundamental rights.[26]

A similar trend can be observed with regard to the principle of proportionality whose main purpose is to limit state interference with rights or freedoms to the minimum necessary to achieve the legitimate goal pursued by the intervention. The Constitutional Court has explicitly linked the principle of proportionality to the Rechtsstaat. It has stressed, however, that this principle is derived from "the very essence" of the basic rights themselves which, as an expression of the general right to freedom of the citizen against the state, may only be limited by the authorities in so far as it is indispensable in the protection of the public interest.[27]

The dominant influence of the concept of fundamental rights on the modern interpretation of the principle of *Rechtsstaat* can finally be seen in the case law on the procedural aspects of fundamental rights guarantees. The Constitutional Court has repeatedly ruled that fundamental rights have a profound impact on the structure of administrative and judicial proceedings through which these rights are implemented or restricted. They must be organized and conducted in such a way as not to render the fundamental liberties at stake meaningless.[28] The idea of (procedural)

[24] BVerfGE 39, 1; 88, 203; compelling reasons which may justify the decision of the legislature to forfeit criminal punishment include the protection of the life and the health of the mother and, in extreme cases, the reasonable fear of a severe deterioration in her conditions of living in extreme cases.

[25] *See also* BVerfGE 46, 160 – *Schleyer.*

[26] BVerfGE 49, 89 – *Kalkar I.*

[27] BVerfGE 19, 342 – *Wencker*; 25, 269 – *Statute of Limitation.*

[28] BVerfGE 37, 132 – *Rent Comparison I*; 53, 30 – *Mühlheim-Kärlich Case.*

"due process" appears from this perspective primarily as a corollary of (substantive) fundamental rights protection.

As a result, the concept of Rechtsstaat has become absorbed to a large extent by the "constitutional state", a term which denotes the peculiarities of post-war German constitutionalism with its heavy emphasis on the substantive principles of human dignity, democracy, social justice and fundamental rights. Here, the effective enforcement of the latter is through an elaborate judicial machinery supervised by a powerful Constitutional Court.[29] While this fundamental shift of paradigm has generally been welcomed by scholars and citizens alike, it has also raised some difficult issues with regard to the relationship between the formal and procedural guarantees of the older notions of Rechtsstaat and the ideal of substantive justice incorporated in the newer versions of the principle.[30]

13.3 The German Rechtsstaat in Comparative Perspective

With its emphasis on human dignity, fundamental rights and social justice, the German Rechtsstaat, as it has developed in the post-war era, clearly belongs to the "thick" or substantive concepts of the rule of law. While the formal theories stress the intrinsic qualities of the law, namely the general character, clarity and certainty of the legal rules and the predictability of their application, the substantive theories move beyond those formal qualities in order to take into account the principles and institutional arrangements which are shaping the substance of the laws.[31] In the words of legal theorist T.R.S. Allan, the rule of law in this sense is:

> an amalgam of standards, expectations, and aspirations: it encompasses traditional ideas about individual liberty and natural justice, more generally, ideas about the requirements of justice and fairness in the relations between government and governed... The idea of the rule of law is also inextricably linked with certain basic institutional arrangements. The fundamental notion of equality, which lies close to the heart of our convictions about justice and fairness, demands an equal voice for all adult citizens in the legislative process: universal suffrage may today be taken to be a central strand of the rule of law.[32]

---

[29] *See* D. Kommers & R. Miller, *The Constitutional Jurisprudence of the Federal Republic of Germany* (3rd ed., 2012) at 48–49. Duke University Press. (the term "Rechtsstaat" nowadays is best translated as "constitutional state").

[30] The Federal Constitutional Court had to come to grips with this issue when it was confronted with the question how to deal with past injustices including grave human rights violations committed by former GDR officials who claimed that their action had been lawful under the relevant GDR legislation in force at the time, *see* P. Kirchof, "Rechtsstaatlichkeit im Umbruch der Wiedervereinigung", in *Teilungsfolgen und Rechtsfriede*, O. Jauernig & P. Hommelhoff eds. (1996) at 145. C.F. Müller.

[31] On this central distinction *see* B. Tamanaha, *On the Rule of Law* (2004) at 91–92. Cambridge University Press.

[32] T.R.S. Allan, *Law, Liberty and Justice: The Legal Foundations of British Constitutionalism* (1993) at 21–22. Clarendon Press.

As the quotation above which refers to the rule of law in the British tradition indicates, this is by no means a development which has been restricted to Germany. To varying degrees, other countries have also recently witnessed a revived interest in the substantive elements of the rule of law. This applies to France, for example, where the rule of law since the establishment of the Third Republic had increasingly been conceived as the rule of law made by Parliament (*principe de légalité*).[33] This veneration of the law owed much to the political philosophy of the Enlightenment which, especially in the writings of Jean-Jacques Rousseau, had attached almost divine qualities to it and was reflected in the famous Declaration of the Rights of Man and of the Citizen of 1789 that left the implementation of the various proclaimed individual rights to the law and expressly recognized its special status as expression of the general will.[34] The deference to the law emanating from the sovereign Parliament also formed the basis of the stricter scrutiny of the legality of administrative action practiced by the Conseil d'Etat in the latter half of the nineteenth century. Not unlike the German Rechtsstaat of the late nineteenth century, the French "principe de légalité" thus focused on the development of a coherent body of legal rules designed to ensure that the administration stayed within the powers conferred upon it by statute. But in contrast to Germany the modern "droit administratif" was developed within a firmly established republican tradition, as enshrined in the Declaration of the Rights of Man and of the Citizen.

However, the political vicissitudes of the first half of the twentieth century showed that the parliamentary statute no longer offered the rock-solid foundation for the rule of law in the republican tradition which the revolutionaries had once supposed it to be. The Conseil d'Etat responded to this "decline of the [parliamentary] law" by recognizing so-called general principles of law ("principes généraux du droit") as unwritten parameters for the control of the legality of administrative action. They do not stem from positive law but are derived from republican tradition and the general principles of legislation, as interpreted by the Conseil d'État. The framing of the general principles has been inspired not only by a variety of sources, including constitutional documents such as the 1789 Declaration of the Rights of Man and the Preamble to the 1946 Constitution, but also by "natural law" ideas of justice and equity. They thus clearly transcend the narrow confines of legal positivism. Nor is the scope of these principles limited to formal or procedural aspects of the law: they also serve to protect a number of substantive rights like freedom of thought and opinion,[35] freedom of movement[36] or the principle of equality before the law.[37] The general principles started to appear in the case-law of the Conseil d'État when public liberties

[33] J. Chevallier, *L'État de droit*, (5th ed., 2010) at 29. Montchrestien.

[34] J.M. Cotteret, *Le pouvoir législatif en France* (1962) at 9; G. Burdeau, *Essai sur l'évolution de la notion de la loi en droit français*, Archives de Philosophie du droit et de Sociologie juridique (1939) at 9. Pichon & Durand-Auzias.

[35] *Chavenau*, CE 1 April 1949, Rec. Leb. 161.

[36] *Vicini*, 20 January 1965, Rec. Leb. 41.

[37] *Société des concerts du Conservatoire*, CE 9 March 1951, Rec. Leb. 151; *Barel*, CE 28 May 1954, Rec. Leb. 308.

came increasingly under threat from the authoritarian rulers of the Vichy regime.[38] However, they did not bind Parliament in the exercise of its legislative powers. The introduction of judicial review of parliamentary laws would have to wait for another two decades. When it finally came, with the establishment of the Conseil Constitutionnel in 1958, it was at first limited to the formal and procedural constitutionality of the laws adopted by Parliament. But, in its famous decision of 1971 "Liberté d'association," the Conseil Constitutionnel asserted its competence to extend the review of constitutionality to the substance of parliamentary statutes on the basis of the fundamental rights provisions contained in the Declaration of the Rights of Man and in the preamble of the Constitution of 1946 which it qualified as legally binding principles.[39] The right to apply for judicial review of parliamentary laws was subsequently extended to members of the political opposition. In 2008, another constitutional reform introduced the right of the parties to a case to ask the court to submit a statutory provision on which the outcome of the case depends to the Conseil Constitutionnel for review of its compatibility with the fundamental liberties guaranteed by the Constitution.[40] The expansion of the scope of application for constitutional review which took place as a result of these developments has been hailed by French scholars as completion of the "État de droit".[41]

The rise of individual rights has also left its mark on the development of the British practice of the rule of law. Under the constitutional settlement of 1688 the protection of civil liberties was left in the hands of Parliament and of the ordinary courts. Parliament would ensure that only such legislation was passed which was not unduly restrictive of civil liberties while the courts would interpret the law to allow the greatest freedom possible, in accordance with the well established principles of the common law. However, with the growing importance of statutory law and the rise of legal positivism in the nineteenth century this arrangement started to look strained. The rule of law was increasingly identified with certain formal qualities of the law, namely with predictability and legal certainty.[42] But on the basis of the principle of parliamentary sovereignty, even the adherence to the formal requirements of the rule of law very much depended on the will on the legislature, as was demonstrated in the *Burmah Oil* case.[43] Not surprisingly, this positivist understanding of the rule of law, which rested less on elaborate constitutional safeguards than on the proper functioning of the democratic political institutions, has not resisted the rise of rights-based litigation in modern times.

---

[38] *See* C.-A. Colliard, *Libertés publiques* (6th ed., 1982) at 113. Dalloz.

[39] CC decision no. 71–44 of 16 July 1971, Rec. 29.

[40] *See* the new article 61–1 in the French Constitution and Sections 23–1 to 23–12 in the amended Act on the Conseil Constitutionnel; G. Carcassonne & O. Duhamel, QPC, La question prioritaire de constitutionnalité, (2011). Dalloz.

[41] L. Favoreu, *Les grandes décisions du Conseil constitutionnel* (12th ed., 2003) at 478. Dalloz.

[42] I. Harden & N. Lewis, *The Noble Lie – The British Constitution and the Rule of Law* (1986) at 32–33. Hutchinson.

[43] The decision of the House of Lords in *Burmah Oil v. Lord Advocate* [1965] AC 75, which ordered the government to pay compensation for the damages suffered by the applicant company as a result of the destruction of its oil installations during the war, was subsequently nullified through the adoption of the War Damage Act 1965 by the British Parliament.

This rise has contributed to a redefinition of the relations between the judiciary and the executive by pushing for an extension of the limits of judicial review of administrative action, which is today openly based on the constitutional mandate of the courts to protect individuals against the abuse of executive power,[44] into areas and matters which had hitherto been seen as immune to judicial review due to their non-justiciable character.[45] But it has also increasingly called into question the doctrine of parliamentary sovereignty itself. The incorporation of the European Convention on Human Rights into British domestic law by virtue of the Human Rights Act 1997 has given this process a new dimension. The Human Rights Act gives the higher courts the power to issue a declaration of incompatibility in cases where it is not possible to construe a domestic statute in accordance with Convention rights,[46] while leaving the final decision to Parliament on the amendments which have to be made to the legislation in order to bring it into line with the Convention, thus formally preserving parliamentary sovereignty. Essentially, however, the new procedure amounts to the introduction of a limited form of judicial review of legislative action previously unknown to British law.[47]

Even in the United States, where the framers of the Declaration of Independence and the United States Constitution had been committed to the idea of rights early on, individual rights have taken on a wholly new dimension in the period following World War II. Prior to that constitutional rights were not a significant constitutional preoccupation, and the federal courts gave them little support.[48] Not only did the Supreme Court, through a radical reinterpretation of the Fourteenth Amendment, effectively incorporate and render applicable to the states the principal provisions of the Bill of Rights; it also proceeded, without formal amendment to the Constitution, to a reconceptualization and expansion of the eighteenth-century rights contained in that Bill. As Louis Henkin put it: "The Constitution has been opened to every man and woman, to the least and the worst of them. Constitutional protection has moved beyond political rights to civil and personal rights, rooted in conceptions of the essential dignity and worth of the individual. The Constitution safeguards not only political freedom but, in principle, also social, sexual, and other personal freedoms, and individual privacy, autonomy, idiosyncrasy."[49]

The post-war trend towards a substantive definition of the rule of law has not been limited to the national level. When international declarations today speak of the rule of law, they often refer to a "thick" version of the concept which includes

---

[44] D. Oliver, "Is the ultra vires rule the basis of judicial review?", *Public Law* (1987) 543.

[45] *R v. Secretary of State for Foreign and Commonwealth Affairs, ex parte Everett* [1989] QB 811 (concerning the powers of the Home Secretary in relation to immigrants which are not statutory and the power to issue passports); *R v. Secretary of State for the Home Department, ex parte Bentley* [1994] QB 349 (concerning the prerogative of mercy). In *R v Ministry of Defence, ex parte Smith* [1995] 4 All ER 427, 446 Brown LJ summed up this development by stating that "only the rarest cases [affecting individual rights] will today be ruled strictly beyond the court's purview."

[46] Section 4 Human Rights Act 1998.

[47] F. Klug & K. Starmer, "Incorporation through the Back Door?", *Public Law* (1997) 230.

[48] L. Henkin, "Constitutional Rights – Two Hundred Years Later", in *The Age of Rights* (1990) at 116. Columbia University Press.

[49] *Id.* at 119.

respect for human dignity, fundamental rights and democratic participation.[50] In this sense, the UN General Assembly in its recent "Declaration on the Rule of Law at the National and International Levels" expressly recognized that "human rights, the rule of law and democracy are interlinked and mutually reinforcing and that they belong to the universal and indivisible core values and principles of the United Nations."[51] This development reflects the rising expectations of an increasing number of people around the world with regard to the promotion of social justice via a substantive concept of the rule of law. The growth of international human rights after World War II as documented in the numerous human rights instruments adopted under the auspices of the UN, the establishment of regional human rights charters and institutions, and the explicit commitment to the protection and promotion of ever-growing catalogues of rights in a huge number of national constitutions around the world are all testimony to this "rights revolution" which constitutes the basis for the transformation of the ideal of rule of law.

This does not mean, however, that the formal theories of the rule of law have lost their practical relevance. They are of considerable interest to political regimes which understand the need to attract investment and promote economic growth by providing a measure of legal stability but shrink from committing themselves to the values and institutions of a genuine pluralist democracy. In some of these countries rule of law rhetoric is also used in order to fill the ideological vacuum left by the demise of communism.[52] However, such rhetoric will only serve its purposes if it is stripped of those elements which could be employed to challenge the monopoly on political power of the ruling elite, namely civil and political rights. A formal understanding of the rule of law goes some way towards meeting this objective. By using the legislative machinery to implement its policies and the judiciary to control their execution, the political regime is able to strengthen its control over the state bureaucracy and regional power centers, but at the same time avoids any legal challenge to the substance of the policies in question. This is "rule by law", i.e. a form of political rule in which the formal qualities of the law are deliberately employed in order to rationalize the way in which administrative power is exercised.[53] "Rule by law" thus enables the political regime to profit both from increased legitimacy as a result of its perceived ability to reign in a rampant bureaucracy by ensuring that it stays within its legally conferred powers and from greater control over centrifugal forces in the state and party bureaucracies, especially in the periphery.

---

[50] Tamanaha, Rule of Law, *supra* note 30, at 111.

[51] Declaration of the High-level Meeting of the General Assembly on the Rule of Law at the National and International Level, U.N.G.A. Document A/67/L.1.

[52] T. Moustafa, *The Struggle for Constitutional Power* (2007) at 39. Cambridge University Press.

[53] That such "rationalization" is a necessary prerequisite for the development of a dynamic capitalist economy, which is today pursued even by some countries which nominally still define themselves as communist or socialist, was already pointed out by the famous German sociologist Max Weber, *see* Trubek, "Max Weber on Law and the Rise of Capitalism", Wisconsin Law Review (1972) 720, 739–745.

In this contest between the formal and the substantive concepts of the rule of law, the German Rechtsstaat constitutes one of the "thickest" versions of the substantive concept. It is not alone: as has rightly been pointed out, and as the brief survey above suggests, the "thick" substantive rule of law likely approximates the common sense of the rule within Western societies today,[54] and has made significant headway in a number of jurisdictions around the world in the last two decades, although it is still in its infancy or virtually non-existent in others. What sets the German version of the substantive concept of rule of law apart from other substantive models, however, is the technical perfectionism with which it has been implemented. Much effort has been put into creating a comprehensive system of rights protection without "gaps". At the procedural level, Art. 19, para. 4 of the Basic Law grants everybody recourse to the courts for the violation of any of his or her rights by an act of public authority. The provision has been hailed as the "keystone" of the ambitious system of rights protection set up by the Basic Law.[55] In addition, the Basic Law has created one of the most powerful constitutional courts of the world. The Federal Constitutional Court's most important head of jurisdiction, which covers more than 90 % of all the cases referred to it each year, is its power to rule on constitutional complaints brought by individuals for alleged violation of their constitutionally protected fundamental rights by any act of public authority, including legislative acts as well as administrative measures and the decisions issued by courts and tribunals, the ordinary courts as well as the tribunals of the specialized jurisdictions (administrative law, tax matters, social security law, labor law).[56] In the latter case, the Court will examine whether the judicial decision rests on an unsound interpretation of the scope and the contents of the applicable fundamental rights.

In terms of substantive law, the Court has interpreted broadly its role as guardian of the Constitution, and especially of the constitutional Bill of Rights, by adopting a very expansive view of the scope and the effects of the protected fundamental rights. In particular, it has substantially extended the scope of protection by construing the right to free development of one's personality in Art. 2, para. 1 of the Basic Law as a catch-all guarantee which protects any kind of activity that is not covered by one of the more specific fundamental rights provisions of the Basic Law against state interference,[57] and has used the former provision in connection with the principle of human dignity in Art. 1, para. 1 as the basis for framing new rights which had not been envisaged in the original text of the Basic Law, such as the right to decide freely on the use of an individual's personal data.[58] It has construed the fundamental rights of the Basic Law as an "objective order of values" and used this concept as a basis for assigning to the former a multiplicity of functions which go

---

[54] Tamanaha, Rule of Law, supra note 30, at 111.

[55] *See* P.M. Huber, Art. 19 Abs. 4 para. 332, in H. v. Mangoldt & F. Klein & C. Starck, Kommentar zum Grundgesetz, vol. 1 (6th ed., 2010). Verlag Franz Vahlen.

[56] A. Voßkuhle, Art. 93 Abs. 1 Nr. 4a para. 175, in H. v. Mangoldt & F. Klein & C. Starck, Kommentar zum Grundgesetz, vol. 3 (6th ed., 2010).

[57] BVerfGE 6, 32 (36–37) – *Elfes*; 80, 139 (153–154) – *Horse riding in the woods*.

[58] BVerfGE 65, 1 – *National Census*.

far beyond their traditional use in defense of individual liberty against state interference. The fundamental rights doctrine developed by the Court over the years is one of the most comprehensive and elaborate to be found anywhere today.

This reconceptualization of the principle of Rechtsstaat, initiated by the Basic Law and carried further by an activist judiciary under the bold leadership of the Federal Constitutional Court, has had far-reaching implications for the balance of powers in the Federal Republic. The judicialization of politics which has taken place as a result is more thorough in Germany than almost anywhere else. It is not that other countries have not also known periods of major judicial activism in the past: the US Supreme Court in the Warren era or, more recently, the Constitutional Courts of South Africa and Hungary are prime examples. Even in countries like Pakistan or Russia the highest courts have been willing to confront, at times, an overbearing executive. However, Germany seems to be one of the few countries in which the expansion of judicial power has been progressing fairly steadily, without major resistance from the political branches and a resulting institutional crisis. While there have been occasionally sharp criticisms of court decisions by the political class,[59] they have not provoked serious attempts by the legislature and the government to curb the powers of the Court. Most importantly, the Court has enjoyed for decades an exceptional high degree of esteem and support by the public. This is an indication of the enormous trust which a strong majority of citizens places in the Court as the guardian of its most cherished rights. This trust goes a long way in explaining the dramatic shifts in the balance of power between the political branches and the constitutional jurisdiction in favor of the latter which have taken place in Germany since the war and which would probably have been unacceptable almost anywhere else.

[59] The court's decision in 1995 that the hanging of the cross (Kruzifix) on the wall of a public school may violate the religious freedom of non-believers (BVerfGE 93, 1) met with criticism and even outrage in certain sectors of the political class and the population and triggered a discussion whether the law should not be changed to require a super-majority for decisions that quash parliamentary statutes. But the storm of indignation subsided as quickly as it had come.

Chapter 14
The Russian Judicial Doctrine of the Rule of Law: Twenty Years After

Gadis A. Gadzhiev

Abstract This Chapter examines the implementation of the rule of law doctrine in Russia. It focuses primarily on the judicial power of the Constitutional Court. It also undertakes a philosophical analysis of the similarities and differences between the rule of law and the legal state doctrines.

14.1 The Rule of Law and the Legal Doctrines: Historical Context

The rule of law is commonly regarded in Russia as an element of a broader legal concept—that of the legal state.[1] Such a perception can be found in textbooks on constitutional law, in legal doctrine, and in judicial decisions.

According to an observation made by N.S. Bondar, the rule of law is the leading principle in constitutional systems of all modern democracies. As it has been repeatedly mentioned in the rulings of the Constitutional Court of the Russian Federation, the rule of law principle, which the legal system of the Russian Federation is based upon, constitutes an integral part of the legal state qualification.[2]

V.D. Zorkin believes that:

> Interpretation of the rule of law principle in the framework of the legal state concept is, to a great extent, determined by the type of legal awareness lying in its foundation. The distinguishing feature of the Russian Constitution is that it quite clearly formulates its conceptual framework as that based on the natural-legal approach to the understanding of law. … Opposite to the legist type of legal awareness, the natural law doctrine proceeds from the

---

[1] Translator's note: sometimes the latter is also called *the rule-of-law state*.

[2] N.S. Bondar, *Sudebnyi konstitucionalizm v Rossii* (Judicial Constitutionalism in Russia) (2012) at 109.

G.A. Gadzhiev (✉)
Constitutional Court of the Russian Federation, Saint Petersburg, Russia
e-mail: barenpetr@mail.ru

J.R. Silkenat et al. (eds.), *The Legal Doctrines of the Rule of Law and the Legal State (Rechtsstaat)*, Ius Gentium: Comparative Perspectives on Law and Justice 38,
DOI 10.1007/978-3-319-05585-5_14,

availability of an objective criterion for the assessment of legal (or non-legal) nature of legislation, thus making it different from any arbitrary state adjudication. Such a criterion, in the framework of this doctrine, appears to be the inherent and inalienable human rights, the compliance with which provides for a truly legal nature of the legislation in question. Therefore, in the interpretation of the natural law doctrine supporters, the rule of law principle "combines in itself the principle of human rights preeminence with that of legal law supremacy".[3]

Solving cognitive tasks from a certain perspective, one cannot but notice a similarity between the *legal state* (*Rechtsstaat*) concept and that of the *rule of law*. However, another cognitive task aimed at looking for differences between these two concepts may appear equally acceptable—that is the difference between the Anglo-Saxon common law and the continental written Roman law.[4]

The latter cognitive task allows examination of the theoretical content of both the rule of law and the legal state concepts from philosophical-legal perspectives, engaging—for the assessment of the degree of universality existing in these two concepts—various ontological and epistemological toolkits (the reality of law and the legal reality; the legal universalism and relativism in law, regarded as manifestations of realism and nominalism, etc.).

This hypothesis assumes that perhaps it is not only the rule of law and legal state concepts that mutually differ, but it is also the rule of law concept that does not (and cannot) exist as a universal, generally binding concept. Most probably, the rule of law concept is rather a community of homogeneous but significantly different judicial doctrines. The Russian judicial doctrine of the rule of law, currently in the early period of its formation, relies for its development mostly on the well-established historical continental legal tradition. At the same time, this doctrine nurtures some healthy ambitions trying to formulate new ideas related to constitutionalism emerging from constitutional economics. One can only hope that such helpful ambitions would not transform into neophyte arrogance.

The rule of law in Russia develops, for the most part, as a judicial doctrine without active legislator participation. In other words, it is not a concept, but a judicial doctrine.

The legal state is, above all, a scientific concept with close spiritual ties to continental philosophical ideas expressed by political writers of the French Enlightenment and philosophers of German idealism. Any philosophical, ethical, and religious views, dominating in a given state at a given time, seem to inevitably permeate its law, however strongly the latter pretends to seek autonomy.

Immanuel Kant is fairly regarded as the founder of the purely legal *Rechtsstaat* (Legal State) concept. In his understanding, the legal state must be bound by law to make it possible for *Vernunft* (Reason), so highly honored by Kant, to permeate all

---

[3] V.D. Zorkin, *Konstitucionno-pravovoe razvitie Rossii* (Constitutional Legal Development of Russia) (2011) at 53.

[4] P.D. Barenboim, *Sootnoshenie doktrin verhovenstva prava i pravovogo gosudarstva kak glavnyi vopros filosofii prava i konstitucionalizma* (The Interrelation of the Rule of Law and the Legal State Doctrines as the Key Issue of Legal Philosophy and Constitutionalism) (2013).

strata of social relations. In fact, Kant by no means sought to substantiate the legal idea of the rule of law. For Kant, it was Law (rather than human rights alone) that paved the way to the embodiment of Reason.[5] It would hardly be fruitful to argue which of the two concepts—that of the rule of law or that of the legal state—is better. In historical perspective, both of them have had their own ups and downs. None of the continental courts of Europe, guided by the legal state concept, has ever had an importance in the nation's political structure or an influence on the nation's public opinion, that could, even in the least degree, be comparable to those enjoyed by the English and North American courts. Alexis de Tocqueville, comparing Switzerland with England, concluded that it was the Anglo-Saxons' inherent love of public justice, together with a peaceful and lawful intervention of judges into the field of politics, that represented the most characteristic features of a free nation.[6]

On the European continent the major efforts were directed at creating positive constitutional law in the form of declarations and constitutions. However, in England, courts had primarily devised the legal means intended to forcefully recognize a right and guarantee it; and then, without resorting to positive constitutional law, provided links between the basic rights *per se* and the means of their guaranteeing by way of judicial rule-making. *Ibi jus ibi remedium!* (For every right there must be a remedy!)

Since Kant was a great deal more preoccupied with the mechanism of the state power than with the individual rights of citizens, his concept was named *Rechtsstaat*. The autonomy of an individual was a good way to produce the criterion—derived from the entirety of Kant's philosophical ideas—of a well-designed state as the Kingdom of Reason. Kant deduces the state order from the individual self-justness (i.e. self-conscious legal awareness of a rational person). Just as in the nineteenth century aprioristic abstract principles of moral philosophy became the legal foundation of state, so later—in the twentieth century—legal principles became the pillars of capitalism.

The German *Rechtsstaat* concept is in thrall to the enthusiastic belief that there exist certain aprioristic principles which are axiomatic by definition. In Russian legal philosophy, these Kantian ideas were developed by Ye.V. Spektorsky who described the ontological problem of the existence of law with the help of such philosophical category as "moral life awareness". In his opinion, both law and morality, given all their difference, inevitably possess a common feature, being special ethical relation of law and morality to people's actions. Both these normative systems are co-subordinated to moral life awareness, which is based on two principles:

1. a belief in the freedom of human will and the ability of each individual to properly choose and decide whether to perform one's moral/legal duty or not;

[5] Translator's note: in Russian, *law* and *right*—as legal terms—are represented by the same word *pravo*, hence the play on words in the original.

[6] A.V. Dicey, "Osnovy gosudarstvennogo prava Anglii", *A Digest of the Law of England* (1907) 210.

2. a belief that both moral and legal standards exist objectively, since there exist common aprioristic paired criteria of the "just-unfair" and the "good-evil". Without resorting to these objective criteria, it becomes impossible to subject the human activity to any ethical and legal qualification.[7]

The ideas of the legal state and the rule of law took shape on the basis of the notion of the "constitution", which, as Jürgen Habermaass once observed, points to the restriction of political domination by way of distributive separation of powers. This notion—embodied already in ancient parliaments or nobility councils, and adapted for collective representation as an idea of reciprocal limitation and balance "of supreme powers"—evolved, in modernistic theories of state, into a notion of distributive "separation of supremacy" or "separation of sovereign's power". This idea then merged with such individualistic concepts as the doctrine of human rights in the English liberalism—and the division of the legislative, executive and judiciary in the German constitutionalism. That led to the emergence of two realizations of the *verhovenstvo prava* (*Vorrangstellung des Rechts*) idea: that of the rule of law and that of the legal state, both of which were aimed at restricting the arbitrariness of power.

These liberal types of constitution, just as those republican constitutions that Kant geared to, both sought the same goal—to give a legal form to political domination.[8]

The belief in aprioristic principles is a distinguishing feature of metaphysics, traditional for philosophical realism. The essence of the dispute on realism and nominalism was formulated by medieval scholars. The same problem, though in a somewhat primitive form, was conceived by Porphyrios as early as the third century. He wondered whether the genera and species existed in reality or only in thought. And, if they existed in reality, did each of them possess a bodily existence which was separate from the tangibly perceived objects or not? Accordingly, scholars inquired whether the general notions were, as the nominalists asserted, nothing more than just a logical generalization, a summation of identical signs, a verbal designation of a group of identical or similar objects.

The North American philosophical tradition develops the English pragmatism of Locke and Hobbes. In the light of modern hermeneutical and postmodernistic philosophical trends, the pragmatism of W. James and the historicism of J. Dewey forms a belief about the necessity of a new philosophical ideology which will sever umbilical ties with the epistemology of Plato, Descartes, and Kant and the view of philosophy as a mere reflection of the world.

Richard MacKay Rorty argues that science does not describe the reality. Rather it adapts to reality with the help of metaphysical visualizations. And the language of science has proved itself to be successful only for the pragmatic purposes of

[7] Ye. Spektorsky, "K sporu o real'nosti prava" (On the Dispute About the Reality of Law), *Yuridicheskii vestnik* (1914), Vol. 5.

[8] Jürgen Habermaass, *Raskolotyi Zapad* (The Divided West) (2008) at 127–128. Noviy Mir.

prediction and monitoring, while scientific progress is just the integration of an ever-growing amount of data into the interconnected cobweb of beliefs.

Rorty is convinced in the falsity of not only the epistemological, but also the ethical tradition. He argues that Kant deduced the moral from the "reason" and considered its rules to be universal, whereas one needs to treat the moral in Darwin's manner, i.e. as the natural rules of human cohabitation which originated as a result of adaptation to the natural and social environment. Therefore, such notions as "universal duty" and "responsibilities" ought to be replaced by notions of "prudence" and "practicability", while such one as "moral progress" should be interpreted in a sense of growing sympathy with the needs of an ever-increasing number of people. This is why Rorty, as a pragmatist, believes that a notion such as "unconditional (absolute) human rights" does not have any universal justification to exist either, since the legal rules fit for some societies are not suited for others. In the history of thought, there existed no impersonal idealistic logic. At different times the same "perpetual problems" were imbued with different meanings. There were only the accidental, epistemologically incomparable utterances of some people and the reaction of others to these. Therefore, Rorty suggests building the presentation of the intellectual past by proceeding from nominalism, instead of realism (i.e. in the form of a description of changing metaphors and images, expressing the *Zeitgeist*).[9]

The spiritual sources of the rule of law doctrine and the legal state concept obviously do not coincide, since they include such deep philosophical differentiations as the dichotomy of realism and nominalism, researched by Ye.V. Spektorsky.[10] The realists professed the primacy of epistemology and metaphysics, the fundamental and ontological superiority of the common and the ideal over the particular and empirical. The nominalists, however, tended to acknowledge the world of empirical facts as the only reality. The whole range of concepts and phenomena of the state life acquired a completely different meaning depending on whether the nominalistic or realistic angle of view was used. So, for example, the constitution of a certain state gets interpreted by a realist as something autotelic and possessing transcendental reality, regardless of the actual correlation of political (or other) powers. For a nominalist, the constitution is something completely different. The nominalist sees it as a monument of legislative scripture or the way Ferdinand Lassalle did in his *Über Verfassungswesen* speech, where he understood the valid constitution of each country as a real correlation of the current factors and forces in its political and cultural life.[11]

For Kant, the ideas of linkage and restriction by law or legal statute (and not only by human rights) constituted the basis of legal state perceptions. Kant had

[9] R. Rorty, *Filosofiya i zerkalo prirody* (Philosophy and the Mirror of Nature) (1997). Publishing House of the Novosibirsk University.

[10] Ye.V. Spektorsky, "Nominalizm i realizm v obschestvennyh naukah" (Nominalism and Realism in Social Sciences), *Yuridicheskii vestnik* (1915), Vol. 9 (1).

[11] *Id.* at 18. When Kant declared as universal such elements of cognition, which were made real not by an *a priori* reality of *ante res* and not by an inductive reality of *in rebus*, he was, to a certain degree, also resolving a dispute between realists and nominalists, and he did so in the spirit of conciliatory conceptualism. *Id.* at 5.

consistently arrived not at the rule of law but at the theory of state supremacy. It meant that the individual was to obey the supreme leadership of the state to which the highest moral principle was granted. This idealism took a bad turn in the twentieth century when the Weimar Republic—in whose constitution the legal state concept was duly recognized—evolved (and quite legally so!) into a Nazi totalitarian state. The German people did not possess any significant experience of democratic movement fostered by the judicial rule of law doctrine. This left a mark on the implementation of the legal state concept in reality. If in England the rule of law was traditionally linked to the supremacy of the Parliament, in the Weimar Republic, thanks to the intellectual efforts of Karl Schmitt, the office of *Reichspräsident*[12] became central in the German system of state power.

The spirit of Roman law, borrowed from the discipline intrinsic to the Roman army, became a legal national tradition.

Why should legislation be discussed as lawful or not? The law must be rigorously obeyed. Avoiding impotence of the state power is the prime requirement. Any such impotence, according to Schmitt, who followed the Machiavellian tradition, should be overcome both by the use of ruse and cruelty. See the Jesuit saying which comes in handy—*Exitus acta probat!* (The end justifies the means!). Today, the ideas of Karl Schmitt have suddenly become quite popular again on the wave of the so-called *Realpolitik*—much in vogue over the recent years. This phenomenon is usually associated with the name of a really effective politician—the Prussian chancellor Otto von Bismarck. Often in the works of political scientists, a target-oriented policy of such type, striving to achieve political ends while disregarding any norms of morality, is indicated with this term. Such policy is implemented by balancing on the brink of permissible and impermissible in the legal and ethical spheres. Again, the most important guidelines of Jesuitism are the Inquisition, the idea of *infallibilitas ex cathedra*[13] and Escobarism—in other words, the rule of "the end justifies the means."

The discussion spawned by Karl Schmitt on the pages of his book *The Concept of the Political* is quite relevant for today's Russia, because it provides a possibility to understand the meaning underlying the Russian constitutionalism and the Russian doctrine of the rule of law. When the new Constitution of Russia was adopted in 1993, everybody was in a state of euphoria, expecting a rapid liberalization to instantly solve all problems. But this euphoria appeared to be accompanied by what Joseph Stalin had once referred to as the "dizziness from success". Then, it suddenly turned out that energetic people with bulging wallets had bent the electoral system to full submission. Adding to the disaster was the fact that a good number of them had a criminal past. But could have it been otherwise? The Soviet Communist ideology had always been strongly opposed to the base spirit of individualist moneymaking. Democratic liberalization in the regions of Russia resulted in an outbreak of crime and corruption, while the rank-and-file citizens started coming to a sad conclusion that liberalism, constitutionalism, and the legal state had all been conceived

[12] A.N. Sokolov, *Id*, at 69.

[13] Infallibility from the [papal] throne (Lat.)

in the interests of criminal godfathers. Such were the sources of a forced change in the parabola of Russia's internal policy. The legal state of the early twenty-first century began to be replaced by a strong state. As the past decade has shown, this strong state, in addition to significant success, also possessed serious disadvantages. Hypocrisy and cynicism have weakened the beneficial potential of the idea of a strong state, which looked so similar to the national ideals of Karl Schmitt. The weakening of parliamentarianism for the purposes of mobilization of state power in the spirit "of political symphonia", as one of the Byzantium's foremost state-legal ideas, very painfully affects the rule of law. It turned out that constitutionalism behaved very much the way the simple model of communicating vessels does when demonstrated in class during physics lessons: if the legislative weakens, so instantly does the judiciary, being an organizational structure required for the rule of law mechanism to function. It is regrettable to admit that just as *genius is incompatible with villainy* (Alexander Pushkin's words), so a strong state is incompatible with strong justice. A strong state is an uncomfortable place not only for parliamentarianism, but also for constitutional justice, which usually resides in the dark space, between the law and politics. The boundaries of constitutional control are located inside the "game zone" of political power, and it is impossible to delineate them with a topographical precision. Judges, as a rule, are patriotic and responsible. As a result, a complex dilemma arises between the maintenance of the rule of law and the realization that a strong state is objectively required for its subsequent gradual transformation into a legal state.

14.2 The Russian Judicial Doctrine of the Rule of Law

So what does the modern Russian judicial doctrine of the rule of law actually represent? Firstly, as a product of the activity of Russian courts (above all, the Constitutional Court of the Russian Federation) and despite all its conflicts with the national legal tradition, it still thrusts its sprouts like the shoots of grass through the asphalt, reaching for the sun. Strange it may seem, it is helpful to start a description of the Russian doctrine of the rule of law from a bit of legalese linguistics. The legal concept of "the rule of law" (*verhovenstvo prava*) emerged in Russia thanks to the new Russian Constitution of 1993, although these words are not expressly found in its text. This constitution recognized that all international treaties signed on behalf of the Russian Federation were an integral part of its legal system. The European Convention for the Protection of Human Rights and Fundamental Freedoms (European Convention), thanks to the Russian Constitution and in accordance with the rulings of the Constitutional Court of the Russian Federation, became not just a legal act exceeding the force of ordinary federal laws, but a subsidiary set of criteria to determine the constitutionality of all Russian laws.

This is how "the rule of law" concept, mentioned in the text of the European Convention, came into legal circulation in Russia. However, some oddities, related to the problem of translation of legal terminology and reflecting serious and deep concepts and doctrines, could not be forgone. Russia failed to immediately understand the significance of the Constitution text's reality. In the text of the Russian Constitution, there are no such words as "the rule of law" (*verhovenstvo prava*). Nonetheless, the judicial doctrine of the rule of law is the basis of Russian constitutional law. So where did it come from, given its clear absence from the text of the Constitution? The constitutional law in Russia is now regarded as a kind of legal, indicative-symbolic, conceptual space. At the foundation of constitutional law's conceptualism lies an idea, according to which the text of Constitution utilizes certain words or word-combinations as symbols or images, producing—in the minds of enlightened lawyers—instant associations with well-known legal concepts and doctrines. These symbols (images) are represented by such terms as "democracy", "republic", "legal state", etc. To better understand this idea, one may compare the text of the constitution to shorthand notes.[14] The reality of the text of constitution and the reality of constitutional law are not the same thing.

In its Resolution No.1594 (2007), entitled "The Rule of Law Principle", the Assembly of the Council of Europe drew special attention to the fact that in some new democratic states of Eastern Europe most lawyers tend to expound "the rule of law" as "the supremacy of statute law" (*verhovenstvo zakona*); actually, it is none other but the latter that is mentioned in Article 4(2) of the Constitution of the Russian Federation. However, "the rule of law" correctly translates into Russian as *verhovenstvo prava*. Further, the EC Resolution emphasizes that the terms *the rule of law* and *la prééminence du droit* are nominal legal concepts which are fully synonymous and must be regarded as such in all English and French language versions of the documents published by the EC Assembly.

The fallacious translation of "the rule of law" as "*verhovenstvo zakona*" (i.e. "the supremacy of statute law") is very much indicative of the fact that such a legal judicial concept as the rule of law has until recently been unused and deprecated in Russia. Although legal terms can technically be translated, one still doubts whether the true understanding of their actual meaning, hidden behind the word shell, can always be rendered. Each national legal language was developed in the framework of a particular legal culture and on the basis of a particular legal theory. Due to this particularity, the target language often does not have adequate terms with which to translate certain foreign (alien) legal concepts.[15]

The rule of law, as a term of legal English, belongs to a legal culture based on *case law* (or *common law*). If in another country this system does not exist, the translation of such term as *the rule of law* may be technically possible; however, in another language, such a translation will be devoid of any real meaning, with the notion having been completely cut off from its roots. Therefore, such term as

[14] G.A. Gadzhiev, *Ontologiya prava* (The Ontology of Law) (2013), at 237. Norma, Infra-M.

[15] A. Nussberger, "Vosstanovlenie Vavilonskoi bashni" in "Edinoe pravovoe prostranstvo Evropy i praktika konstitucionnogo pravosudiya"—Sbornik dokladov ("Rebuildng the Tower of Babel", in "The Common Legal Space of Europe and the Practice of Constitutional Justice" – A Collection of Scientific Papers) (2007) at 22.

verhovenstvo prava will become meaningful only after the appearance of Russia's own judicial doctrine of the rule of law.

But are there in Russia any prerequisites for this? And, if they exist, in what stage is the making of such a doctrine which, even being original, will nevertheless enter the family of similar concepts existing in other countries?

Although the Constitution of the Russian Federation is more than 20 years old, and the new Russian constitutionalism is quickly developing, the judicial concept of the rule of law is only in the beginning of its formation. Its sources may be tracked to the beginning of active judicial rulemaking, which the Constitutional Court of the Russian Federation initiated in the middle of 1990s. The emergence of legal views of the Constitutional Court of the Russian Federation, arising from its interpretation of the Constitution, marked the emergence of judicial constitutionalism.[16]

The second important step in the development of the rule of law concept in Russia was the entry into the Russian legal space of the legal views adopted by the European Court for Human Rights, which followed the ratification by Russia of the European Convention. This is a starting reference point for a grandiose project of Russian participation in the European integration.[17] From the very beginning of formation of the new Russian constitutionalism, Russian lawyers and economists have paid serious attention to the correlation between the process of economic globalization and spontaneous rapprochement of legal systems of various countries, especially, on the European continent. Apparently, the care for economic progress, together with the healthy competition between different national legal systems, became the reason why the ideas of constitutional economics became so popular in Russia. The Constitutional Court of the Russian Federation started actively referring in its decisions to the legal views of the European Court of Human Rights (ECHR). This looked as if it were a retransmission tower broadcasting the signals received from Strasbourg, across the vast expanses of Russia. However, these references are not always relevant to the essence of legal problems discussed by the Constitutional Court of the Russian Federation. This happens because in Russia there was no strong tradition of case law. But still, judicial legislation did exist in the Russian Empire in the second half of the nineteenth century thanks to the activity of the Ruling Senate.[18]

Ten years passed after the ratification by Russia of the European Convention before any essential notions of what was a "fair court" appeared in Russia as an important element of the Russian judicial doctrine of the rule of law.

The Russian legal tradition of the supremacy of statute law (*verhovenstvo zakona*) started being replaced by the rule of law doctrine (*verhovenstvo prava*). The most noteworthy in this process was that it had—and quite properly so—been

---

[16] *See* Bondar, supra note 2.

[17] V. Zorkin, "Integraciya evropeiskogo konstitucionnogo prostranstva: vyzovy i otvety", "Edinoe pravovoe prostranstvo Evropy i praktika konstitucionnogo pravosudiya" – Sborkik dokladov, supra note 15, at 134.

[18] I.M. Tyutryumov, *Zakony grajdanskie s raz'yasneniyami Pravitel'stvuyuschego Senata* (Civil Laws with Clarifications by the Ruling Senate) (1911).

initiated and implemented by Russian courts themselves, practically without participation of the legislative branch of the government.

One can and should criticize the Russian judiciary in a constructive (and, preferably, a friendly) manner. But still it is an indisputable and objective fact that the Russian judiciary has already coped with the most important task. While demonstrating its constitutional status as an independent power (Art. 10 of the Constitution of the Russian Federation), it started—with an active support of the European Court—to create a groundbreaking system of sources of law, including judicial acts of the supreme courts; formed new legal principles and forced the legislator to alter organizational structures of the judiciary.

The most convincing example of the increased constitutional independence of the judiciary is the change in the system of supervision which, being obviously inherited from the Soviet system of public justice, came into direct tension with the principle of legal certainty, as one of the basic elements of the rule of law.

Perhaps, when in 2007 the Constitutional Court was considering a case about the check of constitutional compliance in the norms of procedural law envisaging a system of supervision, it became clear what significance for the Russian legal system bore the words from the Preamble to the Europe Convention, which the ECHR used for the clarification of the right-to-fair-trial content: "…the rule of law is recognized as part of the common [legal] heritage of the contracting states."

Having emerged in the Soviet Union, the system of legislative supervision was, in fact, linked to the tradition of strong prosecution, existing in Russia since the early eighteenth century. It was based on the idea of legality and required the executive to oversee the activity of the judiciary, allowing it after the passage of time to appeal against court decisions which had already become legally effective. In fact, this idea presumed a high probability of judicial mistakes and a considerable degree of mistrust towards courts, which necessitated the procuratorship to constantly supervise their activities. Regulation No. 2-П of February 5, 2007, issued by the Constitutional Court of the Russian Federation, literally having "arisen" from the ECHR's legal views, institutionalized the principle of legal certainty in the Russian legal system. Not only had it destroyed the legislative system of supervision and degraded the power of prosecution, but it had also mandated the legislature to start using the principle of legal certainty in legislation. So after such reloading of the legal system, the judiciary found itself to be the "master", while the legislature became the "slave".

Almost the entire design of the judicial system was changed in a most radical way after the Supreme Arbitration Court of the Russia Federation (SAC-RF) became proactively involved in the process of judicial rulemaking. The Constitutional Court of the Russian Federation, also with references to the legal views of the European Court of Human Rights, confirmed the constitutional compliance of the decision by the SAC-RF to increase the role of judicial rulemaking, once again adopted by the Supreme Arbitration Court without participation of the legislature. In legal resolution No. 1-П of January 21, 2010, the Constitutional Court of the Russian Federation explicitly endorsed the notion that any denial of the right of the Supreme Arbitration Court of the Russian Federation to provide abstract interpretation of the legal norms applied by the courts or to form respective legal views should be treated as derogation both of its constitutional functions and its designation as the highest authority in the system of arbitration courts. Thus it was confirmed that, in the Russian judicial system, the interpretation of law by supreme judicial authorities had a significant impact on the formation of judicial practice. As a general rule, this becomes binding for any subordinated courts in the future. This idea is a most important one. In fact, the emergence of precedent-based (case law) approaches in the Russian legal system, which constitutes a necessary environment for the development of the rule of law, has been carried out in Russia by supreme courts with the tacit consent of other branches of power, which thereby recognized one of the most important principles of constitutionalism: the legislative, the executive and the judiciary must be independent.

Constitutional review of the procedural rules of judicial supervision and provisions used by the Supreme Arbitration Court to develop case law, could be treated as conflicts, which resolved the fundamental antagonism between new principles of the rule of law (such as the rule of legal certainty, the right to fair trial, etc.) and outdated elements of the Russian legal tradition. This resolution marks the formation of the Russian judicial concept of the rule of law.

Another high court—the Supreme Court of Russia—displayed passivity in the recognition of judicial rulemaking which led to a new tension between the supreme courts themselves. It has been resolved by the initiative of the President of the Russian Federation who proposed to merge the Supreme Arbitration Court and the Supreme Court of the Russian Federation. This is how important the rule of law doctrine appears. Advancing with the slow but resonant footsteps of the come-alive statue of *Commendatore* from A.S. Pushkin's poetic tragedy "The Stone Guest", it transforms the Russian legal system by subjecting it to in-depth modernization, quite aside from even the inevitable updates to the Constitution.

One can visualize the Russian doctrine of the rule of law as a honeycomb with bee honey. All of its cells are supposed to be completely filled with honey. However, if the bees are not too active, many cells remain empty. It is difficult to say how well-filled at the moment the comb of the Russian doctrine of the rule of law is.

The rule of law should be regarded as an independent judicial doctrine and, therefore, treating it as an element of the legal state concept and what is worse, equating these two, would most unproductive. The rule of law is also radically different from the system of views represented by such legal notion as *verhovenstvo zakona* (the supremacy of statute law).

The rule of law in Russia has some prerequisites in Russian legal history in the activity of the Russian supreme courts in the second half of the nineteenth century. In the legal culture of Russia, being a lawful heiress to the traditions of Byzantium, there are many things directly antagonistic to the rule of law. It is quite enough to mention the so-called "political symphonia", a system of views, which emerged in the imperial Byzantium and according to which the latter was an *ideological state*, or a *state of concordance*, or a *political symphonia*, as it was called in Byzantium.[19]

[19] V.V. Bibihin, *Vvedenie v filosofiyu prava* (An Introduction to Legal Philosophy) (2005) at 190. Institute of Philosophy of the Russian Academy of Sciences.

But making Russia an heiress to the Byzantine totalitarian traditions, as A. Toynbee attempted to do, can hardly be permissible. Russia possesses the most essential asset necessary for the rule of law to develop successfully: it is her patriotic people who love their country and, as the Preamble to the Russian Constitution says, "recognize themselves as an integral part of the world community." These are well-educated and cultured people belonging to the nation which produced such men of genius as Pushkin, Tolstoy, Dostoevsky, Sholokhov, Korolev, etc. As prerequisites for the emergence of a Russian model of the rule of law, one can also name the solid constitution and the judiciary, developing the principles of case law, and devoted to the idea of constitutionalism and the rule of law. Russia still remembers what irreparable damage may be inflicted on the society by an unlimited power of the totalitarian state. Some of those who had suffered from the atrocities of the Communist state are still alive and their voices are heard.

There is an understanding that one needs to distinguish between legal reality and the reality of law. This means that the text of constitution is a system of conceptual notions open for creative interpretation by the supreme courts. As V.D. Zorkin likes to reiterate, the Russian constitution is not a fossilized text, but a very flexible system of legal principles. In fact, this is a declaration of intent to modernize the traditional statutory positive law and adopt everything valuable from the European and world legal culture. Russians also have a sense of responsibility and a good knowledge of their country, preventing them from recklessly unselective adoption of every legal notion, passed off as universal. There is an ongoing complex intellectual process of conscious perception involving the notions of basic human rights, as seen through a prism of philosophical categories of nominalism—realism. What must prevail in the domestic conceptions of basic human rights—universalism (realism, legal metaphysics) or nominalism (the latter accounts for national cultural originality, though not degraded to a set of historically outdated prejudices)? The search for balance continues; the comb cells are still waiting to be completely filled with honey.

A number of methodological problems, still waiting to be solved for the making of a Russian model of the rule of law, currently remain at an early stage of evolving discussion. These are a set of ontological problems of the reality of human rights. Specifically, this is a question about what these human rights are, whether they become such only after their reflection in the legislation, or can one recognize the legal reality of proto-rights—in other words, the people's claims of freedom as a certain legal reality? Robert Alexy posed a good question concerning the existence of rights.[20] He noted that, if human rights did not exist, then constitutional rights would be limited only to what was contained in the text of constitution. In such a case, constitutional law would possess a solely positivistic nature, with originalism and textualism as the only possible options of the theory of constitutional interpretation. If so, then the constitutional rights are to be understood as a result of constitutional reflection of human rights. But the Constitution of the Russian Federation

[20] Robert Alexy, "Suschestvovanie prav cheloveka" (The Existence of Human Rights), 4 *Pravovedenie* (2011).

consistently presents a whole number of legal ideas, in accordance with which human rights are inalienable and belong to each person from birth, while the enumeration of basic rights and freedoms in the constitution must not be construed as denial of other recognized human and civil rights and freedoms. Courts as agencies of the state must not only protect but also recognize human rights and freedoms (Art. 17(2), 55(1), 2 of the Constitution of the Russian Federation). One can suggest an ontological hypothesis, in accordance with which the proto-rights should be considered the legal reality, while the rights, having undergone positivation, i.e. recognized by the state, would be quite another reality—the reality of rights. Alexy correctly viewed these ontological disputes as directly linked to the most important controversial problems of the world politics. These are problems of the universal nature of basic rights and cultural relativism. If human rights exist, common institutes must exist as well. But the notion of "institutes", the legal standards of rights can be compatible with a quite considerable cultural diversity. Such influential in the legal community judicial thinkers as V.D. Zorkin, A. Nussberger, H.-J. Papier, G. Lübbe-Wolffe—all recognize the need to account for differences in the legal cultures of different countries, without regarding such cultural relativism as a threat to the global law and order. Thus, the rule of law doctrine can easily draw inspiration from legal philosophy.

The rule of law doctrine has especial importance for the judiciary because it formulates in a concentrated form the chief objectives of justice. This is a holistic system of legal ideas, which not only forms the key objectives of justice, but also contains the methodology of actions for each judge deciding a specific case. The nucleus of the rule of law idea in Russia is the belief that the independence of court as a constitutional principle is one of the primary pillars of constitutionalism. If a court is sufficiently independent in its relations with the political bodies of the state, it can engage in an in-court search for legal decisions in a concrete case. This is a development of the idea from Hegel's "Philosophy of Right." He wrote that cognition of right is achieved in each concrete case. This is a special field of epistemology meaning the court's cognition of what the law is, which human rights should be respected, and, when a conflict between equal human rights arises, which thereof needs to be given priority.

By virtue of the rule of law, justice itself acquires great power—that of the extraction of right from the circumstances of a concrete dispute by using aprioristic legal principles. Application of constitutional principles for the creation of new legal norms (i.e. legal views of courts) is not only the means employed by judges, but also the primary goal of justice.

The judiciary cognition in such an interpretation (i.e. in the spirit of legal realism) of which Michel Troper wrote, must rely on the ontological determination of human rights.

It is time to overcome the deontologisation of law accomplished by Hans Kelsen in his "Pure Theory of Law", where he narrowed down legal reality to the already existing reality of positive law.

Since rights exist in the legal reality, the nature of which is non-legal, one needs to especially scrutinize still unrecognized rights, those not specified in constitutions.

There, in the legal reality, exist the subjects who are endowed with initiative, a sense of novelty, a predisposition for legal innovations. They emit the energy capable of creating a new gravitational field, able to convince judges of the necessity to recognize new human rights and freedoms.

Using the approach for the ontological determination of human rights, which predetermines and changes the essence of judicial cognition, it is already impossible to confine oneself to the legal syllogism relying on the "ground rule" of Hans Kelsen. The legal syllogism consists in a simplified understanding of the tasks of justice. At the same time, jurisprudence is regarded as a completely autonomous discipline, well-isolated from economics, philosophy, ethics, and sociology. It is enough to take a premise—and this is a set of vital circumstances having caused the dispute—then find some suitable legal norms (and this is the second premise), then superimpose these circumstances. Finally, obtain a proper conclusion (i.e. a legal syllogism in the form of a court decision). Such an approach utilizes a fiction, which says that sources of law can provide the answers to any legal questions by virtue of the self-sufficiency of law. Sometimes, such an approach engenders what in the practice of the European Court of Human Rights is referred to as "formal justice". Meanwhile, the rule of law doctrine disposes a judge to search not for a formally correct decision but for a rightful and just decision, because the part of this doctrine is the right to fair trial.

Hence, it is the rule of law doctrine that proves to be the most influential for constitutional justice because it demands the economization, socialization, and moralization of justice. That is, it requires the courts not to limit themselves to strictly legal arguments in search of a just decision.

The rule of law represents, therefore, a new concept of law enforcement. As such, it requires the socialization of law. Public justice, to be able to find and take fair decisions, requires extensive non-legal information in the form of sociological, economical and other data. It is particularly important to discover—with the help of analysis of the existing law enforcement practice—any "spontaneously arising" (V.D. Zorkin's term) non-legal methods. Constitutional courts, when checking constitutional compliance of a certain legal norm, cannot be limited only to checking the letter thereof. By applying only the letter of a legal norm, courts and other law enforcers sometimes create entirely different norms, undermining the intent of the source originator. Often, the same legal norm receives different interpretations in different courts across the country. This is exactly what was meant by "spontaneously arising" legal (and sometimes non-legal) methods. Vividly expressing this thought, one can say that, alongside a benign legal norm, "a malignant tumor" may develop. The Constitutional Court must excise all these "malignant tumors." This most important function of constitutional justice also emerged as part of the Russian judicial doctrine of the rule of law.

Here also are discovered new facets of the distinctions between the legal state concept and the rule of law doctrine. The legal state concept focuses on human rights as a result of their reflection in the legislation, while emphasizing the role of the state, in the absence of which these human rights can be neither recognized nor protected. It largely focuses on the nature of state, while the rule of law doctrine is more preoccupied with the ontological nature of human rights and their primacy in the ontological worldview. The rule of law doctrine, in my opinion, must be looking towards the sphere of legal reality, "the factual". The concept of the legal state is more disposed to account not for "the factual", but for "the proper". It seems that in general, the focus on "the factual" reality instead of "the proper" ideal is typical for the spiritual history and legal tradition of Europe. This is why it is so important to find a balance between nominalism and realism. In its endeavor to take into consideration the national legal tradition and the inertial elements of public conscience, modern Russian judicial constitutionalism is also looking towards "the factual". Isensee remarks that a constitution not only codifies the basic legal norms. The real constitution also codifies the ties with the people's past.[21] He also pays attention to the normative significance of the words in the preambles of constitutions. In the Constitution of the Russian Federation, these are the words that the multinational people of Russia are united by its common fate on its native land; that, preserving the historically formed state unity, this people honors the memory of its ancestors who bequeathed their love and respect to their homeland—their faith in the good and the just.

Surely, the ontological methodology of differentiation between the two different realities—legal reality and that of human rights, recognized by the state,—exposes a complex dilemma, the resolution of which is constantly exercised by courts: whether to proceed from the priority of the text of constitution, or to give the priority to the judicial interpretation of this text, together with judicial rulemaking which will require regular updates to the constitution. It seems this dilemma is a simple one, and the choice must be made in favor of the second option. However, allowing to regularly change notions in the constitution text (per the second option) would entail the risk of emergence of judicial views (and even doctrines) antagonistic to the rule of law doctrine. This makes this option comparable in vulnerability to the first one. A desire to coordinate the constitution text with the changing realities of life, new social interests, and volatile balance of political powers can lead to overt revisionism.

But to what extent is such a "living constitution" to be dependent on politics? Or, to the contrary, how autonomous should it be from it? This is yet another complicated and, in many ways, unresolved question. Does constitutional law need to be separated by a high wall from the sphere of the political, economic, religious, ethical—in the spirit of Kelsenian purity; or, vice versa, does the new constitutionalism allow for the influence on the constitutional law by "adjacent" intellectual realms—in the spirit of R. Posner and J. Buchanan? After all, politics can easily "overwhelm" constitutional law—which is nearer to the sphere of the political than all other branches of law—and even completely emasculate the rule of law doctrine. In this connection, another division line, drawn by us between the legal state concept and the rule of law doctrine, may appear important. The former regards—as one of its constructive elements—the principle of proportionality between the goals of rights restriction, introduced by the state, and the legal means, used by it for this

[21] *Gosudarstvennoe pravo Germanii* (German National Law), Vol. 1 (1994) at 12.

purpose. Speaking as a partisan of the legal state concept, J. Isensee acknowledges that the latter "cannot solve the dilemma of how to avoid the mollification of constitutional state without finding oneself in a state frozen in its development and totally unhinged from reality."[22]

In the United States, where the rule of law doctrine is treated with much respect, the principle of proportionality is avoided so as not to stress the risks intrinsic to this judicial technology.[23] It does not mean, however, that United States courts do not engage in balancing competing basic rights. U.S. courts use another technique by applying a fiction, according to which one of the rights is not restricted at all, but they just discover the true limits of its normative content. This shows a more respectful treatment of the rule of law, although this respect is implemented with the help of legal fictions.

Constitutional laws of Europe and Russia allow for restriction of rights. Art. 18 of the European Convention establishes that the restrictions allowed in the Convention with respect to the aforementioned rights and freedoms must not apply for purposes other than those for which they were stipulated. For example, the freedom of expression (Art. 10 of the Convention) can be connected with certain formalities, conditions, restrictions, or sanctions which are provided by law and are necessary in a democratic society to prevent disorder or crime, to protect health and morality, to protect reputation or rights of other persons, to prevent disclosure of information received confidentially, and to protect authority and impartiality of justice. For each of the basic rights in the Convention an independent set of values is stipulated, to ensure the protection of which the respective right can be restricted. A different legal technique is applied in Art. 55 (3) of the Constitution of the Russian Federation.

The essence of the above difference is as follows. In Part 3 of Art. 55 of the Constitution of the Russian Federation, the federal legislature may introduce restrictions on human and civil rights and freedoms by passing a respective law, but only to the extent that it is necessary for the purposes of: (1) protection of foundations of the constitutional system, (2) protection of morality, (3) protection of health, (4) protection of rights, and legitimate interests of other persons, (5) support of national defense, and (6) protection of state security.

Can all these six goals be taken into account to justify the restriction of the constitutional right of dissemination? Or is it admissible to use another interpretation of Part 3, Art. 55 of the Constitution of the Russian Federation which proceeds from the location of Art. 55 in Chapter 2 of the Constitution of the Russian Federation, which is entitled "Human and Civil Rights and Freedoms"? This article completes

---

[22] *Id* at 14.

[23] S. Tsakirakis, "Proportionality: An Assault on Human Rights?", 2 *Comparative Constitutional Review* (2011); Bernhard Schlink, "Proportionality" (to be printed); Moshe Cohen-Eliya, Iddo Porat, "American Method of Weighting Interests and German Test of Proportionality: Historical Roots", 3 *Comparative Constitutional Review* (2011); Madkhav Kosla, "Proportionality: An Assault on Human Rights? Responding to Stavros Tsakirakis", 5 *Comparative Constitutional Review* (2011).

the list of rights and freedoms and, therefore, the order and the regime of legislative restrictions it stipulates is of universal nature. It contains an exhaustive list of the objectives which can justify the restriction of certain human and civil rights and freedoms. The universal nature of this list does not mean that any of the basic rights and freedoms guaranteed by the Russian Constitution can be restricted in view of all six objectives, enumerated in Part 3 of Art. 55 of the Constitution of the Russian Federation. Some of these six goals may be correlated with some other basic right, while some others, if taken into account during the introduction of restrictions, could lead to a derogation of right (Part 2, Art. 55 of the Constitution of the Russian Federation).

The specificity of constitutional law to freely express opinions is such that it can be restricted to achieve such goals as protection of morality, health, rights, and legitimate interests of other persons, support of national defense and protection of national security. As to such a purpose, as protection of foundations of the constitutional system, one might have serious doubts concerning a possibility to restrict the freedom of expression to achieve this goal. The foundations of the constitutional system represent the list of fundamental principles of constitutional law of the Russian Federation. One of them is the principle of free elections (Part 3, Art. 3 of the Constitution of the Russian Federation). If one assumes that this principle from the foundations of the constitutional system is per se sufficient to impose restrictions on the freedom of expression, then the balance between two equal basic rights—the right of dissemination (Part 4, Art. 29 of the Constitution of the Russian Federation) and the right of election—disappears (Part 2, Art. 32 of the Constitution of the Russian Federation).

In the meantime, the ECHR in its ruling of February 19, 1998, on the case "Baughman v. the United Kingdom" proceeds from the fact that the right to free speech must be considered in the light of the right to free elections. In other words, neither of them possesses a priority. Only with such an approach, does the search for the balance between these equivalent basic rights become possible. The force of one basic right in such a case introduces restrictions on another basic right.

As an argument in favor of the proposed interpretation of the normative content of Part 3, Art. 55 of the Constitution of the Russian Federation, may serve a provision in Part 4, Art. 15 of the Constitution of the Russian Federation, according to which international treaties ratified by the Russian Federation should be treated as an integral part of its legal system. This provision of the Constitution stipulates a possibility—when solving a problem as to which of the six purposes specified in Part 3, Art. 55 of the Constitution of the Russian Federation can be used to restrict some basic right or other—to follow the European Convention.

In particular, Art. 10 of the European Convention stipulates that the right to freely express one's opinion can be restricted by law, if such restriction is necessary to the democratic society in the interests of national security, territorial integrity, and public order; for purposes of prevention of disorder or crime, for protection of health and morality, for protection of reputation or rights of other persons, for prevention of disclosure of information received confidentially; or for preservation of authority and impartiality of justice.

The balancing of various social interests is a universal method of judicial cognition. This is a part of legal epistemology. Here, this is similar to a legal situation of extreme necessity, since long ago known in private law. Sometimes, to save a child, one must damage a valuable sculpture. The social value of human life apparently exceeds any material values. In a state of extreme necessity, there is a collision of interests, the protection of which is important and socially significant. The individual acting in a state of extreme necessity "sacrifices" the less significant interest (the statue) to rescue the interest which seems socially more significant (the child). When continental supreme courts apply the principle of proportionality, they willy-nilly accept that one of the rights needs to "sacrificed" to the social, often—public interest. And this does not contradict the legal state concept!

It seems that even here one can find a difference between the legal state and the rule of law. The judicial doctrine of the rule of law must not evolve using such notions as "immolation" or "victory". Balancing is always a compromise. One of the basic rights conflicting with another can be declared by the court—in a particular situation—more "important", but at the same time the court must to the maximum retain the main content, maintain the authority and significance of the "subdued" right. The court should not act like a referee in a boxing match who just counts a prostrate fighter to ten.

In conclusion—the last but not least –the rule of law should be viewed from the constitutional economics standpoint. One of the directions in the development of Russian constitutional law is constitutional economics. The Declaration of the High-level Meeting of the UN General Assembly on the Rule of Law at the National and International Levels (September 19, 2012) expresses a firm belief that the rule of law and economic development are closely interconnected and enhance each other. The Declaration also encourages the rule of law on both national and international level. This has a particularly great importance for a stable and all-encompassing economic growth, sustainable development, eradication of poverty and hunger, and full observance of all human rights and fundamental freedoms, including the right to development,—all and every of which, in turn, strengthen the rule of law. It is for this reason that their interdependence must be considered in the framework of the agenda concerned with the international development after 2015.

This conviction expressed at such a high level gives one optimism and demonstrates powerful potential of constitutional economics, which is intended to deeply explore both the relationship and the mutually reinforcing effects of encouragement of the rule of law for the sake of economic growth. The above international agenda makes constitutionalists ponder about the acceleration of economic growth by way of the rule of law, while economists closely engage in the encouragement of the rule of law, considering this task their own. And then one may also assert the advent of new constitutionalism. So what are its contours, already showing up as at daybreak? In ontological terms, this new constitutionalism is a reflection of what happens not only in the reality of rights that have undergone reflection in legislation, but also in legal reality. When starting the development of new constitutionalism, one must radically change the magnitude of ambition and claims of scientists dealing with constitutionalism and the rule of law. Only those convinced that the rule of law determines economic and social development (but not vice versa) are capable of creating new constitutionalism. Life shows that Rudolf Stammler (1856–1938), representative of the school "of revived natural law" and Neo-Kantian philosopher, was right when he asserted, while criticizing Marxism with its vulgar economic determinism, that law was primary in relation to economic affairs, even if not in the causal or temporal aspect, but surely so on the logical plane.[24] In the twentieth century, the same idea was, in fact, reiterated by the U.S. economists Mancur Olson and James M. Buchanan (the latter received the 1986 Nobel Memorial Prize in Economic Sciences). Buchanan argued that some normative restrictions in the behavior of an individual towards others, such as the repudiation of violence; the status of a person with regard to a possibility of his access to resources, products, and services; as well as the terms of these norms becoming effective –must become focal points in the constitutional contract. Otherwise, one cannot think seriously about a market economy. Therefore, legal norms and the rule of law appear almost as a priority for an extensive and systematic functioning of the market economy. Moreover, they emerged as a public benefit, i.e. as the benefit which could not be produced in conditions of the market itself.[25]

14.3 New Constitutionalism

New constitutionalism is such an attitude towards the most important legal principles of organization of social human life, when these principles are regarded as an object of study by all humanities with the subsequent synthesis. From this standpoint, the rule of law and human rights become the most important factor in economic development. It is necessary to perform the integration of humanitarian knowledge about human rights, considered from a philosophical viewpoint as part of the non-legal reality. At the same time, it is important to find the place of ethics in the development of human rights. New constitutionalism is a general humanitarian doctrine reduced to a positivistic-legal study. With such an approach to constitutionalism, this "synthetic" frame of reference must use the achievements of all humanities. Above all, this involves philosophy, sociology, economics, political science, and culture. New constitutionalism suggests, in particular, further studies in the field of constitutional economics, the ethics of public authority, and world politics.

John B. Rawls, undoubtedly, one of the most distinguished contemporary thinkers, in his *Law of Peoples* expresses an idea that Western democracies may wage "just wars" against "unlawful states", meaning the states, not considering the principles of the rule of law doctrine. Rawls, known as a justice-as-fairness theorist believes that the strict principles of fairness, which all democratic constitutional states must follow,

---

[24] R. Stammler, *Hozyaistvo i pravo s tochki zreniya materialisticheskogo ponimaniya istorii* (Industry and Law in Terms of Materialistic Understanding of History) (2010). Comkniga.

[25] James M. Buchanan, *The Limits of Liberty. Between Anarchy and Leviathan* (1975). The University of Chicago Press, Chicago/London.

should not constrain them in their relations with authoritarian and semi-authoritarian states. Rawls quotes the words of Michael Walzer about the just war and agrees with him. Both thinkers consider justice between nations not only possible but also even desirable. However, there exists a significant difference between their positions—Walzer prefers to entrust the exercise of international justice in each separate case to common resolution by all sovereign states, i.e. by all members of the United Nations Organization, while Rawls leaves this prerogative to the liberal *avant-garde* of the community of states, which was first mentioned by I. Kant.

Walzer argues that protection of the integrity of life, of the habitual ethnos, and of the commonality organized in the state has a priority over the implementation of abstract principles of the world justice (unless the rogue state in question performs genocide against its own citizens).

The German philosopher Jürgen Habermaass, on the other hand, believes that even the liberal *avant-garde* of the community of states cannot appropriate the right at its sole discretion to unleash war against a despotic, totalitarian or criminal state. In the scientific presentation made in Istanbul, Habermaass rightly asserted that impartial assessment can never be produced by a single country or even by a group of liberal countries. The one-sided position, even when taken by the liberal *avant-garde* acting *pro bono*, is non-legal and, therefore, even illegitimate.[26]

Attention should be paid to how this philosophical dispute, conducted by the leading world philosophers, gets permeated by strictly legal ideas and combined into the rule of law doctrine. Philosophers and economists operate with legal concepts! J.B. Rawls builds his conclusions on an assumption that there should exist a group of non-legal states, while J. Habermaass leads his discourse using one of the elements of the rule of law, which is the proportionality between the objective, one needs to achieve, and the used means. From the standpoint of this legal idea, it is none but the approach—chosen by the "liberal *avant-garde* states" which use the slogan "any means to an end"—that is non-legal.

J.B. Rawls is not convincing in this philosophical dispute. However, in the context of reasoning on the rule of law, another observation appears to be more important—no major issue of world politics or economics can ever be resolved without the involvement of that *summa* of top humanitarian ideas which populate and animate the rule of law doctrine.

Translated by Boris Meshcheryakov

---

[26] Jürgen Habermaass, supra note 9, at 92.

Chapter 15
The Law Is a Causeway: Metaphor and the Rule of Law in Russia

Jeffrey Kahn

Abstract This chapter explores how a metaphor for the rule of law created by the playwright Robert Bolt captures the difficulty that Russia has experienced in its self-proclaimed pursuit of a rule-of-law state: "The law is not a 'light' for you or any man to see by; the law is not an instrument of any kind. The law is a causeway upon which, so long as he keeps to it, a citizen may walk safely." In Russia, the failure to build a rule-of-law state has been, among other things, a failure to create what this metaphor describes as the essence of that concept. The essay concludes with a case study taken from the author's experience as an expert invited to submit a report to the Russian President's Council on the Development of Civil Society and Human Rights.

> *We support the aspiration of citizens for the supremacy of law [право] and their demand for the observance of law [закон]. ... Russia does not have the right to repeat mistakes that have occurred at turning points in its History.*
>
> *– Declaration of Members of the Russian President's Human Rights Council, December 9, 2011.*[1]

This essay was completed in fall 2013 while I was an O'Brien Fellow-in-Residence at the Centre for Human Rights and Legal Pluralism, Faculty of Law, McGill University. I wish to thank Ferdinand Feldbrugge, René Provost, Peter Solomon, and Marika Giles Samson for their helpful comments. I alone am responsible for the contents of this essay.

[1] Заявление членов Совета при Президенте Российской Федерации по развитию гражданского общества и правам человека, 09.12.2011. This essay adopts a short form of this official title.

J. Kahn (✉)
Dedman School of Law, Southern Methodist University, Dallas, TX, USA
e-mail: jkahn@mail.smu.edu

J.R. Silkenat et al. (eds.), *The Legal Doctrines of the Rule of Law and the Legal State (Rechtsstaat)*, Ius Gentium: Comparative Perspectives on Law and Justice 38,
DOI 10.1007/978-3-319-05585-5_15,

15.1 Introduction

What did the Russian President's Human Rights Council mean by distinguishing the supremacy of law – using the word *pravo* [право], akin to the Latin *jus* or French *droit* – from the observance of law – using *zakon* [закон], akin to *lex* or *loi*? Do Russian citizens live under either principle? Consider how three Decembers in Moscow shed light on the answer.

In December 2010, Mikhail Khodorkovsky, once Russia's richest man, was convicted of economic crimes.[2] This was Khodorkovsky's second trial, which revisited with new charges many of the claims that led to his first conviction in May 2005.[3] This second verdict was inexplicably postponed on the morning scheduled for its announcement, allowing then Prime Minister Vladimir Putin to discuss the case first on national television, concluding that "a thief should sit in jail."[4] Putin was widely believed to be behind Khodorkovsky's first arrest and conviction, which occurred during his first two terms as president. Khodorkovsky's case had become a cause célèbre, at least among the incipient Russian middle class and the gelded liberal opposition.

What a difference a year seemed to make. In December 2011, Moscow was convulsed by opposition rallies not seen in Russia since the collapse of the Soviet Union. Politicians across the political spectrum – from the billionaire Mikhail Prokhorov to Communist Party leader Gennady Zyuganov – declared their desire to free Khodorkovsky as they angled for advantage in upcoming presidential elections.[5] (The irony of Russia's top communist demanding the release of Russia's top plutocrat underscores the national significance of the case.) They were responding to the pronouncement of the Human Rights Council, which had advised President Medvedev that Khodorkovsky's second conviction should be annulled. The Council's recommendations, more than a year in the making, were the result of detailed analytical reports by six Russian experts and three foreign experts. I was one of the foreign experts.

One year later, the window for change opened by the Bolotnaya Square protests appeared to have closed. For the Khodorkovsky case, this was especially chilling. Putin denied that the case was either personal or political.[6] But in the first year of his

[2] Приговор Хамовнического районного суда г. Москвы от 27.12.2010 г.

[3] Приговор Мещанского районного суда г. Москвы от 16.5.2005 г.

[4] Transcript of "A Conversation with Vladimir Putin," which aired on TV channels "Rossiya" and "Rossiya 24," and radio stations "Mayak," "Vesti FM," and "Radio Rossiya" on Dec. 16, 2010: http://archive.government.ru/docs/13427/

[5] Maria Kuchma, "Russian presidential candidates play Khodorkovsky card," *RIA-Novosti*, Jan. 12, 2012. http://en.ria.ru/analysis/20120112/170725351.html; *see also* Alexandra Odynova, "Rights Council: Free Khodorkovsky," *Moscow Times*, Dec. 22, 2011. http://www.themoscowtimes.com/sitemap/free/2011/12/article/rights-council-free-khodorkovsky/450313.html

[6] News Conference of Vladimir Putin, Moscow, December 20, 2012 (transcript at Johnson's Russia List # 5, January 8, 2013) ("As for Mr Khodorkovsky, there is no personal prosecution in this case. I remember very well how it developed. There still are attempts to present it as a political case. Was Mr Khodorkovsky engaged in politics? Was he a State Duma deputy? Was he a leader of a political party? No, he wasn't any of those things. It's a purely economic offence and the court made a ruling.").

new third term, at least five of the six Russian experts were ordered to appear for questioning by members of the Investigative Committee, the federal agency responsible for the investigation of criminal cases. Many of their homes and offices were searched, their papers, computers, phones and other property seized. Employees of a research institute tangentially associated with some of the experts received the same treatment and the institute was effectively closed down. Oddly, the search warrants were issued as part of the *first* Khodorkovsky case, opened in 2003. The warrants alleged that Khodorkovsky had financed the "deliberately false conclusions of specialists under the guise of independent public expertise by paying those who organized their production as well as the experts."[7]

This essay examines these reprisals as a particular example of Russia's rule-of-law failures. This harassment employed many powerful legal tools – subpoenas, search warrants, tax and regulatory inspections, *etc.* – but in ways that could hardly be considered consonant with the rule of law. Law remains an instrument of power in Russia, not a foundation on which to build (and constrain) government. Russia has become what Vladimir Putin long ago declared his goal: a "dictatorship of law." Putin used the word *zakon*, suggesting the dictatorship of statutes and decrees, not the word *pravo* that conveys a sense of lawfulness and justice beyond mere positivism.[8] It is now clear that Putin meant precisely what he said: the power of the state to rule *through* law, not a state empowered, paradoxically, by the constraining force of the rule of law.

15.2 A Metaphor for the Rule of Law

A metaphor conveys what more formal definitions of the rule of law obscure. The metaphor comes from Robert Bolt's play, A Man For All Seasons, about Thomas More, executed for high treason when he would not support Henry VIII's break with the Roman Catholic Church. More's crime was political, and the charge was as much a weapon used against him as was his executioner's axe. Vladimir Putin is not Henry VIII, nor do the Human Rights Council's experts claim the mantle of Thomas More. But like More, those who have fallen out of favor with the Russian president because of their legal advice find Russian law turned against them.

Although the importance of the rule of law is widely accepted, its precise meaning remains contested (as this book's existence attests). Some definitions emphasize high-level constitutionalism, searching for specific features in founding documents, with little attention to the underlying, everyday legal culture required to support them.[9]

[7] *See* Letter from Mikhail Fedotov, Chairman of the Human Rights Council, to Jeffrey Kahn, Feb. 13, 2013 (quoting warrant).

[8] Открытое письмо Владимира Путина к российским избирателям, 25.02.2000, *Коммерсантъ*, http://www.kommersant.ru/doc/141144

[9] *See*, for example, Juan J. Linz and Alfred Stepan, *Problems of Democratic Transition and Consolidation: Southern Europe, South America, and Post-Communist Europe* (1996). Johns Hopkins University Press, Baltimore, Maryland, at 10.

Others privilege particular institutions (such as courts), substantive rights (such as free expression), characteristics (such as stability), values (such as equality), processes (such as notice and hearing), and sometimes even values *about* processes (like efficient administration).[10] These definitions overlap in some places, and leave gaps in others.

To use a metaphor to examine the marginality of the rule of law in Russia is not to call for an end to the definitional struggle. But metaphor has a special power to advance discussion.[11] Generally speaking, "metaphor enrich[es] the range of phenomena available for systematic philosophical reflection and analysis, and provide[s] hints of the truth which we could not envision if we relied only on the machinery of formal inference."[12] More specifically, Richard Fallon observed (metaphorically): "It is a mistake to think of particular criteria as necessary in all contexts for the Rule of Law. Rather, we should recognize that the strands of the Rule of Law are complexly interwoven, and we should begin to consider which values or criteria are presumptively primary under which conditions."[13]

A few words of history are helpful. In 1529, a legatine court convened in London to determine the validity under canon law of the marriage between Henry VIII and Catherine of Aragon. Henry preferred Anne Boleyn for reasons of both a personal nature and matters of state.[14] He therefore sought legal advice on his "great matter" from the finest lawyer in the realm, Thomas More, whom he named Lord Chancellor after the prior office-holder failed to persuade the Pope to grant an annulment.[15]

More was praised for his legal reasoning, which emphasized the constraint that precedent and legal authority placed on personal judgment. But he also "epitomized, in modern terms, the apparatus of the state using its power to crush those attempting to subvert it."[16] More was an accomplished interrogator, comfortable in the Star

[10] *See*, for example, Rachel Kleinfeld, "Competing Definitions of the Rule of Law," in *Promoting the Rule of Law Abroad: In Search of Knowledge,* Thomas Carothers, ed. (2006). Carnegie Endowment for International Peace, Washington, DC, at 31–73; Martin Krygier, "Rule of Law," *in The Oxford Handbook of Comparative Constitutional Law*, Rosenfeld & Sajó, eds. (2012). Oxford University Press, Oxford.

[11] This claim is contested. *Compare, Berkey v Third Ave. Ry. Co.*, 244 N.Y. 84, 94 (1926) (Cardozo, J.) ("Metaphors in law are to be narrowly watched, for starting as devices to liberate thought, they end often by enslaving it.").

[12] Elizabeth Camp, "Two Varieties of Literary Imagination: Metaphor, Fiction, and Thought Experiments," in *Midwest Studies in Philosophy: Poetry and Philosophy XXXIII*. Howard Wettstein, ed., (2009), at 128.

[13] Richard H. Fallon, Jr., "'The Rule of Law' as a Concept in Constitutional Discourse," 97 *Colum. L. Rev.* (1997) at 6.

[14] Enchanted by Boleyn and needing a son to secure Tudor succession, the King claimed that his heirless marriage contravened Leviticus: he had married his brother's wife (albeit by papal dispensation). Pope Clement VII refused an annulment, perhaps because canon law forbade it or perhaps because he was a virtual prisoner of Catherine's nephew, the Holy Roman Emperor Charles V. This seemingly theological dispute thus raised enormous political and legal issues for England's domestic and international affairs. Peter Ackroyd, *The Life of Thomas More* (1998). Doubleday, USA, at 263–275; Richard Marius. *Thomas More* (1984). Alfred A. Knopf, New York, at 213–16.

[15] Ackroyd, at 266–68; Marius, at 216.

[16] Ackroyd, at 302.

Chamber, who pursued those he feared would destroy the social order. His network of spies, surveillance, and surprise raids would be familiar to present-day spymasters. There is thus irony in using his story as a metaphor for the rule of law.

The King pressed More to endorse his convenient opinion that the Pope lacked any jurisdiction in England. More reports that the king told him "to look and consider his great matter, and well and indifferently to ponder such things as I should find."[17] Unable to agree with his king, More resigned his office only to find himself a defendant in successive specious prosecutions, first for bribery, then for conspiracy with a traitorous nun, and last for his own high treason himself. More easily refuted the first two charges on the evidentiary record alone.

Having refused to swear an oath concerning the King's supremacy, and carefully silent regarding his reasons, More was put on trial for high treason. He relied on a legal defense. The statute setting forth the crime required treasonous "words or writing." More argued that the law required that his silence be construed as loyalty, not treason.[18] Perhaps a century later, Cardinal Richelieu provided the most succinct explanation for such prudence: "If you give me six lines written by the hand of the most honest of men, I will find something in them which will hang him."

Bolt's climactic trial scene prepares us for the metaphor:

CROMWELL The oath was put to good and faithful subjects up and down the country and they had declared His Grace's title to be just and good. And when it came to the prisoner he refused. He calls this silence. Yet is there a man in this court, is there a man in this country, who does not *know* Sir Thomas More's opinion of the King's title? Of course not! But how can that be? Because this silence betokened – nay, this silence was *not* silence at all but most eloquent denial.

MORE Not so, Master Secretary, the maxim is "qui tacet consentire." The maxim of the law is "Silence gives consent." If, therefore, you wish to construe what my silence "betokened," you must construe that I consented, not that I denied.

CROMWELL Is that what the world in fact construes from it? Do you pretend that is what you *wish* the world to construe from it?

MORE The world must construe according to its wits. This Court must construe according to the law.[19]

Now the metaphor. Its focus is not on *definition* of the rule of law, but on its *application*.

CROMWELL I put it to the Court that the prisoner is perverting the law – making smoky what should be a clear light to discover to the Court his own wrongdoing!

[17] Letter from More to Cromwell, March 5, 1534, reprinted in *A Thomas More Source Book*, Gerard Wegemer & Stephen Smith, eds. (2004) at 358.

[18] *Id.*, at 353 (*Paris Newsletter* account of the trial, August 4, 1535).

[19] Robert Bolt, *A Man For All Seasons* (1960), Act II (stage directions omitted).

MORE The law is not a "light" for you or any man to see by; the law is not an instrument of any kind. The law is a causeway upon which, so long as he keeps to it, a citizen may walk safely.[20]

This metaphor describes the essential purpose toward which so many different definitions of the rule of law all aim. In other words, it describes the *how* and the *why* of the rule of law, not the precise *what*.[21]

Contrast this metaphor with another in the play. When his future son-in-law urges him to abuse his office to arrest a "bad" man, More refuses: "And go he should, if he was the Devil himself, until he broke the law!" More rejects the younger man's metaphor of law as a weapon because of its dangerous double edge:

ROPER So now you'd give the Devil benefit of law!
MORE Yes. What would you do? Cut a great road through the law to get after the Devil?
ROPER I'd cut down every law in England to do that!
MORE Oh? And when the last law was down, and the Devil turned round on you – where would you hide, Roper, the laws all being flat? This country's planted thick with laws from coast to coast – man's laws, not God's – and if you cut them down – and you're just the man to do it – d'you really think you could stand upright in the winds that would blow then? Yes, I'd give the Devil benefit of law, for my own safety's sake.[22]

The purpose of the rule of law is not to empower one group over another but to create a safe space for all in which the individual is respected as an intelligent, reasoning creature with inherent value.[23] The causeway metaphor highlights this purpose. Once built, a causeway provides safe passage for *all* who travel it. Its maintenance – the rules and standards for its use, the institutions and processes that make it useful – are part of the state's *raison d'être*.

When law is conceived as an instrument, it has only instrumental value. Such a view devalues the human subjects of law. Law-as-instrument is a selective device for oppression and control; it has no limit but the power of the one who wields it and no values external to the wielder that might constrain his actions. The rule of law is not the rule of *zakon* alone, but a rule imbued with a sense of the state's own limitations, of *law's* limitations, to enter a precious, private sphere uninvited.

---

[20] *Id.*

[21] Others have noted that the rule of law may be approached in this way. *See* Iain Stewart, "From 'Rule of Law' to 'Legal State': A Time of Reincarnation?" *Macquarie Law Working Paper* (Nov. 2007) at 4 ("[I]t appears to be far easier to say what 'the rule of law' does than to state what it is.").

[22] *Id.*, Act I.

[23] Jeremy Waldron, "The Rule of Law and the Importance of Procedure," *New York University School of Law Public Law & Legal Theory Research Paper Series*, Working Paper No. 10-73 (Oct. 2010) at 14 ("Applying a norm to a human individual is not like deciding what to do about a rabid animal or a dilapidated house. It involves paying attention to a point of view and respecting the personality of the entity one is dealing with.").

15.3 The Rule-of-Law Causeway in Russia

One can point to formal principles, institutions, and procedures codified in Russian law that rule-of-law scholars would recognize and approve. One can also identify ordinary Russians willing to trust the legal system with their grievances.[24] One can even recognize lawmaking that assesses proposals against accepted principles, debates publicly, and declares prospective, consistent, general rules for all.

Yet few academic lawyers and practicing attorneys would compare Russia favorably to states long associated with a high degree of conformity to the rule of law. That is because there is no causeway in Russia upon which, so long as he keeps to it, a citizen may walk safely, freely, and with dignity. In other words, law in Russia remains a tool and a weapon. It is this instrumentalism that is the problem of the rule of law in Russia, captured not by precise definitional adjustments but by a metaphor.

The selective use of law-as-weapon creates a "dual state" in Russia in which one may find law and lawlessness, often in the same place. This concept was made famous by Ernst Fraenkel.[25] For ordinary commercial cases or private disputes, the courts are not only functional, but at some levels functioning quite well and professionally. But when a political case arises, or one in which the participants are exceptionally powerful or in league with those in power, one enters a different world. This is not a world of *pravo*, but one of pliable *zakon*, manipulable institutions, and dispensible principles and procedures. All of the elements of every rule-of-law definition may be in place in Russia, from time to time. But they may be disregarded when powerful interests so desire. That is why empirical research and survey data discern an uncanny skill in the average Russian citizen to realize when legal recourse is useful, when it is futile, and when it is dangerous.[26]

Russian aphorisms capture the sense that law is a tool manipulated by powerful forces.[27] All reference *zakon*, not *pravo*. Imperial Russia was known more for the

[24] The best empirical work in this area is by Kathryn Hendley. *See* Kathryn Hendley, "The Puzzling Non-Consequences of Societal Distrust of Courts: Explaining the Use of Russian Courts," 45 *Cornell Int'l L.J.* (2012) at 523.

[25] Ernst Fraenkel, *The Dual State: A Contribution to the Theory of Dictatorship* (1941). I first heard this term used with reference to post-Soviet Russia by Professor Kim Lane Scheppele on a panel I organized, "The Dictatorship of Law: The Khodorkovsky Case, Human Rights, and the Rule of Law in Russia," AALS National Conference, Washington D.C., January 6, 2012. In personal correspondence, Professor Peter Solomon noted to me that in the 1970s specialists on Soviet law debated the applicability to Soviet institutional hierarchies of Fraenkel's divisions between the normative and prerogative states in Nazi Germany.

[26] Kathryn Hendley, "Varieties of Legal Dualism: Making Sense of the Role of Law in Contemporary Russia," 29 *Wis. Int'l L.J.* (2011) at 233.

[27] Consider a few: "Где закон, там и обида" ("Where there is a law, there is an offense.") inverts the classic Latin maxim *Nullum crimen sine lege* ("No crime without law") from a defensive stance against power to an offensive tool of the powerful, emphasizing the use of law to find fault. A similar tone is found in "Если бы не закон, не было бы и преступника" ("If there were no law, then there would be no criminal."). Consider, too, "Закон, что паутина: шмель проскочит, а муха увязнет" ("The law is like a spider's web: the bumble-bee tears through but the fly gets stuck.")

crushing weight of its laws than for their systematic application to protect or promote civil society. In Soviet times, instrumentalism was elevated to the realm of high theory. The first Commissar of Justice, Nikolai Krylenko, explained that a court, like a rifle, is just another weapon of the ruling class.[28] Law-as-weapon applied both to the substance of the laws and to the procedures that governed law-making and judicial activity. The rigid procedural exactitude of Soviet justice provided no succor for the accused or for the society from which they were purged.

Gorbachev came closest to replacing these instrumentalist notions of law with causeway-building ones. His early economic legislation adopted a new approach to the relationship between state and society: "Of the two possible principles, 'You may do only what is permitted' and 'You may do everything that is not forbidden', priority should be given to the latter inasmuch as it unleashes the initiative and activism of people."[29] Gorbachev characterized the concept of subordinating the state to law as a key to his reforms.

Perhaps optimism sparked by such a progressive thought was ill-advised in the face of so much history. As Bernard Rudden evocatively put it, with a simile, "[d]uring the last years of its life the Soviet Union turned to law like a dying monarch to his withered God … and the Congress and Supreme Soviet enact[ed] and amend[ed] statutes with the fervour of one who sees in legislation the path to paradise."[30] A hallmark of the 1990s and first part of the twenty-first century in Russia was the rapid development of new laws and legal codes. This was nothing short of staggering. In the first 10 years of post-Soviet life, there came into being at least fifteen new codes of law, both substantive and procedural.

And yet, such enlightened legal views did not triumph in the aftermath of the collapse of the Soviet Union. The combination of new law-on-the-books with old personnel and practices, mixed together in the economic maelstrom that characterized the first post-Soviet decade, did not produce the rule of law. It could not dislodge an instrumentalist tradition of rule *through* law that Vladimir Putin slowly strengthened. Gorbachev focused on *pravo*, an abstract notion of justice. Putin famously declared that democracy was the dictatorship of law, that is, *zakon*, legislation. This formulation has worked well for him, given his control over institutions beyond the federal executive branch. The result, according to William Partlett, was a "seductively simple" use of law as a weapon and means of control:

> [I]n return for elite adherence to informal rules and personal loyalty, the state tolerates corrupt activities. Meanwhile, the regime closely documents this corruption, building dossiers on key members of the system, which then goes after them. … These formal legal sanctions are a powerful incentive for ensuring elite cohesion and personal loyalty: a

and "Закон – дышло: куда захочешь, туда и воротишь" ("The law is a wagon's shaft: where you want to go, there you turn it."). Владимир Даль, *Пословицы русского народа* (1957) at 245.

[28] Vladimir Gsovski, *Soviet Civil Law System*, Vol. 1 (1948) at 241.

[29] Vladimir Kudryavtsev, Director of the Institute of State and Law and a frequent advisor to Gorbachev, as quoted in Archie Brown, *The Gorbachev Factor* (1996) at 146.

[30] Bernard Rudden, "Civil Law, Civil Society and the Russian Constitution," 110 *L.Q.R.* (1994) at 56.

disobedient individual faces the prospect of jail time as well as full-scale seizure of all of his or her wealth.[31]

A side effect of such a system is a body of law and set of institutions that are fairly effective at resolving commercial disputes and punishing criminals that are of no political interest. There is no disputing that numerous codes of law promulgated in the Yeltsin and Putin presidencies have been great leaps forward (especially in the areas of criminal procedure, property law, and a modernized civil code). Court reform and legal education efforts have improved the quality of bench and bar. But this, at best, has created a system in which the resolution of disputes and the trial of crimes *can* be done according to law, but only if the matter does not pique the interest of a powerful official. When such is the case, law becomes just one option among many, a tool or a weapon at the official's disposal.

Notice that, unlike the use of law in Soviet Russia, this cynical attitude toward law has ceased to be the exclusive possession of the state. New capitalists saw opportunity in the anarchy of weak state enforcement and transitional legal structures. In the worst cases, the unscrupulous or criminal-minded "commissioned" the criminal prosecution of their adversaries by paying off state officials. More intrepid, and more corrupt, law enforcement officials opened specious criminal cases against entrepreneurs as a means of rent extraction.[32] "Corporate raiding" (рейдерство) may combine these techniques with other manipulations of courts and legal processes to strip state or private enterprises of their assets. Thomas Firestone, who as Resident Legal Advisor at the U.S. Embassy-Moscow observed these and other techniques first-hand, described them metaphorically: "Using the law as both sword and shield, the perpetrator turns the victim into a legal defendant, misappropriates the state's legal enforcement power for private ends, and obtains a cover from liability through the claim that he is merely enforcing a legal right."[33]

Firestone (probably the most expert and accomplished Justice Department official to hold the office of resident legal advisor in Moscow was declared *persona non grata* in May 2013 and forced to leave his legal practice in Moscow shortly after leaving public service)[34] does not consider base corruption to be either a necessary or sufficient cause of the proliferation of such legal abuses. Rather, it is the instrumentalist legacy of Soviet law (and, one might say, pre-Soviet Russian law) that Firestone notes as a prime cause: "the notion that law is an instrument of political rule rather than a neutral system for the arbitration of disputes."[35]

[31] William Partlett, "Putin's Artful Jurisprudence," *The National Interest*, Jan. 2, 2013. http://nationalintrest.org/article/putins-artful-jurisprudence-7882

[32] *See* Thomas Firestone, "Armed Injustice: Abuse of the Law and Complex Crime in Post-Soviet Russia," 38 *Denv. J. Int'l L. & Pol'y* 556–59 (2010) at 556–59; Thomas Firestone, "Criminal Corporate Raiding in Russia," 42 *Int'l Law.* (2008) at 1207.

[33] Firestone, "Armed Injustice," *supra* note 31, at 556.

[34] David M. Herszenhorn & Mark Mazzetti, "Russia Expels Former American Embassy Official," *N.Y. Times*, May 19, 2013. http://www.nytimes.com/2013/05/20/world/europe/russia-expels-former-american-embassy-official.html

[35] Firestone, "Armed Injustice," *supra* note 31, at 572.

The causeway metaphor rejects this instrumentalism. A public road is carefully constructed for the use of all. Like all good roads, this causeway provides a safe path to many destinations. All may use it freely and know in advance where it leads. The causeway, as Bolt's More notes, provides a path that the citizen may walk *safely*. This may be understood in several ways. Substantively, the citizen knows the limits of his free movement and can plan life accordingly. Procedurally, the citizen may rely upon the state both to protect the causeway against the harm other travelers may cause him and also to provide redress against interference by the state itself. In addition, as Bernard Rudden observed, "in every human life there are vast areas better left to the conscience of the individual and the sense of the relevant community: there is a precious sphere of non-law." The rule-of-law causeway does not run to every aspect of human life: "[I]f people act in good faith and stay licit, the State will stay away."[36]

Russia seems farther than ever from the causeway conception of the rule of law. The offense of slander, decriminalized in December 2011 by then President Dmitrii Medvedev, returned to the Criminal Code slightly more than a month after Vladimir Putin's May 2012 inauguration as president.[37] A few months later, the crime of treason was both broadened to criminalize more acts and narrowed to require less in the form of proof that the security of the Russian state has been compromised.[38] New laws concerning non-governmental organizations led human rights groups and other monitors of civil society to be officially branded as "foreign agents" (a term redolent with sinister meaning in post-Soviet society) or suffer a range of legal liabilities.[39] Sergei Magnitsky, a lawyer who gained fame first for accusing tax authorities of corruption

---

[36] Rudden, *supra* note 29.

[37] Article 129 (slander) and Article 130 (Insult) were decriminalized in December 2011 under President Medvedev. *See* Article 1(45) in Федеральный закон от 7 декабря 2011 г. N 420-ФЗ. Slander was returned to the Criminal Code under a new Article 128.1 by President Putin roughly 8 months later. *See* Федеральный закон от 28 июля 2012 г. N 141-ФЗ "О внесении изменений в Уголовный кодекс Российской Федерации и отдельные законодательные акты Российской Федерации."

[38] Федеральный закон от 12 ноября 2012 г. N 190-ФЗ "О внесении изменений в Уголовный кодекс Российской Федерации и в статью 151 Уголовно-процессуального кодекса Российской Федерации". In its previous version, Article 275 of the Criminal Code defined treason as "espionage, the delivery of a state secret or other assistance to a foreign state, foreign organization, or their representatives in carrying out hostile acts to damage the foreign security of the Russian Federation." Федеральный закон от 27 декабря 2009 г. N 377-ФЗ. The new law expands treason to include the rendering of "financial, material-technical, consultative, or other assistance to a foreign state, international or foreign organization or their representatives in activity directed against the security of the Russian Federation." The limiting element in the previous version, requiring damage to Russia's "foreign security" ("ущерб внешней безопасности"), has been narrowed by deleting the qualifier to acts "that are directed against the security" of the state.

[39] Федеральный закон от 28 декабря 2012 г. N 272-ФЗ, "О мерах воздействия на лиц, причастных к нарушениям основополагающих прав и свобод человека, прав и свобод граждан Российской Федерации"; Федеральный закон от 20 июля 2012 г. N 121-ФЗ "О внесении изменений в отдельные законодательные акты Российской Федерации в части регулирования деятельности некоммерческих организаций, выполняющих функции иностранного агента".

and then for dying in custody following his accusation, was tried and convicted not just in absentia, but posthumously – a first in recorded Russian history.[40]

The substantive merit of each of these laws and legal actions may be debated. But what matters here is not their normative value but their instrumental use – these are laws and legal processes that are used by the state to project power, not to create a space for the flourishing of individuals and society. Or, to put this metaphorically, there is no path set down by law on which the citizen can walk safely.

15.4 Case Study: The President's Human Rights Council

Thomas More, the King's trusted advisor, found himself accused of treason when his counsel ceased to satisfy the sovereign. So, too, distinguished lawyers and scholars in Russia today find themselves threatened after giving their opinions to their president, by invitation of the President's own Human Rights Council, on his "great matter," the case of Mikhail Khodorkovsky. The Presidential Council on the Development of Civil Society and Human Rights (abbreviated here to the "Human Rights Council") claims a distinguished historical pedigree but possesses no legal independence. Its legal status comes from presidential decree (*ukaz*); it has never known any stronger legal authority than that. Its real authority comes from the reputation of its members.[41]

[40] David M. Herszenhorn, "Russian Court Convicts A Kremlin Critic Posthumously," *N.Y. Times*, July 11, 2013. It is worth noting that the Human Rights Council examined Magnitsky's case immediately prior to its work on the Khodorkovsky case. It gathered experts who wrote a high-quality and methodically rigorous report that returned public attention to the case. The Council's work was cited by the United States Congress. *See* Sergei Magnitsky Rule of Law Accountability Act of 2012, Pub. L. No. 112-208, § 402(8), 126 Stat. 1496, 1503 (2012).

[41] The Council traces its origin to the Human Rights Commission established (by decree) by Boris Yeltsin in 1993 and led by the well-known Soviet-era dissident Sergei Kovalev. *See* http://president-sovet.ru/about/. The author knows of no scholarship published in English or Russian on the Human Rights Council in its current incarnation. Kovalev resigned his post in 1996 in opposition to Yeltsin's war in Chechnya. *See* Sergei Kovalev (trans. by Catherine A. Fitzpatrick), A Letter of Resignation, *New York Review of Books* (Feb. 29, 1996). For much of Vladimir Putin's first two terms in office and the first half of Dmitrii Medvedev's presidency, there existed a Presidential Council on Assistance in the Development of Institutions of Civil Society and Human Rights. But again, the Council lacked real autonomy; its existence depended entirely on presidential decree. *See* Указ Президента Российской Федерации от 6 ноября 2004 г. № 1417 "О Совете при Президенте Российской Федерации по содействию развитию институтов гражданского общества и правам человека". The Council could hardly have been considered overly successful during Putin's first two terms as President. But as Medvedev entered the twilight of his presidential term, the Council appeared to have been given a new lease on life. Mikhail Fedotov was named chair of the Council in October 2010. *See* Указ Президента Российской Федерации от 12 октября 2010 г. № 1234 "О Председателе Совета при Президенте Российской Федерации по содействию развитию институтов гражданского общества и правам человека". And Medvedev signed a new decree in February 2011 that seemed to expand the Council's powers and confirmed a membership composed of the leading lights of the Russian human rights movement. *See* Указ Президента Российской Федерации

As in More's case, the initial allegations seemed easy to bat away. But now, as this chapter is being written, they wait and wonder about their fate. At least one Russian expert has fled Russia in fear for his safety, explaining that "Paris is better than Krasnokamensk," the Siberian location of one of the prison camps that housed Khodorkovsky.[42]

Khodorkovsky was once one of Russia's wealthiest entrepreneurs, the CEO of the Yukos Oil Company.[43] The first of several criminal investigations into his activities and those of his company began in June 2003. In May 2005, Khodorkovsky was convicted of fraud, causing property damage by deceit or breach of trust, and tax evasion. In December 2010, he was convicted of embezzlement and money laundering. Detained since his arrest in October 2003, Khodorkovsky was scheduled to be released in August 2014. In a surprise move, Putin pardoned Khodorkovsky on December 20, 2013; Khodorkovsky immediately left Russia for Germany.

Although the cases were opened separately, the time period and much of the evidence for these different charges were the same. The European Court of Human Rights has issued numerous judgments finding violations of the European Convention on Human Rights concerning the arrest, detention, search, access to counsel, inhumane treatment, and property interests of Khodorkovsky and his fellow defendants.[44] Other judgments by the Court and further applications by various defendants are pending. The Parliamentary Assembly of the Council of Europe expressed its concern for rule-of-law shortcomings revealed by the prosecutions.[45]

Several weeks after the verdict in the second case, President Medvedev met with his Human Rights Council in Ekaterinburg. Several Council members expressed

от 1 февраля 2011 г. № 120 "О Совете при Президенте Российской Федерации по развитию гражданского общества и правам человека".

[42] Christian Neef and Matthias Schepp, Exiled Economic Adviser: "Putin Is Afraid of the Public," Der Spiegel, June 10, 2013. http://www.spiegel.de/international/europe/russian-economist-sergei-guriev-putin-fears-all-opposition-a-905306.html

[43] Detailed factual background may be found in numerous publications, including my report, reprinted in 4 *Journal of Eurasian Law*, No. 3 (2011).

[44] *See* Lebedev v. Russia, App. No. 4493/04 (Oct. 25, 2007); Vasilii Aleksanyan v. Russia, App. No. 46468/06 (Dec. 8, 2008); Khodorkovsky v. Russia, App. No. 5829/04 (May 31, 2011); OAO Neftyanaya Kompaniya Yukos v. Russia, App. No. 14902/04 (September 20, 2011); Khodorkovskiy & Lebedev v. Russia, App. Nos. 11082/06 & 13772/05 (July 25, 2013). It should be noted that, in this latest judgment, the Court did not find a violation of Convention Article 18, which prohibits the restriction of protected rights "for any purpose other than those for which they have been prescribed," *e.g.* political cases. The Court observed that "Article 18 is rarely invoked and there have been few cases where the Court declared a complaint under Article 18 admissible, let alone found a violation thereof," while, with remarkable understatement, it also acknowledged "that the circumstances surrounding the applicants' criminal case may be interpreted as supporting the applicants' claim of improper motives." *Id.* at 898, 901. However, the Court refused to depart from its extremely high standard of direct proof for such allegations and thus declined to find a violation of the Convention. *Id.* at 897–909.

[45] Parliamentary Assembly Resolution 1418 (Jan. 25, 2005), The Circumstances Surrounding the Arrest and Prosecution of Leading Yukos Executives.

concern about the Khodorkovsky case.[46] Tamara Morshchakova, a retired justice of the Russian Constitutional Court, noted the Council's intention to provide the President with "expert legal conclusions" on issues raised by "concrete cases."[47] At the conclusion of the meeting, President Medvedev invited the Council to act:

> You know, I think that practically no one at this table has read the entire case file for Khodorkovsky, Magnitsky, or still others simply because it is not possible. … But it seems to me important, please, here I would be grateful, if the expert community tried to prepare a very legal analysis of these decisions. That would represent something of definite value, because every person who wishes to examine in those things, needs to be guided by the opinions of specialists. … The opinions of different people on these questions is very important for me as the head of state.[48]

This enlightened view was reportedly shared by the chairmen of Russia's three highest courts.[49]

15.4.1 Work of the Human Rights Council and Its Experts

The Human Rights Council took the President's words to heart. A working group chaired by Morshchakova drafted guidelines for this work. The protocol of one of their meetings, in early May, noted that thirteen experts had been invited to participate in the analysis, materials had been sent to them and, "after the anticipated decision of the cassational instance, a session of which is scheduled for May 17, it is expected that the preparation of the experts reports will intensify in order that the work be completed in the course of summer 2011."[50]

---

[46] Стенографический отчёт о заседании Совета по развитию гражданского общества и правам человека, 1 февраля 2011 года, 12:00, Екатеринбург, http://www.president-sovet.ru/meeting_with_president_of_russia/meeting_with_president_in_yekaterinburg_01_02_2011/verbatim_report/index.php. Sergei Karaganov, Tamara Morshchakova, and Irina Yasina raised the issue in their recorded remarks.

[47] *Id.*

[48] *Id.*

[49] Елена Масюк, Тамара Морщакова: "Я не могу оставить свою землю, на которой я выросла," *Новая газета*, 08.06.2013, http://www.novayagazeta.ru/politics/58532.html (Morshchakova: "The Chairmen of the Constitutional Court, Supreme Court, and Supreme Arbitration Court declared, when the Council showed such initiative and announced this to the President, that yes, society has the right to such a public analysis, that courts, like other state structures, are not exempted from public control, that society has the right to know and understand what occurs in the activity of every organ of power."); *see also* Речь члена Совета Т.Г. Морщаковой на пресс-конференции 06 февраля 2013 года, http://president-sovet.ru/structure/group_6/materials/rech_chlena_soveta_t_g_morshchakovoy_na_press_konferentsii_06_fevralya_2013_goda_.php

[50] *See* Протокол заседания Рабочей группы по гражданскому участию в судебно-правовой сфере (совместно с рабочей группой по делу Магнитского), 5 мая 2011 г., at: http://www.president-sovet.ru/structure/group_8/materials/meeting_of_the_working_group.php

As one of those experts, I did not know the identities of the others at the time. This was deliberate and, I now realize, done to protect the integrity of the experts and their work. On April 1, 2011, I received a letter signed by Mikhail Fedotov, the Chairman of the Human Rights Council, and Tamara Morshchakova, as Chairwoman of the Working Group.[51] The letter invited me "to participate in an independent public expert analysis of official documents and proceedings" concerning the second conviction.[52] The analysis would be limited to the text of the verdict, the record of the proceedings which took place in the Khamovnichesky Court, and other court materials. I was invited to write an opinion within my area of expertise concerning any "legal question which you believe to be pertinent within judicial practice in connection with the case at hand."[53]

This was consistent with the principles that the Council had set for itself in this matter, which included a decision that the experts had no mandate to make any "political appraisal" of the case.[54] The Council set itself other principles for the selection of experts, too, including that:

1. The experts should possess high qualifications recognized in law and other academic areas that are confirmed by their published scholarly works;
2. No expert should have a conflict of interest, including past participation in this case;
3. The preparation of the expert reports would be completely voluntary and without any payment by or contract with the Council;
4. The content of the reports were exclusively the prerogative of the individual expert and, regardless of their content, included in the analysis of the Council, presented to the President, and made available to the public.[55]

These principles were put into direct effect, as the letter I received made crystal clear.[56] As promised, I worked without any interference, or even communication, from the Human Rights Council. I was not paid. I did not know the identity of my fellow experts, their opinions, or the Council's recommendations before this information was publicly announced on December 21, 2012.[57] Other experts report

[51] Letter to Jeffrey Kahn from M.A. Fedotov and T.G. Morshchakova, April 1, 2011.

[52] *Id.*

[53] *Id.*

[54] *See* Принципы организации экспертизы (правового анализа) судебных актов по уголовному делу Ходорковского М.Б. и Лебедева П.Л. ("Привлекаемые Советом при Президенте РФ эксперты не имеют мандата на то, чтобы выступить с политической оценкой по поводу состоявшегося процесса."), at: http://www.president-sovet.ru/structure/group_6/materials/principles_of_organization_of_expert_legal_analysis_of_judicial_decisions_in_the_criminal_case_of_mb.php

[55] *Id.*

[56] Letter to Kahn from Fedotov and Morshchakova, *supra* note 50.

[57] Изложение основных тем, составших предмет общественной научной экспертизы по уголвному делу М.Б. Ходорковского и П.Л. Лебедева, 21.12.2012, http://president-sovet.ru/structure/group_6/materials/izlozenie_tem.php

the same experience.[58] When I did learn the identities of my fellow experts, I was pleased to be in the company of such accomplished individuals:

1. Sergei M. Guriev, Rector of the New Economic School (Moscow);
2. Anatolii V. Naumov, Professor at the Academy of the General Procurator's Office (Moscow);
3. Oksana M. Oleinik, Chair of the Department of Entrepreneurial Law, National Research University Higher School of Economics (Moscow);
4. Alexei D. Proshliakov, Chair of the Department of Criminal Procedure, Urals State Law Academy (Ekaterinburg);
5. Mikhail A. Subbotin, IMEMO, Russian Academy of Sciences (Moscow);
6. Astamur A. Tedeev, National Research University Higher School of Economics (Moscow);
7. Ferdinand Feldbrugge, Professor of Law, University of Leiden (the Netherlands);
8. Otto Luchterhandt, Professor of Law, University of Hamburg (Germany).

The experts' reports were evaluated by the Council, which then made its own observations and recommendations.[59] All of these were compiled into a 427-page, three-volume hardbound set that was personally delivered to President Medvedev in the Kremlin by the Chairman of the Council, Mikhail Fedotov, on December 27, 2011, the first anniversary of Khodorkovsky's conviction.[60] Fedotov reminded the President that he himself had directed this work to be done.[61]

The Council recommended a number of substantive and procedural reforms that had been advanced in other forums. Some, it is now clear, were the seeds for reforms subsequently adopted.[62] The Council also made recommendations concerning the

---

[58] Sergei Guriev, "Why I Am Not Returning to Russia," *N.Y. Times*, June 5, 2013. http://www.nytimes.com/2013/06/06/opinion/global/sergei-guriev-why-i-am-not-returning-to-russia.html. Howard Amos, "Russian Scholars Wary After Top Economist Flees Country," *RIA Novosti*, reprinted in Johnson's Russia List # 102 (June 6, 2013). In personal correspondence, Professor Feldbrugge stated to me that in his reply to Mr. Fedotov he had stressed that he had never received directly or indirectly any money or favours from anybody in connection with the experts' reports, that it would in any case be very unlikely that he would ever be selected as the beneficiary of Mr. Khodorkovsky's benevolence, in view of the negative views he had expressed in the past about Khodorkovsky's activities, and that the panel members, including himself, all had written individual reports and there was no co-ordination at any time between the panel members (at least where he was concerned).

[59] Пресс-релиз к заседанию Совета при Президенте Российской Федерации по развитию гражданского общества и правам человека 21.12.2011, http://president-sovet.ru/structure/group_6/materials/ukos_2.php

[60] Рабочая встреча с советником Президента, председателем Совета по развитию гражданского общества и правам человека Михаилом Федотовым, 27 декабря 2011 года, http://news.kremlin.ru/news/14153

[61] *Id.*

[62] The Council recommended expanded use of juries for certain crimes; the elaboration of bases for the exclusion of judges due to conflicts of interests, including the appearance of influence by law enforcement officials; greater rights to confront witnesses and present evidence; limits on prosecution for certain crimes; limits on pre-trial detention; reform of parole and pardon, and an amnesty for those convicted of certain economic crimes. *See* Рекомендации по итогам проведения общественной экспертизы, 21.12.2011, http://president-sovet.ru/structure/group_6/materials/rekomendazii_po_itogam.php

fate of Khodorkovsky himself. Namely, the Council recommended that the Procurator General of the Russian Federation seek the repeal of the 2010 verdict and that the Investigative Committee of the Russian Federation seek reexamination on the basis of newly discovered circumstances, namely, "fundamental violations in the course of the proceedings" resulting in "a miscarriage of justice."[63] The report was referenced by the European Court of Human Rights in its most recent judgment in Khodorkovsky and Lebedev v. Russia.[64]

15.4.2 Reprisals Against the Human Rights Council and Its Experts

On March 4, 2012, Vladimir Putin was elected to a third term as president. Almost immediately, the Council found itself under threat. Its membership was swollen with new members, diluting its ability to act and deliberate. In response, fifteen of the previous members (almost a quarter of the original cadre) – including the highly respected Lyudmila Alexeyeva – resigned.[65]

On April 1, Vladimir Markin, a representative of the Investigative Committee, smeared the integrity of the Council's report, alleging to the mass media in conclusory fashion that some of the participants in the examination of the case may have received funding from Yukos in the past.[66] Around the same time, government authorities conducted an unscheduled audit of the Center for Law and Economic Studies (CLES), a think tank through which a number of members of the Human Rights Council and some of the experts had participated in high-level discussions of law reform in the past.[67]

On July 23, the Basmannyi District Court in Moscow issued a decision permitting investigative searches in the continuation of Criminal Case № 18/41-03 – the first investigation of Khodorkovsky, opened in 2003.[68] The court's order was sought by V.A. Lakhtin, among others, who had been a lead prosecutor in the second Khodorkovsky case.[69] The court's order, by its nature, received no press attention and thus was subject to no public discussion.

---

[63] *See* Рекомендации, *supra* note 61.

[64] *Khodorkovskiy v. Lebedev v. Russia*, App. Nos. 11082/06 & 13772/05 (July 25, 2013).

[65] Tom Balmforth, "Putin Packs Presidential Human Rights Council," *Radio Free Europe/Radio Liberty*, Nov. 12, 2012. http://www.rferl.org/content/putin-appoints-new-members-presidential-human-rights-council-russia/24768384.html

[66] Interfax.ru, "Федотов о заявлении СК РФ по экспертизе дела ЮКОСа: "учите матчасть,"" Apr. 1, 2012, http://www.interfax.ru/news.asp?id=238756; Экспертов СПЧ преследуют за доклад по второму делу "ЮКОСа", 06.02.2013, http://grani.ru/Politics/Russia/yukos/m.211325.html

[67] Леонид Никитинский, Третье дело ЮКОСа, о "печеньках," Новая газета, 08.02.2013, http://www.novayagazeta.ru/politics/56623.html

[68] *Id.*

[69] *Id.*

The searches themselves began in September. The first targets were the CLES offices and three apartments. Investigators seized electronic media and cell phones.[70] The investigators appeared to be searching for connections between the Russian experts, CLES, and Khodorkovsky. CLES had been responsible for a number of progressive legal reform projects in which several of the experts and Council members had participated in the past, including several large monographs on the rule of law.[71] The warrant issued by Judge Skuridina of the Basmannyi Court described the investigators' apparent theory that the Center had received funds from Khodorkovsky that were in turn passed to members of the Council and the experts in exchange for legal opinions favorable to them.[72]

One of the experts targeted was Mikhail Subbotin, a senior researcher at IMEMO and the deputy director of CLES. As he recalled:

> They came at half past eight in the morning on September 7. They presented the search warrant. Typically, a witness is invited, but they do not burst into his house with witnesses. So, evidently, it is all the more serious. … Five warrants (still one more was planned, but did not occur) in one morning in one research center at different addresses.[73]

Subbotin noted how the investigators refused the request of the executive director to call a lawyer. The investigators seized everything from diplomas to a passport, computers, flash drives, professional archives and working papers, bringing the Center's work to a standstill.[74] The CLES accountants and other employees were questioned for several days.[75]

In February 2013, Tamara Morshchakova revealed what was happening at a press conference: "At a minimum, two of the experts have already been subjected to different types of persecution ["преследование"]: one in an official capacity, the other in the form of criminal procedure."[76] Noting the apparent theory of the case – that the NGO used Khodorkovsky's money to fund false expert reports and pervert the course of the criminal proceedings – Morshakova expressed herself forcefully: "The accusation is senseless, fictitious, even more, this Center never conducted any kind of expert examination; it publishes monographs."[77]

---

[70] *Id.*

[71] Речь члена Совета Т.Г. Морщаковой на пресс-конференции 06 февраля 2013 года, http://president-sovet.ru/structure/group_6/materials/rech_chlena_soveta_t_g_morshchakovoy_na_press_konferentsii_06_fevralya_2013_goda_.php

[72] Постановление Басманного районного суда города Москвы о разкушении производства выемки документов, содержащих информазию, составляющую тайну переписки, 9 апреля 2013 года.

[73] Михаил Субботин, "Разбитые зеркала," 08.02.2013, http://www.gazeta.ru/comments/2013/02/08_a_4957537.shtml

[74] *Id.*; "Yukos Report Authors to Face Questioning," *The Moscow Times*, June 26, 2013. http://www.themoscowtimes.com/news/article/yukos-report-authors-to-face-questioning/482250.html

[75] Ellen Barry, "Economist Flees as Russia Aims Past Protesters," *N.Y. Times*, May 29, 2013.

[76] Lenta.ru, СПЧ пожаловался на преследования докладчиков по второму делу "ЮКОСа," 6 февраля 2013, http://lenta.ru/news/2013/02/06/experts/

[77] *Id.*; Мир 24 TV, СПЧ заявили о преследовании экспертов, готовивших доклад по второму делу ЮКОСа, 06.02.2013, http://mir24.tv/news/society/6396581

In April and May, investigators increased their pressure. Russian and Kazakh investigators searched the apartment of Elena Novikova, the Director of CLES, who was caring for her elderly father in Kazakhstan. They seized computers, phones, and papers and questioned Novikova for more than 3 days as a witness. At least once, the session stretched past midnight. Her lawyers complained about the absence of a warrant and their exclusion during the investigative actions, but to no avail.[78]

Another expert to come under pressure was Sergei Guriev, the Rector of one of Russia's premier academic institutions, a member of the Board of Directors for Sberbank, and one of the most prominent and well-respected economists in Russia. After gradually increasing attention, investigators abruptly demanded that he submit 5 years of e-mail correspondence and accede to searches of his office and home.[79] Instead, Guriev fled to Paris in self-imposed exile. "The truth," he wrote in *The New York Times*, "was that I could not come back to Russia because I feared losing my freedom."[80] After describing his work for the Human Rights Council, he turned to his treatment at the hands of investigators:

> As for me, interrogations started in February 2013. After that, I heard that in February, a colleague of Mr. Putin had talked to him about my situation, and the president had reassured the colleague that I had nothing to worry about. This did not stop the investigation – I was interrogated twice and received demands for all sorts of documents and personal information. Moreover, the investigators introduced "operative measures" – the police euphemism for surveillance. … Interestingly, during the interrogations the investigators asked me to produce "alibis," though they did not explain for what, and insisted that I was a "witness," not a "suspect."[81]

Not only Guriev, but also his institution, the Higher School of Economics, was pressured. "Simultaneously with my questioning in the Investigation Committee, a tax audit and a Rosobrnadzor (Federal Education and Science Supervisory Service) inspection were, indeed, performed. They both began at the very time that (my) interrogation began: the tax audit, in January-February, the Rosobrnadzor inspection, in March. We were told that both were normal scheduled inspections. But there had never been anything of the sort earlier."[82]

Guriev noted that his treatment changed for the worst at the end of April. Instead of another scheduled session of questioning, investigators produced a court warrant for all of Guriev's e-mail traffic since 2008: "The warrant gave no specific reasons why my e-mails had to be seized, yet concluded they had to be seized. When I complained to the investigators, one of them said that I was better off than Andrei Sakharov,

[78] Леонид Никитинский, Подробности третьего "дела ЮКОСа": Следственный комитет проводит обыски в Казахстане с санкции Басманного суда, *Новая газета*, 31.5.2013, www.novayagazeta.ru/politics/58386.html

[79] Ellen Barry, "Economist Who Fled Russia Cites Peril in Politically Charged Inquiry," *N.Y. Times*, May 31, 2013.

[80] Sergei Guriev, "Why I Am Not Returning to Russia," *N.Y. Times*, June 5, 2013. *supra* note 57.

[81] *Id.*

[82] Ольга Проскурнина, "Персона – Сергей Гуриев, бывший ректор Российской экономической школы," *Ведомости*, 11.06.2013 (translation from Johnson's Russia List # 107, June 13, 2013, # 11).

the Soviet dissident who was sent to internal exile in Gorky."[83] The investigators suggested that they also had a warrant to search his home, leading Guriev to conclude "the investigators can produce any search warrant they want without any respect for my rights, and [] they can do it without warning."[84] Guriev later told interviewers from Der Spiegel:

> The same mistakes, in terms of names and spelling, were made on both the court order and the documents the investigators presented. In other words, the court in question simply copied the investigators' documents, with their absurd accusations, and will continue to do so in the future. I felt that it was too dangerous for me to stay.[85]

My review of the documents Guriev referenced supports the truth of this allegation. It also resonates with a disturbing fact I noted in my report about the verdict in the second Khodorkovsky case: while ostensibly written by Judge Danilkin, it was riddled with similarly brazen copying, including typographical errors, from the prosecutor's indictment.[86]

After Guriev's departure, the pressure continued to mount. Subbotin was ordered to reappear for more questioning. He estimated that the sum of his interrogations lasted twelve hours.[87] Then, on June 27, Tamara Morshchakova, the retired Constitutional Court justice who chaired the Council's working group on the Khodorkovsky case, was questioned by the Investigative Committee. She summarized the investigators' theory as revealed by their questions to her: "The investigators have formed a definite version in agreement with which the financing of experts occurred through the payment for the publications of their book, participation in scientific conferences and even parliamentary hearings, although such of course is impossible."[88] The efforts of the Investigative Committee were not limited to the Russian experts. Otto Luchterhandt, a professor of law at the University of Hamburg who contributed a report, was warned at the last minute not to board a plane from Hamburg to Moscow because the Investigative Committee had requested the assistance of the German Government to question him.[89]

Tamara Morshchakova summarized the first year of President Putin's third term from the point of view of the experts who had advised his predecessor on his great matter: "Complaints were leveled at Anatoliy Naumov, a classic of Russian criminal

---

[83] *Id.*

[84] *Id.*

[85] Christian Neef and Matthias Schepp, "Exiled Economic Adviser: 'Putin Is Afraid of the Public'," *Der Spiegel*, June 10, 2013. *Supra* note 41.

[86] *See* Report, *supra* note 42. An appendix to the report reveals this cutting-and-pasting between indictment and verdict.

[87] "Yukos Report Authors to Face Questioning," *The Moscow Times*, June 26, 2013. Софья Самохина, "Экспертов допросили по второму делу ЮКОСа," *Коммерсантъ-Online*, 28.06.2013.

[88] Самохина, *supra* note 86.

[89] "Rough Justice: Will Khodorkovsky Face Trial Again?" *Der Spiegel*, 43/2013 (October 21, 2013), http://www.spiegel.de/international/europe/russia-appears-to-be-preparing-a-new-case-against-khodorkovsky-a-929017.html

law – he worked at the Academy of the Office of the Prosecutor General. He has now been dismissed. Searches were carried out at the home of Mikhail Subbotin, Astamur Tedeyev was visited at his department in the Higher School of Economics National Research University. Documents and computers were confiscated. Some of them were questioned. Oksana Oleynik, director of the Higher School of Economics Business Law Department, was also summoned to an investigation, but it has not taken place for some reason or other."[90] With the addition of Sergei Guriev, five of the six Russian experts are publicly known to have been ordered to questioning, subject to search, or both.

15.5 Conclusion

On February 13, 2013, I received another letter from Mikhail Fedotov, the Chairman of the Council. The letter informed me of the investigation, noting that it was ostensibly being conducted under the criminal case opened against Khodorkovsky in 2003 (and for which he had already been convicted in 2005), "but now it is based on the facts of financing by the convicted persons [i.e. Khodorkovsky and Lebedev] of deliberately false conclusions of specialists under the guise of independent public analyses by way of paying those persons who organized its realization and the experts."[91] Fedotov concluded: "I consider it my duty to inform you about this and that the Council will intently follow the developing situation, actively conveying its view to the leaders of the country."[92]

The basis for the warrant that Fedotov identified was patently absurd. The 2003 investigation had been closed after producing 162 volumes of material that served as the basis for a conviction in a case that had been finally adjudicated in 2005. Even if the insinuated payments had occurred (a fact repudiated by numerous members of the Council, as well as several of the experts, including myself),[93] that fact could not possibly constitute a crime under Russian law. The implication – sometimes insinuated and sometimes more overtly stated – that the work of the Council obstructed justice was particularly odd. In an interview Morshchakova gave shortly after President Medvedev charged the Council with its work, she emphasized that analysis of the case "could only begin after the cassational appeal will be completed and the sentence enters into legal force."[94] And so it did.

[90] *See* Проскурнина, *supra* note 81.

[91] *See* Letter from Mikhail Fedotov to Jeffrey Kahn, *supra* note 6.

[92] *Id.*

[93] Jeffrey Kahn, "In Putin's Russia, Shooting the Messenger," *N.Y. Times*, Feb. 25, 2013. http://www.nytimes.com/2013/02/26/opinion/in-putins-russia-shooting-the-messenger.html

[94] Андрей Камакин, "Судите сами," *Журнал "Итоги"*, 21.02.11, http://www.itogi.ru/russia/2011/8/162040.html ("Что же касается дела Ходорковского и Лебедева, то анализ можно начать только после того, как оно пройдет кассационную инстанцию и приговор вступит в законную силу.").

But perhaps the warrant and the theory behind it, like the 2010 verdict that led to the work of the Council in the first place, were not intended to make *legal* sense. Perhaps they were meant to send a message about the use of power. Or, more precisely, the use of law as an instrument of power. Certainly, the investigators' message was not lost on the experts. "I thought that a Russian citizen was entitled to express his viewpoint," Sergei Guriev wrote. "I believe now also that you cannot be afraid to tell the truth. But I know now that such behavior is attended by substantial risk. … I have done nothing wrong and [] there are no grounds for depriving me of freedom. Nonetheless, I disagree [with President Putin] that in present-day Russia this confers guarantees of security."[95]

The message was also not lost on the Council members who organized the work of the experts. On June 6, the Council published an apology:

> We express our apologies to all of the Russian experts invited by us for the anxiety and humiliation that has been caused them by the actions of our country's organs of law enforcement. Unlike these organs, we have no doubts about our conscientiousness in the selection of the experts, nor in their honesty or competence. We underline that their public analysis is not a procedural document, possessing legal effect, nor a final verdict of civil society, but only the result of serious analytical work by those who organized and carried it out. A result of high quality is possible only through guaranteeing to experts the possibility to fearlessly express their independent opinion. In this, in fact, is the essence of the idea of public control and the contract between civil society and power.[96]

Tamara Morshchakova put the matter more bluntly: "The Council does not have the moral right to appeal to experts if it cannot guarantee to them that their free expression will not be punished."[97]

Many scholars would find little difficulty concluding that the aftermath of the Council's expert investigation was an affront to the rule of law. As T.R.S. Allan noted, "those freedoms associated with the citizen's ability to criticise the laws, and question the justice of the government's actions and policies, must be accounted an integral part of the rule of law."[98] Others would label such a claim too normative a conclusion about individual liberty, or otherwise outside the narrower procedural boundaries that contain the concept of the rule of law.

More's metaphor of a causeway redirects these scholarly debates by avoiding precise definitions of the rule of law or prioritizing substance over process, values over institutions, the quotidian over constitutional moments. The law-as-causeway metaphor recognizes that the state must articulate the boundaries of lawful conduct in

---

[95] *See* Проскурнина, *supra* note 81.

[96] Заявление Совета, в связи с ситуацией, сложившейся вокруг Сергея Гуриева и других экспертов, привлеченных Советом для общественной научной экспертизы по "второму делу ЮКОСа", 06.06.2013, http://president-sovet.ru/council_decision/council_statement/v_svyazi_s_situatsiey_slozhivsheysya_vokrug_sergeya_gurieva_i_drugikh_ekspertov.php

[97] Елена Масюк, *supra* note 48.

[98] T.R.S. Allan, The Rule of Law as the Rule of Reason: Consent and Constitutionalism, 115 *L.Q.R.* 225 (1999); *Id.* at 238 ("The rights to receive information and to exchange and debate ideas, whenever such information and ideas concern the content of the laws and the nature of government actions and policies, are integral features of the constitutional interpretation of the rule of law.").

order to construct the social order it desires to create, and the citizen must perceive those boundaries in order to organize his conduct and affairs with a proper understanding of social risk and personal safety. Just as a real causeway provides form and structure, these physical attributes parallel the formal principles and institutions that some rule-of-law definitions prioritize. And just as a real causeway requires travelers to possess a shared understanding of the "rules of the road," the rule-of-law causeway also requires predictable processes, standards as well as rules, and the opportunity to move fluidly within these boundaries. These attributes similarly parallel the emphasis other scholars place on procedure and the opportunity for individuals to be defendants or litigants empowered by legal process and endowed with dignity.

No worse metaphor has been devised for law than to depict it as a sword or a shield, metaphors that emphasize the instrumental use of law. The better metaphor is law as a two-way street, especially in a society struggling under the legacy of recent authoritarian history. The rule-of-law is a causeway. Unfortunately, Russia has always suffered from notoriously bad roads.

Chapter 16
American Constitutional Analysis and a Substantive Understanding of the Rule of Law

Robin Charlow

Abstract Both rule of law and legal state notions developed with the shared goal of promoting peace and freedom by checking excessive concentrations and arbitrary applications of power. Originally both embodied formal requirements for law making and application, to ensure that laws were public, fixed, durable, and uniformly applied. More recently, however, those describing the legal state, and somewhat less universally those advocating for rule of law, seem to have taken these notions in a substantive direction, arguing that compliance requires states to guarantee particular substantive human rights as well. If this substantive concept comes to be accepted as a required aspect of the rule of law, the broadly flexible characteristics of American constitutional interpretation could, perhaps oddly, work against continued American adherence to the rule of law. This is increasingly likely to be the case as the United States deals with the stresses to its safety and security that undoubtedly will arise as it faces the challenges of the twenty-first century.

16.1 Introduction

The twin notions of rule of law, adopted in common law countries, and legal state, prevalent in European and other civil law jurisdictions, appear to have developed along similar lines and to serve essentially the same ends. Both stem from common roots in the political philosophy of the ancient Greeks. Both are intended to control and protect the people from excessive concentrations of power, either in the state or in small groups of individuals, and to prevent consequently arbitrary rule. Ultimately, both are meant to secure a measure of freedom and protection for people and their property, so that we may live together in a peaceful and orderly world.

With thanks to Tianlong You for his exceptionally dedicated research assistance.

R. Charlow (✉)
Maurice A. Deane School of Law, Hofstra University, Hempstead, NY, USA
e-mail: Robin.Charlow@hofstra.edu

J.R. Silkenat et al. (eds.), *The Legal Doctrines of the Rule of Law and the Legal State (Rechtsstaat)*, Ius Gentium: Comparative Perspectives on Law and Justice 38,
DOI 10.1007/978-3-319-05585-5_16, © Springer International Publishing Switzerland 2014

It has been argued that each eventually evolved in at least one major way, to include not only formal requirements for law-making but also certain substantive guarantees as well. While this last development remains more contested in modern accounts of the rule of law than of the legal state, the two constructs nevertheless may be advancing along the same basic trajectory, and they appear to have begun to merge in some discussions within the international arena. The more interchangeably the two notions are used, the greater the possibility that the propriety of adding a substantive aspect to the idea of rule of law, to match that of legal state, while still rather disputed, may gain wider acceptance. If this occurs, then despite their origins in significantly different legal and social environments and despite possible changes in the foundational requirements of each, the modern conceptions of rule of law and legal state may converge not only in terms of goals but also in terms of form. In the meantime, societies might draw on either standard to secure or maintain their basic freedom.

When nations are presented with the challenges they are likely to encounter in the twenty-first century, the success of either one of these constructs in checking governmental or private excess or arbitrariness will likely depend more on the habits and character of the people involved in any given instance than on the particular features of their governing structure or the rights they nominally enjoy. No doubt principles of rule of law or legal state may, over time, influence and even alter the civic and social habits—and therefore the political character—of the populace. Ultimately, it is the latter that will determine the real outcome in terms of genuinely experienced rule of law benefits. In other words, whether any given community actually succeeds in keeping autocracy and irrationality at bay will have more to do with what its constituents expect of their government and of one another, and what they are willing to tolerate from both, than it will depend on alleged adherence to an agreed upon set of rules for governance or list of guaranteed fundamental rights.

In the particular context of rule of law in the United States, the addition of substantive rights guarantees to the accepted canon of rule of law requirements could, perhaps oddly, work against continued adherence to the rule of law. Many of the specific fundamental human rights often considered necessary to a legal state or rule of law regime are contained in, or could be found to reside in, the United States Constitution. There, according to the American tradition of broadly flexible constitutional interpretation and limitation, these human rights are subject to a significant degree of change over time, particularly through an accumulation of incremental interpretive steps. Despite the American character as a generally law-abiding and law-respecting society, when faced with major issues threatening to their sense of national and personal security, Americans may well lapse into complacency in the face of small but cumulative erosion of substantive rights and freedoms. Their traditional process of expansive constitutional interpretation, which seems so natural to Americans at present, could have accustomed them to interpretive change so much so that it effectively enables an almost imperceptible gradual curtailment of rights. Thus, *if* rights are to be considered an indispensable feature of a modern understanding of the rule of law, a significant retraction of rights through interpretive limitation could ultimately mean a significant diminution of American adherence to the rule of law, and both could be facilitated, or at least enhanced, by the well-accepted system of flexible constitutional rights analysis characteristic of United States law.

16.2 Parallel Development of Rule of Law and Legal State

16.2.1 A Substantive Turn in Rule of Law?

The term "rule of law" seems first to appear in the explorations of the ancient Greek philosophers Plato and Aristotle, then to reappear in the work of Christian scholars of the Middle Ages, and finally to be borrowed by European jurists in the late nineteenth century.[1] Although its exact requirements are open to debate, essentially all definitions of the concept emphasize the ideal that law should be promulgated according to pre-established rules, universally and equally applicable, non-arbitrary, and enforced according to its terms (sometimes said to require enforcement by an independent body or judiciary).[2] Until the latter part of the twentieth century, for the most part the idea embodied a formal concept. Law achieved legitimacy by complying with certain prescribed formalities of adoption and application that effectuated the ancient ideals. The goal was to prevent the accretion of broad power in particular individuals or groups of rulers who might be tempted to govern according to their own autocratic policies rather than in the interests of the people generally. Rule of law was rule by pre-set standards, as contrasted with arbitrary and unpredictable rule according to the changing whims of men. In short, rule of law began as a formalistic notion, in which specific procedural features were thought most desirable in order to best ensure against totalitarian exercise of power. Freedom and justice were to be secured by public, fixed, durable laws, uniformly applied (probably by a body independent of the law makers and law enforcers, thus requiring separation of powers, another often-cited feature of conceptions of the rule of law).

During the twentieth century, in countries sharing common law roots, discussion of the rule of law principle began to evolve in some quarters to include a substantive dimension as well, though many noted legal theorists continued—and still

[1] *See* Mark Ellis, "Toward a Common Ground Definition of the Rule of Law Incorporating Substantive Principles of Justice", 72 *University of Pittsburg Law Review* (2010) 193 n.11 (citing Albert Venn Dicey, *An Introduction to the Study of the Law and the Constitution* (1885)); Brian Z. Tamanaha, *On the Rule of Law: History, Politics, Theory* (Cambridge Univ. Press, 2004) at 7, 15, 63.

[2] Ellis, *supra* note 1, at 193; Tamanaha, *supra* note 1, at 63–64 (discussing Dicey's three rule of law requirements: pre-existing laws, equality of application, and judicial enforcement); Brenner M. Fissell, "Jury Nullification and the Rule of Law", draft manuscript at 5 (forthcoming in *Legal Theory*) (citing Lon Fuller, *The Morality of Law* (Yale Univ. Press, 1969) at 38–39, and Matthew Kramer, *Objectivity and the Rule of Law* (Cambridge Univ. Press, 2007) at 104).

continue—to adhere to the original strictly formal notion.[3] It was observed during this period that a number of societies managed to follow to the letter all the procedural dictates of a formal rule of law state and yet failed to establish a truly just government or to provide a meaningful check on the arbitrary imposition of governmental authority.[4] In short, rule of law formality could result in unjust or immoral law. This has led some legal scholars and institutions to amend their understanding of the rule of law principle so that it guarantees not only procedural regularity but also a certain modicum of substantive fairness and/or basic human rights.[5] Although those within the community of reformists may not agree on exactly which rights comprise the necessary minimum to constitute a rule of law, nevertheless for some scholars in the United States and various international arenas the rule of law as a concept has effectively taken on a dual formal plus substantive character.[6] Agreement is assuredly not universal, but there is a growing contingent that reads into the conception of the rule of law this new substantive component.[7]

Adherents to this view present overlapping lists of the specific basic rights and freedoms that comprise the required minimum measure that they consider integral to constitute a rule of law state. As to some rights (such as freedom of speech), there is relatively broad agreement; as to others, perhaps not. In any event, in this twenty-first century, a significant number now seem inclined to embrace the idea that a state must both observe certain procedural formalities for law adoption and application and also conform its law so as to respect particular substantive rights or notions of justice—whatever they might be—in order to warrant designation as a rule of law compliant state.

---

[3] Ellis, *supra* note 1 at 194 n.17 (citing Joseph Raz, "The Rule of Law and its Virtue", 93 *Law Quarterly Review* (1977) 195, 196); Fissell, *supra* note 2 at 9–10 (discussing the author's views and citing Joseph Raz, *The Authority of Law* (Oxford Univ. Press, 1979)).

[4] *See, for example,* Kenneth E. Himma, "What Exactly is the Problem with Judicial Supremacy? The Rule of Law, Moral Legitimacy, and the Construction of Constitutional Law", in *Courts, Interpretation, the Rule of Law—Democracy and the Rule of Law*, Miodrag A. Jovanović and Kenneth E. Himma eds. (Eleven International Publishing, forthcoming 2013), draft manuscript at 10, *available at* http://papers.ssrn.com/sol3/papers.cfm?abstract_id=2288165 (discussing H.L.A. Hart's observation that a strictly formal set of rule of law standards is "compatible with the enactment and enforcement of morally wicked laws").

[5] *Id.* at 9 & n.6 (citing Ronald Dworkin, *Law's Empire* (Harvard Univ. Press, 1986)).

[6] *See* Ellis, *supra* note 1, at 197; Fissell, *supra* note 2, at 6–8 (discussing the work of various American academics).

[7] *See* e.g., Ellis, *supra* note 1, at 194–199; Brian Bix, "Radbruch's Formula, Conceptual Analysis, and the Rule of Law", in *Law, Liberty, and the Rule of Law*, 18 *Ius Gentium: Comparative Perspectives on Law and Justice*, Imer B. Flores & Kenneth E. Himma eds. (Springer, 2013) at 68–69 ("A small number of theorists advocate more substantive conceptions of the rule of law [which] tend to include requirements of democracy and the protection of certain basic human rights"); Gülriz Uygur, "The Rule of Law: Is the Line Between the Formal and the Moral Blurred?", in *Law, Liberty, and the Rule of Law*, 18 *Ius Gentium: Comparative Perspectives on Law and Justice*, Imer B. Flores & Kenneth E. Himma eds. (Springer, 2013) at 118 ("the rule of law has a moral minimum"). *Contra* Himma, *supra* note 4 (rejecting the addition of substantive rights to the notion of rule of law); Fissell, *supra* note 2 (renouncing the idea that rule of law contains any substantive dimension).

16.2.2 The Substantive Turn in Legal State

The idea that "law should have primacy over policy," that is, that people should be ruled by universally-applicable, non-arbitrary laws as opposed to by men (meaning tyrannically), was borrowed from Aristotle not only in countries following the common law but rather throughout the western legal tradition, including in civil law jurisdictions.[8] The German term "Rechtsstaat" or "legal state" similarly derives from critiques of absolute power.[9] It is reported to have first appeared at the end of the eighteenth century in the work of Johann Petersen, nearly 100 years before Albert Dicey resurrected the term rule of law in England in 1885.[10] Petersen considered only a political body based on human rights—a Rechtsstaat, or rights-based state—to be legitimate—thus, a "legal" state—and to stand in contrast to a "Polizeistaat" or policy-based state, in which despotic policy prevailed over human rights.[11] Almost coincident with its origin, this Continental notion of legal state was quickly expanded to encompass Enlightenment values, and therefore to include also a requirement of "Vernunfisstaat" or "rational state."[12] In a rational state, the rationality element translates into a preference for generalized over individuated norms, and thus for statutes over adjudication, and codifications over individual statutes.[13] Rationality thus appears to take up the mantle of non-arbitrariness; outcomes based on fixed, considered statutes containing rules that apply to all are less arbitrary—and therefore more rational—than those that result from the less uniform application of ad hoc, individualized adjudications. Consequently, rule of law and legal state, though somewhat different constructions, in their formal aspect both at least impliedly encompassed notions of the universality, equality, and non-arbitrariness of publicized laws, and both with the goal of preventing autocracy and promoting peace and order.

Also like rule of law, the term Rechtsstaat did not originally require that the people be possessed of certain specific substantive rights. In the early nineteenth century, around the time of its origination, German scholars who were influenced by

---

[8] *See* Iain Stewart, "From 'Rule of Law' to 'Legal State': A Time of Reincarnation?" in *Rule of Law: Transformative Approaches*, K. Padmaja ed. (Icfai Univ. Press, 2008) at 6.

[9] *Id.* at 7 (noting that the term "*Rechtsstaat* ... seems to have found ready translation into every major European language except English").

[10] *Id.*; Ellis, *supra* note 1, at 193 n.11. Others attribute the term to early nineteenth century Hanoverian jurists, influenced by the British, who wished similarly to move from autocratic monarchic rule toward classical liberalism. *See* Hans-Joachim Lauth & Jenniver Sehring, "Putting Deficient Rechtsstaat on the Research Agenda: Reflections on Diminished Subtypes", 8 *Comparative Sociology* (2009) 165, 172–74.

[11] Stewart, *supra* note 8, at 7.

[12] *Id.*

[13] *Id.* at 8. In its preference for codified law over individual statutes, the legal state puts a premium on rationality and regularity, as codifications tend to be less haphazard, more considered bodies of legislation than individual statutes, which might arise in response, for example, to the vagaries of compelling current events.

the reason-based philosophy of Immanuel Kant formulated their notion of a rule of law or legal state that consisted of a set of formal requirements mandating that the state be framed and limited by formally adopted law which, when applied, was subject to judicial review.[14] Notably, they did not provide any specific substantive standards to which the formally adopted law need adhere.[15] This formalistic ideal comprised the understanding of Rechtsstaat so much so that by the turn into the twentieth century, with judicial positivism the dominant paradigm, the notion of rule of law in a legal state completely excluded any substantive, politically-contestable criteria. [16]

But the events of World War II, most especially the Nazi experience, altered this understanding of legal state, just at it changed some theorists' understanding of rule of law. The example of modern totalitarian regimes made it clear that adherence to formal lawmaking and law administration requirements was insufficient to check authoritarian power and unequal application of law. What emerged was a concept of legal state that "was opposed to … formal legal positivism," and instead included "in its core [a] connect[ion] to a culture of universal human rights complemented by a historically grown understanding of social justice."[17] As a consequence, over the course of the twentieth century the concept of legal state, and for some also that of rule of law, evolved in the direction of encompassing dual formal and substantive dimensions. At this juncture, in the twenty-first century, it seems a fairly well accepted view that a legal state requires not only the observance of certain formal procedural principles (separation of powers, public statutes of universal and equal application, etc.) but also the guarantee of respect for a set of particular basic substantive human rights.[18]

---

[14] Matthias Koetter, "*Rechtsstaat* and *Rechtsstaatlichkeit* in Germany", in *Understandings of the Rule of Law: Germany*, Wikis der Freien Universität, (Feb. 28, 2013), *available at* http://wikis.fu-berlin.de/display/SBprojectro/Germany.

[15] *Id.*

[16] In 1928, Hans Kelsen affirmed that the state was "nothing but *Rechtstaat* in a formal sense of the term." *Id.* (citing Kelsen's "Pure Theory of Law"("Reine Rechtslehre")).

[17] Koetter, *supra* note 14.

[18] *See* Ronald Brand, "Promoting the Rule of Law: Cooperation and Competition in the EU-US Relationship", 72 *University of Pittsburgh Law Review* (2010) 163, 164 ("Europeans [attempting to define the rule of law at a recent conference] are much more ready to focus on substantive rights as necessary to the rule of law."); Augusto Zimmermann, "Rule of Law as a Culture of Legality: Legal and Extra-legal Elements for the Realisation of the Rule of Law in Society", 14 *Murdoch University Electronic Journal of Law* (2007)10, 12 n.13 (quoting Ernst Böckenförde, to the effect that Rechsstaat "means primarily recognition of the fundamental civil rights," including such civil liberties as the freedoms of belief, conscience, the press, movement, contract, and occupation, as well as equality before the law and protection of property). Perhaps this was an easier step to take in the case of legal state, as opposed to rule of law, since the term Rechtsstaat itself originally derived from Petersen's privileging of those political units based on human rights.

16.2.3 *Difference and Convergence*

Despite these similarities in their origins, in their goals, and possibly also in their recent development, Iain Stewart observes that the legal state and the rule of law are not one in the same. The law to which policy is subject in a legal state was always statutory law, while the law to which policy is subject in a common law rule of law state was originally judge-made law. However, he explains, the idea that the common law is judge-made is rather nuanced, and to a large extent dated as well. Even in the old days, common law judges were not supposed to (at least if their decisions were to be considered legitimate) fashion judge-made law according to their personal preferences or individual conceptions of proper moral aims, nor according to their ad hoc perception of just results in particular cases. Rather, they searched for universal and widely accepted principles of humanity in determining each interpretation of or advance in the common law, and believed themselves bound by such broad and universally applicable principles in future cases once these were identified as part of the common law.[19] In common law countries today, judge-made common law is, in any event, largely superseded by the primacy of statutory law, which modern common law judges purport to be interpreting and applying in almost all instances.[20]

As a consequence of these developments toward statutory authority in common law jurisdictions, at least in its formal aspect the common law rule of law has moved significantly in the same direction as the civil law legal state. While the common law was earlier conceived as judge-made, and hence not statutory, in much of the common law world today law is now fundamentally codified or at least enacted. In the United States, for example, judges essentially consider themselves to be interpreting and applying legislation either according to its terms and/or in accord with the perceived legislative intention. They do not usually believe themselves to be a lawmaking branch of government, and indeed might describe such behavior as antithetical to their role as legal adjudicators.[21] Thus, in regard to the formal component, both the rule of law and the rational state feature of the legal state depend on the primacy of statutes, which are typically adopted following procedural regularities, publicized, and universally and equally applicable. It can readily be seen that these common formal features of both rule of law and legal state are intended to prevent concentration of power in the few; laws must wend their way through a regular and public process of adoption and promulgation, after which, though perhaps not permanently

[19] *See* Stewart, *supra* note 8, at 8–12.

[20] *Id.* As Kenneth Himma explains, the common law courts' development of governing legal principles operates only at the discretion of the legislature, and their authority in this regard can be revoked at any time by the legislature. Himma, *supra* note 4, at 20.

[21] *See, e.g., National Federation of Independent Business v. Sebelius*, 132 S. Ct. 2566, 2579 (2012) ("Members of this [the United States Supreme] Court are vested with the authority to interpret the law; we possess neither the expertise nor the prerogative to make policy judgments. Those decisions are entrusted to our Nation's elected leaders.... It is not our job to protect the people from the consequences of their political choices.").

entrenched, they stand as the fixed, often long-term rules that are applied the same to all, including government actors.

In the substantive aspect as well, the modern conception of the rule of law and the legal state may also be beginning to converge. While early rule of law descriptions did not include a set of guaranteed substantive rights, and many even decried such a requirement as contrary to the very notion of rule of law, this is no longer the case. Even though clearly not a universally accepted (or some argue even a widely accepted) view, many understand rule of law today to encompass a certain modicum of basic fairness, rights and freedoms. This feature is very much a part of the modern description of the legal state, which it now appears is generally conceived of as a rights-based regime. At least for those who believe a rule of law state and a legal state both envision some set of fundamental human rights that must be respected and enforced by government, these concepts have essentially merged in regard to this substantive aspect as well as in their formal dimension.

Of course, even if both rule of law and legal state contain a substantive requirement, their ultimate convergence would still depend to some extent on what substance must be achieved or which specific rights must be recognized in order to qualify as either a legal or rule of law state, since one's view of the contents of substantive justice could vary quite significantly. The specifics could be a contested feature in both regimes, especially if each encompasses an evolving rather than a fixed list of necessary rights or freedoms. However, to the extent legal state and rule of law theorists have articulated their views of the inventory of necessary substantive guarantees, their lists appear largely to overlap. For example, compilations of required guarantees typically include such fundamental civil rights as freedom of conscience, freedom of speech, freedom of movement, and the right to a fair and impartial legal process, to name a few.[22] It is not especially remarkable to find a fair degree of agreement on the content of required rights because the identification of such rights in both legal and rule of law states would naturally and similarly derive from international norms and other historically common acknowledgements.[23] Therefore, despite some potentially contested particulars, it seems that in their call for the observance of fundamental substantive human rights, as in their requirements for particular procedural formalities, both of which are designed to curb excessive and arbitrary power, the concepts of rule of law (for some) and legal state (for most) are moving along the same path of development, and that, for many they have now effectively merged.

---

[22] *See* Ellis, *supra* note 1, at 202–207 (discussing certain fundamental "non-derogable" rights, including the right to a fair trial; the right to freedom of thought, conscience and religion; and others).

[23] Koetter, *supra* note 14. Mark Ellis suggests that, in the rule of law context, there may be both derogable and non-derogable rights, the latter category containing those that fall within the international consensus of *jus cogens* norms. Ellis, *supra* note 1, at 200–201.

16.3 Culture as Determinative

Despite all the effort that has been expended in determining the necessary and sufficient conditions for adhering to the rule of law or for achieving a legal state, in the end no particular set of features can succeed in identifying those societies in which the essential goals of these constructs have been or will be met.[24] That is because success does not ultimately depend on which formal rules for law making and enforcement are followed, nor on which rights or freedoms are substantively guaranteed. What matters much more than either of these legal characteristics is the character of the subject people.[25] To predict success, it is more important to know whether the citizens typically form, by nature or nurture, a law-abiding culture, or instead its opposite. It is the willingness of the body politic to cooperate in making and enforcing the law, to comply with the law in uncomfortable as well comfortable instances, and to respect the basic civil and human rights of others, that determines how truly peaceful, equitable, orderly, and just any given social group will turn out to be.

A nation's particular structural features of governance and entrenched set of guaranteed rights may influence the political character of its people. The relationship runs in both directions. The people's tendency to adhere to rules and respect rights determines what laws and rules they will adopt and observe. At the same time, over time, the content of their adopted rules and rights may also influence the general character of the people toward the peaceful, equitable, and cooperative goals intended by rule of law and legal state constructs.[26] But no particular institutional characteristics can guarantee achievement of the anticipated objectives of the rule of law, no matter how perfectly the state follows rule of law requirements, be they formal alone or also substantive. It is the willingness of the people to act according to the properly promulgated law, to uphold it, to respect it, to defend it, and to enforce it, even when inconvenient and not in their personal interest, that will determine whether the state, and the society more generally, behave in a non-arbitrary, power-constrained manner. [27] These are characteristics that may be affected by the rules and principles of law, but are not determined by them. The

---

[24] *See* Augusto Zimmermann, "The Politics of Lawlessness in Brazil: How Brazilian Politics Overrides the Rule of Law", 15 *Murdoch University Electronic Journal of Law* (2008) 3 (providing an excellent detailed example of the reasons for Brazil's failure to achieve a rule of law state).

[25] Robin Charlow, "America's Constitutional Rule of Law: Structure and Symbol", in *The Rule of Law in Comparative Perspective*, 3 *Ius Gentium: Comparative Perspectives on Law and Justice*, Mortimer Sellers and Tadeusz Tomaszewski eds. (Springer, 2010) at 93–96 (illustrating this thesis by comparing the different public reactions to contemporary examples of executive excesses in the United States and Russia).

[26] *Id.* at 95–96.

[27] *See* Zimmermann, *supra* note 18, at 24 n. 82 (2007) (quoting John Stuart Mill, *Considerations on Representative Government* (1861, William Benton edition 1952) at 31 (opining that the achievement of the rule of law is "determined by social circumstances")); *id.* at 25 n. 86 (2007) (quoting Martin Krygier expounding on his thesis that the rule of law "depends as much on characteristics of society as of the law, and on their interactions").

political culture of the people has more to do with history and social context, perhaps, than with institutional and constitutional design, though each surely influences the other. [28]

16.4 American Constitutional Rights and Rule of Law in the Twenty-First Century

Since adherence to rule of law or legal state ideals depends on the character of the people, the differing histories of and adversities faced by various jurisdictions will surely determine how each fares in this century. Regimes that have largely achieved and lived under a rule of law for some significant period of time will surely not have to contend with the same difficulties as those that are quite a bit farther from the goal, or have only begun to realize it. Yet, even well-developed democracies that are widely considered paradigms of a rule of law state are subject to stresses that could undermine their achievement, and even more so if the rule of law contains a substantive dimension.

The United States, for example, may encounter challenges that could threaten its seemingly secure hold on the rule of law. One could imagine any number of areas in which potential problems of significant magnitude might arise that could cause sufficient concern to destabilize its rule of law. Dilemmas posed by the "war on terror," the technological revolution and its accompanying dangers, or increasingly frequent and disastrous environmental degradation and climatic events, to name a few, could cause even a sophisticated democratic state to shortchange its historical reliance on the rule of law. Moreover, this problem may be exacerbated by the possible turn to a substantive definition of the rule of law.

There is a peculiarly American wrinkle, introduced by the United States' system of constitutional law interpretation and analysis, in its potential for future success in continuing to adhere to the rule of law. American law operates under an assumption of constitutional supremacy: all statutory law—indeed, all law—is superseded by any contrary rule in the federal Constitution. Unlike many other constitutions, however, the United States Constitution is singularly vague and contains relatively few enumerated rights. It depends for its delineation and enforcement on the interpretation of judges. When engaging in this interpretive enterprise, judges have sometimes enforced unenumerated rights, while at the same time often significantly limiting other rights that are explicitly named. This widely accepted practice of broad-based constitutional interpretation introduces a potentially high degree of discretion and uncertainty to the calculus of rights, just the opposite of what the rule of law or legal state would appear to condone.[29] Americans nevertheless manage to

---

[28] *See id.* at 25 n.88 (noting Krygier's observation that the rule of law is not simply a matter of "detailed institutional design" but also of an "interconnected cluster of values" that may be pursued through different institutional channels).

[29] *See generally* Charlow, *supra* note 25.

adhere to what seems to them to be a rule of law state in large part because their body politic exhibits a very strong law-abiding character.[30] They believe themselves to be universally and equally constrained by law, most especially their federal Constitution as it is interpreted by U.S. courts, even when they may vehemently disagree with what the courts say the law (including the American Constitution) requires, and even when the courts significantly alter their determinations about what the Constitution says.[31] Since there is a great deal of room for constitutional interpretation, and thus for individualizing the understanding and application of U.S. law, this is in itself a striking outcome. It appears that the American national character as a law-abiding and respecting culture combines with the formal components of a rule of law state that are embedded in the American legal and constitutional structure. These work together to mutually reinforce a rather strong, if perhaps somewhat unusual, instantiation of an oddly non-fixed constitutional rule of law.[32]

Yet, even a relatively long-standing rule of law compliant state, such as the United States, with a well-entrenched rule of law oriented culture, is not guaranteed to remain so forever. Americans face different challenges than, for example, some of the emerging democracies struggling to take hold of the rule of law in the wake of unrest after the recent "Arab Spring." However, Americans are not immune from difficulties of their own.[33]

In the next century, one could predict that some of these difficulties may arise in connection with the continuing struggle against terrorism.[34] As a dominant world power, at least for the present, the United States finds itself a favorite target of groups and individuals who resort to violence to express their aims. This has apparently led to a certain degree of complacency on the part of much of the American public with the means its government chooses to fight terrorism. Events such as the attacks on the World Trade Center and the Boston Marathon bombing have left Americans understandably afraid. Recently, the American people learned that their leaders had secured a non-public warrant to collect for potential future use vast quantities of information ("meta-data") about private communications.[35] This occurred despite an express Constitutional right relating to searches that at least on

---

[30] *Id.* at 95.

[31] *See id.* at 98. *Accord* Himma, *supra* note 4, at 24 (pointing particularly to the interpretations of constitutionality by the United States Supreme Court).

[32] *See* Charlow, *supra* note 25, at 93.

[33] *See* Josh Levs, "'Nail in Coffin' for Arab Spring? Experts predict Egypt's Future", *CNN,* July 10, 2013, *available at* http://www.cnn.com/2013/07/10/world/meast/egypt-whats-next (describing a number of daunting obstacles to rule of law in Egypt following that country's early role in the democratic revolutions that recently took hold in many Arab nations).

[34] For example, Bruce Ackerman, among others, argues that the inaccurate nomenclature for and continuing nature of the "war on terror" work to regularize the state of emergency it presents and to inure us to the eventual erosion of our liberty that it occasions. Bruce Ackerman, *Before the Next Attack: Preserving Civil Liberties in an Age of Terrorism* (Yale Univ. Press, 2006) at 13–15.

[35] Glenn Greenwald, "NSA Collecting Phone Records of Millions of Verizon Customers Daily", *The Guardian*, June 5, 2013, *available at* http://www.guardian.co.uk/world/2013/jun/06/nsa-phone-records-verizon-court-order.

its face seems to protect the American people against generalized as opposed to specific government search warrants.[36] What was the public reaction to this enormously general search? Was it to rise up in astonished protest, veritably compelling the American President and Justice Department to explain and apologize for their failure to adhere to the United States Constitution, and to abandon their efforts in this regard? Not only was there not all that much of an outcry, polls actually showed that most Americans were affirmatively unperturbed, at least given what is known to date, and the United States Congress soon decided (albeit by a close vote) against curtailing the government's power in this regard.[37] Of course, it is entirely possible that the relevant constitutional guarantee—the Fourth Amendment right against search and seizure of private information, and against general warrants—could be interpreted so that it permits or does not even to apply to the collection of the private communications data in question in this instance, so that in fact there was and is no intrusion on protected constitutional rights. But even that interpretation simply illustrates the point.

Essentially all American constitutional rights are highly malleable in their interpretive application. This is true not only of rights that are identified as existing under the umbrella of some exceptionally vague standard such as "due process" or "equal protection" of law,[38] but also of rights that seem fairly clearly named and described. Even those rights enumerated in the most emphatic terms are understood, through judicial interpretation, to contain many exceptions. For example, though the United States Constitution says that "Congress shall make *no* law … abridging the freedom of speech, or of the press,"[39] American law allows a wealth of regulation in this regard, including criminal punishment for verbal acts,[40] such as threatening the

---

[36] *See* U.S. Constitution Amendment IV ("The right of the people to be secure in their persons … and effects, against unreasonable searches and seizures, shall not be violated, and no Warrants shall issue, but upon probable cause, … and particularly describing the place to be searched, and the persons or things to be seized.").

[37] Gary Langer, "Most Back NSA Surveillance Efforts—But Also Seek Congressional Hearings", *ABC News*, June 19, 2013, *available at* http://abcnews.go.com/blogs/politics/2013/06/most-back-nsa-surveillance-efforts-but-also-seek-congressional-hearings/. Department of Defense Appropriations Act, 2014, H.R. 2397, H.Amdt. 413, 113th Cong. (2013), *available at* http://amendments-rules.house.gov/amendments/AMASH_018_xml2718131717181718.pdf (proposed amendment to require limiting Foreign Intelligence Surveillance Court warrants so as to bar the collection of metadata); 159 Cong. Rec. H5002, H5028-29 (daily ed. July 24, 2013) (reporting that the amendment was rejected by a vote of 217 to 205), *available at* http://beta.congress.gov/crec/2013/07/24/CREC-2013-07-24-pt1-PgH5002.pdf.

[38] *See Roe v. Wade*, 410 U.S. 113 (1973) (deciding that the right to choose to have an abortion is part of a right of personal privacy contained in the Fourteenth Amendment's express right to "due process of law"); *United States v. Windsor*, 133 S.Ct. 2675 (2013) (invalidating a law that barred federal recognition of same-sex marriages which were valid according to state law because it violated the Fifth Amendment Due Process Clause's implied equal protection principle).

[39] *See* U.S. Constitution Amendment I (emphasis added).

[40] *See Giboney v. Empire Storage & Ice Company*, 336 U.S. 490, 498 (1949) (rejecting the contention that "the constitutional freedom for speech and press extends its immunity to speech or writing used as an integral part of conduct in violation of a valid criminal statute.").

President[41] or possessing child pornography[42]; tort damages for defamation[43]; and regulation of commercial speech,[44] speech of government employees,[45] "fighting words,"[46] and speech considered indecent.[47] Despite these and many other abridgements, the United States may still be among the most strident protectors of free speech rights. Nevertheless, this precedent for judicial delimiting of constitutional rights, though an understandable and perhaps necessary part of even a paradigmatic rule of law state—and considered a perfectly ordinary and acceptable aspect of constitutional interpretation in the U.S.—can at any time become the weak link in the chain supporting the rule of law, if and when events dictate, and if the rule of law contains a substantive component. That is, if Americans are so ready to accept significant impositions on rights in the face of terror, and if they are already accustomed to a system that includes a substantial degree of interpretive flexibility, the very strength of that interpretive openness can eventually turn into the demise of even the most strongly and broadly enumerated rights. Thus, *if* respect for certain substantive rights is a necessary part of the rule of law, as some would have it, American acquiescence and acculturation to constant redefinition of the fundamental rights already enjoyed, even those explicitly entrenched in the United States Constitution, renders their hold on the rule of law that much more tenuous.

Consider another potential point of vulnerability for the rule of law in the United States, rapidly evolving technological development. Like most of the rest of the world, the American people are quick to jump on the bandwagon of technological innovation. But every new electronic gadget or development seems to carry along with it an increasing degree of connectivity, and a concomitant exposure to exploitation, abuse, or even attack. Recent events have revealed how vulnerable the United States is to internet warfare, and how paltry its arsenal is against cyber-crime and cyber-espionage.[48] If the United States were suddenly to find itself facing the

---

[41] 18 U.S.C. § 871 (making it a felony to threaten a United States President).

[42] *Osborne v. Ohio*, 495 U.S. 103 (1990) (ruling that states may outlaw the possession of child pornography even though pornography may be a form of constitutionally protected speech).

[43] *Gertz v. Robert Welch, Inc.*, 418 U.S. 323 (1974) (holding that states may enforce legal remedies for much defamation that injures private individuals).

[44] *Central Hudson Gas and Electric Corporation. v. Public Service Commission*, 447 U.S. 557 (1980) (setting forth an intermediate level of scrutiny standard for review of laws and policies that restrict commercial speech).

[45] *Connick v. Myers*, 461 U.S. 138, 146 (1983) ("When employee expression cannot be fairly considered as relating to any matter of political, social, or other concern to the community, government officials should enjoy wide latitude in managing their offices, without intrusive oversight by the judiciary in the name of the First Amendment.").

[46] *Chaplinsky v. New Hampshire*, 315 U.S. 568 (1942) (holding that "fighting words," such as tend to incite an immediate breach of the peace, are not protected by the First Amendment).

[47] *Federal Communications Commission v. Pacifica Foundation*, 438 U.S. 726, 748 (1978) ("Patently offensive, indecent material presented over the airwaves confronts the citizen, not only in public, but also in the privacy of the home, where the individual's right to be left alone plainly outweighs the First Amendment rights of an intruder.").

[48] *See* Scott J. Shackelford, "From Nuclear War to Net War: Analogizing Cyber Attacks in International Law", 27 *Berkeley Journal of International Law* (2009) 193.

complete erasure of all banking records, the cyber-theft of national wealth, or the long distance shut down of utilities or military defense capabilities, would Americans not similarly be willing to trade many of their fundamental rights for a neat, though currently unconstitutional, remedy? One could envision, once again, a complacent American public, ready to forget privacy and Fourth Amendment guarantees when necessary for effective cyber-law enforcement. If the populace is indeed willing to swap freedom for security, then this could possibly be accomplished—maybe even easily accomplished—without any formal change in the law, but rather under the well-accepted rubric of flexible constitutional interpretation. If this meant altering some right deemed part of the necessary minimum for rule of law to inhere, then once again the American grasp on that construct could be called into question.

The same trade-off of rights for expediency could occur as well in regard to an environmental crisis. Despite a few persistent nay-sayers, it now seems to be the expert consensus that the earth is getting hotter, and that our climate will be significantly affected for the foreseeable future. Different parts of the U.S. have experienced severe climatic events in recent days, and Americans are told to expect more frequent and serious hazards to come.[49] Environmental crises of this proportion, like the threat of terrorism or of cyber-attack on a grand scale, present another, similarly ominous danger that could likewise lead to easy re-interpretation of basic rights, as necessary to meet a looming catastrophe. For example, many Americans might condone the government quartering troops in private homes in peacetime even against the wishes of individual homeowners, despite the Third Amendment's protection against just this,[50] in order to keep the peace in the aftermath of a disastrous storm.[51] After one such horrendous experience, would Americans maybe conclude unwanted billeting is allowed in the *anticipation* of a pending super-storm? And then might they eventually acquiesce to the propriety of similar intrusions perhaps based solely on the general *possibility* of serious storms in the future? To get from the first to the last of these steps, perhaps all that would be needed is a couple of court decisions ruling that the words of the Third Amendment, like much of the rest of the U.S. Constitution, allow for a wide variety of readings, including one that (seemingly contrary to the express words of the text) permits soldiers, in time of peace, to be quartered in any house without the consent of the owner.

This raises another issue with regard to the dilution of rights through interpretation, to wit, the incremental nature of change. Each individual alteration may seem minor and not of particular concern. In the previous account of the American

---

[49] *See* Vicki Arroyo, "Preparing for Future Disasters in the Wake of Sandy", *The Huffington Post*, Nov. 14, 2012, *available at* http://www.huffiingtonpost.com/vick-arroyo/climate-change-preparation_b_2132066.html.

[50] "No soldier shall, in time of peace be quartered in any house, without the consent of the owner, nor in time of war but in a manner to be prescribed by law." U.S. Constitution Amendment III.

[51] *Cf.* Peter Berkowitz, "'We Went into the Mall and Began "Looting"': A Letter on Race, Class, and Surviving the Hurricane", *The Monthly Review*, Sept. 5, 2005, *available at* http://mrzine.monthlyreview.org/2005/berkowitz090905.html (describing the intense ordeal of trying to survive in the wake of Hurricane Katrina in New Orleans, Louisiana).

Government's recent collection of electronic meta-data, many (meaning many law-abiding citizens) concluded that the sheer volume of information collected made it unlikely the Government would actually look at any communications that had anything to do with them personally. They trusted the Government only to examine information about particular individuals when specific facts warranted a suspicion of terrorist connections. However, if courts interpret the Fourth Amendment right to permit the generalized and widespread search and seizure of electronic meta-data, that state of affairs then becomes part of the baseline norm, likely making it a lot easier to justify additional small encroachments going forward. The next time a further expansion of its search capabilities is suggested or considered by the Government, the argument will surely begin with the point that the Fourth Amendment already allows the Government to collect the previously collected meta-data, so that the new intrusive measure is not as far from the existing rule or norm as might otherwise be the case. Once meta-data is surrendered, any rationale for why that perhaps presents a special circumstance not prohibited by the ban on generalized warrants (the compelling case of terrorism, perhaps) begins to fade, so that the next time around it could appear that no special justification is even necessary. For both these reasons, each small increment of interpretation takes Americans farther down the path leading away from a substantive right that some might consider to be an indispensable part of the rule of law.

This is not to suggest that any of the particular hypothesized readings of the U.S. Constitution are correct or incorrect, appropriate or inappropriate. It is only to say that the well-accepted pattern of broad-ranging, open-ended, and frequently changing constitutional interpretation leaves Americans especially vulnerable to rule of law slippage if the rule of law necessitates compliance with rights like those in the U.S. Constitution.

One possible fix for this potential dilemma is to return to the earlier concept of rule of law or legal state, the one that did not contain a substantive dimension. As noted earlier, many have continued to advocate all along that the rule of law has never really changed anyway. Absent the need to adhere to specific rights or a particular substantive conception of what is just, the United States could remain a formally compliant rule of law regime regardless of developments such as those just described. Reinterpretations of substantive rights, as needed to adapt to the perils of the twenty-first century, would not affect a formal rule of law.

For better or worse, however, that does not seem to be the direction in which the world is headed. The reasons for having initially travelled down the current path toward a dual conception of the rule of law and the legal state have not changed. Nor does it appear that the growing modern movement toward the substantive turn on this issue will reverse course any time soon, despite persistent and outspoken dissent in many rule of law quarters. If anything, given the conflation of the two constructs of rule of law and legal state and the latter's hearty embrace of a substantive aspect, proponents of a substantive rule of law are likely only to increase. Thus, if one belongs to the contingent that believes the rule of law must encompass a substantive aspect, the added difficulty in meeting whatever standard that requires would not seem to be appropriate justification for abandoning the requirement as part of the governing concept. This may leave the United States in an especially vulnerable position in terms of meeting the standard going forward, owing to its particular method of expansive constitutional interpretation.

16.5 Conclusion

No one knows how the United States will fare as it faces the challenges outlined, or others of similar stature. The easy and familiar path of reinterpreting settled and even textually strong constitutional rights to accommodate the views and needs of the day, while currently often touted as a special strength of the American system of constitutional law and interpretation, could ironically ultimately spell the demise of the United States as a rule of law compliant state. *If* substantive justice and/or rights are part of the "new" rule of law in the twenty-first century—which appears to be at least the direction we are facing, if not also in which we are marching—and if American constitutional rights someday seem to stand in the way of meeting the compelling exigencies undoubtedly confronting the United States in the years to come, the current American system of broad constitutional interpretive flexibility could work to the disadvantage of the United States in terms of maintaining the rule of law.

In the end, meeting the aspirations of the rule of law will depend, as it always has, less on compliance with specific rule of law requirements—be they formal or also substantive—and more on the character of the American people. The fact that Americans have arguably lived in an essentially rule of law compliant state for over 200 years should serve them well, but it is no guarantee. As has always been true in the past, whether Americans stand up to object or stand by and shrug as rights or any other formalities of the rule of law are potentially gradually eroded is entirely up to them. Having achieved a fairly rule of law compliant state, the American populace can only remain that way if it is vigilant and involved, most especially if that requires adherence to substantive standards of justice. If Americans lapse into complacency, no continuing structure of formal rule of law features, nor even constitutionally guaranteed list of fundamental human rights, will protect them from themselves.

Chapter 17
Building a Government of Laws: Adams and Jefferson 1776–1779

James R. Maxeiner

Abstract America's rule of law is not working well because many American lawyers confound their rule of law with common law and with common law methods. They overlook the contribution of good legislation to good government. They fixate on judges, judge-made law and procedure. America's founders, in particular, John Adams and Thomas Jefferson, did not. They were not entranced by common law and by common law methods. This chapter shows how in the first few years of American independence, Adams popularized the term "government of laws" and how Jefferson drafted statutes for a government of laws. Neither of them assigned common law or common law methods a leading, let alone the preeminent role in governing assumed today. Instead, they looked for a government of laws that anticipated a rule-of-law state. They looked for a path that would lead to good government *and* to liberty in law.

17.1 Introduction

In the United States the rule of law is practically a civil religion. The rule of law is guarantor of Americans' liberties. It protects them from government running amok. Today the American rule of law is under siege. The challenge does not come, however, from a Hitler on the right or a Stalin on the left who would overthrow it.[1] No. The challenge to the rule of law in America comes from the keepers of the faith,

This chapter was supported by The Common Good Institute (Philip K. Howard, President) and by a summer research grant of the University of Baltimore School of Law.

[1] This is not to belittle, however, that developments in terrorism and technology in this century, threaten to undermine the rule of law.

J.R. Maxeiner (✉)
University of Baltimore School of Law, Baltimore, MD, USA
e-mail: jmaxeiner@ubalt.edu

J.R. Silkenat et al. (eds.), *The Legal Doctrines of the Rule of Law and the Legal State (Rechtsstaat)*, Ius Gentium: Comparative Perspectives on Law and Justice 38,
DOI 10.1007/978-3-319-05585-5_17, © Springer International Publishing Switzerland 2014

i.e., from its evangelists, apostles, reformers, and just plain disciples. Americans spread the gospel abroad and question whether they keep it at home.[2] Libertarians think the United States needs better rules rather than fewer rules.[3] Reformers see that the American rule of law undermines individual responsibility.[4] Disciples see that American rules lead to bad decisions rather than to good ones.[5] Even pious parishioners in the pews perceive that, however well they believe that it protects individual liberty against tyrannical heads of state, the American rule of law comes up short in protecting and governing day-to-day.[6] It needs, scholars say, "rethinking."[7]

Doubters of the American rule of law religion discern what true believers do not: the rule of law is not just about liberty. It is also about governing. That thought was in Americans' minds at the beginning of the last century when they sang the second verse of the then recently written and still today popular national hymn, *America the Beautiful*: "America, America, God mend thy every flaw. Confirm thy soul in self-control, Thy liberty in law." Today, liberty in law has lost its ring.[8]

Doubters of the American rule of law religion observe what true believers overlook: an effective rule of law is a law of statutory rules. Judge-made precedents are secondary. That was in the minds of American lawyers already 125 years ago when the American Bar Association resolved: "The law itself should be reduced, so far as its substantive principles are settled, to the form of a statute."[9] Then, even the truest of true believers in judge-made law, James C. Carter, the preeminent nineteenth century opponent of codification, limited his claims for the benefits of common law lawmaking to private law, i.e., claims of rights among individuals, and excluded "our *public* law, our *statutory* law, which relates to the Constitution, organization and administration of the state."[10] Today, however, American lawyers ignore that

[2] *See Promoting the Rule of Law Abroad* (Carnegie Endowment for International Peace, 2006), especially Frank Upham, "Mythmaking in the Rule-of-Law Orthodoxy," *in id.* at 75–104.

[3] Richard A. Epstein, *Design for Liberty: Private Property, Public Administration, and the Rule of Law* (2011). Harvard University Press, Cambridge, MA.

[4] Philip K. Howard, *Rule of Nobody: Saving America from dead laws and senseless bureaucracy* (2014).

[5] Frederick Schauer, *Thinking Like a Lawyer: A New Introduction of Legal Reasoning* (2009). Harvard University Press, Cambridge, MA. *See* James R. Maxeiner, "Thinking Like a Lawyer Abroad: Putting Justice into Legal Reasoning," 11 *Washington U. Global Studies L. Rev.* (2012) at 55.

[6] Ronald A. Cass, *The Rule of Law in America* (2001) at 150–151. The Johns Hopkins University Press, Baltimore.

[7] *See, e.g.*, Robin L. West, "Chapter 2: Rethinking the Rule of Law," *in* Robin L. West, *Re-Imagining Justice: Progressive Interpretations of Formal Equality, Rights and the Rule of Law* (2003), at 13. Ashgate Publishing, Aldershot/Burlington. *See also* "Symposium: Is the Rule of Law Waning in America?," 56 *DePaul L. Rev.* (2007) 223–694 (18 essays by 21 authors).

[8] *See* Michael Kammen, *The Spheres of Liberty: Changing Perceptions of Liberty in American Culture* (2001). University Press of Mississippi, Jackson.

[9] *Report of the Ninth Annual Meeting of the American Bar Association* (1886) at 72–74.

[10] James C. Carter, *Argument of James C. Carter in Opposition to the Bill to Establish a Civil Code, Before the Senate Judiciary Committee, Albany, March 23, 1887* at 26 [emphasis in original].

truth when they celebrate a contemporary common law of judicial lawmaking and ignore statutes of legislatures.[11]

Doubters of the American rule of law see two problems that are, in reality, two sides of the same coin. On the one side of the coin, they see rules of law that are excessively detailed and deny human judgment in their application. Rules and not people end up making decisions in matters that lawmakers never anticipated. The American rule of law today is, says law reformer Philip K. Howard, a "rule of nobody." The language of dead legislators governs because they did not trust judges to carry out less detailed instructions. On the other side of the coin, doubters see judges that assert supremacy over the texts of statutes. Justice Antonin Scalia describes the ills that arise when "judges fashion law rather than fairly derive it from governing texts;" instead of following rules, judges "do what they want."[12] Common law lawmaking undercuts democracy.[13] On the one side of the coin, the law is too certain. On the other side, it is too indeterminate.[14]

Good government depends on well-crafted and routinely applied statutes. Only then can the governed and the governors alike apply laws, to themselves and to others, using their common sense without being perplexed by unfathomable rules or being frustrate- by unending procedure. Professor Richard A. Epstein, a libertarian, prescribes the cure: "make sure that the tasks that are given to the government are both limited and well-defined, and … let the people who are in charge have the degree of flexibility needed to carry out their task."[15]

Americans can structure a government that works, but it requires courage. To limit and to define the tasks given to government, while allowing flexibility in carrying those tasks out, are matters of legislating. American skills with legislation are lacking. American skills in writing statutes are deficient. American skills in interpreting statutes are lacking. American skills in applying statutes are poor. Americans know that. The world knows that.[16] Still, the task is manageable.[17] What doubters seek for

---

[11] *See, e.g.*, American Bar Association, *Common Law, Common Values, Common Rights, Essays on Our Common Heritage by Distinguished British and American Authors* (2000) at viii.

[12] Antonin Scalia & Bryan A. Garner, *Reading Law: The Interpretation of Legal Texts* (2012) at 4 and 9. Thomson, West St. Paul.

[13] *Id.* at 3.

[14] *See* West, *supra* note 7, at 13, 26–31; James R. Maxeiner, "Legal Indeterminacy Made in America: American Legal Methods and the Rule of Law," 41 *Valparaiso U.L. Rev.* (2006) at 517; "Legal Certainty and Legal Methods: A European Alternative to American Legal Indeterminacy?," 15 *Tulane J. Int'l & Comp. L.* (2007) at 541.

[15] Epstein, *supra* note 3, at 6–7. *See* Howard, *supra* note 4 (speaking of "corrals"); James R. Maxeiner, *Policy and Methods in German and American Antitrust Law: A Comparative Study* (1986) at 26 (speaking of "negative binding").

[16] Organisation for Economic Cooperation and Development, *Regulatory Reform in the United States* (1999) at 48. Organisation for Economic Cooperation and Development, Paris ("At the heart of the most severe regulatory problems is the quality of primary legislation. … More so than in other OECD countries, the United States has found it extremely difficult to improve legislative quality and coherence.").

[17] So said iconic contracts scholar Samuel Williston already in 1914. *See* Samuel Williston. "The Uniform Partnership Act with some other remarks on other Uniform Commercial Laws, An

America is reality abroad. It is a part of a legal state. Others can govern according to law: what is to stop the United States from developing good laws?

The rule of law religion and the contemporary common law are the show stoppers. They so dominate American thinking about law and legal methods that they leave no ground for better methods to take root.

17.2 Contemporary Common Law

According to American rule of law religion, the United States is a "common law" country where judicial precedents are the law and where statutes—even today—are occasional interlopers.[18] The American rule of law religion reflects the late nineteenth century rule of law popularized by the English jurist Albert Venn Dicey: common law, common law courts and no discretion in law application.[19] "The common law in the Anglo-American world is synonymous for most people with the rule of law."[20]

In the contemporary common law judges are supreme in lawmaking. Where there is no law or the law is found only in precedents, they have authority to make binding law, *i.e.*, common law precedents binding in future cases (*stare decisis*). Where there are statutes, they have authority to decide whether those laws are consistent with the U.S. Constitution (constitutional or judicial review, sometimes known as judicial supremacy). Moreover, where there are statutes—which today, is just about everywhere—judges assert that they have authority to determine the meaning of statutes not only for the cases they are presently deciding, but for future cases (statutory precedent or statutory *stare decisis*).[21]

Contemporary common law thus extends judicial supremacy over the constitutional validity of statutes to judicial supremacy over the meaning and application of statutes. It makes judicial precedents the starting points for legal reasoning rather

---

Address before the Law Association of Philadelphia December 18, 1914" (1915) at 2, *reprinted in* 63 *U. Pa. L. Rev.* (1915) 196 at 197.

[18] *See* Jane C. Ginsburg, *Introduction to Law and Legal Reasoning, Revised Edition* (2004) at 71. Foundation Press, New York. For views skeptical of common law carryover see, *e.g.*, Calvin Woodard, "Is the United States a Common Law Country?" in *Essays on English Law and the American Experience* (Elisabeth A. Cawthon and David E. Narrett, eds., 1994) at 120. University of Texas, Arlington; Gordon S. Wood, *The Creation of the American Republic, 1776–1787* (1969) at 291–305; For views skeptical of the utility of the common law, see, *e.g.*, Frederick Schauer, "The Failure of the Common Law," 36 *Ariz. St. L. J.* (2004) 765; Frederick Schauer, "Do Cases Make Bad Law?", 73 *U. Chi. L. Rev.* (2006) 883; Gordon Tullock, *The Case Against the Common Law* (1997). Carolina Academic Press, Durham.

[19] Chapter 4 "Rule of Law," in Albert Venn Dicey, *Introduction to the Study of the Law of the Constitution* (1885).

[20] John V. Orth, "Common Law and United States Legal Tradition," in *The Oxford Companion to American Law* (Kermit L. Hall, ed., 2002) 127, 129. Oxford University Press, New York.

[21] *See* Scalia & Garner, *supra* note 12, at 5; Peter L. *Strauss*, "The Common Law and *Statutes*," 70 *U. Colo. L. Rev.* (1998) 225, 243.

than statutory texts. It demonetizes legislation. It encourages legislators to leave to judges the last word in making law: judges will take it anyway.[22] It compromises governing by law.

Contemporary common law concentrates on litigation. In litigation judges are authorized—indeed, they are required—to decide rights between two competing parties before the court. Only in their own world of judicial supremacy, however, do judges in such cases have legal authority or legislative legitimacy to decide, not just the cases before them, but what will be law in future cases decided according to the statutes they apply.[23]

Applying contemporary common law in statutory cases makes a mockery of the idea that law is a set of democratically established rules, applied to the facts of cases, by those subject to law and by those who govern.[24] Contemporary common law in its concentration on litigation dovetails well with the concentration of the American rule of law religion on guaranteeing individual rights to the practical exclusion of good governing. The contemporary common law was a bad choice of American law when judges adopted it gradually in the course of the nineteenth century. That it did not work well was amply proven by American government in the twentieth century. That it should not be the future of American law in the twenty-first century is the challenge that the doubters make.

Faced with the evidence of failure of the contemporary common law, true believers find solace in saying that that is the price we pay for a government under law. No other way can work. Our American ways must be the best—at least for us Americans (American exceptionalism). Received wisdom clings to a view of history that holds that this is the way Americans have always done law. So the late Justice Brennan introduced American law to neophytes with the conventional view of American legal history that American law was largely English common law in the eighteenth century, state common law in the nineteenth century and only in the twentieth century did innovation begin to come through legislation.[25]

---

[22] *See* John V. Orth, "The Persistence of the Common Law," *in* John V. Orth, *How Many Judges does it take to make a Supreme Court? And Other Essays on Law and the Constitution* (2006) at 73, 83, 85. University Press of Kansas, Lawrence. *See also* Scalia, J., dissenting in Sykes v. United States, 564 U.S. 1 (2011).

[23] *See, e.g.*, 1 Joel Prentiss Bishop, *Commentaries on the Law of Criminal Procedure,* (1866) at 704–706 (chap. LIX, §§ 1030–1032); William G. Hammond, "Notes to Laws of England, No. 30," *in* 1 William Blackstone, *Commentaries on the Laws of England* (William G. Hammond, ed., 1890) at 213–226; American Bar Association, *Report of the Committee on Legal Education Presented at the Annual Meeting in Boston, August 26, 1891* (1891) at 44. *See also* Orth, "Can the Common Law Be Unconstitutional?" in Orth, *supra* note 22, at 53, 61–62.

[24] *See* Scalia & Garner, *supra* note 12, at 3–5, 83, 509, 517.

[25] William J. Brennan, Jr., "Introduction" in New York University School of Law, *Fundamentals of American Law* 1, 3 (1996).

Received wisdom is myth. Its view of history is false.[26] Early America was a land of "many legalities."[27] The picture of common law in colonial America was complex. The colonies varied from colony-to-colony in what they adopted. None adopted common law wholesale; each adapted it to local conditions. They chose among common law rules (e.g., land tenures, crimes and punishments, forms of action) and common law institutions (e.g., courts, jury). The rudimentary nature of courts and law practice, as well as limitations on law reporting—there were no printed American law reports and English reports were hard to come by—made adoption of eighteenth century common law methods (known as "declaring law") difficult. Of course, they could not have adopted contemporary common law methods (known as lawmaking), for those methods were yet to be developed.[28] Before the Revolution, there were no published American precedents, but there were many written laws.

Received wisdom ignores centuries of Americans searching for liberty and common good in written law. In the seventeenth century, even before the Pilgrims went ashore on the American Continent, aboard the Mayflower anchored in Massachusetts Bay, they agreed in the *Mayflower Compact* to

> Combine ourselves together into a Civil Body Politic, for our better ordering and preservation and furtherance of the ends aforesaid; and by virtue hereof to enact, constitute and frame such just and equal Laws, Ordinances, Acts, Constitutions and Offices, from time to time, as shall be thought most meet and convenient for the general good of the Colony, unto which we promise all due submission and obedience.

Soon colonists in Massachusetts adopted written laws. The preamble of the *Lawes and Libertyes of Masschusetts* of 1647 colorfully explains why: "a Common-wealth without lawes is like a Ship without rigging and steeradge."[29] They knew that written laws—and not precedents—are how societies run and guide themselves. Their leaders provided a book of laws to "satisfie your longing expectation, and frequent complaints

---

[26] It may be historically inaccurate, but it still has such a hold on the American legal mind that even a judge and scholar who suggests that, relegates that truth to a footnote. Guido Calebresi, *A Common Law for the Age of Statutes* (1980) at 185 n. 10. Harvard University Press, Cambridge, MA.

[27] *See, e.g., The Many Legalities of Early America* (Christopher L. Tomlins & Bruce H. Mann, eds., 2001). University of North Carolina Press, Chapel Hill; William E. Nelson, *The Common Law in Colonial America, Vol. I, The Chesapeake and New England 1607–1660* (2008). Oxford University Press, New York, *Vol. II, The Middle Colonies and the Carolinas, 1660–1730* (2012). Oxford University Press, New York. A century ago Roscoe Pound said: "We must remember that our American law really begins at the Revolution—in fact, not until sometime after. Our reception of the common law is much later than we have commonly thought." [Implicitly suggesting mid-century.] *Proceedings of the Thirteenth Annual Meeting of the Association of American Law Schools, printed in Report of the Thirty-Sixth Annual Meeting of the American Bar Association held at Montreal Canada* (1913) 862 at 869.

[28] *See* Eugene Wambaugh, *The Study of Cases* (2nd ed., 1894) at 75–80. *See also* note 23 *supra* (giving other authorities rejecting theory of common law lawmaking and accepting declaring law theory).

[29] *The Lawes and Libertyes of Massachusetts (1647). See Edmund S. Morgan, The Puritan Dilemma: The Story of John Winthrop (3rd ed., 2007) 156–160.*

for want of such a volume to be published in print: wherin (upon every occasion) you might readily see the rule which you ought to walke by."

In the eighteenth century, founders of the American republic, such as John Adams and Thomas Jefferson, sought a "government of laws and not of men." Their nineteenth century successors, Justice Joseph Story, President Abraham Lincoln and codifier David Dudley Field, looked to written law to govern. Americans legislated. Constitutional conventions created and amended state constitutions: in the first 110 years, to 1887, according to one count, 104 state constitutions and 214 partial amendments.[30] Every state legislature codified, revised or compiled its statutes. Civic leaders celebrated America's heritage of written laws at annual Fourth of July convocations. Civics text books taught of democratically adopted statutes. An "orgy of statute making" is nothing new: that is how modern democratic governments govern.[31]

In 1876, the *North American Review*, then under the editorship of Henry Adams and possibly the nation's most important intellectual magazine, published in its commemoration of the centennial of the American republic: "The *great* fact in the progress of American jurisprudence which deserves special notice and reflection is its tendency towards *organic statute law* and towards the *systematizing of law*; in other words, towards *written constitutions* and *codification*."[32] A competing commemorative volume sponsored by *Harpers Monthly Magazine*, observed that "The art of administering government according to the directions of a written constitution may fairly be named among the products of American thought and effort during our century."[33] "The idea, in its practical development, is American."[34]

With written constitutions go written laws. The *Harper's* commemoration continued: "The readiness of American Legislatures to codify or systematize the laws is a noticeable feature. … There does not appear to be any state, with perhaps the exception of Pennsylvania and Tennessee, which does not possess a codification or revision of the laws made since the commencement of 1860."[35]

Even as most Americans were looking to legislative rules, from the ranks of judges and legal practitioners came another vision: judge-made law and judicial supremacy. According to legal historian Kermit Hall, "the single most significant feature in nineteenth-century American legal culture was the steady rise of judicial authority."[36] In the last quarter of the nineteenth century the newly emerging legal

---

[30] Henry Hitchcock, *American State Constitutions: A Study of their Growth* (1887) at 13–14.

[31] *Contrast*, Guido Calebresi, *A Common Law for an Age of Statutes* (1980) at 1. Harvard University Press, Cambridge, MA.

[32] George Tucker Bispham, "Law in America, 1776–1876," in *North American Review*, vol. 122 (January 1876) 154, at 174 [emphasis in original].

[33] Benjamin Vaughn Abbott, "American Jurisprudence," in *The First Century of the Republic: A Review of American Progress* (1876), at 434, 437.

[34] *Id.* at 438.

[35] *Id.* at 451.

[36] Kermit L. Hall, "History of American Law: Antebellum through Reconstruction, 1801–1877," in *Oxford Companion to American Law* (Kermit Hall, ed., 2002) 374, at 381. Oxford University

professions combined to assert contemporary common law and judicial supremacy. Already in 1870 Oliver Wendell Holmes, Jr. claimed that "It is the merit of the common law that it decides the case first and determines the principle afterwards."[37] Come 1915 Samuel Williston, iconic contracts scholar of the day, reported the triumph of contemporary common law lawmaking over statute lawmaking: "Codification has an ugly sound to most American lawyers. We have been trained to believe that no code can be expressed with sufficient exactness, or can be sufficiently elastic to fulfill adequately the functions of our common law."[38] On the eve of the nation's sesquicentennial in 1926 the consensus of the American Bar Association's meeting in London was that to adopt a code was an un-American attempt "to supplant the parent Common Law" and "to forsake our English heritage and follow the lead of Imperial Rome."[39] In just 50 years between the nation's centennial in 1876 and its sesquicentennial in 1926 lawyers, judges and law teachers took over the legal system to run it as their own.[40]

By the time the bicentennial celebration rolled around in 1976, the ABA commemorative volumes did not even note the triumph of common law over written law; they simply assumed it.[41] At the turn of this century in 2000 the ABA commemorative volume in its "Principles" section at the book's outset claimed that "The common law provides the tools and flexibility to allow the law to continue to serve the

---

Press, New York. Those with foreign experiences did not, however, judge American efforts at statutory lawmaking to be unique or effective. *See, e.g.*, "German Legislation," 10 *Am. L. Rev.* (1875) 270, at 280–281.

[37] Oliver Wendell Holmes, "Codes and the Arrangement of the Law," 5 *Am. L. Rev.* 1 (1870). *See* Frederick Schauer, "Do Cases Make Bad Law?," 73 *U. Chi. L. Rev.* 883 (2006) at 885.

[38] Samuel Williston. *The Uniform Partnership Act with some other remarks on other Uniform Commercial Laws, An Address before the Law Association of Philadelphia December 18, 1914* (1915) at 1–2, reprinted in 63 *U. Pa. L. Rev.* 196 (1915). The new legal "science" of Langdell had no room for statutes, where judicial decisions were the exclusive subject of scientific study.

[39] J. Carroll Hayes, "The Visit to England of the American Bar Association," in *The American Bar Association London Meeting 1924: Impressions of Its Social, Official, Professional and Juridical Aspects as Related by Participants in Contest for Most Enlightening Review of Trip* (1925) 9, at 15.

[40] The shift is evident in the history of the American Bar Association. Article I of its Constitution of 1888 provided that one of the Association's three objects was to promote "the uniformity of legislation throughout the Union." American Bar Association, *Call for a Conference, Proceedings of Conference, First Meeting of the Association; Officers, Members, etc.* (1878) at 16 (as proposed), at 30 (as adopted). Article III required that the President open each annual meeting with an address on the "most noteworthy changes in statute law … during the preceding year." *Id.* at 18, 32. The former was diluted in the new 1919 Constitution; the latter was dropped already in 1913.

[41] *See* Harry W. Jones, "The Common Law in the United States: English Themes and American Variations," *in Political Separation and Legal Community* 91 (American Bar Association, Common Faith and Common Law, Papers Prepared for the Bicentennial Observance, Harry W. Jones, ed., 1976); *Legal Institutions Today: English and American Approaches Compared* (American Bar Association, Common Faith and Common Law, Papers Prepared for the Bicentennial Observance, Harry W. Jones, ed. 1977) at unnumbered vii–viii.

needs of a diverse society in a world of rapid change and technological development."[42] Common law and rule of law are held to be practically one and the same.[43]

Americans need to start over. They need a legal state that works. The failures of the American legal system and the successes of foreign systems are not reasonably deniable.[44] The contemporary common law of judicial supremacy over statutes is not an essential part of American law or of American liberty. Judicial supremacy is not a part of American legal DNA. Legislative supremacy has a better claim. It was present in the legislative work of John Adams and Thomas Jefferson.[45]

17.3 Adams and Jefferson as Legislators

> They formed a system of government, and a code of laws, such as the wisdom of man had never before devised. Sheldon Smith (Eulogy Pronounced at Buffalo New York July 22nd, 1826[46])

The American Declaration of Independence of July 4, 1776 for many people around the world presents the premier principles of protection of individual rights.[47] And in the protection of individual rights, Americans see the essence of the rule of law.[48]

More than any other two people, John Adams and Thomas Jefferson brought the Declaration of Independence into being. They acted to make the republican ideals of the Declaration reality in law. For Adams, it was a frame of government; for Jefferson it was the nuts and bolts of government itself. In fall 1779, Adams drafted the *Constitution and Form of Government of the Commonwealth of Massachusetts*, which is still law today. There he coined the phrase of a "government of laws, not

---

[42] *Common Law, Common Values, Common Rights, Essays on Our Common Heritage by Distinguished British and American Authors* (American Bar Association, 2000) at viii.

[43] *Id.*

[44] *See, e.g.*, "German Legislation," *supra* note 34, at 283; *see also* James R. Maxeiner with Gyooho Lee and Armin Weber, *Failures of American Civil Justice in International Perspective* (2011). Cambridge University Press, New York.

[45] *See* A. London Fell, *Origins of Legislative Sovereignty and the Legislative State, Volume Six: American Tradition and Innovation with Contemporary Import and Foreground, Book I: Foundations (to Early 19th Century)* (2004). Praeger, Westport.

[46] Sheldon Smith, "Eulogy Pronounced at Buffalo New York July, 22nd, 1826," *in A Selection of Eulogies, Pronounced in the Several States, in Honor of those Illustrious Patriots and Statesmen, John Adams and Thomas Jefferson* (1826) at 91, 94.

[47] *See, e.g.*, Ricardo Gosalbo-Bono, "The Significance of the Rule of Law and its Implications for the European Union and the United States," 72 *U. Pitt. L. Rev.* (2010) at 229, 231, 240 and 272 (citation omitted).

[48] American Bar Association Section on International and Comparative Law, *The Rule of Law in the United States: A Statement by the Committee to Cooperate with the International Commission of Jurists* (1958) at 10 (the rule of law is "the body of precepts of fundamental individual rights permeating institutions of government … by which such precepts may be applied to make those rights effective.").

of men" that into the twentieth century described what Americans today call the rule of law. From fall 1776 through spring 1779, Jefferson wrote the laws for a republican government for Virginia. He provided legislation for reformation of the law of the nation's most populous state. James Madison described Jefferson's reformation as "a mine of legislative wealth, and a model of statutory composition."[49]

In the world of Adams and Jefferson, law is about legislation and government is about governing. Written laws decide principles beforehand and authorize governors and governed alike to decide according to those principles. Democratically selected legislatures are supreme and not judges. States have governments of laws and not of men.

True believers in the contemporary common law cannot accept that the founders' world revolved around written law and not around common law, around legislators and not around judges, and around governing and not around resolving disputes. So one wrote not long ago:

> The leaders of the American Revolution, such as John Adams and Thomas Jefferson talked grandly about breaking with the European past and starting "a new order of the world." But when the Constitutional Convention met in a steamy summer in Philadelphia in 1787, it was with the assumption that English common law would continue unchanged in the United States.[50]

Modern scholars look beyond such false received wisdom. I their view the state constitutions of the time, together with the Declaration of Independence "most authentically document the irreversible American commitment to Republicanism in 1776."[51] They perceive in Jefferson's legislation "a rare and comprehensive view of how a founder envisioned an actual republican society."[52]

17.4 Adams' Constitution: The Frame of Government for the Commonwealth of Massachusetts

> You and I, my dear friend, have been sent into life at a time when the greatest lawgivers of antiquity would have wished to live. … When before the present epoch, had three millions of people full power and a fair opportunity to form and establish the wisest and happiest government that human wisdom can contrive? John Adams, *Thoughts on Government* (1776)

---

[49] James Madison to Samuel Harrison Smith, November 4, 1826, *in The Writings of James Madison, Volume 1819–1836* (Gaillard Hunt, 1910) at 256, 257–258.

[50] Norman F. Cantor, *Imagining the Law: Common Law and the Foundations of the American Legal System* (1997) at 354. Harpercollins, New York. *Cf.* William D. Bader, "Mediations on the Original: James Madison, Framer with Common Law Intentions—Ramifications in the Contemporary Supreme Court," 20 *Vt. L. Rev.* 5 (1995).

[51] *See, e.g.*, Willi Paul Adams, "The Liberal and Democratic Republicanism of the First American State Constitutions," *in Republicanism and Liberalism in America and the German States, 1750–1850* (2002) at 127. Cambridge University Press, New York.

[52] Ralph Lerner, *The Thinking Revolutionary: Principle and Practice in the New Republic* (1987) at 62. Cornell University Press, Ithaca.

John Adams wrote the oldest American constitution that is still in force today: the 1780 *Constitution and Form of Government for the Commonwealth of Massachusetts*.[53] In it Adams combined "A Declaration of the Rights of the Inhabitants of the Commonwealth of Massachusetts," as Part the First, and "The Frame of Government," as Part the Second. He placed the idea of "a government of laws and not of men" literally between the two Parts.

17.4.1 Chronicle

That Adams had the opportunity to draft the Massachusetts Constitution is a remarkable story in itself. An earlier attempt at a constitution for the state had failed; Massachusetts was the last state to follow the April 1776 call of the Continental Congress to write a state constitution. But Adams left the United States in 1778 for 10 years in Europe. In that decade, he was home for just 3 months. Yet it was in those 3 months that the Massachusetts Constitutional Convention met and appointed Adams to write the Constitution.

In writing the Constitution, Adams relied on his 1776 pamphlet, *Thoughts on Government: Applicable to the Present State of the American Colonies*.[54] That pamphlet brought him acclaim, contributed to his role in the Declaration of Independence and made him someone for others to consult in drafting their state constitutions. It was there that he wrote that "the very definition of a republic 'is an empire of laws, and not of men'" and that "a republic is the best of governments." He took the term from James Harrington's *Oceana*. For Massachusetts, Adams wrote of a *government* and not an *empire* of laws.

Adams wrote *Thoughts on Government* to give to other Americans advice on how they might create governments for the new states coming into being in 1776. He began by rejecting Pope's famous aphorism "The forms of government let fools contest: That which is best administered is best." Adams said no: "Pope flattered tyrants too much …. Nothing could be more fallacious than this." The form of government does make a difference, he asserted. "Nothing is more certain, from the history of nations and the nature of men, that some forms of government are better fitted for being well-administered than others." And so, Adams asked: "As good

[53] With justification Adams boasted: "I made a constitution for Massachusetts, which finally made the Constitution of the United States." *As quoted in* Robert F. Williams, *The Law of American State Constitutions* (2009) at 36. Oxford University Press, New York. On Adams' Republican thinking generally, see M.N.S. Sellers, *American Republicanism: Roman Ideology in the United States Constitution* (1994), especially at 6, 33–40. NYU Press, New York; M.N.S. Sellers, *The Sacred Fire of Liberty: Republicanism, Liberalism and the Law* (1998) 67–69. NYU Press, New York.

[54] It, together with *The Report of a Constitution, or Form of Government, for the Commonwealth of Massachusetts* (1779), are conveniently reprinted in *The Revolutionary Writings of John Adams, Selected and with a Foreword by C. Bradley Thompson* (2000) at 287–293 and at 297–322 respectively.

government is an empire of laws, how shall your laws be made?" Three years later, he gave his answer in his draft of the Massachusetts Constitution.[55]

17.4.2 Adams' Constitution and Frame of Government

It is anachronistic to describe a document of 1780 in terms that were not to achieve currency for another century. Yet, Adam's Constitution anticipates the balanced approach of a legal state which accommodates individual rights and governing together more than it foreshadows the individual rights-focused American rule of law. It looks more like a legal state founded on statute law and a principle of legality than it does like a rule of law content with judge-made law and inherent authority. It anticipates laws that are integrated and stable that people can follow more than an ever-changing mix of judicial precedents. It is for the legislature to state the laws, for the executive to carry them out, and for the judiciary to accept the reasoned judgments of both.

The preamble of Adams' Constitution begins by stating that government balances common good and individual rights: "The end of the institution, maintenance, and administration of government is to secure the existence of the body-politic, to protect it, and to furnish the individuals who compose it with the power of enjoying, in safety and tranquility, their natural rights and the blessings of life."

The preamble's second paragraph states the means to accomplish this end: "certain laws for the common good." So it is "a duty of the people … *to provide for an equitable mode of making laws, as well as for an impartial interpretation, and a faithful execution of them.*" [Emphasis added.] It is through these written laws, "that everyman may at all times, find his security in them."

Adams' "government of laws and not of men" is part of the statement of the principle of a separation of powers among legislative, executive and judicial branches of government. It occupies a mediating place between individual rights and common good. In the Constitution, it literally stands between two parts, Part the First, Declaration of Rights, and Part the Second, Frame of Government. Adams, in his draft placed it at the beginning of Part the Second, Frame of Government. The Constitutional Convention moved it to the end of Part the First.

17.4.3 Written Law

Adams' Constitution provides a frame for statute law and for governing. Chapter I, Section I, Article IV of Part the Second, the Frame of Government, gives the legislature authority "to make, ordain, and establish all manner of wholesome and reasonable orders, laws, statutes, and ordinances, directions and instructions, either

[55] Except as noted, references here are to the final language of the adopted 1780 constitution and not to that of Adams' 1779 draft. Differences between the two with respect to specific sections cited are believed minor unless discussed.

with penalties or without, so as the same be not repugnant or contrary to this constitution, as they shall judge to be for the good and welfare of this commonwealth, and for the government and ordering thereof, and of the subjects of the same, and for the necessary support and defence of the government thereof." Article XXII of Part the First, the Declaration of Rights, calls on the legislature frequently to assemble "for address[ing] of grievances, for correcting, strengthening, and confirming the laws, and for making new laws, as the common good may require."

Adams' Constitution does not contemplate contemporary judge-made law or judicial supremacy. Article X of Part the First, the Declaration of Rights provides: "In fine, the people of this commonwealth are not controllable by any other laws than those to which their constitutional representative body have given their consent." Article XX adds: "The power of suspending the laws, or the execution of the laws, ought never to be exercised but by the legislature, or by authority derived from it, to be exercised in such particular cases only as the legislature shall expressly provide for."

Adams' Constitution commands "standing laws" to protect the people from rapid changes in law. Article X of Part the First, the Declaration of Rights provides: "Every individual of the society has a right to be protected by it in the enjoyment of his life, liberty, and property, according to standing laws."[56]

Adams' Constitution anticipates laws that are coordinated one with another.[57] Article 6 of Part the Second, the Frame of Government, avoids a gap in law by continuing in force existing laws. To assure consistency Chapter III, Article II gives executive and legislative branches "authority to require the opinions of the justices of the supreme judicial court upon important questions of law, and upon solemn occasions." Article XXIX of Part the First, the Declaration of Rights calls for "an impartial interpretation of the laws, and administration of justice."

17.4.4 Law for Governing

Adams' Constitution looks for a government that will govern according to law. Adams' Constitution comes close to anticipating a requirement of statutory authority for government action, i.e., a principle of legality. Article XVIII of Part the First, the Declaration of Rights, provides that the people "have a right to require of their lawgivers and magistrates an exact and constant observation of them [i.e. fundamental principles of the constitution], in the formation and execution of the laws necessary for the good administration of the commonwealth." It allows for exceptions to rights, such as search warrant may issue, and soldiers may be quartered in homes, but only "with the formalities, prescribed by the laws" or "in a manner

[56] *See* John Adams, *A Defence of the Constitutions of Government of the United States of America* … vol. 1 (3rd ed 1797) at 141 (viewing negatively frequent changes in law).

[57] On the idea generally, see Karl Riesenhuber, "English common law versus German *Systemdenken*? Internal versus external approaches, "7 *Utrecht L. Rev.*, (January 2001) at 117, available at www.utrechtlawreview.org

ordained by the legislature."[58] Government officers are to swear to carry out their duties "agreeably to the rules and regulations of the constitution and the laws of the commonwealth."[59] Carry laws out they must. Later Adams explained: "The executive power is properly the government; the laws are a dead letter until an administration begins to carry them into execution."[60]

Adams' Constitution sets out a frame of a government of laws and not of men, i.e., a legal state. But what would an American legal state look like? Jefferson's legislation suggests one such state.

17.5 Jefferson's Legislation: A Government of Laws for the Commonwealth of Virginia

> When I left Congress in '76, it was in the persuasion that our whole code must be reviewed, adapted to our republican form of government, and, now that we had no negatives of Councils, Governors & Kings to restrain us from doing right, that it should be corrected in all its parts, with a single eye to reason, & the good of those for whose government it was framed. Thomas Jefferson, *Autobiography*[61]

Jefferson's lawmaking from 1776 to 1779 is unparalleled in American history. No American legislator before or since has accomplished so much of such importance in such a short period of time. In 3 weeks in June 1776 he drafted the Declaration of Independence. In 3 years following he drafted the laws for a republican government.[62] In the words of a contemporary biographer Jefferson created "a model for other states" and "invented the United States of America."[63] His vision was of a government of laws, not of judges.

17.5.1 Chronicle

When Jefferson drafted the Declaration of Independence in June 1776, he had on his mind as much building a government of laws as declaring rights and independence.[64] Upon arrival in Philadelphia in May for Congress, he wrote a friend back home that

[58] Declaration of Rights, Arts. XIV and XXVII, respectively.

[59] Frame of Government, Chap. VI.

[60] Adams, *supra* note 56, at 372.

[61] *The Autobiography of Thomas Jefferson, 1743–1790, Together with a Summary of the Chief Events in Jefferson's Life* (Paul Leicester Ford, ed.1914; New Introduction by Michael Zuckerman, 2005) at 67.

[62] Lerner, *supra* note 52, at 61 writes of "Jefferson's grand design to make the promise of the Declaration a reality."

[63] Willard Sterne Randall, *Thomas Jefferson: A Life* (1993), at 306. Henry Holt and Company, New York.

[64] The Declaration itself demonstrates the importance that Jefferson placed on legislation. All of the first named grounds for independence are charges of bad government and not of violations of

the government to be established was "the whole object of the present controversy." If that government were no good, independence would be pointless. It would be just as well to accept "the bad one offered to us from beyond the water without the risk & expence of contest."[65] In distant Philadelphia he worked as hard on a constitution for Virginia as on a declaration of a United States. To his life-long frustration, his draft arrived too late.[66]

In July and August 1776, as Jefferson remained in Philadelphia he was in correspondence with Edmund Pendleton, who would soon be first speaker of the new Virginia House of Delegates. In one letter Pendleton urged Jefferson to return home as Jefferson was needed "much in the Revision of our Laws and forming a new body."[67] In another Pendleton asked Jefferson to elaborate on his plans for changes in land tenures, elections, suffrage and penal law.[68]

No work was of greater urgency for Jefferson than his legislation. He expected the war to be short. He did not stay in Philadelphia a moment longer than he had to. He rushed home to Virginia. A republican state needed republican laws. "It can never be too often repeated," he later wrote, "that the time for fixing every essential right on a legal basis is when our rulers are honest, and ourselves united. From the conclusion of this war we shall be going down hill."[69]

No work had more substance for Jefferson than building a government of laws. He wrote in his autobiography, "I knew that our legislation under the regal government had many vicious points which urgently required reformation, and I thought I could be of more use in forwarding that work. I therefore retired from my seat in Congress on the 2d. day of Sep., resigned it, and took my place in the legislature of my state."[70] When a messenger reached him in Virginia with a Congressional commission to join Benjamin Franklin on the critical mission to France, Jefferson took 3 days to think it over—keeping the messenger waiting—and finally declined the appointment.

From October 1776, when Jefferson joined the state legislature, until June 1779, when he became governor, Jefferson did little else than work on legislation. His work took two forms: (1) drafting bills on particular subjects, e.g., civil justice, property law, the established church, importation of slaves, and naturalization; and (2) systematic review and reform of Virginia law.[71] The latter is known as the

---

individual rights. The very first (of many) reads: "he has refused his assent to laws the most wholesome and necessary for the public good."

[65] Jefferson to Thomas Nelson, May 16, 1776, in 1 *The Papers of Thomas Jefferson (Vol. 1, 1760 to 1776)* (Julian P. Boyd, ed., 1950), at 292.

[66] *See* Merrill D. Peterson, "The Virginia Constitution," in Merrill D. Peterson, *Thomas Jefferson & the New Nation: A Biography* (1970) at 100–107. Oxford University Press, New York.

[67] 1 *The Papers of Thomas Jefferson (1760 to 1776), supra* note 65, at 471, 472.

[68] Pendleton to Jefferson, Aug. 10, 1776, 1 *The Papers of Thomas Jefferson (1760 to 1776), supra* note 65, at 488, 490. *See also* Pendleton to Jefferson, August 3, 1776, *id.* at 484. Jefferson responded to the letter of the 3rd on August 13. *Id.* at 491–494.

[69] Thomas Jefferson, *Notes on the State of Virginia* (London, 1787) at 269.

[70] *Autobiography, supra* note 61, at 57.

[71] *The Papers of Thomas Jefferson (Volume 2, 1777 to 18 June 1779, Including the Revisal of the Laws, 1776–1786)* (Julian P. Boyd, ed., 1950), at 306.

"Revisal." The Revisal was literally two bundles of 126 bills that the Virginia House Committee on Revision under Jefferson's leadership prepared from October 1776 to June 1779.[72]

Jefferson lost no time in getting to work on building a government of laws. Within 2 months of taking his office in early October 1776, he had underway legislation remodeling the state judiciary.[73] Already in early November he achieved adoption of bills overturning the common law of land tenures[74] and authorizing a total overhaul of Virginia law.[75] With respect to the latter, the Assembly in effect made him chair of the five-member committee it appointed to reform Virginia law. The Committee was soon reduced to three; in the end, Jefferson and his former law teacher, George Wythe, did most of the work.[76] The Act creating the Committee gave it "full power and authority to revise, alter, amend, repeal or introduce all or any of the said laws, to form the same into bills, and report them to the next meeting of the General Assembly." The charge to the committee—written by Jefferson—was expansive:

> Whereas the later change which hath of necessity been introduced into the form of government in this country, it is become also necessary to make corresponding changes in the laws heretofore in force, many of which are inapplicable to the powers of government as now organized, others are founded on principles heterogeneous to the republican spirit, others which, long before such change, had been oppressive to the people, could yet never be repealed while the regal power continued, and others, having taken their origin while our ancestors remained in Britain, are not so well adapted to our present circumstances of time and place, and it is also necessary to introduce certain other laws, which, though proved by the experience of other states to be friendly to liberty and the rights of mankind, we have not heretofore been permitted to adopt ....[77]

The Committee presented its report June 18, 1779. Owing to the war and the British invasion of Virginia, the Assembly did not take up the report until years later. In 1784 it ordered the report printed. By then Jefferson was away for a 5 year mission in Europe.

In Jefferson's absence, it was James Madison who brought Jefferson's legislation to the Assembly and took over sponsorship from 1785 to 1787. Madison's central role in presenting Jefferson's anti-common law revision to the Virginia Assembly just months before the 1787 convocation of the U.S. Constitutional Convention contradicts the claim that the Convention convened with the assumption that English

[72] *Id.* at 306–307.

[73] *The Papers of Thomas Jefferson (Vol. 1, 1760 to 1776), supra* note 65, at 605 (for which work he was seen "as the preeminent architect of Virginia's judiciary".)

[74] *The Papers of Thomas Jefferson (Volume 2, 1777 to 18 June 1779, Including the Revisal of the Laws, 1776–1786)* (Julian P. Boyd, ed., 1950) at 560 (Bill to Enable Tenants in Fee Tail to Convey Their Lands in Fee Simple).

[75] *Id.* at 562 (Bill for the Revision of the Laws).

[76] Id. at 313–317.

[77] *Report of the Committee of Advisors Appointed by the General Assembly of Virginia in MDCCLXXVI* (1784) at 3 (available at books.google.com).

common law would continue unchanged in the United States.[78] Madison in those 2 years introduced 118 of the report's 126 bills and achieved adoption of 58. At the end of the later session the un-adopted bills were referred for updating to a new committee of revisers for future action.[79]

17.5.2 *Jefferson's Government of Laws*

Jefferson has rightly been called Jefferson the legislator, Jefferson the lawmaker and Jefferson the lawgiver. Just as Jefferson's contemporaries Catherine the Great, Frederick the Great and Napoleon are remembered for their legislation, so too should Jefferson be remembered for his. His work was no less impressive and no less extensive; except for Catherine and her Proposal for a New Code, he got there first. Moreover, he did the work himself! Yet Jefferson's legislation is unknown among American lawyers. Law schools pay it no mind.[80]

The enormity of the work that Jefferson and Wythe undertook is hard to appreciate even for lawyers. Lawyers work with one case at a time. In counseling, they advise how they see the law in one or a handful of fact situations. In litigating, they argue for one view that they see as benefiting their client. Judges focus on one set of facts and the laws that might apply to it. Law teachers in America assume the role of lawyers. Good lawmakers, on the other hand, must make provision for not one case, but for all possible cases, even though they well know that they cannot anticipate all cases. Good lawmakers must capture in a few understandable words what they want people to do. Good lawmakers must make their laws consistent internally and with other laws. John Austin saw that this, "the technical part of legislation, is incomparably more difficult than what may be styled the ethical".[81]

In legislating, Jefferson was building a government of laws. He was the architect designing a new republic. His designs would demolish old law that was inapplicable, oppressive, contrary to republican sensibilities, or simply not well-adapted to present time. Jefferson intended his designs to rationalize existing laws and institutions and to create new ones. They would create government, guide governors in how to govern and instruct those governed in what was expected of them. He was ripping out common law that he found feudal, offensive or just plain foolish.

Jefferson's Revisal suggests no thought to using contemporary common law methods of lawmaking to bring about the republic of his visions. To the contrary, the Revisal was legislation. Jefferson could hardly have proceeded in any other way. Only statutes can root out old laws, refashion rationally remaining institutions,

[78] *See* text at note 50 *supra*.

[79] *The Papers of Thomas Jefferson (Volume 2, 1777 to 18 June 177), supra* note 71, at 322–323.

[80] The nations' secondary schools may do better. *See, e.g.*, "Jefferson The Legislator (1776–1779)", in *Thomas Jefferson and His World* (American Heritage Junior Library, 1960), at 48–53.

[81] John Austin, *Codification and Law Reform*, in 2 John Austin, *Lectures on Jurisprudence or the Philosophy of Positive Law* 1092, 1099 (5th ed., Robert Campbell, ed., 1885).

create wholly new institutions, and provide direction in how to govern. Jefferson sought to use legislation to do all four. In a democratic republic Jefferson could not decree judicially a new society and new laws. He had to get the assent of the democratically-elected legislature.

17.5.3 The Substance of Jefferson's Legislation[82]

Historians focus—as did Jefferson—on the substance of his legislative work. His biographers take from 25 to 50 pages to describe it. The bills of the Revisal alone were printed in 90 oversized folio pages in tiny type (over 300 pages in a standard type face in a large octavo book). Other legislation he wrote or sponsored was of comparable extent. He was, as the editor of his papers said, "a veritable legislative drafting bureau."[83]

Jefferson worked to build a new society. He designed legislation that struck at the very roots of the common law: the land law, inheritance and criminal law. According to one biographer, Jefferson intended to "completely overthrow the English legal system that had chained Virginia for 170 years."[84] Jefferson abolished primogeniture and completely changed rules of descent. He proposed a new penal law "to proportion crimes and punishments in cases [previously] capital." It failed of passage by a single vote. Jefferson drafted legislation that would end forever the idea that the common law made Christian doctrine a part of law. His legislation disestablished the Anglican Church in Virginia. His bill establishing religious liberty is the best-known of all his legislation.

Jefferson sought to organize and rationalize common law institutions. His legislation restated and reorganized court institutions and procedures both civil and criminal to make, writes one historian, a "mantel of procedural safeguards for all."[85]

Jefferson's legislation reorganized government in all its branches. It provided for a state militia and navy, a board of war, a board of trade and a board of auditors. It districted the legislature and provided for elections and appointments. It created a public land office to administer claims to the western lands.

Jefferson did not know how to treat slavery. Today his legislative proposals look modestly progressive at best and frighteningly racist at worst: gradual emancipation followed by mandatory emigration.[86] His other legislation addressed all

---

[82] The following paragraphs do not generally cite to individual bills from the Revisal. They are found in the Committee's Report, cited above at note 77, and in Boyd's analysis of the Revisal, found in 2 *The Papers of Thomas Jefferson (Volume 2, 1777 to 18 June 1779)*, *supra* note 71.

[83] *The Papers of Thomas Jefferson (Volume 2, 1777 to 18 June 1779)*, *supra* note 71, at 306.

[84] Randall, *supra* note 63, at 285.

[85] Lerner, *supra* note 52, at 64.

[86] *Compare* Lerner, *supra* note 52, at 88 (sympathetic, "society is invited to raise its hopes, even while mired in a system of chattel slavery that promise to swamp or befoul every brave plan") *with* John T. Noonan, Jr., "Chapter 2 "Virginian Liberators"" in John T. Noonan, Jr., *Persons and*

manner of personal status, including slaves, indentured servants, mulattoes, citizens, and aliens.

Jefferson restated and rationalized a nascent regulatory state. His legislation addressed matters as diverse as infection and breeding of animals, licensing and regulating taverns, regulating mill-dams, public store-houses, commodities fraud, unwholesome meat and drink, public health vaccination and quarantine, usury, gaming and what we would call unfair competition.

Jefferson worked at building what we might call a social state. His legislation provided for maintaining and building public roads, establishing ferries, a state postal service, support of the poor, registration of vital statistics, and legal aid in civil court proceedings.

Of all of his proposals for new legislation, Jefferson was most proud of his bills for "the more general diffusion of knowledge." Jefferson wanted to establish universal public schooling. His bill for public education was an American model for a generation. He sought to establish a public research library, to reorganize the College of William and Mary and to establish the University of Virginia.

17.5.4 Jefferson's Dealing with Statutes

Jefferson knew how to deal with statutes. Some of his best practices included:

- *Professional drafting.* In Jefferson's day legislatures acting as a body generally drafted legislation within a single term of few months. The Act that Jefferson wrote took the Revisal out of the normal legislative cycle and gave the work to experts. The Act explained why: "a work of such magnitude, labor and difficulty, may not be effected during the short and busy terms of a session of Assembly."
- *Justifications for bills.* In Jefferson's day legislation usually began simply, "be it enacted," without explanation why. Jefferson, however, for his most important laws, prefaced them with elegant explanations, sometimes called proems, of the basis for the proposed legislation.[87]
- *Publication of the proposed legislation for public comment.* In a day of difficult communication and expensive printing, the legislature took the unusual step of directing printing of the proposed bills. It allowed a comment period of 9 months "for the purpose of affording to the citizens at large, an opportunity of examining

Masks of the Law: Cardozo, Holmes, Jefferson, and Wythe as Makers of the Masks (1976) at 29–64 (critical). *See also* Dumas Malone, "Chapter XIX. Architect of Laws: Slavery and Crime," *in Jefferson the Virginian* (Jefferson and His Time, vol. 1, 1948), at 261–273; Randall, *supra* note 52, at 300–303.

[87] *See* Lerner, *supra* note 52, at 90.

and considering a work which proposes such various and material changes in our legal code."[88]

- *Clarity of statutory language*. Jefferson saw the need for clear and consistent laws. He sought to balance the old and the new in his drafting. He wrote co-draftsman Wythe: "In its style I have aimed at accuracy, brevity and simplicity, preserving however the very words of the established law, wherever their meaning has been sanctioned by judicial decisions or rendered technical by usage."[89] His biographers—laymen—praise his language as "a model of plain, elegant writing"[90] and "comprehensible to laymen."[91]

17.5.5 Jefferson's Legal State

Jefferson's bills respecting education—although not adopted in his day in Virginia—show Jefferson's aspirations for laws that would strike the right balance of defining the tasks of government while allowing the governors sufficient flexibility to govern well.

Government gives direction. Jefferson's proposals give in detail how schools shall be established. They set out not only what shall be done, but who shall do it. "Electors" have their duties, "aldermen theirs," and "overseers" theirs. The latter are to appoint, and remove teachers, and to examine scholars. Summarizing Lerner observes:

> In short, the entire scheme for establishing and maintaining an educational system constitutes in itself an education in responsible self-governance. In lavishing these details upon the bill, Jefferson also gave his fullest explanation by example of what he meant by self-government. … [A] free people must be qualified 'as judges of the actions and designs of men.' Jefferson's bill encompasses that intention at every level.[92]

The ultimate measure of legislation is whether it works. Since much of what Jefferson wrote was not adopted and since much that was adopted addressed soon-to-be-obsolete matters, it is difficult to characterize how well his bills would have worked. But some can be measured. One commentator singled out Jefferson's Statute of Descents of October 1785 a century later. That law "demolished" "every shred of the pre-existing (English) law of descents" and established new law based on contradictory principles. Nonetheless, the admirer wrote: "So precise, so comprehensive and exhaustive, so simple and clear, were the terms in which they were expressed, that in the experience of a completed century *but one single doubt as to the construction and effect of any part of it has arisen.*"[93]

---

[88] As quoted in 2 *The Papers of Thomas Jefferson (Volume 2, 1777 to 18 June 1779), supra* note 71, at 310.

[89] Jefferson to Wythe, Nov 1, 1778, 2 *The Papers of Thomas Jefferson (Volume 2, 1777 to 18 June 1779), supra* note 71, at 229, 230.

[90] Randall, *supra* note 63, at 298.

[91] Mallone, *supra* note 86, at 271.

[92] Lerner, *supra* note 52, at 80–81.

[93] R.G.H. Kean, "Thomas Jefferson as a Legislator," 11 *Virginia L.J.* 705 (1887) at 720 (emphasis in original).

17.6 Conclusion

Ten years ago, Professor Charles Abernathy told a German audience, that although they and Americans might see the roots of the American legal system in English common law and a common law lawmaking, "with respect to constitutional law—America's greatest legal contribution to modern respect for the rule of law, the roots of the U.S. legal system are firmly planted in Europe, not England."[94] This chapter suggests that something of the same might be said of American lawmaking generally.

This chapter does not address where the ideas of Adams and Jefferson came from, but where they might have led. Their government of laws and not of men partakes more of a democratic legal state than it does of the Dicey-like rule of law of contemporary common law. The state they sought is a state based on statutes adopted by democratic legislatures using procedures intended to produce laws that promote the common good. The statutes they wanted are well-crafted and consistent within themselves and with other laws to the end that no one should be forced to break one law in order to follow another. The laws they would have would guide the people—the governed and governors alike—toward making good decisions based on personal responsibility. They would show us a path to good government and to liberty in law.

[94] Charles Abernathy, "The Lost European Aspirations of US Constitutional Law," *in 24. Februar 1803: Die Erfindung der Verfassungsgerichtsbarkeit und ihre Folgen* (Werner Kremp, ed., 2003) at 371. Wissenschaftlicher Verlag, Trier. The occasion was the 100th anniversary of the Supreme Court's decision in *Marbury v. Madison*. For classical roman law ideas in the U.S. constitution, see David J. Bederman, *The Classical Foundations of the American Constitution: Prevailing Wisdom* (2008) Cambridge University Press, New York; M.N.S. Sellers, *American Republicanism: Roman Ideology in the United States Constitution* (1994). NYU Press, New York.

Chapter 18
Rule of Law v. Legal State: Where Have We Come from, Where Are We Going To?

Nadia E. Nedzel

Abstract This article compares the civilian legal state to common law rule of law with regard to economic development and individual liberty. It focuses on the differences in both concept and culture in an effort to tease out what it is about 'Englishness' that has traditionally provided greater stability, greater protection for liberty, and incentives for economic development.

18.1 Introduction

Though the terms rule of law and legal state are used frequently, they are rarely used with precision. Confusion about the historical differences between the terms has made discussion among scholars and policy-makers with varying legal backgrounds difficult, if not impossible.[1] Some scholars and multinational entities have tried to synthesize a definition of the rule of law that encompasses elements of both the

[1] "The Principle of the Rule of Law," *Resolution* 1594, Council of Europe Parliamentary Assembly (2007), at http://assembly.coe.int/main.asp?Link=/documents/adoptedtext/ta07/eres1594.htm [PROPER CITATION PLEASE]: 3. Despite a general commitment to this principle [the rule of law], the variability in terminology and understanding of the term, both within the Council of Europe and in its member states, has elicited confusion. In particular, the French expression *Etat de droit* (being perhaps the translation of the term *Rechtsstaat* known in the German legal tradition and in many others) has often been used but does not always reflect the English language notion of "rule of law" as adequately as the expression *prééminence du droit*, which is reflected in the French version of the Statute of the Council of Europe, in the preamble to the European Convention on Human Rights (ETS No. 5) and in the Strasbourg Court's case law.

N.E. Nedzel (✉)
Reilly Family Professor of Law, Southern University Law Center, Baton Rouge, USA
e-mail: nnedzel@sulc.edu

J.R. Silkenat et al. (eds.), *The Legal Doctrines of the Rule of Law and the Legal State (Rechtsstaat)*, Ius Gentium: Comparative Perspectives on Law and Justice 38,
DOI 10.1007/978-3-319-05585-5_18, © Springer International Publishing Switzerland 2014

traditional common law rule of law and the civilian legal state; others claim that the concepts have been converging since the Second World War.[2]

Though they share a number of the same values, the two legal terms are based in two different legal cultures. The two concepts are different, and a more precise understanding of the difference is needed to further the discussion of good governance. While both emphasize that the law must apply equally to all, the terms *legal state*, *état de droit,* or *rechtsstaat* refer to a state that rules using statutory law enacted by a democratic parliament. Thus, such a state is ruled *through* or *by* law. This is distinct from a state that is itself subject to the rule *of* law, which refers to the use of both customary and institutional means to protect individual liberties and limit governmental powers.[3]

Lon Fuller's eight principles are often stated as necessary characteristics of good law, and hence necessary for both the rule of law and the legal state.[4] Klaus Stern has provided a similar, and perhaps more complete list of characteristics to describe the legal state.[5] Neither list explicitly recognizes those concepts that are specific to the Anglo-American concept: an underlying respect for practice, not legal theory; an understanding that the proper purpose of the government is to protect citizens' rights in a non-instrumental way; and a focus on individual liberty, self government, and the need for effective legal, cultural, and customary controls to protect against a government that will inevitably attempt to infringe on those liberties.[6]

---

[2] Ricardo Gosalbo-Bono, "The Significance of the Rule of Law and its Implications for the European Union and the United States," 72 *U. Pitt. L. Rev.* 229, 360 (2010). Compare the definition and description of the Rule of Law provided by the World Justice Project at http://worldjusticeproject.org/factors/limited-government-powers, which incorporates elements of both rule of law and legal state (including equal application of the law, limited government, protection for fundamental rights, and checks and balances), with the *Resolution of the Council of the International Bar Association* of October 8, 2009, on the Commentary on Rule of Law Resolution (2005) at www.ibanet.org (emphasizing independent judiciary, presumption of innocence, right to a speedy trial, equal application of the law). But *see* the definition in *(S/2004/616) Report of the Secretary-General on the Rule of Law and Transitional Justice in Conflict and Post-Conflict Societies at* http://www.un.org/en/ruleoflaw/index.shtml. The U.N. Secretary General's definition is more consistent with the legal state, as it emphasizes equal application of the law but not limited government.

[3] *See* David Dyzenhaus, "Book Review, The End of the Road to Serfdom", 63 U. Toronto L. Rev. 317–318 (2013).

[4] Lon L. Fuller *The Morality of Law* (Revised ed, Yale University Press, New Haven, 1969) 33–38. Fuller stated the principles negatively, in a parable involving fictional King Rex trying to create a legal system. Stated positively, those eight principles include: 1. *Generality*, 2. *Notice or publicity*, 3. *Prospectivity*, 4. *Clarity*, 5. *Consistency*, 6. Conformability, 7. *Stability*, 8. *Congruency*. Margaret Jane Radin, "Reconsidering the Rule of Law", 69 U. Boston L. Rev. 781, 785 (1989).

[5] Klaus Stern, 1 *Das Staatsrecht der Bundesrepublik Deutschland [The State Law of Germany]* 781 (2nd ed. Munich: CH Beck'sche Verlagsbuchhandlung 1984) (cited and translated by Francois Venter, 'South Africa: A Diceyan Rechtsstaat?,' 57:4 MdGill L. J. 721, 726 (2012): *A constitutional state*: a constitution is the foundational juridical order and supreme legal norm of the state. Stern's list includes 1. Human dignity, liberty, and equality; 2, control of government authority; 3, Legality; 4. Judicial Protection; 5. Reparation, 6. Protection against excessive use of authority.

[6] *See generally* F.A. Hayek, *The Road to Serfdom: Texts and Documents, The Definitive Edition* (ed. Bruce Caldwell, 2007, originally 1944). U. Chicago Press.

Scholars have long noticed that common law countries tend to be more protective of individual liberties. Common law countries have greater economic, business, and labor freedom; greater governmental stability; and faster economic growth than do civil law countries as demonstrated by comparison of the Heritage Fund's *Economic Freedom of the World* map, Transparency International's *Corruption Index*, and the World Justice Project's *Rule of Law Index*.[7] The countries that rate highest on the *Rule of Law Index* are among the richest and most free (Canada, Australia, Denmark, Norway, United States).[8]

This essay discusses the history of both systems and compares some of the resulting effects on economic freedom and liberty as well as cultural reasons for differences in effect. It concludes with a discussion of those attributes, both legal and cultural, that lead to good governance. The thesis of this essay is that study of the historical differences in both concept and culture explains what it is about 'Englishness' that has traditionally provided stability, greater protection for liberty, and incentive for economic development.

18.2 History of the Rule of Law

The Anglo-American conception of the rule of law consists of two interdependent components: (1) a citizen's obligation to obey the law (the law and order component), and (2) the government's subservience to the law (the limited government component). The second component of the Anglo-American concept is more than merely the absence of governmental corruption and the concept that laws must be applied equally to all. It is that the law itself is the ultimate sovereign, not the government, and a government is answerable to its people for any infringement on liberty: "a government of laws, and not of men."[9] The concept, with which many civilians are uncomfortable, includes John Locke's consent theory, that a government is given power through the consent of the people, that its sole purpose is to protect the liberty of the governed, and when it fails to do so, the governed have the right to call it to account.[10] Under the Anglo-American conception, individual rights limit state power (sometimes termed *negative rights'* by scholars); while under the civilian conception, the government is expected to limit itself and provides rights to individuals (sometimes termed 'positive rights' such as a right to a job, health care, etc.).

---

[7] 2013 *Economic Freedom of the World Heat Map*, Heritage Fund, available at http://www.heritage.org/index/heatmap (last visited on July1, 2013), with the *2011 Corruption Perceptions Index*, Transparency International and available at http://www.transparency.org/cpi2011/results. *See also* Nadia E. Nedzel, "The Rule of Law: Its History and Meaning in Common Law, Civil Law, and Latin American Judicial Systems," 10 Richmond J. Global L. & Bus. (2010) 57, 60 (showing composite maps with 2010 data and sources cited therein).

[8] *World Justice Project Rule of Law Index* 2012–2013 Report, available at: http://worldjusticeproject.org/rule-of-law-index-data

[9] *Marbury v. Madison*, 5 U.S. (1 Cranch) 137, 163 (1803).

[10] U.S. Declaration of Independence.

Oxford legal scholar A.V. Dicey used the term rule of law in 1885 to describe the limitations placed on British government:

> The rule of law … remains to this day a distinctive characteristic of the English constitution. In England no man can be made to suffer punishment or to pay damages for any conduct not definitely forbidden by law; every man's legal rights or liabilities are almost invariably determined by the ordinary Courts of the realm, and each man's individual rights are far less the result of our constitution than the basis on which that constitution is founded.[11]

Dicey asserted that the legal positivist movement, developed by Jeremy Bentham, John Austin, and others, which stipulated that the law is what the government says it is, was instrumentalist and inconsistent with the rule of law.[12]

Building on Dicey's description, twentieth century British political philosopher Michael Oakeshott distinguished between two types of governments and two types of cultures: Governments can be either civil or enterprise associations; and cultures can promote either autonomous individuals or anti-individuals.[13]

Civil associations are non-instrumentalist and (except during times of war) consequently encourage individual economic growth. In contrast, a government that is an enterprise association focuses on some collective goal (the general will). A civil association has no collective goal and exists in order to maximize the possibility for autonomous individuals to pursue their personally chosen goals.[14] Autonomous individuals are those who want to choose their own goals, accept responsibility for the consequences of those choices, and are primarily interested in equality of opportunity, not equality of outcome. Anti-individuals are those who are psychologically unwilling to accept responsibility for their own decisions or set their own goals, and who seek a government focused on equality of outcome, which they define as the common good.

Today, it is often assumed that law should be used instrumentally, i.e. as a means to an end, and often that end is some kind of equality – e.g. welfare programs, compulsory participation in various education or social services organizations. Such programs may be adopted by democratic process. Nevertheless, they are inherently inconsistent with the rule of law because the state must give someone the power to determine whether another person merits, or does not merit, the award. In so doing, the state is diminishing individual freedom, is producing laws that give some people privileges which others do not get, and therefore creating laws that do not apply equally to all.[15] Furthermore, such systems are more easily corrupted (because they give those in government the power to distribute political awards) or lead to heightened

---

[11] Albert Venn Dicey, *Introduction to the Study of the Law of the Constitution IV* (1915).

[12] *Id.*

[13] *See* Michael Oakeshott, *On Human Conduct* (1975) at 118–119, 149. Oxford: Clarendon Press. Michael Oakeshott, *Masses in Representative Democracy* (1962) in Rationalism in Politics and Other Essays (Liberty Fund 1991).

[14] *Id.*

[15] *See* F.A. Hayek, "Lecture IV: The Decline of the Rule of Law" in *The Political Idea of the Rule of Law* (National Bank of Egypt, Cairo 1955) at 46–48.

political divisiveness as one or more political factions object to either the means by which the government is trying to achieve a goal or the goal itself. A recent U.S. example could include the political controversy in the U.S. concerning the Patient Protection and Affordable Health Care Act ('Obamacare'). The growth of the bureaucratic state demanded by such programs expands governmental authority, thus further eroding the rule of law.[16]

18.3 The Legal State: Founding Generals, Not Founding Fathers

Chilean economist José Piñera (co-founder of Chile's private pension system) quipped that the United States had Founding Fathers, but Latin America had Founding Generals. His statement was truer than he realized: the Civilian Tradition itself was founded on Roman Emperor Justinian's Digest. One of the predominant concepts in the *Corpus Juris Civilis*, codified by Emperor Justinian in 427 A.D. was that the government (the emperor) was the law[17]: "*Sed quod principi placuit legishabet vigorem*" (what has pleased the prince has the force of law) and "*Princepslegibus solutus est*" (the prince is not bound by the law).[18]

The Civilian tradition, derived as it is from Greek and Roman thought, is focused on deduction from first principles. Thus, it traditionally regards the concept of a government of laws as oxymoronic: laws cannot either create or enforce themselves, there has to be a government that creates them, and therefore, government comes first. The common law/civil law difference here can be analogized to the chicken and egg argument. Common law presumes that in all practicality, it was the egg, the germ of the concept of living in a cooperative society, that came first, not a sovereign government.[19] Under Euclidean deductive logic, civilians would argue that one first has to have a chicken (the government) before one can have an egg (the law).

---

[16] *See* Brian Z. Tamanaha, *How an Instrumental View of Law Corrodes the Rule of Law*, 56 DePaul L. Rev. (2007) 469, 504; A.V. Dicey, *Introduction to the Study of the Law of the Constitution* (1885) ("The ancient veneration for the rule of law has in England suffered during the last thirty years a marked decline."); F.A. Hayek, "Lecture 1: Freedom and the Rule of Law" *A Historical Survey in The Political Ideal of the Rule of Law* (1955) at 3 National Bank of Egypt, Cairo ("[This revolution has gradually whittled away most of the guarantees of individual liberty]").

[17] Gosalbo-Bono, *supra* note 3 (2010) at 229, 235.

[18] Digest 1.4.1 and Digest 1.3.1, cited in Stein, *Roman Law in European History* (1999) at 59.

[19] *See e.g.* Robert Ellickson, *Order Without Law: How Neighbors Settle Disputes* (1991). Harvard U. Press; John Maxcy Zane, *The Story of Law* (1998) at 343. Liberty Fund.

18.3.1 The French Revolution and L'État de Droit

État de droit, the French version of the legal state, developed slowly out of the Enlightenment and the French Revolution's rejection of the prior rigid social structure and turgid legal system, as epitomized by the rallying cry: *"Liberté, Égalité, Fraternité!"* Emmanuel Joseph Sieyès, whose pamphlet "What Is the Third Estate?" became the Revolution's manifesto, envisioned a new nation comprised solely of the Third Estate (the common people). Composed of this one order, his theory was that the nation would possess one single democratic will, and could therefore deliberate and legislate purposefully and effectively.[20] After the Revolution, the focus was on the unity of the Legal State as an embodiment of Rousseau's General Will (*volonté générale*). The Revolutionaries' view of government was necessarily instrumentalist – government was an enterprise association whose proper role was to totally transform France politically, legally, and socially, to overthrow the nation's institutions, and to break with a thousand years of history.[21]

The 1789 French Declaration of the Rights of Man and Citizen, the founding document of the Revolution, proclaimed rights that the French had never previously possessed. It was strikingly different from the U.S. Bill of Rights the purpose of which was to protect individuals and minorities from the tyranny of an oppressive majority or government. The French Declaration was founded on the fear that self-interested individuals and 'particularistic' minorities (factions) could disrupt the General Will (i.e. disrupt the harmony and collective well being of the nation). Thus its purpose was to protect the majority against minorities and individuals.[22] The French revolutionaries feared stagnation, not the concentration of power. They believed that the separation of powers and checks and balances would thwart the radical steps needed to restructure society, and were therefore inappropriate. In 1790, the National Assembly prohibited judicial tribunals from interfering with the exercise of legislative power and from attempting to suspend the execution of the laws.

The result of this instrumentalist view of government led inexorably to the Reign of Terror of 1793–1794, during which 41,594 people were executed as 'enemies of the revolution.' What the French Revolutionaries had overlooked was a principle that even Plato and Aristotle were familiar with: democracy is an inherently unstable form of government and rule by the majority inexorably leads to abuse and repression of minorities.[23] Checks and balances protect individuals as well as minorities and factions from democratically–elected tyrants.

---

[20] Susan Dunn, *Sister Revolutions: French Lightening, American Light* (1999) at 60. Faber & Faber.

[21] *Id.* at 11–12.

[22] *Id.* at 153.

[23] "Democracy will soon degenerate into an anarchy; such an anarchy that every man will do what is right in his own eyes and no man's life or property or reputation or liberty will be secure, and every one of these will soon mould itself into a system of subordination of all the moral virtues and intellectual abilities, all the powers of wealth, beauty, wit, and science, to the wanton pleasures, the capricious will, and the execrable cruelty of one or a very few." John Adams, *An Essay on Man's Lust for Power* (1763).

When Napoleon rose to power, he promulgated yet a third constitution (the Constitution of the Year VIII) and a civil code reflecting the chief accomplishments of the Revolution. Those accomplishments included popular sovereignty, trial by jury (in felony cases), equality before the law, inviolate property ownership, a citizen army, freedom of religion, abolition of feudal privileges, and freedom of the press. His *Code Civile* incorporated a number of traditional principles derived from Justinian's *Corpus Juris Civilis*, updated and organized into a logical, coherent, and transparent system of private law. Law was based on legislation and custom, and was to be predictable, transparent, and apply to all. Thus, it embodied some of the concepts of the legal state. The term *État de droit* developed in the late nineteenth century, long after Napoleon's downfall, and was explicitly introduced by French jurists as a normative principle designed to address perceived governmental deficiencies.[24] French public law had continued to revolve around the concept of the general will,[25] and the issue jurists and law professors were addressing was how to control the legislature.[26]

Influenced by the German *Rechtsstaat*, Carré de Malberg posited that the state was an entity that could act only through law, and could, through the concept of self-limitation, bind itself to its own norms.[27] His theory was that law exists to protect individual rights, and such rights are only partially protected legislated law.[28] French jurists focused specifically on the status of the 1789 *Declaration* of the Rights of Man and the Citizen within the constitutional framework of the Third Republic. Ultimately, Carré de Malberg, as a positivist himself, maintained that without specific appendage to the Constitution, the Declaration could have no legal effect. In contrast, the U.S. Declaration of Independence, a similarly pre-constitutional statement of rights not referenced in the U.S. Constitution, has been cited by the U.S. Supreme Court 212 times (as recently as 2011), and has been cited by federal and state courts in total 2,641 times.[29]

A purely theoretical concept, *État de droit* is defined as (1) "the situation that results, for a society, from its submission to a juridical order that excludes anarchy and private justice, or (2) in a more exact sense, it refers to the respect for rights

[24] Martin Loughlin, "The Rule of Law in European Jurisprudence," *European Commission for Democracy Through Law* Study 512/2009, CDL-JD (2009) (Strasbourg, 29 May 2009) at 7.

[25] *See* Marie-Joëlle Redor, De l'Etat Legal à l'Etat de droit: L'evolution des conceptions de la doctrine publiciste française (Presses universitaires d'Aix-Marseille 1992) at 52–59; Guillaume Bacot, *Carré de Malberg et L'Origine de la Distinction entre Souveraineté du Peuple et Souveraineté Nationale* (1985). Editions du Centre national de la recherche scientifique.

[26] Charles de Gaulle addressed this issue in the Constitution of the Fifth Republic by expanding the power of the presidency: under the pre-existing Fourth Republic, it required an Act of the National Assembly to move a horse trough in Paris. *See* Bernard Chantebout, *The French Constitution: Its Origin and Development in the Fifth Republic*. Translation by David Gruning (1998). Louisiana State U. Press (trans. David Gruning).

[27] Raymond Carré de Malberg, *Contribution à la Théorie générale de l'Etat* (2004), vol.1, 228–243. University of Michigan Library.

[28] Raymond Carre de Malberg, *Contribution à la Théorie générale de l'Etat* (1920–22) at 493–500. University of Michigan Library.

[29] *Stern v. Marshall*, 131 S. Ct. 2594 (2011).

guaranteed to those subjected to a state's laws that they will not be treated arbitrarily."[30] The first is simply the law and order component of the rule of law. The second refers to a guarantee of civil rights that laws will be applied equally. However, it does not indicate that the primary power rests in the people, not the law, or that the government is subservient to both.

18.3.2 Rechtsstaat

In addition to predating it by more than 100 years, the German *Rechtsstaat* is more complex than the French equivalent: German jurists attempted to reconcile modern claims of liberty with traditional authoritarian governing arrangements.[31] Immanuel Kant is generally identified as the spiritual father of the concept by defining the state as the union of a multitude of men under laws of justice with any "lawful state" necessarily being a state governed by the law of reason based on and protecting freedom for every member of society, equality, and individual autonomy.[32] Kant's concept was thus premised on negative freedom – that the government is obligated to not interfere with an individual's liberty, and is also obligated to protect individuals from interference by other people, thus it was predicated on an assumption of the primacy of liberty and limited government.[33] Kant's concept then was consistent with the classical Anglo-American rule of law.

In 1798, Johan Wilhelm Placidus coined the term *Rechtsstaat* which was popularized by Robert von Mohl in 1844.[34] Von Mohl's concept differed from Kant's: in place of Kant's negative freedom, Von Mohl promoted freedom through the state. The law-bound state was to measure governmental action against the general objective of promoting an individual's complete development.[35] Thus, it is premised on 'positive rights' and contrasts with the Kantian and Common law concept that the proper role of government is to prevent interference with liberty and that individuals are in charge of their own development.

After the failed 1848 revolution, Von Mohl's concept was itself redefined by a political compromise between monarchical authoritarianism and liberal constitutionalism.[36] As redefined, the concept was based on three elements: the theory of the

---

[30] Raymond Carré de Malberg, *Contribution à la Théorie générale de l'Etat* (2004), vol.1, 228–243. University of Michigan Library.

[31] *See* Gosalbo-Bono, *supra* note 3, at 247–249 (explaining delay in development of French *l'état de droit*).

[32] History of Political Philosophy, Leo Strauss and Joseph Cropsey eds. (1987) at 581–582,603; Gosalbo-Bono, *supra* note 3.

[33] Martin Loughlin, *Foundations of Public Law* (Press 2012) at 319. Oxford University Press.

[34] Johan Wilhelm Placidus, *Litteratur der Staatslehre, Ein Versuch* (1798); Robert von Mohl, Die *Polizeiwissenschaft nach den Grunds tzen der Rechtstaates* (1844).

[35] Loughlin, *supra* note 38 at 319.

[36] *Id.*

"state's self-limitation," the theory of "subjective rights," and the theory of the "primacy of law."[37] Due to the influence of legal positivism, the state was conceived as a juristic person and rights were created only through legislation.[38] Jhering identified consequential difficulties with respect to the relationship between state and law under this conception: because there is no power above the state, the state must limit itself.[39]

The notion of self-limitation only makes sense in an enterprise association, where there is a collective entity concerned with a collective purpose. In contrast, in a civil association, there is no self-limitation because the law limits legislators, executives, and judges. Furthermore, in contrast with the Anglo-American Rule of Law concept of inalienable rights (life, liberty, and the pursuit of happiness), the rights accorded to individuals by *Rechtsstaat* were given by the state. Though the state was 'obligated' to follow the law, if it did not, individuals did not have a right of resistance, as they do under the U.S. Declaration of Independence. Nineteenth Century *Rechtsstaat* regarded government both as the representative of the general will and as having its own particular will based on the government's subjective right to command in accordance with legislated law. Thus, it was a way to establish the legitimacy of government, not a way to establish rights.

Towards the end of the nineteenth century and through the early part of the twentieth, the term *Rechtsstaat* became so malleable that it was at times regarded as a 'magic box' from which a jurist could obtain any legal principle or claim that was desired. Some jurists did not hesitate to describe Hitler's Third Reich as an exemplary *Rechtsstaat*: If a *Rechtsstaat* is defined as a state based on order, then because Hitler's Third Reich was a legal order, it was a *Rechtsstaat*.[40]

Austrian Hans Kelsen tried to reclaim *Rechtsstaat* by incorporating it into his Pure Theory of Law as legal science rather than legal politics. He asserted that the state was not power but law and the legal system must be hierarchical, with a *Grundnorm*, such as a constitution, at the top.[41] His influence is seen in legal systems, such as those of post World War II Germany and France, which place the constitution as the foundational document with separate constitutional courts having sole responsibility over constitutional disputes.

Rechtsstaat has since been enshrined as a fundamental principle of the 1949 German Basic Law, which states that "[t]he constitutional order in the states must conform to the principles of the republican, democratic and social state under the rule of law (sic)."[42] Thus, *Rechtsstaat* has evolved into a constitutional principle

---

[37] Gosalbo-Bono, *supra* note 3, at 242.

[38] Loughlin, *supra* note 38 at 320.

[39] *Id.*

[40] C. Schmitt, "Nationalsozialismus und Rechtstaat," in *Juristische Wochenschrift* 716 (1934) at 716.

[41] H. Kelsen, *Hauptproleme der Staatsrechtslehre* (1984). Aalen: Scientia-Verlag; H. Kelsen, "Staat und Recht," *Soziologische Hefte* (1922) at 18–27; H. Kelsen, *Rechtsstaat und Staatsrecht* (1913) at 36.

[42] The official English translation uses the term *rule of law*, accessed on June 19, 2013 at http://www.gesetze-im-internet.de/englisch_gg/englisch_gg.html. However, the German version uses the term *Rechtsstaat*: "(1) Die verfassungsmäßige Ordnung in den Ländern muß den Grundsätzen

controlling state activities. It includes fundamental organizational principles such as the separation of powers, judicial review by the German Constitutional Court (the *Bundesvervassungsgericht*), and the principles of legality, fair procedure, legal certainty, and the principle of proportionality.[43] There remains a tension between formal liberal protections of the *Rechtsstaaat* and the social/instrumentalist values implicit in the *Sozialstaat* or 'social state.' As a result, some modern jurists interpret *Rechtsstaat* in highly politicized ways while others jettison it altogether.[44]

Rechtsstaat and the *Rule of Law* differ in two respects: (1) the Anglo-American tradition does not hold that law can be reduced to a logical system supervised solely by a single constitutional court; and (2) it does not regard rights as given by the state. The two concepts indicate an underlying difference in how one should think about law. By regarding law as a rational science with a hidden structure that can be uncovered, European civilians at one time believed, 'almost as an article of faith,' that a single, complete, coherent, and logical system of law to govern all legal relationships is possible and that the human mind is capable of thinking it out.[45] In contrast, the common law mind regards law as empirical and pragmatic as much as rational; thus, common law reasoning is as much inductive as it is deductive. Kelsen's concept of the constitution as a *grundnorm* is consistent with the Anglo-American concept of the constitution as the supreme law of the land. However, the common law concept, as developed in the U.S., is based on inherited inductive habits, rights that pre-exist the state, and a presumed skepticism towards government rather than on a reliance on deductive reasoning or the ability of a government to limit itself.

Under the civilian tradition, the state gives people rights. In common law tradition, the state's power is limited, and it must justify its actions as not infringing on the individual's inalienable rights.

18.4 The Anglo-Americans and the Founding Fathers

In contrast with the Civilian focus on theory, equality before the law, and logical organization, the British concept focused on preserving existing practice and limiting governmental power. The traditional British conception of law was centered on court-made law; legislation was regarded with suspicion and interpreted narrowly – as

des republikanischen, demokratischen und sozialen *Rechtsstaates* im Sinne dieses Grundgesetzes entsprechen" (emphasis added).

[43] Gosalbo-Bono, *supra* note 3, at 244–245.

[44] Loughlin, *supra* note 38 at 321.

[45] Woodfin L. Butte, "Doctrine and Jurisprudence in Mexico," in *The Role of Judicial Decisions and Doctrine in Civil Law and in Mixed Jurisdictions*, Joseph Dainow ed. (1974) at 311, 315. Louisiana State U. Press.

reflected in Dicey.[46] The U.S. tradition contains a similar narrow interpretation, a similar mixture of structural and institutional checks and balances, and a similar focus on the judiciary as supporting the rule of law.[47]

Unlike the violent French Revolution, the U.S. Revolution (1776–1783) was a conservative one. It began as the colonists' demand for the same rights and personal liberties that other British subjects had. Representatives from 12 of the original 13 colonies drafted the U.S. Constitution in the summer of 1787. These Founding Fathers were neither academics nor generals. They were well-read entrepreneurs: businessmen, insurance agents, shipping magnets, farmers, attorneys, bankers, etc. Despite their mandate to propose amendments to the existing Articles of Confederation that would enable the fledgling country to defend itself and pay its army, they instead drafted an entirely new constitution, using the members' experiences in drafting state constitutions and in living with those mistakes. The Founders made a compromise on slavery (i.e. the '3/5 clause') that led inexorably to the Civil War of 1860–65. Nevertheless, the U.S. Constitution has been in place since it was ratified in 1789. In contrast, France, whose revolution occurred shortly after that of the U.S., adopted five constitutions in its first 15 years: a constitutional monarchy, a radical republic, a moderate reaction, a consulate, and finally a dictatorship.[48] France is now on its Fifth Republic. The U.S. currently is the longest continuing constitutional republic in the world.

The U.S. Founders attempted to create a government that functioned not by overcoming human failings, but by using those very human failings in such a way as to create stability and maximize individual liberty. They worried that the federal government would become tyrannical.[49] Having experienced the effects of poorly drafted state legislation and incompetent, corrupt state governments, delegates to the Convention wanted to make it difficult for the U.S. Congress to pass laws. They also wanted to limit executive power to avoid the tyranny they believed they had experienced under British rule. Consequently, they wanted a structure that would require the three branches of government not just to police themselves, but to also have the incentive to police each other. As stated by James Madison:

> [T]he great security against a gradual concentration of the several powers in the same department, consists in giving to those who administer each department the necessary constitutional means and personal motives to resist encroachments of the others … Ambition must be made to counteract ambition.[50]

[46] Martin Loughlin, "The Rule of Law in European Jurisprudence, European Commission for Democracy through Law", Venice Commission, CDL-AD (2011).

[47] Dicey commented that the U.S. had "shown unrivalled skill in providing means for giving legal security to the rights declared by American Constitutions." The rule of law is as marked a feature of the United States as of England. Dicey, supra *note* 14 at 119.

[48] Constitution of 3 September 1791; Constitution of 24 June 1793; Constitution of 26 August 1795; Constitution of 13 December 1799; and Constitution of 18 May 1804.

[49] *See generally* the Anti-Federalist Papers.

[50] James Madison, *Federalist Papers* #51.

The Founders developed a governmental structure based on experience and their understanding of human behavior as much as theory.

In keeping with the *Declaration of Independence*, they believed that government's power is premised on the consent of the governed and that individual rights are primary and inalienable – not given by government. It is government's job to protect the individual's inalienable rights to life, liberty, and property against incursions by the government itself, by the majority, or by other individuals.[51]

With the understanding that a democracy is inherently unstable, and in contrast with the French belief that factions would hamper a vigorous government, the drafters of the U.S. Constitution believed that a compound republic with a bicameral legislature would be more stabile precisely because a multiplicity of factions would prevent it from being pulled in one direction or another and would slow-down or prevent the passage of unjust, ineffective, or poorly-drafted laws.[52] Consequently, the American solution encourages both factions and congressional deadlock, and it includes an Electoral College rather than direct election as a way to balance rural versus urban states. The concept is similar to the child's game in which a group of children pull a circular piece of fabric taut from multiple directions so that a playmate can bounce in the stabile, secure middle of it.

18.4.1 Organic Checks and Balances: Stare Decisis and the Jury System

A primary difference between common law and civilian legal systems has been that civilians generally limit the authority of judicial decisions. Civilians (with some justification) regard *stare decisis* as having led to convoluted legal doctrine, and believe that common law is non-transparent and hence inconsistent with the legal state.[53] Common law supporters regard stare decisis as being more flexible, better able to distinguish among different factual situations, and easier to adapt to societal changes.[54] *Stare decisis* adds predictability: a judge must adhere to prior decisions unless he explains in a well-reasoned opinion why the precedent should not apply and that explanation is affirmed by a reviewing court.[55]

---

[51] James Madison, *Federalist Papers* #10.

[52] James Madison, *Federalist Papers* #10.

[53] *See* J.W. Tubbs, *The Common Law Mind: Medieval & Early Modern Conceptions* (2002) at 173. Johns Hopkins U. Press.

[54] *See* Hayek, Law, Legislation & Liberty (1983) at 115–122. U. Chicago Press.

[55] The value of maintaining consistency in jurisprudence has been recognized in international law, *see e.g.* the U.S. Convention on the International Sale of Goods, art. 7(1) "(1) In the interpretation of this Convention, regard is to be had to its international character and to the need to promote uniformity in its application and the observance of good faith in international trade," which has led to a database of international decisions, available on line at www.cisg.law.pace.edu. See also the WTO appellate body opinions.

Common law adversarial procedure and the jury system provide another way to protect against governmental intrusion. Under U.S. adversarial procedure, the judge acts as an umpire or referee until he or the jury reaches the final decision. The jury's sole job is to determine the facts, using an ordinary understanding of human nature, and to apply the facts they find to the law given them by the judge. Because the adversaries stand at a level below the judge and jury to argue their cases, neither defense nor the prosecution nor plaintiff appears to be favored. Thus, common law procedure is consistent with values underlying both the rule of law and the legal state in the sense that both sides are to be treated equally by the law. U.S. adversarial procedure provides further checks on governmental power: the right not to be forced to testify against oneself, the right to testify on one's own behalf, the presumption of innocence until proven guilty, the right to representation by counsel, and the right not to be tried twice for the same crime.[56]

The role of a lay jury (a jury composed of ordinary citizens) as a check on government is most easily seen in criminal trials, and in the U.S., civil trials may use juries as well. In either case, the jury is seated separately from the judge. After both sides have presented their cases, the jury is sent to a private room to deliberate, and those deliberations are secret and protected, not even the judge can participate in or listen to the jury's deliberations. This secrecy means that the jury is insulated from the judge's opinion. It is also insulated from attempted corruption (whether by the judge or by the parties themselves). It is free to discuss the evidence presented at trial candidly. Even if a jury suspects that the defendant is guilty, it can acquit the defendant if it believes the government's actions were unjustifiable. That decision cannot be appealed.

This concept of *jury nullification* is commonly understood as the reason O.J. Simpson, a famous African-American former football player and actor, was acquitted of killing his ex-wife and her friend: the jury was so offended by perceived racism in the Los Angeles police department that it refused to find him guilty despite DNA evidence to the contrary. That secrecy also means that the jury's decision may be insulated from media and political pressure. This is not to say that all Americans agreed with the decision; however, the decision was made not by a government official, but by ordinary citizens based on the evidence presented by both parties at trial. Citizens who participate as jurors gain an experiential understanding of how the system works,[57] and consequently often find the experience empowering.

[56] U.S. Constitution Amendment V.

[57] Andrew Guthrie Ferguson, "Jury Instructions as Constitutional Education", 84 U. Col. L. Rev. 233 (2013); Nancy S. Marder, "Introduction to the Jury at a Crossroad: The American Experience", 78 Chi.-Kent L. Rev. 909 (2003).

18.4.2 Judicial Review

Judicial review is only one of a number of institutional mechanisms that force U.S. governments to police themselves.[58] Now widely accepted as necessary to both the rule of law and the legal state,[59] judicial review is an additional check on the legislature. As is well known, Chief Justice John Marshall adopted the concept in *Marbury v. Madison*.[60] What isn't so well known, however, is that it demonstrates more about how political disputes among factions can stabilize a republic, as posited by Madison in the *10th Federalist Paper*, than it does about the utilization of judicial review as a check on the other two branches.

Marbury v. Madison involved a vigorous political battle between outgoing President John Adams and his Federalist Party, and incoming president Thomas Jefferson and the Democratic-Republican Party.[61] Shortly before leaving office, Adams appointed 42 justices of the peace to new posts authorized by the Judiciary Act of 1789, passed while his party controlled Congress.[62] The appointments were made so late the night before Adams left office that those appointed were called "midnight" judges.[63] Marshall, formerly Adams' Secretary of State, had just been seated as Chief Justice of the Supreme Court and faced probable impeachment by Jefferson's administration if he decided the case against them.[64] Marbury, one of the 'midnight' judges and a political opponent of Jefferson's, asked the Court for a writ of mandamus, demanding that Madison (Jefferson's newly appointed Secretary of State) be forced to deliver his appointment.

In a brilliant – and quirky – piece of judicial reasoning, Marshall held that, if the issue is raised in a case before it, the Supreme Court has the power to verify that statutes passed by Congress dealing with judicial powers are within the limitations set by the Constitution, that the Act of 1789 expanding the Court's powers by giving it original jurisdiction over writs of mandamus was unconstitutional, and therefore though Marbury was due his appointment, the Supreme Court had no power to grant the writ.[65] Marshall avoided impeachment and tiptoed around a political morass by issuing a decision consistent with the desires of his political foes, and yet did so in a decision that was consistent with the strictures and intent of the Constitution. The language Marshall used has since been interpreted as a broad power by any court in the U.S. to determine the constitutionality of any

[58] Under the U.S. compound republic system, each state has its own government which is completely separate from (and not accountable to) the U.S. Federal Government.

[59] *See* Gosalbo-Bono, *supra* note 3, at 245.

[60] 5 U.S. 137 (1803).

[61] *See* James Étienne Viator, "Marbury & History: What Do We Really Know About What Really Happened?", 37 *Revue Juridique Themis* (2003) 329, 335–43*; see also* William Michael Trennor, "Judicial Review before Marbury," 58 *Stanford L. Rev.* (2005)455.

[62] Viator, *supra* note 71, at 338.

[63] *Id.* at 338–339.

[64] John F. Preis, "Constitutional Enforcement by Proxy," 995 *Virginia L. Rev.* (2009)1663, 1693.

[65] *Marbury*, 5 U.S. (Cranch 1) 137.

statute brought before it.[66] More to the point, the political story behind this most famous of U.S. Supreme Court decisions demonstrates that Madison was correct in his view that the very factions the French most feared could be used to stabilize, rather than destabilize, a republic.

18.5 Rule of Law Reform and Judicial Independence

The most recent round of international initiatives attempted to strengthen protection for human rights and the rule of law by encouraging the development of independent judiciaries, among other things. This reform movement used the term *rule of law* in the sense of *rechsstaat* to mean effective government. As such, it appealed to bureaucrats in both governments and multinational organizations. Like the previous such attempts, this third round of top-down reform initiatives has been criticized as being largely a failure.[67] Nevertheless, there has been some convergence of the two types of judicial systems, as well as increased judicial independence brought about by internal effort in developing countries.

Civilian and common law legal systems, though starting from two different fundamental legal philosophies, have come to recognize the importance of good governance, and their conceptions of the rule of law and the legal state have undergone a certain rapprochement, particularly with regard to the concept of judicial independence. Some of the advantages of the adversarial tradition can be adapted to different legal traditions.

Chile has successfully implemented a new criminal justice system that combines elements of both common law and civilian procedure, and did it from within. Prior to 1997, under the inquisitorial system Chile inherited from colonial Spain, a criminal proceeding was written rather than oral, a single judge was responsible for the entire proceeding from investigation to sentencing, and defense counsel had almost no role.[68] The power to investigate, accuse, and decide was concentrated in one person – the judge.[69] The problems with this system included biased judges, ineffective investigation, substantial delays, lack of transparency, lack of protection for defendants, lack of delegation of investigatory functions between the police and court clerks, lack of control over the police, and incipient corruption of the system.[70]

---

[66] *See* David E. Marion, "Judicial Faithfulness or Wandering Indulgence? Original Intentions and the History of Marbury v. Madison", 57 Ala. L. Rev. (2006) 1041 (discussing the interpretation *Marbury*).

[67] William C. Prillaman, *The Judiciary and Democratic Decay in Latin America: Declining Confidence in the Rule of Law* (2000). Praeger Publishers.

[68] Carlos Rodrigo de la Barra Cousino, "Adversarial vs. Inquisitorial Systems: The Rule of Law and Prospects for Criminal Procedure Reform in Chile", 5 Sw. J. L. & Trade Am. (1998)323, 325.

[69] E-mail from Alejandro Silva, Associate Dean and Associate Professor of Law, Universidad de los Andes, to Nadia E. Nedzel (Jan. 2010) (on file with author).

[70] De la Barra Cousino, *supra* note 77, at 325.

The consensus among all Chilean political parties in the 1990s was that Chile's criminal legal system was ineffective at both deterring criminal activity and protecting human rights. In 1997, Chile's Congress enacted a constitutional amendment and began to substantially change its criminal justice system.[71]

Chile's new system was designed by Chileans with advice from outside experts. It changed the role of the judge to that of an umpire and arbitrator, created a public prosecutor's office charged with investigating and prosecuting crimes, and created a public defender's office with discovery power.[72] Trials are oral and encourage open debate and logical presentations from each attorney.[73] All parties have access to the files, and trials are open to the public and are video-recorded.[74] Thus, the changes incorporated checks and balances as well as transparency in an effort to deter corruption, increase efficiency, promote equal application of the law and fairness, and strengthen independence.

Furthermore, the changes were implemented in a manner that maximized effectiveness. Though they consulted with outside help, Chileans themselves designed, paid-for, and implemented the new institutions. Starting with ambitious law students and using simulated trials, Chileans trained young defense attorneys, prosecutors, judges, and court clerks in the new system.[75] Pilot programs in two regions tested and tweaked the process.[76] The new system was then instituted in the entire country, but only for new cases,[77] and the public was made aware of their new rights through several methods.[78]

The changes to Chile's criminal justice system have significantly improved transparency, speed, due process, impartiality, and professionalism.[79] The average duration of prosecutions has gone from 3.5 years to a maximum of 10.4 months.[80] The new system eliminated the corrupt actuaries and bailiffs prevalent in the old system.[81] By providing judges who have no part in the prosecution, and a speedy and oral trial, the new system protects defendants' rights, including the presumption of innocence, the right to a speedy trial, the right to a quality defense, the right to confront witnesses and evidence, and the right to an impartial and honest judge.[82] The new system is both more protective of defendants' rights and more effective. At the same time, conviction rates have increased significantly, thus improving the law and order component of the rule of law.

---

[71] *Id.* at 327.

[72] Cousino, *supra* note 77 at 328, 356; Rafael Blanco et al., "Reform to the Criminal Justice System in Chile: Evaluation and Challenges", 2 Loy. *U. Chi. Int'l L. Rev.* (2005) 253, 255–259.

[73] Blanco, *supra* note 79, at 256.

[74] Blanco, *supra* note 79, at 262.

[75] James M. Cooper, "Proyecto Acceso: Using Popular Culture to Build the Rule of Law in Latin America", 5 Rutgers J.L. & Pub. Pol'y 378, 383 (2008); Bianco *supra* note 79, at 259.

[76] Blanco, *supra* note 81 at 259.

[77] *Id.* at 260.

[78] Cooper, *supra* note. 130 at 383–384.

[79] Blanco, *supra* note 81 at 263.

[80] *Id.*

[81] *Id.* at 263–64.

[82] *Id.*

18.6 Economic Freedom and the Rule of Law

Economic freedom provides incentive for commerce and healthy commerce provides a strong economy. A strong economy, in turn, provides the means for a functional criminal justice system and provides support for the rule of law by producing necessary funds, in the form of taxes, for an effective criminal justice system.[83] Economic freedom also encourages economic growth.

The U.S. colonists inherited mercantilism from the British, not laissez-faire capitalism. From the sixteenth to the eighteenth century, it was assumed that the amount of gold and silver amassed indicated a nation's wealth and power, and that the world's capital was static. Thus, a nation could increase its power only at the expense of rival nations. Monopolies and subsidies granted by the crown enabled some merchants while prohibiting others from entering the market.[84]

Colonies were used as captive markets for exports and suppliers of raw materials to England, a policy that fanned resentment of Britain in North America. By the 1770s, the East India Company, a monopoly originally chartered by Queen Elizabeth I, held a massive surplus of tea and was struggling financially. In 1773, in an effort to improve its financial condition, Parliament authorized the East India Company to sell its surplus tea directly to the North American colonies subject to an additional tax assessed only against the colonists. Bostonians, enraged that Parliament would demand that they pay a tax that other British citizens did not have to pay, boarded three ships and threw the taxed tea overboard into the Boston Harbor. This reaction to an unequal application of the law – a violation of either the rule of law or the legal state – is known as the 'Boston Tea Party,' and was one of the events that sparked the American Revolution.[85]

In addition to mercantilism, the agrarian tradition, a belief system widespread in the eighteenth century, held that farming was the best pursuit for citizens of the new U.S. republic: "those who labor in the earth are the Chosen people of God," and "the mobs of great cities add just so much to the support of pure government as sores do to the strength of the human body."[86] This belief system led to the passage of laws contrary to capitalistic interests and cities such as the requirement that voters and office holders own land. Such qualifications insured that agricultural interests would dominate government at the expense of commercial, manufacturing, and financial interests.[87]

---

[83] *See* Alexander Hamilton, *Federalist Paper* #12 (1787).

[84] *See* Sir George Clark, *The Seventeenth Century* (2nd ed., 1961) at 24. Oxford U. Press.

[85] The rallying cry of the Boston Tea Party was 'no taxation without representation': Boston Tea Party members were objecting not only to the tax itself, but also to the fact that it was passed without their being represented in Parliament. The current U.S. 'Tea Party' conservative/libertarian movement was originally founded in 2009 by a group opposing increased federal spending and increased federal taxes.

[86] Forrest MacDonald, "The Founding Fathers and the Economic Order," Speech before the Economic Club of Indianapolis (2006).

[87] *Id.*

Adam Smith, in the *Wealth of Nations* (1776), challenged mercantilism. He argued that rather than the wealth of a nation being based on its accumulation of riches, it is based instead on the production of goods and services and therefore is not static: with the industrial revolution, nations do not increase wealth by invading others. Instead their wealth is based on gross national product and is increased by producing goods that are in demand. Thus, if left alonc, free of governmental interference, markets allocate resources optimally, and labor, motivated by wealth-maximizing self-interest and efficient specialization, responds accordingly. This causes the marketplace to expand and attracts competition and lower prices. The flow of goods and the flow of the money to pay for them determines prices and exchange rates and thus free trade benefits all participants.[88] Consequently, Smith believed that given a free market, self-interest would emerge as a major motivating force for economic development.[89]

The British regarded Adam Smith's ideas as radical. However, he was widely read by a number of the Founders.[90] Smith's thoughts on banking influenced Alexander Hamilton, treasury secretary of the U.S. from 1789 to 1795, who was faced with resolving the U.S. government's post-revolutionary debt. The new country was near bankruptcy, had no currency, no sources of national revenue, no monetary or fiscal system, and no sources of credit.[91] Hamilton persuaded Congress to pay the post-revolutionary debt in full in order to establish international credibility.[92] He persuaded it to create a new currency, a tax-collection system, and form a central bank that stabilized and fortified American finances by 1795. He also set up a system of protective tariffs to discourage product imports and encourage industry in the U.S. By that time, wealthy Europeans, looking for a safe place to put their money during the Napoleonic wars, chose the U.S. because of its quick rise to financial respectability.[93]

Hamilton's reasons for adopting Adam Smith's capitalism, however, were based on more than just a vision of increased wealth for the new United States. He believed that encouraging private enterprise was an effective way to encourage both human freedom and moral values as well.

> "Minds of the strongest and most active powers," [Hamilton] wrote, "fall below mediocrity and labour without effect, if confined to uncongenial pursuits. ...The spirit of enterprise, useful and prolific as it is, must necessarily be contracted or expanded in proportion to the simplicity or variety of the occupations and productions, which are to be found in a Society."
>
> And so we return to the original question. Did the Founding generation contemplate the creation of a capitalistic, free – market economy? No, the majority did not. Had the will of

[88] Roy C. Smith, *Adam Smith and the Origins of American Enterprise: How the Founding Fathers Turned to A great Economist's Writings and Created the American Economy* (2002) at 21. St. Martin's Griffin.

[89] *Id.* at 147.

[90] *Id.*

[91] *Id.* at 118–124.

[92] *Id.*; *see also* MacDonald, *supra* n. 91.

[93] *Id.* at 124.

> the majority prevailed, ... the United States would have remained an agrarian, colonial economy destined to become a collection of banana republics.[94]

Thomas Jefferson, in his first message to Congress as President, stated: "Agriculture, manufacture, commerce and navigation, the four pillars of our prosperity, are the most thriving when left most free to individual enterprise."[95] Against this backdrop of non-interference with economic activity, U.S. entrepreneurs began to thrive and a new business class began to develop in the early nineteenth century, which included entrepreneurs such as Robert Morris (organized the first bank), Steven Girard (early shipping magnate), and John Jacob Astor (fur merchant). Later in the century, after the Civil War, titans of industry such as J.P. Morgan (finance), Cornelius Vanderbilt (railroads), John D. Rockefeller (oil), George Westinghouse (electricity), and Andrew Carnegie (steel) changed the U.S. into a powerhouse of production.[96] The U.S. became a land of opportunity because there were no special privileges, no system of "influence" to determine one's success. Instead, an extraordinary new system of equal opportunity allowed enterprising people to become wealthy and self-sufficient.

As Hayek explained,[97] where economic freedom is limited, governmental controls on commerce and industry cause economic dysfunctionality. Without potential profit motivating them to be efficient, both stagnate and atrophy. Those same policies provide incentive to develop a black market or shadow economy, where entrepreneurs make (and keep) untaxed illegal gains. Such markets encourage the growth of criminal enterprises: e.g. the underground economy in the former Soviet Union, the U.S. Prohibition of alcohol markets in the 1920s, and the illegal drugs markets in the U.S. The latter affects both the U.S. and Latin America: the U.S. now has the highest incarceration rate in the world; Latin America is seeing tremendous carnage caused by drug-trafficking organizations.

In addition to discouraging economic growth, governmental control over the economy encourages governmental violation of individual rights. As Hayek, in discussing Central Europe in 1944 noted: "the almost boundless possibilities for a policy of discrimination and oppression provided by such apparently innocuous principles as 'government control of the development of industry' have been amply demonstrated."[98]

---

[94] Forrest MacDonald, The Founding Fathers and the Economic Order, Speech before the Economic Club of Indianapolis (April 19, 2006).

[95] Smith, *supra* note 96 at 149.

[96] *See e.g. The Men who Built America* series, The History Channel, available at http://www.history.com

[97] F.A. Hayek, "The Use of Knowledge in Society," in XXXV #4 *American Economic Review* (1945) at 519–30, available at http://www.econlib.org/library/Essays/hykKnw1.html; *Hayek on Socialism*, available at http://www.youtube.com/watch?v=CNbYdbf3EEc; F. A. Hayek, "The Fatal Conceit: The Errors of Socialism in 1 The Collected Works of Friedrick August Hayek" pp 84–88 (1988) at 84–88, available at http://www.libertarianismo.org/livros/fahtfc.pdf

[98] F.A. Hayek, "The Road to Serfdom: Text and Documents, the Definitive Edition", U. Chicago Press (2007) at 122–23.

The fact that government control of commerce is ineffective and dangerous does not mean that government does not have a proper role in the economy. Its proper role is to enable inexpensive, simple, and effective systems to register business entities and property ownership, thus enabling entrepreneurship. Hernando de Soto, the Peruvian economist, in his empirical work *The Mystery of Capital: Why Capitalism Triumphs in the West and Fails Everywhere Else*,[99] showed how red tape makes it difficult for start-up entrepreneurs to survive and how forcing them to operate in a black-market economy prevents them from thriving. As part of his research, he attempted to register and open a one-person garment workshop in Lima, Peru: an effort that required 289 6-hour days for registration, and cost $1,231 (which was 31× Peru's monthly minimum wage). Obtaining legal authorization to build a home in Peru took almost 7 years and 207 administrative steps in 52 government offices, but was even worse in the Philippines, Egypt, and Haiti.

As with Prohibition and the War on Drugs, over-regulation of property and business ownership provides enterprising people with the incentive to find ways to getting around the law. Peruvians illegally subdivided state-owned land into smaller, privately held parcels and as a result, few if any landholders had valid title. Extralegal housing results in dead capital and unprotected owners. (Dead capital refers to property which is not legally recognized, thus decreasing both its value and the ability to lend or borrow against it.) The effect of the over-abundance of red-tape means that the official registry system becomes inaccurate, so most people's resources are commercially and financially invisible: No one knows who owns what or where, who is accountable for the performance of obligations, who is responsible for losses or fraud, or what mechanisms are available to enforce payment for services and goods delivered.[100] Insurance is unavailable. Holders cannot raise capital by obtaining loans for improvements or investments, and there is little likelihood that buildings will be safely built (e.g. Haiti's 2010 earthquake). As a result, although the laws may provide for private ownership of property, there is no effective legal protection for ownership, and no rule of law.

As with inefficient property registration, over-regulation of business results in dead capital. Small entrepreneurs who lack legal ownership of their business cannot easily get credit, sell the business, or expand. They cannot seek legal remedies, nor can the government collect taxes on their income. Over-regulation facilitates corruption as governmental agents take advantage of potential entrepreneurs' attempts to cut through the red tape. Consequently, De Soto's primary thesis is that no nation can have a strong, free market economy without a simple, effective system that records property and business ownership:[101] "The existence of such massive exclusion generates two parallel economies, legal and extra legal. An elite minority enjoys the economic benefits of the law and globalization, while the majority of

[99] Hernando de Soto, *The Mystery of Capital: Why Capitalism Triumphs in the West and Fails Everywhere Else* (2000). Basic Books.

[100] *Id.* at 32.

[101] "The Destruction of Economic Facts", by Hernando de Soto. April 28, 2011. Bloomberg *BusinessWeek*, available at: http://www.businessweek.com/magazine/content/11_19/b4227060634112.html

entrepreneurs are stuck in poverty, where their assets –adding up to more than US$ 10 trillion worldwide– languish as dead capital in the shadows of the law."

Economic freedom is a fundamental right to control one's own labor and property, it empowers the individual, resulting in nondiscrimination and open competition, and allows free movement of capital and goods.[102] A lack of economic freedom leads to a failure of the rule of law. The two most basic areas covered by law are property and contract: if societies regulate nothing else, they will still have laws in these two areas.[103] The more highly regulated licensing or ownership become, the more likelihood that people will be frustrated by such laws and unlikely to follow them[104] – and the more incentive there will be for bureaucrats to seek bribes.

18.7 Culture and Liberty

> The central conservative truth is that it is culture, not politics, that determines the success of a society. The central liberal truth is that politics can change a culture and save it from itself.[105]

Outside-in and top-down legal transplants do not work. However, legal systems can successfully adapt ideas gleaned from elsewhere, as evidenced by Chile's new criminal justice system. Nevertheless, one cannot intentionally change an entire legal system unless one also changes the underlying legal and popular culture. Established judges and governmental officials will not want to give up powers they have enjoyed for decades, lose political capital, or learn an entirely new system. They are unlikely to believe that an untested new system will actually work. Professors comfortable with training lawyers for an existing system will not be comfortable training students for a new system. Even if changes are made to the legal system, the public may well be unaware of them. Their cultural habits may need to change in order for the changes to become effective.

International law and policy analysts avoid discussing cultural problems for fear of being accused of being imperialistic or paternalistic, and also because of the current view that law should avoid the imposition of moral values on society – a view inherited from the positivist views developed by Jeremy Bentham, adopted by Oliver Wendall Holmes, and since spread through law schools both in the U.S. and abroad. However, a study of history reveals the extent to which cultures evolve as a result of contact with other cultures, self-criticism, and other factors: "No culture dictates its

---

[102] *FAQ: "What is Economic Freedom,"* at http://www.heritage.org/index/about (accessed on July 2, 2013).

[103] Garrett Barden & Tim Murphy, *Law and Justice in Community* 253–264 (2010 Oxford U. Press) at 253–264.

[104] *See generally* Hernando de Soto: *The Mystery of Capital: Why Capitalism Triumphs in the West and Fails Everywhere Else* (2000). Basic Books.

[105] Daniel Patrick Moynihan, quoted in Samuel P. Huntington, "Foreword, Cultures Count," *Culture Matters* at xiv.

own future. Human beings are always free to accept, reject, or redeploy their inheritance."[106] In implementing its new criminal court system, a number of vehicles were used to make Chile's citizenry aware of new rights, thus leading gradually to cultural change in their expectations. Similarly, during the 1960s civil rights era, segregation in the U.S. ended due to vehement grass-roots objections, resulting legislation, executive enforcement of that legislation, and judicial decisions. While racism still exists in the U.S., it is typically treated with ridicule, legal action, or both: the culture has changed, and what was once acceptable behavior is now Unacceptable.

18.7.1 Anglo-American Protestant Culture and U.S. Values

> To suppose that any form of government will secure liberty or happiness without any virtue in the people, is a chimerical idea.[107]

As Madison espoused, a virtuous citizenry is essential in a political order where the people are self-governing.[108] Self governance refers to two separate ideas: it refers to a people's ability to govern themselves (rather than being governed by a monarch); but it also refers to an individual's ability to regulate his own behavior, ambitions, and passions, and it is in this sense that Madison was discussing virtue. The Anglo-Protestant culture traditionally values individuality and personal responsibility – Oakeshott's autonomous individual. Protestant sects required their followers to read the Bible for themselves and examine their own sins rather than confessing to a priest, and thus began the concept of the autonomous individual. As Kant defined it, a person is free to the extent that he imposes rules on himself. Weber described the same concept as the inner-directed individual. De Tocqueville described it as 'self-interest, rightly understood,'[109] by which he meant that it is in the interest of every man to be virtuous, to make sacrifices for his fellow man not because it is noble to do so, but because such sacrifices ultimately benefit the one who makes them as much or more than they do the recipient.

The Protestant ethic, says Max Weber, leads to a secular code of behavior valuing hard work, honesty, seriousness, the thrifty use of money and time, values which help business and capital accumulation.[110] Alexander Hamilton found that many of his compatriots did not share these values and the United States was not classless,

---

[106] Nicholas Capaldi, "Philosophical Amnesia," in *Conceptions of Philosophy* (2009), vol. 65 at 93, 102–03 & note 32. Cambridge U. Press.

[107] James Madison, Virginia Ratifying Convention (June 20, 1788) Papers 11:163, available at http://press-pubs.uchicago.edu/founders/documents/v1ch13s36.html

[108] *See The Federalist Papers No. 55*, at 346 (James Madison) (Clinton Rossiter ed., 1961); Gordon S. Wood, T*he Creation of the American Republic*, 1776–1787 (1969) at 426–29. U. North Carolina Press.

[109] Alexis de Tocqueville, *Democracy in America.*

[110] Max Weber, "The Protestant Ethic and the Spirit of Capitalism," as discussed in David Landes, "Culture Makes Almost All the Difference", *Culture Matters* 11. (2010). Oxford U. Press (trans. Kalberg).

in contrast with the classlessness de Toqueville found 50 years later. Hamilton believed that provincialism and lassitude would hold the country back.[111] While society was more fluid than in the Old World, under the agrarian system, status and substantial wealth were vested in a small number of intermarried, land-owning, families. Those who were not landowners or members of such families, such as immigrants, were dependent on them.

As an immigrant himself, Hamilton vehemently abhorred dependency, servility, narrow provincialism, and exclusivity. He further believed that status derived from family connections and personal relationships discouraged industry, self-reliance, and work ethic and encouraged sloth, indifference, drunkenness, and dissipation.[112] Hamilton believed that monetizing the economy would encourage diligence and production. While the agrarian majority disdained money and made do with personal obligations, barter, and credit (as do shadow economies), Hamilton believed that making industry both rewarding and necessary would make society more fluid: money is oblivious to class, status, color, and inherited social position. Money can be used to stimulate growth, change, and national strength.

The stark difference between Hamilton's capitalism and Jefferson's agrarianism would eventually be seen in the split between north and south during the Civil War. The industrial North grew rapidly due to immigration, while the agrarian, slave-holding South of large land-owning families and small farmers saw its political and economic power dwindle. Furthermore, many Americans in the North found it impossible to reconcile slavery with Christianity and the Declaration of Independence. The South may have had the best-trained soldiers, but the North had all the cannon factories. The result was an un-avoidable and horrific war killing more Americans than did the First and Second World Wars combined.[113] The North won the Civil War ultimately because of its economic strength and industrialization, which developed because Hamilton's policies encouraged individual endeavor.

The development of the rule of law in the United States has been attributed to its classless society, its focus on individual rights, and the Protestant ethic that fostered commerce. As Max Weber noted, the virtues entrepreneur Ben Franklin espoused in both his *Autobiography* and his *Poor Richard's Almanac* were consistent with capitalism: honesty (useful because it assures credit), as well as punctuality, industry, frugality, and the appearance of modesty.[114] The individual must conform to the capitalistic rules of action, or ultimately be economically marginalized.[115]

The Protestant work ethic promoted the notion of the self-governing, autonomous individual. It emphasized work, equality before the law, and achievement. The Protestant conception of capitalism involves self-discipline and reinvesting to create

---

[111] MacDonald, *supra* note 104.

[112] *Id.*

[113] Civil war: approximately 625,000 killed; World War I: approximately 116,000; World War II: approximately 470,000.

[114] Max Weber, The Protestant Ethic & the Spirit of Capitalism 19–20 (1930). Charles Scribner (trans. Parsons).

[115] *Id.*

more growth and make the world a better place. It involves the creation, marketing, and sale of a desirable good to others who find it useful. It is not greed, a desire for riches at the expense of others. Greed, like corruption, may always be present, but it is not a part of capitalism as properly defined. The Protestant entrepreneur avoids ostentation and unnecessary expenditure, conscious enjoyment of his powers, and is embarrassed by outward signs of the social recognition he receives.[116]

Whether one likes or dislikes Walmart, its low prices and wide variety of products attract customers. It claims 245 million customers, 10,800 stores in 27 countries, e-commerce websites in 10 countries, fiscal year 2013 sales of approximately $466 billion, and 2.2 million employees worldwide.[117] Consistent with the image of an autonomous individual, Sam Walton (the founder of Walmart), who went from a salary of $85 per month to a fortune of $6 billion, listed his 'Commandments' for success, which include industry, treating both customers and employees well, and concern for an appearance of modesty.[118] His personal frugality was described as follows:

> [H]e lives in a modest house in a small town in Arkansas a few blocks from one of his warehouses. He keeps a dusty pickup truck in the driveway, a dusty Chevy sedan in the garage and a couple of muddy bird dogs in the yard. Each weekday, after breakfast at a local Days Inn, he drives the pickup, missing two hubcaps, to his office, a cubicle 8 by 12 feet. There, beside the secretarial pool, amid stacks of papers, he settles in at his desk, furniture that one visitor describes as having an "early Holiday Inn" look.[119]

In addition to emphasizing frugality, industry, and honesty, the Protestant Ethic focuses on covenants and contracts including the consent theory of government, and the basic understanding that one should keep one's word and perform what one promised to do. The faith in covenant is balanced by a practical understanding of the corruptible nature of man and government officials in particular.[120] Many Americans still regard government as a necessary evil.[121] Furthermore, Americans are a litigious society and quick to protest against those who intrude on their liberty,

---

[116] *Id.* at 33.

[117] *Walmart Launches New Advertising Campaign 'The Real Walmart'*, available at: http://news.walmart.com/news-archive/2013/05/04/walmart-launches-national-advertising-campaign-to-show-the-real-walmart; New Ad Campaign Promotes 'The Real Walmart,' Forbes (5/06/2013), available at http://www.forbes.com/sites/lauraheller/2013/05/06/new-ad-campaign-promotes-the-real-walmart/

[118] Michael Bergdahl, *The 10 Rules of Sam Walton Success Secrets for Remarkable Success* (2006). Wiley.

[119] John Anderson, "The Frugal Lifestyle of the King of Thrift," *Chicago Tribune* (Dec. 17, 1990) book review of Vance H. Trimble, *Sam Walton: The Inside Story of America's Richest Man*. Available at: http://articles.chicagotribune.com/1990-12-17/features/9004140388_1_sam-waltonwal-mart-discount-stores-vance-h-trimble

[120] *See e.g.* the maxim commonly quoted in the U.S.: "Power tends to corrupt and absolute power corrupts absolutely." Sir John Emerich Edward Dalberg-Acton, Essays on Freedom & Power 364 (Beacon Press 1949) (quotation by prominent nineteenth century British Catholic referring to the powers of popes and kings.)

[121] See generally Garry Wills: A Necessary Evil: A History of American Distrust of Government, Introduction (Simon & Schuster 2008) (discussing the pervasive and historical distrust of government in the U.S.)

whether other citizens or government officials. The American judicial system is effective in part because citizens use it so often and can be counted upon to object loudly when they feel they have been treated unfairly whether by an fellow citizen or by the government.

Two additional values may help account for the prominence of the Protestant culture in countries that rank highly in terms of the rule of law: the emphasis on literacy and the importance accorded to time.[122] The emphasis on instruction and literacy, a by-product of Bible Reading, led to greater literacy from generation to generation. The making and buying of clocks and watches, and the use of them to measure time was stressed in Britain and Holland; consequently, efficiency became a value. Parental styles reflect individualism, autonomy, self-reliance, and self-expression. The statistical result has been that countries with a greater percentage of Protestants and a British colonial history are associated with lower levels of national corruption coupled with a strong GDP.[123]

18.8 Russian Culture and the Legal State

Just as the French *l'état de droit* differs from the German *Rechtsstaat*, Russia is developing its own definition for the term legal state. The Russian Federation, whose legal system is in part grounded in the German legal tradition, adopted the term legal state in the first substantive sentence of its 1993 Constitution: "The Russian Federation – Russia is a democratic federal legal state with a republican form of governance." ("Российская Федерация – Россия есть демократическое федеративное правовое государство с республиканской формой правления.")[124] Although Russia's laws may have some grounding in the German legal tradition, just as the U.S., England, France, and Germany have each developed their own definitions. However, the Russian Federation is itself in the process of developing its own definition for the term "*Правовое государство.*" By embracing the study constitutional economics in law schools, Russian leaders have shown an understanding that one cannot isolate law from economics and expect to develop a functional, efficient government. In fact, the first characteristic of the Russian model identifies constitutional economics as a bridge between the legal state and economics.[125]

Progress towards the rule of law or the legal state is painful and difficult, as shown by the experiences of France, the U.S., and Chile. Some of the problems facing

---

[122] *Id.* at 12.

[123] Lipset & Menz, Corruption, Culture, and Markets 116, in Culture Matters. See also Jeffrey Sachs, A Cultural Typology of Economic Development 47–53 in Culture Matters.

[124] Art. 1, Constitution of the Russian Federation, trans. author.

[125] Peter Barenboim, Natalya Merkulova. "The 25th Anniversary of Constitutional Economics: The Russian Model and Legal Reform in Russia," *The World Rule of Law Movement and Russian Legal Reform,* (Francis Neate and Holly Nielsen eds.; Justitsinform, Moscow (2007) at 174. Moscow City Chamber of Advocates.

the Russian Federation as identified in the 2007 Symposium included managing the governmental budget so as to create an independent yet accountable judiciary, provide protection for individual rights, and improve public health and education.[126] Furthermore, Valery Zorkin, President of the Constitutional Court of Russia, recognizes that the legal state cannot exist without support from society and that Russia needs to develop public legal awareness.[127] Sadly, Russians historically do not expect law and justice to coincide, and thus have not demanded more of their legal system: "[L]aws aren't all that important to us [Russians]. To produce and observe laws-it's just another culture. Like cockroaches, we try to creep away to some chink where the law won't reach us."[128]

18.9 Conclusion

> The rule of law is an ideal, it bakes no bread, it is unable to distribute loaves or fishes (it has none), and it cannot protect itself against external assault, but it remains the most civilized and least burdensome conception of a state yet to be devised.[129]

Under the common law definition of the rule of law, the law is above the government and the government is beholden to the people. This, coupled with shared values and economic freedom, is the result of a series of historical accidents. It anticipates that governmental officials will be prone to corruption. The advantages of the rule of law can only be realized through procedural, structural, political, and cultural characteristics, rather than through mere substantive changes in the law. As attorneys, in working to improve the rule of law, we need to be aware that legal changes can only be effective if accompanied by economic and cultural change. Otherwise we become like the person who only has a hammer and therefore sees everything as a nail. The *rule of law* differs from the *legal state* in two significant respects: (1) it puts inalienable rights above the government, and (2) it limits governmental powers through external, not just internal, controls.

Acknowledgement The author would like to thank the Southern University Law Center for the 2013 summer research stipend that made this project possible, and I would like to thank James Silkenat for inviting me to participate in this Symposium.

---

[126] *Id.* at 181.

[127] Anna Zakatnova, "Fronde In Judges Robes and Without," *Rossiskaya Gazeta* (July 9, 2007), *Reproduced in The World Rule of Law Movement and Russian Legal Reform*, at 243–244.

[128] Ellen Carnaghan, *Thinking About Democracy: Interviews With Russian Citizens*, Studies in Pub. Pol'y 322 (1999); cited and quoted in Kathryn Hendley, "Assessing The Rule of Law in Russia," 14 Cardozo J. Int'l & Comp. L. 347, 377 (2006).

[129] Michael Oakeshott, "The Rule of Law", in *On History and Other Essays* (Oxford 1983) (new: Liberty Fund 1999) 178.

Chapter 19
The Rule of Law in the Middle East

Hossein Esmaeili

Abstract This chapter analyses the nature of the rule of law in the Middle East, and the transition towards civil societies and the rule of law within the specific historical, cultural and political contexts of the region. The chapter examines the reasons for the lack of effective rule of law systems in the Middle East from economic, historical, and cultural perspectives, as well as in light of colonisation and external factors. Different approaches taken by various countries of the Middle East in relation to establishing rule of law systems, including secular approaches and traditional and Islamic directions, are also discussed. The chapter proposes approaches which deeply consider historical, religious, and cultural traditions of the region, and a gradual transition towards the rule of law and civil societies from within Middle Eastern societies.

19.1 Introduction

Establishing and promoting the rule of law in the Middle East has become an important and complex issue in the region and globally. It is an especially complex problem given the diversity of the region, its history, the role of religion, tribal structures and the development of modern institutions particularly since the Arab Spring. Generally, the region is slowly moving towards the rule of law but most Middle Eastern countries still do not have effective independent judicial systems with control over the State and powerful institutions. Despite the slow and gradual movement towards the establishment of rule of law systems, an effective rule of law system is as yet unavailable in most Middle Eastern countries.

H. Esmaeili (✉)
Flinders Law School, Flinders University, Adelaide, Australia
e-mail: hossein.esmaeili@flinders.edu.au

J.R. Silkenat et al. (eds.), *The Legal Doctrines of the Rule of Law and the Legal State (Rechtsstaat)*, Ius Gentium: Comparative Perspectives on Law and Justice 38,
DOI 10.1007/978-3-319-05585-5_19,

Various Middle Eastern countries and societies have taken different approaches towards modernising their legal systems and establishing the rule of law. These include for example, Turkey's adoption of a modern Western legal system and progress towards secularisation, Saudi Arabia's espousal of 'purified' traditional Islamic law, Egypt's reliance on a mix of Islamic and modern systems, while Iran's system consists of a theocracy with some modern legal institutions. In any case, it seems that Islam as a whole and its legal system has a special place in the establishment of the rule of law institutions and systems in the Middle East.

This chapter analyses theoretical discussions on the concept of the rule of law in Muslim traditions, discusses the reasons behind the lack of the rule of law in the region, and examines different approaches towards the establishing the rule of law and its institutions in the Middle East.

19.2 The Current Status of the Rule of Law in the Middle East

There is no well-established or effective legal and political system in the Middle East that incorporates the rule of law. In 2007, Chibli Mallat claimed that "none of the Middle Eastern jurisdictions has reached the critical mass under which I am comfortable describing it as a state where the rule of law prevails".[1] In the 6 years since Mallat made that proposition, the Middle East has witnessed some developments, including the Arab Spring and the removal of a number of totalitarian regimes. Nonetheless, there is still no effective rule of law in the Middle East. This does not mean that certain aspects of the rule of law do not exist in the Middle East, such as working legal systems, elections, federalism, parliamentary systems, and some protection of human rights.

In Turkey, the polarisation of politics, the parliamentary system, and the constitutional reform process are evident.[2] In Jordan, Kuwait, Qatar and the United Arab Emirates, parliamentary elections are held and the property interests of national and international corporations are effectively protected. Presidential, parliamentary and local government elections are held regularly in Iran, and although the judiciary is independent of the executive, it is ultimately answerable to the *Velayat Faghi* (the Supreme Leader). The post-Arab Spring states of Tunisia and Egypt held elections recently and some disruptions occurred recently in Egypt, where the first democratically elected President was removed by the military. In Lebanon and Israel,

[1] Chibli Mallat, *Introduction to Middle Eastern Law* (2007) at 6. Oxford University Press; Mark Tessler and Eleanor Gao, "Gauging Arab Support for Democracy", 16(3) *Journal of Democracy* (2005) 83–97, at 84.

[2] A 2010 assessment report by a joint initiative of the OLED and the European Union (financed by the EU) expressed concern about the independence of the judiciary in Turkey. See Assessment, Turkey, Democracy and the Rule of Law, SIGMA, 2010 *available at* http://www.oecd.org/site/sigma/publicationsdocuments/47075640.pdf

the rule of law exists to some degree with some caveats in relation to the existence of armed parties in Lebanon and the high risk of religious and political violence, as well as Israel's occupation of Palestinian territories and the treatment of Palestinians. Some civil unrest arose in Bahrain in 2011 after the government, aided by troops from Saudi Arabia, cracked down on pro-democracy protests. In Iraq, Afghanistan, and Yemen, authorities are battling Al-Qaeda linked militants and other sources of unrest in their countries. In Libya, despite parliamentary elections held in 2012, large parts of the country are still ruled by tribal leaders. Unrest is also rife in Syria where a civil war is being waged between the regime and the oppositions and there is little prospect of resolution in favour of democracy and the rule of law.

The World Justice Project (WJP) in 2011[3] made an assessment of the extent to which countries and regions of the world adhered to the rule of law in practice. The project covered a number of subject elements of the rule of law, including limited government powers, fundamental rights, open government, access to civil justice, effective criminal justice absence of corruption, order and security, and regulatory enforcement. The WJP included five Middle Eastern countries: Iran, Jordan, Lebanon, Morocco and the United Arab Emirates. In most of the areas assessed, particularly in areas of limited government powers, fundamental rights, open government, access to civil justice, and effective criminal justice, Middle Eastern countries displayed average scores with serious weaknesses in the areas of accountability, check and balances on the executive branch, transparency, and respect for fundamental rights, particularly freedom of opinion, belief, and religion.[4]

19.3 Islamic Law and the Modern Concept of the Rule of Law

The modern concept of the rule of law evolved as part of the doctrine of limited government and is closely linked with the doctrines of the separation of powers and constitutional government.[5] In the Western tradition, 'the law' is an autonomous system that is primarily produced by human interaction and is conceptually distinct from morality, custom and religion.[6]

Sharia, the Islamic legal system, has influenced the legal systems of almost every Middle Eastern country. Under the Islamic legal tradition, 'law' has certain unique characteristics that are fundamentally different from the Western concept of law. Four of these unique characteristics are discussed below.

---

[3] Mark David Agrast, Juan Carlos Botero and Alejandro Ponce, *WJP Rule of Law Index 2011* (2011).

[4] *Id* at 32, 34.

[5] Hossein Esmaeili, "The Nature and Development of Law in Islam and The Rule of Law Challenge in the Middle East and the Muslim World", 26(2) *Connecticut Journal of International Law* (2011) 329–366, at 332–333.

[6] Patrick Parkinson, *Tradition and Change in Australian Law* (2010) at 23. Thomson Reuters.

First, unlike the Western tradition, law in Islam is not a product of social contracts or a political process. Rather, law is created by classical religious texts, namely the Quran and the Sunnah (the sayings and traditions of the Prophet of Islam collected in a number of volumes) and other sources of law, such as analogical reason (*qiyas*) and the consensual opinion of Muslim jurists (*ijma*). Law is produced through the interpretation of the original sources by qualified Muslim jurists (*foqaha*). The science of producing legal principles from original sources of sharia is known as *fiqh,* and in English is termed Islamic jurisprudence. Although Muslim jurists may arrive at new legal principles, they are constrained in the degree to which they can adjust sharia principles. Therefore, secular institutions, such as modern parliaments, may not declare a law if it is inconsistent with sharia. For example, Iran's legal system is two-tiered. It has a parliament, which can enact legislation, and a 'Council of Guardian' that is comprised of a number of highly-ranked Muslim jurists who are specialists in *fiqh*. The Council's responsibility is to make sure all laws passed by parliament are consistent with sharia principles.

Secondly, while Western law is produced through political processes or by sovereign authorities, the dominant and traditional view of Muslim scholars is that Islamic law is divinely inspired. Seyyed Hossein Nasr posits that:[7]

> in the Islamic perspective, divine law is to be implemented to regulate society and the actions of its members rather than society dictating what laws should be. The injunctions of divine law are permanent, but the principles can also be applied to new circumstances as they arise. But the basic thesis is one of trying to make human order conform to the divine norm, not vice-versa.

Thirdly, whereas Western law is often subject to critical examination by academics, jurists and the general public, the divine basis of Islamic law means that critical analysis of certain legal principles may not be allowed and those who question it may be subject to criminal sanctions of blasphemy or apostasy. Indeed, it is a principal of traditional Islamic law that rejecting or casting doubt on certain 'sacred' rules, which are followed by all Islamic schools of thought, amounts to *kofr* (rejection of Islam) and may be a crime under Islamic criminal law.[8] This means that in a Muslim country, religious authorities and/or the state may have a special privilege because of their status under religious law. As a result, they can be put beyond the reach of the law. By contrast, in a rule of law system, everyone, particularly powerful individuals and the State, are subject to restrictions imposed on them by the law.

Fourthly, under Western legal tradition, there is a clear distinction between law applicable to the public and the private spheres. This makes the legal system able to protect individual rights from arbitrary interference by the State or powerful individuals, particularly in relation to the freedom of an individual's beliefs, speech and actions.[9] On the other hand, under Islamic legal tradition, the distinction

[7] Seyyed Hossein Nasr, *The Heart of Islam: Enduring Values for Humanity* (2002) at 117–119. HarperOne.

[8] Seyyed Al Sabiq, *Fiq al Sunna [The Sunni Jurisprudence] Vol. 2* (1998) at 304. darelfkr@cyberia.net.lb

[9] Spencer Zifcak, "Western and Islamic Conceptions of the Rule of Law", in *Islam Beyond Conflict, Indonesian Islam and Western Political Theory*, Azyumardi Azara and Wayne Hudson eds. (2008) at 37. Ashgate.

between the public and private realms of life is not significant. Law in Islam is part of a comprehensive religious system in which legal principles, rituals and beliefs merge and all may be the subject of sanctions by the Islamic state. As a result, Islamic law recognises no such a distinction between the public and private realms. Under Islamic law all human conduct comes under one of five classifications: those which are obligatory (*wajib*), recommended (*mustahab*), permitted (*mubah*), disliked (*makruh*), and forbidden (*haram*). The first and the last categories, *wajib* and *haram*, must be complied with or risk sanctions. This means that omitting rituals such as prayer and fasting can lead to punishment. In modern Muslim countries however, non-observance of rituals is seldom enforced by the state. Nevertheless, Islamic belief systems still influence the political culture of the Muslim world, and a clear distinction between private and public spheres is yet to get full recognition in Middle Eastern cultures. Given that the protection of human rights is fundamental to the rule of law, this poses a problem for Muslim countries that might want to consider establishing such a system.

Despite these unique characteristics that differ from the Western concept of law, there are certain other characteristics of the Islamic legal system that suggest that Islamic law could accommodate a limited version of the rule of law. One key concept of Islamic public law is the doctrine of *shura*, a consultative process by which people choose leaders of the society and manage the community's public affairs. The *shura* doctrine is expressly mentioned in the Quran.[10] After the death of the Prophet Mohammad, early Muslim caliphs were elected through the process of *shura*, which entails consultation and voting (*biat*). For example, the concept of *shura* is implemented in the Iranian constitution in the form of elections of local governments, the parliament, the president, and the Council of Experts that appoints the Supreme Leader. In addition to *shura* and *biat*, there are other concepts in Islam that can be used to established Islamic forms of parliamentary democracy, representative elections, and some other civil institutions,[11] such as *ijma* (the source of law based on the consensus of Muslim jurists), *qiyas* (analogical reasoning), *istihsan* (equity or juristic preference), *istishab* (presumptions of continuity), *sadd al-dharai* (blocking the means),[12] *ijtihad* (the process of personal interpretation of religious texts), and *maslahah* (expediency as a source of law). While certain legal principles of Islam may be fixed, many others are produced based on the process of interpretation by Muslim jurists over the last 15 centuries, which are

[10] The Quran 3:159 and 42:38. For further discussion of the role of *shura* in Islamic governance, *see*, Ann Black, Hossein Esmaeili and Nadirsyah Hosen, *Modern Perspectives on Islamic Law* (2013) at 43–44. Edward Elgar.

[11] John Esposito, "Practice and Theory" in *Islam and the Challenge of Democracy*, Joshua Cohen and Deborah Chasman eds. (2004) at 96. Princeton University Press.

[12] The doctrine of *sadd al-dharai* allows Muslim jurists or Islamic authorities to prohibit certain acts that may lead to crimes and corruption (preventative measures). In practice, this doctrine can be used in expanding the power of the state, but it may give flexibility in making and un-making of Islamic legal rules. For further discussion of this principle and other principles mentioned here, see Mohammad Hashim Kamali, *Principles of Islamic Jurisprudence* (2003) at Chapter 16. The Islamic Texts Society.

largely similar to modern secular legal systems, and can only be reformed and changed if necessary.

Further, there are a number of Islamic legal principles, maxims, and presumptions that, to some extent, are similar to modern legal principles. These include the principle of non-retroactivity, the principle of legality, and the presumption of innocence.[13] Also, under Islamic law, the lives, reputations, and properties of individuals are protected. Pre-trial detention is not permitted and the power of authorities to arrest and detain individuals before a trial and conviction is also limited.

Another aspect of the Islamic legal tradition is the relatively well-developed system of Islamic jurisprudence (*fiqh*). The Islamic jurisprudence has undergone many developments since its inception, almost a millennia ago. The sharia legal system was an effective legal system in the eleventh century. In contrast, England did not have an effective legal system in place when it was conquered by the Normans in 1066, but relied instead on rudimentary Anglo-Saxon customs. By then, sharia law had a developed structure on contracts, criminal law, property law and civil and criminal procedures. Various Islamic schools of law had developed legal theories, jurisprudential theories and extensive legal principles.

Finally, in almost every Muslim society, including Saudi Arabia, one of the most traditional Muslim states, proponents of reform, civil society and the rule of law can be found among Muslim intellectuals, jurists and scholars. Since the ninth century, there have been many calls for the traditional sources of Islamic law, the Quran and the Sunnah, to be re-interpreted. One such demand originally came from the theological group known as *Mutazilah* which took a rationalist approach to the interpretation of certain sharia principles. Among the great reformist scholars to approach sharia and Islamic thought in a rational way were Ghazali and Mawardi (eleventh century), Ibn Khaldun (fourteenth century), Shah Wali Allah (eighteenth century), and Allamah Mohammad Iqbal (twentieth century).

In practice, elements of pluralism, diversity and democracy are evident not only in the modern Muslim world but also in historical accounts of the Islamic caliphate. The history of Muslim societies includes various dictatorships and tyrannical states along with some moderate and autonomous states existing in different parts of the Muslim world. Several Muslim countries—Turkey, Pakistan, Bangladesh, Malaysia, Indonesia, the United Arab Emirates, Jordan, and Iran—have adopted certain elements of civil society, diversity, pluralism, federalism and constitutional structures. However, the move by the Middle East towards civil societies and the rule of law is very gradual and given the complexity of Middle Eastern society, culture, religion and politics, this move should naturally be slow. Further, institutionalising the rule of law and civil society in the Middle East needs to be within the framework of existing Islamic traditions and cultures. While Muslim traditions, particularly sharia law, need substantial reform and restructuring, modern democratic institutions and principles may need to be slightly adjusted in order to be incorporated within Middle Eastern countries.

---

[13] *See also*, Esmaeili, *supra* note 5. At 359.

19.4 Reasons for the Lack of the Rule of Law

There have been extensive discussions by political scientists, legal experts, jurists, sociologists and other scholars, regarding the lack of the rule of law in the region. According to Blaydes and Lo, the failure of Middle Eastern societies to make the transition from authoritarian systems to democratic government is puzzling.[14] The literature and scholarship on the Middle East and the Muslim world have attempted to explain the lack of effective rule of law systems based on a number of reasons, including structural economic justifications, historical reasons specific to the Middle East, colonisation and external factors, as well as cultural and religious factors.

In regard to the economic reasons, Kazem Alamdari argues that all reasons for the lack of democracy and the rule of law in the Middle East are linked to the lack of available water resources.[15] Also it has been said that countries that derive their funds from non-taxable resources and revenues, such as oil, tend to be arbitrary and lack an adversarial link with their people.[16]

As a further example, Timur Kuran claimed that Islamic principles of law, particularly the inheritance law and the institution of *waqf* (charitable trust), obstructed capital accumulation and the development of big corporations and hence prevented the establishment of accountable government and the rule of law in the Middle East.[17]

Addressing historical reasons specific to the Middle East, Jamal ad-Din al-Afghani, among others, argues that the development and dominance of superstitious beliefs and practice, as well as existing racial, tribal and ethnic prejudice all help to account for the underdevelopment of Muslim societies.[18]

A large number of Middle Eastern intellectuals, both leftist and traditional elites, blame colonialism, external invasions, and the sudden introduction of European legal codes into the Middle East for the underdevelopment and lack of democracy and the rule of law.[19]

Others blame Islamic political culture for the lack of democratic institutions and the rule of law. For example, Samuel Huntington argued that "the Islamic concept of politics differs from, and contradicts, the premise of democratic politics".[20] Sexism and the role of women in the Muslim societies have also been cited as

---

[14] Lisa Blaydes and James Lo, "One man, one vote, one time? A model of democratization in the Middle East" 24 *Journal of Theoretical Politics* (2011) 110–146, at 111.

[15] Kazem Alamdari, *Chera Iran Aghab Mand Va Gharb Pish Raft [Why the West Progressed and Iran Stayed Undeveloped]* (2001) at 198.

[16] Blaydes and Lo, *supra* note 14. At 113.

[17] *See* Timur Kuran, *The Long Divergence: How Islamic Law Held Back the Middle East* (2012). Princeton University Press.

[18] *See* Seyyed Ahmad Movassaghi, *Elal Va Avamel Zaf Va Enhetat Moslemin Dar Andishehaye Siasi Va Araye Eslahi Seyyed Jamal al-din Asadabadi [Reasons for the Dismal of Muslim Societies According to Al-Afghani's Doctrines]* (1994). Dafter Nashr Farhamg Islami (Tehran).

[19] *See*, the writings of Edward Said and Seyyed Hossein Nasr.

[20] Samuel Huntington, *The Third Wave: Democratization in the Late Twentieth Century* (1991) at 307. University of Oklahoma Press.

explanations for the underdevelopment and failure of civil society institutions in the Middle East.[21]

As stated, some scholars point to very limited water resources, land ownership systems and issues about natural resources as reasons for the Middle East not having civil institutions, democratic government and the rule of law.[22] They argue that the lack of rainfall and water resources and, therefore, the use of complex systems for water collection resulted in the development of a hierarchal power structure in the Middle East. This is due to water resources, such as bore water systems, canals, and small rivers being subject to the control of States, tribal leaders and powerful individuals who would take control of water resources by force. In practice, individuals always were dependant on the rulers and tribal chiefs for access to water. As a result, unlike European societies, the power structure developed from top to bottom in the Middle East. Discovery of oil in the Middle East in the early twentieth century in places such as Saudi Arabia, Iran, Iraq and the Arab countries surrounding the Persian Gulf, further strengthened the power structure as it existed traditionally in the Middle East where individual members of the societies were dependent on the resources to the authorities, rulers and tribal chiefs. Michael Ross, in an extensively quoted 2001 article 'Does Oil Hinder Democracy?', claimed that dependency on oil and mineral resources has strong negative effects on the development of democracy and civil society institutions.[23] Ross' hypothesis is supported by a number of studies.[24] However, others such as Sven Oskarsson and Eric Ottosen dismissed Ross' theory and argued that "the jury appears to be out concerning the generality of the oil hinders democracy hypothesis".[25] It seems that the issue of natural resources in the Middle East, such as the limitation of water resources, complicity of water management and use, and the discovery of huge oil resources in the early part of the twentieth century, are just some of the factors that have influenced the power structures and relationship between members of society, the State and powerful individuals. Before the discovery of oil in the Middle East and the commercial use of oil from the 1950s onwards, similar problems in relation to the lack of democracy and the rule of law existed. Further, Middle Eastern countries without oil resources, such as Syria and Jordan, are no different in terms of arbitrary power structures and undemocratic institutions.

---

[21] *See,* M. Steven Fish, "Islam and authoritarianism", 55 *World Politics* (2002) 4–37.

[22] *See,* Ann Lambton, *Continuity and Change in Medieval Persia: Aspects of Administrative, Economic and Social History, 11th -14th Century* (1988). State University of New York Press; and Ann Lambton, *Landlord and Peasant in Persia: A Study of Land Tenure and Land Revenue Administration* (1991). I.B. Tauris.

[23] Michael Ross, "Does Oil Hinder Democracy?", 53(3) *World Politics* (2001) 325–361.

[24] N Jenson and L Wantchekon, "Resource Wealth and Political Regimes in Africa", 37 *Comparative Political Studies* (2004) 816–841; B Smith, "Oil Wealth and Regime Survival in the Developing World, 1960–1999", 48 *American Journal of Political Science* (2004) 232–246; J Ulfelder, "Natural Resource Wealth and the Survival of Autocracy", 40 *Comparative Political Studies* (2007) 995–1018.

[25] Sven Oskarsson and Eric Ottosen, "Does Oil Still Hinder Democracy?", 46(6) *Journal of Development Studies* (2010) 1067–1083, at 1067.

As to the proposal that Islamic law is a barrier to economic development, there is limited evidence that the religion of Islam and its legal system have contributed significantly to the underdevelopment of the Middle East. A number of studies have failed to present conclusive evidence of the connection between Islam and the underdevelopment of economies.[26] In fact, many centuries ago, the Muslim society was a pioneer of science of economic development for centuries. However, over the last several centuries, principles of land ownership, the Islamic law of inheritance and the institution of charitable trusts have been important in developing the private and public principles of sharia law that relate to property law and the economy. Low rainfall and limited water supplies led to complicated water management systems put in place whereby local people are dependant on their water allocations and other economic benefits on the state, as powerful warrior and tribal chiefs have taken control of the wells and deep water canals. This process was repeated when huge oil reserves were discovered in the Middle East and were subsequently owned and controlled by the state. Once again, ordinary people became subject to the will of chiefs, warriors and the state, unlike the situation in Europe where states were dependent on revenue and taxes paid by the people who owned land and water resources.

For various historical reasons, from the thirteenth century onwards superstitious and irrational notions and practices emerged in Muslim societies along with alien ideas and doctrines. Gradually, the legal system of Islam and the religion of Islam became rigid, inflexible, sexist and in some areas, superstitious. While Islamic law was relatively dynamic and progressive at the time of the Prophet Mohammad and the righteous caliphs, and during the early periods of the Abbasid Empire, by the eighteenth century, or even earlier, it became largely ineffective and frozen. The legal system was unable to limit and influence the conduct of caliphs, sultans, shahs, local rulers and tribal chiefs. However, the reformist movements that sought to fix these problems largely failed to produce important outcomes, and in some instances led to even more inflexible and fundamentalist movements. For example, early reformists such as Ghazali, had a positive influence for centuries on the Islamic world, but in more recent times efforts by proponents of change such as Ibn Taymyah, Muhammad Ibn Abd Al-Wahab, Muhammad Abdu, and Maoududi have resulted in a fundamentalist backlash (e.g. Wahabism in Arabia and Ikhvan al-Muslimin in Egypt and North Africa). Again, while these historical factors are important to the development of legal systems in the Middle East, they are not the only considerations, as elaborated by many recent Muslim intellectuals.

Colonisation, along with external factors such as invasions and extensive wars have influenced the social, economic, and political structures of Middle Eastern societies, but these factors are not solely confined to that region alone. Similar

---

[26] *See*, Marcus Noland, "Religion and Economic Performance", 33(8) *World Development* (2005) 1215–1232; Frederick Pryor, "The Economic Impact of Islam on Developing Nations", Working Paper, Swathmore College (USA) (2004); Robert Barro and R.M. McCleary, "Religion and Economic Growth Across Countries" 68(1) *American Sociological Review* (2003) 760–781; Adeel Malik, "Was the Middle East's economic descent a legal or political failure? Debating the Islamic Law Matters Thesis", Working Paper, Oxford Centre for Islamic Studies (UK) (2011).

events have occurred in other parts of the world, including India, South America, and Asia. It is particularly notable that all major nationalities in the Middle East (Arabs, Persians, Turks, and Jews) blame each other for their troubles and for the stagnation of their civilisations. However, in more recent years all of them blame European colonisation, Western imperialism, and modern cultural invasions for the problems in the Middle East relating to the development of social, economic, and political structures. The rapid introduction of European legal codes into the Middle East after the collapse of the Ottoman Empire created tensions and made the establishment of effective legal systems problematic. However, it can be argued that external factors have played a minor role in accounting for the lack of rule of law and democracy in the Middle East. Elsewhere, certain countries, such as in India, Malaysia and certain African countries that were colonised by European powers, have successfully established some kind of rule of law system, as well as some democratic and civil institutions.

Some researchers inside and outside the Middle East have argued that Arab and Islamic political culture obstructs liberalisation and legal development, and the religion of Islam in particular is blamed for the current political, legal and cultural problems in the Middle East.[27] However, as demonstrated rightly by Alamdari, Islam, the dominant religion of the Middle East, is the religion of underdeveloped societies rather than Islam being the reason for underdevelopment in the Middle East.[28] Blades and Lo argue that the transition in the Middle East towards democracy and the rule of law, does not arise from some immutable attributes of Muslim or Arab culture but, "has been hindered by concern on the part of regime liberalisers regarding the preferences of an emerging civil society and that these preferences are often conflated with culture".[29] Nevertheless, the religion of Islam and Arab, Turkish, Persian and Muslim cultures, together with other cultural aspects of the Middle East, such as tribal systems, influence the current status of these societies. However, the important point is that the current status of the rule of law and democracy in the Middle East cannot solely be attributed to one factor, such as religion or a specific cultural norm. There have been other cultures that have had inconsistencies with principles of democracy, such as Catholicism and Confucianism. Nonetheless, a number of Catholic and Confusion nations throughout Europe, Latin America, and East Asia have successfully transitioned towards the rule of law and democracy.[30]

Although all of the above factors are relevant in explaining the absence of rule of law systems, civil institutions, and democratic norms, none of those factors are the

---

[27] For example, *see,* Huntington, *supra* note 20; and, Timur Kuran, "Islam and Underdevelopment: An Old Puzzle Revisited", 153(1) *Journal of Institutional and Theoretical Economics (JITE)* (1997) *41–71.*

[28] Kazem Alamdari, *Chera Iran Aghat Mand Va Ghardb Pish Raft [Why the West Progressed and Why Iran Did Not]* (2001) at 499.

[29] Blaydes and Lo, *supra* note 14. At 115.

[30] *See,* Eva Bellin, "Coercive institutions and coercive leaders", in *Authoritarianism in the Middle East: Regimes and Resistance*, Marsha Pripstein Posusney and Michele Penner Angris eds. (2005). Marsha Pripstein Posiusney.

sole reason for Middle Eastern exceptionalism with respect to the lack of rapid movement towards the rule of law. Indeed, all of those factors have contributed to the inefficiencies of existing modern political systems in the Middle East in relation to the rule of law.

19.5 Existing Approaches to the Rule of Law in the Middle East

As discussed earlier, calls for the rule of law to be established in the Middle East and the rest of the Muslim world are becoming more dominant. However, approaches differ in regard to the nature of rule of law system and which model will best serve the transition from totalitarian structures to rule of law systems. The views differ as to how to manage the transition from totalitarianism to the rule of law. A number of practical models exist: countries such as Saudi Arabia, the United Arab Emirates and Qatar have traditional systems; those in Turkey and to some extent Tunisia are secular; Iran is based on Islamic theocratic principles in combination with some modern institutions such as parliamentary elections and law making; and a mixed model is emerging in Egypt. The Iraqi and Afghan models are also significant, as when foreign forces occupied these countries there were attempts made to establish the rule of law and modern constitutions.

All the Arab countries of the Persian Gulf, such as Saudi Arabia, the United Arab Emirates, Kuwait, Qatar, Oman, and Bahrain, along with Jordan and Morocco in Northern Africa, are classified in this chapter as traditional systems. These nations appear to be slowly adopting some basic elements of civil society and the rule of law, although the degree of transition is stronger in Jordan and the United Arab Emirates, for example, than in Saudi Arabia. Every one of these countries has been ruled for decades or centuries by traditional Arab and Muslim monarchies established by strong, non-elected tribal families. While the governments of these countries are not elected and are occasionally brutal, some degree of consultation and power sharing occurs with various tribal groups—rather like the processes modern political parties employ.

Another significant aspect of these traditional societies is the continuation of their traditional culture and practices (including the application of certain aspects of sharia) without much significant foreign invasion and introduction of sudden alien legal systems. In practice, while these countries appear to be stuck in the past and lack modern democratic fundaments such as free and fair elections, independent judiciaries and human rights protection, there is substantially less tension in these societies, particularly between the government and the people. Further, the process of transition in these countries is being undertaken more peacefully. The process of establishing a limited rule of law system in some of these countries, notably in Saudi Arabia, may take decades or even another century.[31]

[31] *See* Hossein Esmaeili, "On a Slow Boat Towards the Rule of Law: The Nature of Law in the Saudi Arabian Legal System", 26(1) *Arizona Journal of International and Comparative Law* (2009) 1–47.

The secular systems are comprised of two groups—the Turkish and to some extent, Tunisian models, and totalitarian, socialist regimes such as those in Algeria, Iraq before the 2002 invasion, and Syria, Libya and Yemen before the Arab Spring and changes of government. Violence against citizens was rife in most of these predominantly secular, totalitarian republics. Islamist parties are the most dominant opposition groups in many of these countries.

Turkey emerged as a secular society after World War I and has perhaps, the most successful, liberal and effective rule of law system in the Middle East, although it has been riven by rivalry between hard-line Kemalists and more liberal republicans for decades. A third group, the liberal Islamic parties, emerged during the 1980s. The Turkish army is the fourth major power player in this secular Muslim country. Gradual, non-violent rivalry helped to foster the current semi-democratic system in Turkey that provides some human rights protection including women's rights and a stronger and efficient legal and political system. Although the secularisation of the Turkish system saw the establishment of a partial democracy and limited rule of law, the same results may not necessarily occur in other secular Middle Eastern societies given that Turkey is unique in terms of its proximity to Europe and as a result its culture has been greatly influenced by European ideas and practices.

The second secular group (Iraq, Syria, Algeria, and Libya) do not possess the values common to Turkey's democratic liberal values and in the last few decades have experienced considerable instability, violence and lack of power-sharing.

With the Islamic revolution in 1979, Iran moved from a totalitarian state to an Islamic republic based on Islamic theocracy. The new constitution of Iran established that governance would be managed by the principle of *velayat faghih*, whereby a high-ranking *faghih*, a Muslim cleric, had absolute authority to rule the country based on his interpretation of sharia, the sole source of law in Iran. However, certain features of democracy exist, such as elections, the tenure of judges, and the separation of powers between the judiciary, the legislative branch and the executive government. Yet, despite the separation of powers of the three branches of government, it does not apply to the supreme authority of the *velayat faghih*. While the system in Iran has been in place for over 34 years and has influenced the Middle East and Islamic worlds, it has created some tensions within the country. However, the system is not totally authoritarian and while it opposes many democratic principles, some pro-civil society ideas are tolerated. The rivalry between opposing groups (such as conservatives and reformists) is helping to further a culture of democracy and dialogue, in much the same way that rivalry between the army and liberals in Turkey led to the establishment of a more democratic state.

The Egyptian model is also unique in terms of its legal and political system. Egypt moved from being a moderate monarchy to a republic in 1960, but although it was a dictatorship, it was not predominantly violent and the political system was opened occasionally unlike Iraq, Syria and Libya. While the army and the judiciary were corrupt, they had some degree of independence from the ruling party. The legal system adopted some modern principles from European laws but maintained traditional Islamic law in relation to personal law of Muslim citizens. The sizeable Coptic Christian minority, approximately 10 % of Egypt's population, has made Egypt a more pluralistic society in comparison to its Arab and North African neighbours.

The Arab Spring of 2011 resulted in the first free election in Egypt in 2012, in which the powerful traditional Muslim Brotherhood came into power, and Mohamed Morsi was elected President. Although Morsi's government made several mistakes, was incompetent and became increasingly unpopular, there is no doubt that the coup was a significant setback for the rule of law and democracy in Egypt. The country may now follow Turkey's example in which the army assumes the role of the guardian of secularism and enters into power sharing, competition, and occasional conflicts with liberals and Islamists, until such time as civilian governments and institutions become the dominant force in Egypt. Alternatively, the country may fall prey to violence and disarray as happened in Algeria in 1991 after the army deposed the first democratically elected government in the Arab world where the Islamic party, National Liberation Front, won the election.

Two other significant cases of transition in the Middle East are Afghanistan and Iraq. Both these countries were ruled by very extremist regimes: the secular dictatorship of Saddam Hussein and the radical Islamic Taliban. These countries were occupied by foreign forces that involved operations led by the United States in 2001 (Afghanistan) and 2003 (Iraq). Afghanistan and Iraq have now modern constitutions in which the rule of law, multiple political parties, and basic human rights are recognised. Under both constitutions, sharia is a source of law (not the source of law). However, both countries are the subject of extensive sectarian violence and terrorism led by Al-Qaeda and other extremist groups. It seems that foreign occupation and imposing modern constitutions, may have improved the legal and political systems in Afghanistan and Iraq. However, given the significant violence and sectarian conflicts resulting from the process, it has not been an overall success, and would probably not work in other countries throughout the Middle East.

Given that every Middle Eastern country has its own unique history, culture, political situation, it is very likely that different means need to be found by each country for making the transition towards democracy and the rule of law, rather than simply looking to a single model. It is also worth noting that desire for the introduction of the rule of law and democratic institutions is not shared equally by all Middle Eastern societies. For example, people in Turkey and Iran have struggled for democratic governance, the rule of law and human rights for much longer than their counterparts in Saudi Arabia and Qatar.

19.6 Looking into the Future

There are significant similarities, as well as differences, between the Middle East and Europe. The two regions have had interactions, conflicts and war, trade and commerce, as well as the transfer of ideas and opinions with each other. While Europe was the birthplace of Western civilisation, the heart of Islamic civilisation is embedded in the Middle East from where the three major Abrahamic religions emerged—Judaism, Christianity and Islam. Democracy, the rule of law, and modern human rights originated in Europe, but have been introduced to other parts of the world, such as Japan, India, South America, and Africa.

Western and Islamic thinking diverges significantly around the relationship between religion, law and politic. While issues about that relationship have been more or less settled in Europe, questions concerning religion and secularism fluctuate constantly in Middle Eastern societies and are the subject of extensive intellectual and political debate. While the majority of people, intellectuals, political parties, and institutions in the Middle East aspire increasingly to the rule of law and democratic values, Middle Eastern countries may adopt rule of law systems that reflect their own unique history and culture. This however, does not mean that the nature of democracy and the rule of law can significantly be different in the Middle East or elsewhere. However, the process of transition may be different. While concepts involving the law, legal systems and the rule of law may not sit comfortably with religion and ideology, the views espoused by Islam and Muslim parties cannot be ignored and they must have an important role in the process of their countries making the transition from totalitarian states to democratic systems.

Another important factor to be considered—if Middle Eastern countries are to move away from dictatorial, totalitarian, and tyrannical regimes to systems marked by the rule of law, democracy and the protection of human rights—is the sheer complexity of a region which gave birth to the oldest civilisations in the world and three major religions. The process of moving away from the weight of the history and tradition may take generations. For example, it took nearly 80 years before Turkey's civil institutions and governments were able to uphold the rule of law and prevent arbitrary interference by the Army. Since the first constitutional revolution in the early 1900s, Iran has also struggled for the establishment of the rule of law and responsible governments. Arabs in the Middle East have also struggled for justice and democracy, which have been hindered by military interventions in Egypt and Algeria, as well as by conflicts in Iraq, Syria, and Lebanon. The Arab Spring started by citizens in Arab countries rejected violence and called for freedom, justice, and the rule of law. However, the conflicts that have arisen post-Arab Spring in Syria, Libya, Bahrain, and Egypt seem to indicate that a changeover to the rule of law and democratic institutions may take longer than was first thought.

The battle for the rule of law, justice, democracy and human rights has a long history in the Middle East, and has existed in the modern world since the early twentieth century. In 1910, an Iranian legal scholar in a monograph titled, 'One Term' stated that "the fundamental basis of Western civilisation is one term, and all achievements in the West result from one term: the rule of law".[32] Between 2001 and 2007, the Gallop organisation conducted a comprehensive survey totalling 5,000 h, of nationals from more than 50 Muslim countries. Substantial majorities of nearly all the nations surveyed, said that in the event of drafting a new constitution, they would like the guarantee of freedom of speech, equal rights for women and men,

[32] Mirza Yusuf Moustashar al-Douleh Tabrizi, *Yek Kalama ('One Term')* (1985).

and the right to vote without interference.[33] Between 2000 and 2004 a number of national surveys in six Arab countries showed that 90 % or more of those interviewed would like to see a democratic political system in their country.[34] According to the 2012 Global Attitudes Project carried out by the Pew Research Centre, the clear majority of people from Lebanon, Turkey, Egypt, Tunisia and Jordan believe democracy is the best form of government.[35]

19.7 Conclusion

The rule of law, and its institutions, is one of the foundations of modern democratic societies. Although modern effective rule of law systems may not yet exist in most Middle Eastern societies, this topic is discussed extensively in the Middle East and the Muslim world. However, it must be emphasised that the desire by Middle Eastern societies for democratic systems and the rule of law is conditional on these sitting alongside existing traditions and cultures. Islam and sharia law are a major pillar of the Middle Eastern tradition, culture, and politics. While some aspects of Islamic law may be inconsistent with democratic principles and the rule of law, some other characteristics of the Islamic legal system are potentially accommodating to the rule of law.

Experts and scholars have proposed various reasons for the lack of effective of rule of law in the Middle East: economic structures, historical context, colonisation, and cultural and religious values. However, given the complex nature of Middle Eastern societies, it is fair to say that the cause lies with a combination of factors, not just one.

Besides the different views on the nature and limits of a rule of law system in the Middle East, in practice there are different models and cases in the implementation of a rule of law system, including traditional models, secular models, the theocracy cases, and a combination of traditional and modern cases. Again, no single approach may be prescribed for all Middle Eastern societies, and each society may have its own model of transition towards the rule of law.

In any case, the establishment of the rule of law systems and transition towards democracy and civil societies in the Middle East is very slow, gradual, and must be initiated from within societies.

---

[33] John L. Esposito and Dalia Mogahed, *Who Speaks for Islam? What a Billion Muslims Really Think* (2007) at 47 and 62. Gallup Press.

[34] Mark Tessle and Eleanor Gao, *supra* note 1. At 87.

[35] Pew Research Centre, Global Attitudes Project, "Most Muslims Want Democracy, Personal Freedoms, and Islam in Political Life", July 10, 2012, *available at* http://www.pewglobal.org/2012/07/10/most-muslims-want-democracy-personal-freedoms-and-islam-in-political-life/

Chapter 20
Waiting for the Rule of Law in Brazil: A Meta-legal Analysis of the Insufficient Realization of the Rule of Law in Brazil

Augusto Zimmermann

"Para os amigos tudo, para os indiferentes nada, e para os inimigos a lei!"

("For my friends, everything; for strangers, nothing; for my enemies – the law!") – traditional Brazilian saying

Abstract This chapter provides a broad account of the manifold deficiencies in the implementation of the rule of law in Brazil, offering both legal and extra-legal explanations for this. In doing so, it is contended that it is impossible to properly comprehend and appreciate the obstacles facing the realization of the rule of law in Brazil if confined simply to the observation of legal phenomena. Rather, a proper understanding can be achieved if a more ambitious interdisciplinary analysis is undertaken, addressing the legal, institutional, political and cultural issues of Brazilian society.

20.1 Introduction

A survey of Brazil's reality shakes one's faith in 'legal recipes' that may be proffered to realize the rule of law. And yet, there is little research in the legal field containing empirical investigation of the extra-legal obstructions to the realization of the rule of law in Brazil's context. This chapter provides a basic account of some of these obstructions. In doing so, it is argued that it is not possible to comprehend and appreciate the obstacles facing the realization of the rule of law in that country

I would like to thank Frank Gashumba for his comments on an earlier draft of this chapter.

A. Zimmermann (✉)
School of Law, Murdoch University, Murdoch, WA, Australia
e-mail: a.zimmermann@murdoch.edu.au

J.R. Silkenat et al. (eds.), *The Legal Doctrines of the Rule of Law and the Legal State (Rechtsstaat)*, Ius Gentium: Comparative Perspectives on Law and Justice 38,
DOI 10.1007/978-3-319-05585-5_20,

if one is confined simply to the more formalistic observation of legal phenomena. Rather, we must also turn attention to the many patterns of social behaviour that inhibit regular respect for legal rules, principles and institutions.

This chapter, therefore, provides an interdisciplinary analysis of Brazil's legal culture and general attitudes toward the formal legal system. It is thus an explanation of the manner in which Brazilian law operates in practice as opposed to solely in theory. Due to the manifest chasm that separates law on paper and 'law' in practice, anyone wishing to understand how the country really operates will need to consider the ways in which people are able to exempt themselves from the application of laws. Accordingly, an empirical analysis of the reality in Brazil reveals a deeply inter-relational society that is profoundly regulated by *contra-legem* (anti-legal) rules. These are not the formal rules taught in the law schools but rather socially defined rules that may vary quite remarkably from state codes and statutes, as well as the rulings of the courts.

20.2 Defining the Rule of Law

Although the meaning of a concept such as the rule of law is open to debate, there is a general agreement that this is essentially concerned with protecting the individual from unpredictable and arbitrary interference with their vital interests. Such interference may come from the government or other individuals. Thus, a community is said to be under the rule of law if citizens are protected from arbitrary violence and if laws exist that are established to maintain peace and avoid that which may be called a *Hobbesian* state of "war of every man against every man".[1]

There is also a broad understanding that the rule of law means something more than the sanction by law of every governmental action. In contrast to the rule of men, which implies arbitrary rule, the ideal of the rule of law is designed to minimize public and private arbitrariness so that the rights of the individual may be formally recognized and substantially protected. As such, the rule of law seems to involve a liberal principle of considerable delimitation of governmental functions, so that these functions can be exercised in accordance with clear, stable and general rules of law. Such rules must be promulgated in advance and enforced by an independent and impartial judiciary. By forcing the state to follow legal rules and procedures, law operates to reduce the possibility of government being able to excessively coerce, obstruct or otherwise unreasonably interfere with the life, liberty and property of the individual.

In this sense, a society truly living under the rule of law must deny its government any 'right to destroy, enslave, or designedly to impoverish the subjects'.[2] Instead,

[1] Thomas Hobbes, *Leviathan* (1651), Ch XIII, para 62.

[2] John Locke, *Second Treatise on Civil Government* (1689), Sec 135.

the state shall act only through law and law must check the power of government.[3] Hence, the concept of the rule of law has been historically linked to 'an ideal undoubtedly connected with individual freedom understood as freedom from [unduly arbitrary] interference on the part of everybody, including the authorities'.[4] As the late English constitutionalist, O Hood Phillips, pointed out: "Historically, the phrase [the rule of law] was used with reference to a belief in the existence of law possessing higher authority – whether divine or natural – than that of the law promulgated by human rulers which imposed limits on their power".[5] In this context, the term 'rule of law' was first coined by the Greek philosophers Plato and Aristotle and then rediscovered and elaborated by Christian scholars, notably Saint Thomas Aquinas, during the Middle Ages, as "an umbrella concept for a number of legal and institutional instruments to protect citizens against the power of the state".[6]

Amongst the nations of continental Europe, the rule of law is classically connected with a constitutional perspective whereby the state is "bound by the law in its dealings with citizens: its power is, in other words, limited by the individual rights of the people".[7] For example, the German equivalent of the English concept of the rule of law is *Rechtsstaat*, which was conceived in the nineteenth century by R von Mohl, E Brandes, A W Rehberg and F C Dahlmann and other Hanoverian jurists who wished to promote classical liberal principles of limited government and individual rights in their Germanic principality. In those days the prince of Hanover was also the English monarch and so there was a visible link between these two nations. Inspired by the English Whig tradition, von Mohl coined the term *Rechtsstaat* to advocate the prevalence of principles that, in his opinion, "irrevocably determines and secures the directions and the limits of state activity".[8] According to Professor Ernst-Wolfgang Böckenförde, such idea of *Rechtsstaat* still remains a leading principle of German constitutionalism. Böckenförde explains that this principle is "primarily" associated with "the recognition of fundamental civil rights … such as civil liberty (protection of personal freedom, freedom of belief and conscience, freedom of the press, freedom of movement, freedom of contract, and freedom of occupation), equality before the law, and the guarantee of (acquired) property".[9]

---

[3] Schor, Miguel, *The Rule of Law, in* D. Clark (ed.), *Encyclopedia of Law and Society: American and Global Perspectives* (London/UK: Sage, 2005) at 231.

[4] Leoni, Bruno, *Freedom and the Law* (Los Angeles/CA: Nash Publishing, 1972) at 76.

[5] Phillips, Owen H., and Jackson, Paul, *O Hood Phillips' Constitutional and Administrative Law* (7th ed., London/UK: Sweet & Maxwell, 1987) at 37.

[6] Adriaan Bedner, 'An Elementary Approach to the Rule of Law' 2 *Hague Journal on the Rule of Law* (2010) 50.

[7] van Caenegen, R.C., *An Historical Introduction to Western Constitutional Law* (Cambridge/UK: Cambridge University Press, 1995) at 15.

[8] Robert von Mohl, *Die Philosophie des Rechts* (1837) Vol II, Pt II, quoted in Friedrich A. Hayek, *Constitution of Liberty* (1960) at 483.

[9] Böckenförde, Ernst-Wolfgang, *State, Society and Liberty: Studies in Political Theory and Constitutional Law* (New York: Berg, 1991) at 50.

Emulating the same tradition of *Rechtsstaat*, Brazilian legal theorists have described their version of the rule of law, called *Estado de Direito*, in the light of values and principles associated with the classical liberal ideal of "government under the rule of law".[10] According to Carlos Ari Sundfeld, *Estado de Direito* implies the development by positive law of principles of separation of powers and protection of "fundamental human rights".[11] In his book *Fundamentos de Direito Público* ('Foundations of Public Law'), Professor Sundfeld characterises the basic elements of *Estado de Direito* as follows: (a) supremacy of the law; (b) separation of powers; and (c) legal-institutional protection of individual rights. Thus, he states that the first two characteristics, legal supremacy and separation of powers, comprise the principles by which an "effective, permanent, and indestructible" protection of the fundamental rights can be guaranteed against all forms of governmental arbitrariness.[12]

This is the prevailing understanding of the subject in Brazil. For Manoel Gonçalves Ferreira Filho, in its most classic definition, *Estado de Direito* is related to a liberal tradition of legality that seeks to prevent arbitrariness so that the basic rights and freedoms of the individual are protected. These rights and freedoms are said to comprise the following: (a) formal equality of citizens before the law; (b) freedom of belief and conscience; (c) freedom of the press; (d) freedom of movement; (e) freedom of contract; and (f) freedom of association.[13] But the enjoyment of these rights and freedoms, Professor Ferreira Filho concludes, can only be secured if a certain form of government is achieved, namely government under the rule of law.[14]

20.3 Rule of Law as a Culture of Legality

As seen above, legal academics in Brazil have a fairly good idea of what the rule of law traditionally implies, at least in its classical liberal perspective. These legal theorists have embraced a substantive conception of the rule of law as opposed to a more formalist conception, thus linking the phrase with the values of limited government and individual rights.[15] And yet, a good theoretical understanding might

---

[10] *See* Caenegem, *supra* note 7. At 15.

[11] Sundfeld, Carlos A., *Fundamentos de Direito Público* (4th ed., São Paulo/SP: Malheiros Editores, 2008) at 37–58.

[12] *Id.*, at 48.

[13] Ferreira Filho, Manoel Gonçalves, *Curso de Direito Constitutional* (São Paulo/SP: Saraiva, 1999) at 13.

[14] For a more comprehensive analysis of *Estado de Direito*, see: Zimmermann, Augusto, *Curso de Direito Constitucional* (4th ed., Rio de Janeiro/RJ: Lumen Juris, 2006) at 59–71 & 228–231; *see also*, Reale, Miguel, *O Estado Democrático de Direito e o Conflito das Ideologias* (São Paulo: Saraiva, 1999) at 1–13.

[15] For an analysis of formal and substantive conceptions of the rule of law, see: Paul Craig, "Formal and Substantive Conceptions of the Rule of Law", 16 *Public Law* (Autumn 1997) 467; *see also* Paul Craig, "Constitutional Foundations, the Rule of Law and Supremacy", 22 *Public Law* (Spring 2003) 93; *see also* Augusto Zimmermann, *Western Legal Theory: History, Concepts and Perspectives* (Sydney/NSW: LexisNexis Butterworths, 2013) at 85–91.

not be enough for the realization of the rule of law. After all, every legal system needs to operate in a dynamic relationship with its surrounding social, political and cultural context.

To become a reality in practice and not merely in theory, the rule of law must rest on a proper relationship between legal rules and social behaviour. Accordingly, any option for anti-legal behaviour must, as a matter of general principle, be rejected, otherwise the entire edifice of legality may well collapse.[16] Regardless of which conception of the rule of law is embraced, its practical achievement requires a *culture of legality* in which both ordinary citizens and public officials evidence a commitment to law by generally complying with legal rules, principles and institutions, insisting on their compliance, criticizing those who fail to comply with them, and finally taking whatever action is necessary to correct any lack of compliance.

Unfortunately, it seems that some societies are not entirely qualified to accept all the moral implications of government under the law. In his *Considerations on Representative Government* (1861), John Stuart Mill speculated that the achievement of the rule of law is actually "determined by social circumstances".[17] Because Mill assumed that these circumstances are malleable and can be changed for either better or worse, he observed that people can be taught to behave democratically and according to principles of the rule of law. And yet, Mill kept on insisting that some patterns of behaviour are fundamental in determining the realization of the rule of law. As he explained:

> The people for whom the form of government is intended must be willing to accept it; or at least not so unwilling as to oppose an insurmountable obstacle to its establishment... A rude people ... may be unable to practice the forbearance which... [the rule of law] demands: their passions may be too violent, or their personal pride too exacting, to forego private conflict, and leave to the laws the avenging of their real or supposed wrongs.[18]

Many lawyers today appear to have a tendency to make rather exaggerated claims for what positive laws can deliver in terms of providing for the rule of law. Martin Krygier has called attention to the intrinsic correlation between the rule of law and its socio-politico-cultural milieu.[19] As Krygier notes, the realization of the rule of law "depends as much on characteristics of society as of the law, and on their interactions".[20] He explains that the rule of law is not merely a matter of "detailed

---

[16] Reale, Miguel, *O Estado Democrático de Direito e o Conflito das Ideologias* (São Paulo: Saraiva, 1999) at 9.

[17] John Stuart Mill, *Considerations on Representative Government* (1861) at 31.

[18] *Id.*, at 29.

[19] *See* Martin Krygier, *Ethical Positivism and the Liberalism of Fear, in* T. Campbell and J. Goldsworthy (eds.), *Judicial Power, Democracy, and Legal Positivism* (Ashgate: Aldershot, 2000) at 64; *see also* Martin Krygier, "Transitional Questions about the Rule of Law: Why, What, and How?" Paper delivered at the conference *East Central Europe: From Where to Where?* East Central Institute for Advanced Study, Budapest, February 15–17, 2001. See also: Martin Krygier, *Institutional Optimism, Cultural Pessimism and the Rule of Law, in* M. Krygier and A. Czarnota (eds.), *The Rule of Law After Communism: Problems and Prospects in East-Central Europe* (Aldershot: Ashgate, 1999).

[20] Martin Krygier, "False Dichotomies, True Perplexities, and the Rule of Law". Paper Presented at the *Center for the Study of Law and Society*, University of California, Berkeley, 2003, at 11.

institutional design" but also an "interconnected cluster of values" that can be pursued in a variety of institutional ways.[21] Rather, the counter-intuitive fact that the rule of law has "thrived best where it was least designed"[22] appears to provide the best (empirical) evidence that this ideal of legality is more about social outcome (i.e., the restriction of government arbitrariness) than a simple legal mechanism.[23] In essence, to be achieved, the rule of law would rest primarily with extra-legal circumstances of social predictability and not simply formal-institutional mechanisms.[24]

It is valuable to consider that law is not necessarily the primary source of political legitimacy.[25] There are other ways in which government can be socially legitimised other than through positive law. On the basis of charismatic leadership, for example, the late German sociologist, Max Weber, explained that political power is endorsed primarily by means of "devotion to the exceptional sanctity, heroism, or exemplary character of an individual person, and of the normative patterns or order revealed or ordained by him".[26] Such development results in a social context in which charisma becomes more important than compliance with legal rules, and so the rule of law is not seen by society as the most acceptable element of power recognition. Sir Ivor Jennings noted:

> If it is believed that the individual finds his greatest happiness, or best develops his soul, in a strong and powerful State, and that government implies… the unity of the nation behind a wise and beneficent leader, the rule of law is a pernicious doctrine.[27]

What seems to give real life to the rule of law lies in the social environment, which, according to Friedman, "is constantly at work on the law – destroying here, renewing there; invigorating here, deadening there; choosing what parts of law will operate, which parts will not; what substitutes, detours, and bypasses will spring up; what changes will take place".[28] Hence, even if an enlightened legislator drafts a "perfect" rights-based democratic constitution, still a further problem is for the society to which such law is the recipient, to develop a culture of legality whereby the ideal of the rule of law is not trumped by extra-legal (political) premises informing, for example, that "whoever wins election to the presidency is thereby entitled to govern as he or she sees fit".[29]

---

[21] Martin Krygier, "Rule of Law", in *International Encyclopedia of the Social & Behavioral Sciences*, N.J. Smelser and P.B. Baltes eds. (2001) at 13404.

[22] Martin Krygier, "Compared to What? Thoughts on Law and Justice", *Quadrant Magazine*, December 1993, at 52.

[23] Krygier, *supra* note 21. At 13404.

[24] *Id.*

[25] Tamanaha, Brian Z., *A General Jurisprudence of Law and Society* (Oxford/UK: Oxford University Press, 2001) at 140.

[26] Weber, Max, *Theory of Social and Economic Organization* (New York/NY, MacMillan, 1948) at 215.

[27] Jennings, Ivor, *The Law and the Constitution* (London/UK: University of London Press, 1959) at 46.

[28] Friedman, Lawrence M., *The Legal System: A Social Science Perspective* (New York: Russell Sage, 1975) at 193–194.

[29] Guillermo O'Donnell, "Delegative Democracy", 5 Democracy (1994) at 54.

The observation above leads to the moral question regarding the compliance with laws. If compliance with laws does not rest on a firm element of public morality, then the rule of law ultimately becomes "an impracticable and even undesirable ideal, and... society will quickly relapse into a state of arbitrary tyranny".[30] Indeed, the rule of law appears to rest upon "an attitude of restraint, an absence of arbitrary coercion by governments or by other individuals or groups".[31] The rule of law can only subsist in a social environment where the citizens take their legal rights seriously, considering the respect to legal rules, principles and institutions as a matter of highest moral obligation.[32] By contrast, the absence of any such recognition to the supremacy of law over personal will might explain the constant failure of certain societies to resist arbitrary (non-legal) governmental attempts over the life, liberty, and property of their citizens. As Reynolds asserts:

> The rule of law does poorly in cultures where it is not the fundamental expectation that a people has of its government... If people do not expect the rule of law and insist on it when officials move to compromise its effect, it is soon corrupted and replaced by rule of will. Rule of law seems to require this virtue of any populace that will enjoy its benefits.[33]

20.4 Ineffectiveness of Laws in Brazil

The Brazilian legal system is based on the civil law tradition of Continental Europe. Accordingly, the legislator introduces statutes in an attempt to predict, in advance, every scenario of social conflict. The legislator looks upon society as an artificial creation, as inert matter that receives all its life, organization, and morality from the state's legislative power. A corollary of this is the tendency of legislators to regulate every aspect of human life.[34] Consequently, Brazilians have acquired a tendency to soften laws by not applying them properly. On the other hand, they have inherited from their Portuguese colonizers the rather naïve belief or hope that laws can function as panaceas for every sort of social disease.[35] This hope maintains that one

---

[30] Hayek, *supra* note 8. At 206.

[31] Walker, Geoffrey de Q., *The Rule of Law: Foundations of Constitutional Democracy* (Melbourne/Vic: Melbourne University Press, 1988) at 2.

[32] Selzenick, Philip, *Legal Cultures and the Rule of Law*, in M. Krygier and A. Czarnota (eds.), *Rule of Law after Communism* (Ashgate: Adershot, 1998) at 37.

[33] Noel B. Reynolds, "Grounding the Rule of Law", 2 *Ratio Juris* (March 1989) 7.

[34] Keith Rosenn comments: "The Brazilian legal culture is highly legalistic; that is, the society places great emphasis upon seeing that all social relations are regulated by comprehensive legislation. There is a strong feeling that new institutions or practices ought not to be adopted without a prior law authorizing them. As has been said with reference to German legalism, there is a 'horror of a legal vacuum'. Brazil has reams of laws and decrees regulating with great specificity seemingly every aspect of Brazilian life, as well as some aspects of life not found in Brazil. It often appears that if something is not prohibited by law, it must be obligatory". Keith S. Rosenn, "The Jeito, Brazil's Institutional Bypass of the Formal Legal System and Its Developmental Implications", 19 *American Journal of Comparative Law* (1971) 528.

[35] Rosenn, Keith, *O Jeito na Cultura Jurídica Brasileira* (Rio de Janeiro/RJ: Renovar, 1998) at 54.

day everybody will start respecting the existing laws, and when this miracle occurs, laws will solve all the country's problems. Therefore, a common witticism in Brazil states that the only thing the country needs is a new law to put all the existing ones into practice!

Without doubt, the Brazilian legislator exhibits the quite undesirable practice of introducing new laws that are often too abstract and unrealistic to be put into practice. During colonial times, laws in Brazil were merely copied from those already applied in Portugal without being adequately adapted to the new destination. For three centuries, the main Portuguese law adopted in the country was the *Ordenações Filipinas* (1603).[36] This codified body of legislation was notorious for its confused and contradictory provisions. Although it was not designed with Brazil's conditions in mind, it remained the nation's basic civil law until the adoption of a new civil code in 1917.[37] As Nardoff indicates:

> The Portuguese fondness for form over substance, rooted firmly in Roman and Canon law, resulted in an incredibly formalistic legal system… Under the Portuguese legal system, the Crown pretended to rule and the subjects pretended to obey… Lisbon found great comfort in issuing reams of esoteric and unrealistic laws, while its Brazilian subjects took equal pleasure in finding ways around these ill-conceived edicts from the state.[38]

One may argue that the case has ever since been that legislators in Brazil often fail to consider the social context in which laws are to be applied.[39] The result is an abysmal distance between law and reality, with copycat laws introduced without a more careful attention as to the prospects of their practical implementation.[40] One would not be wrong in asserting that some laws have been introduced in Brazil almost with the certain knowledge that they will never be observed. Thus, as Rosenn explains, "Brazilians refer to law much in the same manner as one refers to vaccinations. There are those who take, and those who do not".[41] He gives the insightful example of a Minister of Justice, Francisco Campos, who in the 1930s responded to criticisms about the enactment of a new legislation that was identical to another enacted by the same government only a year earlier by saying: "There is no harm done, my son. We are going to publish this one because the other *não pegou* (did not take hold)".[42]

The problem of laws not taking hold in Brazil may be attributed to a lack of realism that causes pragmatic solutions to be sacrificed on the altar of utopian postulations.

---

[36] The Portuguese law was codified, or rather compiled, first in the *Ordenações Afonsinas* (1446–1457), revised in 1521 as the *Ordenações Manuelinas*, and finally in the *Ordenações Filipinas* (1603), also known as the *Código Filipino*.

[37] Rosenn, *supra* note 35. At 35–36.

[38] Norman Nardoff, "Book Review: O Jeito na Cultura Jurídica Brasileira", 32 *University of Miami Inter-American Law Review* (Fall 2001) 607.

[39] Duarte, Nestor, *A Ordem Privada e a Organização Política Nacional* (São Paulo/SP: Cia. Editora Nacional, 1950) at 221–22.

[40] Faoro, Raymundo, *Os Donos do Poder: Formação do Patronato Político Brasileiro* (Porto Alegre/RS: Globo, 1975) at 745.

[41] Rosenn, *supra* note 34. At 530.

[42] *Id.*, at 531.

The late historian José Honório Rodrigues once commented that 'the most persistent element in Brazilian political life seems to have been the habit of adopting solutions that fit principles rather than situations'.[43] According to Rodrigues, this lack of realism is caused by the legislator's incapacity for meeting challenges with real solutions, not with theories.[44] Indeed, the problem with utopian legislation has occurred even at the level of the nation's most fundamental law, the constitution. In countries like Brazil, Rosenn points out:

> Constitutions typically contain a substantial number of aspirational or utopian provisions that are either impossible or extremely difficult to enforce. Some of these provisions contain social rights that seem far more appropriate in a political platform or a sermon than in a constitution.[45]

This is particularly true about the current Brazilian Constitution. Although the document recognises a vast array of 'fundamental rights', it is quite evident that these rights are often trumped by the less egalitarian structure of society. When analysing the state of human rights in Brazil, it is not difficult to recognize the vivid contrast between rights on paper and how these rights work in practice. The great paradox is that despite its rights-based constitution, basic human rights are not necessarily respected in Brazil. Clearly, positive law may deem a right fundamental but it does not follow that any such right will be guaranteed; it may simply be abused or ignored by the authorities, and even other citizens.[46] Of course one of the leading causes for the violation of constitutional rights is the problem of impunity, which is a critical factor contributing to the declining faith in the rule of law in Brazil.[47] Curiously, Brazilians often say among themselves that there is only one law that is always respected if you are rich or influential: *a lei da impunidade* (the law of impunity).

20.5 Subordination of Law to Social Status

Brazil is a nation suffering from a substantial lack of commitment to legality. Most of what happens in a country like Brazil lies outside the statute books and law reports. There is a sharp contrast between, on the one hand, statutes and the written

---

[43] Rodrigues, José Honório, *The Brazilians: Their Character and Aspirations* (Austin/TX: University of Texas Press, 1967) at 57.

[44] *Id.*, at 63.

[45] Keith S. Rosenn, "The Success of Constitutionalism in the United States and Its Failure in Latin America: An Explanation", 22 *University of Miami Inter-American Law Review* (1990) 36.

[46] *See* Zimmermann, Augusto, "Constitutions without Constitutionalism: The Failure of Constitutionalism in Brazil" *in* Mortimer Sellers and Tadeusz Tomaszewski (eds.), *The Rule of Law in Comparative Perspective* (Springer, 2010), at 101–145; *see also* Augusto Zimmermann, "Constitutional Rights in Brazil: A Legal Fiction?" 14(2) *Murdoch University Law Review* (2007) 28–55.

[47] Prillaman, William C., *The Judiciary and Democratic Decay in Latin America: Declining Confidence in the Rule of Law* (London/UK: Praeger, 2000) at 76.

texts of the constitution, and, on the other hand, the daily life as demonstrated in the regular dealings between individuals and public authorities.[48]

Due to the extent to which positive law is not properly respected, Roberto DaMatta explains that Brazilian society is pervaded by a double ethic. Whereas, in theory, Brazilians seem ruled by general and abstract rules of law, in practice they are far more regulated by the unwritten rules of society, which "promulgate and protect the ethic of privilege and those who act on it".[49] Such rules derive from a range of factors but are generally related to extra-legal conditions of wealth, social status, and ties of family and friendship.[50] They are based on historical and cultural precedents which have led to social practices by which some people regard themselves as being above the law.[51] As Rodrigues observed, in Brazil, "personal liking is above the law".[52] And so, the familiar Brazilian maxim: *Para os amigos tudo, para os indiferentes nada, e para os inimigos a lei* (For my friends, everything; for strangers, nothing; for my enemies – the law!).[53]

Brazil's society stresses direct relations based on personal liking as opposed to formal relations. Since personal liking is more relevant than respecting the written law, the greatest fear of every citizen is that of becoming an isolated individual. The isolated individual is that person reduced to the inferior condition of being only under the law. Such a person will have only the law on which to depend; whereas anyone with good friends can actually be far more than just a citizen, and obtain some special treatment from both government and institutions of prestige. Indeed, it is universally known in Brazil that certain bureaucratic inconveniences can only be solved through favors provided by public servants in state agencies. As such, part of the importance given by Brazilians to relationship ties stems from the undeniable failure of the bureaucratic sector to operate satisfactorily. But state agencies can, of course, work extremely well for those with the right connections.[54]

Unlike a country such as the United States, where its first European settlers possessed a real commitment to the rule of law, the first European settlers in Brazil tried to disrespect the law and did not even acknowledge the most basic notions of public service and public trust. These first colonizers, explains Rosenn, "bequeathed the Brazilians a weak sense of loyalty and obligation towards the body politic, and

---

[48] Eder, Phanor J., *Law and Justice in Latin America* (New York/NY: New York University Press, 1937) at 57.

[49] *Id.*, at 296.

[50] DaMatta, Roberto, *Carnivals, Rogues, and Heroes: An Interpretation of the Brazilian Dilemma* (Notre Dame/IN: University of Notre Dame Press, 1991) at 187–88.

[51] DaMatta, Roberto, *'The Quest for Citizenship in a Relational Universe'*, *in* J.D. Wirth, E.O. Nunes, and T.E. Bogenschild (eds.), *State and Society in Brazil: Continuity and Change* (London/UK: Westview, 1987) at 317.

[52] Rodrigues, *supra* note. At 57.

[53] DaMatta, *supra* note 51. At 319.

[54] Miller, Charlotte I., 'The Function of Middle-Class Extended Family Networks in Brazilian Urban Society', *in* M.L. Margolis and W.E. Carter (eds.), *Brazil: Anthropological Perspectives: Essays in Honor of Charles Wagley* (New York/NY: Columbia University Press, 1979) at 136.

a strong sense of loyalty and obligation towards family and friends".[55] During the colonial period, the Portuguese Crown was largely dependent on the landed aristocracy for the development of Brazil's economy and for its military security. Landowners administered justice across their lands and possessed their own private militias for the purposes of maintaining public order.[56] Being independent of the law, they became paternal protectors of all those surrounding their homes.[57] As Valença states:

> The patron-client relationship was based on mutual exchange and the expectation of both sides that it would provide future yields. The *patrão* provided resources, protection and links to the outside world... The 'client' offered support and obedience... The patron-client system depended on the interaction between individuals and favored informal flexible relationships.[58]

When Dom Pedro I, the eldest son of the Portuguese king, declared Brazil's independence on September 7, 1822, the new monarch organized a powerful bureaucracy recruited from members of the landed aristocracy. But as early as 1885, liberal politician Joaquim Nabuco complained of bureaucrats producing a "rotten system" that sucked all the nation's resources so as to "redistribute them to its clients".[59] Unfortunately, the situation remained the same after the fall of monarchy on November 15, 1889, with local rural bosses maintaining their traditional power and demanding loyalty of all those under their paternal protection.[60] An individual's economic security and social wellbeing flowed directly from their bosses' personal dominion. There was a sense of *noblesse oblige* on the part of these local bosses, with their vassals developing an attitude of loyalty to them. As Wagley observed:

> Frequently the local political boss ... was a sort of *patrão* to his followers, who received favors and expected future favors. A lower-class worker without a *patrão* of the kind or another was a man without a protector in time of need. The *patrão* provided some measure of social security – generally the only form available to the worker.[61]

The process of industrialization initiated in the 1930s appeared to make this reality no longer a possibility, because it now created a large urban class which developed apart from the old influence of the landed aristocracy. In the 1930s, about

---

[55] Rosenn, *supra* note 34. At 523.

[56] C.R. Boxer, "The Bay of All Saints", in *History of Latin American Civilization – Vol. 2.*, L. Hanke ed. (1967) at 164.

[57] Freire, Gilberto, 'The Patriarchal Basis of Brazilian Society'. in J. Maier and R. W. Weatherhead (eds.), *Politics of Change in Latin America* (New York/NY: Praeger, 1964) at 164.

[58] Márcio M. Valença, "Patron-Client Relations and Politics in Brazil: An Historical Overview", Paper presented at the London School of Economics and Political Science, January 2000, at 8, available at: http://www.lse.ac.uk/collections/geographyAndEnvironment/research/Researchpapers/rp58.pdf

[59] Robert M. Levine, *Jeitinho Land.* Brazzil Magazine, January 1998, available at: http://www.brazzil.com/content/view/8072/75/

[60] Chevigny, Paul, *Edge of the Knife: Police Violence in the Americas* (New York/NY: New Press, 1995) at 151.

[61] Wagley, Charles, *An Introduction to Brazil* (New York/NY: Columbia University Press, 1971) at 99.

70 % of Brazilians lived in rural areas while today roughly 85 % of the country's population live in urban areas. Brazil is today one of most heavily industrialised nations in the world. This new socio-economic reality, however, has not altered traditional patterns of clientelistic behaviour, since the people who moved from the countryside to the cities preserved the tendency to view all relationships, including with public officials, in deeply personal rather than impersonal (legal) terms.

Curiously, the first politician to capitalise on the preservation by new urban classes of this paternalist mind-set inherited from the countryside was a wealthy landowner himself. And yet, Getúlio Vargas, a lawyer and landowner who began his political career with the support of other rural oligarchs from his native southern state of Rio Grande do Sul, was wise enough to understand that the continuing process of urbanization would dramatically reduce the power of landowners. Thus, in 1937 he masterminded a coup that installed the *Estado Novo* (New State), a personal dictatorship where Vargas assumed the role of paternal ruler who directly appealed to the popular masses as the great benefactor of the working people. As Page explains:

> Upon assuming the presidency ... he set about creating a relationship of dependency not only between government and private enterprise... but also between government and labor. This relationship turned out to be a mirror image of the traditional tie between haves and have-nots in rural Brazil. Peasants who moved to the cities encountered a social structure quite different from the one to which they were accustomed. They have to live in amorphous slums and, as Brazil industrialized, to toil in impersonal workplaces. Thus it was easy for Vargas to substitute the government as the authority figure that would take care of the needs of employees, just as the landlord... had done in the countryside.[62]

President Vargas constructed an image of himself as a paternal ruler modelled on the *pater familias*. He posed as the great benevolent leader and protector of the working classes, and expected absolute loyalty from them to such an extent that, from 1937 to 1945, laws in Brazil were little more than a tool for the imposition of his arbitrary will. With no elections, no judicial independence, and not even a functioning legislature, Vargas was virtually free to order the state apparatus to kill, arrest, and torture anyone he wished. Playing the role of "father of the poor", he established labor legislation based on Mussolini's *Carta del Lavoro*, and for this act of generosity, he attracted the absolute loyalty of workers who often verged on veneration to the leader.[63] After visiting the country in 1938, Karl Loewenstein commented that the greatest asset of the Brazilian dictatorship was the dictator himself, who carried the regime "on his shoulders'"

> The dictatorship is personalistic in character. In that, it is altogether different from the European totalitarian pattern. No government party protects it, and no coercive ideology supports it. The regime rests on no visible props, except the army; it is based [not on law but] on the popularity of one man alone.[64]

---

[62] Page, Joseph A., *The Brazilians* (Reading/MA: Addison-Wesley, 1995) at 203.

[63] Burns, E. Bradford, *A History of Brazil* (New York/NY: Columbia University Press, 1970) at 298.

[64] Lowenstein, Karl, *Brazil made Tremendous Advances, in* L. Hanke (ed.), History of Latin American Civilization, Vol. 2 (Irvine/CA: University of California Press, 1967) at 446.

In today's Brazil, many are those who still believe that their political leaders are morally bound to provide supporters with extra-legal favors. Brazilians seem to expect just about everything from their government. These expected favors can come in the form of such things as t-shirts, bags of basic foodstuff, bags of cement, beer, telephone lines, musical instruments, paint for buildings, stable prices, credit, subsidies for carnival masquerades, etc. As Rosenn observes, "there is hardly anything for which the government is not expected to provide".[65] And yet, without doubt, one of the most common favors these voters ask of their politicians is the provision of a public job. Public jobs are common currency in Brazilian politics, serving as a type of income-generating property to pay off supporters and place them within positions in the state machinery that can be quite useful to the political bosses.[66] As Rosenn also points out:

> Political clientage, whose roots go back to the *patrão* system of traditional rural Brazil, still dominates the bureaucratic structure. One who owes his job to political clientage is less likely to be averse to doing favors for family and friends. Moreover, the influx of large numbers of untrained and unqualified personnel has itself generated more red tape, partially to give superfluous employees something to do, partially to diffuse responsibility so that fixing blame for incompetence becomes more difficult... Large numbers of civil servants have at least one other daytime job; substantial numbers show up only to collect their paychecks.[67]

20.6 Omnipotence of the Brazilian State

One should note that the state is the main agent of social transformation in Brazilian society. It is not that the ruling elite in Brazil comprises only bureaucrats, but rather that the state bureaucracy is the base to which all other groups adhere, either through alliance or dependence. Since the state is the ultimate provider of all existing resources, "the citizenry expects to live at government expense and under full protection".[68] Consequently, statism is strongly supported and fully endorsed by all sorts of individuals, including old-fashioned socialists, neo-mercantilist businesspeople, reactionary conservatives who oppose free-market capitalism, the authoritarian military, privileged bureaucrats, intellectuals who seek after state subvention, and a plethora of compassionate individuals who believe that only a more powerful government can generate progress and reduce social inequalities.[69]

---

[65] Rosenn, *supra* note 34. At 526.

[66] Claphan, Christopher; *Clientelism and the State, in* C. Claphan (ed.), Private Patronage and Public Power (London/UK: Francis Pinter, 1982) at 25.

[67] Rosenn, *supra* note 34. At 535.

[68] Heitor de Paola, "The Concept of Democracy in Latin America", Hispanic American Center for Economic Research – HACER, July 2006, available at: http://www.hacer.org/current/Brazil109.php

[69] Prado, Ney, *Razões das Virtudes e Vícios da Constituição de 1988* (São Paulo/SP: Inconfidentes, 1994) at 59. For the purposes of this chapter, statism is defined as an ideology which provides a preferential role for the state in society, placing the state as the main agent of social action and transformation.

To better understand the correlation between statism and the perversion of the rule of law, one needs first to consider the reality of a state that has historically been above society.[70] Statism is a by-product of an old spoils-system inherited from Portugal, a country where the monarch granted to his staff and preferred subjects all sorts of graces and favours at the expense of the rule of law. This is a reality that has existed in Brazil since its very first day as a Portuguese colony.[71] Indeed, when seafarer Pero Vaz de Caminha wrote to Portugal's King D. Manuel on April 22, 1500, to inform him of the country's discovery, he considered the occasion opportune to request of the monarch "a good job for his nephew".[72]

The lack of the rule of law in Brazil also finds its early roots in Portugal's disdain for individual freedom and initiative. In Portugal's traditional Catholic hierarchy, the class of entrepreneurs (traders) was ranked lowest on the social scale. In that small country of the Iberian peninsula, "as in Communist China and Marxist Russia, the merchant was regarded as a parasitic and profiteering middle-man, resolved to enrich himself at the expanse of his fellow-men".[73] During colonial times, therefore, the Portuguese Crown possessed an enormous variety of commercial monopolies, ranging from the importation of sugar to the control of the soap industry. Regional and district monopolies were granted to favored individuals and courtiers arbitrarily.[74] According to Boxer:

> It would take too long to enumerate all the overseas sources of wealth which were exploited by the Crown at one time or another, whether in the form of a (theoretically) rigorous monopoly, or a percentage of the profits, or in the way of Customs duties and export and import dues … Perhaps more than any other country, it was a long-established practice in Portugal for the Crown … to farm out the smallest public offices which might be expected to produce any revenue; and the same procedure was followed in Portuguese Brazil.[75]

After the country's independence from Portugal, on September 7, 1822, complaints over excessive state interference and regulation were still commonplace. As early as 1853, exasperated entrepreneurs like the Viscount of Mauá often complained that "everything is expected from the government and that individual initiative does not exist".[76] He argued that economic activities entirely depended on official sensibilities to continue their existence, and that people were much inclined to regard the state as the tutor or paternal protector of society.[77] As a result, even the most successful businesspeople were no more than clients of the landed gentry who controlled the state, and who expected to receive "unbearable tutelage of the government".[78] Such individuals saw this as an easier means of acquiring wealth than through work and production. Thus, in 1870, a prominent politician, Tavares Bastos, explained that there existed amongst his fellow Brazilians a certain fear of companies, which he

---

[70] DaMatta, *supra* note 51. At 296.

[71] Clapham, *supra* note 65. At 5.

[72] Emilio E. Dellasoppa, *Corruption in Brazilian Society: An Overview* (2001) at 2.

[73] Boxer, C.R., *The Portuguese Seaborne Empire (1415–1835)* (London: Hutchinson, 1969) at 319.

[74] *Id.*, at 321.

[75] *Id.*, at 322.

[76] Graham, Richard; *Britain and the Onset of Modernization in Brazil: 1815–1914* (Cambridge: Cambridge University Press, 1968) at 223.

[77] *Id.*, at 216.

[78] José Ignácio Silveira da Motta, *Degeneração do Sistema Representativo* (1869) at 21.

directly associated with an "anachronistic tradition of despotism that denies the modern spirit of liberty".[79]

This reality has not substantially changed over the years. Indeed, the country's most successful businesspeople remain the neo-mercantilists, who practice any sort of cartel capitalism with the state. Under the pretext of protecting so-called national interest, these supposed entrepreneurs often request privileged conditions from the Brazilian government, such as preferential interest rates and special loans from state banks and other public agencies, which they quite often do not have to repay. As a result, writes William Prillaman, "aspiring entrepreneurs are unable to seek relief, because economic decision-making is based on political concerns rather than rational dictates of the rule of law".[80]

20.7 Statism and Corruption

There is a visible link in Brazil between statism and corruption.[81] Everybody knows that too much state intervention may lead to more opportunities for corruption, since a big government may provide a fertile breeding ground for the abuse of power. This is particularly true in societies like Brazil's, where true power seems to reside in the ability of some individuals to operate above the law. As Montaner observes, when speaking about the reality of Latin American countries such as Brazil, "it is as if politicians were not elected to obey the laws but rather to be autocrats who measure their prestige by the laws they are able to violate".[82] According to Dellasoppa:

> In Brazil, we can say that [corruption] is endemic, closely related with the political system, especially with clientelistic relations; it pervades all of Brazilian society at different levels of institutions and officials and is extremely difficult to fight, so impunity is the probable end of most cases, even the most noted scandals.[83]

Once again, the problem has deep historical roots. Portuguese colonizers were, more than any other people, adherents of the rule that "a gift makes room for a person".[84] Colonial documents reveal that most public officers, including high-ranking authorities, were constantly engaged in robberies, injuries, murders, rapes, etc. All such things, reports an official document of the time, were inflicted upon the population "without

---

[79] Aureliano Candido Tavares Bastos, *A Província: Estudo sobre a Descentralização no Brasil* (1870) at 264.

[80] Prillaman, *supra* note 47. At. 9.

[81] The etymological root of the word corruption comes from the Latin *corruptus*, which literally means the act of breaking an object. Conceptually, it describes any situation of abuse of power for private gains by means of fraud, bribery, extortion (payment for favourable government decisions) and embezzlement (theft of state funds).

[82] Montaner, Carlos Alberto, *Culture and the Behaviour of Elites in Latin America*, From: L.E. Harrison and S. Huntington (eds.); 'Culture Matters: How Values Shape Human Progress' (New York: Basic Books, 2000) at 58.

[83] Dellasopa, Emilio E.; *Corruption in Brazilian Society: An Overview* (Rio de Janeiro: FSS/UERJ, 2001) at 3.

[84] Boxer, *supra* note 72. At 209.

fear of God and the King".[85] Such complaints, indeed, were a common theme in official correspondence over three centuries of colonial rule in Brazil. Thus, when King John IV (1640–56) asked Antônio Vieira in the 1640s whether or not the region of Maranhão should be separated from the province of Pará, the outspoken Jesuit advised the king to keep things just as they were, reminding him that "one thief in a public office is a lesser evil than two".[86] Likewise, an English woman commented in the 1820s that the abuse of power on the part of the colonial rulers "was an evil that affected Brazil generally". She then explained that "the Governors [of Brazil] were … virtually free from any responsibility", and that "the corrupt administration of the laws kept pace with the vices and irregularities of the government".[87]

Since even the colonial governors behaved in such an appalling way, most of the judges, magistrates, bailiffs, and treasury officials did also.[88] It is commonly said that even a morally upright Portuguese would abandon his morals upon migrating to Brazil, only to behave again in a decent manner if he were ever to return to Europe.[89] As a result, Brazilians became accustomed to the prevalence of widespread corruption and impunity. Both in folklore and in practice, they have 'traditionally regarded a degree of corruption as normal'.[90] Curiously, one of the principal reasons proffered by military leaders for ousting President João Goulart on March 31, 1964, was the need to end corruption. Nevertheless, two decades after their coup it would seem that corruption had increased all the more during their watch. Those army officers took power promising to eliminate corruption, but they were forced 20 years later to relinquish that power, due, among other things, to "increased levels of corruption, and the erosion of the armed forces institutional prestige".[91]

Since the new democratic period began, in March 1985, corruption has not diminished but rather probably increased. Indeed, corruption reached unprecedented levels during the administration of President Lula da Silva (2002–2010).[92] No other government in the country's history had more top party-leaders, congressmen, ministers, and functionaries under investigation for fraud in such a brief period of time.[93]

---

[85] *Id.*, at 144.

[86] *Id.*, at 324.

[87] Maria Dundas Graham (Lady Maria Calcott), *Journal of a Voyage to Brazil and Residence There. During Part of the Years 1821, 1822, 1823* (1969) at 30.

[88] Diffie, Bailey W. and Winius, George D.; *Foundations of the Portuguese Empire 1415–1580* (Minneapolis: Minnesota University Press, 1977) at 419.

[89] *Id.*

[90] Gordon, Lincoln; *Brazil's Second Chance: En Route Toward the First World* (Washington, D.C.: Brookings Institution Press, 2001) at 159.

[91] Alana Gutierrez, "Bush Should Use Brazil's Corruption to Show Real Friendship", Brazzil Magazine, September 14, 2005, available at: http://www.brazzil.com/content/view/9399/76/

[92] John Otis, "Government Corruption at New Heights in Brazil", Houston Chronicle, October 16, 2005, available at: http://www.chron.com/cs/CDA/ssistory.mpl/headline/world/3399089

[93] According to sociology professor James Petras, "every sector of President Lula's Workers' Party [was] implicated in bribery, fraud, vote buying, theft of public funds, failure to report illicit campaign financing, and a host of other felonious behaviour … All of Lula's closest and most important advisers, congressional leaders and party bosses [were involved in] illegal large-scale transfers of funds into electoral campaigns, private enrichment, and financing full time functionaries" – James

Day after day, the local media is full of reports on corruption involving politicians and public officers. Although this might be considered a positive sign that the country still has a free and investigative press to denounce corruption, its persistence after all these years of formal democracy "indicates rather the high degree of impunity due to a generalised tolerance of an complicity with the phenomenon".[94] Unfortunately, in Brazil, as Gutierrez correctly states,

> there truly is no deterrence from venality because the political elite is rarely charged or punished for it. This indicates that there is a serious failing when it comes to respecting the rule of law. As a result, political credibility and respect for policy-making, as well as compliance with already existing laws that act as a shield against unlawful behavior, become invalid. In the end, an inefficient state is born from the ashes of immorality and injustice.[95]

20.8 Conclusion

This chapter is a modest attempt to explain significant aspects of Brazil's legal culture and society. It focused on explaining how the informal rules of society can differ remarkably from what one may have supposed had they simply looked at the statute books. Whereas in all countries one may observe certain gaps separating the written law and the law as it is practiced, these gaps are much wider in a country like Brazil than in countries like Australia and the United States. Hence, the problem facing the rule of law in Brazil stems not only from the absence of "good" laws, though there are indeed many bad laws in the country; the problem, rather, stems far more from factors that are extra-legal and, ultimately, sociological in nature, which confirms the assumption that the realization of the rule of law depends less on a "recipe for detailed institutional design" than on a 'cluster of values' that entails a willingness by everyone to fulfil their general legal obligations.[96]

This chapter offers a broad account of the intrinsic relationship between law, politics and culture within the context of Brazilian society. The intention has been to establish whether the significant absence of the rule of law in Brazil might be as much a socio-political problem as it is a legal-institutional one.[97] It explores the many instances in which certain values have created considerable obstacles to the realization of the rule of law in the country. As a matter of empirical fact, these values have not assisted Brazilians to develop a culture of legality to underpin the ideal of the rule of law. Instead, they seem to provide manifold incentives for widespread corruption, influence-peddling, and red tape. Such values need to be more seriously reconsidered and remedial action needs to be taken. This situation has benefitted only a small minority of privileged individuals at the expense of the rule of law and society as a whole.

Petras, "Lula's Workers Regime Plummets in Stew of Corruption", Counterpunch, July 30–31, 2005, available at: http://www.counterpunch.org/petras08012005.html

[94] Carvalho, José Murilo de, *The Struggle for Democracy in Brazil: Possible Lessons for Nigeria*, (Port Harcourt: SEPHIS/University of Port Harcourt, 2000) at 11.

[95] *Id.*

[96] Krygier, *supra* note 21. At 13404.

[97] Krygier, *supra* note 22. At 52.

Chapter 21
The Rule of Law and the United Nations

Edric Selous and Giovanni Bassu

Abstract This chapter explores the evolution of the rule of law from the perspective of the United Nations. The chapter describes the foundations of the principle, its role at both international and national levels and its importance across all three pillars of the organization: peace and security, human rights and development. The history of the rule of law is described through the work of the General Assembly and the Security Council, and the policy and programmatic activities of the United Nations system. The chapter concludes by looking at the Secretary-General's initiatives to enhance coordination in rule of law support and to ensure consideration of the rule of law as a horizontal theme and not a vertical pillar of intervention.

21.1 The Foundations

The rule of law is a universal concept which existed long before the United Nations. Around the world and throughout history, individuals, communities and States have worked towards containing individual and state power through laws. The Code of Hammourabi, promulgated by the King of Babylon around 1760 BC, is one of the first examples of the codification of law, publicly promulgated and of application to the ruler. In the Arab world, a rich tradition of Islamic law embraced the notion of the supremacy of law. Core principles of holding government authority to account and placing the wishes of the populace before the rulers, can be found amid the

The views expressed herein are those of the authors and do not necessarily reflect the views of the United Nations.

E. Selous (✉) • G. Bassu
Rule of Law Unit, Executive Office of the Secretary-General
at the United Nations, New York, USA
e-mail: selous@un.org; bassu@un.org

J.R. Silkenat et al. (eds.), *The Legal Doctrines of the Rule of Law and the Legal State (Rechtsstaat)*, Ius Gentium: Comparative Perspectives on Law and Justice 38,
DOI 10.1007/978-3-319-05585-5_21,

main moral and philosophical traditions across the Asian continent, including in Confucianism. In the Anglo-American context, the Magna Carta of 1215 emphasized the importance of the independence of the judiciary and the role of judicial process as fundamental characteristics of the rule of law. In continental Europe, notions of rule of law focused on the nature of the State, particularly on the role of constitutionalism. The rule of law has developed as a concept in opposition to the "rule of man"; governance based on non-arbitrary rules and power constrained by laws.

In the twenty-first century, the rule of law has come to describe a complex set of social, political and economic realities that govern human and state interaction and the exercise of power. Rule of law is synonymous with global governance founded in the principles of the United Nations Charter and is closely linked to the principles of justice, accountability, and fairness in the protection and vindication of rights and the prevention and punishment of wrongs. It is also closely tied to the human rights doctrine, to constitutionalism and to democracy.

21.2 The Rule of Law at the International and National Levels

The rule of law applies within and between States. At the international level, the rule of law means that States do not act arbitrarily towards each other, but in conformity with pre-agreed rules of international law. At the heart of these rules, akin to an international constitution, is the United Nations Charter.

In the Preamble to the United Nations Charter, one of the aims of the United Nations is to "establish conditions under which justice and respect for the obligations arising from treaties and other sources of international law can be maintained". Under Article 1, one of the primary purposes of the Organization is "to maintain international peace and security… and to bring about by peaceful means, and in conformity with the principles of justice and international law, adjustment or settlement of international disputes or situations which might lead to a breach of the peace." This is the normative basis for friendly relations between States.

Aside from the Charter, the United Nations has played a central role in developing the wider corpus of international law, which guides the actions of States in all realms, from as diverse subjects as extradition to commercial relations. The body of international norms and standards developed under the auspices of the United Nations remains one of the Organization's greatest achievements. The Secretary-General is the repository of numerous treaties, and the United Nations' International Law Commission, together with the Sixth Committee of the General Assembly are the inter-governmental entities in which international treaty-based law is principally developed. A comprehensive multilateral system based on agreed laws is essential to addressing the multifaceted and interconnected challenges facing our world. The United Nations is truly at the centre of this work.

One of the central features of the rule of law at the international level is the ability of Member States to have recourse to international adjudicative mechanisms to settle disputes peacefully and without recourse to the use of force. The International Court of Justice is established as the principal judicial organ of the United Nations and remains the only judicial forum before which Member States can bring virtually any legal dispute concerning international law. No other forum's jurisdiction is potentially as far-reaching as that of the Court. Yet, it is competent to hear a case only if the States concerned have accepted its jurisdiction. Such an acceptance can take the form of the conclusion of an *ad hoc* agreement to submit a specific dispute to the Court or of a jurisdictional clause of a treaty. The Court's jurisdiction can also derive from the optional declarations accepting such jurisdiction as compulsory. Such optional declarations are the best way of ensuring that all inter-State disputes are settled peacefully. To date, however, only 70 Member States have accepted as compulsory the jurisdiction of the Court. For this reason, the Secretary-General has consistently and regularly called on those States who have not yet done so to accept the compulsory jurisdiction of the Court.

In addition, the General Assembly and the Security Council have the ability to refer any legal question to the Court for an advisory opinion, as do other organs of the United Nations and the specialized agencies when authorized to do so by the General Assembly.[1] This enables the principal organs of the United Nations to ensure that any action that they take is in accordance with the Charter and international law, increasing the legitimacy of their actions. In practice, however, these advisory opinions are rarely sought. The Secretary-General has therefore also recommended that the General Assembly, the Security Council and other organs of the United Nations commit themselves to making greater use of their ability to request advisory opinions from the International Court of Justice. Indeed, it is important for the principal organs of the United Nations to fully adhere to applicable international law and basic rule of law principles to ensure the legitimacy of their actions.

The rule of law at the international level is closely connected with the rule of law at the national level. Much of international law, for instance treaties relating to human rights, relies on being implemented nationally for its effectiveness. For the United Nations, adhering to the rule of law at the national level means that all persons and institutions, including the State, are accountable to laws that must be equally applied to all, and must equally protect all without discrimination.

These laws should be administered by an independent and impartial judicial system, which creates a separation of powers in the structure of the State. Laws must also be just, fair and equitable, and therefore in conformity with international human rights norms. Finally, laws must be publicly consulted and promulgated, which brings in a strong democratic element.

[1] Charter of the United Nations, Article 96.

21.3 The Rule of Law, Peace and Security, Human Rights and Development

The rule of law is central to all of the work of the United Nations: peace and security, development and human rights. In the peace and security area, it is increasingly recognised that States marked by ineffective governance, repressive policies, poverty, high rates of violent crime and impunity pose significant threats to international peace and security. Deep capacity deficits in state justice and security institutions, exacerbated by widespread corruption and political interference, lead to diminishing levels of citizen security and economic opportunity. Resentment, distrust and hostility towards the Government grow. Radicalised movements often stand ready to mobilise and incite marginalised groups, unemployed youth and criminal elements to challenge the established order through violent means. Transnational organized crime emerges in parallel with increasing instability, increasing violence, and further undermining the legitimacy and capacity of state institutions. Such transnational criminal networks escape national borders and sow instability across entire regions.

In the last years, we have seen this playing out in the Middle East which continues to be over-run by civil conflict, from Tunisia, to Egypt to Syria. These break-downs in governance, violation of rights and cycles of violence, all of which impact national, regional and international peace and security, are underpinned by weak institutions and an absence of the rule of law. The establishment and maintenance of the rule of law within states is therefore fundamental to the maintenance of peace and security.

Similarly, the role of the rule of law in sustainable development at the national level has been clearly acknowledged. Progress in the rule of law furthers development, which in turn furthers the rule of law. The rule of law is essential for inclusive economic growth. It is both a goal in itself and a framework for development outcomes. The rule of law provides legal systems that increase contractual security, lowers levels of corruption, and allows for the timely, transparent and predictable resolution of disputes. The rule of law enhances personal security and good governance; widens access to public services; and improves a sustainable environment and natural resource management.

These linkages are widely recognised. All States agree that the rule of law and development are strongly interrelated and mutually reinforcing. The High-level Panel of Eminent Persons on the Post-2015 Development Agenda convened by the Secretary-General to advise him has endorsed this approach, and has included the rule of law as an issue supporting a number of development outcomes in its final Report to the Secretary-General.[2] The Secretary-General's subsequent report to the General Assembly, "A Life of Dignity for All", also calls for building peace and effective governance based on the rule of law and sound institutions. After consideration of the Secretary-General's Report, the Outcome Document adopted at the

[2] Report of the High-Level Panel of Eminent Persons on the Post-15 Development Agenda, *A New Global Partnership: Eradicate Poverty and Transform Economies Through Sustainable Development,* May 2013, particularly Goals 1, 2, 10, and 11.

September 2012 Special Event of the General Assembly on the MDGs also reaffirms "the importance of promoting human rights, good governance, the rule of law, transparency and accountability at all levels."[3] Finally, an Economic and Social Council (ECOSOC) resolution passed by the Third Committee of the General Assembly reaffirms the place of the rule of law, crime prevention and criminal justice in the development agenda beyond 2015.[4]

In addition, a number of non-governmental organizations, other international organizations and academics have similarly supported this important linkage. In 2008, the International Commission on Legal Empowerment of the Poor estimated that as many as four billion people live outside the protection of the law.[5] People are threatened by violence in countries in which governance has broken down and conflict has erupted, and are unable to access criminal justice systems that are lacking in capacity, are overloaded or corrupt. Additionally, for many citizens of our world, a weak or absent rule of law means that they live daily in poverty, lack recognition of their political, civil, social or economic rights, and do not have the dignity nor the opportunity to which all are entitled.

The importance of the rule of law in underpinning inclusive growth is especially salient in countries affected by conflict and fragility, as recognised by the 2011 World Bank Development Report.[6] The Report makes clear that conflict, crime and violence are major barriers to development in conflict affected and fragile settings. On the one hand, perceptions of injustice that arise across sectors are major sources of stress that can lead to conflict. On the other hand, justice systems play an important role in providing both the legitimate processes for the resolution of disputes that may otherwise lead to violence, and disincentives for crime.

Finally, in the area of human rights, where international norms fundamentally implicate the individual, the rule of law is inherently necessary. Rights are empty words in the absence of a legal order in which they can be realised. The rule of law provides a framework in which the arbitrary exercise of power is subjected to agreed rules, guaranteeing protection of both collective and individual civil, political, cultural, social and economic rights. Where rights are violated, the rule of law provides a means of redress. The rule of law is the vehicle for the promotion and protection of all human rights.

This clear inter-connection with the human rights framework is the reason why the phrase "rule of law" first appeared in United Nations history in the Universal Declaration of Human Rights of 1948, the historic international recognition that all human beings have fundamental rights and freedoms. In its preamble, the Declaration recognizes that "… it is essential, if man is not to be compelled to have

[3] Outcome Document, 2012 Special Event of the General Assembly on the MDGs.

[4] 'The rule of law, crime prevention and criminal justice in the United Nations development agenda beyond 2015', A/RES/68/188.

[5] Commission on Legal Empowerment of the Poor (2008), Making the Law Work for Everyone, Volume I in the Report of the Commission, United Nations, New York. WDR (2011), 218–220.

[6] The World Bank, World Development Report 2011: Conflict, Security and Development (2011).

recourse, as a last resort, to rebellion against tyranny and oppression, that human rights should be protected by the rule of law…"[7]

21.4 The Rule of Law and the General Assembly

Picking up the reference to the rule of law in the Universal Declaration, the United Nations General Assembly first considered the rule of law at its World Conference on Human Rights in Vienna in 1993, when a programme of action was adopted calling on the United Nations to establish a comprehensive programme to strengthen national structures that have a direct impact on the observance of human rights and the maintenance of the rule of law.[8] Following the Vienna World Conference, the Third Committee of the General Assembly, dedicated to human rights, adopted yearly resolutions on the rule of law until 2002.

Whilst this intrinsic link with the human rights agenda was drawn early, the General Assembly also considered the importance of the rule of law in respect of its other business. The Millennium Declaration, highlighted the importance of the rule of law for international peace and security, identifying key objectives of "strengthen[ing] respect for the rule of law in international as in national affairs and, in particular, to ensure compliance by Member States with the decisions of the International Court of Justice, in compliance with the Charter of the United Nations, in cases to which they are parties" and "ensur[ing] the implementation, by States Parties, of treaties in areas such as arms control and disarmament and of international humanitarian law and human rights law."[9] The Declaration also affirmed that Member States would "spare no effort to promote democracy and strengthen the rule of law, as well as respect for all internationally recognized human rights and fundamental freedoms, including the right to development."[10]

The United Nations World Summit in September 2005 unanimously recognized the need for "universal adherence to and implementation of the rule of law at both the national and international levels" and reaffirmed Member States commitment to "an international order based on the rule of law and international law."[11] The rule of law was acknowledged as an essential component of development, as well as peace and security, human rights and good governance. Member States recognized that the rule of law belongs to the universal and indivisible core values and principles of the United Nations.

---

[7] Universal Declaration of Human Rights, General Assembly resolution 217 A (III), Preamble.

[8] Vienna Declaration and Programme of Action, adopted by the World Conference on Human Rights in Vienna, 25 June 1993, paragraph 69.

[9] United Nations General Assembly, 'United Nations Millennium Declaration', A/RES/55/2, 18 September 2000, paragraph 9.

[10] *Id.*, paragraph 24.

[11] United Nations General Assembly, '2005 World Summit Outcome', A/RES/60/1, 24 October 2005, paragraph 134(a).

The General Assembly has also played a central role in developing a normative framework for the prevention of atrocities in developing the notion of the Responsibility to Protect. The commission of the most serious international crimes, such as genocide and crimes against humanity, breach the rule of law at its most fundamental level, and require a response at both the national and at the international levels. The concept of humanitarian intervention, to put a stop to these atrocity crimes, was first raised by the United Kingdom in the context of NATO's intervention in Kosovo in 1999. In order to ensure that international law was in a position to respond to similar situations in the future, the Canadian Government put together an International Commission on Intervention and State Sovereignty, which developed the outline of a Responsibility to Protect. This was further discussed at the 2005 World Summit, and in its Outcome document Member States agreed that "[e]ach individual State has the responsibility to protect its populations from genocide, war crimes, ethnic cleansing and crimes against humanity"[12] and that "[t]he international community, through the United Nations, also has the responsibility… to help to protect populations" from those crimes.[13]

In 2009, the Secretary-General provided a report on the need to develop a United Nations strategy to implement the responsibility to protect, outlining three pillars for advancing the issue: pillar one on the responsibility of States to protect their own populations; pillar two on international assistance and capacity-building to assist States to protect their populations; and pillar three on a timely and decisive response where States are not able or willing to protect their populations. The rule of law is critical to supporting each of these three identified pillars. In terms of the first, it is important that States become parties to relevant international instruments on human rights, international humanitarian law and refugee law, and to the ICC Statute, and international obligations need to be reflected in national laws. Under the second pillar, United Nations rule of law assistance at the national level can help build capacity to support the rule of law. Finally, under the third pillar, it is important to emphasize all of the tools available to Member States under the Charter, in Chapters VI, VII and VIII. The responsibility to protect does not create a new basis for the use of force outside of those contained in international law but provides a robust framework for national priorities and international cooperation to address the worst crimes known to humankind.

The work of the General Assembly on the rule of law reached a high point on 24 September 2012, when it held the first ever High-level Meeting specifically devoted to the rule of law, and adopted a Declaration on the Rule of Law at the National and International Levels (A/RES/37/1). More than 30 Presidents and Prime Ministers, and more than 30 Ministers of Government attended this important plenary meeting of the General Assembly.

The Declaration reaffirms Member States' commitment to the rule of law and its fundamental importance for political dialogue and cooperation among all States.

---

[12] United Nations General Assembly, '2005 World Summit Outcome', A/RES/60/1, 24 October 2005, paragraph 138.

[13] *Id.*, paragraph 139.

Notably, Member States agreed to the building blocks of the rule of law, acknowledging that adhering to the rule of law means that "all persons, institutions and entities, public and private, including the State itself, are accountable to just, fair and equitable laws and are entitled without discrimination to equal protection of the law."[14] They also agreed that laws should be administered by an independent and impartial judicial system.

The Declaration was also important in tracing the contours of the rule of law at both the national and international levels and in exploring its breadth, as it covers areas such as humanitarian law and human rights, informal justice systems and transitional justice, support for international courts and tribunals, and domestic criminal justice processes, transnational organized crime and terrorism, corruption and international trade.

The High-level Meeting reaffirmed the importance of the rule of law in the international agenda, and the Declaration that was adopted is a new, essential tool in the diplomatic toolbox of the United Nations for its work across the spectrum of its activities.

Notably, the Declaration also recognized that the rule of law applied to the United Nations itself, and that respect for and promotion of the rule of law and justice should guide all of its activities and accord predictability and legitimacy to its actions.[15] This reference was called for especially by some States which query how much the United Nations' principal organs, including the Security Council are bound by the rule of law.

21.5 The Rule of Law and the Security Council

Aside from a preambular reference to the deterioration of law and order in the Congo in 1961, the Security Council first used the concept of the "rule of law" in 1996 in resolution 1040 where it expressed its support for the Secretary-General's efforts to promote "national reconciliation, democracy, security and the rule of law" in Burundi. Since that time, the rule of law has become a standard tool in the Security Council's peacebuilding toolbox and numerous peace operations have had important rule of law components.

The rule of law has featured in the work of the Security Council in three principal ways: first, as noted above, the rule of law has been incorporated into the Council's work on country-specific issues; secondly, the Council has used the rule of law in support of thematic issues on which there have been resolutions and statements; and finally, the Council has been guided more generally by the rule of law in the course of its work.

[14] Declaration of the High-level Meeting of the General Assembly on the Rule of Law at the National and International Levels (A/RES/37/1), paragraph 2.

[15] *Id.*, paragraph 2.

The use of the rule of law by the Council to support its peacebuilding work stands to reason, as particularly in post-conflict States, the rule of law is crucial to consolidating political settlements and enabling a fragile peace to take hold. It fosters the development of norms and social practices, and ensures the growth of strong institutions central to good governance.

The Council has mandated support for the rule of law in many peacekeeping and political missions, including in Afghanistan, Burundi, the Central African Republic, Chad, Cote d'Ivoire, the Democratic Republic of the Congo, Guinea-Bissau, Haiti, Iraq, Liberia, Sierra Leone, South Sudan, the Sudan and Timor-Leste. There are currently 18 Security Council mission mandates that include strengthening the rule of law. In two situations, Kosovo and Timor-Leste (1999–2002), the United Nations has had direct responsibility for the administration of justice, including control of police and prison services.[16]

Rule of law activities have also been integrated into thematic Council resolutions and presidential statements, as well as reports of the Secretary-General to the Council. The Council held its first thematic debate on the rule of law in 2003 on "Justice and the Rule of Law: The United Nations Role".[17] In the presidential statement from the United Kingdom, following the debate, the Council highlighted the relevance of the rule of law in its work in areas such as protection of civilians, peacekeeping and international criminal justice, and welcomed the preparation of a report by the Secretary-General. In 2004, the Secretary-General submitted his report on "The Rule of Law and Transitional Justice in Conflict and Post-Conflict Societies",[18] including recommendations for further work of the Council. Similar debates followed in 2006, 2010, 2011 and 2012. The most recent report of the Secretary-General to the Security Council looks at measuring the effectiveness of the support provided by the United Nations system for the promotion of the rule of law in conflict and post-conflict situations.[19]

The Security Council has also been central to strengthening the rule of law by promoting accountability for the most serious international crimes. In the aftermath of such crimes, ensuring accountability and providing victims with the right to an effective remedy (giving redress and adequate reparations for the atrocities committed against them) are key to increasing public trust in justice and security institutions, and to building the rule of law and sustainable peace.

The conflicts in the early to mid-1990s in the former Yugoslavia and Rwanda sparked a global outrage at the lack of effective tools to both prevent, and to deal with the aftermath of the horrible crimes that were perpetrated on those civilian populations. The Security Council was at the centre of these difficult debates, and ended up playing a fundamental role in ensuring accountability for the perpetrators of these crimes. Acting under Chapter VII of the Charter, and picking up where

[16] Similar powers were exercised in Bosnia and Herzegovina through the Office of the High Representative from 1996.

[17] S/PV.4833.

[18] S/2004/616.

[19] S/2013/341.

Nuremberg left off, the Security Council established the International Criminal Tribunals for the former Yugoslavia and Rwanda, finding that accountability was essential for the maintenance of international peace and security. The Security Council developed the jurisdiction and mandates of the *ad hoc* tribunals, making a historic contribution to the development of international criminal law.

Whilst the centre of gravity for accountability efforts has now shifted to the International Criminal Court, the role of the Security Council in moving forward the principle of accountability for serious international crimes, and for highlighting their link with international peace and security cannot be underestimated. In addition, the Security Council still has a place within the new system of international criminal justice set up under the Rome Statute, with its power to refer cases to the International Criminal Court; a power which they have exercised in respect of the situations in Darfur and in Libya. Article 16 of the Rome Statute of the International Criminal Court also allows for a deferral of investigation or prosecution by the Security Council in a resolution under Chapter VII of the Charter. These crucial connections will guarantee that the issue of criminal accountability for serious crimes is closely linked to international peace and security in the future.

The Security Council has also been guided by the rule of law in the course of other resolutions, taking into account the due process rights of those affected by Council measures, such as resort to sanctions under Chapter VII. In 2009, the Security Council established an Ombudsperson to review requests from individuals, groups, undertakings or entities seeking to be removed from the Al-Qaida sanctions list of the Security Council's Al-Qaida Sanctions Committee. The mandate of the Ombudsperson was most recently extended in December 2012. This is an area of continued evolving practice as the Council faces pressure from States and others to ensure the rule of law is respected in its own work.

21.6 The Rule of Law and the United Nations System

Much of the operational work of assisting Member States in strengthening the rule of law is done by the United Nations Secretariat, together with its Funds and Programmes and their extensive network of field presences. The United Nations provides rule of law assistance to over 150 Member States. These activities take place in several contexts, including development, conflict, post-conflict and peacebuilding situations. Three or more United Nations entities currently engage in rule of law activities in at least 70 countries, and 5 or more entities in over 25 countries.

The breadth of the work in the area of the rule of law undertaken by the United Nations system in-country is wide; it includes support for the domestic implementation of international normative frameworks, drafting of constitutions and legislative reform, the strengthening of institutions, including in the areas of policing, justice and corrections, as well as the provision of and support to transitional justice processes.

The work of the United Nations is based operationally on technical assistance and capacity-building carried out for the benefit of Member States, at their request or as mandated by the Security Council, and in accordance with national policies and priorities. The United Nations works to eschew one-size-fits-all formulas and foreign imported models, and instead to base support on local aspirations and national priorities. The guiding principles for United Nations rule of law assistance include basing assistance on international norms and standards, taking into account the political context and basing assistance on the unique country context. Assistance aims to advance human rights and gender justice, ensure national ownership, and support national reform constituencies. The United Nations works to ensure a coherent and comprehensive approach to assistance and to engage in effective coordination and partnerships.

21.7 Enhanced Coordination in Rule of Law Support

Given the number of tasks and United Nations actors involved, there has been a growing need to ensure a coordinated and strategic approach to the work of the United Nations. In the past, institutional arrangements have not allowed the organization to deliver as efficiently or effectively as it might have. In 2012, the Secretary-General created a new three-tier system to strengthen the Organization's ability to support the rule of law. At the field level, support was fragmented and did not have an overall lead for United Nations rule of law assistance. United Nations field leadership are now responsible and accountable for guiding and overseeing United Nations rule of law strategies, resolving political obstacles and coordinating United Nations country support on the rule of law. While responsibility for programme implementation is left firmly in the hands of the different United Nations entities, these entities are also required to cooperate with senior field leadership.

At the Headquarters level, support to the field was also fragmented by entity, with different organizations leading on different components of the rule of law. The Secretary-General has now designated the Department of Peacekeeping Operations and the United Nations Development Programme (UNDP) as the joint Global Focal Point for the police, justice and corrections areas in the rule of law in post-conflict and other crisis situations, to provide support to the field.

At the highest strategic level, the Deputy Secretary-General heads the inter-agency Rule of Law Coordination and Resource Group and has been given the overall leadership role for the rule of law. This structure will ensure that the United Nations is able to foresee new opportunities, address new challenges and develop linkages with a broad range of stakeholders.

21.8 Conclusion

The rule of law permeates all of the work of the Organization. United Nations support has typically focused on traditional rule of law areas, such as justice and security needs including infrastructure and capacity building in courts, police and corrections institutions. All such rule of law support is critical. However, rule of law challenges in the twenty-first century are of far greater breadth. The new frontier of rule of law support is to ensure that the rule of law is considered as a horizontal theme, not as a vertical pillar of intervention.

In furtherance of this, the Secretary-General has made it a priority to mainstream the rule of law in all the work of the United Nations. He is engaging the whole United Nations system so that it can deliver more effectively by systematically considering the rule of law as a cross-cutting theme in its support to Member States in the areas of peace and security, development and human rights.

Editors

James R. Silkenat, a partner in Sullivan & Worcester's New York office, is a member of the firm's Corporate Department and is President of the 400,000 member American Bar Association. His primary focus is on international joint ventures, mergers and acquisitions, privatizations, project finance transactions (in developed and developing countries) and private equity investment funds. Mr. Silkenat has substantive industry experience in energy, hotels, manufacturing, transportation and telecommunications. Mr. Silkenat is a member of the Council on Foreign Relations and of the American Law Institute, has served as a Fellow in the U.S. State Department Scholar/Diplomat Program, and was a Fellow of the National Endowment for the Humanities. He is also a Life Fellow of the American Bar Foundation and has served as National Chair of the Fellows. He is a director of the World Justice Project. In 2000, he received the Outstanding Alumni Award for Career Achievement from Drury University and in 2007 he received the Lifetime Achievement Award from the ABA Section of International Law.

James E. Hickey, Jr. is Professor of Law and former Director of International Programs at Maurice A. Deane School of Law, Hofstra University, where he teaches energy and international law courses. He has twice been a Visiting Fellow at the Lauterpacht Centre for International Law at Cambridge University. He has practiced energy and international law with two Washington D.C. law firms. He is past Chair of the ABA Special Committee on Electric Industry Restructuring. He has been a Consultant to the Energy Charter Secretariat in Brussels and a Special Assistant to the National Petroleum Council. He sits on the Book Publications Board of the ABA Section of Environment, Energy and Resources and is a Fellow of the American Bar Foundation. He has over 60 publications including four books. He holds a JD degree from the University of Georgia and a Ph.D. in International Law from the University of Cambridge (Jesus College) where he also taught international law. He has visited and taught at numerous universities around the world.

J.R. Silkenat et al. (eds.), *The Legal Doctrines of the Rule of Law and the Legal State (Rechtsstaat)*, Ius Gentium: Comparative Perspectives on Law and Justice 38,
DOI 10.1007/978-3-319-05585-5,

Peter D. Barenboim is an attorney whose areas of practice include criminal law, constitutional law, and banking law. He earned his law degree and Ph.D. in Law from Moscow State University. He is currently Council Member of the International Bar Association (London), First Vice President of the International Union (Commonwealth) of Advocates (Moscow) and Chairman of the International Commission of the Moscow City Chamber of Advocates. His publications include 30 books and over 250 other articles. He has lectured at law schools in the USA, France and Russia.

Contributors

T.R.S. Allan is the author of many books and papers on legal and constitutional theory including *Law, Liberty, and Justice: The Legal Foundations of British Constitutionalism* (Oxford: Clarendon Press, 1993), *Constitutional Justice: A Liberal Theory of the Rule of Law* (Oxford: Oxford University Press, 2001), and *The Sovereignty of Law: Freedom, Constitution, and Common Law* (Oxford: Oxford University Press, 2013). He has taught public law and jurisprudence at Cambridge since 1985.

Giovanni Bassu is the Senior Rule of Law Officer in the Rule of Law Unit in the Executive Office of the Secretary-General at the United Nations. Mr. Bassu has previously worked as the Special Adviser on External relations and Cooperation at the International Criminal Court, and with the Special Representative of the Secretary-General on the Extraordinary Chambers in the Courts of Cambodia, as well as with the UN Office of Legal Affairs. He spent time in Colombia with the United Nations High Commissioner for Refugees, and with the Delegation of the European Commission in Kenya. Mr. Bassu is a qualified solicitor in England and Wales, and has a Masters in Economics and Law from the University of Edinburgh, and in International Studies from the Johns Hopkins University School of Advanced International Studies.

Robin Charlow is a Professor of American Constitutional and Criminal Law at the Maurice A. Deane School of Law of Hofstra University, where she has received an award for her teaching. She has lectured and published in the United States and abroad on a wide range of topics, including rule of law, equality, law and religion, discrimination, and culpable mental states. She previously served as a federal appellate clerk, a criminal defense attorney, a legislative analyst, and a consultant on the formulation of the United States Sentencing Guidelines, and she currently sits on the Board of Directors of the Federal Defenders of New York.

Dmitry Dedov is a Judge of the European Court of Human Rights of the Council of Europe. He has been a Professor at Moscow State University and at the Center for Transnational Legal Studies and has served as an expert at the Russian

J.R. Silkenat et al. (eds.), *The Legal Doctrines of the Rule of Law and the Legal State (Rechtsstaat)*, Ius Gentium: Comparative Perspectives on Law and Justice 38,
DOI 10.1007/978-3-319-05585-5, © Springer International Publishing Switzerland 2014

Constitutional Court. He also has been a Judge at Russian Supreme Commercial Court. He completed his law studies and earned his PhD at Moscow State University Law School.

Hossein Esmaeili studied law at the University of Tehran and the University of New South Wales in Sydney, Australia. He is an Associate Professor of Law at Flinders University in Adelaide, Australia. He teaches, among other subjects, international law, comparative law, and property law. He has published articles on international law, and Islamic and Middle Eastern law, in leading law journals in Australia, Europe, and the United States. He is the author of *The Legal Regime of Offshore Oil Rigs in International Law* (Ashgate 2001), and the co-author of *Modern Perspectives on Islamic Law* (Edward Elgar, 2013).

Gadis A. Gadzhiev is a Judge on the Constitutional Court of the Russian Federation. He earned his PhD and graduated from the Lomonosov Moscow State University.

Rainer Grote is a Senior Research Fellow at the Max Planck Institute for Public Comparative Law and Public International Law in Heidelberg, Germany, and Adjunct Professor of Public Law at the University of Göttingen. He studied law at the universities of Bielefeld, Geneva, Göttingen and Edinburgh and holds a PhD from the University of Göttingen and a LL.M. from the University of Edinburgh. He teaches and writes in the fields of constitutional law, comparative law and public international law.

Jeffrey Kahn is an Associate Professor of Law at the Dedman School of Law at Southern Methodist University. He received his doctorate in politics from Oxford University and his degree in law from the University of Michigan. He is the author of *Federalism, Democratization, and the Rule of Law in Russia* (Oxford University Press) and numerous scholarly articles on Russian law, legal reform, and human rights.

Stephan Kirste is professor for Legal and Social Philosophy at the Department for Economic and Social Sciences in the Faculty of Law of the Paris Lodron University of Salzburg, Austria. He is president of the German Section of the International Association for Legal and Social Philosophy (IVR). He studied law, philosophy and history at the University of Freiburg i.Br., where he was promoted Dr. iur. and received the venia legendi for public law, philosophy of law, history of public law and sociology of law on the basis of his second thesis on public administrative law at the University of Heidelberg in 2004.

Matthias Kötter, Dr. jur. is a research associate at the WZB Social Science Center Berlin. His research focus is on German public law and on the social conditions of governance and the rule of law in diverse societies.

Dmitry V. Kravchenko is an Advocate of the Law Firm, Asnis and Partners (Russia). He is Vice-President of the Inter-Regional Non-governmental Foundation (Law Development Foundation – Russia) and is Head of the Young Lawyers Division of the Moscow Branch of the Association of Lawyers of Russia. He previously worked for the Deposit Insurance Agency of Russia. He earned his PhD from the Kutafin Moscow State Law Academy.

Martin Krygier is Gordon Samuels Professor of Law and Social Theory at the University of New South Wales, Adjunct Professor at the Regulatory Institutions Network, Australian National University, and a Fellow of the Australian Academy of Social Sciences. He writes extensively on the rule of law. He has edited and contributed to *Spreading Democracy and the Rule of Law?* (2006); *Rethinking the Rule of Law after Communism* (2005); *Community and Legality* (2002), *The Rule of Law after Communism* (1999), *Marxism and Communism. Posthumous Reflections on Politics, Society, and Law* (1994). His most recent book is *Philip Selznick. Ideals in the World,* (2012).

Aniceto Masferrer teaches legal history and comparative law as a Professor at the Faculty of Law, University of Valencia. He is the author of seven books (including *Spanish Legal Traditions: A Comparative Legal History Outline* (2nd ed. 2012,)) and the editor of 4, and more than 50 book chapters and articles. He has published extensively on criminal law from an historical and comparative perspective, as well as on the codification movement and fundamental rights in the Western legal tradition. He is the Chief Editor of *GLOSSAE. European Journal of Legal History* (http://www.glossae.eu) and the current president of the 'European Society for Comparative Legal History' (http://esclh.blogspot.com/).

James R. Maxeiner is Associate Professor of Law at the University of Baltimore, School of Law. In addition to law degrees in international legal affairs from Cornell and Georgetown, he holds a doctorate in law (Dr. jur.) from the University of Munich obtained while he was Max Rheinstein Fellow of the Alexander von Humboldt Foundation at the Max Planck Institute for Foreign and International Patent, Copyright and Competition Law. His email is jmaxeiner@ubalt.edu.

Nadia E. Nedzel is tenured professor teaching commercial law, both common law and civil law, at Southern University Law Center in Baton Rouge, Louisiana. She has written on comparative and international topics including Good Faith, Eminent Domain, and Unfair Trade actions. Her primary scholarship focuses on the Rule of Law as compared to its civilian counterparts. After receiving an undergraduate degree in English, French, Spanish, and Russian literature, Nadia studied Louisiana's civil law receiving her J.D. Magna Cum Laude. She clerked for Hon. Carl E. Stewart at the U.S. Fifth Circuit Court of Appeals, obtained her LL.M. from Northwestern University with honors, and practiced Admiralty and International Trade law. As Director of LL.M. Programs at Tulane Law School, she wrote a widely used textbook: Legal Reasoning, Research, and Writing for International Graduate Students.

Gianluigi Palombella (professor of Legal Philosophy, University of Parma and Distinguished Schuman Fellow, 2013, EUI) held visiting positions in U.S., Europe, Australia, and was Inaugural Fellow at the "Straus Institute" (NYU); published extensively on fundamental rights, constitutionalism, the rule of law. His last book is *E' possibile una legalità globale?* (Il Mulino, 2012), Among his recent works: *The Rule of law as an Institutional Ideal* (in Morlino & Palombella (eds), *Rule of law and Democracy*, Brill 2010); *The (re) Constitution of the Public in a Global Arena,* in Michelon, Walker (eds.), *After Public Law* (O.U.P. 2013).

Gunnar Folke Schuppert, Prof. Dr. jur. is professor emeritus at Humboldt-University of Berlin and former managing director of the WZB Rule of Law Center at the Social Science Center Berlin. His research focus is on German public law and theory of governance.

Mortimer N.S. Sellers is Regents Professor of the University System of Maryland and Director of the University of Baltimore Center for International and Comparative Law. He is president of the American branch of the International Society for the Philosophy of Law and Social Philosophy and co-editor (with Elizabeth Andersen) of the Cambridge University Press book series ASIL Studies in International Legal Theory.

Edric Selous is the Director of the Rule of Law Unit in the Executive Office of the Secretary-General at the United Nations. Mr Selous' background is as a practicing attorney in the UK. He joined the United Nations in 1993 and has held legal and policy positions both at Headquarters and in the Field. Mr. Selous has worked with the Department of Peacekeeping Operations and with the OECD on conflict affected and fragile States in the Balkans region and as a legal adviser with UNRWA in Gaza. He has also worked in the UN Office of Legal Affairs for 9 years, establishing a Unit handling judicial cooperation and accountability issues.

Yury A. Sharandin is Deputy Secretary General-Head of the legal Department at the Council of Federation of the Federal Assembly of the Russian Federation (High Chamber of the Russian Parliament). Previously, he was a Senator and the Chairman of the Constitutional Committee of the Council of Federation. He earned his PhD from the Lomonosov Moscow State University.

Anna Taitslin holds a PhD (University of Tasmania, 2004) and a JD (University of Canberra, 2011). Dr Taitslin is the author of *Controversies in Natural Law from Zeno to Grotius* (2010). Her recent publications include "The Competing Sources of Aquinas' Natural Law: Aristotle, Roman Law and the Early Christian Fathers", in *The Treads of Natural Law,* ed. F. J. Contreras (2013); "Private Law in the Shadow of Public Law", *Archiv für Rechts-und Sozialphilosophie-Beiheft*, II (2011) [with Murray Raff].

Paul Tiedemann, Dr. iur. Dr. phil. is a judge at the Administrative Court Frankfurt am Main, Honorable Professor at Justus-Liebig-University in Gießen and apl. Professor at Özyeğin University, Istanbul. He is director of the IARLJ Database (International Association of Refugee Law Judges) and founder and acting manager of the Refugee Law Clinic at the University Giessen. He is founding member of the Neue Richtervereinigung (New Association of Judges) and member of the International Association for Philosophy of Law and Social Philosophy (IVR).

Francois Venter has taught law since 1974 in the Faculty of Law in Potchefstroom, South Africa. During the constitutional negotiations and drafting process in 1993, which resulted in constitutionalism being established in South Africa, he served as convenor of the Technical Committee on Constitutional Affairs of the Multiparty Negotiation Process. He was president of the South African Law Deans' Association for 2009–2010. He publishes primarily in the field of constitutional comparison.

Dietmar von der Pfordten, is professor for philosophy of law and social philosophy at the University of Göttingen, Germany, and the director of the Section for Philosophy of Law and Social Philosophy. He was visiting scholar at Harvard, Columbia and New York University and visiting professor in the Netherlands and Italy. He is the author of several books, e. g. "Description, Evaluation, Praeskription", 1993, "Rechtsethik", 2. ed. 2011, "Menschenwürde, Recht und Staat bei Kant", 2009, "Normative Ethik", 2010, "Suche nach Einsicht", 2010, "Rechtsphilosophie. Eine Einführung", 2013. He has edited with Jaap Hage "Concepts in Law", 2009.

Dr. Augusto Zimmermann (LLB (PUC-Rio), LLM *cum laude* (PUC-Rio), PhD (Monash University)) is Senior Lecturer and formerly Associate Dean (Research) at the School of Law at Murdoch University. He is also a Commissioner with the Law Reform Commission of Western Australia and Adjunct Professor of Law at Universitas Kristen Maranatha in Indonesia. A prolific writer of many academic articles and books, Dr Zimmermann has been awarded the *Vice Chancellor's Award for Excellence in Research*, in 2012.

CPSIA information can be obtained at www.ICGtesting.com
Printed in the USA
BVOW02*1103050914

365650BV00008B/20/P

9 783319 055848